Macroeconomic Theory

Macroeconomic Theory

A Dynamic General Equilibrium Approach

Michael Wickens

Princeton University Press
Princeton and Oxford

ISBN: 978-0-691-11640-2 (alk. paper)

Library of Congress Control Number: 2007939554

British Library Cataloguing-in-Publication Data is available

This book has been composed in Lucida
Typeset by T&T Productions Ltd, London
Printed on acid-free paper ∞
press.princeton.edu

Printed in the United States of America

10 9 8 7 6 5 4 3 2

Contents

Preface

No subject with a foot in both the academic and public domains like macro-economics remains unchanged for long. The search for improved explanations, and the challenge of new problems and new circumstances, keeps such subjects in a constant state of flux. Dynamic general equilibrium (DGE) macroeconomics has emerged in recent years as the latest step in the development of macroeconomics from its origins in the work of Keynes in the 1930s. It is largely an attempt to integrate macroeconomics with microeconomics by providing microfoundations for macroeconomics. Most modern research in macroeconomics now adopts this approach. The purpose of this book is to provide an account of the DGE approach to modern macroeconomic theory and, in the process, make DGE macroeconomics accessible to both a new generation of students and older generations brought up on earlier approaches to macroeconomics, particularly those charged with giving policy advice to government, central banks, or business.

A feature of the DGE approach to macroeconomics is that it considers the whole economy at all times. Consequently, instead of viewing the economy as a collection of features to be studied separately at first, before perhaps being assembled into a complete picture of the economy, the focus of DGE macroeconomics is the economy as a whole. This is especially helpful when formulating economic policy, where one wants to know the wider effects of any given measure. It is essential knowledge for a policy advisor.

DGE macroeconomics evolved from neoclassical macroeconomics and real-business-cycle (RBC) theory to include virtually every aspect of the aggregate economy, including the open economy, exchange rates, and monetary and fiscal policy. It incorporates both Keynesian and New Keynesian economics, with the latter's emphasis on the microfoundations of macroeconomics and the role of monopolistic competition: key elements in modern theories of inflation targeting.

Once the preserve of finance, through DGE macroeconomics, asset pricing is now reclaimed as part of macroeconomics. A particular feature of this book is the inclusion of asset pricing theory as part of macroeconomics. It is shown that exactly the same model used to determine macroeconomic aggregates like consumption and capital accumulation also provides an explanation of stock and bond prices, and foreign exchange, based on economic fundamentals. This enables the sources of risk to be identified, as well as priced.

The virtue of DGE macroeconomics is brought out in the following encounter with a frustrated student. He protested that he knew there were many theories of macroeconomics, so why was I teaching him only one? My reply was that this was because only one theory was required to analyze the economy, and it seemed easier to remember one all-embracing theory than a large number of different theories.

I give the credit for my own conversion to DGE macroeconomics to the first edition of Robert Barro's undergraduate textbook *Macroeconomics* (Barro 1997). This was the first textbook to present macroeconomics using a general equilibrium approach. Many years ago, when visiting the University of Florida, I was asked to teach a section of Macroeconomics II. As my research area at the time was primarily econometrics, I had not taught macroeconomics before. Since I had strongly disliked the Keynesian approach to macroeconomics, even from my undergraduate days at the London School of Economics (LSE), partly as a learning device I chose *Macroeconomics* as the course book. Although the students found *Macroeconomics* far too hard, together with Kydland and Prescott's RBC analysis, I found it to be a most revealing way to think about both macroeconomics and econometrics.

It made me realize that the traditional way of doing macroeconometrics, equation by equation, had largely failed to engage the interest of macroeconomic theorists because the emphasis was too much on the dynamic specification of the model and too little on the key macroeconomic parameters, or the general equilibrium implications of the estimated model. Since any variable can be closely approximated by a univariate time-series representation, the danger in traditional macroeconometrics is that, in trying to improve goodness of fit by using a general dynamic specification, the omission of (possibly important) variables may be obscured. This indicated to me that macroeconomic theory should be given a much more important role in macroeconometric model building, and the reliance on time-series methods should be rethought. This is still not a popular view in the United Kingdom, and was heretical for an ex-postgraduate student from the LSE, particularly one brought up in "the LSE tradition" of econometrics.

Although Barro's *Macroeconomics* uses little mathematics, in this book the aim is to provide a more formal demonstration of the results. In my view, it is only by going into such details that one can obtain a proper understanding of the strengths and weaknesses of the theory. This was beautifully shown in the classic Blanchard and Fischer book *Lectures in Macroeconomics*, which gave the first technical textbook treatment of DGE macroeconomics. The present book may even be regarded simply as a more mathematical exposition of *Macroeconomics* with extensions to more recent research, and an updated version of *Lectures in Macroeconomics*.

In order to maintain the flow of the argument in the book, I have tried to avoid unnecessary clutter by keeping footnotes and references to a minimum. I should therefore like to acknowledge my enormous debt to the writings of others whose work I have drawn on without giving them explicit recognition. Some of the material in the book is original, usually with the purpose of filling in gaps in the literature in order to make the coverage of topics more comprehensive.

The immediate motivation for this book will be familiar to many teachers who have tried to innovate by including recent research ideas in their lectures. Having decided to change radically the content of macroeconomics in the M.Sc. degree at the University of York, I found that there was no single book that I could recommend to the students that covered all of the material I wished to include. The students soon complained that there was no book for the course and asked me to photocopy and distribute my lectures notes, which I did. The next cohort of students complained that they couldn't read my handwritten lecture notes, so why didn't I type them out, which I did. Subsequent cohorts complained that notes were all very well but they would be even more useful if they were written up properly with all of the argument included. So I did. I then received requests from old students, who had heard about this latest development, to send them the notes too. At this point I decided that I might as well turn my notes into a book, and so redeem a pledge made long ago to Richard Baggaley of Princeton University Press to write a book for him. I then provided my students with chapters of the book instead of lecture notes. Their complaint now is that the course seems to contain rather a lot of material and some of it is rather technical. So thanks for bringing about this book go especially to my students, who have been right at every stage and have prompted me to do better by them. Even so, without Richard Baggaley's constant support and encouragement, I doubt if I would have made the required effort.

I would also like to thank Gulcin Ozkan for reading and commenting on large parts of the book and my wife Ruth for not grudging the many weekends spent writing—in all honesty, I cannot call it work, as it has proved such a stimulating project. I hope that the reader will share my enthusiasm, and the enlightenment that this way of doing macroeconomics brings.

Macroeconomic Theory

1
Introduction

1.1 Dynamic General Equilibrium versus Traditional Macroeconomics

Modern macroeconomics seeks to explain the aggregate economy using theories based on strong microeconomic foundations. This is in contrast to the traditional Keynesian approach to macroeconomics, which is based on ad hoc theorizing about the relations between macroeconomic aggregates. In modern macroeconomics the economy is portrayed as a dynamic general equilibrium (DGE) system that reflects the collective decisions of rational individuals over a range of variables that relate to both the present and the future. These individual decisions are then coordinated through markets to produce the macroeconomy. The economy is viewed as being in continuous equilibrium in the sense that, given the information available, people make decisions that appear to be optimal for them, and so do not make persistent mistakes. This is also the sense in which behavior is said to be rational. Errors, when they occur, are attributed to information gaps, such as unanticipated shocks to the economy.

A distinction commonly drawn is between short-run and long-run equilibria. The economy is assumed to always be in short-run equilibrium. The long run, or the steady state, is a mathematical property of the macroeconomic model that describes its path when all past shocks have fully worked through the system. This can be either a static equilibrium, in which all variables are constant, or, more generally, a growth equilibrium, in which in the absence of shocks, there is no tendency for the economy to depart from a given path, usually one in which the main macroeconomic aggregates grow at the same rate. It is not, therefore, the economy that is assumed to be in long-run equilibrium, but the macroeconomic model. The equilibrium—short or long—is described as general because all variables are assumed to be simultaneously in equilibrium, not just some of them, or a particular market, which is a situation known as partial equilibrium.

Individual decisions are assumed to be based on maximizing the discounted sum of current and future expected welfare subject to preferences and four constraints: budget or resource constraints, endowments, the available technology, and information. A central issue in DGE macroeconomics is the intertemporal nature of decisions: whether to consume today, or save today in order to consume in the future. This entails being able to transfer today's income for future use, or future income for today's use. These transfers may be achieved by holding financial assets or by borrowing against future income. The different decisions are then reconciled through the economy-wide market system, and by market prices (including asset prices). The focus of modern macroeconomics, therefore, is on the individual's responses to shocks and how these are likely to affect multiple markets simultaneously both in the present and in the future.

Three main types of decision are taken by economic agents. They relate to goods and services, labor, and assets: physical assets (the capital stock, durables, housing, etc.) or financial assets (money, bonds, and equity)—each has its own economy-wide market. It is convenient to consider the decisions of individuals according to whether they are acting, in economic terms, as a household, a firm, or a government. Broadly, the decisions of the household relate to consumption, labor supply, and asset holdings. The firm determines the supply of goods and services, labor demand, investment, productive and financial capital, and the use of profits. Government determines its expenditure, taxation, transfers, base money, and the issuance of public debt.

The starting point for DGE macroeconomic models is a small general equilibrium model, but one that includes the main macroeconomic variables of interest. It is based on a single individual who produces a good that can either be consumed or invested to increase future output and consumption. It is commonly known either as the Ramsey (1928) model or as the representative-agent model. This is a surprisingly useful characterization of the economy as it permits the analysis of a number of its key features—consumption and saving, saving and investment, investment and dividend payments, technological progress, the intertemporal nature of decisions, the nature of economic equilibrium, the short-run and long-run behavior of the economy (the business cycle and economic growth), and how prices, such as real wages and interest rates, are determined—but without having to introduce them explicitly.

The basic Ramsey model can be roughly interpreted as that of a closed economy without a market structure in which the decisions are coordinated by a central planner. A first step toward greater realism is to allow decisions to be decentralized. This requires us to add markets—which act to coordinate decisions, and thereby enable us to abandon the device of the central planner—and financial assets. Subsequent steps are to include a government, and hence fiscal policy, to introduce money, and hence a distinction between real and nominal variables, and to allow a foreign dimension (the current account, the balance of payments, and real and nominal exchange rates). At each stage the economy is analyzed as a general equilibrium system and the significance for the economy of each added feature can be studied. Because it highlights individual behavior, one of the main attractions of this approach is that it provides a suitable framework for analyzing economic policy through respecting the "deep structural" parameters of the economy, which are not usually changed by policy—unless, of course, they are policy parameters that are changed. This too is in contrast to traditional macroeconomic models, like the Keynesian model, which are not specified in terms of the deep structural parameters but by coefficients which may be changed by policy in a manner that is unspecified, or unknown.

1.2 Traditional Macroeconomics

Views on how best to analyze macroeconomic variables such as aggregate consumption, total output, and inflation have changed much in the last twenty-five years. Under the influence of Keynesian macroeconomics, the emphasis was on the short-run behavior of the economy, why the economy seemed to persist in a state of disequilibrium, and how best to bring it back to equilibrium, i.e., how to stabilize the economy. In studying these issues, it was common for each macroeconomic variable to be modeled one at a time in separate equations; only then were they combined to form a model of the whole economy. The Brookings macroeconometric model was constructed in exactly this way (Duesenberry 1965): in the first stage individual aggregate variables were allocated to separate researchers and then, in the second stage, their equations were collected together to form the complete macroeconometric model. As a result, macroeconomics tended to focus on the short-run behavior of the economy and did so using a partial-equilibrium approach which led to a compartmentalization of thought in which it was difficult to acquire an overall view of how the system as a whole was likely to behave in response, for example, to a change in an exogenous variable, such as a policy instrument, or to a shock. Consequently, it was sometimes difficult to take into account the wider and longer-run effects of policy—policies which may even have been designed to combat the shock. There was, therefore, a tendency for policy to be too narrowly conceived and analyzed.

The study of macroeconomics was prompted in large part by the Great Depression—the worldwide recession of the 1930s. One of Keynes's original objectives in *The General Theory* (Keynes 1936) was to understand how such sustained periods of high unemployment could occur. From the beginning, therefore, interest was directed not so much to how the economic system behaved in long-run equilibrium, but to why it seemed to be misbehaving by generating long periods of apparent disequilibrium—in particular, departures from full employment—and to what, if anything, could be done about this. Until the last few years macroeconomic theory (and especially macroeconomic textbooks) has focused mainly on constructing models to explain this so-called disequilibrium behavior in the economy with a view to formulating appropriate stabilization policies to return the economy to equilibrium. The grounds for stabilization policy are that the economic system departs from equilibrium and, left to itself, would not return to equilibrium, or would do so too slowly. The aim of the policy intervention is to restore equilibrium, or to return the economy to equilibrium (or close to equilibrium) more quickly. This disequilibrium approach to macroeconomics tends to focus on individual markets and not the system as a whole. It also emphasizes the demand side of the economy. The outcome was a piecemeal, partial-equilibrium approach to macroeconomics. A corollary of the emphasis on disequilibrium was that equilibrium came to be regarded as a special, and less important, case.

1.3 Dynamic General Equilibrium Macroeconomics

The traditional approach to macroeconomics may be contrasted with the conception of DGE macroeconomics that economic agents are continuously reoptimizing subject to constraints with the result that the macroeconomy is always in some form of equilibrium, whether short run or long run. According to this view, the short-run equilibrium of the economy may differ from its long-run equilibrium but, if stable, the short-run equilibrium will be changing through time and will over time approach the long-run equilibrium; but the only sense in which the economy can be in disequilibrium at any point in time is through basing decisions on the wrong information. From this perspective, even the view sometimes expressed that disequilibrium is a special case of DGE macro-economics is misleading. DGE models assume that *ex ante* the economy is always in equilibrium.

Although for most economies macroeconomics has retained a focus on short-run behavior and stabilization, inspection of the path followed by gross domestic product (GDP) shows that the dominant feature is the growth in the trend of potential output; the loss of output due to recessions is almost trivial by comparison. This suggests that it is far more important to raise the rate of growth of potential output through supply-side policies than to move the economy back toward the trend path of potential output by demand-side stabilization policies.

The origins of DGE macroeconomics lie in the work of Lucas (1975), Kydland and Prescott (1982), and Long and Plosser (1983) on real business cycles. Their aim was to explain the dynamic behavior of the economy (notably the autocovariances of real output and the covariances of output with other aggregate macroeconomic time series) based on a competitive rational-expectations equilibrium model that took its inspiration from models of economic growth. The initial focus was on the role of technology shocks in generating the business cycle. The model used by Kydland and Prescott was, in essence, the model of Ramsey; that of Lucas included, in addition, government expenditures and money. Subsequent work extended the model in various ways in order to examine the effects of other types of shocks. We consider the principal results of this research in chapter 14. These issues are not, however, the sole concern of DGE macroeconomics, or of this book.

A frequent motivation for constructing macroeconomic models, and one of the first questions usually asked of a model, is what it implies for economic policy. (A recent discussion of the usefulness of DGE models in formulating policy is Chari and Kehoe (2006).) Nonetheless, it is important to realize that the aim of macroeconomics is not just to study policy issues. There are prior questions that should be asked, such as how the economy behaves in equilibrium, and how it responds to changes in exogenous variables and to shocks. Finding the answers to these questions is a sufficient reason to study macroeconomics. Although it is common to ask what the policy implications of a macroeconomic theory are, with the implicit assumption that we are forever seeking to interfere in the economy, it is not always necessary to search for policies that alter the equilibrium solution, especially if we are unclear what the broader consequences might be. Arguably, simply trying to understand how the economy behaves is sufficient justification.

Much of our analysis will be on considering what sort of factors might disturb an economy's equilibrium, and how the economy responds to these. They may be changes in exogenous variables or shocks. They may be permanent or temporary, anticipated or unanticipated, real or nominal, demand or supply, domestic or foreign, and the response of the economy may be different in each case. The conclusions we reach are often very different from those based on traditional macroeconomic models. Shocks may be serially uncorrelated, but the intrinsic dynamic structure of the economy may result in them having persistent effects on macroeconomic variables. This is the cause of short-term fluctuations in the economy, and hence the basis of business-cycle theory.

DGE models are forward looking and hence intertemporal. Current decisions are affected by expectations about the future. As a result, we use intertemporal dynamic optimization, in which people are treated as rationally processing current information about the future when making their decisions. There is a premium on obtaining the correct information and on deciding how best to use it. These concerns are linked to the concept of rationality—another key feature of DGE macroeconomics. The willingness of macroeconomists to make the assumption of rationality rapidly divided professional opinion into two camps. Traditional macroeconomics was based on the assumption of myopic decision making in which mistakes, even when realized, were often persisted in. The central idea behind rational expectations is that people do not make persistent mistakes once they are identified. This does not necessarily imply, as is often assumed, that people have more or less complete knowledge—for the mistakes are largely the result of unanticipated information gaps or shocks. It is sufficient to suppose that mistakes are not repeated. As forward-looking decisions must be based on expectations of the future, they may be incorrect; decisions that seem correct *ex ante* may not therefore be correct *ex post*. As previously noted, only as a result of this type of mistake might it be appropriate to think of the economy as being in disequilibrium.

Recent research has suggested that a policy of intervention by the government tends to be most successful when the government has an informational advantage over the private sector. If the private sector is able to fully anticipate the intervention, then the policy may be less successful. This is mostly true when the intervention involves private rather than public goods. As the private sector would substitute public for private goods, in effect, households would be paying for these goods from taxes instead of after-tax income. In contrast, the provision of public goods leads to a net increase in output as total private benefits exceed total private costs. These arguments about government expenditures apply more generally, of course, and will be developed further.

Another attraction of this intertemporal approach to macroeconomics is that it resolves a long-standing flaw in Keynesian economics. This concerns the way equilibrium is defined in dynamic macroeconomics. The problem goes back to Keynes's (1930) *Treatise on Money*, in which the concept of equilibrium used was that of a flow equilibrium (savings equals investment). Keynes realized that his formulation of equilibrium was incorrect and so he wrote *The General Theory* partly in an attempt to correct this error (Keynes 1936). In the *Treatise on Money*, one variable (the interest rate) had the task of equilibrating two variables (savings and investment). Keynes's solution in *The General Theory* was to introduce a second variable (income). This allowed savings to be equal to investment for any possible values of savings and investment. Unfortunately, Keynes was still using an inappropriate concept of equilibrium, namely, flow equilibrium. It is suggested by Skidelski (1992) that Keynes was never entirely happy with *The General Theory*. Perhaps this was because he realized that he had still not fully solved the problem of macroeconomic equilibrium.

The correct concept of equilibrium, which eluded Keynes, is that of stock equilibrium; perhaps this was because he was principally interested in the short run and not in long-run equilibrium. In DGE macroeconomic models individual preferences relate to consumption (a flow variable), but equilibrium in the economy is defined with reference to capital (a stock). There are an infinite number of possible flow equilibria—sometimes called temporary (or short-term) equilibria—but only one of these is consistent with the stock equilibrium. The problem is how to obtain this flow equilibrium. (We show that this is usually the unique saddlepath to equilibrium.) It is common in DGE macroeconomics to start by deriving the stock equilibrium.

A crucial feature of the stock equilibrium is that it involves a forward-looking component, and is not just backward looking. This introduces a vital distinction between economics and the natural sciences that in some ways makes economics harder. Because people look forward when making decisions there may be opportunities for others to manipulate strategically for their own benefit the information on which these decisions are based. The inanimate natural sciences, such as physics and chemistry, do not have such a forward-looking component in their dynamic structure, and therefore do not have this strategic dimension.

Stocks, or capital, consist of physical and financial capital. This provides a natural link between macroeconomics and finance. The theory of finance is largely concerned with pricing financial assets, notably bonds and equity. As financial assets play a crucial role in macroeconomics, and are sometimes substitutes in wealth portfolios for physical assets, asset-pricing theory is an essential component of macroeconomics and not something that may be omitted as in the past, or allowed to become a different discipline from macroeconomics.

Two complaints are sometimes made about macroeconomics. The first is that macroeconomics employs models that are far too simple to capture the full complexity of the economy, and as a result are of dubious value. The second, a comment made by some who are familiar with engineering, is that macroeconomic models are far too complex to be useful. The first opinion is easier for most people to sympathize with than the second. However, engineering has found that it is necessary to find a way of simplifying matters in order to make progress. There may be a lesson in this for macroeconomics. It may provide a justification for the use of models that are designed to capture key features of the economy while retaining their simplicity by abstracting from unnecessary detail. The simplicity of macroeconomic models, commonly seen as a major weakness, may therefore be a potential strength. It is true that virtually all macroeconomic policy is based on a simplified model of the economy, and there is an obvious danger in applying the conclusions obtained from such models to situations where the simplifying assumptions are too distorting. This makes it advisable to take care to establish the robustness of the conclusions to departures from the model assumptions. Nonetheless, as in engineering, the simple models of macroeconomics can often be remarkably robust and hence useful. DGE macroeconomic models tend to be more complex than Keynesian models, but are still essentially highly stylized. For another view of the relation between macroeconomics and engineering, see Mankiw (2006).

1.4 The Structure of This Book

This book is organized as a sequence of steps that extend the basic model in order to produce, by the end, a general picture of the economy that can be used to analyze its main features. The sequence starts with the basic closed-economy model and is followed by the introduction of growth, markets, government, the real open economy, money, price stickiness, asset price determination, financial markets, the international monetary system, nominal exchange rates, and monetary policy. The book concludes with a discussion of some empirical evidence on DGE models. In view of the above strictures on the advantages of using simple models, rather than retaining each added feature for each subsequent step, thereby finishing up with a complex general model of the economy, we aim to return to the original model as closely as we can and add the new feature to that. In this way we aim to provide a toolbox that is suitable for understanding how the economy works and that is useful for macroeconomic analysis, rather than a fully specified macroeconomic model so complex that it can only be studied using numerical methods.

Our starting point, in chapter 2, is the basic centralized DGE model for a closed economy expressed in real terms. Its purpose is to introduce the methodology of DGE macroeconomics. Although the setting is simple, it provides a remarkably powerful representation of an economy that has been used to study a wide variety of problems in macroeconomics, including real business cycles. It captures the key problem of DGE macroeconomics: namely, the intertemporal decision either to consume today or to invest in order to accumulate capital and produce more for extra consumption in the future. This simple model illustrates the important distinction between stock equilibrium and the sequence of flow equilibria that bring this about subject to suitable stability conditions.

The steady-state solution of the basic model of chapter 2 is a static equilibrium. In chapter 3 we show how the basic model can be modified so that in steady state the economy may achieve balanced economic growth. As a result, we are able to reinterpret the basic static solution as a description of the behavior of the economy about its steady-state growth path. As it is simpler to analyze a model with a static equilibrium, in later chapters we ignore, where possible, growth in the knowledge that we can focus on the deviations of the economy from its growth path. If we require the full solution, we can add the growth path to the deviations from it.

We decentralize decision making in chapter 4 and include markets to coordinate these decisions. In this way we are able to study the joint decisions of households and firms and their interaction in goods, labor, and capital markets. We show that various prices—notably wages and the rate of return on capital—although not included explicitly in the basic model, are nonetheless present implicitly. We also discuss the relationship between households and firms, and how the profits of the firm generate the firm's total value, the value of a share, and dividend income to households who are the owners of firms.

We introduce government into the model in chapter 5. We discuss the basis of government expenditures and how best to finance them with debt and taxes. In the process we consider optimal debt and taxation policy and the sustainability of the fiscal stance. This discussion is extended in chapter 6 to cover the problem of time inconsistency in fiscal policy, and to introduce the overlapping-generations model. This is particularly useful for fiscal and other decisions involving time periods that are very long, such as that of a generation. We use this to study the increasingly important issue of how to finance pensions.

In chapter 7 we introduce the foreign sector. This has important consequences for the economy as it alters the economy's resource constraint. The economy is no longer constrained to consume only what it can produce itself. Domestic residents can then borrow from and/or invest abroad. All of this should result in a welfare improvement for the economy. Making the economy open introduces many new issues and variables, and so greatly complicates the basic model. For example, there is the allocation problem between domestic and foreign goods and services and the determination of their associated relative price (the terms of trade), the relative costs of living of different countries (the real exchange rate), and the sustainability of current-account deficits.

So far all variables have been defined in real terms. This is partly to show that money plays a minor role in most of the real decisions of the economy. In chapter 8 we study nominal magnitudes—including the general price level and the optimal rate of inflation—by introducing money into the closed economy. Our focus here is on what determines the demand for money and why this might be affected by interest rates. We also discuss the use of credit instead of money. Although in a partial-equilibrium view of the economy money appears to impose a real cost, we show that in general equilibrium money is far more likely to be neutral in its effect on real variables. This chapter paves the way for the later discussion of monetary policy as it covers a key channel in the monetary transmission mechanism, namely, how money and interest rates affect other variables via the money market. Later we consider whether money has real effects in the short run.

Up to this point it has been assumed that prices are perfectly flexible and adjust so that markets clear each period. This is often regarded as a major weakness of DGE models compared with Keynesian models, which tend to stress the imperfect flexibility of prices, arguing that this causes a consequent lack of market clearing. In chapter 9 we show how to introduce imperfect price flexibility into the DGE model. We show how monopolistic competition in goods and labor markets may cause imperfect price flexibility and result in a cost to the economy in terms of lost output. In this way we are able to incorporate price stickiness yet retain the benefits and insights of the DGE model. Such models are sometimes known as New Keynesian models. The principal remaining difference between Keynesian and DGE macroeconomics is that in the DGE framework we continue to assume that the economy is always in equilibrium—albeit a temporary, and not necessarily a long-run, equilibrium. Thus economic agents always expect to be in their preferred positions subject to the constraints they face, one of which is the information they possess. In this sense, even prices are chosen optimally. Having introduced price stickiness, we then consider how this affects the determination of the aggregate supply function, a key equation in the determination of inflation.

Chapters 10 and 11 are a notable departure from traditional treatments of macroeconomics as they consider the determination of asset prices and the behavior of financial markets. Once the preserve of finance, these issues are now increasingly recognized as essential components of economics and, in particular, of DGE theory. The same basic DGE model that we have used to determine consumption, savings, and capital accumulation can be solved for financial assets and asset prices. This provides an explanation of asset prices based on economic fundamentals as opposed to the usual approach in finance, namely, relative asset pricing. Consequently, asset prices are determined in conjunction with macroeconomic variables instead of in relation to other asset prices. The general equilibrium theory of asset pricing is set out in chapter 10 and it is specialized to apply to the bond, equity, and foreign exchange (FOREX) markets in chapter 11.

Until chapter 10, we have, for the most part, ignored the fact that intertemporal decisions involve uncertainty about the future and are based on forecasts of the future formed from current information. Our analysis has therefore been conducted using nonstochastic, rather than stochastic, intertemporal optimization. This has allowed us to use Lagrange multiplier analysis instead of the more complicated stochastic dynamic programming. In general equilibrium asset pricing, uncertainty about future payoffs is a central feature of the analysis. The degree of uncertainty about each asset can be different. It ranges from certain to highly uncertain payoffs. Assets with certain payoffs have risk-free returns; those with uncertain payoffs have risky returns which incorporate risk premia in order to provide compensation for bearing the risk. Asset pricing may be characterized as the problem of determining the size of the risk premium that is required in order for risk-averse investors to hold a risky asset, i.e., the expected return on a risky asset in excess of the return on a risk-free asset.

In our previous discussion of the economy, in effect, we treated savings as being invested in a risk-free asset. It may seem, therefore, that we must rework many of our previous results in order to allow for investing in risky assets. This would, of course, greatly complicate the analysis as it would necessitate the inclusion of risk effects throughout. We show in chapter 10 that this is not, in fact, necessary as all we need do is risk-adjust all returns, i.e., adjust all risky returns by subtracting their risk premium. This implies that we can continue to work with only a risk-free asset and to use nonstochastic optimization. Hence, most of the time we are able to ignore such uncertainty.

In chapter 7 we treat the nominal exchange rate as given and consider only the determination of the real exchange rate. In chapter 12 we analyze the determination of nominal exchange rates. As the exchange rate is an asset price (the relative price of domestic and foreign currency), we must use the asset pricing theory developed in chapters 10 and 11. The no-arbitrage condition for FOREX is the uncovered interest parity condition, which relates the exchange rate to the interest differential between domestic and foreign bonds. Macroeconomic theories of the exchange rate are based on how macroeconomic variables affect interest rates and, through these, the exchange rate. Before embarking on our analysis of exchange rates in chapter 12, we discuss the effect of different international monetary arrangements on the determination of exchange rates.

We complete our development of the DGE model in chapter 13 by studying monetary policy. Our analysis is based on the New Keynesian model of inflation. To bring out its new features, we contrast this with the traditional Keynesian analysis of inflation. We consider alternative ways of conducting monetary policy: via exchange rates, money-supply targets, and inflation targeting. We then focus solely on inflation targeting. We examine the optimal way to conduct inflation targeting both in a closed economy and in an open economy with a floating exchange rate. We conclude our discussion of monetary policy by proposing a simple model of monetary policy in the euro area, where there are independent economies but a single currency, and hence a single interest rate for all economies.

In the final chapter, chapter 14, we present a brief account of how well simple DGE models perform in explaining the main stylized facts of the economy, and we try to identify some of their shortcomings. We base our discussion on a small selection of studies of the real business cycle that is designed to illustrate the principal issues. The main focus in this literature is the ability of these models, whether they are for a closed or an open economy, to explain the business cycle solely by productivity shocks. We complete this discussion by examining a DGE model of the economy that compares the effects of a large number of different types of shock, including monetary-policy shocks.

Finally, we provide a mathematical appendix in which we explain the main mathematical results and techniques we have used in this discussion of contemporary macroeconomic theory based on DGE models.

There are also exercises (with solutions) for students, and these will be available on the Princeton University Press web site at

http://press.princeton.edu/titles/8595.html

from March 2008.

2

The Centralized Economy

2.1 Introduction

In this chapter we introduce the basic dynamic general equilibrium model for a closed economy. The aim is to explain how the optimal level of output is determined in the economy and how this is allocated between consumption and capital accumulation or, put another way, between consumption today and consumption in the future. We exclude government, money, and financial markets, and all variables are in real, not money, terms. Although apparently very restrictive, this model captures most of the essential features of the macroeconomy. Subsequent chapters build on this basic model by adding further detail but without drastically altering the substantive conclusions derived from the basic model.

Various different interpretations of this model have been made. It is sometimes referred to as the Ramsey model after Frank Ramsey (1928), who first introduced a very similar version to study taxation (Ramsey 1927). The model can also be interpreted as a central (or social) planning model in which the decisions are taken centrally by the social planner in the light of individual preferences, which are assumed to be identical. (Alternatively, the social planner's preferences may be considered as imposed on everyone.) It is also called a representative-agent model when all economic agents are identical and act as both a household and a firm. Another interpretation of the model is that it can be regarded as referring to a single individual. Consequently, it is sometimes called a Robinson Crusoe economy. Any of these interpretations may prove helpful in understanding the analysis of the model. This model has also formed the basis of modern growth theory (see Cass 1965; Koopmans 1967). Our interest in this model, however interpreted, is to identify and analyze certain key concepts in macroeconomics and key features of the macroeconomy. The rest of the book builds on this first pass through this highly simplified preliminary account of the macroeconomy.

2.2 The Basic Dynamic General Equilibrium Closed Economy

The model may be described as follows. Today's output can either be consumed or invested, and the existing capital stock can either be consumed today or used to produce output tomorrow. Today's investment will add to the capital stock and increase tomorrow's output. The problem to be addressed is how best to allocate output between consumption today and investment (i.e., to accumulating capital) so that there is more output and consumption tomorrow.

The model consists of three equations. The first is the national income identity:

$$y_t = c_t + i_t, \tag{2.1}$$

in which total output y_t in period t consists of consumption c_t plus investment goods i_t. The national income identity also serves as the resource constraint for the whole economy. In this simple model total output is also total income and this is either spent on consumption, or is saved. Savings $s_t = y_t - c_t$ can only be used to buy investment goods, hence $i_t = s_t$.

The second equation is

$$\Delta k_{t+1} = i_t - \delta k_t. \tag{2.2}$$

This shows how k_t, the capital stock at the beginning of period t, accumulates over time. The increase in the stock of capital (net investment) during period t equals new (gross) investment less depreciated capital. A constant proportion δ of the capital stock is assumed to depreciate each period (i.e., to have become obsolete). This equation provides the (intrinsic) dynamics of the model.

The third equation is the production function:

$$y_t = F(k_t). \tag{2.3}$$

This gives the output produced during period t by the stock of capital *at the beginning* of the period using the available technology. An increase in the stock of capital increases output, but at a diminishing rate, hence $F > 0$, $F' > 0$, and $F'' \leqslant 0$. We also assume that the marginal product of capital approaches zero as capital tends to infinity, and approaches infinity as capital tends to zero, i.e.,

$$\lim_{k \to \infty} F'(k) = 0 \quad \text{and} \quad \lim_{k \to 0} F'(k) = \infty.$$

These are known as the Inada (1964) conditions. They imply that at the origin there are infinite output gains to increasing the capital stock whereas, as the capital stock increases, the gains in output decline and eventually tend to zero.

If we interpret the model as an economy in which the population is constant through time, then this is like measuring output, consumption, investment, and capital in per capita terms. For example, if there is a constant population N, then $y_t = Y_t/N$ is output per capita, where Y_t is total output for the whole economy.

Output and investment can be eliminated from the subsequent analysis, and the model reduced to just one equation involving two variables. Combining the three equations gives the economy's resource constraint:

$$F(k_t) = c_t + \Delta k_{t+1} + \delta k_t. \tag{2.4}$$

This is a nonlinear dynamic constraint on the economy.

Given an initial stock of capital, k_t (the endowment), the economy must choose its preferred level of consumption for period t, namely c_t, and capital at the start of period $t + 1$, namely k_{t+1}. This can be shown to be equivalent to choosing consumption for periods $t, t + 1, t + 2, \ldots$, with the preferred levels of capital, output, investment, and savings for each period derived from the model.

Having established the constraints facing the economy, the next issue is its preferences. What is the economy trying to maximize subject to these constraints? Possible choices are output, consumption, and the utility derived from consumption. We could choose their values in the current period or over the long term. We are also interested in whether a particular choice for the current period is sustainable thereafter. This is related to the existence and stability of equilibrium in the economy. We consider two solutions: the "golden rule" and the "optimal solution." Both of these assume that the aim of the economy (the representative economic agent or the central planner) is to maximize consumption, or the utility derived from consumption. The difference is in attitudes to the future. In the golden rule the future is not discounted whereas in the optimal solution it is. In other words, any given level of consumption is valued less highly if it is in the future than if it is in the present. We can show that, as a result, the golden rule is not sustainable following a negative shock to output but the optimal solution is.

2.3   Golden Rule Solution

2.3.1   The Steady State

Consider first an attempt to maximize consumption in period t. This is perhaps the most obvious type of solution. It would be equivalent to maximizing utility $U(c_t)$. From the resource constraint, equation (2.4), c_t must satisfy

$$c_t = F(k_t) - k_{t+1} + (1 - \delta)k_t. \tag{2.5}$$

To maximize c_t the economy must, in period t, consume the whole of current output $F(k_t)$ plus undepreciated capital $(1-\delta)k_t$, and undertake no investment so that $k_{t+1} = 0$. In the following period output would, of course, be zero as there would be no capital to produce it. This solution is clearly unsustainable. It would only appeal to an economic agent who is myopic, or one who has no future.

We therefore introduce the additional constraint that the level of consumption should be sustainable. This implies that in each period new investment is required to maintain the capital stock and to produce next period's output. In effect, we are assuming that the aim is to maximize consumption *in each period*. With no distinction being made between current and future consumption, the problem has been converted from one with a very short-term objective to one with a very long-term objective.

The solution can be obtained by considering just the long run and we therefore omit time subscripts. In the long run the capital stock will be constant and long-run consumption is obtained from equation (2.5) as

$$c = F(k) - \delta k. \tag{2.6}$$

Consumption in the long run is output less that part of output required to replace depreciated capital in order to keep the stock of capital constant. Thus the only investment undertaken is that to replace depreciated capital. The output that remains can be consumed.

The problem now is how to choose k to maximize c. The first-order condition for a maximum of c is

$$\frac{\partial c}{\partial k} = F'(k) - \delta = 0 \tag{2.7}$$

and the second-order condition is

$$\frac{\partial^2 c}{\partial k^2} = F''(k) \leqslant 0.$$

Equation (2.7) implies that the capital stock must be increased until its marginal product $F'(k)$ equals the rate of depreciation δ. Up to this point an increase in the stock of capital increases consumption, but beyond this point consumption begins to decrease. This is because the output cost of replacing depreciated capital in each period requires that consumption be reduced. The solution can be depicted graphically. Figure 2.1 shows straightforwardly that the marginal product of capital falls as the stock of capital increases. Given the rate of depreciation δ, the value of the capital stock can be obtained. The higher the rate of depreciation, the smaller the sustainable size of the capital stock.

We can determine the optimal level of consumption from figure 2.2. The curved line is the production function: the level of output $F(k)$ produced by the capital stock k that is in place at the beginning of the period. The straight line is replacement investment δk. The difference between the two is consumption plus net investment (capital accumulation), i.e.,

$$F(k) - \delta k = c + \Delta k,$$

which is simply equation (2.5). The maximum difference occurs where the lines are furthest apart. This happens when $F'(k) = \delta$, i.e., when the slope of the tangent to the production function—the marginal product of capital $F'(k)$— equals the slope of the line depicting total depreciation, δ. For ease of visibility, in the diagram the size of δ (and hence of depreciated capital) has been exaggerated.

Figure 2.3 provides another way of depicting the solution. The curved line represents consumption plus net investment (i.e., net output or the vertical distance between the two lines in figure 2.2) and is plotted against the capital stock. Points above the line are not attainable due to the resource constraint $F(k) - \delta k \geqslant c + \Delta k$. The maximum level of consumption plus net investment

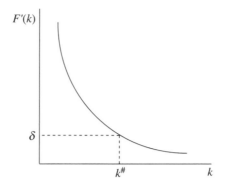

Figure 2.1. The marginal product of capital.

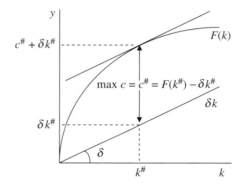

Figure 2.2. Total output, consumption, and replacement investment.

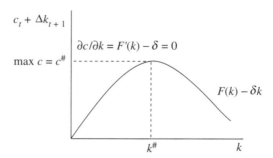

Figure 2.3. Net output.

occurs where the slope of the tangent is zero. At this point net investment $F'(k) - \delta = 0$.

We can now find the sustainable level of consumption. This occurs when the capital stock is constant over time, implying that $\Delta k = 0$ and that net investment is zero. The maximum point on the line is then the maximum sustainable level of consumption $c^{\#}$. This requires a constant level of the capital stock $k^{\#}$. This solution is known as the golden rule.

2.3.2 The Dynamics of the Golden Rule

Due to the constraint that the capital stock is constant, $c^\#$ is sustainable indefinitely *provided there are no disturbances to the economy.* If there are disturbances, then the economy becomes dynamically unstable at $\{c^\#, k^\#\}$. To see why the golden rule is not a stable solution, consider what would happen if the economy tried to maintain consumption at the maximum level $c^\#$ even when the capital stock differs from $k^\#$ due to a negative disturbance.

If $k < k^\#$ then the level of output would be $F(k) < F(k^\#)$. In order to consume the amount $c^\#$, it would then be necessary to consume some of the existing capital stock, with the result that $\Delta k < 0$, and the capital stock would no longer be constant, but would fall. With less capital, future output would therefore be even smaller and attempts to maintain consumption at $c^\#$ would cause further decreases in the capital stock. Eventually the economy would no longer be able to consume even $c^\#$ as there would be too little capital to produce this amount.

An important implication emerges from this: an economy that consumes too much will, sooner or later, find that it is eroding its capital base and will not be able to sustain its consumption. In practice, of course, it is not possible to switch to consuming capital goods, except in a few special cases. The analysis can, however, be interpreted to mean that switching resources from producing capital goods to consumption goods will eventually undermine the economy, and hence consumption. Thus, the apparently small technical point concerning the stability of the solution turns out to have profound implications for macroeconomics.

There is, however, a simple solution. The economy can reduce its consumption temporally and divert output to rebuilding the capital stock to a level that restores the original equilibrium. This would mean that negative shocks to the system would impact heavily on consumption in the short term. Trying to achieve the maximum level of consumption in each period may not, therefore, result in maximizing consumption in the longer term. The solution is to suspend the consumption objective temporarily.

It may be noted that if, as a result of a positive disturbance, $k > k^\#$ and hence output is raised, it would be possible to increase consumption temporarily until the capital stock returns to the lower, but sustainable, level $k^\#$. We make further observations on the stability of the economy under the golden rule below after we have considered the optimal solution.

2.4 Optimal Solution

2.4.1 Derivation of the Fundamental Euler Equation

Instead of assuming that future consumption has the same value as consumption today, we now assume that the economy values consumption today more than consumption in the future. In particular, we suppose that the aim is to maximize the present value of current and future utility,

$$\max_{\{c_{t+s}, k_{t+s}\}} V_t = \sum_{s=0}^{\infty} \beta^s U(c_{t+s}),$$

where additional consumption increases instantaneous utility $U_t = U(c_t)$, implying $U_t' > 0$, but does so at a diminishing rate as $U_t'' \leqslant 0$. Future utility is therefore valued less highly than current utility as it is discounted by the discount factor $0 < \beta < 1$, or equivalently at the rate $\theta > 0$, where $\beta = 1/(1 + \theta)$. The aim is to choose current and future consumption to maximize V_t subject to the economy-wide resource constraint equation (2.4).

As the problem involves variables defined in different periods of time it is one of dynamic optimization. This sort of problem is commonly solved using either dynamic programming, the calculus of variations, or the maximum principle. But because, as formulated, it is not a stochastic problem, it can also be solved using the more familiar method of Lagrange multiplier analysis. (See the mathematical appendix for further details of dynamic optimization by these methods.)

First we define the Lagrangian constrained for each period by the resource constraint

$$\mathcal{L}_t = \sum_{s=0}^{\infty} \{\beta^s U(c_{t+s}) + \lambda_{t+s}[F(k_{t+s}) - c_{t+s} - k_{t+s+1} + (1 - \delta)k_{t+s}]\}, \qquad (2.8)$$

where λ_{t+s} is the Lagrange multiplier s periods ahead. This is maximized with respect to $\{c_{t+s}, k_{t+s+1}, \lambda_{t+s}; s \geqslant 0\}$. The first-order conditions are

$$\frac{\partial \mathcal{L}_t}{\partial c_{t+s}} = \beta^s U'(c_{t+s}) - \lambda_{t+s} = 0, \qquad\qquad s \geqslant 0, \qquad (2.9)$$

$$\frac{\partial \mathcal{L}_t}{\partial k_{t+s}} = \lambda_{t+s}[F'(k_{t+s}) + 1 - \delta] - \lambda_{t+s-1} = 0, \quad s > 0, \qquad (2.10)$$

plus the constraint equation (2.4) and the transversality condition

$$\lim_{s \to \infty} \beta^s U'(c_{t+s}) k_{t+s} = 0. \qquad (2.11)$$

Notice that we do not maximize with respect to k_t as we assume that this is predetermined in period t.

To help us understand the role of the transversality condition (2.11) in intertemporal optimization, consider the implication of having a finite capital stock at time $t + s$. If consumed this would give discounted utility of $\beta^s U'(c_{t+s}) k_{t+s}$. If the time horizon were $t + s$, then it would not be optimal to have any capital left in period $t + s$; it should have been consumed instead. Hence, as $s \to \infty$, the transversality condition provides an extra optimality condition for intertemporal infinite-horizon problems.

The Lagrange multiplier can be obtained from equation (2.9). Substituting for λ_{t+s} and λ_{t+s-1} in equation (2.10) gives

$$\beta^s U'(c_{t+s})[F'(k_{t+s}) + 1 - \delta] = \beta^{s-1} U'(c_{t+s-1}), \quad s > 0.$$

For $s = 1$ this can be rewritten as

$$\beta \frac{U'(c_{t+1})}{U'(c_t)} [F'(k_{t+1}) + 1 - \delta] = 1. \tag{2.12}$$

Equation (2.12) is known as the Euler equation. It is the fundamental dynamic equation in intertemporal optimization problems in which there are dynamic constraints. The same equation arises using each of the alternative methods of optimization referred to above.

2.4.2 Interpretation of the Euler Equation

It is possible to give an intuitive explanation for the Euler equation. Consider the following problem: if we reduce c_t by a small amount dc_t, how much larger must c_{t+1} be to fully compensate for this while leaving V_t unchanged? We suppose that consumption beyond period $t + 1$ remains unaffected. This problem can be addressed by considering just two periods: t and $t + 1$. Thus we let

$$V_t = U(c_t) + \beta U(c_{t+1}).$$

Taking the total differential of V_t, and recalling that V_t remains constant, implies that

$$0 = dV_t = dU_t + \beta\, dU_{t+1} = U'(c_t)\, dc_t + \beta U'(c_{t+1})\, dc_{t+1},$$

where dc_{t+1} is the small change in c_{t+1} brought about by reducing c_t. Since we are reducing c_t, we have $dc_t < 0$. The loss of utility in period t is therefore $U'(c_t)\, dc_t$. In order for V_t to be constant, this must be compensated by the discounted gain in utility $\beta U'(c_{t+1})\, dc_{t+1}$. Hence we need to increase c_{t+1} by

$$dc_{t+1} = -\frac{U'(c_t)}{\beta U'(c_{t+1})}\, dc_t. \tag{2.13}$$

As the resource constraint must be satisfied in every period, in periods t and $t + 1$ we require that

$$F'(k_t)\, dk_t = dc_t + dk_{t+1} - (1 - \delta)\, dk_t,$$
$$F'(k_{t+1})\, dk_{t+1} = dc_{t+1} + dk_{t+2} - (1 - \delta)\, dk_{t+1}.$$

As k_t is given and beyond period $t + 1$ we are constraining the capital stock to be unchanged, only the capital stock in period $t + 1$ can be different from before. Thus $dk_t = dk_{t+2} = 0$. The resource constraints for periods t and $t + 1$ can therefore be rewritten as

$$0 = dc_t + dk_{t+1},$$
$$F'(k_{t+1})\, dk_{t+1} = dc_{t+1} - (1 - \delta)\, dk_{t+1}.$$

These two equations can be reduced to one equation by eliminating dk_{t+1} to give a second connection between dc_t and dc_{t+1}, namely,

$$dc_{t+1} = -[F'(k_{t+1}) + 1 - \delta]\, dc_t. \tag{2.14}$$

This can be interpreted as follows. The output no longer consumed in period t is invested and increases output in period $t + 1$ by $-F'(k_{t+1})\,\mathrm{d}c_t$. All of this can be consumed in period $t + 1$. And as we do not wish to increase the capital stock beyond period $t + 1$, the undepreciated increase in the capital stock, $(1 - \delta)\,\mathrm{d}c_t$, can also be consumed in period $t + 1$. This gives the total increase in consumption in period $t + 1$ stated in equation (2.14). The discounted utility of this extra consumption as measured in period t is

$$\beta U'(c_{t+1})\,\mathrm{d}c_{t+1} = -\beta U'(c_{t+1})[F'(k_{t+1}) + 1 - \delta]\,\mathrm{d}c_t.$$

To keep V_t constant, this must be equal to the loss of utility in period t. Thus

$$U'(c_t)\,\mathrm{d}c_t = \beta U'(c_{t+1})[F'(k_{t+1}) + 1 - \delta]\,\mathrm{d}c_t.$$

Canceling $\mathrm{d}c_t$ from both sides and dividing through by $U'(c_t)$ gives the Euler equation (2.12).

2.4.3 Intertemporal Production Possibility Frontier

The production possibility frontier is associated with a production function that has more than one type of output and one or more inputs. It measures the maximum combination of each type of output that can be produced using a fixed amount of the factor(s). The result is a concave function in output space of the quantities produced. The *intertemporal* production possibility frontier (IPPF) is associated with outputs at different points of time and is derived from the economy's resource constraint. This gives the second relation between c_t and c_{t+1}. It is obtained by combining the resource constraints for periods t and $t + 1$ to eliminate k_{t+1}. The result is the two-period intertemporal resource constraint (or IPPF)

$$\begin{aligned}
c_{t+1} &= F(k_{t+1}) - k_{t+2} + (1 - \delta)k_{t+1} \\
&= F[F(k_t) - c_t + (1 - \delta)k_t] - k_{t+2} + (1 - \delta)[F(k_t) - c_t + (1 - \delta)k_t].
\end{aligned}$$
$$(2.15)$$

This provides a concave relation between c_t and c_{t+1}.

The slope of a tangent to the IPPF is

$$\frac{\partial c_{t+1}}{\partial c_t} = -[F'(k_{t+1}) + 1 - \delta]. \tag{2.16}$$

As noted previously, this is also the slope of the indifference curve at the point where it is tangent to the resource constraint. Hence, the IPPF also touches the indifference curve at this point. And as

$$\frac{\partial^2 c_{t+1}}{\partial c_t^2} = F''(k_{t+1}) < 0,$$

the tangent to the IPPF flattens as c_t decreases, implying that the IPPF is a concave function. We use this result in the discussion below.

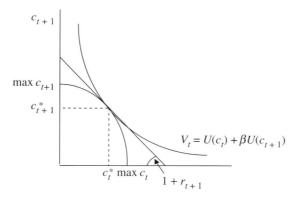

Figure 2.4. A graphical solution based on the IPPF.

2.4.4 Graphical Representation of the Solution

The solution to the two-period problem is represented in figure 2.4. The upper curved line is the indifference curve that trades off consumption today for consumption tomorrow while leaving V_t unchanged. It is tangent to the resource constraint. The lower curved line represents the trade-off between consumption today and consumption tomorrow from the viewpoint of production, i.e., it is the IPPF. It touches the indifference curve at the point of tangency with the budget constraint. This solution arises as in equilibrium equations (2.13) and (2.14), and (2.16) must be satisfied simultaneously so that

$$-\frac{dc_{t+1}}{dc_t}\bigg|_{V_{\mathrm{const.}}} = F'(k_{t+1}) + 1 - \delta = 1 + r_{t+1} = -\frac{\partial c_{t+1}}{\partial c_t}\bigg|_{\mathrm{IPPF}}.$$

The net marginal product $F'(k_{t+1}) - \delta = r_{t+1}$ can be interpreted as the implied real rate of return on capital after allowing for depreciation. An increase in r_{t+1} due, for example, to a technology shock that raises the marginal product of capital in period $t + 1$ makes the resource constraint steeper, and results in an increase in V_t, c_t, and c_{t+1}.

2.4.5 Static Equilibrium Solution

We now return to the full optimal solution and consider its long-run equilibrium properties. The long-run equilibrium is a static solution, implying that in the absence of shocks to the macroeconomic system, consumption and the capital stock will be constant through time. Thus $c_t = c^*$, $k_t = k^*$, $\Delta c_t = 0$, and $\Delta k_t = 0$ for all t. In static equilibrium the Euler equation can therefore be written as

$$\frac{\beta U'(c^*)}{U'(c^*)}[F'(k^*) + 1 - \delta] = 1,$$

implying that

$$F'(k^*) = \frac{1}{\beta} + \delta - 1 = \delta + \theta.$$

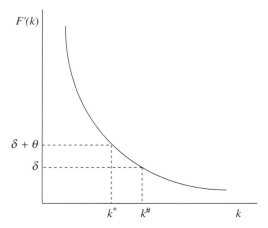

Figure 2.5. Optimal long-run capital.

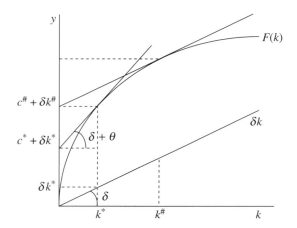

Figure 2.6. Optimal long-run consumption.

The solution is therefore different from that for the golden rule, where $F'(k) = \delta$. Figure 2.1 is replaced by figure 2.5. This shows that the optimal level of capital is less than for the golden rule. The reason for this is that future utility is discounted at the rate $\theta > 0$.

   The implications for consumption can be seen in figures 2.5 and 2.6. In figure 2.5 the solution is obtained where the slope of the tangent to the production function is $\delta + \theta$. As the tangent must be steeper than for the golden rule, this implies that the optimal level of capital must be lower. Figure 2.6 shows that this entails a lower level of consumption too. Thus $c^* < c^\#$ and $k^* < k^\#$.

   We have shown that discounting the future results in lower consumption. This may seem to be a good reason for not discounting the future. To see what the benefit of discounting is we must analyze the dynamics and stability of this solution.

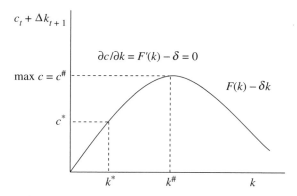

Figure 2.7. Optimal consumption compared.

2.4.5.1 An Example

Suppose that utility is the power function

$$U(c) = \frac{c^{1-\sigma} - 1}{1 - \sigma}.$$

It can be shown that $\sigma = -cU''/U'$ is the coefficient of relative risk aversion. Suppose also that the production function is Cobb–Douglas so that

$$y_t = Ak_t^\alpha.$$

Then the Euler equation (2.12) is

$$\beta \frac{U'(c_{t+1})}{U'(c_t)} [F'(k_{t+1}) + 1 - \delta] = \beta \left(\frac{c_{t+1}}{c_t} \right)^{-\sigma} [\alpha A k_{t+1}^{-(1-\alpha)} + 1 - \delta] = 1.$$

Hence the steady-state level of capital is

$$k^* = \left(\frac{\alpha A}{\delta + \theta} \right)^{1/(1-\alpha)}$$

and the steady-state level of consumption is

$$c^* = Ak^{*\alpha} - \delta k^*$$

$$= \left(\frac{A}{\delta + \theta} \right)^{1-\alpha} \left(\frac{(1 - \alpha)\delta + \theta}{\alpha^\alpha} \right).$$

2.4.6 Dynamics of the Optimal Solution

The dynamic analysis that we require uses a so-called phase diagram. This is based on figure 2.7. To construct the phase diagram, we must first consider the two equations that describe the optimal solution at each point in time. These are the Euler equation and the resource constraint. For convenience they are reproduced here:

$$\frac{\beta U'(c_{t+1})}{U'(c_t)} [F'(k_{t+1}) + 1 - \delta] = 1,$$

$$\Delta k_{t+1} = F(k_t) - \delta k_t - c_t. \tag{2.17}$$

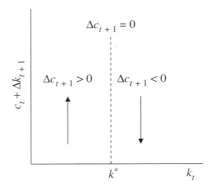

Figure 2.8. Consumption dynamics.

A complication is that both equations are nonlinear. We therefore consider a local solution (i.e., a solution that holds in the neighborhood of equilibrium) obtained through linearizing the Euler equation by taking a Taylor series expansion of $U'(c_{t+1})$ about c_t. This gives

$$U'(c_{t+1}) \simeq U'(c_t) + \Delta c_{t+1} U''(c_t).$$

Hence

$$\frac{U'(c_{t+1})}{U'(c_t)} \simeq 1 + \frac{U''}{U'} \Delta c_{t+1}, \quad \frac{U''}{U'} \leqslant 0,$$

and

$$\Delta c_{t+1} = -\frac{U'}{U''} \left[1 - \frac{1}{\beta[F'(k_{t+1}) + 1 - \delta]} \right]. \tag{2.18}$$

Thus we have two equations that determine the changes in consumption and capital: equations (2.17) and (2.18).

These equations confirm the static-equilibrium solution as when $c_t = c^*$ and $k_t = k^*$, we have $\Delta c_{t+1} = 0$, $\Delta k_{t+1} = 0$, and $F'(k^*) = \delta + \theta$. From equation (2.18) we note that when $k > k^*$ we have $F'(k) < F'(k^*)$, and therefore $F'(k) + 1 - \delta < F'(k^*) + 1 - \delta$. It follows that if $k = k^*$ we have $\Delta c = 0$, i.e., consumption is constant, and if $k > k^*$ then $\Delta c < 0$, i.e., consumption must be decreasing. By a similar argument, if $k < k^*$ then $\Delta c > 0$ and consumption is increasing. Thus, $\Delta c \lesseqgtr 0$ for $k \gtreqless k^*$. This is represented in figure 2.8.

The dynamic behavior of capital is determined from equation (2.17). When $c_t \gtreqless F(k_{t+1}) - \delta k_t$ we have $\Delta k_{t+1} \lesseqgtr 0$. This is depicted in figure 2.9. Above the curve consumption plus long-run net investment exceeds output. The capital stock must therefore decrease to accommodate the excessive level of consumption. Below the curve there is sufficient output left over after consumption to allow capital to accumulate.

Combining figures 2.8 and 2.9 gives figure 2.10, the phase diagram we require. Note that this applies in the general nonlinear case and is not a local approximation. The optimal long-run solution is at point B. The line SS through B is known as the saddlepath, or stable manifold. Only points on this line are attainable. This is not as restrictive as it may seem, as the location of the saddlepath

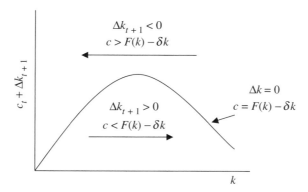

Figure 2.9. Capital dynamics.

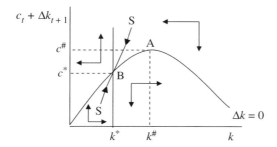

Figure 2.10. Phase diagram.

is determined by the economy, i.e., the parameters of the model, and could in principle be in an infinite number of places depending on the particular values of the parameters. The arrows denote the dynamic behavior of c_t and k_t. This depends on which of four possible regions the economy is in. To the northeast, but on the line SS, consumption is excessive and the capital stock is so large that the marginal product of capital is less than $\delta + \theta$. This is not sustainable and therefore both consumption and the capital stock must decrease. This is indicated by the arrow on SS. The opposite is true on SS in the southwest region. Here consumption and capital need to increase. As the other two regions are not attainable they can be ignored. The economy therefore attains equilibrium at the point B by moving along the saddlepath to that point. At B there is no need for further changes in consumption and capital, and the economy is in equilibrium. Were the economy able to be off the line SS—*which it is not and cannot be*—the dynamics would ensure that it could not attain equilibrium. When there are two regions of stability and two of instability like this the solution is called a saddlepath equilibrium.

2.4.7 Algebraic Analysis of the Saddlepath Dynamics

An algebraic analysis of the dynamic behavior of the economy may be based on the two nonlinear dynamic equations describing the optimal solution, namely, the Euler equation and the resource constraint:

$$\frac{\beta U'(c_{t+1})}{U'(c_t)}[F'(k_{t+1}) + 1 - \delta] = 1, \tag{2.19}$$

$$\Delta k_{t+1} = F(k_t) - \delta k_t - c_t. \tag{2.20}$$

The static (or long-run) equilibrium solutions $\{c^*, k^*\}$ are obtained from

$$F'(k^*) = \delta + \theta, \tag{2.21}$$

$$c^* = F(k^*) - \delta k^*. \tag{2.22}$$

As equations (2.19) and (2.20) are nonlinear in c and k, our analysis is based on a local linear approximation to the full nonlinear model. The linear approximation to equation (2.19) is obtained as a first-order Taylor series expansion about $\{c^*, k^*\}$:

$$\beta\left[F'(k^*) + 1 - \delta + \frac{U''(c^*)}{U'(c^*)}\Delta c_{t+1} + F''(k^*)(k_{t+1} - k^*)\right] \simeq 1.$$

Using the long-run solutions (2.21) and (2.22), this can be rewritten as

$$\frac{U''(c^*)}{U'(c^*)}(c_{t+1} - c^*) + F''(k^*)(k_{t+1} - k^*) \simeq \frac{U''(c^*)}{U'(c^*)}(c_t - c^*). \tag{2.23}$$

The linear approximation to (2.20) is

$$\Delta k_{t+1} \simeq F(k^*) + F'(k^*)(k_t - k^*) - \delta k_t - c_t$$

or

$$k_{t+1} - k^* \simeq -\{c_t - [F(k^*) - \delta k^*]\} + [F'(k^*) + 1 - \delta](k_t - k^*)$$
$$= -(c_t - c^*) + \theta(k_t - k^*). \tag{2.24}$$

We can now write equations (2.24) and (2.23) as a matrix equation of deviations from long-run equilibrium:

$$\begin{bmatrix} c_{t+1} - c^* \\ k_{t+1} - k^* \end{bmatrix} = \begin{bmatrix} 1 + \dfrac{U'F''}{U''} & -(1+\theta)\dfrac{U'F''}{U''} \\ -1 & 1 + \theta \end{bmatrix}\begin{bmatrix} c_t - c^* \\ k_t - k^* \end{bmatrix}.$$

This is a first-order vector autoregression, which has the generic form

$$x_{t+1} = Ax_t,$$

where $x_t = (c_t - c^*, k_t - k^*)'$.

The next step is to determine the dynamic behavior of this system. As shown in the mathematical appendix, this depends on the roots of the matrix A or, equivalently, the roots of the quadratic equation

$$B(L) = 1 - (\operatorname{tr} A)L + (\det A)L^2 = 0.$$

If the roots are denoted $1/\lambda_1$ and $1/\lambda_2$, then they satisfy

$$(1 - \lambda_1 L)(1 - \lambda_2 L) = 0.$$

If the dynamic structure of the system is a saddlepath, then one root, say λ_1, will be the stable root and will satisfy $|\lambda_1| < 1$ and the other root will be unstable and will have the property $|\lambda_2| \geqslant 1$. It is shown in the mathematical appendix that approximately the roots are

$$\{\lambda_1, \lambda_2\} \simeq \left\{ \frac{\det A}{\operatorname{tr} A}, \operatorname{tr} A - \frac{\det A}{\operatorname{tr} A} \right\}$$
$$= \left\{ \frac{1 + \theta}{2 + \theta + (U'F''/U'')}, 2 + \theta + \frac{U'F''}{U''} - \frac{1 + \theta}{2 + \theta + (U'F''/U'')} \right\}.$$

Thus, as $U'F''/U'' \geqslant 0$, we have $0 < \lambda_1 < 1$ and $\lambda_2 > 1$. The dynamics of the optimal solution are therefore a saddlepath, as already shown in the diagram. We note that in the previous example

$$\frac{U'F''}{U''} = \frac{\alpha(1-\alpha)cy}{\sigma k^2} > 0.$$

2.5 Real-Business-Cycle Dynamics

2.5.1 The Business Cycle

In practice an economy is continually disturbed from its long-run equilibrium by shocks. These shocks may be temporary or permanent, anticipated or unanticipated. Depending on the type of shock, the equilibrium position of the economy may stay unchanged or it may alter; and optimal adjustment back to equilibrium may be instantaneous or slow. The path followed by the economy during its adjustment back to equilibrium is commonly called the business cycle, even though the path may not be a true cycle. Although the economy will not be in long-run equilibrium during the adjustment, it is behaving optimally during the adjustment back to long-run equilibrium. In effect, it is attaining a sequence of temporary equilibria, each of which is optimal at that time.

The traditional aim of stabilization policy is to speed up the return to equilibrium. This is more relevant when market imperfections due to, for example, monopolistic competition and price inflexibilities have caused a loss of output, and hence economic welfare, than it is in our basic model, where there are neither explicit markets nor market imperfections. We return to these issues in chapters 9 and 13.

Real-business-cycle theory focuses on the effect on the economy of a particular type of shock: a technology (productivity) shock. We already have a model capable of analyzing this. The previous analysis has assumed that the economy is nonstochastic. In keeping with this assumption we presume that the technology shock is known to the whole economy the moment it occurs. A technology shock shifts the production function upwards. Thus for every value of the stock of capital k there is an increase in output y and hence in the marginal product of capital $F'(k)$. We consider both permanent and temporary technology shocks.

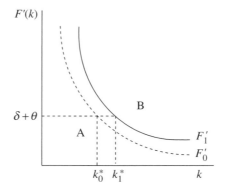

Figure 2.11. The effect on capital of a positive technology shock.

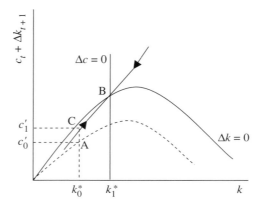

Figure 2.12. The effect on consumption of a positive technology shock.

2.5.2 Permanent Technology Shocks

A positive technology shock increases the marginal product of capital. This is depicted in figure 2.11 as a shift from F'_0 to F'_1. As $\delta + \theta$ is unchanged, the equilibrium optimal level of capital increases from k^*_0 to k^*_1.

The exact dynamics of this increase and the effect on consumption is shown in figure 2.12. A positive technology shock shifts the curve relating consumption to the capital stock upwards. The original equilibrium was at A, the new equilibrium is at B, and the saddlepath now goes through B. As the economy must always be on the saddlepath, how does the economy get from A to B? The capital stock is initially k^*_0 and it takes one period before it can change. As the productivity increase raises output in period t, and the capital stock is fixed, consumption will increase in period t so that the economy moves from A to C, which is on the new saddlepath. There will also be extra investment in period t. By period $t + 1$ this investment will have caused an increase in the stock of capital, which will produce a further increase in output and consumption. In period $t + 1$, therefore, the economy starts to move along the saddlepath—in geometrically declining steps—until it reaches the new equilibrium at B. Thus a permanent positive technology shock causes both consumption and capital to increase, but in the first period—the short run—only consumption increases.

2.5.3 Temporary Technology Shocks

If the positive technology shock lasts for just one period, then there is no change in the long-run equilibrium levels of consumption and capital. The increase in output in period t is therefore consumed and no net investment takes place. In period $t + 1$ the original equilibrium level of consumption is restored. If the shock is negative, then consumption would decrease.

This can also be interpreted as roughly what happens when there is a temporary supply shock. Business-cycle dynamics can be explained in a similar way, though in a deep recession there is usually time for the capital stock to change too. As the economy comes out of recession the level of the capital stock is restored.

2.5.4 The Stability and Dynamics of the Golden Rule Revisited

Further understanding of the stability and dynamics of the golden rule solution can now be obtained. The golden rule equilibrium occurs at point A in figure 2.10. It will be recalled that the golden rule does not discount the future and therefore implicitly sets $\theta = 0$. As a result the vertical line dividing the east and west regions now goes through A, which is an equilibrium point.

The model appropriate for the golden rule can be thought of as using a modified version of the Euler equation (2.12) in which the marginal utility functions are omitted. The Euler equation therefore becomes $F'(k) = \delta$, in which there are no dynamics at all. This equation determines k_t. The other equation is the resource constraint, equation (2.17), and this determines c_t. Thus the only dynamics in the model are those associated with equation (2.17), and these concern the capital stock.

At every point on the curved line in figure 2.10—except the point $\{c^\#, k^\#\}$—we have $\Delta k_{t+1} < 0$. At the point $\{c^\#, k^\#\}$ we have $\Delta k_{t+1} = 0$. This point is therefore an equilibrium, but, as we have seen, it is not a stable equilibrium because achieving maximum consumption at each point in time requires absorbing all positive shocks through higher consumption and all negative shocks by consuming the capital stock, which reduces future consumption. Thus, after a negative shock the economy is unable to regain equilibrium if it continues to consume as required by the golden rule.

The lack of stability of the golden rule solution can be attributed to the impatience of the economy. By trading off consumption today against consumption in the future, and by discounting future consumption, the optimal solution is a stable equilibrium.

We now consider two extensions to the basic model that involve labor and investment.

2.6   Labor in the Basic Model

In the basic model labor is not included explicitly. Implicitly, it has been assumed that households are involved in production and spend a given fixed
amount of time working. In an extension of the basic model we allow people to
choose between work and leisure, and how much of their time they spend on
each. Only leisure is assumed to provide utility directly; work provides utility
indirectly by generating income for consumption. This enables us to derive a
labor-supply function and an implicit wage rate. In practice, people can usually
choose whether or not to work, but have limited freedom in the number of
hours they may choose. We take up this point in chapter 4.

Suppose that the total amount of time available for all activities is normalized
to one unit—in effect it has been assumed in the basic model considered so far
that labor input is the whole unit. We now assume instead that households have
a choice between work n_t and leisure l_t, where $n_t + l_t = 1$. Thus, in effect, in
the basic model, $n_t = 1$. We now allow n_t to be chosen by households.

We assume that households receive utility from consumption and leisure and
so we rewrite the instantaneous utility function as $U(c_t, l_t)$, where the partial
derivatives $U_c > 0$, $U_l > 0$, $U_{cc} \leqslant 0$, and $U_{ll} \leqslant 0$. In other words, there is
positive, but diminishing, marginal utility to both consumption and leisure. For
convenience, we assume that $U_{cl} = 0$, which rules out substitution between consumption and leisure. We also assume that labor is a second factor of production, so that the production function becomes $F(k_t, n_t)$, with $F_k > 0$, $F_{kk} \leqslant 0$,
$F_n > 0$, $F_{nn} \leqslant 0$, $F_{kn} \geqslant 0$, $\lim_{k \to \infty} F_k = \infty$, $\lim_{k \to 0} F_k = 0$, $\lim_{l \to \infty} F_n = \infty$, and
$\lim_{l \to 0} F_n = 0$, which are the Inada conditions.

The economy maximizes discounted utility subject to the national resource
constraint

$$F(k_t, n_t) = c_t + k_{t+1} - (1 - \delta)k_t$$

and the labor constraint $n_t + l_t = 1$. Often it will be more convenient to replace
l_t by $1 - n_t$ but, for the sake of clarity, here we introduce the labor constraint
explicitly.

The Lagrangian is therefore

$$\mathcal{L}_t = \sum_{s=0}^{\infty} \{\beta^s U(c_{t+s}, l_{t+s}) + \lambda_{t+s}[F(k_{t+s}, n_{t+s}) - c_{t+s} - k_{t+s+1} + (1 - \delta)k_{t+s}]$$
$$+ \mu_{t+s}[1 - n_{t+s} - l_{t+s}]\},$$

which is maximized with respect to $\{c_{t+s}, l_{t+s}, n_{t+s}, k_{t+s+1}, \lambda_{t+s}, \mu_{t+s}; s \geqslant 0\}$.
The first-order conditions are

$$\frac{\partial \mathcal{L}_t}{\partial c_{t+s}} = \beta^s U_{c,t+s} - \lambda_{t+s} = 0, \quad s \geqslant 0, \tag{2.25}$$

$$\frac{\partial \mathcal{L}_t}{\partial l_{t+s}} = \beta^s U_{l,t+s} - \mu_{t+s} = 0, \quad s \geqslant 0, \tag{2.26}$$

$$\frac{\partial \mathcal{L}_t}{\partial n_{t+s}} = \lambda_{t+s} F_{n,t+s} - \mu_{t+s} = 0, \qquad\qquad s \geqslant 0, \qquad (2.27)$$

$$\frac{\partial \mathcal{L}_t}{\partial k_{t+s}} = \lambda_{t+s}[F_{k,t+s} + 1 - \delta] - \lambda_{t+s-1} = 0, \quad s > 0. \qquad (2.28)$$

From the first-order conditions for consumption and capital we obtain the same solutions as for the basic model. The consumption Euler equation for $s = 1$ is as before:

$$\beta \frac{U_{c,t+1}}{U_{c,t}}[F_{k,t+1} + 1 - \delta] = 1. \qquad (2.29)$$

Eliminating λ_{t+s} and μ_{t+s} from the first-order conditions for consumption, leisure, and employment gives, for $s = 0$,

$$U_{l,t} = U_{c,t} F_{n,t}. \qquad (2.30)$$

This has the following interpretation. Consider giving up $dl_t = -dn_t < 0$ units of leisure. The loss of utility is $U_{l,t}\, dl_t < 0$, which is the left-hand side of equation (2.30). This is compensated by an increase in utility due to producing extra output of $F_{n,t}\, dn_t = -F_{n,t}\, dl_t$. When consumed, each unit of output gives an extra $U_{c,t}$ in utility, implying a total increase in utility of $-U_{c,t}F_{n,t}\, dl_t > 0$, which is the right-hand side of equation (2.30) when $dl_t = -1$.

The long-run solution is obtained sequentially. In steady-state equilibrium the long-run solution for capital is obtained from

$$F_k = \theta + \delta,$$

where $\beta = 1/(1 + \theta)$. The long-run solution for consumption is then obtained from the resource constraint. So far this is the same as for the basic model. Given c and k, we solve for l_t and n_t from equation (2.30) and the labor constraint. The short-run solutions for c_t and k_t are the same as before. The short-run dynamics for l_t are similar to those for c_t.

We can now obtain expressions for the wage rate and the total rate of return to capital, which are implicit in the model but have not been defined explicitly. If the production function is a homogeneous function of degree one (implying that the production function has constant returns to scale), then we can show that[1]

$$F(k_t, n_t) = F_{n,t} n_t + F_{k,t} k_t. \qquad (2.31)$$

Recalling that the general price level is unity, equation (2.31) says that the total value of output is shared between labor and capital. The first term on the right-hand side is the share of labor and the second is the share of capital. If labor is paid its marginal product, then this is also the implied wage rate, i.e., $F_{n,t} = w_t$, with each unit of labor having a cost (receiving a return) equal to the wage rate. Similarly, if capital is paid its (net) marginal product, then $F_{k,t} - \delta = r_t$ is the

---

[1] A function $f(x, y)$ that is homogeneous of degree α satisfies $\lambda^\alpha f(x, y) = f(\lambda x, \lambda y)$. Alternatively, we could take a first-order expansion of the production function $F(k_t, n_t)$ about $k_t = n_t = 0$, which would give the approximation $F(k_t, n_t) \simeq F_{n,t} n_t + F_{k,t} k_t$.

return on capital. Thus, $F_{n,t}$ and $F_{k,t} - \delta$ are the implicit wage and rate of return to capital in the basic model.

Consequently, we can write equation (2.31) as

$$F(k_t, n_t) = w_t n_t + (r_t + \delta)k_t.$$

It follows that the real wage can also be expressed as

$$w_t = \frac{F(k_t, n_t) - (r_t + \delta)k_t}{n_t}.$$

In the steady state, when $r_t = \theta$, these become

$$F(k^*, n^*) = wn^* + (\theta + \delta)k^*,$$
$$w^* = \frac{F(k^*, n^*) - (\theta + \delta)k^*}{n^*}.$$

As previously noted, labor was not included explicitly in the basic model. But if we assume that $n_t = 1$, then, in effect, labor was included implicitly. The implied real wage is then

$$w_t = F(k_t, 1) - F_{k,t}k_t$$
$$= F(k_t) - (r_t + \delta)k_t.$$

In equilibrium this is

$$w^* = F(k^*) - (\theta + \delta)k^*.$$

To summarize, we have found that when we allow people to choose how much to work and we determine the wage rate and the rate of return to capital explicitly, the solutions for consumption and capital are virtually unchanged from those of the basic model. This suggests that where appropriate and convenient we may continue to omit labor explicitly from the analysis knowing that it is present implicitly. Moreover, the wage rate and the rate of return to capital, although not explicitly included either, are also defined implicitly.

2.7 Investment

Investment is included explicitly in the basic model, but the emphasis is on the capital stock, not investment. We have assumed previously that there are no costs to installing new capital. We now consider investment and capital accumulation when there are installation costs. Although we focus on Tobin's (1969) q-theory of investment (see also Hayashi 1982), which has the effect of complicating the dynamic behavior of the economy, there are other ways to account for the effects of investment on dynamic behavior. One alternative examined below is to assume that it takes time to install new investment. This is the approach adopted by Kydland and Prescott (1982) and they called it "time to build."

2.7.1 *q*-Theory

In the basic model the focus was on obtaining the optimal levels of consumption and the capital stock. As the change in the stock of capital equals gross investment net of depreciation, this also implies a theory of net investment. We saw that following a permanent change in the long-run equilibrium level of capital, it is optimal if the actual level of capital adjusts to its new equilibrium over time along the saddlepath. The adjustment path for capital implies an optimal level of investment each period. This optimal level of investment will differ each period until the new long-run general equilibrium level of capital is attained. At this point investment is only replacing depreciated capital. Although capital takes time to adjust to its new steady-state level, investment in the basic model adjusts instantaneously to the level that is optimal for each period. In practice, however, due to costs of installation, it is usually optimal to adjust investment more slowly. As a result, the dynamic behavior of capital reflects both adjustment processes.

To illustrate, suppose that new investment imposes an additional resource cost of $\frac{1}{2}\phi i_t/k_t$ for each unit of investment, where $\phi > 0$. In other words, the cost of a unit of investment depends on how large it is in relation to the size of the existing capital stock. We choose this particular functional form due to its mathematical convenience and the consequent ease of interpreting the results. The resource constraint facing the economy now becomes nonlinear in i_t and k_t and is given by

$$F(k_t) = c_t + \left(1 + \frac{\phi}{2}\frac{i_t}{k_t}\right)i_t, \quad \phi \geqslant 0, \tag{2.32}$$

where for simplicity we have reverted to the assumption that capital is the sole factor of production and we ignore leisure. Since our primary interest here is investment we do not combine the resource constraint with the capital accumulation equation, but treat them as two separate constraints.

The Lagrangian for maximizing the present value of utility is therefore

$$\mathcal{L}_t = \sum_{s=0}^{\infty} \left\{ \beta^s U(c_{t+s}) + \lambda_{t+s}\left[F(k_{t+s}) - c_{t+s} - i_{t+s} - \frac{\phi}{2}\frac{i_t^2}{k_t}\right] \right.$$
$$\left. + \mu_{t+s}[i_{t+s} - k_{t+s+1} + (1-\delta)k_{t+s}] \right\}.$$

The first-order conditions are

$$\frac{\partial \mathcal{L}_t}{\partial c_{t+s}} = \beta^s U_{c,t+s} - \lambda_{t+s} = 0, \qquad\qquad s \geqslant 0,$$

$$\frac{\partial \mathcal{L}_t}{\partial i_{t+s}} = -\lambda_{t+s}\left(1 + \phi\frac{i_t}{k_t}\right) + \mu_{t+s} = 0, \qquad\qquad s \geqslant 0,$$

$$\frac{\partial \mathcal{L}_t}{\partial k_{t+s}} = \lambda_{t+s}\left[F_{k,t+s} + \frac{\phi}{2}\left(\frac{i_t}{k_t}\right)^2\right] - \mu_{t+s-1} + (1-\delta)\mu_{t+s} = 0, \quad s > 0.$$

The first-order condition for investment implies that

$$i_{t+s} = \frac{1}{\phi}(q_{t+s} - 1)k_{t+s}, \quad s \geqslant 0, \tag{2.33}$$

where the ratio of the Lagrange multipliers

$$q_{t+s} = \frac{\mu_{t+s}}{\lambda_{t+s}} \geqslant 1 \tag{2.34}$$

is called Tobin's q. It follows that investment will take place in period $t + s$ provided $q_{t+s} > 1$.

q can be interpreted as follows. An extra unit of capital raises output, and hence consumption and utility, and λ is the marginal benefit in terms of the utility of sacrificing a unit of current consumption in order to have an extra unit of investment, and hence the extra capital. Similarly, μ is the marginal benefit in terms of utility of an extra unit of investment. Thus q measures the benefit from investment per unit of benefit from capital. Expressing utility in terms of units of output, q can also be interpreted as the ratio of the market value of one unit of investment to its cost.

Combining the three first-order conditions, we obtain the following nonlinear dynamic relation when $s = 1$:

$$F_{k,t+1} = \frac{U_{c,t}}{\beta U_{c,t+1}} q_t - (1 - \delta)q_{t+1} - \frac{1}{2\phi}(q_{t+1} - 1)^2. \tag{2.35}$$

This equation together with equations (2.32)–(2.34) and the capital accumulation equation form a system of four nonlinear dynamic equations that we can solve for the decision variables c_t, k_t, i_t, and q_t.

2.7.1.1 Long-Run Solution

In the steady-state long run we have $\Delta c_t = \Delta k_t = \Delta i_t = \Delta q_t = 0$. In the long run the capital accumulation equation and equation (2.33) imply that

$$\frac{i}{k} = \delta = \frac{1}{\phi}(q - 1).$$

Hence, the long-run value of q is

$$q = 1 + \phi\delta \geqslant 1. \tag{2.36}$$

The long-run level of the capital stock is obtained from the steady-state solution of equation (2.35). From $\beta = 1/(1 + \theta)$, and using the long-run solution for q, equation (2.35) can be written as

$$F_k = \theta + \delta + \phi\delta(\theta + \tfrac{1}{2}\delta) \geqslant \theta + \delta. \tag{2.37}$$

In the absence of costs of installation, $\phi = 0$, and so $q_t = 1$ and $F_k = \theta + \delta$, which is the same result as that obtained in the basic closed-economy model. From figure 2.5, in order for $F_k \geqslant \theta + \delta$, a lower level of capital is required, implying that installation costs reduce the optimal long-run level of the capital stock and hence also the optimal long-run levels of consumption and investment. This is because installation costs reduce the resources available for consumption and investment.

2.7.1.2 Short-Run Dynamics

Introducing installation costs affects the short-run dynamic behavior of the economy as well as its long-run solution. To gain some insight into the effects of installation costs on dynamic behavior we analyze an approximation to equation (2.35) obtained by assuming that consumption is at its steady-state level and using a linear approximation to the quadratic term in q_{t+1} about q, its steady-state level given by equation (2.36). As a result, we are able to approximate equation (2.35) by the forward-looking equation

$$q_t = \beta q_{t+1} + \beta(F_{k,t+1} - \delta - \tfrac{1}{2}\phi\delta^2).$$

Using the steady-state level of $F_{k,t+1}$ given by equation (2.37), this equation can be rewritten in terms of deviations from long-run equilibrium as

$$q_t - q = \beta(q_{t+1} - q) + \beta(F_{k,t+1} - F_k). \tag{2.38}$$

Solving this forwards, the solution for q_t is

$$q_t - q = \sum_{s=0}^{\infty} \beta^{s+1}(F_{k,t+s+1} - F_k).$$

A further interpretation of q_t can now be provided. It is the present value of the extra output produced by undertaking one more unit of investment. The greater this is, the more investment will be undertaken in period t. Since the price of one unit of investment is one, $q_t - 1$ is the increase in the implied value of the firm.

In practice, the measurement of q_t presents a problem. Although q_t can be interpreted as the ratio of the market value of one unit of investment to its cost, it is often estimated by the ratio of the market value of a firm to its book value. This implies using the average value of current and past investment instead of the marginal value of new investment.

Consider next the dynamic interaction between k_t and q_t. Two equations capture this. The first is equation (2.38). The second is obtained by using (2.33) to eliminate i_t from the capital accumulation equation to give

$$i_t = \frac{1}{\phi}(q_t - 1)k_t = k_{t+1} - (1 - \delta)k_t.$$

We therefore have two nonlinear equations:

$$q_t - q = \beta(q_{t+1} - q) + \beta(F_{k,t+1} - F_k),$$
$$(q_t - q + \phi)k_t = \phi k_{t+1}.$$

These can be linearly approximated about the steady-state levels of k_t and q_t as

$$(1 - \beta)(q_t - q) - \beta F_{kk}(k_t - k) = \beta \Delta q_{t+1} + \beta F_{kk} \Delta k_{t+1}, \tag{2.39}$$
$$k(q_t - q) = \phi \Delta k_{t+1}, \tag{2.40}$$

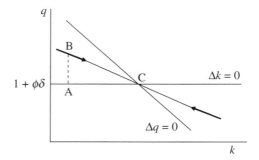

Figure 2.13. Phase diagram for q.

where k is the steady-state level of k_t. Thus, as $F_{kk} < 0$, in steady state k_t is negatively related to q_t through

$$k_t - k = \frac{\theta}{F_{kk}}(q_t - q). \tag{2.41}$$

2.7.1.3   The Effect of a Productivity Increase

The dynamic behavior of k_t and q_t can be illustrated by considering the effect of a permanent increase in capital productivity. In figure 2.13 the line $\Delta q = 0$ depicts the long-run relation between k_t and q_t given by equation (2.41). This was derived from equation (2.39) by setting $\Delta k_{t+1} = \Delta q_{t+1} = 0$. The line $\Delta k = 0$ gives the long-run equilibrium level of k_t and is obtained from equation (2.40) by setting $\Delta k_{t+1} = 0$. Before the productivity increase these two lines intersected at A. Note that at this initial equilibrium $q_t = 1$. Following the productivity increase there is a "jump" increase in q_t so that $q_t > 1$. This induces a rise in investment above its normal replacement level δk. Initially, k_t remains unchanged and so the economy moves to point B. New investment increases the capital stock each period until the economy reaches its new long-run equilibrium at C by moving along the saddlepath from B. At this point q_t is restored to its long-run equilibrium level of one and the equilibrium capital stock, output, and consumption are permanently higher.

2.7.2   Time to Build

An alternative way of reformulating the basic model that results in more general dynamics is to assume that it takes time to install new investment. Kydland and Prescott (1982) were the first to incorporate this idea from neoclassical investment theory into their real-business-cycle DGE macroeconomic model (see also Altug 1989).

   Taking account of time-to-build effects results in a respecification of the capital accumulation equation (2.2). Consider two ways of doing this. Suppose, first, that investment expenditures recorded at time t are the result of decisions to invest i_t^s made earlier. Moreover, suppose that a proportion φ_i of recorded investment in period t is investment starts made in period $t - i$, then we can write

$$i_t = \sum_{i=0}^{\infty} \varphi_i i^s_{t-i}. \tag{2.42}$$

If there is a lag in installation, the initial values of φ_i may be zero; and if the lag is finite, then $\varphi_i = 0$ for some $i > J > 0$. The capital accumulation equation (2.2) remains unchanged. We now carry out the optimization of discounted utility with respect to i_t and i^s_t as well as consumption and capital subject to the extra constraint, equation (2.42). This is the Kydland and Prescott approach.

An alternative possible formulation is to assume that a proportion φ_i of investment undertaken in period t is installed and ready for use as part of the capital stock by period $t + i$. Equation (2.2) may therefore be rewritten as

$$\Delta k_{t+1} = \sum_{i=0}^{\infty} \varphi_i i_{t-i} - \delta k_t, \tag{2.43}$$

where $\sum_{i=0}^{J} \varphi_i = 1$. The shape of the distributed lag function will reflect the costs of installation. A modification of this is to incorporate depreciation in φ_i and assume that it reflects the proportion of investment undertaken in period t that contributes to productive capital in period $t + i$. Equation (2.43) can then be rewritten with $\delta = 0$. As a result, using the national income identity (2.1) and the production function, the economy's resource constraint becomes

$$\Delta k_{t+1} = \sum_{i=0}^{\infty} \varphi_i [F(k_{t-i}) - c_{t-i}]. \tag{2.44}$$

We may now maximize $\sum_{s=0}^{\infty} \beta^s U(c_{t+s})$ subject to equation (2.44).

2.8 Conclusions

In this highly simplified account of macroeconomics we have developed a skeleton model that provides the basic framework that will be built on in the rest of the book. The framework itself will need little change, but more detail will be required.

The key features of the macroeconomy that we have represented are the economy's objectives (its preferences), the resource constraint facing the economy (which is derived from the production function, the capital accumulation equation, and the national income identity), and the endowment of the economy (its initial capital stock). We have shown that the central issues are intertemporal: whether to consume today or in the future, and whether to maximize consumption each period or take account of future consumption. Consumption in the future is increased by consuming less today and by saving today's surplus and investing it in additional capital in order to produce, and hence to consume, more in the future. Trying to maximize today's consumption without considering future consumption, or preservation of the capacity to produce in the future, is shown to destabilize the economy, leaving it vulnerable to negative output shocks.

We have found that the dynamics of the basic model derive from just two sources: the intertemporal utility function and the presence of the change in stocks in the resource constraint. An important issue in macroeconomics is the extent to which the dynamic behavior of the macroeconomy can be attributed to these two factors, or whether accounting for business cycles requires additional features.

We have extended the basic model in two ways. One allowed people flexibility in their choice between work and leisure. We were then able to derive a labor-supply function and to obtain an implicit measure of the wage rate. We found that the solutions for consumption and capital were virtually unchanged from those of the basic model. This suggests that, where appropriate and convenient, we may continue to omit labor explicitly, recognizing that it is present implicitly.

The second extension was to take account of the cost of installing capital. As a result, we were able to derive the investment function. In the absence of costs of installing capital, investment takes place instantaneously, even though it takes time for capital to adjust to the desired level. Introducing installation costs for new investment has the effect of delaying the completion of new investment and slowing down the adjustment of the capital stock even more. Having considered the theory of investment that arises from the presence of costs of installing capital and noted the extra complexity it brings to the analysis of the short-run behavior of the economy, for simplicity we will assume hereafter that there are no capital installation costs.

The basic model provides a centralized analysis of the economy. In chapter 4 we decentralize the decisions of households and firms and introduce goods and labor markets to coordinate their decisions.

For further discussion of the basic model see Blanchard and Fischer (1989) and Intriligator (1971).

3

Economic Growth

3.1 Introduction

In our analysis of the basic model we have assumed that in long-run equilibrium the economy will be static. A more realistic description of most economies is that they are growing through time and that in the long run the rate of growth is constant and positive. In other words, the steady state is a path involving growth. In this chapter we consider how to modify the previous analysis to accommodate steady-state growth. We are then able to reinterpret the basic model as representing the behavior of the economy about its steady-state growth path. This decomposition of the dynamic behavior of the economy into a steady-state growth path and deviations from it is retained only implicitly in subsequent chapters as we omit explicit discussion of the growth path and focus only on the deviations from it. We do so in the knowledge that this is not a full description of the economy. The key references on the theory of growth are Cass (1965), Koopmans (1967), Shell (1967), Solow (1956), and Swan (1956). For more recent surveys see Aghion and Howitt (1998), Howitt (1999), and Barro and Sala-i-Martin (2004).

There are three main causes of economic growth: increases in the stock of capital; technological progress embodied in new capital equipment; and growth in labor input due primarily to population growth, immigration, changes in participation rates, and human capital. Hours of work have tended to decline slowly over time in more developed countries, but we assume that they are constant. It could be argued, with good reason, that technological change simply reflects advances in human knowledge acquired from education and research and development. Economic growth should therefore be ascribed to labor and not to capital. This is the basis of endogenous theories of economic growth. Nonetheless, our discussion will proceed as though technical progress appears exogenously at a constant rate μ. Population growth has affected different countries at different times. For example, in the United States, population growth brought about by immigration has always been an important source of growth. In Europe and Japan population growth has been much less important than capital accumulation. More recently, immigration into the United Kingdom as a result of the expansion of the European Union (EU) has contributed to raising

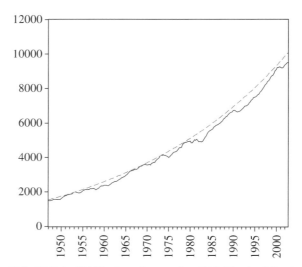

Figure 3.1. U.S. GDP (solid line) and capacity GDP (dashed line) 1947–2002.

the United Kingdom's rate of growth of GDP. We assume that the population grows in our economy at the constant rate n.

The importance of economic growth is revealed in figure 3.1, which plots GDP and an estimate of full-capacity GDP for the United States in the period 1947:1–2002:4. The main feature of this graph is the growth of full-capacity GDP. In comparison, deviations of GDP from full capacity are relatively minor. Insofar as economic welfare depends on output, this suggests that the gains from growth are far more important than those from stabilization, yet historically macroeconomics has been much more concerned with stabilization than with growth. A rough estimate of the relative importance of stabilization is the ratio of cumulative actual output over the period to cumulative capacity output. This is 94.8%, implying that only 5.2% of output was lost as a result of not operating at full capacity. This measure of the output loss is likely to be an underestimate as capacity output is endogenous and is linked to the level of the capital stock and investment. As the capital stock and investment are expected to be higher when the economy is operating close to full capacity, with perfect stabilization capacity output is likely to have been larger than implied by figure 3.1.

3.2 Modeling Economic Growth

We now turn to the issue of how to modify our previous analysis, which assumed a zero rate of long-run growth. We make three changes to the model. All affect the production function, which is now specified as

$$Y_t = F(K_t, N_t, t).$$

In this chapter, we use capital letters for total output, capital, and labor, and lowercase letters for the corresponding per capita values. Previously, output and capital were measured in per capita terms. First, we take account of the size of the population, N_t, and assume that the entire population work. Second, we introduce the total level of output in the economy, Y_t, and the total capital stock, K_t. Third, we allow the production function to shift with time at the constant rate μ, hence the inclusion of t in the production function. This is designed to capture technological progress. In this formulation, technical progress occurs exogenously; it is not the result of an explicit economic decision and there are no resource costs. A more realistic model of technological development would be to assume that it requires resources to produce it such as human capital, which is created in part by educational investment, and research and development expenditures. This would imply that technical progress is endogenous to the economy, and not exogenous. We examine this case later in the chapter.

To make matters more transparent, we make the convenient and widely used assumption that the production function has the constant-returns Cobb–Douglas form:

$$Y_t = (1 + \mu)^t K_t^\alpha N_t^{1-\alpha}.$$

This implies that technical progress is neutral and not factor-augmenting or biased. Thus it raises the productivity of both factors. In practice, technical progress is also likely to be embodied in new capital, making new capital more productive, and hence raising the marginal product of labor.

The production function can be rewritten in per capita terms as

$$y_t = (1 + \mu)^t k_t^\alpha,$$

where $y_t = Y_t/N_t$ and $k_t = K_t/N_t$.

The national income identity becomes

$$Y_t = C_t + I_t,$$

where C_t is total consumption, I_t is total investment, and the capital accumulation equation is

$$\Delta K_{t+1} = I_t - \delta K_t.$$

As $\Delta N_{t+1}/N_t = n$,

$$N_t = (1 + n)^t N_0,$$

where N_0 is the population level in the base period.

We consider two approaches: the Solow–Swan theory of growth and the "theory of optimal growth." The Solow–Swan theory is akin to the golden rule and the theory of optimal growth is a generalization of the optimal solution. We show that the key difference between the two theories reduces to their treatment of savings.

3.3   The Solow–Swan Model of Growth

3.3.1   Theory

The original aim of the Solow–Swan theory of growth was to provide a model of balanced growth under exogenous technological change. It can also be used to discuss optimization of the rate of growth of output per capita, y_t, each period (see Solow 1956; Swan 1956). We can see from the production function that this is equivalent to maximizing capital per capita, k_t.

The savings rate for the economy is

$$s_t = 1 - \frac{C_t}{Y_t}$$
$$= 1 - \frac{c_t}{y_t}.$$

The key assumption in the Solow–Swan model is that the economy has a constant savings rate so that $s_t = s$.

If all savings are invested, then

$$s_t = \frac{I_t}{Y_t} = i_t.$$

As the savings rate is constant, so is the investment rate.

The rate of growth of capital is

$$\frac{\Delta K_{t+1}}{K_t} = \frac{I_t}{K_t} - \delta$$
$$= \frac{I_t / Y_t}{K_t / Y_t} - \delta$$
$$= s\frac{Y_t / N_t}{K_t / N_t} - \delta$$
$$= s\frac{y_t}{k_t} - \delta.$$

Hence the rate of growth of capital per capita is

$$\frac{\Delta k_{t+1}}{k_t} = \frac{\Delta K_{t+1}}{K_t} - \frac{\Delta N_{t+1}}{N_t}$$
$$= s\frac{y_t}{k_t} - (\delta + n),$$

and so the capital accumulation equation is

$$\Delta k_{t+1} = sy_t - (\delta + n)k_t. \tag{3.1}$$

Equation (3.1) says that the change in capital per capita equals gross investment per capita (which is equal to savings sy_t) less depreciation and an adjustment that allows for the fact that capital has to grow extra fast to keep ahead of population growth.

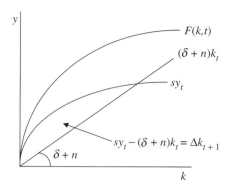

Figure 3.2. Total output and saving.

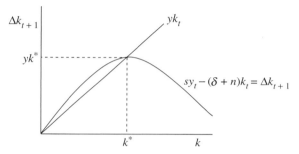

Figure 3.3. Capital accumulation.

What is the maximum rate of change in capital per capita, k_t, that the economy can sustain? Consider figures 3.2 and 3.3, in which all variables are measured in per capita terms.

Figure 3.2 depicts the production function, gross investment per capita, and the drag on growth in capital per capita caused by depreciation and population growth. Δk_{t+1} is measured by the distance between sy_t and $(\delta + n)k_t$.

Figure 3.3 plots Δk_{t+1} against k_t. The slope of a straight line through the origin, which can be written as $\Delta k_{t+1} = yk_t$, denotes the rate of growth of capital, namely, y. The maximum rate of growth is at the origin when $k_t = 0$. The highest point on the curve denotes the maximum value of Δk_{t+1} that is achievable, but not the maximum rate of growth. The line from the origin is drawn through this point. Let the value of capital per capita at this point be k^*. Choosing a $k_t > k^*$ would be suboptimal as the rate of growth of k_t would be lower than is necessary. Choosing $k_t < k^*$ would generate a higher rate of growth in k_t but this would not be sustainable because output would be at too low a level.

The relation between the rate of growth of capital and its level can be shown more formally using the fact that the rate of growth of the capital stock is a function of the size of the capital stock, i.e.,

$$y(k_t) = s\frac{y_t}{k_t} - (\delta + n).$$

We then find that

$$\frac{dy(k_t)}{dk_t} = \frac{s}{k_t}\left[\frac{\partial y_t}{\partial k_t} - \frac{y_t}{k_t}\right] = -\frac{sy_t}{k_t^2}\left[1 - \frac{k_t}{y_t}\frac{\partial y_t}{\partial k_t}\right] < 0,$$

because the capital elasticity

$$\frac{k_t}{y_t}\frac{\partial y_t}{\partial k_t} < 1.$$

Thus, due to the declining marginal product of capital, the larger the capital stock, the lower the rate of growth.

3.3.2 Growth and Economic Development

We can now draw some very important implications for economic development.

1. As $\partial y/\partial k < 0$, less developed (lower k) countries grow faster than more developed (higher k) countries.

2. As $\partial y/\partial s = y/k > 0$ and $\partial y/\partial\delta = \partial y/\partial n < 0$, a higher savings rate and lower rates of depreciation and population growth would increase y.

3. Technical progress would shift the production function up in each period and would increase y/k. As $\partial y/\partial(y/k) = s > 0$, it would therefore increase y.

Developed countries tend to have higher savings rates and more technical progress; developing countries tend to have higher rates of population growth. In practice, the growth advantage of developing countries due to having a higher marginal product of capital is often offset in per capita terms by higher population growth. Higher rates of technical progress in developed countries often sustain their economic growth rates.

3.3.3 Balanced Growth

The rate of growth of per capita output is

$$\frac{\Delta y_{t+1}}{y_t} = \frac{\Delta Y_{t+1}}{Y_t} - \frac{\Delta N_{t+1}}{N_t}$$

$$= \mu + \alpha\left[\frac{\Delta K_{t+1}}{K_t} - \frac{\Delta N_{t+1}}{N_t}\right]$$

$$= \mu + \alpha\frac{\Delta k_{t+1}}{k_t}$$

$$= \mu + \alpha\left[s\frac{y_t}{k_t} - (\delta + n)\right]$$

$$= \mu + \alpha y.$$

As $c_t = (1 - s)y_t$, the rate of growth of consumption per capita is given by

$$\frac{\Delta c_{t+1}}{c_t} = \frac{\Delta y_{t+1}}{y_t}.$$

Thus while the growth rates of per capita output and consumption are the same, the growth rate of capital per capita may be different. Such a situation is called unbalanced growth.

Balanced growth in the economy requires that per capita output, consumption, and capital all grow at the same rate. Since

$$\frac{\Delta y_{t+1}}{y_t} = \frac{\Delta c_{t+1}}{c_t} = \mu + a y,$$

$$\frac{\Delta k_{t+1}}{k_t} = y,$$

balanced growth requires that

$$y = \frac{\mu}{1 - \alpha}.$$

Thus, in this model, balanced growth is not possible unless there is technical progress.

3.4 The Theory of Optimal Growth

3.4.1 Theory

Instead of considering how to maximize output per capita we now turn our attention to the optimal level of consumption per capita when there is technical progress and population growth. This is rather like our earlier discussion comparing the golden rule with the optimal solution. In the basic static model we assumed implicitly that there was neither technical progress nor population growth. As a result, the long-run solution was a static equilibrium—now it will be a growth equilibrium. In other words, the previous solution $\{c^*, k^*\}$ becomes $\{c_t^*, k_t^*\}$ as the equilibrium is growing over time.

The key to obtaining the growth solution is to reinterpret the previous closed-economy model to take account of the changes we have made to the model. Having done this, it can be shown that the two solutions are essentially the same. For reasons that will become clear shortly, first we rewrite the production function as

$$Y_t = K_t^\alpha [(1 + \mu)^{t/(1-\alpha)} N_t]^{1-\alpha}$$
$$= K_t^\alpha (N_t^\#)^{1-\alpha},$$

where $N_t^\# = (1 + \mu)^{t/(1-\alpha)} N_t$ can be interpreted as effective labor input. Implicitly, this is equivalent to assuming that technical progress is labor augmenting, i.e., it improves the productivity of labor. We recall that every member of the population is assumed to work and that labor still satisfies $N_t = (1 + n)^t N_0$, hence we can write

$$N_t^\# = (1 + \mu)^{t/(1-\alpha)} N_t = [(1 + \mu)^{1/(1-\alpha)}]^t (1 + n)^t N_0 = (1 + \eta)^t N_0,$$

where we have used the approximation

$$[(1 + \mu)^{1/(1-\alpha)}]^t (1 + n)^t \simeq (1 + \eta)^t,$$

$$\eta \simeq n + \frac{\mu}{1 - \alpha}.$$

We now define output and capital per effective unit of labor (either current or base-period labor) to obtain

$$y_t^\# = \frac{Y_t}{N_t^\#} = \frac{Y_t}{[(1 + \mu)^{1/(1-\alpha)}]^t N_t} = \frac{Y_t}{(1 + \eta)^t N_0},$$

$$k_t^\# = \frac{K_t}{N_t^\#} = \frac{K_t}{[(1 + \mu)^{1/(1-\alpha)}]^t N_t} = \frac{K_t}{(1 + \eta)^t N_0}.$$

The production function can then be rewritten as

$$y_t^\# = k_t^{\#\alpha}.$$

Thus, by working in output and capital per effective unit of labor, the production function has been converted to the same form as we used previously. This was the reason for introducing the transformations.

The national income identity is unaffected and can be written as

$$y_t^\# = c_t^\# + i_t^\#,$$

where

$$c_t^\# = \frac{C_t}{N_t^\#} = \frac{C_t}{(1 + \eta)^t N_0},$$

$$i_t^\# = \frac{I_t}{N_t^\#} = \frac{I_t}{(1 + \eta)^t N_0}.$$

By dividing the capital accumulation equation

$$K_{t+1} = I_t + (1 - \delta)K_t$$

through by $N_t^\#$, it can be rewritten in terms of effective units of labor as

$$\frac{K_{t+1}}{[(1 + \mu)^{1/(1-\alpha)}]^{t+1} N_{t+1}} \frac{[(1 + \mu)^{1/(1-\alpha)}]^{t+1} N_{t+1}}{[(1 + \mu)^{1/(1-\alpha)}]^t N_t}$$

$$= \frac{I_t}{[(1 + \mu)^{1/(1-\alpha)}]^t N_t} + (1 - \delta) \frac{K_t}{[(1 + \mu)^{1/(1-\alpha)}]^t N_t},$$

or

$$[(1 + n)(1 + \mu)^{1/(1-\alpha)}]k_{t+1}^\# = i_t^\# + (1 - \delta)k_t^\#.$$

Hence,

$$(1 + \eta)k_{t+1}^\# = i_t^\# + (1 - \delta)k_t^\#.$$

The economy seeks to maximize

$$\sum_{s=0}^{\infty} \beta^s U(C_{t+s})$$

subject to

$$F(K_t) = C_t + K_{t+1} - (1 - \delta)K_t.$$

The utility function $U(C_t)$ can be rewritten in terms of c_t. Consider the power utility function

$$
\begin{aligned}
U(C_t) &= \frac{C_t^{1-\sigma} - 1}{1 - \sigma} \\
&= \frac{[(1 + \eta)^t N_0 c_t^{\#}]^{1-\sigma} - 1}{1 - \sigma} \\
&= \left[\frac{c_t^{\#1-\sigma} - [(1 + \eta)^t N_0]^{-(1-\sigma)}}{1 - \sigma} \right][(1 + \eta)^t N_0]^{(1-\sigma)}.
\end{aligned}
$$

Setting $N_0 = 1$ for convenience, but without loss of generality, the problem facing the economy can now be formulated as

$$\max_{c_{t+s}, k_{t+s}} \sum_{s=0}^{\infty} \tilde{\beta}^s \left[\frac{c_{t+s}^{\#1-\sigma} - [(1 + \eta)]^{-(1-\sigma)t}}{1 - \sigma} \right][(1 + \eta)]^{(1-\sigma)t},$$

where $\tilde{\beta} = \beta(1 + \eta)^{1-\sigma}$, subject to

$$k_t^{\#\alpha} = c_t^{\#} + (1 + \eta)k_{t+1}^{\#} - (1 - \delta)k_t^{\#}.$$

The Lagrangian is

$$
\begin{aligned}
\mathcal{L}_t = \sum_{s=0}^{\infty} \Bigg\{ \tilde{\beta}^s & \left[\frac{c_{t+s}^{\#1-\sigma} - (1 + \eta)^{-(1-\sigma)t}}{1 - \sigma} \right](1 + \eta)^{(1-\sigma)t} \\
& + \lambda_{t+s}[k_{t+s}^{\#\alpha} - c_{t+s}^{\#} - (1 + \eta)k_{t+s+1}^{\#} + (1 - \delta)k_{t+s}^{\#}] \Bigg\}.
\end{aligned}
$$

Thus the first-order conditions are

$$\frac{\partial \mathcal{L}_t}{\partial c_{t+s}^{\#}} = \tilde{\beta}^s c_{t+s}^{\#-\sigma}(1 + \eta)^{(1-\sigma)t} - \lambda_{t+s} = 0, \qquad\qquad s \geqslant 0,$$

$$\frac{\partial \mathcal{L}_t}{\partial k_{t+s}^{\#}} = \lambda_{t+s}[\alpha k_{t+s}^{\#\alpha-1} + 1 - \delta] - \lambda_{t+s-1}(1 + \eta) = 0, \quad s > 0.$$

Noting that for power utility

$$\frac{\tilde{\beta} U_{t+1}'}{U_t'} = \tilde{\beta}\left(\frac{c_{t+1}^{\#}}{c_t^{\#}}\right)^{-\sigma},$$

the Euler equation can be shown to be

$$\tilde{\beta}\left(\frac{c_{t+1}^{\#}}{c_t^{\#}}\right)^{-\sigma}[\alpha k_{t+1}^{\#\alpha-1} + 1 - \delta] = 1 + \eta.$$

This is similar in form to the Euler equation for the static economy that was derived previously, and reduces to the same Euler equation if $\eta = 0$.

In the presence of growth, the steady-state equilibrium condition is that the rates of growth of consumption and capital per effective unit of labor are zero. Thus $\Delta c_{t+1}^{\#} = \Delta k_{t+1}^{\#} = 0$ for each time period. In the absence of growth this

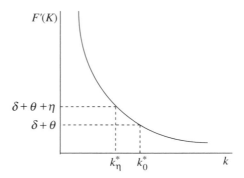

Figure 3.4.   Optimal capital in a growth equilibrium.

reduces to $\Delta c_{t+1} = \Delta k_{t+1} = 0$, the equilibrium condition for a static economy. Hence, in steady-state growth we obtain

$$\tilde{\beta}[\alpha k_{t+1}^{\#\alpha-1} + 1 - \delta] = 1 + \eta.$$

This implies that

$$F'(k^{\#*}) = \alpha(k^{\#*})^{\alpha-1} = \delta - 1 + \frac{1+\eta}{\beta(1+\eta)^{1-\sigma}} \simeq \delta + \theta + \sigma\left(n + \frac{\mu}{1-\alpha}\right),$$

where we have used a first-order Taylor series approximation:

$$\eta = n + \frac{\mu}{1-\alpha} \quad \text{and} \quad \beta = \frac{1}{1+\theta}.$$

The solution of $k^{\#*}$ is depicted in figure 3.4. The optimal level of $k^{\#*}$ can be compared with the model with no growth by setting $n = \mu = 0$. This would give $F'(k^{\#*}) = \delta + \theta$ once again.

We have specified the model in sufficient detail to be able to derive an expression for $k^{\#*}$ explicitly. Approximately, this is

$$k^{\#*} \simeq \left(\frac{\sigma(n + (\mu/(1-\alpha))) + \delta + \theta}{\alpha}\right)^{-1/(1-\alpha)}.$$

Although capital per effective unit of labor is constant along the equilibrium path, K_t/N_t, the capital stock per capita of the economy is growing through time. As

$$k_t^{\#} = \frac{K_t}{[(1+\mu)^{1/(1-\alpha)}]^t N_t},$$

it follows that the optimal path for capital per capita is

$$\frac{K_t}{N_t} = \left(\frac{\sigma(n + (\mu/(1-a))) + \delta + \theta}{\alpha}\right)^{-1/(1-\alpha)}[(1+\mu)^{1/(1-\alpha)}]^t.$$

Thus K_t/N_t grows at a rate of approximately $\mu/(1-\alpha)$.

The optimal growth rate of output per capita, Y_t/N_t, is determined from

$$y_t^{\#} = \frac{Y_t}{[(1+\mu)^{1/(1-\alpha)}]^t N_t}.$$

As $y_t^{\#} = k_t^{\#\alpha}$ and $\Delta k_{t+1}^{\#} = 0$, it follows that $\Delta y_{t+1}^{\#} = 0$ too. Consequently, the growth rate of Y_t/N_t is also approximately $\mu/(1-\alpha)$. The optimal growth rate of consumption per capita, C_t/N_t, can be obtained from the condition that $\Delta c_{t+1} = 0$ and $c_t^{\#} = C_t/([(1+\mu)^{1/(1-\alpha)}]^t N_t)$. Hence the growth rate of C_t/N_t is also approximately $\mu/(1-\alpha)$. The optimal growth rates of total output, total capital, and total consumption are obtained by taking into account population growth. Adding on the growth rate of the population, we obtain their common rate of growth $\eta = n + (\mu/(1-\alpha))$. As the growth rates of output, capital, and consumption are the same, the optimal solution is a balanced growth path.

3.4.2 Additional Remarks on Optimal Growth

The technical details of the solution to the problem of optimal growth may obscure how simple an extension it is to the static solution. Because growth is balanced, the steady-state growth paths of consumption, capital, output, and investment are the same; all are growing at the constant rate η. The per capita effective measures of these variables that we have introduced can be reinterpreted as proportional to deviations from their optimal growth paths. For example, if output on the optimal growth path is

$$
\begin{aligned}
Y_t^* &= (1+\eta)^t Y_0 \\
&= (1+\eta)^t N_0 \frac{Y_0}{N_0} \\
&= N_t^{\#} \frac{Y_0}{N_0},
\end{aligned}
$$

then

$$
y_t^{\#*} = \frac{Y_t}{N_t^{\#}} = \frac{Y_t}{Y_t^*} \frac{Y_0}{N_0}.
$$

As a result, the solution is essentially the same as that for the zero-growth case examined previously. These deviations have a static-equilibrium solution, and the short-run dynamics of the original variables of the model are now defined as deviations from the optimal growth path instead of about static equilibrium. This observation suggests that we do not need to consider the full solution about optimal growth paths in subsequent analysis. We can adopt the simplification of working in terms of static solutions, and presume that this would also describe dynamic behavior relative to the balanced steady-state growth path of the economy.

Comparing the Solow–Swan model with the optimal growth solution, the main similarity is that in equilibrium both have constant savings rates. This is because the savings rate along the optimal growth path is given by

$$
s_t = 1 - \frac{C_t}{Y_t} = 1 - \frac{c_t^{\#}}{y_t^{\#}}.
$$

Hence, the behavior along the optimal growth paths is the same. The main difference is that whereas the Solow–Swan model *assumes* a constant savings rate at all times, and this rate is determined exogenously, the savings rate in the optimal growth model is not determined exogenously, but is the result of preferences, technology, and the rates of depreciation and population growth. To see this, we note that, along the optimal growth path,

$$y_t^{\#} = k_t^{\#\alpha},$$
$$c_t^{\#} = k_t^{\#\alpha} - (\eta + \delta)k_t^{\#},$$
$$k_t^{\#} = \left(\frac{\sigma\eta + \delta + \theta}{\alpha}\right)^{-1/(1-\alpha)}.$$

Hence, the savings rate is the constant

$$s_t = \frac{\alpha(\eta + \delta)}{\sigma\eta + \delta + \theta} = \frac{\alpha(n + (\mu/(1 - \alpha)) + \delta)}{\sigma(n + (\mu/(1 - \alpha))) + \delta + \theta}.$$

Another difference between the two theories is in their implications for the short run. In the optimal growth model, in the short run the savings rate can deviate from its optimal level, whereas in the Solow–Swan model the savings rate is held constant in the short run. The dynamic behavior of the optimal growth model can be analyzed using the effective per capita definitions of consumption and capital, or in terms of the proportional deviations of total consumption and capital from their optimal growth paths. It follows that the dynamic behavior of these deviations is a saddlepath. The Solow–Swan model has the same type of short-run dynamics as the golden rule, and hence is an unstable solution.

3.5 Endogenous Growth

The theories above attribute economic growth to exogenous technical progress and to population increases. The rate of technical progress is treated as beyond the control of a country—it just happens. This is a useful simplification, but it is not, of course, a correct account of growth. Most countries probably acquire much of their new technology by importing it from other countries in the form of new products, and by adopting new processing methods developed elsewhere. Nonetheless, someone somewhere is developing the new technology.

Due to the diffusion of new technology through the world, with the consequence that different countries can adopt the same technology, countries with low unit costs of production—notably lower wage costs—will drive out those with higher costs. The only way for high-wage countries to compete is for them to innovate further, creating new products over which they have a degree of monopoly pricing power and new technologies that are labor saving and hence reduce unit costs. The implications are that technical progress is largely embodied in new products, especially new capital investments, and that technical progress occurs largely in developed countries, but that its advantages may not be long lasting.

In order to produce a steady stream of innovations it is necessary to invest in research and development activities and in human capital skills. In this way technical progress ceases to be exogenous, and becomes an endogenous economic decision. Modern theories of growth are of this sort: see, for example, Romer (1986, 1987, 1990), Rebelo (1991), and the surveys of Aghion and Howitt (1998) and Barro and Sala-i-Martin (2004). There are many models of endogenous growth.

3.5.1 The AK Model of Endogenous Growth

We consider the AK model (see Jones and Manuelli (1990) and also McGrattan (1998)). The name derives from the assumption that the production function takes the simple form

$$Y_t = AK_t, \quad A > 0,$$

where K_t is interpreted here to mean all capital, including human capital. We also note that technical progress may be embodied in new capital investment, thereby making new capital more productive than old capital. Computers are an obvious example. The key features of this model are that there is no exogenous technical progress and that there are constant returns to scale with respect to K_t.

We denote output per capita by y_t and capital per capita by k_t. Hence

$$y_t = Ak_t.$$

It follows from earlier results (equation (3.1)) that the rate of growth of k_t is

$$\gamma(k_t) = s_t \frac{y_t}{k_t} - (\delta + n)$$

$$= s_t A - (\delta + n).$$

If $s_t = s$, a constant, then the growth rate is constant. If $sA > \delta + n$, then the growth rate is constant and positive. Thus, unlike the earlier case, the rate of growth is not falling as the capital stock increases. This result is due to the assumption of a constant-returns-to-scale production function. Note also that the rate of growth is independent of the initial level of the capital stock. This implies that all countries, no matter their state of development (in particular, the current level of the capital stock), can achieve a constant rate of growth. The rate itself will depend upon the parameters s, A, δ, and n.

We have therefore shown that exogenous technical progress is not required to achieve growth when output has constant returns to scale with respect to total capital—physical and human. This result holds for both the Solow–Swan theory and the theory of optimal growth.

3.5.2 The Human Capital Model of Endogenous Growth

A more transparent treatment of human capital and its role in economic growth is obtained if we separate human capital from physical capital. Let h_t

denote human capital per capita and k_t physical capital and suppose that the production function per capita is

$$y_t = Ak_t^\alpha h_t^{1-\alpha}, \quad 0 \leqslant \alpha \leqslant 1.$$

Note that there is no exogenous technical progress. We assume that capital accumulation takes place as before, and that real resources are needed for human capital accumulation. Accordingly we write

$$\Delta k_{t+1} = i_t^k - \delta k_t,$$
$$\Delta h_{t+1} = i_t^h - \delta h_t,$$

where i_t^k and i_t^h are the levels of investment in physical and human capital, respectively. For convenience, we assume that the rate of population growth is zero and that the rate of depreciation δ for human capital is the same as that for physical capital. The national resource constraint satisfies

$$y_t = c_t + i_t^k + i_t^h.$$

The instantaneous utility function is power utility.

The optimal solution is given by maximizing the Lagrangian

$$\mathcal{L}_t = \sum_{s=0}^{\infty} \left\{ \beta^s \frac{c_{t+s}^{1-\sigma} - 1}{1 - \sigma} \right.$$
$$\left. + \lambda_{t+s}[Ak_{t+s}^\alpha h_{t+s}^{1-\alpha} - c_{t+s} - (k_{t+s+1} + h_{t+s+1}) + (1 - \delta)(k_{t+s} - h_{t+s})] \right\}.$$

The first-order conditions are

$$\frac{\partial \mathcal{L}_t}{\partial c_{t+s}} = \beta^s c_{t+s}^{-\sigma} - \lambda_{t+s} = 0, \qquad\qquad\qquad s = 0, 1, 2, \ldots,$$

$$\frac{\partial \mathcal{L}_t}{\partial k_{t+s}} = \lambda_{t+s}[\alpha Ak_{t+s}^{\alpha-1} h_{t+s}^{1-\alpha} + 1 - \delta] - \lambda_{t+s-1} = 0, \qquad s = 1, 2, \ldots,$$

$$\frac{\partial \mathcal{L}_t}{\partial h_{t+s}} = \lambda_{t+s}[(1 - \alpha) Ak_{t+s}^\alpha h_{t+s}^{-\alpha} + 1 - \delta] - \lambda_{t+s-1} = 0, \quad s = 1, 2, \ldots.$$

It follows that the Euler equation is

$$\beta \left(\frac{c_{t+1}}{c_t} \right)^{-\sigma} \left[\alpha A \left(\frac{k_{t+1}}{h_{t+1}} \right)^{-(1-\alpha)} + 1 - \delta \right] = 1$$

and that

$$\frac{k_{t+1}}{h_{t+1}} = \frac{\alpha}{1 - \alpha},$$

a constant. Thus, in equilibrium we may write $k_t/h_t = k/h$, and hence

$$\beta \left(\frac{c_{t+1}}{c_t} \right)^{-\sigma} \left[\alpha A \left(\frac{k}{h} \right)^{-(1-\alpha)} + 1 - \delta \right] = 1,$$

and so the rate of growth of consumption $y(c_t)$ is constant and is given by

$$y(c_t) = \Delta \ln c_{t+1}$$

$$= \frac{1}{\sigma} \left[\alpha A \left(\frac{k}{h} \right)^{-(1-\alpha)} - \delta - \theta \right].$$

If we define

$$r^k = \alpha A \left(\frac{k}{h} \right)^{-(1-\alpha)} - \delta = A\alpha^\alpha(1-\alpha)^{1-\alpha} - \delta,$$

where r^k can be interpreted as the net rate of return to capital, then

$$y(c_t) = \frac{1}{\sigma}(r^k - \theta).$$

We also note that as k_t/h_t is constant the rates of growth of the two types of capital are the same and, as growth is balanced, they are equal to the rate of growth of consumption.

Finally, we note that if we substitute into the production function the result that the optimal ratio of physical to human capital is constant, we obtain the AK production function

$$y_t = A^* k_t,$$

with $A^* = A(\alpha/(1-\alpha))^{1-\alpha}$.

3.6 Conclusions

We have argued that the behavior of most economies can be described as fluctuations around a steady-state growth path and that economic welfare arises largely as a result of growth. In comparison, the economic benefits from stabilizing the economy so that it does not deviate much from the growth path are small. We have shown that growth comes principally from three sources: technological progress, labor force growth, and education (human capital formation). We have found that balanced economic growth is not possible without technological progress. We have also shown that self-sustaining growth is possible without exogenous technological progress by investing in human capital; in effect, therefore, human capital accumulation is another way of describing technical progress.

4

The Decentralized Economy

4.1 Introduction

So far we have considered a stylized model of the economy in which a single economic agent makes every decision: consumption, saving, leisure, work, investment, and capital accumulation. An alternative interpretation we gave to this model was that a central planner was making all of these decisions for each person in the economy and was taking the same decision for everyone so that there was, in effect, a single household (or person) or, more generally, representative economic agent. In this interpretation there is no need for a market structure as all decisions are automatically coordinated.

We now generalize this model by introducing a distinction between households and firms. Households will take consumption decisions, they will own firms (and will therefore receive dividend income from firms), they will supply labor to firms, and they will save in the form of financial assets. Firms act as the agents of households. They make output, investment, and employment decisions, determine the size of the capital stock, borrow from households to finance investment, pay wages to households, and distribute their profits to households in the form of dividends. In separating the decisions of households and firms we introduce a number of additional economic variables. In order to coordinate the separate decisions of households and firms, we also need to introduce product, labor, and capital markets.

As a result of making these changes, the model is becoming more recognizable as a macroeconomic system. The model is also becoming considerably more complex. To simplify the analysis, we delay considering labor issues. First we consider household decisions on consumption and savings, taking the supply of labor as fixed. We then make the work/leisure decision endogenous. Next we derive the firm's decisions on investment, capital accumulation, debt finance, and, after these, employment. We then show how markets coordinate the separate decisions of households and firms to bring about general equilibrium in the economy. In the process we require markets for goods, labor, equity, and bonds. We find that the behavior of the decentralized economy when in general equilibrium is remarkably similar to that of the basic representative-agent model discussed previously.

4.2 Consumption

4.2.1 The Consumption Decision

It is assumed that the representative household seeks to maximize the present value of utility,

$$\max_{\{c_{t+s}, a_{t+s}\}} V_t = \sum_{s=0}^{\infty} \beta^s U(c_{t+s}), \tag{4.1}$$

subject to its budget constraint

$$\Delta a_{t+1} + c_t = x_t + r_t a_t, \tag{4.2}$$

where, as before, c_t is consumption, $U(c_t)$ is instantaneous utility ($U'_t > 0$ and $U''_t \leqslant 0$), the discount factor is $0 < \beta = 1/(1 + \theta) < 1$. a_t is the (net) stock of financial assets at the beginning of period t; if $a_t > 0$ then households are net lenders, and if $a_t < 0$ they are net borrowers. r_t is the interest rate on financial assets during period t and is paid at the beginning of the period, and x_t is household income, which is assumed for the present to be exogenous. At this point we do not need to specify what a_t and x_t are. Later, in the absence of government, we show that a_t is solely corporate debt and x_t is income from labor plus dividend income from the ownership of firms. All of these variables continue to be specified in real terms.

At the beginning of period t the stock of financial assets (and firm capital, which is not a variable chosen by households) is given. Thus households must choose $\{c_t, a_{t+1}\}$ in period t, $\{c_{t+1}, a_{t+2}\}$ in period $t + 1$, and so on. This is equivalent to choosing the complete path of consumption, i.e., current and all future consumption, $\{c_t, c_{t+1}, c_{t+2}, \dots\}$. The main changes compared with the basic model, therefore, are the replacement of the capital stock with the stock of financial assets, the introduction of the interest rate explicitly, and the replacement of the national resource constraint with the household budget constraint.

The solution to this problem can be obtained, as before, using the method of Lagrange multipliers. The Lagrangian is defined as

$$\mathcal{L} = \sum_{s=0}^{\infty} \{\beta^s U(c_{t+s}) + \lambda_{t+s}[x_{t+s} + (1 + r_{t+s})a_{t+s} - c_{t+s} - a_{t+s+1}]\}. \tag{4.3}$$

The first-order conditions are

$$\frac{\partial \mathcal{L}}{\partial c_{t+s}} = \beta^s U'(c_{t+s}) - \lambda_{t+s} = 0, \qquad s \geqslant 0,$$

$$\frac{\partial \mathcal{L}}{\partial a_{t+s}} = \lambda_{t+s}(1 + r_{t+s}) - \lambda_{t+s-1} = 0, \quad s > 0,$$

together with the budget constraint.

Solving the first-order conditions for $s = 1$ to eliminate λ_{t+s} gives the Euler equation:

$$\frac{\beta U'(c_{t+1})}{U'(c_t)}(1 + r_{t+1}) = 1. \tag{4.4}$$

Equation (4.4) is identical to the Euler equation derived for the basic model if $r_{t+1} = F'(k_{t+1}) - \delta$. This is why previously we interpreted the net marginal product of capital, $F'(k_{t+1}) - \delta$, as the real interest rate.

4.2.2 The Intertemporal Budget Constraint

The household's problem can be expressed in another way. This uses the intertemporal budget constraint, which is derived from the one-period budget constraints by successively eliminating $a_{t+1}, a_{t+2}, a_{t+3}, \ldots$. The budget constraints in periods t and $t + 1$ are

$$a_{t+1} + c_t = x_t + (1 + r_t)a_t,$$
$$a_{t+2} + c_{t+1} = x_{t+1} + (1 + r_{t+1})a_{t+1}.$$

Combining these to eliminate a_{t+1} gives the two-period intertemporal budget constraint

$$a_{t+2} + c_{t+1} + (1 + r_{t+1})c_t = x_{t+1} + (1 + r_{t+1})x_t + (1 + r_{t+1})(1 + r_t)a_t. \quad (4.5)$$

This can be rewritten as

$$\frac{a_{t+2}}{1 + r_{t+1}} + \frac{c_{t+1}}{1 + r_{t+1}} + c_t = \frac{x_{t+1}}{1 + r_{t+1}} + x_t + (1 + r_t)a_t. \quad (4.6)$$

Further substitutions of $a_{t+2}, a_{t+3}, \ldots$ give the wealth of the household as

$$W_t = \frac{a_{t+n}}{\prod_{s=1}^{n-1}(1 + r_{t+s})} + \sum_{s=0}^{n-1} \frac{c_{t+s}}{\prod_{s=1}^{n-1}(1 + r_{t+s})} \quad (4.7)$$

$$= \sum_{s=0}^{n-1} \frac{x_{t+s}}{\prod_{s=1}^{n-1}(1 + r_{t+s})} + (1 + r_t)a_t. \quad (4.8)$$

Thus wealth can be measured either in terms of its source as the present value of current and future income plus initial financial assets (equation (4.8)), or in terms of its use as the present value of current and future consumption plus the discounted value of terminal financial assets (equation (4.7)).

Taking the limit of wealth as $n \to \infty$ gives the infinite intertemporal budget constraint. When the interest rate is constant (equal to r), wealth can be written as

$$W_t = \sum_0^\infty \frac{c_{t+s}}{(1 + r)^s} = \sum_0^\infty \frac{x_{t+s}}{(1 + r)^s} + (1 + r)a_t. \quad (4.9)$$

An alternative way to express the household's problem would be to maximize V_t (equation (4.1)) subject to the constraint on wealth (equation (4.9)). This would then involve a single Lagrange multiplier.

We note that we also need an extra optimality condition, namely, the transversality condition, which is

$$\lim_{n \to \infty} \beta^n a_{t+n} U'(c_{t+n}) = 0. \quad (4.10)$$

Financial assets in period $t + n$ if consumed would give a discounted utility of $\beta^n a_{t+n} U(c_{t+n})$. Equation (4.10) implies that as $n \to \infty$ their discounted value goes to zero. Since $U'(c_{t+n})$ is positive for finite c_{t+n}, this implies that $\lim_{n \to \infty} \beta^n a_{t+n} = 0$. And as

$$\beta^n = \frac{1}{\prod_{s=1}^{n-1} (1 + r_{t+s})}$$

in the steady state, we obtain

$$\lim_{n \to \infty} \frac{a_{t+n}}{\prod_{s=1}^{n-1} (1 + r_{t+s})} \geqslant 0. \tag{4.11}$$

This is known as the no-Ponzi-game (NPG) condition. It implies that households are unable to finance consumption indefinitely by borrowing, i.e., by having negative financial assets.

4.2.3 Interpreting the Euler Equation

An interpretation similar to that proposed in chapter 2 can be given to the Euler equation. Again we reduce the problem to two periods, and then consider reducing c_t by a small amount dc_t and asking how much larger c_{t+1} must be to fully compensate for this, i.e., in order to leave V_t unchanged. Thus we let

$$V_t = U(c_t) + \beta U(c_{t+1}).$$

Differentiating V_t, and recalling that V_t remains constant, implies that

$$0 = dV_t = dU_t + \beta \, dU_{t+1} = U'(c_t) \, dc_t + \beta U'(c_{t+1}) \, dc_{t+1},$$

where dc_{t+1} is the small change in c_{t+1} brought about by reducing c_t. The loss of utility in period t is therefore $U'(c_t) \, dc_t$. In order for V_t to be constant, this must be compensated by the discounted gain in utility $\beta U'(c_{t+1}) \, dc_{t+1}$. Hence we need to increase c_{t+1} by

$$dc_{t+1} = -\frac{U'(c_t)}{\beta U'(c_{t+1})} \, dc_t. \tag{4.12}$$

All of this is the same as for the centralized model.

We now use the two-period intertemporal budget constraint, equation (4.5). Assuming that the interest rate, exogenous income, and the asset holdings a_t and a_{t+2} are unchanged, the intertemporal budget constraint implies that

$$dc_{t+1} = -(1 + r_{t+1}) \, dc_t,$$

and hence that

$$-\frac{dc_{t+1}}{dc_t} = 1 + r_{t+1}. \tag{4.13}$$

Combining (4.12) and (4.13) gives

$$-\frac{dc_{t+1}}{dc_t} = \frac{U'(c_t)}{\beta U'(c_{t+1})} = 1 + r_{t+1}, \tag{4.14}$$

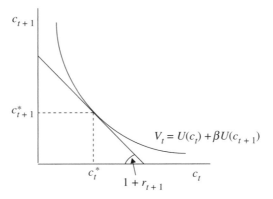

Figure 4.1. Two-period solution.

implying that

$$U'(c_t)(-dc_t) = \beta U'(c_{t+1})[1 + r_{t+1}]\,dc_t.$$

Thus the reduction in utility in period t due to cutting consumption and increasing saving, $-U'(c_t)\,dc_t$, is compensated by the discounted increase in utility in period $t+1$ created by the interest income generated from the additional saving, $\beta U'(c_{t+1})[1 + r_{t+1}]\,dc_{t+1}$.

Solely for the sake of convenience, we consider the case where the interest rate is a constant equal to r in depicting the solution in figure 4.1. The maximum value of c_t occurs when $c_{t+1} = 0$ and we consume the whole of next period's income by borrowing today and repaying the loan with next period's income. The maximum value of c_{t+1} occurs when $c_t = 0$ and we save all of the current period's income. Thus, from equations (4.5) and (4.6),

$$\max c_t = x_t + \frac{x_{t+1}}{1 + r} + (1 + r)a_t,$$
$$\max c_{t+1} = (1 + r)x_t + x_{t+1} + (1 + r)^2 a_t.$$

These determine the points at which the budget constraint touches the two axes. The slope of the budget constraint is $-(1 + r)$. The optimal solution occurs where the budget constraint is tangent to the highest attainable indifference curve.

An increase in income in either period t or $t + 1$ shifts the budget constraint to the right and results in higher c_t, c_{t+1}, and V_t.

An increase in the interest rate (from r_0 to r_1) makes the budget constraint steeper, as shown in figure 4.2. It also affects the maximum values of c_t and c_{t+1}. If $a_t = 0$, then there is a decrease in the maximum value of c_t (from $c_{t,0}^*$ to $c_{t,1}^*$) because the amount that can be borrowed on future income falls; and there is an increase in the maximum value of c_{t+1}, because the interest earned by saving current income rises. The result is an intertemporal substitution of consumption in which c_t falls and c_{t+1} rises. The effect on V_t is ambiguous: the point of tangency of the budget constraint may be on the same indifference

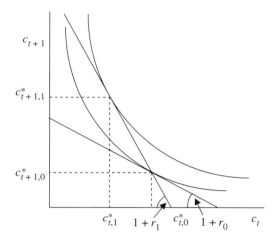

Figure 4.2. The effect of an increase in the interest rate.

curve, one to the left (implying a loss of discounted utility), or one to the right (implying a gain in discounted utility).

When $a_t < 0$, we obtain the same outcome, except that V_t is unambiguously reduced. When $a_t > 0$, max c_{t+1} still increases, and if $x_{t+1}/(1 + r) < (1 + r)a_t$, then max c_t now increases. This would then result in higher c_t, c_{t+1}, and V_t; this case is depicted in figure 4.2. In practice, as most of household financial wealth is in the form of pension entitlements, and this is sufficiently far in the future to be heavily discounted, households—especially those with large mortgages—probably behave in the short run as though they are net debtors (i.e., as if $a_t < 0$). We conclude, therefore, that in practice an increase in r is likely to cause c_t to fall and c_{t+1} to rise.

4.2.4 The Consumption Function

What factors affect the behavior of consumption? We have shown already that consumption in period t increases if income or net assets increase, and it is likely to decrease if the interest rate increases. We now examine the behavior of consumption in more detail. We consider the traditional consumption function—the behavior of consumption in period t—together with the future behavior of consumption along the economy's optimal path.

First we examine the behavior of consumption on the optimal path. Exactly what this means will become clear. First we take a linear approximation to the Euler equations, (2.12) and (2.12). Using a first-order Taylor series expansion of $U'(c_{t+1})$ about c_t we obtain

$$\frac{U'(c_{t+1})}{U'(c_t)} \simeq 1 + \frac{U''}{U'}\Delta c_{t+1}$$

$$= 1 - \sigma\frac{\Delta c_{t+1}}{c_t}, \qquad (4.15)$$

where $\sigma = -cU''/U'$ is the coefficient of relative risk aversion (CRRA). In general the CRRA will be time-varying, but, again for convenience, we consider the case where it is constant. Solving (2.12) and (4.15) we obtain the future rate of growth of consumption along the optimal path as

$$\frac{\Delta c_{t+1}}{c_t} = \frac{1}{\sigma}\left[1 - \frac{1}{\beta(1 + r_{t+1})}\right] \simeq \frac{r_{t+1} - \theta}{\sigma(1 + r_{t+1})}. \tag{4.16}$$

Thus, if $r_{t+1} = \theta$, then optimal consumption in the future will remain at its period t value. In this case households are willing to save until the rate of return on savings falls to equal the rate of time discount θ. This is the long-run general equilibrium solution. For interest rates below θ households prefer to consume than save. In the short run, the interest rate will typically differ from θ. If $r_{t+1} > \theta$ consumption will be growing along the optimal path, but this will not be sustained due to the rate of return to saving falling. This is a result of the diminishing marginal product of capital.

Consumption in period t—the consumption function—is obtained by combining equation (4.16) with the intertemporal budget constraint (4.7). Again for convenience we assume that the interest rate is the constant r. The generalization to a time-varying interest rate is straightforward. We also assume that $r = \theta$, its steady-state value, when optimal consumption in the future remains at its period t value. This enables us to replace c_{t+s} ($s > 0$) in equation (4.9) by c_t to obtain

$$W_t = \sum_0^\infty \frac{c_{t+s}}{(1 + r)^s} = \frac{1 + r}{r}c_t$$

$$= \sum_0^\infty \frac{x_{t+s}}{(1 + r)^s} + (1 + r)a_t.$$

Hence

$$c_t = \frac{r}{1 + r}W_t = r\sum_0^\infty \frac{x_{t+s}}{(1 + r)^{s+1}} + ra_t. \tag{4.17}$$

Equation (4.17) implies that consumption in period t is proportional to wealth. This solution for c_t is forward looking. It implies that an anticipated change in income in the future will have an immediate effect on current consumption. In general equilibrium, income is determined by labor and capital so this solution is similar to that for the basic model. This solution has been called the "life-cycle hypothesis" for reasons that will be explained later (see Modigliani and Brumberg 1954; Modigliani 1970). It has also been called the "permanent income hypothesis," as the present-value term in income can be interpreted as the amount of wealth that can be spent each period without altering wealth (see Friedman 1957). It also implies that temporary increases in wealth should be saved and temporary falls should be offset by borrowing.

In the special case where $x_{t+s} = x_t$ ($s \geqslant 0$), the consumption function, equation (4.17), becomes

$$c_t = x_t + ra_t. \tag{4.18}$$

Thus, c_t is equal to total current income, i.e., income from savings, ra_t, plus income from other sources, x_t. Equation (4.18) can be interpreted as the familiar Keynesian consumption function. We note that it implies that the marginal and the average propensities to consume are unity.

We now have a complete description of consumption. The optimal path determines how consumption will behave in the future relative to current consumption. The consumption function determines today's consumption, and hence where the optimal path is located. The same information is contained in the consumption functions for periods $t, t+1, t+2, \ldots$. Hence together they are an equivalent representation to current consumption and the optimal path.

4.2.5 Permanent and Temporary Shocks

In our discussion of the effects on consumption of changes in income and interest rates we have made no distinction between whether the changes are permanent or temporary. It is vital to make this distinction as the results are quite different. The policy implications of this are of great importance. First we consider shocks to income.

4.2.5.1 *Income*

If, for convenience, we assume that the real rate of interest is constant, then, in general, consumption is determined by equation (4.17). A permanent change in income in period t will affect $x_t, x_{t+1}, x_{t+2}, \ldots$. If, again for convenience, we assume that $x_{t+s} = x_t$ ($s \geqslant 0$), then we can analyze the effect of a change in x. In this case the consumption function simplifies to become equation (4.18). It follows that both the marginal and the average propensities to consume following a permanent change in income are unity, i.e., none of the increase in income is saved. A permanent change in income is the prevailing state for an economy that is growing through time.

A temporary change in income is analyzed using equation (4.17). We rewrite the equation as

$$c_t = \frac{r}{1+r}x_t + \frac{r}{(1+r)^2}x_{t+1} + \cdots + ra_t.$$

It follows that a change in x_t (but not in $x_{t+1}, x_{t+2}, \ldots$) has a marginal propensity to consume of only $r/(1+r)$. Hence, most of the increase in x_t is saved rather than consumed. We also note that an expected increase in x_{t+1} will also cause c_t to increase, but the marginal propensity to consume out of x_{t+1} is $r/(1+r)^2$, which is lower due to discounting income in period $t+1$ by $1/(1+r)$. The effect on consumption of a permanent shock to income is the discounted sum of current and expected future income effects.

Thus the Keynesian marginal propensity of unity implicitly assumes that the change in income is permanent, not temporary. The importance of this distinction for policy is clear. A policy change (such as a temporary cut in income tax) that is designed to affect income only temporarily will have little effect on consumption.

4.2.5.2 Interest Rates

First, we recall that the interest rate r_t is the real interest rate. A permanent change in real interest rates implies that $r_t, r_{t+1}, r_{t+2}, \ldots$ all increase. This can be analyzed using equation (4.18) and treated as an increase in r. The effect on consumption depends on whether the household has net assets or net debts (i.e., on whether $a_t > 0$ or $a_t < 0$). If $a_t > 0$ then interest income—and hence total income—is increased permanently. The marginal propensity to consume from this increase is unity as none of the additional interest income is saved. But if $a_t < 0$ then debt service payments increase permanently and total income decreases. Consumption will therefore fall.

A temporary increase in interest rates will be treated by households as though it were a temporary change in income. For example, equation (2.1) shows that an increase in r_t just affects current interest earnings (or debt service payments). Hence, most of the additional interest income is saved, not consumed. In contrast, an expected increase in r_{t+1} requires us to use equation (4.16). It affects consumption by causing a substitution of consumption across time (i.e., an intertemporal substitution). This was analyzed earlier. We recall that the response of consumption depends on whether a_t is positive or negative. If it is negative, and hence the household is a net debtor, then there is an unambiguous decrease in c_t and increase in c_{t+1}. Thus, once again, there is an important difference between a permanent and a temporary change.

In practice, real interest rates tend to fluctuate about an approximately constant mean. This implies that a permanent increase in real interest rates is improbable. At best, it might prove a convenient way of analyzing a change in interest rates that is thought will last for many periods. The sustained rise in stock market returns in the 1990s is a possible example. This continued for so long that households may have treated it as more or less permanent. This may explain why the savings rate fell over this period and why consumption did not turn down when the stock market did. Perhaps consumers took the view that the fall in the stock market would be temporary and so they tried to maintain their level of consumption. Apart from relatively rare cases like this, it will usually prove more useful, especially for policy analysis, to treat the analysis of a change in real interest rates as being temporary, and to suppose that the effect of an increase in real interest rates will be to reduce current consumption.

4.2.5.3 Anticipated and Unanticipated Shocks to Income

Because consumption depends on wealth, and wealth is forward looking, unanticipated future changes in income and interest rates will have no effect on current consumption. But changes that are anticipated at time t will affect current consumption. The distinction between anticipated and unanticipated future changes in income helps to explain a confusion that prevailed for a time in the literature.

It was claimed that (4.16) was a rival consumption function to equation (4.17). As equation (4.16) appeared to suggest that consumption would be unaffected by income, it was seen as an inferior theory. For example, if $r_{t+1} = r = \theta$, then equation (4.16) implies that

$$c_{t+1} = c_t, \tag{4.19}$$

which does not involve income explicitly; c_{t+1} is just determined from knowledge of c_t.

To see why this interpretation is incorrect consider the effect on consumption of a permanent but unanticipated increase in income in period $t + 1$. Thus there is an increase in $x_{t+1}, x_{t+2}, \ldots$. Taking the first difference of equation (4.18) and noting that the stock of assets is unchanged, the consumption function for period $t + 1$ can be written

$$
\begin{aligned}
c_{t+1} &= x_{t+1} + r a_{t+1} \\
&= c_t + (x_{t+1} - x_t) + r(a_{t+1} - a_t) \\
&= c_t + (x_{t+1} - x_t).
\end{aligned}
$$

If income remains unchanged ($x_{t+1} = x_t$), then consumption would be unchanged too and would satisfy equation (4.19). But if $x_{t+1} > x_t$, then $c_{t+1} > c_t$. Thus consumption in period $t + 1$ has responded to the unanticipated increase in income in period $t + 1$. From equation (4.17), if the increase in x_{t+1} had been anticipated in period t, then c_t would have changed too. As a result, knowledge of c_t would be sufficient for determining c_{t+1} as in equation (4.19), and there would be no *additional* information possessed by income.

This illustrates the limitations of working with the assumption of perfect foresight when, strictly, we should allow for uncertainty about the future. Accordingly, we should write equation (4.19) as

$$E_t c_{t+1} = c_t, \tag{4.20}$$

where E_t is the expectation conditional on information available up to and including period t. If expectations are rational, then the expectational error

$$e_{t+1} = c_{t+1} - E_t c_{t+1}$$

is unpredictable from information dated at time t, i.e., $E_t e_{t+1} = 0$. This would imply that consumption is a martingale process. (In the special case where $\text{var}_t(\Delta c_{t+1})$ is constant the martingale process is given the more familiar name of a random walk.) Equation (4.20) was first derived by Hall (1978).

We have shown therefore that equation (4.19) is not an alternative theory of consumption, but is a description of the anticipated future behavior of consumption relative to today's consumption. Current consumption is given by the consumption function, equation (4.17) or, when income is expected to be constant, by equation (4.18). A complete description of consumption requires both equation (4.17) and equation (4.19). Equation (4.19) is not therefore a rival consumption function to equation (4.18).

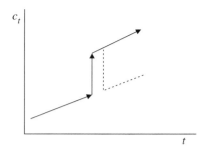

Figure 4.3. The effect on consumption of
permanent and temporary shocks to income.

Figure 4.3 illustrates the argument. We plot the behavior of (log) consumption against time. It has two features: its slope (which is upwards if $r > \theta$) and its location. Consider the lower segment. The movement of consumption along this segment is determined from the Euler equation; it is at a constant rate. The location of the segment (i.e., its level) is determined by the consumption function. Suppose that after a while there is a permanent positive shock to consumption due perhaps to an increase in income. This will cause consumption to jump to the higher segment. Consumption will then move along this segment, continuing to grow at the same rate as before because the Euler equation is unaffected by the jump. In contrast, a temporary positive shock to consumption would cause consumption to rise above the lower segment briefly before returning to it and then continuing along it at the old rate of growth, as shown by the dotted line. And if the permanent increase in income had been anticipated earlier, then consumption would have started to increase at that time. The path of consumption would then be above the lower segment of figure 4.3 from the date when the income change was anticipated and would join the upper segment smoothly when the increase in income takes place.

4.3 Savings

We have been considering consumption—now we briefly consider savings. We assume that the interest rate is the constant r. Savings are then

$$s_t = x_t + r a_t - c_t.$$

Eliminating c_t using equation (4.17) we obtain

$$s_t = x_t - r \sum_{s=0}^{\infty} \frac{x_{t+s}}{(1+r)^{s+1}}$$

$$= -\frac{r}{1+r} \sum_{s=1}^{\infty} \frac{x_{t+s} - x_t}{(1+r)^s}$$

$$= -\sum_{s=1}^{\infty} \frac{\Delta x_{t+s}}{(1+r)^{s+1}}.$$

This has a very interesting interpretation. It shows that saving is undertaken in order to offset (expected) future falls in income. These could be temporary—for example, due to spells of unemployment—or permanent—for example, due to retirement. Thus, abstracting from an economy that is growing, saving enables consumption to be kept constant throughout life.

4.4 Life-Cycle Theory

We have assumed so far that households are identical and live for ever. In fact, due to the finiteness of lives, the age of households is one of the main causes of differences in their behavior. A young household, possibly with dependants and many years of work before retirement, will have different consumption and savings patterns from old households, possibly already in retirement. Most obviously, a typical household with young children will have high expenditures relative to income, and so will have a low savings rate. A middle-aged household will usually save more in order to generate an income in retirement. An old household in retirement is likely to be dependent on past savings, such as a (contributed) pension, and to dissave. Clearly, the theory above does not capture all of these features. It can easily be modified, however, to reflect the main point that consumption and savings depend on age. Further, if the age distribution of the whole population is relatively stable, then, to a first approximation, we may be able to ignore age when analyzing aggregate consumption and savings.

4.4.1 Implications of Life-Cycle Theory

Before modifying the theory, we note how it can be interpreted to reflect some of these considerations. The key result is that consumption is in general a function of wealth (equation (4.17)). Since wealth is the discounted sum of expected future income over a person's life plus current financial assets, it may be expected to be fairly stable over time. This implies that consumption in each period would be stable too and would be independent of a person's age. Thus, fluctuations in income due to unemployment or retirement, when income from employment is zero, should not in theory affect current consumption. This is why the theory above is called the life-cycle theory; in principle, it automatically takes account of each household's position in its life cycle.

Life-cycle theory makes a number of strong assumptions. In particular, it assumes that the future can be anticipated reasonably accurately. Alternatively, we could make the strong assumption that households hold assets whose pay-offs vary between good and bad times in such a way as to offset unexpected changes in income and, as a result, leave wealth unaffected.

Another critical assumption is that households are able to borrow to maintain consumption even when current income and financial assets are insufficient to pay for current consumption. In practice, a possibly substantial proportion of households face a borrowing constraint that prevents them from doing this.

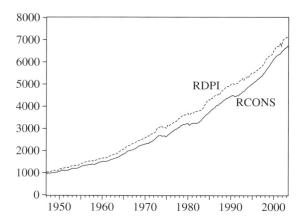

Figure 4.4. U.S. total real consumption and real disposable income 1947–2003.

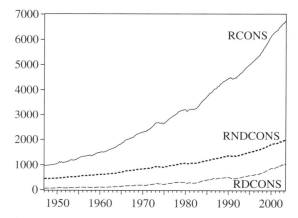

Figure 4.5. U.S. total, nondurable, and durable real consumption 1947–2003.

Consequently, their consumption would be limited to their current income. Their consumption would therefore tend to fluctuate with their income, rather than be smoothed over time as life-cycle theory predicts. What does empirical evidence show? Figures 4.4 and 4.5 give a rough guide. Figure 4.4 plots disposable (after-tax) income against total consumption for the United States for the period 1947–2003. Figure 4.5 shows total, real nondurable, and durable consumption.

Figure 4.4 suggests that total consumption is somewhat smoothed but still fluctuates. The fluctuations in total consumption are not dissimilar to those in income. Figure 4.5 reveals that the fluctuations in total consumption are due much more to variations in durable consumption than to those in nondurable consumption. Table 4.1 gives the standard deviations of the growth rates.

The table reveals that the standard deviation of total consumption is 66% of that of disposable income, but the standard deviation of nondurable consumption expenditures is 54% of that of disposable income. Significantly, the

Table 4.1. Standard deviations in growth rates.

	%
Disposable income	1.12
Total consumption	0.74
Nondurables and services	1.22
Nondurables	0.60
Durables	17.13

standard deviation of nondurable consumption is only 3.5% of that of durable expenditures. We conclude that there is evidence of consumption smoothing, but only of nondurable expenditures. Neither service nor durable expenditures appear to be smoothed relative to income. We note, however, that unlike nondurables and services, durables are not a flow variable but a stock; it is the services from the durable stock that are a flow. Strictly speaking, therefore, the theory derived above does not apply to durables. We therefore reexamine the determination of durable consumption below.

4.4.2 Model of Perpetual Youth

A modification to life-cycle theory that explicitly recognizes the household's finite tenure on life is the Blanchard and Fischer (1989) and Yaari (1965) theory of perpetual youth. Each individual is assumed to have a constant probability of death in each period of ρ, which is independent of age. The probability of not dying in any period is therefore $1 - \rho$. The probability of dying in s periods' time is the joint probability of not dying in the first $s - 1$ periods multiplied by the probability of dying in period s, i.e.,

$$f(s) = \rho(1 - \rho)^{s-1}, \quad s = 1, 2, \ldots.$$

Thus, expected lifetime is

$$E(s) = \sum_{s=1}^{\infty} s\rho(1 - \rho)^{s-1} = \rho^{-1}.$$

Hence, in the limit as $\rho \to 0$, lifetime is infinite, as in the basic model. If newborns have the same probability of dying in each period, then, for the population size to be constant, births must exactly offset deaths. In practice, the average lifespan has increased over time, implying that ρ has been falling over time.

As the date of death is unknown, households must make consumption and savings decisions under uncertainty. We must therefore replace utility in period $t + s$ by the expected utility *given that the household will still be alive*. The probability of being alive in period $t + s$ is $(1 - \rho)^s$. The present value of *expected* utility is then

$$V_t = \sum_{s=0}^{\infty} \beta^s (1 - \rho)^s U(c_{t+s})$$

$$= \sum_{s=0}^{\infty} \tilde{\beta}^s U(c_{t+s}),$$

where $\tilde{\beta} = \beta(1 - \rho)$. Thus, the household objective function has the same form as previously; only the discount rate has changed. We note that the optimal rate of growth of consumption is then given by

$$\frac{\Delta c_{t+1}}{c_t} = \frac{1}{\sigma}\left[1 - \frac{1}{\tilde{\beta}(1 + r_{t+1})}\right] \simeq \frac{r_{t+1} - (\theta + \rho)}{\sigma(1 + r_{t+1})}.$$

Thus, the prospect of death raises the minimum rate of return required to induce saving, cuts the optimal rate of consumption growth, and raises consumption levels. Since, in practice, the probability of death is not constant but increases with age, we may expect relatively higher consumption by older households, and net dissaving, especially among retired households.

To sum up, we can therefore proceed as before. We do not need to change the previous analysis, but we should be aware of what interpretation we give to the discount rate.

4.5   Nondurable and Durable Consumption

The key difference between nondurables and durables is that the former is a flow variable while the latter is a stock that provides a flow of services in each period. Moreover, the stock of durables depreciates over time due to wear and tear and obsolescence. We now modify our previous analysis of household consumption to incorporate these features.

In this section we denote real nondurable consumption by c_t, the stock of durables by D_t, and the total investment expenditures on durables by d_t. The accumulation equation for durables can be written as

$$\Delta D_{t+1} = d_t - \delta D_t, \tag{4.21}$$

where δ is the rate of depreciation. The household budget constraint is altered to reflect the fact that the household purchases both nondurables and durables. It is now written as

$$\Delta a_{t+1} + c_t + p_t^D d_t = x_t + r_t a_t,$$

where p_t^D is the price of durables relative to nondurables and $p_t^D d_t$ is the total expenditure on durables measured in terms of nondurable prices. Thus the budget constraint becomes

$$\Delta a_{t+1} + c_t + p_t^D [D_{t+1} - (1 - \delta)D_t] = x_t + r_t a_t. \tag{4.22}$$

Utility is derived by households from the services of nondurable and durable consumption through $U(c_t, D_t)$, where $U_c, U_D > 0$, $U_{cc}, U_{DD} \leqslant 0$. This reflects the fact that the greater the stock of durables, the greater the flow of services from durables. If $U_{cD} > 0$ nondurables and durables are complementary, and if $U_{cD} < 0$ they are substitutes.

The problem becomes that of maximizing

$$V_t = \sum_{s=0}^{\infty} \beta^s U(c_{t+s}, D_{t+s}),$$

with respect to $\{c_{t+s}, D_{t+s+1}, a_{t+s+1}; s \geqslant 0\}$, subject to equation (4.22) and the durable accumulation equation (4.21). The Lagrangian is

$$\mathcal{L} = \sum_{s=0}^{\infty} \{\beta^s U(c_{t+s}, D_{t+s}) + \lambda_{t+s}[x_t + (1 + r_{t+s})a_{t+s} - c_{t+s}$$
$$- p_{t+s}^D D_{t+s+1} + p_{t+s}^D (1 - \delta)D_{t+s} - a_{t+s+1}]\}.$$

The first-order conditions are

$$\frac{\partial \mathcal{L}}{\partial c_{t+s}} = \beta^s U_{c,t+s} - \lambda_{t+s} = 0, \qquad\qquad s \geqslant 0,$$

$$\frac{\partial \mathcal{L}}{\partial D_{t+s}} = \beta^s U_{D,t+s} + \lambda_{t+s} p_{t+s}^D (1 - \delta) - \lambda_{t+s-1} p_{t+s}^D = 0, \quad s > 0,$$

$$\frac{\partial \mathcal{L}}{\partial a_{t+s}} = \lambda_{t+s}(1 + r_{t+s}) - \lambda_{t+s-1} = 0, \qquad\qquad s > 0.$$

The first and third equations give the usual Euler equation, but now defined in terms of nondurable consumption:

$$\frac{\beta U_{c,t+1}}{U_{c,t}}(1 + r_{t+1}) = 1.$$

From all three equations we obtain

$$U_{D,t+1} = U_{c,t+1} p_{t+1}^D (r_{t+1} + \delta). \tag{4.23}$$

If, for example, utility is Cobb–Douglas and given by

$$U(c_t, D_t) = c_t^\alpha D_t^{1-\alpha},$$

then the Euler equation becomes

$$\beta \left(\frac{c_{t+1}/D_{t+1}}{c_t/D_t} \right)^{-(1-\alpha)} (1 + r_{t+1}) = 1 \tag{4.24}$$

and equation (4.23) can be written as

$$\frac{c_{t+1}}{p_{t+1}^D D_{t+1}} = \frac{\alpha}{1 - \alpha}(r_{t+1} + \delta). \tag{4.25}$$

Equation (4.25) implies that an increase in the real rate of interest reduces the value of the stock of durables relative to nondurable expenditures.

In steady state, when $\Delta c_{t+1} = \Delta D_{t+1} = 0$, we have $r_{t+1} = \theta$. Hence

$$\frac{c}{p^D D} = \frac{\alpha}{1-\alpha}(\theta + \delta)$$

and the ratio of expenditures on nondurable consumption to durables in the long run is

$$\frac{c}{p^D d} = \frac{\alpha}{1-\alpha}\frac{\theta + \delta}{\delta}.$$

Short-run behavior is affected by the lag in the adjustment of the stock of durables. Although nondurable and durable expenditures can instantly respond to a period t shock, the stock of durables is given in period t and cannot respond until period $t + 1$. For example, a permanent increase in income from period t causes a permanent increase in expenditures on both nondurables and durables from period t. The relative response of nondurable to durable expenditures is obtained as follows. From equations (4.21) and (4.24) the expenditure on durables relative to nondurables is

$$\frac{p_t^D d_t}{c_t} = \frac{c_{t+1}}{c_t}\frac{P_t^D D_{t+1}}{c_{t+1}} - (1-\delta)\frac{P_t^D D_t}{c_t}$$

$$= \left[\frac{c_{t+1}}{c_t}\left(\frac{1+r_{t+1}}{1+\theta}\right)^{-1/(1-\alpha)} - 1 + \delta\right]\frac{P_t^D D_t}{c_t}$$

$$\simeq \left[\frac{\Delta c_{t+1}}{c_t} - \frac{1}{1-\alpha}(r_{t+1} - \theta) + \delta\right]\frac{P_t^D D_t}{c_t}.$$

The effect on this relative expenditure of an increase in c_t, with D_t given, is therefore determined by the sign of the term in square brackets. If this is negative, then the relative expenditure on durables in period t is greater. This result seems to be supported by the evidence, which shows that the volatility of durables is larger than that of nondurables.

4.6 Labor Supply

So far we have focused on the consumption and savings decisions of households, taking noninterest income x_t as given. We now consider the household's labor-supply decision. This is a first step toward endogenizing noninterest income. This will be followed by a discussion of the demand for labor by firms and the coordination of these decisions in the labor market.

In the basic model of chapter 2 we assumed initially that households work for a fixed amount of time. In the extension to the basic model we distinguished between work and leisure, allowing a choice between the two. The wage rate was only included implicitly. We now assume an explicit wage rate w_t. Time spent in employment n_t generates labor income and therefore contributes to consumption c_t, but it is at the expense of leisure l_t, which is also assumed to be desirable to households. The total time available to households is unity, so $n_t + l_t = 1$. In contrast to our previous analysis of labor, we now write the instantaneous utility function as

$$U(c_t, l_t) = U(c_t, 1 - n_t),$$

where $U_c > 0$, $U_l < 0$, $U_{cc} \leqslant 0$, $U_{ll} \leqslant 0$, $U_{n,t} = -U_{l,t}$, and the household budget constraint is

$$\Delta a_{t+1} + c_t = w_t n_t + x_t + r_t a_t, \tag{4.26}$$

where w_t is the real-wage rate per unit of labor time, x_t is still treated as exogenous income but now excludes labor income, and r_t is the real rate of interest on net asset holdings a_t held at the beginning of period t.

The Lagrangian is

$$\mathcal{L} = \sum_{s=0}^{\infty} \{\beta^s U(c_{t+s}, 1 - n_{t+s})$$

$$+ \lambda_{t+s}[w_t n_t + x_t + (1 + r_{t+s})a_{t+s} - c_{t+s} - a_{t+s+1}]\}.$$

Maximizing with respect to $\{c_{t+s}, n_{t+s}, a_{t+s+1}; s \geqslant 0\}$ gives the first-order conditions

$$\frac{\partial \mathcal{L}}{\partial c_{t+s}} = \beta^s U_{c,t+s} - \lambda_{t+s} = 0, \qquad s \geqslant 0,$$

$$\frac{\partial \mathcal{L}}{\partial n_{t+s}} = -\beta^s U_{l,t+s} + \lambda_{t+s} w_{t+s} = 0, \qquad s \geqslant 0,$$

$$\frac{\partial \mathcal{L}}{\partial a_{t+s}} = \lambda_{t+s}(1 + r_{t+s}) - \lambda_{t+s-1} = 0, \qquad s > 0,$$

along with the budget constraint.

Solving the first two conditions for $s = 0$ and eliminating λ_t gives

$$\frac{U_{l,t}}{U_{c,t}} = w_t. \tag{4.27}$$

Once consumption is determined, the supply of labor can be derived from this as a function of consumption and the wage rate.

Consumption is derived much as it was before. From the first and third conditions we obtain the same Euler equation as before, namely equation (2.12), which for convenience we repeat:

$$\frac{\beta U_{c,t+1}}{U_{c,t}}(1 + r_{t+1}) = 1. \tag{4.28}$$

This is then combined with the intertemporal budget constraint associated with the new instantaneous budget constraint (4.26). Assuming that the interest rate is constant, we can show that

$$c_t = \frac{r}{1+r} W_t = r \sum_{0}^{\infty} \left[\frac{w_{t+s} n_{t+s}}{(1+r)^{s+1}} + \frac{x_{t+s}}{(1+r)^{s+1}} \right] + r a_t, \tag{4.29}$$

where wealth is

$$W_t = \sum_0^\infty \left[\frac{w_{t+s} n_{t+s}}{(1+r)^s} + \frac{x_{t+s}}{(1+r)^s} \right] + (1+r)a_t.$$

Hence, wealth includes discounted current and future labor income. Equations (4.27) and (4.29) and the labor constraint are three simultaneous equations in $\{c_{t+s}, l_{t+s}, n_{t+s}\}$, from which the optimal levels of consumption and the supply of labor can be obtained.

Consider the special case where $w_{t+s} = w_t$ and $x_{t+s} = x_t$ ($s \geqslant 0$). The consumption function then becomes

$$c_t = w_t n_t + x_t + r a_t. \qquad (4.30)$$

Thus c_t is once more equal to total current income, i.e., income from labor $w_t n_t$ as well as from savings $r a_t$ and x_t. The supply of labor is derived from equations (4.27) and (4.30).

To illustrate, suppose that instantaneous utility is the separable power function

$$U(c_t, l_t) = \frac{c_t^{1-\sigma} - 1}{1-\sigma} + \ln l_t,$$

where $\sigma > 0$, then

$$U_{c,t} = c_t^{-\sigma} \quad \text{and} \quad U_{l,t} = \frac{1}{l_t}.$$

Equation (4.27) becomes

$$\frac{1/(1-n_t)}{c_t^{-\sigma}} = w_t,$$

implying that the supply of labor is

$$n_t = 1 - \frac{c_t^\sigma}{w_t}. \qquad (4.31)$$

Consequently, given c_t, an increase in w_t will increase labor supply and hence total labor income. However, from (4.29) an increase in labor income will increase consumption, and from (4.31) an increase in consumption will reduce the labor supply. This implies that the sign of the net effect of an increase in the wage rate on the labor supply is not determined. This can also be shown by combining equations (4.30) and (4.31) to eliminate c_t and give the labor-supply function:

$$n_t = N^s(w_t, x_t, r, a_t).$$

It follows that

$$\frac{\partial n_t}{\partial w_t} = \frac{1}{w_t} \left(\frac{1}{\sigma c_t^{\sigma-1} + 1} - n_t \right),$$

where the sign is still not clear. However, the smaller consumption is, the more likely it is that the sign will be positive. In contrast, an increase in x_t, a_t, or r will cause an unambiguous increase in c_t, and hence a fall in the labor supply.

4.7 Firms

Next we consider the decisions of the representative firm. Firms make decisions on output, factor inputs (capital and labor), and product prices. They also determine their financial structure—that is, whether to use equity or debt finance—and the proportion of profits to disburse as dividends. We assume that the representative firm seeks to maximize the present value of current and future profits by a suitable choice of output, investment, the capital stock, labor, and debt finance. In effect we are assuming that firms use debt, rather than equity finance, and borrow from households. Consequently, firm debts are household assets.

First we consider the problem in the absence of costs of adjustment of labor. We then examine the effects of including labor costs of adjustment. We recall that in chapter 2 we considered the cost of adjustment of capital in the centralized model of the economy.

4.7.1 Labor Demand without Adjustment Costs

The present value of the stream of real profits discounted using a constant real interest rate r is

$$\mathcal{P}_t = \sum_{s=0}^{\infty} (1 + r)^{-s} \Pi_{t+s}, \tag{4.32}$$

where the firms's real profits (net revenues) in period t are

$$\Pi_t = y_t - w_t n_t - i_t + \Delta b_{t+1} - r b_t,$$

where w_t is the real-wage rate, n_t is labor input, and b_t is the stock of outstanding firm debt at the beginning of period t, i.e., b_t is corporate debt and it is held by households. As we are still working in real terms we have set the price level to unity.

The production function depends on two factors of production,

$$y_t = F(k_t, n_t),$$

and capital is accumulated according to

$$\Delta k_{t+1} = i_t - \delta k_t.$$

Thus the net revenue of the firm is

$$\Pi_t = F(k_t, n_t) - w_t n_t - k_{t+1} + (1 - \delta)k_t + b_{t+1} - (1 + r)b_t.$$

Firms seek to maximize the present value of their profits with respect to $\{n_{t+s}, k_{t+s+1}, b_{t+s+1}; s \geqslant 0\}$. Hence they maximize

$$\mathcal{P}_t = \sum_{s=0}^{\infty} (1 + r)^{-s} \{ F(k_{t+s}, n_{t+s}) - w_{t+s} n_{t+s} - k_{t+s+1}$$
$$+ (1 - \delta)k_{t+s} + b_{t+s+1} - (1 + r)b_{t+s} \}.$$

The first-order conditions are

$$\frac{\partial \mathcal{P}_t}{\partial l_{t+s}} = (1 + r)^{-s}\{F_{n,t+s} - w_{t+s}\} = 0, \qquad s \geqslant 0,$$

$$\frac{\partial \mathcal{P}_t}{\partial k_{t+s}} = (1 + r)^{-s}[F_{k,t+s} + 1 - \delta] - (1 + r)^{-(s-1)} = 0, \quad s > 0,$$

$$\frac{\partial \mathcal{P}_t}{\partial b_{t+s}} = (1 + r)^{-s}(1 + r) - (1 + r)^{-(s-1)} = 0, \qquad s > 0.$$

The demand for labor is obtained from the usual condition that the marginal product of labor equals the real wage,

$$F_{n,t} = w_t,$$

and will depend on the stock of capital. For a given stock of capital and a given technology, an increase in the wage rate will reduce the demand for labor.

The demand for capital is derived from

$$F_{k,t+1} = r + \delta$$

using the inverse function $F_{k,t+1}^{-1}(r + \delta)$. Hence gross investment is

$$i_t = F_{k,t+1}^{-1}(r + \delta) - (1 - \delta)k_t.$$

Consequently, an increase in the rate of interest reduces investment. An increase in the marginal product of capital due, for example, to a permanent technology shock raises the optimal stock of capital and investment. We note that this solution implicitly assumes that there are no lags of adjustment in investment. Investment and the capital stock instantaneously achieve their optimal levels for each period. If there are additional costs to investing, as in Tobin's q-theory, then firms will prefer to take more time to adjust their capital stock to the long-run desired level. As we saw in chapter 2, this introduces additional dynamics into the investment and capital accumulation decisions, and through these into the economy as a whole.

In the short term, the firm chooses the capital stock so that the net marginal product of capital equals the cost of financing. This is also the opportunity cost of holding a bond instead. In the long term (i.e., in general equilibrium), households will be willing to save until the return to savings falls to the household rate of time preference θ. At this point $F_{k,t+1} - \delta = \theta$, the same result we obtained for the basic centralized model.

The condition $\partial \mathcal{P}_t / \partial b_{t+s} = 0$ is independent of b_t, and hence is satisfied for all values of b_t, including zero. Since any value of debt is consistent with maximizing profits, the firm can choose between using debt finance or its profits (i.e., retained earnings) when financing new investment. This is a version of the Modigliani–Miller theorem (see Modigliani and Miller 1958).

4.7.2 Labor Demand with Adjustment Costs

In effect, we have assumed that labor consists of the number of hours worked per worker. A generalization of this would be to decompose labor into the number of workers and the hours they work. Individuals may choose whether or not to work (the participation decision), and how many hours to work. In practice, household choice may be constrained by firms to working full time, part time, and/or overtime. Thus, it is firms that dominate the balance between the number of workers employed and the hours worked. The indivisible labor model of Hansen (1985) assumes that hours of work are fixed by firms and individuals simply decide whether or not to participate in the labor force. We modify this by assuming that households can choose whether or not to work, but if they do decide to participate in the labor force, the number of hours is chosen by firms.

Since working more hours often involves having to pay a premium overtime hourly wage rate, and hiring and firing entails additional costs, when adjusting labor input, firms must trade off the cost of changing the workforce against that of altering the number of hours worked. Intuitively, it may be less costly to meet a temporary increase in labor demand by raising the number of hours worked, while it may be cheaper to meet a permanent increase in labor demand by increasing the number of workers. We construct a simple model of the firm that illustrates how one might incorporate these features of the labor market. For convenience we abstract from the capital decision and firm borrowing.

We assume that the firm's production function is

$$y_t = F(n_t, h_t),$$

where n_t is the numbers of workers and h_t the number of hours each person works, and $F_n, F_h > 0$, $F_{nn}, F_{hh} \leqslant 0$, and $F_{nh} \geqslant 0$. Wages for each person are $W(h_t)$ with $W' \geqslant 0$, $W'' \geqslant 0$ to reflect the need to pay higher hourly wage rates the greater the number of hours worked by each person.

We also assume that there are costs to hiring and firing. The change in the workforce can be written as

$$n_t = v_t - q_t + n_{t-1},$$

where v_t represents total new hires and q_t total quits. There are costs associated both with taking on new employees and with firing existing workers. If $v_t = q_t$ there is no change in the labor force, yet there may still be hiring and firing costs due to turnover in each period. These could vary over time. For example, during a boom more workers may quit to find a better job and this may result in further hires to replace them. For convenience, however, we simply assume that there is a cost to changes in the total workforce, whether the workforce is increasing or decreasing, and we ignore the problem of turnover. Accordingly, we assume that the firm maximizes present value $\mathcal{P}_t$, equation (4.32), where the firms's net revenues in period t are given by

$$\Pi_t = F(n_t, h_t) - W_t(h_t)n_t - \tfrac{1}{2}\lambda(\Delta n_{t+1})^2.$$

The last term reflects the cost of hiring and firing during period t. Our discussion of turnover could be addressed by allowing λ to be higher when there is a lot of labor turnover in the boom phase of the business cycle and lower in recession when there is less turnover, but we assume that λ is constant.

The first-order conditions for maximizing $\mathcal{P}_t$ with respect to $\{n_{t+s}, h_{t+s};$ $s \geqslant 0\}$ are

$$\frac{\partial \mathcal{P}_t}{\partial n_{t+s}} = (1 + r)^{-s}(F_{n,t+s} - W_{t+s} + \lambda \Delta n_{t+s+1}) + (1 + r)^{-(s-1)}\lambda \Delta n_{t+s} = 0,$$

$$\frac{\partial \mathcal{P}_t}{\partial h_{t+s}} = (1 + r)^{-s}(F_{h,t+s} - W'_{t+s}n_{t+s}) = 0.$$

From the second first-order condition,

$$\frac{F_{h,t}}{n_t} = W'_t. \tag{4.33}$$

This implies that the marginal product of an extra hour per worker is equal to the marginal hourly wage. We note that adjustment is instantaneous in equation (4.33). Given the number of workers, the equation gives their number of hours of work. If there is only a single hourly wage rate, then W'_t does not depend on h_t.

The second first-order condition gives the level of employment and can be written as

$$\Delta n_t = \frac{1}{1+r}\Delta n_{t+1} + \frac{1}{\lambda(1+r)}(F_{n,t} - W_t) \tag{4.34}$$

$$= \frac{1}{\lambda(1+r)} \sum_{s=0}^{\infty} (1+r)^{-s}(F_{n,t+s} - W_{t+s}). \tag{4.35}$$

Equation (4.35) shows that there will be an increase in the number of employees if the marginal product of workers exceeds their total wages either today or in the future. In steady state we have $\Delta n_t = 0$ when $F_{n,t} = W_t$. This is the usual marginal productivity condition for labor, i.e., each worker is paid their marginal product for the total number of hours worked.

Equation (4.34) can also be written in terms of the level of employment as

$$n_t = \frac{1}{2+r}n_{t+1} + \frac{1+r}{2+r}n_{t-1} + \frac{1}{\lambda(2+r)}(F_{n,t} - W_t). \tag{4.36}$$

This shows that the firm's adjustment of its number of employees takes place over time. The greater the turnover of workers, the higher λ is and the slower the adjustment of employment is.

Consider now the response of hours and employment to a permanent increase in labor demand as measured by an increase in the marginal products $F_{n,t}$ and $F_{h,t}$. To make matters clearer, assume that the production function can be expressed in terms of total hours as $F(n_t h_t)$. Thus, an increase in the number of total hours is required. Noting that $F_{h,t} = F'_t n_t$ and $F_{n,t} = F'_t h_t$, in the long run

$$\frac{F_{h,t}}{n_t} = F_t' = W_t',$$

$$F_{n,t} = F_t' h_t = W_t.$$

Due to the convexity of the wage function, $W_t' \geqslant W_t/h_t$. Hence, it is more costly to raise the number of hours per worker than to increase the number of workers. Thus, in the long run, hours will stay constant and employment will increase. But in the short run, as employment takes time to adjust, there will be a temporary increase in the number of hours. The response of hours and employment to a temporary increase in labor demand depends on the cost of hiring and firing relative to the cost of increasing hours worked.

4.8 General Equilibrium in a Decentralized Economy

General equilibrium is attained through markets coordinating the decisions of households and firms. The goods market coordinates households' consumption decisions and firms' output and investment decisions. The labor market coordinates firms' demand for labor and households' supply of labor with the real-wage rate equating labor demand and supply. Financial markets coordinate households' savings decisions and firms' borrowing requirements through the real interest rate. The bond market coordinates the savings in financial assets of households and the borrowing by firms. In the absence of considerations of risk, the price of bonds is determined by equating their rate of return in the long run to the rate of time preference of households. And the stock market prices the capital of firms so that its rate of return is the same as that on bonds.

4.8.1 Consolidating the Household and Firm Budget Constraints

Before examining general equilibrium in further detail, we consider what the results so far imply for the various constraints on households and firms, and how they can be combined, or consolidated. This enables us to determine a number of the variables defined above, such as exogenous income x_t, household assets a_t, firm debt b_t, and profits Π_t.

The national income identity is

$$y_t = c_t + i_t = F(k_t, n_t).$$

The household budget constraint is

$$\Delta a_{t+1} + c_t = w_t n_t + x_t + r_t a_t.$$

This includes labor income, exogenous income, and interest income. Combining these with the capital accumulation equation

$$\Delta k_{t+1} = i_t - \delta k_t$$

gives

$$x_t = F(k_t, n_t) - w_t n_t - \Delta k_{t+1} - \delta k_t + \Delta a_{t+1} - r a_t. \tag{4.37}$$

For the firm, profits are

$$\Pi_t = F(k_t, n_t) - w_t n_t - \Delta k_{t+1} - \delta k_t + \Delta b_{t+1} - r b_t. \tag{4.38}$$

Subtracting equation (4.38) from equation (4.37) gives

$$x_t - \Pi_t = \Delta(a_{t+1} - b_{t+1}) - r(a_t - b_t).$$

Since households' financial assets are firms' debts, $a_t = b_t$. This is the condition for equilibrium in the bond market. (If firms issue no debt, then $a_t = 0$.) It then follows that $x_t = \Pi_t$. Consequently, instead of x_t being exogenous, as has been assumed so far, we have shown that x_t is the distributed profit of the firm, the profits being distributed in the form of dividends.

As $F_{n,t} = w_t$ and $F_{k,t} = r + \delta$ for all t (as r and δ are constant) we can rewrite firm profits as

$$\Pi_t = F(k_t, n_t) - F_{n,t} n_t - \Delta k_{t+1} - (F_{k,t+1} - r) k_t + \Delta b_{t+1} - r b_t$$
$$= F(k_t, n_t) - F_{n,t} n_t - F_{k,t} k_t - \Delta(k_{t+1} - b_{t+1}) + r(k_t - b_t).$$

If the production function has constant returns to scale (or, alternatively, approximating using a Taylor series expansion about $n_t = k_t = 0$),

$$F(k_t, n_t) = F_{n,t} n_t + F_{k,t} k_t.$$

Hence,

$$\Pi_t = -(k_{t+1} - b_{t+1}) + (1 + r)(k_t - b_t), \tag{4.39}$$

where $k_t - b_t$ can be interpreted as the net value of the firm.

From equation (4.39), the net value of the firm can be rewritten as the forward-looking difference equation

$$k_t - b_t = \frac{\Pi_t + (k_{t+1} - b_{t+1})}{1 + r}.$$

As $1/(1 + r) < 1$ we solve this equation forwards to obtain

$$k_t - b_t = \sum_{s=0}^{\infty} \frac{\Pi_{t+s}}{(1 + r)^{s+1}},$$

where we assume that the transversality condition

$$\lim_{s \to \infty} \frac{k_{t+s} - b_{t+s}}{(1 + r)^s} = 0$$

holds, implying that the discounted net value of the firm tends to zero. Thus the value of the firm is the discounted value of current and future profits. If profits are constant, and equal to Π, then this simplifies to

$$k_t - b_t = \frac{\Pi}{r}.$$

In other words, the net value of the firm, $k - b$, equals the present value of profits, Π/r. Further, as $x = \Pi$ and $a = b$, total household asset income is $x + ra = rk$.

If all profits are distributed as dividends and not retained to finance investment, then $k - b$ also equals the present value of total dividend payments. Dividing $k - b$ and Π/r by $n_{s,t}$, the number of shares in existence at time t, gives the standard formula for the value of a share, namely, the present value of current and expected future profits (commonly called earnings) per share. If all profits are distributed as dividends, and assuming that dividends per share d_t are expected to be the same in the future, the value of a share can also be written as

$$\frac{k_t - b_t}{n_{s,t}} = \frac{d_t}{r}. \tag{4.40}$$

Thus, $d_t = r((k_t - b_t)/n_{s,t})$, implying that dividend income is the permanent income provided from the net value of the firm. The rate of return to capital is $r = F_k - \delta$, the net marginal product of capital. r is also the rate of return to bonds and, as we have seen, in the long run this is equal to θ, the rate of time preference of households, which limits their willingness to save, i.e., to lend to firms. Financial markets therefore equate the rate of return on all forms of capital and determine the income flows from assets. Later, in chapter 10, we examine other aspects of the determination of asset prices and returns such as risk considerations and the concept of no-arbitrage.

If some profits are retained for investment, then the value of a share will also depend on the discounted net value of the firm at some point $T > t$ in the future and can be written

$$\frac{k_t - b_t}{n_{s,t}} = \sum_{s=0}^{T-1} \frac{d_{t+s}}{n_{s,t}(1+r)^{s+1}} + \frac{k_T - b_T}{n_{s,t}(1+r)^{T+1}}. \tag{4.41}$$

If we assume that all profits are eventually distributed as dividends, then, as $T \to \infty$, equation (4.41) reduces to equation (4.40).

4.8.2 The Labor Market

Abstracting from labor market adjustment costs and a nonlinear wage function, the demand and supply for labor are determined, respectively, from

$$F_{n,t} = w_t,$$
$$U_{n,t} = -w_t U_{c,t}.$$

Real wages adjust to clear the market so that

$$w_t = F_{n,t} = \frac{U_{n,t}}{U_{c,t}}.$$

This is a partial-equilibrium solution for labor as the marginal product of labor and the two marginal utilities will, in general, depend upon other endogenous variables, i.e., variables that are also determined within the economy.

The full general equilibrium solution requires that each endogenous variable is determined in terms of the exogenous variables.

This may be clearer if we employ particular functional forms. If, for example, the production function is Cobb–Douglas with constant returns to scale, then

$$y_t = Ak_t^\alpha n_t^{1-\alpha}$$

and so

$$F_{n,t} = (1-\alpha)A\left(\frac{k_t}{n_t}\right)^\alpha,$$

implying that the demand for labor is

$$n_t^d = \left[\frac{w_t}{(1-\alpha)A}\right]^{-\alpha} k_t,$$

where k_t is given at time t. If the utility function is that considered previously, namely,

$$U(c_t, l_t) = \frac{c_t^{1-\sigma}-1}{1-\sigma} + \ln(1-n_t),$$

then the labor supply is

$$n_t^s = 1 - \frac{c_t^\sigma}{w_t}.$$

Thus, the supply of labor depends on an endogenous variable, c_t. The equilibrium quantity of labor is

$$n_t = \left[\frac{w_t}{(1-\alpha)A}\right]^{-\alpha} k_t = 1 - \frac{c_t^\sigma}{w_t}.$$

The equilibrium real wage can be derived from this. It does not have a closed-form solution, but will depend on c_t and k_t. If the equilibrium real wage is

$$w_t = w(c_t, k_t),$$

then the equilibrium quantity of labor is

$$n_t = \left[\frac{w(c_t, k_t)}{(1-\alpha)A}\right]^{-\alpha} k_t$$
$$= n(c_t, k_t).$$

It also follows that, in equilibrium, labor income is

$$w_t n_t = w_t - c_t^\sigma$$
$$= f(c_t, k_t).$$

4.8.3 The Goods Market

Equilibrium in the goods market requires that aggregate demand equals aggregate supply. Aggregate demand is

$$y_t^d = c_t + i_t$$
$$= c_t + k_{t+1} - (1-\delta)k_t$$
$$= c_t + F_{k,t}^{-1}(r+\delta) - (1-\delta)k_t,$$

where we have used the result that consumption is proportional to wealth, the net marginal product of capital $F_{k,t} - \delta = r$, and hence k_{t+1} is the inverse function of $r + \delta$. Assuming a Cobb–Douglas production function,

$$F_{k,t}^{-1}(r + \delta) = \left[\frac{\alpha A}{r + \delta}\right]^{1/(1-\alpha)} n_t.$$

Hence,

$$y_t^d = c_t + \left[\frac{\alpha A}{r + \delta}\right]^{1/(1-\alpha)} n_t - (1 - \delta)k_t.$$

We note that c_t is proportional to wealth and so could be substituted.

Aggregate supply is obtained from the production function. Accordingly, goods-market equilibrium can be expressed as

$$A k_t^\alpha n_t^{1-\alpha} = c_t + \left[\frac{\alpha A}{r + \delta}\right]^{1/(1-\alpha)} n_t - (1 - r - \delta)k_t.$$

In steady state we have shown that

$$c_t = w_t n_t + x_t + r a_t$$
$$= w_t n_t + \Pi_t + r a_t$$
$$= w_t n_t + r k_t.$$

Aggregate supply is obtained from the production function. Consequently, goods-market equilibrium becomes

$$A k_t^\alpha n_t^{1-\alpha} = \left\{ w_t + \left[\frac{\alpha A}{r + \delta}\right]^{1/(1-\alpha)} \right\} n_t - (1 - r - \delta)k_t.$$

This involves three variables: k_t, n_t, and w_t. It can be solved together with the three equations

$$w_t = w(c_t, k_t) = w^*(k_t, n_t, r),$$
$$n_t = n(c_t, k_t) = n^*(k_t, n_t, r),$$
$$k_t = \left[\frac{\alpha A}{r + \delta}\right]^{1/(1-\alpha)} n_t.$$

We then have the complete solution.

4.9 Comparison with the Centralized Model

We may summarize the similarities between the basic centralized model and the decentralized model as follows. In the basic centralized model labor was not included explicitly, although, in effect, there was a single unit of labor. Despite this, the capital stock is determined in both the basic centralized model and the decentralized model from the marginal product of capital, investment is derived from the capital accumulation equation, and consumption is obtained from the national income identity.

In the centralized model capital is determined from the condition

$$F'(k_{t+1}) = \theta + \delta.$$

In the decentralized solution it is obtained from

$$F_{k,t+1} = r + \delta.$$

As there is just one unit of labor in the basic model, $n_t = 1$. Hence either $F_{k,t+1}$ does not depend upon labor or, equivalently, $F'(k_{t+1})$ includes labor implicitly. Further, in steady state, $r = \theta$ as households will continue to save, and firms will continue to accumulate capital, until the return obtained falls to θ, when households will not save any more and firms will no longer wish to accumulate more capital. Thus, in the centralized model, there is an implicit real interest rate, which is given by the net marginal product of capital:

$$r = F'(k_{t+1}) - \delta.$$

Although there is no explicit wage rate in the basic model, there is an implicit wage rate. As there is just one unit of labor in the basic model, the wage rate is also equal to the total cost of labor. From

$$F(k_t, n_t) = F_{n,t} n_t + F_{k,t+1} k_t$$

and from the condition that the marginal product of labor is the real wage, and also as $n_t = 1$, we obtain the following expression for the implicit real wage in the basic model:

$$w_t = F(k_t) - F'(k_{t+1})k_t. \tag{4.42}$$

In the basic centralized model there are no debts or financial assets; there is only capital, which is equity. An implicit measure of profits in the basic model can be obtained from the definition of profits in the decentralized model. If we define w_t as in equation (4.42), set $n_t = 1$, and $b_t = 0$, then firm profits are

$$\Pi_t = F(k_t) - [F(k_t) - F'(k_{t+1})k_t] - \Delta k_{t+1} - \delta k_t.$$

Substituting $F'(k_{t+1}) = \theta + \delta$ gives

$$\Pi_t = -k_{t+1} + (1 + \theta)k_t.$$

Consequently, the value of the capital stock (equity) in the basic model is

$$k_t = \frac{\Pi_t + k_{t+1}}{1 + \theta}$$

$$= \sum_{s=0}^{\infty} \frac{\Pi_{t+s}}{(1 + \theta)^{s+1}},$$

namely, the discounted value of current and future profits. If profits are denoted by the constant Π, then

$$k_t = \frac{\Pi}{\theta}.$$

Consumption is obtained in the basic model from the resource constraint:

$$c_t = F(k_t) - k_{t+1} + (1 - \delta)k_t.$$

When $n_t = 1$, it is also obtained from this equation in the decentralized model.

4.10 Conclusions

We have now seen how decisions can be decentralized and how markets, particularly labor and financial markets, coordinate decisions. This generalization has added useful detail to the basic centralized model and it has allowed us to include further variables such as saving, financial assets, the interest rate, labor, and the real-wage rate, and it has made it easier to examine a number of issues in greater depth. The analysis has also shown that the essential insights of the basic centralized model are unchanged. As it is often easier to analyze general equilibrium by using the basic centralized model than by using a decentralized model, which tends to lead to an increase in detail without altering the main conclusions, when it is convenient and the results are little affected, we will revert to using a centralized model in preference to a decentralized model. Further, we note that including labor caused only minor changes to the previous results; consequently, we shall also exclude labor where appropriate and feasible.

The decentralized general equilibrium model provides a benchmark against which later models may be compared. This is not to say that the model is suitable for analyzing every situation. We have still not introduced government, money, nominal values, or taken account of economic transactions with the rest of the world. Moreover, we have assumed that households and firms have perfect foresight and that there are no market imperfections due, for example, to monopoly power or frictions. It is the presence of these features that causes most of the complications in setting monetary and fiscal policy: inflation control and macroeconomic stabilization. Without these it is debatable whether active monetary and fiscal policy would even be required.

5

Government: Expenditures and Public Finances

5.1 Introduction

We now introduce government into our general equilibrium model. In this chapter we focus largely on the role of government in steady-state equilibrium: its expenditures and the implications of the government budget constraint for financing these expenditures through taxes and debt. For completeness, we include money and the general price level in the model at this stage but we defer the analysis of money demand, monetary policy, and inflation until later chapters.

The principal role of government is to provide public goods and services. Most governments also transfer income from one group to another, usually in pursuit of goals such as social equality or, less ambitiously, simply to improve the welfare of the poorest. These expenditures must be paid for. This can be achieved through taxation, or by borrowing (issuing debt to the public), or by printing money (in effect, borrowing from the central bank). In reality, all three financing methods are just different forms of taxation. Borrowing is deferred taxation as debt must be repaid in the future, together with any interest payments. Printing money generally creates inflation, which imposes a tax due to the loss of real purchasing power of nominal money holdings as prices rise.

A number of important new issues now arise. Ignoring the question of social equity, why should government, rather than the private sector, provide goods and services? What sort of goods and services should government provide, and what sort should the private sector provide for itself? As debts must be repaid in the future, in the longer term the current generation's borrowing is paid for from the taxes of tomorrow's generation. This gives rise to the notion that long-term borrowing involves intergenerational transfers. In what circumstances, therefore, is it justified for government to finance expenditures using debt finance (deferred taxation) rather than current taxation?

A pure public good is one whose consumption by one person does not exclude its consumption by others. The examples that are closest to being pure public goods are defense, the legal system, policing, environmental protection, and roads. Who should provide the public goods: the private sector or the government? Since private provision by one person implies provision for all, and public

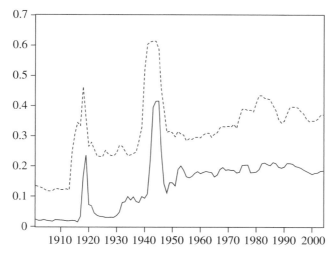

Figure 5.1. U.S. (solid line) and U.K. (dashed line) government
expenditures as a proportion of GDP, 1901–2005.

goods are costly to produce, there is little or no incentive for any one individual to make the provision if someone else will do so instead. This suggests that altruistic individuals would be necessary for any provision to be made. Everyone else would then become a "free rider." The outcome of leaving individuals to supply public goods would be fewer—possibly far fewer—public goods than would be required to maximize the welfare of the economy as a whole. One of the main reasons for having a government is to solve this problem. The role of the political system is to enable individuals to reveal their preferences about the type and quantity of public goods that they want. Governments then make the provision and share the cost among households. How cost is shared depends on the method of financing.

Many states also provide goods and services that are not pure public goods. For these government-supplied goods one person's consumption may well be at the cost of less consumption of these (or of other goods) by someone else. Examples are government-provided education, health, and some forms of transport. These goods and services are often provided by the state on the grounds of equity or efficiency due to economies of scale. Frequently, their public provision is a source of political controversy. Apart from government expenditures on goods and services, there are also government transfers arising from social security benefits, such as unemployment compensation, family benefits, and state pensions.

Most people take it for granted that government expenditures form a substantial proportion of GDP, yet this is a relatively recent phenomenon, as can be seen from figure 5.1 which plots government expenditures as a proportion of GDP for the United States and the United Kingdom since 1901. Real government expenditures on goods and services and real social security benefits as a proportion of GDP have increased considerably over the last century. In 1901 they were only 2.3% of GDP for the United States and 13.5% for the United Kingdom. In most Western countries they increased from around 10–20% of GDP prior to World War I to around 40–50% after World War II. The wars themselves were the times of the greatest expansion in government expenditures. Since World War II, the shares of government expenditures in GDP have not changed much, and are not much affected by the business cycle. In contrast, real unemployment benefits vary countercyclically over the business cycle. On average, the expenditures on goods and services and on transfers are roughly equal in size. Total government expenditures also include interest payments on government debt.

Government revenues are primarily tax revenues: direct taxes on incomes and expenditure, social security taxes, and corporate taxes. The balance varies somewhat between countries, but for most developed countries direct taxes and social security taxes—which are in effect taxes on incomes—are about 60% of total tax revenue, consumption taxes are about 25%, and corporate taxes are about 10%. The average tax rate on incomes (including social security) is around 42%.

As previously noted, governments can raise additional revenues through borrowing from the public or borrowing from the central bank, i.e., by printing money. The government simply extends its overdraft on its account with the central bank, which cashes checks issued to the public by the government.

It is common in macroeconomics without microfoundations, such as Keynesian macroeconomics, to treat government expenditures as having no welfare benefits. They are included simply to allow fiscal policy to be included in the analysis and to allow the size of the fiscal multiplier to be calculated. In the standard Keynesian model this is the effect on GDP of a discretionary change in government expenditures. As this is tantamount to buying goods and services and then throwing them away—or, as Keynes himself noted, burying them—this is not a satisfactory formulation of fiscal policy. In our analysis we start by including government expenditures in the household's utility function. We can then discuss the issue of the optimal level of government expenditures. This is followed by an analysis of public finances: how best to pay for government expenditures and satisfy the government budget constraint. We examine optimal tax policy, optimal debt, and the sustainability of fiscal deficits (the fiscal stance) in the longer term.

5.2   The Government Budget Constraint

5.2.1   The Nominal Government Budget Constraint

We begin by considering the government budget constraint (GBC), the sustainability of the fiscal stance, and the implications of various fiscal rules, such as the European Union's Stability and Growth Pact. The nominal GBC can be written as

$$P_t g_t + P_t h_t + B_t^G = P_t^B B_{t+1}^G + \Delta M_{t+1} + P_t T_t, \tag{5.1}$$

where g_t is real government expenditure, h_t is real transfers to households, T_t is total real taxes, and M_t is the stock of base, or outside, nominal money, i.e., non-interest-bearing money in circulation that is supplied by the government (the central bank) at the start of period t. The total stock of money consists of outside and inside money; inside money (mainly credit) is provided by the commercial banking system.

If the government issues only one-period bonds with a face value (value at maturity) of unity, then B_t^G is both the number of bonds issued at the start of period $t-1$ and the nominal expenditure made at the start of period t to redeem these bonds. Thus B_t^G is the value at maturity of the stock of nominal government debt held by the public (households) during period $t-1$. At the start of period t the government issues B_{t+1}^G new bonds at a price of P_t^B. As a result, it borrows $P_t^B B_{t+1}^G$.

The price of bonds can be written as

$$P_t^B = \frac{1}{1 + R_t},$$

where R_t is the rate at which one unit of currency is discounted in the next period. It is also the nominal interest rate on government debt issued at the start of period t but paid on the maturity of the bond in period $t+1$. Excluding default risk (the risk that the government fails to redeem the bond despite its promise to do so), R_t is a *risk-free return* that is known at time t. In practice, in each period a government usually issues bonds that mature at different times in the future. For convenience, here we assume that all bonds are issued for one period.

More generally, bonds may be of longer maturity, and may pay a coupon v each period that is a proportion of the face value of the bond at maturity. Bonds may also be sold prior to maturity. In this case we would define the return on the bond through

$$1 + R_{t+1}^B = \frac{P_{t+1}^B + v}{P_t^B}.$$

At the time of purchase, in period t, P_{t+1}^B is unknown and so, therefore, is the return on this investment, R_{t+1}^B. This is why the return R_{t+1}^B is dated at time $t+1$ and not t. As a result, R_{t+1}^B would be a risky return. We discuss the pricing of bonds in more detail in chapter 10.

The left-hand side of equation (5.1) is total nominal expenditures and the right-hand side is total revenues plus additions to the current financial resources of the government. Although the central bank supplies the additional money, we treat the central bank as an arm of government by consolidating the central bank's account with the government budget constraint.

5.2.2 The Real Government Budget Constraint

The real government budget constraint can be derived from the nominal GBC
by dividing through the nominal GBC by the general price level P_t. This gives

$$
g_t + h_t + b_t^G = T_t + P_t^B \frac{P_{t+1}}{P_t} \frac{B_{t+1}^G}{P_{t+1}} + \frac{P_{t+1}}{P_t} \frac{M_{t+1}}{P_{t+1}} - \frac{M_t}{P_t}
$$

$$
= T_t + \frac{1 + \pi_{t+1}}{1 + R_t} b_{t+1}^G + (1 + \pi_{t+1}) m_{t+1} - m_t
$$

$$
= T_t + \pi_{t+1} m_t + \frac{1}{1 + r_{t+1}} b_{t+1}^G + (1 + \pi_{t+1}) \Delta m_{t+1},
$$

where $\pi_{t+1} = \Delta P_{t+1}/P_t$ is the rate of inflation, $b_t^G = B_t^G/P_t$ is the real stock of
government debt, $m_t = M_t/P_t$ is the real stock of money, and r_t is the real rate
of interest defined by

$$
1 + r_{t+1} = \frac{1 + R_t}{1 + \pi_{t+1}},
$$

which implies that $r_{t+1} \simeq R_t - \pi_{t+1}$.

The term $\pi_{t+1} m_t$ measures the real resources accruing to the government
from holders of nominal non-interest-bearing money. It is known as "seigniorage" and is in effect a tax. A government unable to raise revenues from any other
source can usually do so from seigniorage. The higher the inflation rate, the
more seigniorage the government obtains. At some point, of course, the inflation rate may reach such a high level that people would cease to hold money,
in which case seigniorage revenues would collapse.

A very high rate of inflation is often thought to be due to a failure of monetary policy. In fact it is more likely to signal a failure of fiscal policy. Countries
without an adequate tax base, like many of the ex-Soviet Union states in the
1990s and more recently Zimbabwe in 2007, were obliged to pay for expenditures by printing money. In most low-inflation developed countries seigniorage
provides negligible revenue to the government.

To illustrate the relation between inflation and the pure-money financing of
fiscal expenditures, consider an economy in which the ratio of (base) money to
GDP is 0.2 and the proportion of GDP spent by government is 50%. To generate
sufficient seigniorage revenues the rate of inflation would have to be $\pi = [(g + h)/y]/[m/y] = 250\%$. This is typical of the rates of inflation that some ex-
Soviet Union states experienced before they established a conventional taxation
framework.

5.2.3 An Alternative Representation of the GBC

It is convenient for subsequent analysis to express the debt component of the
GBC so that it includes an explicit term for interest payments on government
debt. Accordingly, we rewrite the government revenue from bond sales in period
t as B_{t+1} instead of $P_t^B B_{t+1}^G$, and we denote expenditures in period t by $(1 + R_t)B_t$

instead of B_t^G. We can now interpret $R_t B_t$ as interest payments made at the start of period t on government debt that was issued in period $t-1$.

The nominal GBC therefore becomes

$$P_t g_t + P_t h_t + (1 + R_t)B_t = B_{t+1} + \Delta M_{t+1} + P_t T_t, \tag{5.2}$$

and the real GBC can be written as

$$g_t + h_t + (1 + R_t)b_t = T_t + (1 + \pi_{t+1})(b_{t+1} + m_{t+1}) - m_t, \tag{5.3}$$

where $b_t = B_t/P_t$. We shall use equation (5.3) in further analysis.

5.3 Financing Government Expenditures

We now consider alternative ways of financing government expenditures and some of the implications for fiscal policy. We ignore money finance and focus on tax and debt finance. The balanced-budget multiplier, a well-known result derived from the traditional Keynesian model, is that a tax-financed permanent increase in government expenditure permanently raises output and consumption. We consider whether this result also holds in our dynamic general equilibrium model. We also examine the effects of temporary fiscal policies and whether using debt finance makes a difference. For simplicity, we ignore issues related to money and inflation, and hence we assume that the interest rate is constant.

5.3.1 Tax Finance

Consider first a permanent increase of Δg_t in government expenditures from period t that is financed by an increase in lump-sum taxes of ΔT_t in period t. Noting that $b_{t-1} = b_t$ in all of the following examples, the GBCs for periods $t-1$, t, and $t+1$ are

$$t - 1: \qquad g_{t-1} + Rb_t = T_{t-1},$$
$$t: \quad g_{t-1} + \Delta g_t + Rb_t = T_{t-1} + \Delta T_t,$$
$$t + 1: \quad g_{t-1} + \Delta g_t + Rb_t = T_{t-1} + \Delta T_t.$$

Thus, if government expenditures are raised permanently by Δg_t, then taxes must be raised permanently by the same amount to satisfy the GBC. We now examine the effect on consumption and GDP.

We have seen previously that consumption in the DGE model is proportional to wealth, and not income as in the Keynesian model. If inflation is zero, consumption and household wealth are (omitting transfers)

$$c_t = \frac{R}{1 + R} W_t,$$
$$W_t = \sum_{s=0}^{\infty} \frac{(x_{t+s} - T_{t+s})}{(1 + R)^s} + (1 + R)b_t,$$

where x_t is income before taxes, which is assumed to be exogenous. If future income and taxes are expected to remain at their time t and $t - 1$ levels, then $x_{t+s} = x_t = x_{t-1}$ and $T_{t+s} = T_t$ for all $s \geqslant 0$. This implies that consumption is determined by current total income:

$$c_t = x_t - T_t + Rb_t. \tag{5.4}$$

We now introduce a permanent increase in government expenditures in period t. Since taxes also increase permanently by ΔT, consumption in periods $t - 1$ and t is

$$c_{t-1} = x_{t-1} - T_{t-1} + Rb_t,$$
$$c_t = x_t - (T_{t-1} + \Delta T_t) + Rb_t$$
$$= c_{t-1} - \Delta T_t$$
$$= c_{t-1} - \Delta g_t.$$

The increase in government expenditure has therefore been fully offset by a reduction in private consumption due to a fall in wealth caused by extra taxes. If the national income identity at time $t - 1$ is

$$y_{t-1} = c_{t-1} + g_{t-1},$$

then

$$y_t = c_{t-1} + \Delta c_t + g_{t-1} + \Delta g_t = y_{t-1}.$$

As $\Delta c_t = -\Delta g_t$, GDP is unchanged. The fiscal stimulus has therefore been totally ineffective as the injection of expenditure has been completely crowded out by expected increases in taxes.

If the fiscal expenditure increase takes the form of an increase in transfers, then higher taxes would completely offset the higher transfer income. There would therefore be no change in wealth, consumption, or GDP because, for unchanged income x_t and a permanent increase in transfers of Δh_t, wealth in period t would be

$$W_t = \frac{(1 + R)(x_t + h_{t-1} + \Delta h_t - T_{t-1} - \Delta T_t)}{R} + (1 + R)b_t = W_{t-1}.$$

We contrast this result with the standard Keynesian balanced-budget multiplier. The standard Keynesian consumption function assumes that consumption is a proportion $0 < \mu < 1$ of total income, so that instead of equation (5.4) we have

$$c_t = \mu(x_t - T_t + Rb_t).$$

It then follows that after the expenditure increase,

$$y_t = \mu(x_t - T_{t-1} - \Delta T_t + Rb_t) + g_{t-1} + \Delta g_t$$
$$= y_{t-1} + (1 - \mu)\Delta g_t > y_{t-1}.$$

Thus, if $0 < \mu < 1$, then GDP would increase and fiscal policy would be effective in the Keynesian model.

5.3.2 Bond Finance

We now assume that pure bond finance is used. Issuing more bonds raises government expenditures through the additional interest payments. We distinguish between a permanent and a temporary increase in government expenditures.

5.3.2.1 A Permanent Increase of Δg_t in Period t

The sequence of government budget constraints in periods $t - 1$, t, $t + 1$, etc., following a permanent increase in government expenditures is

$$
\begin{aligned}
t-1: &\quad g_{t-1} + Rb_t = T_{t-1}, \\
t: &\quad g_t + \Delta g_t + Rb_t = T_{t-1} + \Delta b_{t+1}, \\
t+1: &\quad g_t + \Delta g_t + R(b_t + \Delta b_{t+1}) = T_{t-1} + \Delta b_{t+2}, \\
&\qquad\qquad\vdots \\
t+n-1: &\quad g_t + \Delta g_t + Rb_t + R\sum_{s=1}^{n-1} \Delta b_{t+s} = T_{t-1} + \Delta b_{t+n}.
\end{aligned}
$$

Hence,

$$
\Delta b_{t+n} = (1 + R)^{n-1}\Delta g_t
$$

and so

$$
b_{t+n} = b_t + \sum_{s=1}^{n} \Delta b_{t+s} = b_t + (1 + R)\left[\frac{(1 + R)^{n-1} - 1}{R}\right]\Delta g_t.
$$

Therefore,

$$
\frac{b_{t+n}}{(1 + R)^n} = \frac{b_t}{(1 + R)^n} + \left[\frac{1}{R} - \frac{1}{R(1 + R)^{n-1}}\right]\Delta g_t
$$

and

$$
\lim_{n \to \infty} \frac{b_{t+n}}{(1 + R)^n} = \frac{1}{R}\Delta g_t \neq 0.
$$

As discounted debt is not zero, it follows that debt grows without bound. This violates the intertemporal budget constraint. Hence, a bond-financed permanent increase in government expenditures is not sustainable.

5.3.2.2 A Temporary Increase of Δg_t (Or a Fall in T) Only in Period t

The sequence of government budget constraints in periods $t - 1$, t, $t + 1$, etc., is now

$$
\begin{aligned}
t-1: &\quad g_{t-1} + Rb_t = T_{t-1}, \\
t: &\quad g_{t-1} + \Delta g_t + Rb_t = T_{t-1} + \Delta b_{t+1}, \\
t+1: &\quad g_{t-1} + R(b_t + \Delta b_{t+1}) = T_{t-1} + \Delta b_{t+2}, \\
&\qquad\qquad\vdots \\
t+n-1: &\quad g_{t-1} + R\left(b_t + \sum_{s=1}^{n} \Delta b_{t+s}\right) = T_{t-1} + \Delta b_{t+n},
\end{aligned}
$$

where

$$\Delta b_{t+1} = \Delta g_t,$$
$$\Delta b_{t+2} = R\Delta g_t,$$
$$\Delta b_{t+3} = R(1 + R)\Delta g_t,$$
$$\vdots$$
$$\Delta b_{t+n} = R(1 + R)^{n-2}\Delta g_t.$$

Hence

$$b_{t+n} = b_t + \sum_{s=1}^{n} \Delta b_{t+s}$$
$$= b_t + \left[1 + R \sum_{s=0}^{n-2} (1 + R)^s\right]\Delta g_t$$
$$= b_t + (1 + R)^{n-1}\Delta g_t,$$
$$\frac{b_{t+n}}{(1 + R)^n} = \frac{b_t}{(1 + R)^n} + \frac{1}{1 + R}\Delta g_t,$$

and so

$$\lim_{n \to \infty} \frac{b_{t+n}}{(1 + R)^n} = \frac{1}{1 + R}\Delta g_t \neq 0.$$

As discounted debt is not zero, fiscal policy is still not sustainable.

Suppose, however, that the temporary change in government expenditures was a random shock, and that in each period there is a random shock with zero mean, we can then write $\Delta g_t = e_t$, where $E(e_t) = 0$ and $E(e_t e_{t+s}) = 0$. As a result, we now consider the *average* discounted value of debt, which is

$$\lim_{n \to \infty} E\left[\frac{b_{t+n}}{(1 + R)^n}\right] = \frac{1}{1 + R}E[\Delta g_t] = 0.$$

Hence debt no longer explodes. We have shown, therefore, that bond-financing temporary increases in government expenditures that are expected to be zero on average (i.e., fiscal policy shocks) is a sustainable policy because positive shocks are expected to be offset over time by negative shocks.

A similar argument can be made with respect to the business cycle, where the shocks may be serially correlated over time. If increases in expenditures during periods of recession are offset by decreases in expenditures during boom, and if these cancel out over a complete cycle, then debt finance can be used. In particular, there is no need to raise taxes during a recession, as many governments seem to do, just because the government deficit is increasing. It is, however, important that, when fiscal surpluses reappear in the upturn, these are used to redeem debt and are not used to cut taxes. There are often strong pressures on government to cut taxes during a boom, but it may be necessary to resist these to avoid the accumulation of debt across cycles and hence to keep public finances on a sustainable path in the longer term.

5.3.3 Intertemporal Fiscal Policy

Suppose the government wants to provide a temporary stimulus to the economy. One possible policy is to cut taxes today, finance this by borrowing today, and then, as the stimulus is temporary, to restore tax revenues tomorrow. In this way fiscal policy will be sustainable. What is the effect of this on the GBC and on consumption?

Let the tax cut occur in period t, and assume that in period $t + 2$ the GBC of period $t - 1$ is to be restored. Consequently, the GBCs for periods $t - 1, t, t + 1$, and $t + 2$ are

$$
\begin{aligned}
t - 1: && g_{t-1} + Rb_t &= T_{t-1}, \\
t: && g_{t-1} + Rb_t &= T_{t-1} + \Delta T_t + \Delta b_{t+1}, \\
t + 1: && g_{t-1} + R(b_t + \Delta b_{t+1}) &= T_{t-1} + \Delta T_{t+1} + \Delta b_{t+2}, \\
t + 2: && g_{t-1} + Rb_t &= T_{t-1},
\end{aligned}
$$

where, due to the tax cut, $\Delta T_t < 0$. Thus

$$
\begin{aligned}
\Delta b_{t+1} &= -\Delta T_t, \\
\Delta b_{t+2} &= -\Delta b_{t+1}, \\
\Delta T_{t+1} &= R\Delta b_{t+1} - \Delta b_{t+2} = -(1 + R)\Delta T_t.
\end{aligned}
$$

Hence, for b_{t+2} to be restored to b_{t-1}, taxes must be increased in period $t + 1$ by $-(1 + R)\Delta T_t$.

It can be shown that wealth is unaffected by this as its values in periods $t - 1$ and t are

$$
W_{t-1} = \sum_{s=0}^{\infty} \frac{x_{t+s-1} - T_{t+s-1}}{(1 + R)^s} + (1 + R)b_{t-1},
$$

$$
\begin{aligned}
W_t &= \sum_{s=0}^{\infty} \frac{x_{t+s} - T_{t+s}}{(1 + R)^s} + (1 + R)b_t \\
&= W_{t-1} - \Delta T_t - \frac{1 - (1 + R)}{(1 + R)}\Delta T_t = W_{t-1} - \frac{1}{1 + R}\Delta T_t.
\end{aligned}
$$

As $\Delta T_t < 0$, wealth and hence consumption increase in period t. In period $t + 1$ wealth returns to its period $t - 1$ value as higher taxes exactly offset the increase in financial assets. Thus the stimulus to consumption of the bond-financed tax cut is only temporary.

5.3.4 The Ricardian Equivalence Theorem

In the two examples above, fiscal policy has been shown to be ineffective in raising consumption in the long run. This is because the public has anticipated the future tax increases required to balance the budget and has revised its current wealth estimates accordingly. Thus, neither a government expenditure increase funded by a lump-sum tax increase nor a temporary decrease in taxes funded initially by borrowing are effective ways to stimulate the economy. These examples are illustrations of what is known as the "Ricardian equivalence theorem," due to Barro (1974, 1989; see also Woodford 1995, 2001). Barro posed the question of whether government bonds are net wealth to the private sector, and took the view that they were not due to the public correctly anticipating the implied future tax liabilities. The theorem is associated with David Ricardo, the nineteenth-century economist, because Barro thought that Ricardo was the first to put forward the idea that taxation and debt are equivalent in their effects on the economy. Whether Ricardo really did believe this is a matter of dispute (see Buchanan 1976; O'Driscoll 1977).

The prevailing view at the time, which was in contrast to the Ricardian equivalence theorem, was based on the Keynesian model: it was that current consumption depended only on after-tax current income and not on wealth. It would then follow that if current income increases, then so would consumption and GDP. The Keynesian model therefore assumes that future tax increases have no effect on current consumption. This implies either that households are shortsighted or that they face a borrowing constraint so that in each period their consumption is limited to their current income, which they spend in full even though they would prefer to borrow in order to consume more than this.

A counterexample to the Ricardian equivalence theorem is the overlapping-generations (OLG) model, which is discussed in more detail in chapter 6. The distinguishing feature of the OLG model is the length of a time period. Typically people live for only two periods. The young pay taxes in both periods, but the old only pay taxes in the first period. Both generations receive the current benefits of the fiscal expansion (the tax cut), but only the young generation expects to have to pay the tax increase when it takes place next period. In this case, the old generation would increase their consumption in period t as their wealth is increased by the tax cut. Assuming that next period there is a new generation to share the tax burden with the current young generation and that, as a result, the current tax cut is fully offset by higher taxes next period so that the wealth of the current young generation is unchanged, then they would maintain their existing level of consumption. As a result, today's total consumption and GDP would increase.

More generally, time spent working is longer than time spent in retirement and so more than two time periods are required. This permits the tax burden to be shared with future generations, which would reduce the tax burden on today's young generation, and hence result in the current tax cut giving an even greater stimulus to the economy. Moreover, the further in the future the tax increase takes place, the greater the tax burden is on future generations and the less it is on the current young generation and so, once again, the greater is the current stimulus to the economy.

The OLG model is often a convenient analytic vehicle as it simplifies the dynamics. Its main drawback is that it may distort time too much. For example, unless the tax increase is expected to occur far into the future, all generations

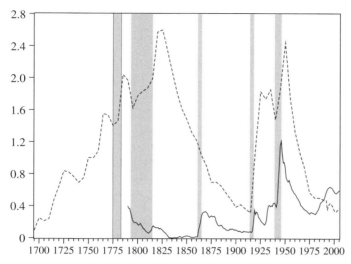

Figure 5.2. U.S. (solid line) and U.K. (dashed line)
government debt–GDP ratio, 1695–2005.

would expect to have to pay the increase. In contrast, for reasons of intergenerational equity, government expenditures (typically capital expenditures) that
are expected to have long-lasting benefits for later generations should be partly
borne by these later generations rather than be paid for in full by the current
generation. This can be accomplished by financing the expenditures partly by an
increase in current taxes and partly by government borrowing to be redeemed
by the taxes of future generations. In this way, all generations would share the
cost.

   We have seen that the greatest increases in government expenditures occur
during and immediately following wars. Since wars tend to be financed through
debt, there is usually also a substantial increase in the level of government debt:
see figure 5.2, which plots the debt–GDP ratios for the United States since 1790
and for the United Kingdom since 1695; the shaded areas are periods of war. U.S.
debt was high in 1790 following the American War of Independence (1775–83).
It increased substantially during the Civil War (1861–65) and World War I (U.S.
participation was from 1917 to 1918); it also increased during World War II
(U.S. participation was from 1942 to 1945) and more recently during the 1980s.
U.K. government debt rose steadily during the eighteenth century, especially
during the American War of Independence, and peaked during and after the
Napoleonic Wars (1792–1815). It is still possible to purchase consols issued to
finance the Napoleonic Wars. It then rose very sharply during and after World
War I (1914–18) and again during and immediately after World War II (1939–45).
After this, U.K. debt has been rapidly redeemed. The last loans from the United
States were paid off during 2006. One rationale for the use of debt to finance
wars is that, as future generations benefit from victory, they should share the
cost.

Whatever Ricardo's views and the general applicability of the Ricardian equivalence theorem, it has become a key proposition in DGE models of the economy as it focuses attention both on the effectiveness of a debt-financed fiscal stimulus to the economy and the relation between government debt and future net government revenues. It has even influenced government policy. For example, recently, the U.K. government proposed a "golden rule" for public finance that says that debt finance not associated with the business cycle may only be used for government investment (but not consumption). Ultimately, of course, the investment is tax financed. What is not stated is that this policy is equitable only if future taxpayers also benefit from the investment. If the current generation also obtain benefit from the investment, then they too should make a tax contribution. We now consider the longer-term sustainability of public finances in more detail.

5.4   The Sustainability of the Fiscal Stance

Government expenditures can be financed either from taxes or by borrowing. Whatever the balance between the two, the government budget constraint must be satisfied at all times. In the short run this is usually achieved through debt finance. For the private sector to be willing to hold government debt, especially in the longer term, it must be confident that the debt will be redeemed. In other words, the fiscal stance (public finances) must be sustainable. If the debt–GDP ratio is expected to rise indefinitely, then concern that government would be unable to meet its debt obligations without having to resort to monetizing the debt—which carries with it the threat of generating high inflation, or even hyperinflation—would be likely to cause the private sector to be unwilling to hold government debt. Such a situation would arise if fiscal expenditures persistently exceeded revenues by a sufficient margin. This could happen due to either high government expenditures or low tax revenues as a result of a poor tax base. If the private sector were unwilling to hold government debt, then the government would have to print money. If this situation continued, before long it would lead to hyperinflation. As previously noted, this was what happened in many of the former Soviet republics immediately after their independence. More generally, it can be shown that a necessary condition for the sustainability of the current fiscal stance is that government debt and the debt–GDP ratio are expected to remain finite.

The European Union's Stability and Growth Pact (SGP) and the United Kingdom's golden rule of public expenditures are attempts to achieve a sustainable fiscal stance. According to the SGP, no EU government is allowed a government deficit in excess of 3% of GDP or a level of debt in excess of 60% of GDP. The United Kingdom's golden rule requires a balanced budget over the business cycle. In other words, the ratio of debt to GDP should be constant over a complete cycle. It also stipulates that the government will borrow only to finance investment, not consumption, expenditures. We now consider the conditions required for the fiscal stance to be sustainable and whether the EU and U.K. fiscal rules make sense.

We begin by rewriting the government budget constraint in terms of proportions of GDP. This is more convenient for a growing economy as these proportions are likely to remain constant over time. The ratio of taxes to output can then be interpreted as the average effective tax rate. Dividing through the nominal government budget constraint, equation (5.2), by nominal GDP $P_t y_t$ gives

$$\frac{P_t g_t}{P_t y_t} + \frac{P_t h_t}{P_t y_t} + \frac{(1 + R_t) B_t}{P_t y_t} = \frac{P_t T_t}{P_t y_t} + \frac{B_{t+1}}{P_t y_t} + \frac{M_{t+1}}{P_t y_t} - \frac{M_{t+1}}{P_t y_t}. \tag{5.5}$$

This can be rewritten as

$$\frac{g_t}{y_t} + \frac{h_t}{y_t} + (1 + R_t)\frac{b_t}{y_t}$$
$$= \frac{T_t}{y_t} + (1 + \pi_{t+1})(1 + y_{t+1})\left(\frac{b_{t+1}}{y_{t+1}} + \frac{m_{t+1}}{y_{t+1}}\right) - \frac{m_t}{y_t}, \tag{5.6}$$

where y_t is the rate of growth of GDP and T_t/y_t is the average tax rate.

The total nominal government deficit (or public-sector borrowing requirement, PSBR) is defined as

$$P_t D_t = P_t g_t + P_t h_t + R_t B_t - P_t T_t - \Delta M_{t+1}; \tag{5.7}$$

hence D_t/y_t, the real government deficit as a proportion of GDP, is

$$\frac{D_t}{y_t} = \frac{g_t}{y_t} + \frac{h_t}{y_t} + R_t\frac{b_t}{y_t} - \frac{T_t}{y_t} - (1 + \pi_{t+1})(1 + y_{t+1})\frac{m_{t+1}}{y_{t+1}} + \frac{m_t}{y_t}$$
$$= (1 + \pi_{t+1})(1 + y_{t+1})\frac{b_{t+1}}{y_{t+1}} - \frac{b_t}{y_t}. \tag{5.8}$$

The right-hand side shows the net borrowing required to fund the deficit expressed as a proportion of GDP.

We also define the nominal primary deficit $P_t d_t$ (the total deficit less debt interest payments) as

$$P_t d_t = D_t - R_t B_t. \tag{5.9}$$

Hence the ratio of the primary deficit to GDP is

$$\frac{d_t}{y_t} = \frac{g_t}{y_t} + \frac{h_t}{y_t} - \frac{T_t}{y_t} - (1 + \pi_{t+1})(1 + y_{t+1})\frac{m_{t+1}}{y_{t+1}} + \frac{m_t}{y_t}$$
$$= -(1 + R_t)\frac{b_t}{y_t} + (1 + \pi_{t+1})(1 + y_{t+1})\frac{b_{t+1}}{y_{t+1}}. \tag{5.10}$$

Equations (5.8) and (5.10) are both difference equations that determine the evolution of b_t/y_t. One is expressed in terms of the total deficit, the other in terms of the primary deficit. Since the nominal rate of growth $\pi_{t+1} + y_{t+1}$ is nearly always strictly positive, equation (5.8) is an unstable difference equation and hence must be solved forwards. In contrast, equation (5.10) could be a stable or an unstable difference equation, depending on whether

$$\frac{1 + R_t}{(1 + \pi_{t+1})(1 + y_{t+1})}$$

is greater than (unstable) or less than (stable) unity. If the difference equation is stable, then b_t/y_t will remain finite. But if it is unstable, then b_t/y_t could be finite or infinite. A finite debt–GDP ratio is necessary (but not sufficient) for the private sector to be willing to hold government debt. An exploding debt–GDP ratio is sufficient for the fiscal stance to be unsustainable. We therefore wish to find the conditions under which b_t/y_t remains finite.

We begin by examining equation (5.10). For simplicity, we assume that R_t, π_t, and y_t are constant. A more general analysis that allows these variables to be time-varying can be found in Polito and Wickens (2007). It then follows that

$$\begin{aligned}
\frac{d_t}{y_t} &= \frac{g_t}{y_t} + \frac{h_t}{y_t} - \frac{T_t}{y_t} - (1 + \pi)(1 + y)\frac{m_{t+1}}{y_{t+1}} + \frac{m_t}{y_t} \\
&= -(1 + R)\frac{b_t}{y_t} + (1 + \pi)(1 + y)\frac{b_{t+1}}{y_{t+1}}.
\end{aligned}$$

The debt–GDP ratio therefore evolves according to the difference equation

$$\frac{b_t}{y_t} = -\frac{1}{1 + R}\frac{d_t}{y_t} + \frac{(1 + \pi)(1 + y)}{1 + R}\frac{b_{t+1}}{y_{t+1}}. \tag{5.11}$$

5.4.1 Case 1: $[(1 + \pi)(1 + y)]/(1 + R) > 1$ (Stable Case)

In this case the rate of growth of nominal GDP is greater than the nominal rate of interest, i.e., $R < \pi + y$. We therefore write the GBC, equation (5.11), as the difference equation

$$\frac{b_{t+1}}{y_{t+1}} = \frac{1 + R}{(1 + \pi)(1 + y)}\frac{b_t}{y_t} + \frac{1}{(1 + \pi)(1 + y)}\frac{d_t}{y_t}. \tag{5.12}$$

As $0 < (1 + R)/[(1 + \pi)(1 + y)] < 1$, this is a stable difference equation, and hence can be solved *backwards* by successive substitution. For $n > 0$ we obtain

$$\begin{aligned}
\frac{b_{t+n}}{y_{t+n}} &= \left(\frac{1 + R}{(1 + \pi)(1 + y)}\right)^n \frac{b_t}{y_t} \\
&\quad + \frac{1}{(1 + \pi)(1 + y)}\sum_{s=0}^{n-1}\left(\frac{1 + R}{(1 + \pi)(1 + y)}\right)^{n-s-1}\frac{d_{t+s}}{y_{t+s}}.
\end{aligned}$$

Taking the limit as $n \to \infty$ and noting that

$$\lim_{n\to\infty}\left(\frac{1 + R}{(1 + \pi)(1 + y)}\right)^n \frac{b_t}{y_t} = 0,$$

we obtain

$$\lim_{n\to\infty}\frac{b_{t+n}}{y_{t+n}} = \frac{1}{(1 + \pi)(1 + y)}\sum_{s=0}^{\infty}\left(\frac{1 + R}{(1 + \pi)(1 + y)}\right)^{n-s-1}\frac{d_{t+s}}{y_{t+s}}. \tag{5.13}$$

We now examine the implications of equation (5.13).

5.4.2 Implications

(1) In the special case where the ratio of the primary deficit to GDP is expected to remain unchanged in the future, i.e.,

$$\frac{d_{t+s}}{y_{t+s}} = \frac{d_t}{y_t} \quad \text{for } s \geqslant 0,$$

equation (5.13) becomes

$$\lim_{n \to \infty} \frac{b_{t+n}}{y_{t+n}} = \frac{1}{(1+\pi)(1+y) - (1+R)} \frac{d_t}{y_t}$$

$$\simeq \frac{1}{\pi + y - R} \frac{d_t}{y_t} > 0. \tag{5.14}$$

Hence, if $\pi + y > R$, the debt–GDP ratio will remain finite regardless of the initial value of d_t/y_t. Hence fiscal policy is sustainable for any value of d_t/y_t. There can even be a permanent primary deficit (i.e., $d/y > 0$) and the debt–GDP ratio will be constant.

(2) In principle, fiscal sustainability only requires that the debt–GDP ratio remains finite and that the market is willing to hold government debt. In general, therefore, $d_{t+s}/(y_t + s)$ can vary over time. As the debt–GDP ratio rises, however, fears of default may increase. Prudential reasons therefore tend to limit the acceptable size of this ratio. As a result, it is common in practice to impose an upper limit on the debt–GDP ratio, as in the SGP. The precise choice of upper limit is inevitably somewhat arbitrary. The market has shown that it is willing to continue to hold government debt for higher values of the debt–GDP ratio than that prescribed by the SGP. When fiscal policy is not sustainable at the announced limit, there may be a temptation to raise the limit. The drawback is that doing this repeatedly would damage the credibility of fiscal policy.

(3) Although not strictly necessary, in order to give fiscal policy greater clarity—and hence make it more accountable—a government might wish to achieve a particular debt-GDP ratio in period $t + n$. This might be the same value as for period t. The government might even go a step further and want both b_t/y_t and d_t/y_t to be constant for all future t. From equation (5.14) this would imply that the following condition should be satisfied:

$$\frac{b_t}{y_t} \geqslant \frac{1}{\pi + y - R} \frac{d_t}{y_t}. \tag{5.15}$$

The equality sign in equation (5.14) has been replaced by an inequality sign as the fiscal stance is sustainable provided the evolution of debt (as given by the right-hand side) does not exceed the target debt–GDP ratio. More generally, this enables us to find the debt-GDP ratio for any constant d_t/y_t and any constant value of $\pi + y - R$ that is positive. In other words, fiscal sustainability may be satisfied, but at a different value of the debt-GDP ratio from the one that was wanted.

(4) We could have obtained this result directly from the GBC, equation (5.11), by rewriting it as

$$(1 + \pi)(1 + y)\Delta\frac{b_{t+1}}{y_{t+1}} = -(\pi + y - R)\frac{b_t}{y_t} + \frac{d_t}{y_t} = 0.$$

If the debt–GDP ratio is constant, then $\Delta(b_{t+1}/y_{t+1}) = 0$. We then obtain equation (5.15).

(5) Not only may the fiscal stance be sustainable when there is a permanent primary deficit, there may also be a permanent *total* deficit. As

$$\frac{D_t}{y_t} = \frac{d_t}{y_t} + R\frac{b_t}{y_t}$$

we have

$$\begin{aligned}
\frac{b_t}{y_t} &\geqslant \frac{1}{\pi + y - R}\frac{d_t}{y_t} \\
&\geqslant \frac{1}{\pi + y - R}\left(\frac{D_t}{y_t} - R\frac{b_t}{y_t}\right) \\
&\geqslant \frac{D_t/y_t}{\pi + y}.
\end{aligned} \tag{5.16}$$

$D_t > 0$ implies that fiscal sustainability is also consistent with having a permanent total deficit. In particular, although often regarded as a requirement for sound fiscal policy, a balanced budget is unnecessary for fiscal sustainability.

5.4.3   Case 2: $0 < [(1 + \pi)(1 + y)]/(1 + R) < 1$ (Unstable Case)

In this case $R > \pi + y$: the nominal rate of interest is greater than the rate of growth of nominal GDP. The GBC is now an unstable difference equation. It must therefore be solved *forwards*, not backwards, as follows:

$$\begin{aligned}
\frac{b_t}{y_t} &= \left(\frac{(1 + \pi)(1 + y)}{1 + R}\right)\frac{b_{t+1}}{y_{t+1}} - \frac{1}{1 + R}\frac{d_t}{y_t} \\
&= \left(\frac{(1 + \pi)(1 + y)}{1 + R}\right)^n\frac{b_{t+n}}{y_{t+n}} - \frac{1}{1 + R}\sum_{s=0}^{n-1}\left(\frac{(1 + \pi)(1 + y)}{1 + R}\right)^s\frac{d_{t+s}}{y_{t+s}}.
\end{aligned}$$

Taking limits as $n \to \infty$, if

$$\lim_{n \to \infty}\left(\frac{(1 + \pi)(1 + y)}{1 + R}\right)^n\frac{b_{t+n}}{y_{t+n}} = 0, \tag{5.17}$$

then

$$\frac{b_t}{y_t} \leqslant \frac{1}{1 + R}\sum_{s=0}^{\infty}\left(\frac{(1 + \pi)(1 + y)}{1 + R}\right)^s\left(\frac{-d_{t+s}}{y_{t+s}}\right), \tag{5.18}$$

where $-d_t > 0$ is the primary *surplus*. We introduce the inequality sign because a present value of current and future surpluses that exceeds the current debt–GDP ratio is also consistent with fiscal sustainability. The terminal condition, equation (5.17), is known as the no-Ponzi condition. It rules out funding debt interest payments by issuing more debt. (A Ponzi game is a pyramid system in which contributors are paid interest on their investments and the interest payments are paid from the investments of new contributors. At some point the pyramid will, of course, collapse due to an insufficient number of new investors.)

5.4.4 Implications

(1) The right-hand side of equation (5.18) is the present value of current and future primary *surpluses* as a proportion of GDP. Thus, for fiscal sustainability, these must be sufficient to meet current debt obligations. This allows d_t/y_t to vary through time. One of the factors that causes d_t/y_t to vary is the business cycle; d_t/y_t tends to be positive in a recession and negative in a boom. A practical way to interpret the condition for fiscal sustainability is to require that the present value of primary surpluses over a complete business cycle is zero. As a result, the debt–GDP ratio would rise during a recession, fall during a boom, but remain constant over the whole cycle. This is the basis of the U.K. government's golden rule for fiscal policy.

(2) In the special case where

$$\frac{d_{t+s}}{y_{t+s}} = \frac{d_t}{y_t} \quad \text{for all } s > 0$$

we find that

$$\frac{b_t}{y_t} \leqslant \frac{1}{1+R} \sum_{s=0}^{\infty} \left(\frac{(1+\pi)(1+y)}{1+R} \right)^s \left(\frac{-d_t}{y_t} \right) \simeq \frac{1}{R-\pi-y} \left(\frac{-d_t}{y_t} \right). \tag{5.19}$$

When the equality sign holds this is the same result as in the stable case, except that because the sign of $R-(\pi+y)$ is now reversed, the sign of d is also reversed (i.e., we need surpluses to pay off the debt). The inequality sign reflects the fact that a positive present value will also allow current debts to be paid off. We note that the inequality sign in the unstable case is the opposite of that in the stable case. The reason for the difference is that in the stable case future primary deficits must not cause the *future* debt–GDP ratio to exceed a given upper limit, whereas in the unstable case future primary surpluses must be large enough to meet *current* debt liabilities.

(3) Again, although it is necessary to have primary surpluses, it is still possible to have a total deficit. As

$$\frac{D_t}{y_t} = \frac{d_t}{y_t} + R\frac{b_t}{y_t}$$

we have

$$\frac{b_t}{y_t} \leqslant \frac{1}{R-\pi-y} \left(\frac{-d_t}{y_t} \right) \tag{5.20}$$

$$\leqslant \frac{1}{R-\pi-y} \left(R\frac{b_t}{y_t} - \frac{D_t}{y_t} \right)$$

$$\geqslant \frac{D_t/y_t}{\pi+y}. \tag{5.21}$$

This is identical to equation (5.16)—even the inequality sign is the same. Three cases may be distinguished:

$$\frac{b}{y} > \frac{1}{\pi + y}\frac{D}{y}, \quad \text{falling debt–GDP ratio,}$$

$$\frac{b}{y} = \frac{1}{\pi + y}\frac{D}{y}, \quad \text{constant debt–GDP ratio,}$$

$$\frac{b}{y} < \frac{1}{\pi + y}\frac{D}{y}, \quad \text{rising debt–GDP ratio.}$$

The first two are sustainable fiscal stances, but the third—where the debt–GDP ratio is rising—is ultimately unsustainable.

(4) Consider what would happen if a government had existing debts but maintained a zero primary deficit (i.e., $d_t/y_t = 0$). In order to meet the interest charges on existing debt, the government must issue more debt. Debt would therefore accumulate without limit. In this case the budget constraint can be written as

$$\frac{b_t}{y_t} = \frac{(1 + \pi)(1 + y)}{1 + R}\frac{b_{t+1}}{y_{t+1}}$$

and hence

$$\frac{b_t}{y_t} = \lim_{n \to \infty}\left(\frac{(1 + \pi)(1 + y)}{1 + R}\right)^n\frac{b_{t+n}}{y_{t+n}}.$$

This no-Ponzi game condition implies that only zero initial debt would be consistent with this limit tending to zero, and hence satisfy equation (5.17). If initial debt is not zero, then a primary surplus is required, otherwise debt will grow too fast.

5.4.5 The Optimal Level of Debt

As a final observation on these results we note that although they tell us how to run fiscal policy to sustain a given level of debt, and what the debt consequences will be of running a given deficit, they do not tell us what the optimal level of debt is. In effect, we are taking the current debt–GDP ratio as given; sustainable fiscal policy simply seeks to maintain this debt–GDP ratio. In practice, countries have different debt–GDP ratios. This suggests that a country can change its debt–GDP ratio if it wishes, and this too would be sustainable at an appropriate level of the fiscal deficit compatible with the sustainability condition above.

Sargent and Wallace (1981), in an article entitled "Some unpleasant arithmetic," have suggested that there is an upper limit to the debt–GDP ratio above which financial markets would not be willing to hold more government debt. Beyond this point, they argue, the government would need to use money finance. The title of their paper reflects the possibility that the resulting rate of growth of the money supply may exceed the target set by the monetary authority. This is an example of how fiscal policy may destabilize monetary policy.

Further references on fiscal sustainability are Bohn (1995), Polito and Wickens (2007), and Wilcox (1989).

5.5 The Stability and Growth Pact

The European Union's SGP sets upper limits on the debt–GDP ratio and the total deficit as a proportion of GDP. The maximum value of $b/y = 0.6$ (60% of GDP) and the maximum value of $D/y = 0.03$ (3% of GDP). What implications does this have for fiscal sustainability? From equation (5.16),

$$\frac{b_t}{y_t} \geqslant \frac{1}{\pi + \gamma} \frac{D_t}{y_t},$$

$$60 \geqslant \frac{1}{\pi + \gamma} 3,$$

$$\pi + \gamma \geqslant \frac{3}{60} \equiv 5.$$

Thus, even if the debt and deficit limits of the SGP are achieved, for the fiscal stance to be sustainable, the nominal rate of growth must not be less than 5%. If nominal growth were less than this, then debt would rise above 60% even if the deficit limit were satisfied. It follows that the SGP is not sufficient for the sustainability of the fiscal stance.

Nor is the SGP necessary for a sustainable fiscal policy either. Even if the deficit or debt limits were exceeded, there is a rate of nominal growth that would be consistent with fiscal sustainability. For example, if the deficit exceeds 3%, it is still possible for the debt–GDP ratio to meet the 60% limit if nominal growth exceeds 5%. And if the debt–GDP ratio exceeds 60%, but the deficit satisfies 3%, then sustainability could be satisfied with a nominal growth rate less than 5%.

Consider the case of Belgium in 1993, when the SGP was first enshrined in the Maastricht Treaty. Belgium's fiscal stance was

$$\frac{b}{y} = 145\%, \qquad \frac{D}{y} = 6.5\%, \qquad R = 7.8\%, \qquad \pi + \gamma = 4.$$

Clearly Belgium broke both the debt and deficit limits and therefore did not satisfy the SGP. But was its fiscal stance nonetheless sustainable? The answer is no, as

$$\frac{b_t}{y_t} = 1.45 \geqslant \frac{1}{\pi + \gamma} \frac{D_t}{y_t} = \frac{0.065}{0.04} = 1.63.$$

Belgium did not satisfy fiscal sustainability—it would have done so had its rate of growth of nominal GDP been a little higher at 4.5%, or had the deficit been only 5.8%.

Since we have data on the nominal interest rate, and this exceeds the nominal rate of growth of GDP (as $7.8 > 4$), we can calculate the primary deficit and evaluate the sustainability condition expressed in terms of the present value of current and future primary surpluses. The primary deficit is

$$\frac{d_t}{y_t} = \frac{D_t}{y_t} - R \frac{b_t}{y_t}$$

$$= 0.065 - 0.078 \times 1.45 = -0.048.$$

Table 5.1. Fiscal sustainability of France and Germany in 2002.

	France (%)	Germany (%)
D/y	3.1	3.6
b/y	59.1	60.8
π	1.9	1.3
y	1.2	0.2
$\dfrac{1}{\pi + y}\dfrac{D}{y}$	100	240

Hence, in 1993 Belgium had a primary surplus. The present-value condition for fiscal sustainability is

$$\frac{b_t}{y_t} \leqslant \frac{1}{R - \pi - y}\left(\frac{-d_t}{y_t}\right).$$

For Belgium in 1993 we have $b/y = 1.45$ and the present value of future primary surpluses equal to 1.26, implying that the present value of current and future primary surplus is not expected to be sufficient to pay off current debt. The present-value condition has therefore given the same result as the total-deficit condition. Had the nominal interest rate been 3.6%, a considerably lower figure, then fiscal sustainability would have been satisfied. To sum up, in 1993 not only did Belgium not satisfy the Maastricht conditions or the SGP, it did not have a sustainable fiscal policy stance, however measured. We have also seen that a small increase in the rate of growth of nominal GDP, a small reduction in the deficit, or a considerably lower nominal interest rate would have made fiscal policy sustainable. Nevertheless, despite failing these tests, Belgium has continued to be able to sell its debt.

More recently, France and Germany have had difficulties meeting the requirements of the SGP. This led to attempts to impose substantial fines on them in accordance with the enforcement provisions of the SGP. Data for 2002 are given in table 5.1.

For fiscal sustainability we require that the value in the last row of the table should be less than the current debt–GDP ratio. We note that this is not satisfied for either country. The problem for each country is that although the SGP is almost satisfied, the rate of growth of nominal GDP is too low. The rates of nominal growth would need to be 5.2% for France and 5.9% for Germany. Given the prevailing rates of growth of nominal GDP in France and Germany, they would have needed to reduce their deficits below 3% to satisfy the debt–GDP limit. Thus although they meet the debt and deficit criteria of the SGP, the fiscal positions of France and Germany did not satisfy fiscal sustainability.

5.6   The Fiscal Theory of the Price Level

We have interpreted the condition for fiscal sustainability when $R > \pi + y$ as the requirement that current liabilities (i.e., outstanding debt) match the expected present value of net revenues (primary surpluses). An implicit assumption is that to achieve this a government may need to alter its fiscal stance in order to generate appropriate primary surpluses and reduce the total deficit. A policy that accomplishes this has been named "Ricardian." In contrast, a "non-Ricardian" policy is said to be one in which the current fiscal stance is taken as given—even though it may not satisfy the government's intertemporal budget constraint—yet despite this, equilibrium is automatically maintained. This is said to come about due to the "fiscal theory of the price level" (FTPL).

The FTPL asserts that the government's intertemporal budget constraint will be satisfied automatically for some value of the current price level, and that the price level will adjust instantly to this level to achieve this (see Sims 1994; Woodford 1995, 2001). Moreover, this is said to be true even when there is no money in the system. According to FTPL the price level is determined, therefore, not by the quantity of money in the economy, but by fiscal considerations, hence the name of the theory.

To illustrate this, consider the government's intertemporal budget constraint: equation (5.18). This can be rewritten as

$$\frac{B_t}{P_t} = \frac{y_t}{1+R} \sum_{s=0}^{\infty} \left(\frac{1+\pi+y}{1+R}\right)^s \left(\frac{-d_{t+s}}{y_{t+s}}\right),$$

and can be solved for P_t for any given values of $\{B_t, d_t, y_t, \pi, R\}$. We then obtain

$$P_t = \frac{B_t}{\dfrac{y_t}{1+R} \sum_{s=0}^{\infty} \left(\dfrac{1+\pi+y}{1+R}\right)^s \left(\dfrac{-d_{t+s}}{y_{t+s}}\right)}.$$

Consequently, if the outstanding nominal value of government debt exceeds the denominator, then the FTPL says that the price level would automatically, and instantaneously, increase. In this way, the government's intertemporal budget constraint would always be satisfied.

The intriguing aspect of this theory is that the price level is determined by fiscal policy, not monetary policy. How plausible is this theory? It is implicitly assumed that the price level is perfectly flexible so that it can adjust instantaneously. In practice, however, price adjustment is not instantaneous. Rather, prices are sticky, taking time to adjust. This is one of the main reasons why monetary policy has strong real effects in the short run. The FTPL does not, therefore, seem a useful theory of price determination in the short term. In the long run all variables in the intertemporal budget constraint are endogenous, and adjust to achieve general equilibrium, not just the price level.

5.7 Optimizing Public Finances

So far our discussion of fiscal policy has focused on issues related to the government budget constraint, and whether the current fiscal stance is sustainable in the sense that it satisfies the intertemporal budget constraint. We have seen that the answer to this depends on the choice of fiscal instruments: the levels of government expenditures, tax revenues, tax rates, and government debt. We now discuss the optimal choice of these instruments for a government seeking to maximize household welfare while constrained to satisfy the GBC. We also constrain the government to respect the decision framework of the private sector. We then ask whether optimal government policy distorts the decisions of the private sector by altering its behavior. As we wish to impose the optimal decision framework of the private sector on the government, we carry out the analysis using, in the main, a decentralized model of the economy.

To start with, however, we examine the optimal level of government expenditures, funded either by lump-sum or proportional taxes, using a centralized model of the economy in which a social planner is assumed to optimize all decisions on behalf of each individual. We then consider a decentralized economy in which the private sector and the government act separately. The analysis is considerably more complicated in a decentralized economy because of the need to take account of the sequence of decision making between the private sector and government. The private sector makes its decisions given government expenditures and tax rates; the government then chooses the rates of taxation of consumption, income, and capital earnings to maximize social welfare taking into account how the private sector responds to taxes. After this we revisit the issue of the optimal level of debt. Finally, we summarize these findings through a discussion of the key ingredients that make up an optimal fiscal policy.

5.7.1 Optimal Government Expenditures

5.7.1.1 *Lump-Sum Taxation*

We assume that the government chooses its level of expenditures to maximize household utility and it satisfies its budget constraint by the use of lump-sum taxes. Government debt may be set to zero, at which point the government budget constraint becomes $g_t = T_t$. To keep the analysis as simple—and hence as transparent—as possible, first we derive the optimal solution based on a centralized version of the economy. It can be shown that the same solution occurs in a decentralized economy.

We assume that households gain utility from both private and public expenditures. As a result, we write the household's utility function as

$$U(c_{t+s}, g_{t+s}), \quad U_c > 0, \ U_{cc} \leqslant 0, \ U_g > 0, \ U_{gg} \leqslant 0, \ U_{cg} \leqslant 0.$$

This implies that c_t and g_t are substitutes. In a centralized economy, the government's problem is to choose c_t, k_t, and T_t to maximize

$$\sum_{s=0}^{\infty} \beta^s U(c_{t+s}, g_{t+s})$$

subject to the economy's resource constraint

$$F(k_t) = c_t + k_{t+1} - (1 - \delta)k_t + g_t$$

and the government budget constraint. It is unnecessary to introduce the GBC explicitly as it is already incorporated into the national resource constraint, but we do so to illustrate what happens if we do.

The Lagrangian for this problem is

$$\mathcal{L} = \sum_{s=0}^{\infty} \{\beta^s U(c_{t+s}, g_{t+s}) + \lambda_{t+s}[F(k_{t+s}) - k_{t+s+1} + (1 - \delta)k_{t+s} - c_{t+s} - g_{t+s}]$$

$$+ \mu_{t+s}(g_{t+s} - T_{t+s})\}.$$

The first-order conditions are

$$\frac{\partial \mathcal{L}}{\partial c_{t+s}} = \beta^s U_{c,t+s} - \lambda_{t+s} = 0, \qquad s \geqslant 0,$$

$$\frac{\partial \mathcal{L}}{\partial k_{t+s}} = \lambda_{t+s}(F_{k,t+s} + 1 - \delta) - \lambda_{t+s-1} = 0, \quad s > 0,$$

$$\frac{\partial \mathcal{L}}{\partial g_{t+s}} = \beta^s U_{g,t+s} - \lambda_{t+s} + \mu_{t+s} = 0, \qquad s \geqslant 0,$$

$$\frac{\partial \mathcal{L}}{\partial T_{t+s}} = -\mu_{t+s} = 0, \qquad s \geqslant 0.$$

The last first-order condition implies that, as $\mu_{t+s} = 0$ for $s \geqslant 0$, using lump-sum taxation does not affect the other marginal conditions, and hence is said to be nondistorting of household behavior. Lump-sum taxes are simply set so that $T_t = g_t$.

The first-order conditions for consumption and capital are familiar and lead to the usual solutions for c_t and k_t, but with the additional presence of g_t. The Euler equation is

$$\frac{\beta U_{c,t+1}}{U_{c,t}}(F_{k,t+1} + 1 - \delta) = 1.$$

In the long run $F_{k,t} - \delta = \theta$ and c_t is obtained from

$$c_t = F(k_t) - \delta k_t - g_t.$$

Our present interest, however, lies more in the optimal solution for g_t. This is obtained from the first-order conditions for consumption and government expenditures, which imply that

$$U_{g,t} = U_{c,t}.$$

In general, therefore, the optimal level of g_t is a function of only c_t.

We consider two special cases.

1. c_t and g_t are perfect substitutes.

   In this case the utility function can be written as $U(c_t + g_t)$. Households are therefore indifferent about the division between c_t and g_t. As households would provide these goods for themselves, there appears to be no good reason why government should provide them instead. And if it were more costly for government to provide them—possibly due to dead-weight administrative costs—then it would certainly not be optimal for government to do so.

2. g_t is a public good.

   In the case of a pure public good, providing a level of real expenditures of g_t for one household is equivalent to providing g_t for all households. Thus, instead of duplicating the good or service for all households, they can be provided just once. This reduces the cost of provision. Assuming government can avoid the free-rider problem, this cost can be shared among all households. As a result, the level of tax revenues that would support government expenditure on pure public goods is a fraction of the cost that households would face if they provided them themselves.

In practice, government expenditures have a mixture of private-good and public-good characteristics. Services such as health and education tend to have a higher private-good component; policing and defense have a higher public-good content. The greater the public-good content, the higher should be the proportion supplied by government.

5.7.1.2 Proportional Taxation

In principle, taxes may be lump-sum or proportional, and these may be levied at a fixed or time-varying rate. The main attraction of lump-sum taxes is that they do not affect the marginal conditions of households and, as a result, are nondistorting. The fact that they are not distorting is also the source of their main disadvantage. As lump-sum taxes are the same for all, irrespective of income or wealth, they are regressive and hence take a higher proportion of the total income (or expenditures, in the case of consumption taxes) of lower-income households than of higher-income households. In practice, therefore, governments raise tax revenues almost entirely through proportional taxes.

Consider imposing a proportional tax on output. The GBC is then

$$g_t = \tau_t F(k_t),$$

where τ_t is the rate of tax. It can be shown that this would produce the same outcome as for lump-sum taxes, and hence would be nondistorting. The first-order condition with respect to τ_t replaces that with respect to T_{t+s} and is

$$\frac{\partial \mathcal{L}}{\partial \tau_{t+s}} = -\mu_{t+s} F(k_{t+s}) = 0.$$

Hence, for $k_{t+s} > 0$, once more we have $\mu_{t+s} = 0$ for $s \geqslant 0$. The tax rate τ_{t+s} must therefore be set so that the government budget constraint is satisfied each period. The optimal solution is $\tau_t = g_t / f(k_t)$ and hence varies with the proportion of output purchased by government.

If $\tau_t = \tau$, a constant, then, unless the ratio of government expenditures to GDP remains constant, in general the government budget constraint would not be satisfied without government borrowing. In this case, the first-order condition with respect to a constant rate of tax τ would be

$$\frac{\partial \mathcal{L}}{\partial \tau} = -\sum_{s=0}^{\infty} \mu_{t+s} F(k_{t+s}) = 0.$$

This may be satisfied even if $\mu_{t+s} \neq 0$ for some s, which would then affect the optimal solution. We conclude, therefore, that having a constant proportional tax rate will, in general, be distorting.

5.7.2 Optimal Tax Rates

We have previously noted that, in most countries, over half of total tax revenue comes from labor income (income and social security taxes) and just under a third comes from consumption (sales) taxes. The rest is made up mainly from taxes on capital income (profits and savings taxes). We therefore consider the optimal rates of tax for labor income, consumption, and capital.

There is now an important difference in our method of analysis that marks a further step toward greater realism. Instead of using the centralized model in which a social planner acts on behalf of each individual, the analysis is now based on a decentralized model of the economy in which decisions are taken sequentially. First the private sector determines consumption, labor, and capital, etc., taking the government's decisions on expenditure and taxation as given. The government then chooses its expenditure and taxation to optimize social welfare subject to its budget constraint and the marginal conditions derived by the private sector. In equilibrium, the private sector correctly anticipates the government's decisions. Our analysis is based on Chari et al. (1994) and Chari and Kehoe (1999). (See also Chamley (1986), Judd (1985), and Ljungqvist and Sargent (2004).)

5.7.2.1 The Household's Problem

We begin by considering the decisions of households, taking tax rates as given. Distinguishing between the various types of taxation, the household budget constraint can be written as

$$(1 + \tau_t^c)c_t + k_{t+1} + b_{t+1} = (1 - \tau_t^w)w_t n_t + [1 + (1 - \tau_t^k)r_t^k]k_t + (1 + r_t^b)b_t, \quad (5.22)$$

where c_t is consumption, k_t is equity capital, b_t is government debt, w_t is the average wage rate, n_t is employment (leisure is $l_t = 1 - n_t$), $r_t^k = F_{k,t} - \delta$ is the rate of return to equity capital, and r_t^b is the rate of return on government debt. All variables are real. τ_t^c, τ_t^w, and τ_t^k are the rates of tax on consumption, wage income, and capital income, respectively. The real rate of return to capital was determined in our earlier discussion of the decentralized economy. We can either think of government debt as not being taxed because its rate of return is determined by the government, or we can interpret r_t^b as an after-tax rate of return where the rate of tax is chosen by the government.

As we have introduced taxes on labor, we include leisure in the household utility function and we include labor in the production function. For convenience, we no longer include government expenditures explicitly in the utility function. We assume that the production function is homogeneous of degree one and that factors are paid their marginal products. Hence,

$$F(k_t, n_t) = F_{k,t} k_t + F_{n,t} n_t$$
$$= (r_t^k + \delta) k_t + w_t n_t.$$

The resource constraint can therefore be written as

$$r_t^k k_t + w_t n_t = c_t + k_{t+1} - k_t + g_t. \tag{5.23}$$

The household's problem is to maximize intertemporal utility subject to its budget constraint. The Lagrangian for this problem can be written as

$$\mathcal{L} = \sum_{s=0}^{\infty} \left\{ \beta^s U(c_{t+s}, l_{t+s}) + \lambda_{t+s} [(1 - \tau_{t+s}^w) w_{t+s} n_{t+s} + [1 + (1 - \tau_{t+s}^k) r_{t+s}^k] k_{t+s} \right.$$
$$\left. + (1 + r_{t+s}^b) b_{t+s} - (1 + \tau_{t+s}^c) c_{t+s} - k_{t+s+1} - b_{t+s+1}] \right\}.$$

The first-order conditions are

$$\frac{\partial \mathcal{L}}{\partial c_{t+s}} = \beta^s U_{c,t+s} - \lambda_{t+s} (1 + \tau_{t+s}^c) = 0, \qquad s \geqslant 0,$$

$$\frac{\partial \mathcal{L}}{\partial n_{t+s}} = -\beta^s U_{l,t+s} + \lambda_{t+s} (1 - \tau_{t+s}^w) w_{t+s} = 0, \qquad s \geqslant 0,$$

$$\frac{\partial \mathcal{L}}{\partial k_{t+s}} = \lambda_{t+s} [1 + (1 - \tau_{t+s}^k) r_{t+s}^k] - \lambda_{t+s-1} = 0, \quad s > 0,$$

$$\frac{\partial \mathcal{L}}{\partial b_{t+s}} = \lambda_{t+s} (1 + r_{t+s}^b) - \lambda_{t+s-1} = 0, \qquad s > 0.$$

From the first-order conditions for consumption and leisure we obtain

$$\frac{U_{l,t+s}}{U_{c,t+s}} = \frac{(1 - \tau_{t+s}^w) w_{t+s}}{1 + \tau_{t+s}^c}, \quad s \geqslant 0. \tag{5.24}$$

From the first-order conditions for capital and bonds we obtain

$$\frac{\lambda_{t+s-1}}{\lambda_{t+s}} = 1 + (1 - \tau_{t+s}^k) r_{t+s}^k = 1 + r_{t+s}^b, \quad s > 0. \tag{5.25}$$

Hence, the no-arbitrage condition between equity and bonds is

$$(1 - \tau_{t+s}^k) r_{t+s}^k = r_{t+s}^b, \quad s > 0. \tag{5.26}$$

In other words, investment in equity takes place until the after-tax rate of return on equity capital $(1 - \tau_{t+s}^k) r_{t+s}^k$ equals the rate of return on government bonds r_{t+s}^b—in effect the cost of borrowing.

The Euler equation can be obtained from the first-order conditions for consumption and capital as

$$\frac{\beta U_{c,t+1}}{U_{c,t}} \frac{1 + \tau_t^c}{1 + \tau_{t+1}^c} [1 + (1 - \tau_{t+1}^k) r_{t+1}^k] = 1.$$

Hence, in the long run, either

$$\beta[1 + (1 - \tau^k) r^k] = 1 \qquad (5.27)$$

or $(1 - \tau^k) r^k = r^b = \theta$, the rate of time preference.

In contrast to lump-sum taxes, or just proportional taxes on output, these proportional taxes affect the marginal relations from which the household's decisions for consumption, labor, and capital are derived, and hence are distorting. Equation (5.24) shows that the consumption and labor income taxes drive a wedge between the ratio of the marginal utilities and the real wage. If we write the equation as

$$\frac{U_{c,t}}{1 + \tau_t^c} = \frac{U_{l,t}}{(1 - \tau_t^w) w_t},$$

it is clear that a consumption tax causes households to reduce consumption. A labor income tax causes households to require a higher wage to induce the same supply of labor; if the wage is unchanged, then labor supply is reduced (leisure is increased). Equation (5.27) implies that a tax on capital raises the rate of return on the marginal investment in capital. Since $r^k = F_k - \delta$ and $F_{kk} < 0$, it also implies a lower optimal level of capital and hence lower output and consumption.

5.7.2.2 The Government's Problem

We now consider the optimal choice of rates of taxation by the government. We assume that this is constrained by the government's wish to take into account the optimality conditions of households. We can capture the constraint imposed by households on government decisions through what is known as the implementability condition. This is derived as follows.

Substituting the rates of return for capital and bonds into the household budget constraint using equation (5.25) we obtain

$$(1 + \tau_{t+s}^c) c_{t+s} + k_{t+s+1} + b_{t+s+1} = (1 - \tau_{t+s}^w) w_{t+s} n_{t+s} + \frac{\lambda_{t+s-1}}{\lambda_{t+s}} (k_{t+s} + b_{t+s}).$$

This can be solved forwards to give the intertemporal household budget constraint

$$\lambda_{t-1}(k_t + b_t) = \sum_{s=0}^{\infty} \lambda_{t+s} [(1 + \tau_{t+s}^c) c_{t+s} - (1 - \tau_{t+s}^w) w_{t+s} n_{t+s}], \qquad (5.28)$$

provided the transversality conditions

$$\lim_{n \to \infty} \lambda_{t+n} k_{t+n+1} = 0,$$

$$\lim_{n \to \infty} \lambda_{t+n} b_{t+n+1} = 0$$

hold. Using the first-order conditions for consumption and work, equation (5.28) can be rewritten as

$$\lambda_{t-1}(k_t + b_t) = \sum_{s=0}^{\infty} \beta^s (U_{c,t+s}c_{t+s} - U_{l,t+s}n_{t+s}). \tag{5.29}$$

This equation is known as the implementability condition. We note that the left-hand side is predetermined at time t.

The government budget constraint at time t is now

$$g_t + (1 + r_t^b)b_t = \tau_t^c c_t + \tau_t^w w_t n_t + \tau_t^k r_t^k k_t + b_{t+1}. \tag{5.30}$$

As we can derive the economy's resource constraint from the household and government budget constraints, the government's problem can be expressed as maximizing the intertemporal utility of households subject to the implementability condition (5.29) and the economy's resource constraint, equation (5.23). We note that although the three tax rates appear in the government budget constraint equation (5.30), they do not all appear in the resource constraint or in the Lagrangian, which can be written as

$$\mathcal{L} = \sum_{s=0}^{\infty} \{\beta^s U(c_{t+s}, l_{t+s}) + \phi_{t+s}[r_{t+s}^k k_{t+s} + w_{t+s}n_{t+s} - c_{t+s} - k_{t+s+1} + k_{t+s} - g_{t+s}]\}$$

$$+ \mu \left[\sum_{s=0}^{\infty} \beta^s (U_{c,t+s}c_{t+s} - U_{l,t+s}n_{t+s}) - \lambda_{t-1}(k_t + b_t) \right].$$

This problem can be expressed more compactly if we define

$$V(c_{t+s}, l_{t+s}, \mu) = U(c_{t+s}, l_{t+s}) + \mu(U_{c,t+s}c_{t+s} - U_{l,t+s}n_{t+s}). \tag{5.31}$$

The Lagrangian is then

$$\mathcal{L} = \sum_{s=0}^{\infty} \{\beta^s V(c_{t+s}, l_{t+s}, \mu)$$
$$+ \phi_{t+s}[r_{t+s}^k k_{t+s} + w_{t+s}n_{t+s} - c_{t+s} - k_{t+s+1} + k_{t+s} - g_{t+s}]\}$$
$$- \mu\lambda_{t-1}(k_t + b_t).$$
$$\tag{5.32}$$

The first-order conditions for consumption, labor, and capital are

$$\frac{\partial \mathcal{L}}{\partial c_{t+s}} = \beta^s V_{c,t+s} - \phi_{t+s} = 0, \qquad\qquad s \geqslant 0,$$

$$\frac{\partial \mathcal{L}}{\partial n_{t+s}} = -\beta^s V_{l,t+s} + \phi_{t+s}w_{t+s} = 0, \qquad s \geqslant 0,$$

$$\frac{\partial \mathcal{L}}{\partial k_{t+s}} = \phi_{t+s}(1 + r_{t+s}^k) - \phi_{t+s-1} = 0, \quad s > 0.$$

We now consider the implications of these conditions for the optimal choice of the three tax rates.

5.7.2.3 Capital Taxation

We consider the implications for capital taxation both in the long run and the short run. The Euler equation is now

$$\frac{\beta V_{c,t+1}}{V_{c,t}}(1 + r_{t+1}^{k}) = 1.$$

Hence, the Euler equation implies that in the long run

$$\beta(1 + r^{k}) = 1, \tag{5.33}$$

which gives the familiar result that $F_k - \delta = r^k = \theta$.

Equation (5.33) can be compared with equation (5.27), which says that $\beta[1 + (1 - \tau^k)r^k] = 1$. For simultaneous household and government optimization both equations must hold. It therefore follows that the optimal rate of capital taxation in the long run—the rate that is consistent with both equations—is $\tau^k = 0$. This result was first derived by Chamley (1986). The implication is that a zero rate of capital taxation is optimal for all periods *after period t*.

In period t, the first period, both capital k_t and bonds b_t are already given and therefore cannot respond to their rate of taxation. We have assumed that there is a zero tax on capital in period t. If the government were able to tax capital in period t, then the last term in the Lagrangian, equation (5.32), would be $\mu\lambda_{t-1}(\tau_t^k k_t + b_t)$. Maximizing with respect to τ_t^k gives

$$\frac{\partial \mathcal{L}}{\partial \tau_t^k} = -\mu\lambda_{t-1}k_t,$$

which, due to the use of distortionary taxation, is strictly positive if $\mu > 0$.

Without distortionary taxation, $\mu = 0$. This implies that the present-value budget constraint does not affect household decisions. To avoid using distortionary taxation—and hence allow all current and future proportional tax rates to be set to zero—the government would need to be able to raise sufficient revenues solely from taxing k_t. It would then follow that $\mu = 0$. This result is due to k_t and b_t being given and is related to the well-known proposition that goods and services in fixed supply yield only economic rents and, in the absence of intertemporal considerations, the optimal rate of taxation of economic rents is 100%. (We note that an economic rent should not be confused with rents on housing. An economic rent is the revenue arising from the vertical section of a supply curve, where supply no longer responds to a higher price.)

If the private sector had worked out beforehand that capital would be taxed at 100%, there would, of course, be no incentive to invest in new capital in the first place. Such a policy would therefore only be effective if the government could persuade the private sector that it does not intend to implement it. Once it is implemented, the private sector would believe that it will always be implemented, which would completely deter private capital accumulation. Hence, for this policy of taxing initial capital to work, the private sector is required not to learn from the past. Since this is not credible, we may conclude that the optimal rate of capital taxation for all periods, including the first, is zero.

5.7.2.4 Consumption and Labor Taxation

From the first-order conditions and the marginal condition for labor,

$$\frac{V_{l,t}}{V_{c,t}} = w_t. \tag{5.34}$$

We wish to know how the tax rates on consumption and labor can be chosen so that both this equation and the equivalent equation for the household, equation (5.24), are satisfied. From equation (5.31) it can be shown that equation (5.34) can be rewritten as

$$\frac{V_{l,t}}{V_{c,t}} = \frac{(1+\mu)U_{l,t} + \mu(U_{cl,t}c_t - U_{ll,t}n_t)}{(1+\mu)U_{c,t} + \mu(U_{cc,t}c_t - U_{lc,t}l_t)} = w_t.$$

Hence, from equation (5.24),

$$\frac{V_{l,t}}{V_{c,t}} = \frac{(1+\mu)U_{l,t} + \mu(U_{cl,t}c_t - U_{ll,t}l_t)}{(1+\mu)U_{c,t} + \mu(U_{cc,t}c_t - U_{lc,t}l_t)} = \frac{1+\tau_t^c}{1-\tau_t^l}\frac{U_{l,t}}{U_{c,t}}. \tag{5.35}$$

It can be shown that if the utility function is homothetic, i.e., if, for any θ,

$$\frac{U_c[\theta c, \theta l]}{U_l[\theta c, \theta l]} = \frac{U_c(c, l)}{U_l(c, l)}, \tag{5.36}$$

then differentiating (5.36) with respect to θ and evaluating at $\theta = 1$ gives

$$\frac{U_{cc,t}c_t - U_{lc,t}l_t}{U_{c,t}} = \frac{U_{cl,t}c_t - U_{ll,t}l_t}{U_{l,t}}. \tag{5.37}$$

Substituting (5.37) into (5.35) gives

$$\frac{V_{l,t}}{V_{c,t}} = \frac{U_{l,t}}{U_{c,t}} = \frac{1+\tau_t^c}{1-\tau_t^w}\frac{U_{l,t}}{U_{c,t}}.$$

The optimal rates of tax are therefore either $\tau_t^c = \tau_t^w = 0$ or $\tau_t^c = -\tau_t^w$.

   The first solution arises from the fact that, as both taxes are distorting, it is optimal to set them to zero. The second condition implies that it is optimal to compensate for taxes on consumption ($\tau_t^c > 0$) by subsidizing wages ($\tau_t^w = -\tau_t^c < 0$). The household and government budget constraints then become

$$(1 + \tau_t^c)(c_t - w_t n_t) + k_{t+1} + b_{t+1} = [1 + (1 - \tau_t^k)r_t^k]k_t + (1 + r_t^b)b_t,$$

$$g_t + (1 + r_t^b)b_t = \tau_t^c(c_t - w_t n_t) + \tau_t^k r_t^k k_t + b_{t+1}.$$

Hence, government receives tax revenues (and households pay tax) only if consumption exceeds wage income. Borrowing undertaken in order to spend more than current wage income would therefore be taxed, but saving wage income would be subsidized.

   In practice, as the government must satisfy its budget constraint, it must collect taxes. We have shown that lump-sum taxes, or proportional taxes on total output, would not be distorting, but proportional taxes on consumption, wages, or capital would be distorting. To be optimal, taxes should therefore be lump-sum or on total output. Despite this result, most taxation is not lump-sum but proportional. Moreover, tax rates commonly rise with income. This is called progressive taxation. The aim is to place more of the tax burden on higher-income households and, by implication, redistribute income to low-income households. As most capital income is received by higher-income households, a similar argument is used to justify taxing capital. In our analysis, progressive taxation is not optimal because household utility functions are assumed to be independent of each other. One way to justify progressive taxation formally would be to assume instead that higher-income households are deriving satisfaction from raising the utility—or consumption levels—of lower-income households. This is the purpose of government transfers; they reflect the collective altruism of people.

5.7.2.5 Tax Smoothing

We have argued that in the long run, considerations of fiscal sustainability determine that government expenditures must be paid for by taxes. We have examined which taxes to impose in the long run and, if we rule out initial capital taxation on credibility grounds, we have found that it is optimal for the government to tax output and labor, with the government free to choose the balance between the two. Although we have said that, in the short run, debt must then be issued or retired in order that the government budget constraint is satisfied each period, we have not determined what the optimal mix of tax revenues and debt is each period. Should shocks be absorbed in the short run by varying taxes or through debt? We draw on the analysis of Barro (1979) to answer this question (see also Chari and Kehoe 1999).

There are clearly administrative costs to changing taxes frequently and it is optimal for the government to minimize these. Assume that these costs are an increasing (i.e., nonlinear) function of the level of total tax revenues so that

$$\Phi(T_t) = \phi_1 T_t + \tfrac{1}{2}\phi_2 T_t^2, \qquad \Phi'(T_t) \geqslant 0$$

and assume that the government seeks to minimize $\sum_{s=0}^{\infty} \beta^s \Phi(T_{t+s})$, the present value of these costs, with respect to T_t and b_t subject to its budget constraint

$$\Delta b_{t+1} = g_t - T_t + r_t^b b_t, \tag{5.38}$$

where g_t and r_t^b are taken as given.

The Lagrangian for this problem is

$$\mathcal{L} = \sum_0^{\infty} \{\beta^s [\phi_1 T_{t+s} + \tfrac{1}{2}\phi_2 T_{t+s}^2] + \mu_{t+s}[g_{t+s} - T_{t+s} - b_{t+s+1} + (1 + r_t^b)b_{t+s}]\}.$$

The first-order conditions are

$$\frac{\partial \mathcal{L}}{\partial T_{t+s}} = \beta^s [\phi_1 + \phi_2 T_{t+s}] - \mu_{t+s} = 0,$$

$$\frac{\partial \mathcal{L}}{\partial b_{t+s}} = \mu_{t+s}(1 + r_t^b) - \mu_{t+s-1} = 0.$$

Hence

$$T_{t+1} = \frac{\phi_1[1 - (1 + r_t^b)\beta]}{\phi_2(1 + r_t^b)\beta} + \frac{1}{\beta(1 + r_t^b)} T_t. \tag{5.39}$$

If the government's discount rate is the rate of time preference of households, then $\beta = 1/(1 + \theta)$, and if the government chooses $r_t^b = \theta$, then $\beta(1 + r_t^b) = 1$, and equation (5.39) becomes

$$T_{t+1} = T_t.$$

In other words, it is optimal to keep T_t constant, and for debt to absorb any shocks.

This analysis has assumed a deterministic world. Suppose instead that we allow government expenditures to be a random variable, and assume that government seeks to minimize $E_t[\sum_{s=0}^{\infty} \beta^s \Phi(T_{t+s})]$. It can be shown that the optimal tax rule becomes

$$T_t = E_t T_{t+1}.$$

This implies that the aim is to set taxes today so that they are expected to stay constant in the future. If expectations are rational, we can define the innovation to taxes e_{t+1} through

$$T_{t+1} = E_t T_{t+1} + e_{t+1},$$
$$E_t e_{t+1} = 0.$$

Hence optimal tax revenues should follow the random walk (or, more strictly, the martingale process):

$$\Delta T_{t+1} = e_{t+1}.$$

We now consider the implications for debt. The GBC, equation (5.38), can be written as

$$b_t = \frac{T_t - g_t}{1 + \theta} + \frac{1}{1 + \theta} E_t b_{t+1}$$

$$= E_t \sum_{s=0}^{\infty} \frac{T_{t+s} - g_{t+s}}{(1 + \theta)^{s+1}}.$$

If $T_t = E_t T_{t+1}$ then $E_t T_{t+s} = T_t$ and debt is given by

$$b_t = \frac{T_t}{\theta} - E_t \sum_{s=0}^{\infty} \frac{g_{t+s}}{(1 + \theta)^{s+1}}.$$

A Temporary Increase in Government Expenditures.   Suppose that g_t is subject to temporary and unforecastable shocks in every period such that

$$g_t = g + \varepsilon_t,$$
$$E_t \varepsilon_{t+1} = 0,$$

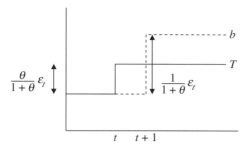

Figure 5.3. The response of debt and taxes to a temporary shock.

then

$$b_t = \frac{T_t}{\theta} - E_t \sum_{s=0}^{\infty} \frac{g_{t+s}}{(1+\theta)^{s+1}}$$

$$= \frac{T_t}{\theta} - \frac{g}{\theta} - \frac{\varepsilon_t}{1+\theta}.$$

As b_t is given, it follows that in period t

$$T_t = g + \theta b_t + \frac{\theta}{1+\theta}\varepsilon_t.$$

T_t must therefore increase by $(\theta/(1+\theta))\varepsilon_t$ in order that the GBC is satisfied.

In period $t+1$, noting that $E_t\varepsilon_{t+1} = 0$ and $E_t T_{t+1} = T_t$, it follows that

$$b_{t+1} = \frac{T_{t+1}}{\theta} - \frac{g}{\theta} - \frac{\varepsilon_{t+1}}{1+\theta}$$

and so

$$E_t b_{t+1} = \frac{E_t T_{t+1}}{\theta} - \frac{g}{\theta}$$

$$= \frac{T_t}{\theta} - \frac{g}{\theta}$$

$$= b_t + \frac{\varepsilon_t}{1+\theta},$$

implying that there is now an increase in debt. In subsequent periods,

$$E_t b_{t+n} = b_t + \frac{\varepsilon_t}{1+\theta} \quad \text{for } n > 0.$$

Thus, it is optimal to raise debt permanently by $\varepsilon_t/(1+\theta)$. Future shocks $\varepsilon_{t+1}, \varepsilon_{t+2}, \ldots$ will cause future debt to be further affected. But since the mean shock is zero, the shocks will on average cancel each other out, and so the average level of debt will be constant at the initial level b_t.

To summarize, we have shown that although the plan is to smooth taxes so that $T_t = E_t T_{t+1}$, this does not mean that T_t is unaffected by the shock ε_t. A proportion $\theta/(1+\theta)$ of the shock is absorbed by T_t and the rest, $1/(1+\theta)$, is absorbed by debt. Since θ is small, debt absorbs most of the shock. In figure 5.3 we depict the time paths of T_t and b_t following a shock ε_t.

A Permanent Increase in Government Expenditures. We assume that government expenditures increase by Δg in period t and that this is expected to be permanent. Suppose that in period $t - 1$

$$b_{t-1} = \frac{T_{t-1}}{\theta} - \frac{g}{\theta}.$$

In period t, when the permanent expenditure shock occurs,

$$b_t = \frac{T_t - (g + \Delta g)}{1 + \theta} + \frac{1}{1 + \theta} E_t b_{t+1}.$$

Due to tax smoothing, $T_t = E_t T_{t+1}$ and so

$$E_t b_{t+1} = \frac{E_t T_{t+1}}{\theta} - \frac{(g + \Delta g)}{\theta}$$

$$= \frac{T_t}{\theta} - \frac{(g + \Delta g)}{\theta} = b_t.$$

Hence, the GBC at time t can be written as

$$b_t = \frac{T_t}{\theta} - \frac{(g + \Delta g)}{\theta}.$$

It follows that

$$T_t = T_{t-1} + \Delta g$$

$$= E_t T_{t+n}, \quad n \geqslant 0.$$

Consequently, a permanent increase of Δg causes T_t and $E_t T_{t+n}$ to be raised by Δg, but b_t and $E_t b_{t+n}$ are unchanged. This shows that it is optimal to absorb a permanent expenditure shock entirely by taxes.

If we reinterpret this result so that it applies to the business cycle by assuming that fiscal shocks are serially correlated, then we reinforce conclusions obtained previously about how to conduct fiscal policy. The implication of this result is that over the business cycle fiscal deficits and surpluses should be financed almost entirely by debt. The average level of debt, from one cycle to the next, should therefore be approximately constant. This requires that increases in debt during recessions, when a fiscal deficit occurs, should be redeemed during the boom phase when the aim should be to generate fiscal surpluses. Consequently, governments, observing a fiscal surplus, should not immediately increase expenditures or cut taxes. In contrast, a permanent increase in government expenditures, expected to persist over more than one business cycle, should be tax financed. This implies that permanent expenditures, health care and education for example, should be tax financed, but temporary expenditures, such as unemployment benefit, should be debt financed.

This prescription for healthy public finances has been interpreted by the U.K. government as using debt finance over the business cycle so that at the end of the cycle debt is restored to its previous level. This is not, however, what the rule says; only if temporary expenditures are associated with the business cycle, and most are, is such an interpretation valid. Emergency expenditures, due, for example, to a natural disaster, are not associated with the business cycle, but may be debt financed insofar as they are random events with a zero mean.

5.7.2.6 Simulation Evidence

Chari et al. (1994) have compared the welfare outcomes of alternative taxation policies of capital and labor using simulation methods based on a DGE model. They found that the greatest welfare benefits occurred for a high initial capital tax and a negative initial labor tax. Thereafter, they found that capital taxes should be close to zero and labor taxes should be positive, but not fluctuate much. However, they also found that the benefits from having a zero capital tax were small. This suggests that the temptation for government to tax capital in later periods, despite the promise not to do so, is considerable. This temptation would be greatest following an unexpected increase in government expenditures, or a shortfall in tax revenues. Giving in to such a temptation would, of course, permanently destroy the credibility of the government's promise not to tax future returns to capital. Once the private sector believes that capital will be taxed, there may be a substantial loss of welfare.

In chapter 6, in our discussion of time-inconsistent economic policy, we take up the issue of pursuing a different policy from that announced. And in chapter 14 we comment on evidence about the effectiveness of fiscal policy, and how this is influenced by the method of financing, based on a theoretical DGE macroeconomic model.

5.8 Conclusions

What can we conclude from this analysis about how best to conduct fiscal policy? The following is a list of our conclusions.

1. From an economic (as opposed to purely political) perspective, government expenditures should be undertaken for three reasons: to provide public, not private, goods; as automatic stabilizers; for (intergenerational) equity of welfare.

2. Permanent increases in government expenditures should be financed by higher taxes; temporary increases, possibly due to recession, should be financed by debt, due to the desirability of smoothing taxes.

3. Lump-sum taxation is nondistorting, but proportional taxes on consumption, labor, and capital are distorting. The justification for distorting taxes derives from the need to finance expenditures and the wish to do so fairly.

4. It is optimal in the long run for capital taxes to be very low, or even zero. The temptation to tax capital heavily in the short term should be avoided as this would quickly undermine the government's credibility and so prove counterproductive.

5. The fiscal stance, and, in particular, a fiscal deficit, is sustainable if the present value of current and expected future primary fiscal surpluses is sufficient to meet current government debt liabilities.

6. The European Union's Stability and Growth Pact appears to be neither necessary nor sufficient to achieve a sustainable fiscal stance.

7. Optimal fiscal policy consists of first determining the optimal level of government expenditures. Long-run taxation levels should be set to pay for long-run government expenditures. In the short term, debt finance should be used for temporary increases in the deficit. In the longer term, debt should be used to achieve intergenerational equity; this is mainly for capital projects. At all times the fiscal stance should be seen to be sustainable.

6

Fiscal Policy: Further Issues

6.1 Introduction

In this chapter we consider two further issues in fiscal policy: time inconsistency and pensions policy. Governments sometimes announce a policy for the future but find it optimal to carry out a different policy when the future arrives, perhaps because the conditions are different from those that were expected to prevail. This change of mind is called the problem of time inconsistency. A policy that it is not optimal to change in the future is called time consistent. The mathematical appendix includes a discussion of the general problem of time inconsistency. In this chapter the general theory is used to examine the circumstances under which time-consistent and time-inconsistent fiscal policies are optimal.

Many problems in macroeconomics involve a period of time so long that conventional dynamic analysis is no longer appropriate. An example is where the time period is that of a generation, as opposed to the calendar time that is conventionally used, such as a month or a year. A decision taken by one generation may affect subsequent generations, but later generations would have had no say in the decision. Many fiscal decisions are of this sort; for example, pensions and some public investments. In order to analyze these issues we may need to use the overlapping-generations (OLG) model. In this chapter, we discuss the OLG model and then we illustrate its use by analyzing the issue of pensions. We examine the relative merits of funded and unfunded pension schemes.

By way of a warning, the reader may find that some of the analysis of these issues is technically more complex than most of the other material in this book.

6.2 Time-Consistent and Time-Inconsistent Fiscal Policy

According to Chari and Kehoe (2006), optimal policy in an intertemporal context has three components: a model to predict how people will behave under alternative policies; a welfare criterion to rank the outcomes of alternative policies; and a description of how policies will be set in the future. Such policies are usually contingent on the conditions expected to prevail in the future. If these conditions change, then it may be optimal to alter the policy, thereby making the policy time inconsistent. This problem has its origins in the public-finance literature and, in particular, in Ramsey's (1927) work on taxation. As a result, a sequence of optimal policies over time is sometimes referred to as Ramsey policies, and its associated outcomes as Ramsey outcomes (see also Chari et al. 1989).

We encountered the problem of the time inconsistency of fiscal policy in our discussion of the optimal rate of capital taxation in chapter 5. A seminal treatment of time-consistent and time-inconsistent fiscal policies is that of Fischer (1980). We consider a slightly modified version of this that is designed to illustrate many of the arguments about fiscal policy discussed previously, as well as the differences between time-consistent and time-inconsistent fiscal policies. We show the differences between nondistortionary and distortionary taxation, between taxing labor and capital, and why a time-inconsistent policy involving taxing capital, but not labor, may sometimes be better than a policy of precommitment.

The problem Fischer considers is highly stylized through being simplified to bring out the key features of time inconsistency. It is assumed that there are two periods only. The intertemporal utility of the private sector is given by

$$\mathcal{U}_t = U(c_t, l_t, g_t) + \beta U(c_{t+1}, l_{t+1}, g_{t+1}),$$

$$U(c_t, l_t) = \ln c_t + \alpha \ln l_t + \gamma \ln g_t,$$

where c_t is consumption, $l_t = 1 - n_t$ is leisure, n_t is employment, and g_t is government expenditure. To simplify the analysis, it is assumed that in the first period there is no production because the private sector undertakes no work, but lives off its endowment of capital k_t, which it can either consume or save. As a result, the budget constraint of the private sector in the first period is

$$c_t + \Delta k_{t+1} = r k_t, \tag{6.1}$$

where k_t, the capital stock, is taken as predetermined with an implied rate of depreciation of zero, and r is the rate of return on capital. Another simplifying assumption is that the government makes no expenditures in period t. Hence n_t and g_t are constrained to be zero in period t.

In the second period, the private sector works, producing an output of y_{t+1} using the linear production function

$$y_{t+1} = w n_{t+1} + r k_{t+1},$$

where w and r are the (constant) marginal products of labor and capital, respectively. The government now spends g_{t+1}. The resource constraint for the economy in the second period is therefore

$$c_{t+1} + g_{t+1} = w n_{t+1} + r k_{t+1}. \tag{6.2}$$

The government satisfies its budget constraint by taxing the private sector either through lump-sum taxes T_{t+1}, or through taxes on labor and capital. The government budget constraint is therefore either $g_{t+1} = T_{t+1}$ or

$$g_{t+1} = \tau^w w n_{t+1} + (R - R^\tau) k_{t+1}, \tag{6.3}$$

where τ^w is the proportional tax rate on wages and $w^\tau = (1 - \tau^w)w$ is the after-tax wage rate. If $R = 1 + r$ is the gross return to capital and R^τ is the after-tax gross return, then the tax rate of capital is $R - R^\tau$. Capital taxes can consist of taxing the rate of return to capital at the rate τ^r so that $r^\tau = (1 - \tau^k)r$ is the after-tax rate of return, or of taxing the stock of capital at the rate τ^k when

$$R - R^\tau = \tau^k + \tau^r r.$$

The private sector's budget constraint in the second period is therefore either

$$c_{t+1} + \Delta k_{t+2} + T_{t+1} = wn_{t+1} + rk_{t+1} \tag{6.4}$$

or

$$c_{t+1} + \Delta k_{t+2} = w^\tau n_{t+1} + R^\tau k_{t+1}, \tag{6.5}$$

where $k_{t+2} = 0$.

For each type of financing—lump-sum taxation and proportional tax rates—we consider the central planning or command solution in which the government chooses the optimal solutions for the economy as a whole. We then consider the decentralized solution in which first the private sector makes its decisions in the expectation of the government's choice in period $t + 1$, and second the government is free to reoptimize in the second period taking the private sector's first-period decisions and outcomes as given, including the assumption that the private sector correctly anticipates period $t + 1$ taxes and expenditures. Finally, we allow both the private sector and the government to reoptimize in period $t + 1$ taking the outcomes of period t as given. This is where the issue of time consistency could arise.

6.2.1 Lump-Sum Taxation

6.2.1.1 The Central Planning Solution

The government's problem is to maximize intertemporal utility $\mathcal{U}_t$ subject to the economy's intertemporal resource constraint, which is

$$(1 + r)c_t + c_{t+1} + g_{t+1} = wn_{t+1} + (1 + r)^2 k_t.$$

The Lagrangian is

$$\mathcal{L} = \ln c_t + \alpha \ln l_t + \beta(\ln c_{t+1} + \alpha \ln l_{t+1} + \gamma \ln g_{t+1})$$
$$+ \lambda[wn_{t+1} + (1 + r)^2 k_t - (1 + r)c_t - c_{t+1} - g_{t+1}].$$

We note that $l_t = 1 - n_t$ could be omitted as it is assumed that there is no production in period t. The first-order conditions are

$$\frac{\partial \mathcal{L}}{\partial c_t} = \frac{1}{c_t} - \lambda(1 + r) = 0,$$

$$\frac{\partial \mathcal{L}}{\partial c_{t+1}} = \beta \frac{1}{c_{t+1}} - \lambda = 0,$$

$$\frac{\partial \mathcal{L}}{\partial n_{t+1}} = -\alpha\beta\frac{1}{1 - n_{t+1}} + \lambda w = 0,$$

$$\frac{\partial \mathcal{L}}{\partial g_{t+1}} = \beta\gamma\frac{1}{g_{t+1}} - \lambda = 0,$$

implying that

$$
\begin{aligned}
c_t &= \frac{((w - g_{t+1})/(1 + r)) + (1 + r)k_t}{1 + (1 + \alpha)\beta} \\
&= \frac{(w/(1 + r)) + (1 + r)k_t}{1 + (1 + \alpha + \gamma)\beta},
\end{aligned}
\tag{6.6}
$$

$$c_{t+1} = \beta(1 + r)c_t, \tag{6.7}$$

$$l_{t+1} = (\alpha/w)c_{t+1}, \tag{6.8}$$

$$g_{t+1} = T_{t+1} = \gamma c_{t+1}, \tag{6.9}$$

$$k_{t+1} = (1 + r)k_t - c_t. \tag{6.10}$$

6.2.1.2   The Decentralized Solution

The Intertemporal Solution

(i) The private sector's problem.   In the first period the private sector maximizes $\mathcal{U}_t$ subject to its intertemporal budget constraint, taking government expenditures and lump-sum taxation as given. The intertemporal budget constraint can be written as

$$(1 + r)c_t + c_{t+1} + g_{t+1} = wn_{t+1} + (1 + r)^2 k_t.$$

The Lagrangian is

$$
\begin{aligned}
\mathcal{L} = {}&\ln c_t + \alpha\ln l_t + \beta(\ln c_{t+1} + \alpha\ln l_{t+1} + \gamma\ln g_{t+1}) \\
&+ \lambda[wn_{t+1} + (1 + r)^2 k_t - (1 + r)c_t - c_{t+1} - g_{t+1}]
\end{aligned}
$$

and the first-order conditions are

$$\frac{\partial \mathcal{L}}{\partial c_t} = \frac{1}{c_t} - \lambda(1 + r) = 0,$$

$$\frac{\partial \mathcal{L}}{\partial c_{t+1}} = \beta\frac{1}{c_{t+1}} - \lambda = 0,$$

$$\frac{\partial \mathcal{L}}{\partial n_{t+1}} = -\alpha\beta\frac{1}{1 - n_{t+1}} + \lambda w = 0,$$

implying that

$$c_{t+1} = \beta(1 + r)c_t, \tag{6.11}$$

$$l_{t+1} = (\alpha/w)c_{t+1}, \tag{6.12}$$

$$c_t = \frac{w - g_{t+1} + (1 + r)^2 k_t}{[1 + (1 + \alpha)\beta](1 + r)}, \tag{6.13}$$

$$k_{t+1} = (1 + r)k_t - c_t. \tag{6.14}$$

This is exactly the same solution as under central planning.

(ii) **The government's problem.** As the government takes the first-period outcomes as given, its problem is to choose g_{t+1} to maximize utility in period $t+1$ subject to the economy's resource constraint in period $t+1$ and to the period t outcomes. This implies taking account of equation (6.12) and taking c_t and k_{t+1} as given. The Lagrangian can be written as

$$\mathcal{L} = \ln c_{t+1} + \alpha \ln l_{t+1} + \gamma \ln g_{t+1}$$
$$+ \lambda \left[l_{t+1} - \frac{\alpha}{w} c_{t+1} \right] + \mu [w n_{t+1} + (1+r) k_{t+1} - c_{t+1} - g_{t+1}].$$

The first-order conditions are

$$\frac{\partial \mathcal{L}}{\partial c_{t+1}} = \frac{1}{c_{t+1}} - \lambda \frac{\alpha}{w} = 0,$$

$$\frac{\partial \mathcal{L}}{\partial n_{t+1}} = -\alpha \frac{1}{1 - n_{t+1}} + \lambda w = 0,$$

$$\frac{\partial \mathcal{L}}{\partial g_{t+1}} = \gamma \frac{1}{g_{t+1}} - \mu = 0.$$

Hence,

$$g_{t+1} = \gamma c_{t+1}.$$

Again this is the same as for the centrally planned economy.

We now consider whether there are any benefits to reoptimization by the government in period $t+1$.

Reoptimization in Period $t+1$

(i) **The private sector's problem.** If the private sector reoptimizes in period $t+1$ taking k_{t+1}, the outcome from period t, as given, then it maximizes $U(c_{t+1}, l_{t+1}, g_{t+1})$ subject to the resource constraint in period $t+1$ (equation (6.4)). The Lagrangian is

$$\mathcal{L} = \ln c_{t+1} + \alpha \ln l_{t+1} + \gamma \ln g_{t+1} + \lambda [w n_{t+1} + (1+r) k_{t+1} - c_{t+1} - g_{t+1}].$$

The first-order conditions are

$$\frac{\partial \mathcal{L}}{\partial c_{t+1}} = \frac{1}{c_{t+1}} - \lambda = 0,$$

$$\frac{\partial \mathcal{L}}{\partial n_{t+1}} = -\alpha \frac{1}{1 - n_{t+1}} + \lambda w = 0,$$

$$\frac{\partial \mathcal{L}}{\partial g_{t+1}} = \gamma \frac{1}{g_{t+1}} - \lambda = 0.$$

These give the same solutions as before.

(ii) **The government's problem.** The problem facing the government in the second period is therefore also the same. Consequently, there is no time inconsistency for policy using lump-sum taxes.

Taken together with the private sector's decisions, we conclude that in a decentralized economy reoptimization by the government in period $t+1$ simply duplicates both the centrally planned solution and the optimal policy. Policy under lump-sum taxes is therefore time consistent.

6.2.2 Taxes on Labor and Capital

6.2.2.1 The Central Planning Solution

The government maximizes intertemporal utility $\mathcal{U}_t$ subject to the economy's intertemporal resource constraint and the government budget constraint in period $t + 1$. The Lagrangian is

$$\mathcal{L} = \ln c_t + \alpha \ln l_t + \beta(\ln c_{t+1} + \alpha \ln l_{t+1} + \gamma \ln g_{t+1})$$
$$+ \lambda[w n_{t+1} + R^2 k_t - R c_t - c_{t+1} - g_{t+1}]$$
$$+ \mu[\tau^w w n_{t+1} + (R - R^\tau)(R k_t - c_t) - g_{t+1}].$$

The first-order conditions are

$$\frac{\partial \mathcal{L}}{\partial c_t} = \frac{1}{c_t} - \lambda(1 + r) - \mu(R - R^\tau) = 0,$$

$$\frac{\partial \mathcal{L}}{\partial c_{t+1}} = \beta\frac{1}{c_{t+1}} - \lambda = 0,$$

$$\frac{\partial \mathcal{L}}{\partial n_{t+1}} = -\alpha\beta\frac{1}{1 - n_{t+1}} + \lambda w + \mu \tau^w w = 0,$$

$$\frac{\partial \mathcal{L}}{\partial g_{t+1}} = \beta\gamma\frac{1}{g_{t+1}} - \lambda - \mu = 0,$$

$$\frac{\partial \mathcal{L}}{\partial \tau^w} = \mu w n_{t+1} = 0,$$

$$\frac{\partial \mathcal{L}}{\partial R^\tau} = -\mu(R k_t - c_t) = 0.$$

It follows that $\mu = 0$ and hence

$$c_{t+1} = \beta R c_t = \beta(1 + r)c_t, \tag{6.15}$$

$$l_{t+1} = \frac{\alpha}{w}c_{t+1}, \tag{6.16}$$

$$g_{t+1} = \gamma c_{t+1}. \tag{6.17}$$

These are the same as for lump-sum taxation, namely, equations (6.7)–(6.9). As the budget constraint is different, however, there is a different solution for c_t. This is

$$c_t = \frac{(w/R) + R k_t}{1 + \beta(1 + \alpha + \gamma)}. \tag{6.18}$$

6.2.2.2 Decentralized Solution

Intertemporal Solution

(i) The private sector's problem. In the first period the private sector maximizes $\mathcal{U}_t$ subject to its intertemporal budget constraint taking government expenditures and the taxes on labor and capital as given. The private sector's intertemporal budget constraint is

$$R^\tau c_t + c_{t+1} = w^\tau n_{t+1} + R R^\tau k_t.$$

The Lagrangian is

$$\mathcal{L} = \ln c_t + \alpha \ln l_t + \beta(\ln c_{t+1} + \alpha \ln l_{t+1} + \gamma \ln g_{t+1})$$
$$+ \lambda[w^\tau n_{t+1} + RR^\tau k_t - R^\tau c_t - c_{t+1}].$$

The first-order conditions are

$$\frac{\partial \mathcal{L}}{\partial c_t} = \frac{1}{c_t} - \lambda R^\tau = 0,$$

$$\frac{\partial \mathcal{L}}{\partial c_{t+1}} = \beta \frac{1}{c_{t+1}} - \lambda = 0,$$

$$\frac{\partial \mathcal{L}}{\partial n_{t+1}} = -\alpha \beta \frac{1}{1 - n_{t+1}} + \lambda w^\tau = 0,$$

implying that

$$c_t = \frac{(w^\tau / R^\tau) + Rk_t}{(1 + \alpha)\beta}, \tag{6.19}$$

$$c_{t+1} = \beta R^\tau c_t, \tag{6.20}$$

$$l_{t+1} = \frac{\alpha}{w^\tau} c_{t+1}, \tag{6.21}$$

$$k_{t+1} = (1 + r)k_t - c_t. \tag{6.22}$$

Comparing the solution involving lump-sum taxes with this solution, w is replaced by w^τ and R is replaced by R^τ, i.e., the after-tax wage rate and the after-tax return to capital are now used. This implies that this type of taxation of labor and capital is distorting.

(ii) The government's problem. The government takes the first-period outcomes as given. Its problem is to choose g_{t+1} and labor and capital taxes to maximize utility in period $t+1$ subject to the economy's resource constraint in period $t+1$, and to the period t outcomes. This implies taking account of equation (6.12) and taking c_t and k_{t+1} as given. The Lagrangian can be written as

$$\mathcal{L} = \ln c_{t+1} + \alpha \ln l_{t+1} + \gamma \ln g_{t+1} + \lambda\left[l_{t+1} - \frac{\alpha}{w^\tau} c_{t+1}\right]$$
$$+ \mu[\beta R^\tau c_t - c_{t+1}] + \phi[\tau^w w n_{t+1} + (R - R^\tau)k_{t+1} - g_{t+1}].$$

The first-order conditions are

$$\frac{\partial \mathcal{L}}{\partial c_{t+1}} = \frac{1}{c_{t+1}} - \lambda \frac{\alpha}{w^\tau} - \mu = 0,$$

$$\frac{\partial \mathcal{L}}{\partial n_{t+1}} = -\alpha \frac{1}{1 - n_{t+1}} - \lambda + \phi \tau^w w = 0,$$

$$\frac{\partial \mathcal{L}}{\partial g_{t+1}} = \gamma \frac{1}{g_{t+1}} - \phi = 0,$$

$$\frac{\partial \mathcal{L}}{\partial \tau^w} = -\lambda \frac{\alpha w}{(w^\tau)^2} c_{t+1} + \phi w n_{t+1} = 0,$$

$$\frac{\partial \mathcal{L}}{\partial R^\tau} = \mu \beta c_t - \phi k_{t+1} = 0.$$

These equations can be solved for the optimal taxes, but the solution is complex and highly nonlinear. With taxes on labor and capital, the solution in a decentralized economy is therefore different from that in a centrally planned economy.

Reoptimization in Period $t + 1$

(i) The private sector's problem. The private sector now reoptimizes in period $t+1$ taking k_{t+1}, g_{t+1}, and the tax rates as given. It maximizes $U(c_{t+1}, l_{t+1}, g_{t+1})$ subject to its budget constraint in period $t + 1$ (equation (6.5)). The Lagrangian is

$$\mathcal{L} = \ln c_{t+1} + \alpha \ln l_{t+1} + \gamma \ln g_{t+1} + \lambda(w^\tau n_{t+1} + R^\tau k_{t+1} - c_{t+1}).$$

The first-order conditions are

$$\frac{\partial \mathcal{L}}{\partial c_{t+1}} = \frac{1}{c_{t+1}} - \lambda = 0,$$

$$\frac{\partial \mathcal{L}}{\partial n_{t+1}} = -\alpha \frac{1}{1 - n_{t+1}} + \lambda w^\tau = 0.$$

Hence, we obtain

$$c_{t+1} = \frac{w^\tau + R^\tau k_{t+1}}{1 + \alpha}, \tag{6.23}$$

$$l_{t+1} = \frac{\alpha}{w^\tau} c_{t+1}. \tag{6.24}$$

(ii) The government's problem. The government maximizes $U(c_{t+1}, l_{t+1}, g_{t+1})$ subject to its budget constraint in period $t + 1$ (equation (6.3)) and to equations (6.23) and (6.24). The Lagrangian is

$$\mathcal{L} = \ln c_{t+1} + \alpha \ln l_{t+1} + \gamma \ln g_{t+1} + \lambda \left(l_{t+1} - \frac{\alpha}{w^\tau} c_{t+1} \right)$$

$$+ \mu \left(c_{t+1} - \frac{w^\tau + R^\tau k_{t+1}}{1 + \alpha} \right) + \phi(\tau^w w n_{t+1} + (R - R^\tau) k_{t+1} - g_{t+1}).$$

The first-order conditions are

$$\frac{\partial \mathcal{L}}{\partial c_{t+1}} = \frac{1}{c_{t+1}} - \frac{\alpha}{w^\tau} \lambda + \mu = 0,$$

$$\frac{\partial \mathcal{L}}{\partial n_{t+1}} = -\alpha \frac{1}{1 - n_{t+1}} - \lambda + \phi \tau^w w = 0,$$

$$\frac{\partial \mathcal{L}}{\partial g_{t+1}} = \gamma \frac{1}{g_{t+1}} - \phi = 0,$$

$$\frac{\partial \mathcal{L}}{\partial \tau^w} = -\lambda \frac{\alpha w}{(w^\tau)^2} c_{t+1} + \mu \frac{w}{1 + \alpha} + \phi w n_{t+1} = 0,$$

$$\frac{\partial \mathcal{L}}{\partial R^\tau} = -\mu \frac{k_{t+1}}{1 + \alpha} - \phi k_{t+1} = 0.$$

It can be shown that these imply that $l_{t+1} = (\alpha/w)c_{t+1}$. This is different from the constraint $l_{t+1} = (\alpha/w^\tau)c_{t+1}$ unless $\tau^w = 0$. It follows, therefore, that the optimal value of the labor tax rate is zero. Thus, despite the private sector's expectation that wages will be taxed in period $t + 1$, when period $t + 1$ arrives it is optimal not to do so, but to encourage employment and output.

The optimal rate of taxation of capital must satisfy the government budget constraint. As the optimal level of government expenditure is given by

$$g_{t+1} = \gamma c_{t+1},$$

which is the same as for lump-sum taxes, the optimal after-tax gross rate of return to capital is

$$R^\tau = \frac{(1 + \alpha)R - (\gamma w / k_{t+1})}{1 + \alpha + \gamma}, \tag{6.25}$$

implying that the rate of taxation of capital is

$$R - R^\tau = \frac{\gamma (R - (w / k_{t+1}))}{1 + \alpha + \gamma}.$$

Recalling that $R - R^\tau = \tau^k + \tau^r r$, this can be raised from taxing either the stock of capital or the rate of return to capital, or, if necessary in order to satisfy the government budget constraint, both.

With these taxes the solution for c_{t+1} becomes

$$c_{t+1} = \frac{w + R k_{t+1}}{1 + \alpha + \gamma}.$$

It can be shown that the solution for c_t is equation (6.18), the centrally planned solution.

We conclude that in a decentralized economy with labor and capital taxes, reoptimization by the government in period $t + 1$ results in a time-inconsistent solution as it produces a different outcome from the intertemporal solution without reoptimization. However, the reoptimized time-inconsistent solution is the same as the solution under central planning. The reason for this is that taxing capital differently in period $t + 1$ from what was expected by the private sector in period t is equivalent to using lump-sum taxes in period $t + 1$.

6.2.2.3 A Time-Consistent Solution

It is possible to derive an optimal solution for the decentralized economy in the presence of distortionary taxation that the government would not want to deviate from in period $t + 1$. This is called the time-consistent solution. It is obtained using the "principle of optimality" of dynamic programming. Dynamic programming reverses the order in which the full solution for the two periods is derived. First, in period $t + 1$ both the private sector and the government optimize, taking k_{t+1} as given. This is the same solution that was derived above and is based on reoptimization in period $t + 1$. Taking this solution as given (i.e., given the values for τ^w, R^τ, and g_{t+1}), the private sector optimizes intertemporal utility over the two periods, by choosing k_{t+1}. We then have the full solution.

The intertemporal utility function to be maximized in period t is now

$$\mathcal{U}^* = \ln c_t + \alpha \ln l_t + \beta(\ln c_{t+1} + \alpha \ln l_{t+1} + \gamma \ln g_{t+1}),$$

where c_{t+1}, l_{t+1}, and g_{t+1} are the optimal solutions derived for period $t + 1$. Once more, l_t could be omitted as it is assumed that there is no production in period t. The private sector maximizes $\mathcal{U}^*$ subject to equations (6.23) and (6.24) and to the first-period budget constraint, equation (6.1), taking τ^w, R^τ, and g_{t+1} as given. Instead of using Lagrangian multipliers, we substitute the three constraints into $\mathcal{U}^*$ to obtain

$$\mathcal{U}^* = \ln(Rk_t - k_{t+1}) + \alpha \ln l_t$$
$$+ \beta(1 + \alpha)[\ln(w^\tau + R^\tau k_{t+1}) - \ln(1 + \alpha)] + \alpha \ln \frac{\alpha}{w^\tau} + \gamma \ln g_{t+1}.$$

The only decision left is the choice of k_{t+1}. The first-order condition is

$$\frac{\partial \mathcal{U}^*}{\partial k_{t+1}} = -\frac{1}{Rk_t - k_{t+1}} + \frac{\beta(1 + \alpha)R^\tau}{w^\tau + R^\tau k_{t+1}} = 0.$$

Consequently,

$$k_{t+1} = \frac{(1 + \alpha)\beta Rk_t - (w^\tau/R^\tau)}{1 + (1 + \alpha)\beta}, \qquad (6.26)$$

and so

$$c_t = \frac{Rk_t + (w^\tau/R^\tau)}{1 + (1 + \alpha)\beta}. \qquad (6.27)$$

In order to obtain the time-consistent optimal capital tax R^τ, we must combine equations (6.26) and (6.25) to eliminate k_{t+1}. The result is the solution to the following quadratic equation in R^τ:

$$(R^\tau)^2(1 + \alpha + \gamma)\beta Rk_t - R^\tau[w(1 - \beta\gamma) + R^2(1 + \alpha)\beta k_t] + wR = 0.$$

The assumption in the time-consistent solution when optimizing in period t is that the private sector takes the government decisions in period $t+1$ concerning τ^w, R^τ, and g_{t+1} as given, and the government takes the decisions of the private sector for period $t + 1$ as given when optimizing in period $t + 1$. This results in a welfare loss compared with a cooperative solution—were cooperation possible. The optimal level of the capital tax R^τ depends on how the private sector acts in the first period: if the private sector cooperates, then the tax would be low, which would encourage capital accumulation; but if the private sector does not act cooperatively, then capital taxes would be high.

A ranking can be given to these various policy scenarios concerning labor and capital taxes. The first-best welfare outcome is the centrally planned solution; the time-inconsistent solution is second; the intertemporal solution, in which the government takes account of the constraints on its decisions following the private sector's intertemporal optimization, is third; and the time-consistent solution is last.

6.2.3 Conclusions

We have shown how policymaking over more than one period may lead to a desire by government to change its original plan. Moreover, this may be optimal for the economy as a whole. The analysis is complicated. Consequently, there are few examples of the problem in the literature, and Fischer's paper has become a key reference, even though the model is highly stylized. Nonetheless, the results are very sensitive to the outcomes for the different types of policy scenarios. A key assumption was that the policy problem was for two periods. In practice, it will be a repeated problem involving many periods. If it is best for the government to reoptimize each period, then only the first period of the plan will ever be carried out, however many periods each plan is for. The private sector, realizing this, will act accordingly in making their own decisions, and ignore any statement from the government that refers to periods beyond the current period. Consequently, the multiperiod problem is effectively reduced to a series of one-period problems.

6.3 The Overlapping-Generations Model

6.3.1 Introduction

The models considered so far are all representative-agent models, in which all households and firms are assumed to be identical. Moreover, the representative agent is assumed to live forever. Even the Blanchard–Yaari model, where there is a constant, finite, nonzero probability of dying in each period, was shown in chapter 4 to reduce to an infinite-life model with a redefined discount rate. The infinite-life representative-agent model is convenient when analyzing most problems. It does, however, have some strong implications for the behavior of the economy that may not always be appropriate. It removes most of the effects of ageing, particularly as they relate to intergenerational effects. For example, it eliminates the possibility of intergenerational transfers. This is particularly relevant for the analysis of pensions, a major reason for household saving. It also affects some of our earlier conclusions about fiscal policy.

In practice, the obligations of governments tend to be indefinite, whereas those of people are limited to their lifetimes. The probability that a government assumes that its actions would result in it having a finite time in office seems to be negligible and may for most practical purposes be ignored. Suppose, however, that today's old generation voted themselves lower taxes, higher benefits, or larger expenditures, and financed this by borrowing from today's young generation. Since the old generation would not be alive to redeem the debt, the burden of doing this would fall on tomorrow's old generation (today's young generation). Today's old generation has therefore benefited at the expense of the current young generation. This could, of course, be repeated with next period's old generation (today's young generation) redeeming the debt by borrowing from the following period's young generation.

In order to analyze the issues arising from this we switch from the representative-agent model to the overlapping-generations (OLG) model. We begin our study of the OLG model by considering it solely as an alternative representation of the intertemporal macroeconomic model used previously. Our discussion of the OLG model is developed from Diamond (1965) (which adds a supply side to Samuelson's (1958) original pure-exchange OLG model), Blanchard and Fischer (1989), Barro and Sala-i-Martin (2004), and Michel and de la Croix (2002). We then apply the OLG model to analyze different ways of financing pensions. Finally, we consider how the OLG model affects some of our previous conclusions about fiscal policy.

6.3.2 The Basic Overlapping-Generations Model

For simplicity and transparency, our basic OLG model is also highly stylized. The key assumption is that each person's life has two time periods: youth and old age. Hence in every time period there are two types of people: the young and the old. Both make intertemporal decisions: the young for two periods and the old for one period. Clearly, a time period in the OLG model is different from before, being a matter of a generation rather than months.

It is assumed that only the young work; the old are retired. If the total population is N_t, then in time t there are N_{1t} young people and N_{2t} old people. Hence,

$$N_t = N_{1t} + N_{2t}.$$

This period's old are last period's young and so

$$N_{2t} = N_{1,t-1}.$$

Thus

$$N_t = N_{1t} + N_{1,t-1}.$$

We assume that the population grows at the fixed rate n. Hence

$$N_{1,t} = (1 + n)N_{1,t-1} \tag{6.28}$$

and

$$N_t = N_{1,t} + \frac{1}{1 + n}N_{1,t}.$$

If c_{1t} and c_{2t} are the respective consumptions per head of the young and the old, then total consumption by the young and old in period t is

$$C_{it} = c_{it}N_{it}, \quad i = 1, 2.$$

The current generation of young consume $c_{2,t+1}$ per capita in period $t + 1$ when they become old. Total consumption at time t is

$$C_t = C_{1t} + C_{2t}$$

$$= \left(c_{1t} + \frac{1}{1 + n}c_{2t}\right)N_{1t}.$$

The national income identity is

$$Y_t = C_t + I_t,$$

where I_t is investment. The capital accumulation condition is

$$\Delta K_{t+1} = I_t - \delta K_t,$$

where the rate of depreciation will be much closer to unity than in the previous representative-agent model. The resource constraint for the economy can therefore be written as

$$Y_t = \left(c_{1t} + \frac{1}{1+n}c_{2t}\right)N_{1t} + K_{t+1} - (1-\delta)K_t. \tag{6.29}$$

The resource constraint expressed in per capita terms is

$$y_t = \frac{N_{1t}}{N_t}\left(c_{1t} + \frac{1}{1+n}c_{2t}\right) + \frac{N_{1t}}{N_t}\frac{N_{1,t+1}}{N_{1t}}\frac{K_{t+1}}{N_{1,t+1}} - (1-\delta)\frac{N_{1t}}{N_t}\frac{K_t}{N_{1t}}$$

$$= \frac{1}{1+(1/n)}\left[c_{1t} + \frac{1}{1+n}c_{2t} + (1+n)k_{t+1} - (1-\delta)k_t\right],$$

where $k_t = K_t/N_{1t}$.

Only the young work. We assume that the production function is

$$Y_t = F(K_t, N_{1t})$$

and has constant returns to scale. Thus output per head is

$$y_t = \frac{Y_t}{N_t} = \frac{N_{1t}}{N_t}F\left(\frac{K_t}{N_{1t}}, 1\right)$$

$$= \frac{1}{1+(1/n)}f(k_t),$$

where $k_t = K_t/N_{1t}$. The resource constraint per capita is therefore

$$f(k_t) = c_{1t} + \frac{1}{1+n}c_{2t} + (1+n)k_{t+1} - (1-\delta)k_t. \tag{6.30}$$

Profit maximization implies that r_t, the rate of return to capital, equals the net marginal product of capital,

$$f'(k_t) - \delta = r_t, \tag{6.31}$$

and that the young are paid their marginal product. Given the assumption of constant returns, their wage rate (also the income per young person) is

$$w_t = f(k_t) - k_t f'(k_t). \tag{6.32}$$

The young generation consumes c_{1t} and saves

$$s_{1t} = w_t - c_{1t}. \tag{6.33}$$

Due to investing savings, they generate an income when old of $(1+r_{t+1})s_{1t}$. As the old generation consumes the whole of their income and saves nothing, the intertemporal budget constraint is

$$c_{2,t+1} = (1+r_{t+1})(w_t - c_{1t}). \tag{6.34}$$

We note that this can also be written in the more familiar form of the two-period intertemporal budget constraint:

$$c_{1t} + \frac{c_{2,t+1}}{1 + r_{t+1}} = w_t.$$

From the resource constraint for the total economy at time t, net investment is

$$\Delta K_{t+1} = Y_t - c_{1t}N_{1t} - c_{2t}N_{1,t-1} - \delta K_t$$
$$= w_t N_{1t} + r_t K_t - c_{1t}N_{1t} - c_{2t}N_{1,t-1}.$$

Using $c_{1t} = w_t + s_t$ and $c_{2t} = (1 + r_t)s_{t-1}$ we obtain

$$K_{t+1} - s_t N_{1t} = (1 + r_t)(K_t - s_{t-1}N_{1,t-1}).$$

This unstable difference equation is satisfied for all t only by the degenerate solution

$$K_{t+1} = s_t N_{1t}. \tag{6.35}$$

In other words, the total demand for capital must equal the total supply of savings. Saving is undertaken only by the young, who own next period's capital stock. If we assume that they do not want to be left with any assets when they die, then, in the following period, when they are old, they sell this capital to the new young generation. Equation (6.35) can be written in per capita terms as

$$s_t = \frac{K_{t+1}}{N_{1t}} = (1 + n)k_{t+1}. \tag{6.36}$$

Accordingly, consumption when old can be related to next period's capital stock through

$$c_{2,t+1} = (1 + r_{t+1})(1 + n)k_{t+1}. \tag{6.37}$$

The two generations are assumed to be identical in their preferences. The difference lies in how many years of life they have left. Hence consumption decisions depend on the age of the individual. The young live for two periods, and so in period t their intertemporal utility function is

$$\mathcal{U} = U(c_{1t}) + \beta U(c_{2,t+1}).$$

Taking w_t and r_{t+1} as given, the young maximize $\mathcal{U}$ subject to their intertemporal constraint. The Lagrangian for this problem is

$$\mathcal{L} = U(c_{1t}) + \beta U(c_{2,t+1}) + \lambda[c_{2,t+1} - (1 + r_{t+1})(w_t - c_{1t})].$$

The first-order conditions are

$$\frac{\partial \mathcal{L}}{\partial c_{1t}} = U_{c_1,t} + \lambda(1 + r_{t+1}) = 0, \tag{6.38}$$

$$\frac{\partial \mathcal{L}}{\partial c_{2,t+1}} = \beta U_{c_2,t+1} + \lambda = 0. \tag{6.39}$$

Hence

$$\frac{\beta U_{c_{2,t+1}}(1 + r_{t+1})}{U_{c_{1,t}}} = 1. \tag{6.40}$$

This is the OLG equivalent of the Euler equation in the basic representative-agent model and it relates consumption next period to consumption this period. Writing $\beta = 1/(1 + \theta)$, where θ is the discount rate, we obtain

$$\frac{U_{c_{2,t+1}}}{U_{c_{1,t}}} = \frac{1 + \theta}{1 + r_{t+1}}.$$

If, for example, we have power utility so that

$$U(c_{it}) = \frac{c_{it}^{1-\sigma} - 1}{1 - \sigma}, \quad i = 1, 2,$$

then $U_{c_{it}} = c_{it}^{-\sigma}$ and

$$c_{2,t+1} = \left(\frac{1 + r_{t+1}}{1 + \theta}\right)^{1/\sigma} c_{1t}. \tag{6.41}$$

Assuming that $U'' < 0$ we find that $c_{1t} \gtreqless c_{2,t+1}$ as $r_{t+1} \lesseqgtr \theta$. Consumption when young exceeds consumption when old if the real return to saving is less than the rate of time discount, i.e., if the incentive to save for the future is insufficient to offset the discounting of future utility.

6.3.3 Short-Run Dynamics and Long-Run Equilibrium

The dynamic behavior of the economy and its steady-state solution may be derived from equations (6.32), (6.33), (6.37), and (6.41). Eliminating c_{1t} from equation (6.33) using equation (6.41) gives

$$s_t = w_t - \left(\frac{1 + r_{t+1}}{1 + \theta}\right)^{-1/\sigma} c_{2,t+1}.$$

Substituting for s_t into equation (6.34) and simplifying gives

$$\left[1 + \frac{(1 + r_{t+1})^{1-1/\sigma}}{(1 + \theta)^{-1/\sigma}}\right] c_{2,t+1} = (1 + r_{t+1}) w_t.$$

Substituting $c_{2,t+1}$ into equation (6.37) and recalling the solution for wages (equation (6.32)) gives the following nonlinear difference equation in k_t:

$$k_{t+1} = (f(k_t) - f'(k_t)k_t) \Big/ \left((1 + n)\left[1 + \frac{(1 + r_{t+1})^{1-1/\sigma}}{(1 + \theta)^{-1/\sigma}}\right]\right), \tag{6.42}$$

where $r_t = f'(k_t) - \delta$ is also a function of k_t.

A general closed-form solution for k_t is not available, due to the nonlinearity of this equation of motion. We therefore consider a specific solution. A particularly convenient assumption is that the utility function is logarithmic. This implies that $\sigma = 1$, which eliminates r_{t+1} from equation (6.42). We also assume a

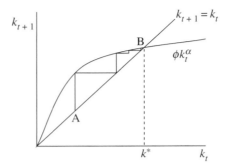

Figure 6.1. The adjustment path of capital.

Cobb–Douglas production function where $f(k_t) = k_t^\alpha$, giving $f'(k_t) = \alpha k_t^{-(1-\alpha)}$. As a result, equation (6.42) can be written as

$$k_{t+1} = \frac{1}{(1+n)(2+\theta)}[f(k_t) - f'(k_t)k_t]$$
$$= \phi k_t^\alpha, \tag{6.43}$$

where $\phi = (1-\alpha)/((1+n)(2+\theta))$.

The condition for the existence and the stability of long-run equilibrium is that

$$-1 < \frac{dk_{t+1}}{dk_t} < 1,$$

and, from equation (6.43),

$$\frac{dk_{t+1}}{dk_t} = \alpha \phi k_t^{-(1-\alpha)}.$$

The dynamic behavior of capital can be analyzed algebraically or graphically. First we examine local stability. Assuming that there is a long-run solution, this is given by

$$k^* = \left[\frac{1-\alpha}{(1+n)(2+\theta)}\right]^{1/(1-\alpha)}.$$

Using a Taylor series expansion about k^* of the right-hand side of equation (6.43), we obtain

$$\Delta k_{t+1} = -(1-\alpha)(k_t - k^*),$$

which is a partial adjustment model. We note that $dk_{t+1}/dk_t = \alpha < 1$. Hence equation (6.42) is locally stable.

Alternatively, we may use figure 6.1. The curve is equation (6.42). Along the 45° line $k_{t+1} = k_t$. The intersection of the lines gives k^* at point B. At B the slope of the curve is less than that of the 45° line, hence $0 < dk_{t+1}/dk_t < 1$, and so the long-run solution is globally stable. Figure 6.1 also depicts the adjustment path from A to B following a permanent shift upwards in the curve, which, we note, raises the equilibrium value of capital.

From equation (6.33), and noting that $c_2^* = ((1 + r^*)/(1 + \theta))c_1^*$, it can be shown that

$$c_1^* = \frac{1 + \theta}{2 + \theta} w^*,$$

$$s^* = \frac{1}{2 + \theta} w^*,$$

$$c_2^* = (1 + r^*)s^* = \frac{1 + r^*}{2 + \theta} w^*,$$

where an asterisk denotes the long-run equilibrium value. Hence

$$c_2^* - c_1^* = \frac{r^* - \theta}{2 + \theta} w^*.$$

Since we expect $r^* \geqslant \theta$, we have $c_2^* \geqslant c_1^*$.

In the more general solution that does not assume logarithmic utility, the more σ exceeds unity, the smaller k^* is for $r_{t+1} > \theta$. Also, the greater n is, the smaller k^* is. Although we have introduced n as the rate of population growth of the young, we could give it another interpretation. It could be regarded as the rate of growth of the productivity of labor, possibly through improved knowledge. N_1 would then be interpreted as effective labor, and consumption and capital would be measured per effective unit of labor.

6.3.4 Comparison with the Representative-Agent Model

In the static-equilibrium representative-agent model consumption is the same for everyone. A question of interest is whether this level of consumption is more or less than the young and old generations of the OLG model. In the OLG model, the income of the old is due to saving when young, whereas in the representative-agent model, people receive wage income throughout their lives. The intertemporal model aims to smooth consumption by saving today to offset reductions in future income. This suggests that households in the OLG model will save far more than those in the representative-agent model. Consequently, we would expect the capital stock in the OLG model to be greater. Given the same capital stock, and the opportunity to save a lower proportion of income, we would expect consumption in the representative-agent model to be greater than that of the young generation in the OLG model. A larger capital stock in the OLG model could reverse this.

In making a more formal comparison, we assume that $n = 0$ in the OLG model and that the production function in the representative-agent model is $f(k) = k^\alpha$. We assume logarithmic utility in both. The optimal solution in the representative-agent model is

$$k^\# = \left(\frac{\alpha}{\delta + \theta}\right)^{1/(1-\alpha)},$$
$$w^\# = (1 - \alpha)k^{\#\alpha},$$
$$c^\# = w^\#.$$

In the OLG model with $n = 0$ it is

$$k^* = \left[\frac{1-\alpha}{2+\theta}\right]^{1/(1-\alpha)},$$

$$w^* = (1-\alpha)k^{*\alpha},$$

$$c_1^* = \frac{1+\theta}{2+\theta}w^*,$$

$$c_2^* = \frac{1+r^*}{2+\theta}w^*.$$

It can be shown that $k^\# \gtreqless k^*$ and $w^\# \gtreqless w^*$ as

$$\delta \lesseqgtr \frac{\alpha(2+\theta)}{1-\alpha} - \theta.$$

In general, it is not clear what the sign will be. However, if $\alpha = 0.25$ then $\delta \lesseqgtr \frac{2}{3}(1-\theta)$. It is probable, therefore, that $k^\# < k^*$ and $w^\# < w^*$. If capital fully depreciates during a generation so that $\delta = 1$, then $k^\# < k^*$. This would accord with our intuition. Even then, however, it is still not possible to determine the relative sizes of $c^\#$ and c_1^*.

6.3.5 Fiscal Policy in the OLG Model: Pensions

The OLG model is particularly suitable for analyzing fiscal policy issues involving a different treatment of young and old. Examples are the provision of funded and unfunded pensions, welfare benefits to the young such as unemployment benefit or state aid for education, and government investment projects that mainly benefit future generations. We begin by considering a generic problem in which the government taxes the young and old differently through lump-sum taxes. We allow the taxes to be negative so that they may also be a benefit. We also permit the government to issue one-period bonds to cover any deficit. These are purchased only by the young.

The principal reason for saving is to provide a pension in retirement. A fully funded pension is one in which the whole pension is due to past savings. In many countries pensions are paid for out of current taxation and not savings. This is called an unfunded pension, or a pay-as-you-go (PAYG) system. Longer lifetimes and lower population growth are currently causes of considerable concern because unfunded pensions then impose a growing tax burden. The OLG model is particularly suited to an analysis of pensions, funded or unfunded.

6.3.5.1 *Fully Funded Pensions*

If fully funded pensions are provided for from personal savings, then there is no need to bring government into the analysis. The income of the old generation in the previous analysis of the OLG model is, in effect, a pension generated from savings. The situation changes if there is, in addition, a state pension. If the state pension is fully funded, then the government taxes the young generation, invests this contribution and pays out the proceeds to the young generation when they are old. The government seems, therefore, to be forcing the young to save more than they would choose to on their own. We examine this case in greater detail.

Suppose that the government imposes a tax of τ_t on each member of the young generation which it then invests. The proceeds from the investment are returned to them when they are old in the form of a pension p_{t+1}. For this fully funded scheme,

$$p_{t+1} = (1 + r_{t+1})\tau_t.$$

Hence, in a stochastic economy, p_{t+1} is not known with certainty.

The budget constraint for the young generation is

$$s_{1t} = w_t - c_{1t} - \tau_t$$

and their consumption when old is

$$\begin{aligned} c_{2,t+1} &= (1 + r_{t+1})s_t + p_{t+1} \\ &= (1 + r_{t+1})(s_t + \tau_t). \end{aligned}$$

The intertemporal budget constraint therefore remains

$$c_{2,t+1} = (1 + r_{t+1})(w_t - c_{1t}) \tag{6.44}$$

and the Euler equation (2.12) is also the same.

The resource constraint for the total economy at time t is now

$$\begin{aligned} \Delta K_{t+1} &= w_t N_{1t} + r_t K_t - c_{1t} N_{1t} - c_{2t} N_{1,t-1} \\ &= w_t N_{1t} + r_t K_t - (w_t - s_t - \tau_t)N_{1t} - (1 + r_t)(s_{t-1} + \tau_{t-1})N_{1,t-1}. \end{aligned}$$

Hence,

$$K_{t+1} - (s_t - \tau_t)N_{1t} = (1 + r_t)[K_t - (s_{t-1} + \tau_{t-1})N_{1,t-1}],$$

which has the per capita solution

$$s_t + \tau_t = (1 + n)k_{t+1}. \tag{6.45}$$

In effect, therefore, s_t has been replaced by $s_t + \tau_t$.

Recalling that τ_t is determined exogenously by the government, provided $\tau_t < (1 + n)k_{t+1}$, i.e., it does not exceed total savings when there is no government intervention, the desired capital stock, and hence total savings, are therefore the same as when there is no fully funded government pension. In this case, there would be little point in having a state pension. Individuals would simply make an equal cut in their voluntary savings one-for-one to offset the state pension and so when old finish up with the same income as before.

6.3.5.2 Unfunded Pensions

Under a PAYG system, pensions to the old generation are paid from current tax receipts. Assuming a poll tax on both generations, the government budget constraint for time t can be written as

$$\tau_t (N_{1t} + N_{2t}) = p_t N_{2t}.$$

Recalling that $N_{2t} = N_{1,t-1} = N_{1t}/(1+n)$, the pension after tax is

$$p_t - \tau_t = (1+n)\tau_t.$$

Consumption when old is now

$$
\begin{aligned}
c_{2,t+1} &= (1+r_{t+1})s_t + (p_{t+1} - \tau_{t+1}) \\
&= (1+r_{t+1})s_t + (1+n)\tau_{t+1}.
\end{aligned}
\tag{6.46}
$$

Thus the rate of return to private savings is r_{t+1}, but the effective rate of return on the enforced pension contributions is n. The intertemporal budget constraint becomes

$$c_{2,t+1} = (1+r_{t+1})(w_t - c_{1t} - \tau_t) + (1+n)\tau_{t+1},
\tag{6.47}$$

which is different from (6.44).

The resource constraint for the total economy at time t is now

$$
\begin{aligned}
\Delta K_{t+1} &= w_t N_{1t} + r_t K_t - c_{1t} N_{1t} - c_{2t} N_{1,t-1} \\
&= w_t N_{1t} + r_t K_t - (w_t - s_t - \tau_t)N_{1t} - [(1+r_t)s_{t-1} + (1+n)\tau_{t-1}]N_{1,t-1}.
\end{aligned}
$$

Hence,

$$K_{t+1} - (s_t + \tau_t)N_{1t} = (1+r_t)[K_t - (s_{t-1} + \tau_{t-1})N_{1,t-1}] - (n - r_t)\tau_{t-1}N_{1,t-1}$$

or

$$(1+n)k_{t+1} - (s_t + \tau_t) = \frac{1+r_t}{1+n}[(1+n)k_t - (s_{t-1} + \tau_{t-1})] - \frac{n - r_t}{1+n}\tau_{t-1}.$$

The solution to this difference equation depends on whether r_t is greater than or less than n. The steady-state solution for given constant taxes τ_t and interest rates r_t is

$$s_t = (1+n)k_{t+1},$$

which is the same relation as for the economy without state pensions. This does not imply, however, that savings or the capital stock are at the same level.

The problem for the young is to maximize U subject to this intertemporal budget constraint for given wages, interest rates, and taxes. The Lagrangian is

$$\mathcal{N} = U(c_{1t}) + \beta U(c_{2,t+1}) + \lambda[c_{2,t+1} - (1+r_{t+1})(w_t - c_{1t} - \tau_t) - (1+n)\tau_{t+1}].$$

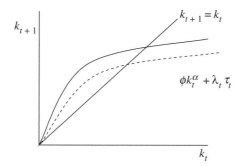

Figure 6.2. The effect on capital of an increase in taxes.

The first-order conditions for consumption and the resulting Euler equation have the same form as those without pensions, namely, equations (6.38), (6.39), and (2.12). Assuming power utility, we obtain

$$c_{2,t+1} = (1 + r_{t+1})(w_t - c_{1t} - \tau_t) + (1 + n)\tau_{t+1}$$

$$= (1 + r_{t+1})\left[w_t - \left(\frac{1 + r_{t+1}}{1 + \theta}\right)^{-1/\sigma} c_{2,t+1} - \tau_t\right] + (1 + n)\tau_{t+1}.$$

Hence for $\sigma = 1$ and constant taxes,

$$c_{2,t+1} = \frac{1 + r_{t+1}}{2 + \theta} w_t + \frac{n - r_{t+1}}{2 + \theta} \tau_t. \tag{6.48}$$

From equation (6.46),

$$s_t = (1 + n)k_{t+1},$$

and assuming that $f(k_t) = k_t^\alpha$, we obtain

$$w_t = (1 - \alpha)k_t^\alpha \quad \text{and} \quad r_t = \alpha k_t^{-(1-\alpha)} - \delta.$$

The left-hand and right-hand sides of equation (6.48) can therefore be written as

$$(1 + r_{t+1})(1 + n)k_{t+1} = \frac{1 + r_{t+1}}{2 + \theta}(1 - \alpha)k_t^\alpha + \frac{n - r_{t+1}}{2 + \theta}\tau_t;$$

hence

$$k_{t+1} = \frac{1 - \alpha}{(2 + \theta)(1 + n)}k_t^\alpha - \frac{1}{2 + \theta}\left[\frac{1 + \theta}{1 + r_{t+1}} + \frac{1}{1 + n}\right]\tau_t$$

$$= \phi k_t^\alpha + \lambda_t \tau_t,$$

where

$$\lambda_t = \frac{1}{2 + \theta}\left[\frac{1 + \theta}{1 + r_{t+1}} + \frac{1}{1 + n}\right] > 0.$$

This equation is represented in figure 6.2.

Consequently, an increase in the unfunded state pension shifts the curve downward. This results in a lower equilibrium capital stock and lower savings. Therefore, only the current old generation benefits, not future old generations—in particular, not the current young generation.

We conclude, therefore, that an unfunded pension scheme with a static or slowly growing population is likely to reduce economic welfare in the longer term. For such a population a fully funded scheme is clearly preferable. Unfunded schemes are feasible only for fast-growing populations.

6.3.5.3 Fiscal Policy with Debt

The government pension policies considered so far involve a balanced budget as pension payments to the old generation are paid for in each period by pension contributions from the young generation. Suppose, however, that the government also uses debt finance. More generally, the government budget constraint (GBC) can be written as

$$\Delta B_{t+1} = \tau_{1t} N_{1t} + \tau_{2t} N_{2t} + r_t B_t,$$

where τ_{1t} and τ_{2t} are taxes (or, if negative, subsidies) for the young and old generations, respectively. B_{t+1} is one-period government debt held by the young generation of period t. It is determined by the need to satisfy the GBC and to pay the given interest rate. In per capita terms the GBC is

$$(1+n)b_{t+1} = \tau_{1t} + \frac{\tau_{2t}}{1+n} + (1+r_t)b_t, \tag{6.49}$$

where $b_t = B_t / N_{1t}$.

The budget constraint for the young generation is

$$s_{1t} = w_t - c_{1t} - \tau_{1t} - (1+n)b_{t+1}$$

and their consumption when old is

$$c_{2,t+1} = (1+r_{t+1})[s_t + (1+n)b_{t+1}] - \tau_{2,t+1}.$$

The intertemporal budget constraint is therefore

$$c_{2,t+1} = (1+r_{t+1})[w_t - c_{1t} - \tau_{1t}] - \tau_{2,t+1}.$$

We note the absence of debt. Consequently, the optimal decision takes the same form as before.

The resource constraint for the total economy at time t is

$$\begin{aligned}
\Delta K_{t+1} &= w_t N_{1t} + r_t K_t - c_{1t} N_{1t} - c_{2t} N_{1,t-1} \\
&= w_t N_{1t} + r_t K_t - [w_t - s_t - \tau_{1t} - (1+n)b_{t+1}]N_{1t} \\
&\qquad - \{(1+r_t)[s_{t-1} + (1+n)b_t] - \tau_{2,t}\}N_{1,t-1}.
\end{aligned}$$

Hence,

$$\begin{aligned}
K_{t+1} &- [s_t + (1+n)b_{t+1}]N_{1t} \\
&= (1+r_t)\{K_t - [s_{t-1} + (1+n)b_t]N_{1,t-1}\} + \tau_{1t} N_{1t} + \tau_{2,t} N_{1,t-1}
\end{aligned}$$

or

$$(1+n)(k_{t+1} + b_{t+1}) - s_t = \frac{1+r_t}{1+n}[(1+n)(k_t + b_t) - s_{t-1}] + \tau_{1t} + \frac{\tau_{2,t}}{1+n}.$$

Using the government budget constraint, equation (6.49), gives

$$(1+n)k_{t+1} - s_t = \frac{1+r_t}{1+n}[(1+n)k_t - s_{t-1}].$$

Hence the steady-state solution is $s_t = (1+n)k_{t+1}$, the same as for an economy with no government.

If government debt plays no role in either the intertemporal budget constraint or the determination of savings, then it will not affect the optimal solution either. We conclude that there is no advantage in not balancing the budget. Let us therefore reconsider our previous analysis of pensions. In the case of unfunded pensions the GBC has $\tau_{1t} = \tau_t$, $\tau_{2t} = \tau_t - p_t$, and no debt. For fully funded pensions $\tau_{1t} = \tau_t$ and $\tau_{2t} = -p_t = -(1+r_t)\tau_{t-1}$. The GBC is then

$$(1+n)b_{t+1} = \tau_t - \frac{(1+r_t)\tau_{t-1}}{1+n} + (1+r_t)b_t$$

or

$$(1+n)b_{t+1} - \tau_t = \frac{1+r_t}{1+n}[(1+n)b_t - \tau_{t-1}].$$

Hence, $\tau_t = (1+n)b_{t+1}$. Consequently, pension contributions are equivalent to purchasing government debt, and pension payments are equivalent to the redemption value of this debt.

6.3.6 Conclusions

The OLG model is useful for analyzing economic problems involving periods of time that are quite long, in which people are assumed to live for only a few of these—usually only two. A key feature of the OLG model is that people born in a later period have no control over decisions taken in an earlier period. Unfortunately, problems involving OLG models soon become quite complex and so the economic models used are usually simplified, and hence somewhat stylized. Hence the usual assumption of only two periods. It is common in economic problems for the time period to be more than a matter of months, or even years, but less than a generation, say twenty-five years. This suggests the need to have more than two generations. The difficulty is that, as the number of generations increases, so does the complexity of the analysis. As a result, it is then usually more convenient to assume an infinite number of periods. Even so, we have found that it is not easy to compare the solutions of a two-period OLG model with an infinite-horizon model.

We have used the OLG model to compare funded and unfunded pensions. We concluded that the slower population growth is, the stronger the case is for having fully funded pensions. We also concluded that financing unfunded pensions through government debt is equivalent to having a funded scheme in which pension payments are used to purchase government debt.

7

The Open Economy

7.1 Introduction

The key distinction between closed and open economies is that they have different constraints. In an open economy there is international trade in goods and services, and international capital flows. Imports remove the restriction that consumption and investment in the domestic economy are limited to what the domestic economy can produce. Exports remove the restriction that firms' sales are limited by domestic demand. International capital flows allow the domestic economy to borrow from abroad and to hold foreign assets. In principle, by being less constrained, an open economy ought to be able to attain a higher level of welfare than a closed economy. For example, borrowing from abroad should assist in smoothing consumption in bad times.

The distinction usually emphasized between a closed and an open economy relates to domestic and foreign goods and services. The importance of this distinction depends on the extent to which they are substitutes. This will affect their relative consumption and their relative price, i.e., the (real) terms of trade: strictly speaking, the price of imports relative to exports where both are expressed in domestic currency. If, for example, all goods and services are traded, and if domestic and foreign goods and services were perfect substitutes, then the terms of trade would be constant (or, ignoring transport costs, unity). There would then be a single world price for goods and services. Nonetheless, it would be important to take into account the distinction between domestic and foreign goods and services.

Not all goods and services are traded internationally. We therefore differentiate between traded and nontraded goods and services (i.e., between tradeables and nontradeables). We also distinguish between the terms of trade (which refers only to tradeables) and the real exchange rate, which is the (trade-weighted) average of the price levels of trading partners relative to the general price level of the domestic economy. The more a single world price exists for tradeables, the more likely it is that the main cause of differences between the real exchange rate and the terms of trade is the relative price of domestic and foreign nontradeables.

The real exchange rate is also different from the nominal exchange rate; in fact, in the conventional sense, it is not an exchange rate at all. The real exchange rate is the price of goods and services at home compared with the price abroad—both price levels being expressed in domestic currency. In calculating the real exchange rate, the average foreign price level is converted into domestic currency by being multiplied by the nominal effective exchange rate. The price levels could be either the consumer price index (CPI) or the product-based GDP deflator. Using the CPI the real exchange rate is more a measure of the relative costs of living than an exchange rate; using the GDP deflator it is more a measure of the relative costs of production. Thus the two ways of measuring the real exchange rate convey different information. In contrast, the nominal exchange rate is the relative price of currencies: it is the price of foreign currency in terms of domestic currency. The nominal exchange rate is a bilateral rate, i.e., the price of one currency in terms of another. The effective nominal exchange rate is a (trade-weighted) average of the bilateral exchange rates of trading partners.

In an open economy, a distinction also arises between domestic and foreign assets. In the absence of capital market imperfections such as capital controls, or incomplete markets which may cause assets to be discounted—and hence valued—differently in different countries, the choice of which to hold will depend mainly on their relative rates of return. In the absence of capital controls, any potential profits arising from differences in domestic and foreign rates of return (when expressed in the same currency) would result in large capital flows between countries. This would cause an appreciation (an increase in value) of the nominal exchange rate of the country with the higher return, which would tend to eliminate the interest differential. As a result, the capital account tends to dominate the current account in the determination of a flexible exchange rate. The imposition of capital controls was a large factor in the stability of the Bretton Woods fixed-exchange-rate system. In the flexible-exchange-rate regimes that replaced Bretton Woods, capital controls were found to be unnecessary. In this chapter we take the nominal exchange rate as given, leaving discussion of the determination of flexible exchange rates to chapter 12. We focus instead on the choices between domestic and foreign tradeables and between tradeables and nontradeables, the determination of the terms of trade and the real exchange rate, the implications for net asset holding of the current account, and whether a current-account deficit is sustainable. In other words, we consider the open economy expressed in real, not nominal, terms.

For a more detailed and general account of the open economy see Obstfeld and Rogoff (1996). For recent surveys see Lane (2001) and Obstfeld (2001).

7.2 The Optimal Solution for the Open Economy

7.2.1 The Open Economy's Resource Constraint

As a result of introducing international trade and capital flows, the resource constraint for the open economy is different from that of the closed economy.

It is derived from the national income identity for the open economy and the balance of payments identity. The national income identity becomes

$$y_t = c_t + i_t + x_t - Q_t x_t^{\mathrm{m}}, \tag{7.1}$$

where x_t denotes exports and x_t^{m} denotes imports expressed in foreign real prices. At this stage we assume that the domestic economy produces a single good, as does the rest of the world. As a result, Q_t will initially denote both the terms of trade (the price of imports relative to exports expressed in terms of domestic currency) and the real exchange rate when it is measured by the GDP deflator (the foreign producer price level expressed in terms of domestic currency relative to the domestic producer price level). We also assume that Q_t is exogenous, but we allow it to vary over time. We could have assumed that there is a single world price, in which case the terms of trade would be fixed over time; we could then have defined $Q_t = 1$. We retain Q_t purely to show where it would enter the analysis if it were to change. Subsequently, Q_t becomes an endogenous variable in the analysis. The domestic price level is assumed to be unity at all times. $Q_t x_t^{\mathrm{m}}$ is imports expressed in terms of domestic prices. $x_t - Q_t x_t^{\mathrm{m}}$ is net trade. We note that c_t and i_t, which measure domestic expenditures, both include an import component. As domestic output is the sum of domestic consumption and investment expenditures on domestic production (plus foreign expenditures on domestic production), $Q_t x_t^{\mathrm{m}}$ must be subtracted from total domestic expenditures to obtain domestic output.

The balance of payments (BOP) in nominal terms may be written as

$$CA_t = P_t x_t - S_t P_t^* x_t^{\mathrm{m}} + R_t^* S_t B_t^* - R_t B_t^{\mathrm{F}} = S_t \Delta B_{t+1}^* - \Delta B_{t+1}^{\mathrm{F}}, \tag{7.2}$$

where CA_t is the current-account balance expressed in terms of nominal domestic currency, R_t and R_t^* are the domestic and foreign nominal interest rates, respectively, B_t^* is the domestic nominal holding of foreign assets expressed in foreign currency, B_t^{F} is the foreign holding of domestic assets expressed in domestic currency, $F_t = S_t B_t^* - B_t^{\mathrm{F}}$ is the net asset position expressed in domestic currency, and $R_t^* S_t B_t^* - R_t B_t^{\mathrm{F}}$ is net foreign asset income expressed in domestic currency.

S_t is the nominal exchange rate (the domestic price of foreign exchange, or the price of a unit of foreign currency). An increase in S_t implies a depreciation of domestic currency as foreign currency then costs more. Strictly speaking, S_t is the nominal *effective* exchange rate rather than a bilateral nominal exchange rate. It is, therefore, a weighted average of bilateral rates, where the weights for each currency represent the proportion of trade involving countries using that currency. We frequently refer to the *exchange rate*, usually meaning the nominal exchange rate. In chapter 12, where we consider the role of the capital account in the determination of flexible exchange rates, we deal with bilateral exchange rates. In this chapter we are concerned primarily with the trade account, which involves the effective exchange rate. $P_t x_t - S_t P_t^* x_t^{\mathrm{m}}$ is the trade account expressed in terms of domestic currency and $x_t - Q_t x_t^m$ is the trade account expressed in real terms, where $Q_t = S_t P_t^* / P_t$.

To obtain the BOP in real terms we deflate by the domestic price level, P_t, obtaining

$$x_t - \frac{S_t P_t^*}{P_t} x_t^m + (1 + R_t^*) S_t \frac{B_t^*}{P_t} - (1 + R_t) \frac{B_t^F}{P_t} = \frac{S_t}{P_t} B_{t+1}^* - \frac{B_{t+1}^F}{P_t},$$

$$x_t - \frac{S_t P_t^*}{P_t} x_t^m + (1 + R_t^*) \frac{S_t P_t^*}{P_t} \frac{B_t^*}{P_t^*} - (1 + R_t) \frac{B_t^F}{P_t} = \frac{P_{t+1}}{P_t} \frac{S_t}{S_{t+1}} \frac{P_{t+1}^* S_{t+1}}{P_{t+1}} \frac{B_{t+1}^*}{P_{t+1}^*},$$

where lowercase letters denote the equivalent real variables with $f_t = F_t/P_t = Q_t b_t^* - b_t^F$ and where $\pi_{t+1} = \Delta P_{t+1}/P_t$ is the inflation rate. The BOP then becomes

$$x_t - Q_t x_t^m + (1 + R_t^*) Q_t b_t^* - (1 + R_t) b_t^F = (1 + \pi_{t+1}) \left[\frac{Q_{t+1} b_{t+1}^*}{1 + \Delta s_{t+1}} - b_{t+1}^F \right]$$

(7.3)

or

$$x_t - Q_t x_t^m + (1 + R_t^*) f_t - (R_t - R_t^*) b_t^F = \left(\frac{1 + \pi_{t+1}}{1 + \Delta s_{t+1}} \right) \left(f_{t+1} - \Delta s_{t+1} b_{t+1}^F \right),$$

(7.4)

where f_t is the net holding of foreign assets expressed in terms of domestic prices at the beginning of period t; f_t can be positive (net holdings) or negative (net debts) and $s_t = \ln S_t$; consequently, Δs_{t+1} is the proportional rate of change of the exchange rate between periods t and $t + 1$.

It is convenient for our analysis of the real open economy to assume that inflation is zero and that the nominal effective exchange rate is constant. Therefore, $\Delta s_{t+1} = 0$ and nominal interest rates are also real interest rates. Accordingly, they are renamed r_t and r_t^*. We also assume that $r_t = r_t^*$. Equation (7.4) can now be written more simply as

$$x_t - Q_t x_t^m + r_t^* f_t = ca_t = \Delta f_{t+1},$$

(7.5)

where $ca_t = CA_t/P_t$ is the real current account.

We assume that the domestic economy has no capital controls and that it is small enough to be able to borrow from (and lend to) world capital markets without affecting r_t^*. Thus $r_t^* f_t$ denotes interest income (or payments) on net foreign capital holdings (or debts), and is also expressed in domestic prices. The left-hand side of equation (7.4) is the current-account position. This is identical to the change in the net foreign asset position Δf_{t+1}, i.e., the capital account. Thus, in order for the economy to increase net savings, it must run a current-account surplus. If it wants to have a current-account deficit in order to consume more today than it would if the economy were closed, thereby easing the constraint provided by the production possibility frontier, it must borrow from the rest of the world. And if the rest of the world wishes to hold more domestic assets, then it must accept that the domestic economy will either have a larger current-account deficit (or a smaller current-account surplus) or that the shift in asset demand will be absorbed in a revaluation of domestic assets with no change in the current account. This has been the situation of the United States since the 1990s: the rest of the world wants to hold U.S. assets, and so the United States has to run a current-account deficit.

The budget constraint facing the open economy is obtained by combining the national income identity, equation (7.1), and the balance of payments identity, equation (7.4), by eliminating net trade $x_t - Q_t x_t^m$. This gives

$$(y_t + r_t^* f_t - c_t) - i_t = \Delta f_{t+1}, \tag{7.6}$$

where $y_t + r_t^* f_t - c_t$ can be interpreted as national savings (total income less consumption). Thus the budget constraint says that the current account is national savings minus investment (i.e., net national savings) and this equals the net increase in the open economy's holding of foreign assets—in other words, the capital account of the balance of payments.

7.2.2   The Optimal Solution

The optimal solution for the centralized open economy involves maximizing the present value of current and future utility

$$\max_{\{c_{t+s}, k_{t+s}, f_{t+s}\}} V_t = \sum_{s=0}^{\infty} \beta^s U(c_{t+s})$$

with respect to c_{t+s}, k_{t+s}, f_{t+s} subject to the budget constraint, equation (7.6), the capital accumulation equation

$$\Delta k_{t+1} = i_t - \delta k_t, \tag{7.7}$$

and the production function

$$y_t = F(k_t). \tag{7.8}$$

The open-economy budget constraint can therefore be rewritten as

$$F(k_t) = c_t + k_{t+1} - (1 - \delta)k_t + f_{t+1} - (1 + r_t^*)f_t. \tag{7.9}$$

The Lagrangian is

$$\mathcal{L} = \sum_{s=0}^{\infty} \{\beta^s U(c_{t+s})$$

$$+ \lambda_{t+s}[F(k_{t+s}) - c_{t+s} - k_{t+s+1} + (1 - \delta)k_{t+s} - f_{t+s+1} + (1 + r_{t+s}^*)f_{t+s}]\}.$$

The first-order conditions with respect to $\{c_{t+s}, k_{t+s+1}, f_{t+s+1}; s \geqslant 0\}$ are

$$\frac{\partial \mathcal{L}}{\partial c_{t+s}} = \beta^s U'(c_{t+s}) - \lambda_{t+s} = 0, \qquad\qquad s \geqslant 0,$$

$$\frac{\partial \mathcal{L}}{\partial k_{t+s}} = \lambda_{t+s}[F'(k_{t+s}) + 1 - \delta] - \lambda_{t+s-1} = 0, \quad s > 0,$$

$$\frac{\partial \mathcal{L}}{\partial f_{t+s}} = \lambda_{t+s}[1 + r_{t+s}^*] - \lambda_{t+s-1} = 0, \qquad\qquad s > 0,$$

plus the budget constraint (7.9).

Combining the first-order conditions for consumption and net foreign assets in order to eliminate the Lagrange multipliers gives the open-economy Euler equation:

$$\frac{\beta U'(c_{t+1})}{U'(c_t)}(1 + r^*_{t+1}) = 1. \tag{7.10}$$

Compared with the decentralized closed economy, therefore, the foreign rate of return replaces the domestic rate of return. Combining the first-order conditions for capital and net foreign assets gives the equation determining the optimal capital stock:

$$F'(k_{t+1}) = \delta + r^*_{t+1}. \tag{7.11}$$

Substituting in the Euler equation that the net marginal product of capital is equal to the world interest rate, i.e., $F'(k_{t+1}) - \delta = r^*_{t+1}$, would yield the same Euler equation as that for the closed economy. The optimal solution for capital is like that for the decentralized solution but with the world interest rate replacing the domestic interest rate.

7.2.3 Interpretation of the Solution

Consider just two periods t and $t + 1$, and suppose that c_t is cut by a small amount dc_t with c_{t+1} increasing by dc_{t+1} so that V_t is unchanged, where

$$V_t = U(c_t) + \beta U(c_{t+1}).$$

It was shown in chapter 4 that the slope of the resulting indifference curve is

$$\frac{dc_{t+1}}{dc_t} = -\frac{U'(c_t)}{\beta U'(c_{t+1})}.$$

The open-economy budget constraints for periods t and $t + 1$ are

$$ca_t = \Delta f_{t+1} = y_t + r^*_t f_t - c_t - i_t,$$
$$ca_{t+1} = \Delta f_{t+2} = y_{t+1} + r^*_{t+1} f_{t+1} - c_{t+1} - i_{t+1}.$$

Assuming that $f_t = f_{t+2} = 0$ and eliminating f_{t+1} gives the two-period inter-temporal budget constraint

$$(y_t - i_t) + \frac{(y_{t+1} - i_{t+1})}{1 + r^*_{t+1}} = c_t + \frac{c_{t+1}}{1 + r^*_{t+1}}.$$

The slope of this budget constraint is

$$\frac{dc_{t+1}}{dc_t} = -(1 + r^*_{t+1}).$$

At the point where the budget constraint is tangent to the indifference curve their slopes are the same, implying that

$$-\frac{dc_{t+1}}{dc_t} = \frac{U'(c_t)}{\beta U'(c_{t+1})} = 1 + r^*_{t+1}.$$

This gives the open-economy Euler equation (7.10).

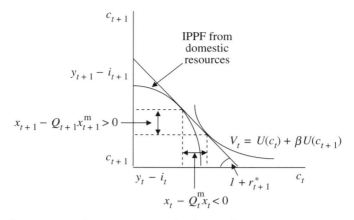

Figure 7.1.   The intertemporal solution for an open economy.

We depict the solution in figure 7.1. We have assumed that there is a trade deficit in period t. The optimal values $\{c_t, c_{t+1}\}$ are where the budget constraint is tangent to the indifference curve. Also depicted is the domestic economy's intertemporal production possibility frontier (IPPF), representing the consumption possibilities in periods t and $t+1$ based only on domestic production and with no international trade. The budget constraint is a tangent to this too but, unlike the closed economy, in general the point of tangency is now different: it is at $(y_t - i_t, y_{t+1} - i_{t+1})$. From the national income identity for the open economy, equation (7.1),

$$(y_t - i_t) - c_t = x_t - Q_t x_t^{\mathrm{m}},$$

implying that the difference between $y_t - i_t$ and c_t is the trade surplus $x_t - Q_t x_t^{\mathrm{m}}$.

Consequently, in the case shown in figure 7.1, there is a trade deficit in period t and there is a trade surplus in period $t+1$. This is achieved by consuming more in period t than if it were a closed economy dependent solely on domestic production. In period $t+1$, the economy must pay for this by consuming less than it would if it were a closed economy. To finance the trade deficit in period t it is necessary to borrow (or reduce net assets) during period t with the result that net foreign assets at the start of period $t+1$ are reduced. This is reversed during period $t+1$ by running a trade surplus which restores the stock of net foreign assets at the start of period $t+2$ to its original level. We could have depicted an alternative situation in which the economy runs a trade surplus in period t, and a deficit in period $t+1$. The key point is that, through trade and foreign borrowing (or lending), the economy may be able to achieve a higher level of welfare, V_t, than it could if it were a closed economy.

7.2.4 Long-Run Equilibrium

Long-run equilibrium in the open economy depends on the world real rate of return r_t^*, which all but the largest economies, such as the United States, will be too small to affect. If we assume that there is a common rate of time preference θ at home and abroad, then, due to capital mobility, in the long run $r_t = r_t^* = \theta$. The long-run capital stock, investment, and output for the open economy are then constant with the capital stock being determined from equation (7.11), where the net marginal product equals the world real rate of interest.

The equilibrium level of consumption is obtained by eliminating trade from the national income identity (7.1) using the balance of payments (7.5), and noting that in equilibrium $i_t = \delta k_t$. Thus

$$
\begin{aligned}
c_t &= y_t + r^* f_t - i_t \\
&= F(k_t) + r^* f_t - \delta k_t.
\end{aligned}
\tag{7.12}
$$

Although imports are part of total consumption, we are unable to obtain an expression for the equilibrium level of imports from this model. This is because we have implicitly assumed that imports are perfect substitutes for other components of consumption. We return to this issue below when we allow home-produced goods to be imperfect substitutes for foreign goods.

Finally, consider the long-run equilibrium net stock of foreign assets. From the balance of payments identity, equation (7.5), the initial net asset holding, which is taken as given, must satisfy

$$
\begin{aligned}
f_t &= \frac{1}{1 + r^*} (Q_t x_t^m - x_t + f_{t+1}) \\
&= \frac{1}{1 + r^*} \sum_{s=0}^{\infty} \left[\frac{Q_{t+s} x_{t+s}^m - x_{t+s}}{(1 + r^*)^s} \right],
\end{aligned}
\tag{7.13}
$$

provided the transversality condition

$$
\lim_{n \to \infty} \sum_{s=1}^{n} \frac{f_{t+s}}{(1 + r^*)^s} = 0
$$

holds. If Q_t and x_t are constant, and as x_t^m is part of total consumption, which is also constant, equation (7.13) implies that in the steady state net foreign asset holdings satisfy

$$
f_t = -\frac{x_t - Q_t x_t^m}{r^*},
\tag{7.14}
$$

which may be rewritten as

$$
x_t - Q_t x_t^m + r^* f_t = 0.
$$

Hence, in the steady state, the stock of net foreign assets is constant at its initial level and the current account must be in balance.

In interpreting equation (7.14) we recall that f_t and r^* are given. The equation therefore determines the long-run trade surplus or deficit. If the initial net stock of foreign assets is positive, the equation shows the size of the permanent trade deficit that a country may sustain given its current interest income from foreign assets. If the trade deficit is smaller than this, then, in effect, the country has too large a stock of foreign assets for its level of consumption. It is then said to be dynamically inefficient. The implication is that it can increase its domestic consumption of foreign goods and services. If the trade deficit is larger than this, then the current-account position is commonly said to be unsustainable. We examine these issues in greater detail below.

7.2.5 Shocks to the Current Account

The open economy is affected by both external and domestic shocks. To illustrate, we consider the effects of temporary and permanent external exogenous shocks to exports. These could be due, for example, to a change in foreign income or tastes. We continue to assume that the economy is initially in equilibrium and that $r_t^* = r^* = \theta$ and $Q_t = Q$.

7.2.5.1   A Temporary Shock to Exports

Consider a temporary negative shock to exports of $\Delta x < 0$ in period t. From the balance of payments (7.5),

$$f_{t+1} = x_t + \Delta x - Q x_t^m + (1 + r^*) f_t$$
$$= f_t + \Delta x < f_t.$$

Hence there is a temporary fall in net asset holdings f_{t+1}. In subsequent periods both imports and the net stock of foreign assets will be affected. Assuming that imports are proportional to consumption, such that

$$c_t = \phi Q x_t^m, \quad 0 < \phi < 1,$$

then, from equation (7.12), imports will fall as

$$x_{t+1}^m = \frac{F(k_{t+1}) + r^* f_{t+1} - \delta k_{t+1}}{\phi Q}$$
$$= x_t^m + \frac{r^* \Delta x}{\phi Q} < x_t^m,$$

and so

$$f_{t+2} = x_t - Q\left(x_t^m + \frac{r^* \Delta x}{\phi Q}\right) + (1 + r^*)(f_t + \Delta x)$$
$$= f_{t+1} + r^*\left(1 - \frac{1}{\phi}\right)\Delta x > f_{t+1}$$
$$= f_t + \left[1 + r^*\left(1 - \frac{1}{\phi}\right)\right]\Delta x < f_t,$$

assuming that $0 < [1 + r^*(1 - 1/\phi)] < 1$. More generally,

$$f_{t+s} = f_t + \left[1 + r^*\left(1 - \frac{1}{\phi}\right)\right]^{s-1}\Delta x,$$

and so $\lim_{s \to \infty} f_{t+s} = f_t$. Thus, although the stock of financial assets falls initially, in the next period it begins a process in which it returns to the original equilibrium. We note that the capital stock k_t remains unchanged throughout as neither θ nor δ have altered.

7.2.5.2 A Permanent Shock to Exports

We distinguish between two cases: one in which the terms of trade is fixed, as above, and another in which it is allowed to change to restore steady-state equilibrium.

Q Fixed. Suppose that exports increase permanently from x_t to $x_t + \Delta x$. For a given level of imports this would result in an increase in the net stock of foreign assets such that

$$
\begin{aligned}
f_{t+1} &= x_t + \Delta x - Q x_t^{\mathrm{m}} + (1 + r^*) f_t \\
&= f_t + \Delta x, \\
f_{t+s} &= f_t + \frac{(1 + r^*)^s - 1}{r^*} \Delta x.
\end{aligned}
$$

Hence, f_{t+s} would explode if imports were fixed. However, the increase in net foreign assets would cause an increase in consumption and hence imports. This increase must be equal to the increase in exports for net foreign assets to be stable. Thus, the outcome is that imports must increase permanently by $Q\Delta x^m = \Delta x$ and the net asset position remains unchanged. The question that then arises is how the increase in imports occurs. Since, in general, imports will depend on Q, one answer is through a change in Q which so far has been assumed to be fixed. We now consider what change in Q is required.

Q Flexible. We assume that both exports and imports are functions of Q_t. Suppose that the export function is

$$
x_t = x(Q_t) + z_t, \quad x' > 0,
$$

where z_t is an exogenous effect on exports, and the import function is

$$
x_t^{\mathrm{m}} = x^m(Q_t), \quad x^{m\prime} < 0.
$$

We also recall that $f_t = Q_t b_t^* - b_t^{\mathrm{F}}$. From equation (7.14),

$$
r^* f_t = r^* (Q_t b_t^* - b_t^{\mathrm{F}}) = Q_t x_t^{\mathrm{m}}(Q_t) - x_t(Q_t) - z_t.
$$

If Δz denotes a permanent exogenous increase in exports, then, assuming that b_t^* and b_t^{F} are given,

$$
r^* \Delta f = r^* b^* \Delta Q = (x^m + Q x^{m\prime}) \Delta Q - (x' \, dQ + \Delta z).
$$

Therefore,

$$
\begin{aligned}
\Delta z &= (x^m + Q x^{m\prime} - x' - r^* b^*) \Delta Q \\
&= -[(\epsilon^x + \epsilon^m - 1) x^m + r^* b^*] \Delta Q \\
&= -\frac{1}{\psi} \Delta Q,
\end{aligned}
$$

where $\psi = [(\epsilon^x + \epsilon^m - 1)x^m + r^*b^*]^{-1}$, ϵ^x and $-\epsilon^m$ are the price elasticities of exports and imports, respectively, and we have assumed that $x \simeq Qx^m$. We note that if trade is initially in balance, then

$$\frac{\partial(x - Qx^m)}{\partial Q} = (\epsilon^x + \epsilon^m - 1)x^m \gtreqless 0 \quad \text{as } \epsilon^x + \epsilon^m \gtreqless 1. \tag{7.15}$$

This is known as the Marshall–Lerner condition. Consequently, if the trade elasticities sum to greater than or equal to unity, in order for the fall in exports not to cause an outflow of capital, Q_t would need to increase because $\psi > 0$. The increase in Q would raise interest income from abroad but would only improve the trade balance if the elasticities sum to greater than one.

More generally, the long-run effects on exports, imports, and hence trade following a permanent exogenous increase in exports, but no change in the long-run net asset position, would be

$$\Delta x = (1 - \psi\epsilon^x x^m)\Delta z,$$
$$\Delta(Qx^m) = -(1 - \epsilon^m)x^m\psi\Delta z,$$
$$\Delta(x - Qx^m) = r^*b^*\psi\Delta z.$$

As we discuss below, Q_t is determined in the short run far more by the behavior of the nominal exchange rate S_t than by relative prices, and S_t is determined in the short run almost entirely by short-run capital-account considerations and not by the trade account. Consequently, this long-run result for Q_t should not be regarded as a good guide to the behavior of Q_t in the short run.

7.3 Traded and Nontraded Goods

We have assumed so far that all goods and services are traded internationally. In fact, some goods such as buildings and roads are not traded, and nor are most services. Financial services are a notable exception as they are sold internationally. We shall now draw a formal distinction between traded and nontraded goods, which are denoted using the superscripts "T" and "N," respectively.

Apart from this, the specification of the model is similar in structure to the open-economy model above. It is summarized in table 7.1, where i_t^T and i_t^N refer to total investment in traded and nontraded capital goods, respectively.

As a result of making the distinction between traded and nontraded goods, we need to take account of their relative price. For clarity, we allow each to have a price, rather than just consider their relative price. (Alternatively, we could have just set one price to unity when the other would become the relative price.) We will also need the general price level of the economy, which we denote by P_t.

Utility now depends on both types of goods. In general, it can be written $U(c_t^T, c_t^N)$. It is, however, more convenient to assume that c_t^T and c_t^N are intermediate goods and services that are involved in producing total consumption

Table 7.1. The model and notation.

	Traded	Nontraded
Output	$y_t^T = F(k_t^T, k_t^N)$	$y_t^N = G(k_t^T, k_t^N)$
Consumption	c_t^T	c_t^N
Capital	k_t^T	k_t^N
Investment	$i_t^T = \Delta k_{t+1}^T + \delta^T k_t^T$	$i_t^N = \Delta k_{t+1}^N + \delta^N k_t^N$
Prices	P_t^T	P_t^N

services c_t. This enables us to retain the earlier assumption that utility is $U(c_t)$. In particular, we assume that the power utility function is given by

$$U(c_t) = \frac{c_t^{1-\sigma} - 1}{1 - \sigma}, \quad \sigma > 0,$$

and define total consumption via the constant elasticity of substitution (CES) function

$$c_t = [\alpha(c_t^T)^{1-1/\gamma} + (1 - \alpha)(c_t^N)^{1-1/\gamma}]^{1/(1-1/\gamma)}, \quad 0 < \alpha < 1, \ \gamma > 0, \quad (7.16)$$

where $\gamma \geqslant 1$ is the elasticity of substitution between traded and nontraded goods.[1] We choose a CES function in preference to a Cobb–Douglas function in order to illustrate the role of substitutability.

Total real expenditures on consumption can be written as follows:

$$P_t c_t = P_t^T c_t^T + P_t^N c_t^N.$$

Although we have three prices, there are only two that are independent. We could therefore set the third to unity. It is more instructive if we do not add this restriction at this stage. Similarly, total real expenditures on investment and output are

$$P_t i_t = P_t^T i_t^T + P_t^N i_t^N,$$
$$P_t y_t = P_t^T y_t^T + P_t^N y_t^N.$$

---

[1] The elasticity of substitution between c^T and c^N is defined as

$$\sigma^{ES} = \frac{d \ln(c^T/c^N)}{d \ln(MP_{c^T}/MP_{c^N})} \geqslant 0,$$

where

$$MP_{c^T} = \frac{\partial c}{\partial c^T} \quad \text{and} \quad MP_{c^N} = \frac{\partial c}{\partial c^N}.$$

In other words, it is the proportional change in the ratio of the inputs c^T and c^N divided by the proportional change in the ratio of their marginal products. The more restrictive Cobb–Douglas function $c = (c^T)^\alpha (c^N)^{1-\alpha}$ has $\sigma^{ES} = 1$. As $\sigma^{ES} \to \infty$, (i.e., $\gamma \to \infty$), the function tends to linearity. As $\sigma^{ES} \to 0$, (i.e., $\gamma \to 1$), c^T and c^N are consumed in fixed proportions.

The economy's real resource constraint is a generalization of equation (7.9) and may be written as

$$
\frac{P_t^T}{P_t} F(k_t^T, k_t^N) + \frac{P_t^N}{P_t} G(k_t^T, k_t^N)
$$

$$
= \frac{P_t^T}{P_t} [c_t^T + k_{t+1}^T - (1 - \delta^T) k_t^T]
$$

$$
+ \frac{P_t^N}{P_t} [c_t^N + k_{t+1}^N - (1 - \delta^N) k_t^N] + \Delta f_{t+1} - (1 + r_t^*) f_t. \qquad (7.17)
$$

We can now express the open economy's problem as that of maximizing $\sum_{s=0}^{\infty} \beta^s U(c_{t+s})$ with respect to $\{c_{t+s}^T, c_{t+s}^N, k_{t+s+1}^T, k_{t+s+1}^N, f_{t+s+1}; s \geqslant 0\}$ subject to the various production functions, the capital accumulation equations, and the national resource constraint (7.17). The Lagrangian can be written as

$$
\mathcal{L} = \sum_{s=0}^{\infty} \left\{ \beta^s U(c_{t+s}) + \lambda_{t+s} \left[\frac{P_{t+s}^T}{P_{t+s}} [F(k_{t+s}^T, k_{t+s}^N) - c_{t+s}^T - k_{t+s+1}^T + (1 - \delta^T) k_{t+s}^T] \right.\right.
$$

$$
\left.\left. + \frac{P_{t+s}^N}{P_{t+s}} [G(k_{t+s}^T, k_{t+s}^N) - c_{t+s}^N - k_{t+s+1}^N + (1 - \delta^N) k_{t+s}^N] - f_{t+s+1} + (1 + r_{t+s}^*) f_{t+s} \right] \right\}.
$$

The first-order conditions are

$$
\frac{\partial \mathcal{L}}{\partial c_{t+s}^T} = \beta^s c_{t+s}^{-\sigma} \alpha \left(\frac{c_{t+s}}{c_{t+s}^T} \right)^{1/\gamma} - \lambda_{t+s} \frac{P_{t+s}^T}{P_{t+s}} = 0, \qquad\qquad s \geqslant 0,
$$

$$
\frac{\partial \mathcal{L}}{\partial c_{t+s}^N} = \beta^s c_{t+s}^{-\sigma} (1 - \alpha) \left(\frac{c_{t+s}}{c_{t+s}^N} \right)^{1/\gamma} - \lambda_{t+s} \frac{P_{t+s}^N}{P_{t+s}} = 0, \qquad\qquad s \geqslant 0,
$$

$$
\frac{\partial \mathcal{L}}{\partial k_{t+s}^T} = \lambda_{t+s} \left\{ \frac{P_{t+s}^T}{P_{t+s}} [F_{k^T, t+s} + 1 - \delta^T] + \frac{P_{t+s}^N}{P_{t+s}} G_{k^T, t+s} \right\} - \lambda_{t+s-1} \frac{P_{t+s-1}^T}{P_{t+s-1}} = 0,
$$
$$
s > 0,
$$

$$
\frac{\partial \mathcal{L}}{\partial k_{t+s}^N} = \lambda_{t+s} \left\{ \frac{P_{t+s}^N}{P_{t+s}} [G_{k^N, t+s} + 1 - \delta^N] + \frac{P_{t+s}^T}{P_{t+s}} F_{k^N, t+s} \right\} - \lambda_{t+s-1} \frac{P_{t+s-1}^N}{P_{t+s-1}} = 0,
$$
$$
s > 0,
$$

$$
\frac{\partial \mathcal{L}}{\partial f_{t+s}} = \lambda_{t+s} [1 + r_{t+s}^*] - \lambda_{t+s-1} = 0, \qquad\qquad s > 0.
$$

From the conditions for $\partial \mathcal{L}/\partial c_t^T$ and $\partial \mathcal{L}/\partial c_t^N$, and setting $s = 0$, we obtain the relative consumption of traded and nontraded goods as a function of their relative price:

$$
\frac{c_t^T}{c_t^N} = \left(\frac{\alpha}{1 - \alpha} \frac{P_t^N}{P_t^T} \right)^{\gamma}.
$$

Thus an increase in the relative price of traded goods reduces their consumption relative to nontraded goods. As the elasticity of substitution $\gamma \to 0$, traded and nontraded goods are consumed in fixed proportions, and as $\gamma \to \infty$, when traded and nontraded goods become perfect substitutes, P_t^N becomes a fixed proportion of P_t^T.

We can therefore write total real consumption as

$$c_t = [\alpha(c_t^T)^{1-1/\gamma} + (1-\alpha)(c_t^N)^{1-1/\gamma}]^{1/(1-1/\gamma)}$$

$$= \alpha^{1/(1-1/\gamma)} c_t^T \left[1 + \left(\frac{1-\alpha}{\alpha} \right)^\gamma \left(\frac{P_t^N}{P_t^T} \right)^{1-\gamma} \right]^{1/(1-1/\gamma)}$$

and total consumption expenditures as

$$P_t c_t = P_t^T c_t^T + P_t^N c_t^N$$

$$= P_t^T c_t^T \left[1 + \left(\frac{1-\alpha}{\alpha} \right)^\gamma \left(\frac{P_t^N}{P_t^T} \right)^{1-\gamma} \right].$$

Eliminating c_t^T / c_t from these two equations we obtain an expression for the general price level as

$$P_t = P_t^T \frac{c_t^T}{c_t} \left[1 + \left(\frac{1-\alpha}{\alpha} \right)^\gamma \left(\frac{P_t^N}{P_t^T} \right)^{1-\gamma} \right]$$

$$= [\alpha^\gamma (P_t^T)^{1-\gamma} + (1-\alpha)^\gamma (P_t^N)^{1-\gamma}]^{1/(1-\gamma)}. \tag{7.18}$$

The general price level is therefore a function of traded and nontraded goods' prices, where the aggregator function is also a CES function. Note that we can still arbitrarily set one of these prices to unity.

It now follows that the individual consumption functions are

$$\frac{c_t^T}{c_t} = \alpha^\gamma \left(\frac{P_t^T}{P_t} \right)^{-\gamma},$$

$$\frac{c_t^N}{c_t} = (1-\alpha)^\gamma \left(\frac{P_t^N}{P_t} \right)^{-\gamma}.$$

Thus, the share of tradeables (nontradeables) in total consumption decreases as the relative price of tradeables (nontradeables) increases; the size of the response increases with the substitutability of tradeables for nontradeables (the elasticity of substitution γ).

The short-run dynamics are obtained from the Euler equation and these two consumption equations. For tradeable goods, for example, the first-order condition for net assets can be rewritten as

$$\frac{\partial \mathcal{L}}{\partial c_{t+s}^T} = \frac{P_{t+s}^T}{P_{t+s}} \beta^s c_{t+s}^{-\sigma} - \lambda_{t+s} \frac{P_{t+s}^T}{P_{t+s}} = 0, \quad s \geqslant 0.$$

Hence, from the first-order condition that $\partial \mathcal{L} / \partial f_{t+1} = 0$, we can show that the Euler equation for consumption takes the usual form:

$$\beta \left(\frac{c_{t+1}}{c_t} \right)^{-\sigma} (1 + r_{t+1}^*) = 1.$$

We could obtain an identical result using the nontradeables equations.

The solutions for the two types of capital stock, which are affected by the choice of production function, can be obtained from the first-order conditions for $\partial \mathcal{L}/\partial k_{t+1}^{\mathrm{T}}$, $\partial \mathcal{L}/\partial k_{t+1}^{\mathrm{N}}$, and $\partial \mathcal{L}/\partial f_{t+s}$. We find that

$$\frac{P_{t+1}^{\mathrm{T}}/P_{t+1}}{P_t^{\mathrm{T}}/P_t}\left\{[F_{k^{\mathrm{T}},t+1} + 1 - \delta^{\mathrm{T}}] + \frac{P_{t+1}^{\mathrm{N}}}{P_{t+1}^{\mathrm{T}}}G_{k^{\mathrm{T}},t+1}\right\} = 1 + r_{t+1}^*,$$

$$\frac{P_{t+1}^{\mathrm{N}}/P_{t+1}}{P_t^{\mathrm{N}}/P_t}\left\{[G_{k^{\mathrm{N}},t+1} + 1 - \delta^{\mathrm{N}}] + \frac{P_{t+1}^{\mathrm{T}}}{P_{t+1}^{\mathrm{N}}}F_{k^{\mathrm{N}},t+1}\right\} = 1 + r_{t+1}^*.$$

These two equations can be solved simultaneously to obtain the long-run solutions for the two capital stocks.

In the special case where only traded capital goods are used in the production of traded goods and vice versa, the second term in braces would disappear. The two equations would then look very like that for the basic closed-economy model apart from the presence of the world instead of the domestic interest rate. Consequently, we would obtain

$$F_{k^{\mathrm{T}},t+1} = r_{t+1}^* + \pi_{t+1} - \pi_{t+1}^{\mathrm{T}} + \delta^{\mathrm{T}},$$

$$G_{k^{\mathrm{N}},t+1} = r_{t+1}^* + \pi_{t+1} - \pi_{t+1}^{\mathrm{N}} + \delta^{\mathrm{N}},$$

where π_t^{T}, π_t^{N}, and π_t are the inflation rates of traded and nontraded goods, and the general price level. If the inflation rates are equal, as we would expect in steady state, then the inflation terms could be omitted.

7.3.1   The Long-Run Solution

In long-run equilibrium all variables are constant and we can therefore omit the time subscript. From the consumption Euler equation, $r^* = \theta$, i.e., the foreign rate of return equals the domestic rate of time preference. As becomes clear in chapter 10, this result implicitly assumes that world markets are "complete," i.e., that domestic and foreign preferences are the same.

The net marginal products of capital of traded and nontraded goods and services are equal and satisfy

$$F_{k^{\mathrm{T}}} - \delta^{\mathrm{T}} + \frac{P^{\mathrm{N}}}{P^{\mathrm{T}}}G_{k^{\mathrm{T}}} = G_{k^{\mathrm{N}}} - \delta^{\mathrm{N}} + \frac{P^{\mathrm{T}}}{P^{\mathrm{N}}}F_{k^{\mathrm{N}}} = r^* = \theta.$$

From this we can derive the optimal steady-state levels of the capital stocks k^{T} and k^{N}. In the special case where traded goods capital consists only of traded goods, and nontraded goods capital consists only of nontraded goods, we obtain the simpler condition

$$F_{k^{\mathrm{T}}} - \delta^{\mathrm{T}} = G_{k^{\mathrm{N}}} - \delta^{\mathrm{N}} = r^* = \theta.$$

Here, on the margin, both capital stocks are increased until their net marginal products equal the cost of borrowing, which in long-run equilibrium is the rate of time preference of savers.

The long-run equilibrium values for the other variables are

$$c^T = F(k^T) - \delta^T k^T, \tag{7.19}$$

$$c^N = G(k^N) - \delta^N k^N, \tag{7.20}$$

$$\frac{P^T}{P^N} = \frac{\alpha}{1-\alpha}\left(\frac{c^T}{c^N}\right)^\gamma, \tag{7.21}$$

$$P = [\alpha^\gamma (P^T)^{1-\gamma} + (1-\alpha)^\gamma (P^N)^{1-\gamma}]^{1/(1-\gamma)}, \tag{7.22}$$

$$c = \alpha^{-\gamma}\left(\frac{P^T}{P}\right)^\gamma c^T = (1-\alpha)^{-\gamma}\left(\frac{P^N}{P}\right)^\gamma c^N. \tag{7.23}$$

We now have a complete long-run solution. The logic behind this solution is that the capital stocks are determined first, followed by the consumption of traded and nontraded goods and services, and hence total consumption. The relative consumption of traded and nontraded goods and services determines their relative prices. To determine individual prices we need to introduce the normalization rule discussed earlier. We could, for example, set $P = 1$ and we can then solve simultaneously for the other two prices from the last two equations.

The long-run solution will be disturbed by productivity shocks to the production of traded and nontraded goods and services. A permanent productivity increase to $F(k^T)$ will increase c^T, and hence raise P^N/P^T, implying that P^T will fall. Similarly, a permanent productivity increase to $G(k^N)$ will increase c^N, and hence reduce P^N/P^T, implying that P^N will fall.

7.4 The Terms of Trade and the Real Exchange Rate

We recall that the terms of trade is the price of imports (expressed in terms of domestic currency) relative to exports, and the real exchange rate is the ratio of the world price level (expressed in terms of domestic currency) to the home price level. Thus the terms of trade involves only traded goods and services, whereas the real exchange rate involves traded and nontraded goods and services. The real exchange rate is therefore not so much an exchange rate, as exchange may not be involved, as a comparison of price levels (producer costs or costs of living). If there are no nontraded goods and services, the real exchange rate is the same as the terms of trade.

We denote the terms of trade by

$$Q^T = \frac{SP^{T*}}{P^T},$$

where P^T and P^{T*} are the prices of domestic and foreign tradeables, respectively, and S is the nominal (effective) exchange rate; SP^{T*} is then the price of imports in domestic currency terms. We now denote the real exchange rate by

$$Q = \frac{SP^*}{P},$$

where P and P^* are the home and world price levels. An increase in Q^T implies a real depreciation, i.e., an increase in competitiveness. An increase in Q can be interpreted as an increase in the purchasing power of domestic residents, or a fall in the domestic cost of living, relative to the rest of the world. We now consider some of their properties, including some special cases.

7.4.1 The Law of One Price

According to the law of one price (LOOP) there is a single price throughout the world for each tradeable when prices are expressed in the same currency (see Isard 1977). This is brought about by goods arbitrage, i.e., buying where the good is cheapest and selling where it is highest. If this holds for all tradeables— and if tastes are identical across countries, there are no constraints on trade or monopolies, and if prices adjust instantaneously—then trade weights would be the same in each country and the terms of trade would be constant over time and identical for each country. We could then write

$$P^T = SP^{T*}$$

when $Q^T = 1$. More generally, the LOOP does not imply constant terms of trade if home and foreign countries produce different goods. These are, of course, strong assumptions but they are commonly made implicitly in open-economy macroeconomics, especially in the determination of floating exchange rates.

7.4.2 Purchasing Power Parity

Purchasing power parity (PPP) is where the purchasing power of domestic residents relative to the rest of the world is constant. In other words, the real exchange rate is constant. A strong version of PPP asserts that the real exchange rate is the same at each point in time; a weak version assumes that it is constant only in the long run. Relative PPP assumes that the change in the real exchange rate is constant.

In principle, there is no reason why Q should be constant, even in the long run. To see this, consider the causes of changes to Q implied by the theory above. They could be due to changes in the prices of tradeables, nontradeables, or the nominal exchange rate. At this stage, as we are still working in real terms and not focusing on the determination of nominal prices, we also assume that any change in the nominal exchange rate S is exogenous. If, for convenience, we assume that foreign and domestic parameters are identical, so that $\alpha = \alpha^*$ and $y = y^*$, then it follows from equation (7.22) that

$$
\begin{aligned}
Q &= \frac{SP^*}{P} \\
&= S \left[\frac{\alpha^y (P^{T*})^{1-y} + (1-\alpha)^y (P^{N*})^{1-y}}{\alpha^y (P^T)^{1-y} + (1-\alpha)^y (P^N)^{1-y}} \right]^{1/(1-y)} \\
&= \frac{SP^{T*}}{P^T} \left[\left(1 + \left(\frac{1-\alpha}{\alpha} \right)^y \left(\frac{P^{N*}}{P^{T*}} \right)^{1-y} \right) \Big/ \left(1 + \left(\frac{1-\alpha}{\alpha} \right)^y \left(\frac{P^N}{P^T} \right)^{1-y} \right) \right]^{1/(1-y)}.
\end{aligned}
$$

The first factor on the right-hand side is the terms of trade. Thus Q depends on the terms of trade and on the relative prices of domestic and foreign nontraded and traded goods: P^N/P^T and P^{N*}/P^{T*}.

If the terms of trade is constant, the real exchange rate could be rewritten as

$$Q = \left[\left(1 + \left(\frac{1-\alpha}{\alpha} \right)^y \left(\frac{SP^{N*}}{P^T} \right)^{1-y} \right) \Big/ \left(1 + \left(\frac{1-\alpha}{\alpha} \right)^y \left(\frac{P^N}{P^T} \right)^{1-y} \right) \right]^{1/(1-y)}, \quad (7.24)$$

indicating that it is the relative nontraded goods' prices when expressed in the same currency, and not traded goods prices, that determine the real exchange rate in the long run. The dependence of the real exchange rate on the relative price of nontradeables is even more apparent if the elasticity of substitution $y = 1$. Using l'Hôpital's rule, we can show that in this case,

$$\lim_{y \to 1} Q = \left[\frac{SP^{N*}}{P^N} \right]^{1-\alpha}. \quad (7.25)$$

If we were to take the notion that Q is an exchange rate literally, then it would no doubt appear counterintuitive to have an exchange rate being determined by nontraded economic activity which is not exchanged. Consider, therefore, the effect of an improvement in productivity in domestic relative to foreign nontraded production. This would reduce domestic nontraded prices. It would therefore cause an improvement in the real exchange rate (an increase in Q). It will also increase the attractiveness in the domestic economy of nontraded goods relative to traded goods, which will reduce the demand for traded goods, whether of domestic or foreign origin. Traded goods therefore become less competitive compared with nontraded goods and so a switch of expenditure occurs between traded and nontraded goods. It is this that is being reflected in the increase in the real exchange rate. This is an example of what is known as a Balassa–Samuelson effect (see Balassa 1964): a factor causing Q to change in the long run.

7.4.3 Some Stylized Facts about the Terms of Trade and the Real Exchange Rate

Although PPP implies that Q is constant and the LOOP could give rise to a constant terms of trade, the empirical evidence shows overwhelmingly that neither are constant, either in the short run or in the long run. The key empirical facts are these (see Froot and Rogoff (1995), Froot et al. (1995), Goldberg and Knetter (1997), Engel (2000), Obstfeld and Rogoff (2000), or, for a summary, Obstfeld (2001)).

- *For most countries with a freely floating (i.e., not managed) nominal exchange rate the statistical properties of the real exchange rate and the terms of trade are very similar.*

- *Shocks to the real exchange rate take a long time to disappear. It has been estimated that they have a half-life of 2–4.5 years, i.e., after this time only half the total effect of the shock is complete.*

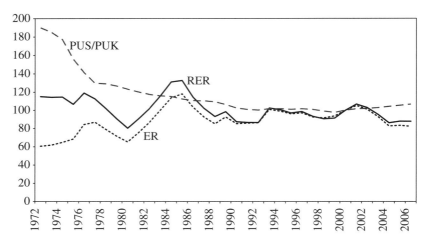

Figure 7.2. Stylized facts about the real exchange rate and the terms of trade.

- *The real exchange rate and the terms of trade are almost as volatile as the nominal exchange rate S.*

- *The correlation coefficients between the real exchange rate and the terms of trade and the relative prices of nontradeables when expressed in the same currency (i.e., SP^{N*}/P^{N}) lie in the range 0.92–1.00 for most OECD countries and are close to unity after five years.*

- *The correlation between the real exchange rate and the terms of trade increases with the volatility of S.*

There are two possible explanations for these findings. Either they all indicate that changes in the nominal exchange rate dominate movements in the real exchange rate, the terms of trade, and goods prices, whether traded or not, whereas, in comparison, goods prices are slow to change, i.e., they are sticky. Or, less plausibly, the evidence is consistent with home and foreign countries conducting their monetary policies by targeting their price levels in ways that cause the real exchange rate to behave as above.

Figure 7.2 provides some further evidence. It shows for the period 1972–2006 the real-exchange-rate (RER) index based on the CPI between the United States and the United Kingdom, their nominal exchange rate (ER), and the relative price levels of the United States and the United Kingdom (PUS/PUK), both also expressed as an index, with all indices based on 2000 = 100. It reveals that, following the floating of exchange rates in 1973 and the removal of capital controls by the United Kingdom in 1981, the real and nominal exchange rates quickly converged. By comparison, their relative price level (the ratio of U.K. to U.S. prices and also the ratio of the real to the nominal-exchange-rate indices) is far less volatile and has fallen smoothly. This fall reflects the decline in the high U.K. inflation rates of the 1970s compared with those of the United States, and the subsequent similarity of their inflation rates afterwards; both price levels have, of course, risen steadily over the period. Thus, monetary policy since 1990 seems to have resulted in a convergence of the two exchange rates and has confirmed that fluctuations in the real exchange rate are due almost entirely to those in the nominal exchange rate.

7.5 Imperfect Substitutability of Tradeables

Previously we have considered imperfect substitutability between tradeables and nontradeables. We now examine imperfect substitutability among tradeables. First we discuss some pricing implications of the degree of substitutability between tradeables. We then develop a model which allows imperfect substitutability both among tradeables and between tradeables and nontradeables.

7.5.1 Pricing-to-Market, Local-Currency Pricing, and Producer-Currency Pricing

Economies typically consume both their own and foreign traded goods and services. In the absence of restrictions on trade, this suggests that they must in general be imperfect substitutes. If domestic and foreign tradeables were close substitutes, then for the typical small economy both export and import prices would be determined by world prices. In this case a depreciation of domestic currency, or an increase in world prices, would result in higher export and import prices measured in domestic currency.

If, however, the domestic economy is large, then domestic tradeables prices are more likely to dominate foreign tradeables prices. The price of imports would then be determined largely by the price of local competing products. This is known as pricing-to-market or local-currency pricing (LCP). An exchange-rate depreciation would then have little effect on domestic prices.

Now suppose that domestic and foreign tradeables have a low elasticity of substitution. In this case, domestic and foreign producers would have monopoly power both in their own and in foreign markets, which would enable them to set prices in each market. This has been called producer-currency pricing (PCP) by Betts and Devereux (1996) and Devereux (1997) (see also Knetter 1993). An exchange-rate depreciation would not then necessarily affect the domestic currency price of exports or imports. The terms of trade would not then increase.

7.5.2 Imperfect Substitutability of Tradeables and Nontradeables

We now develop a model which allows imperfect substitutability both among tradeables and between tradeables and nontradeables. We retain the assumption that utility is $U(c_t) = (c_t^{1-\sigma} - 1)/(1 - \sigma)$, but we assume that total consumption c_t is the two-level Cobb–Douglas function

$$c_t = \frac{(c_t^{\mathrm{T}})^\gamma (c_t^{\mathrm{N}})^{1-\gamma}}{\gamma^\gamma (1 - \gamma)^{1-\gamma}}, \tag{7.26}$$

$$c_t^{\mathrm{T}} = \frac{(c_t^{\mathrm{H}})^\alpha (c_t^{\mathrm{F}})^{1-\alpha}}{\alpha^\alpha (1 - \alpha)^{1-\alpha}}, \tag{7.27}$$

where, as before, c_t^T and c_t^N are the consumption of tradeables and nontradeables and c_t^H and c_t^F are tradeables consumption produced at home and abroad. In terms of the first model in this chapter, this notation is equivalent to denoting exports as $x_t = c_t^{F*}$ and imports as $x_t^m = c_t^F$. The use of the Cobb–Douglas function is more restrictive than the CES function used before as it assumes a unit elasticity of substitution but this simplifies the analysis, as does the particular form of the Cobb–Douglas function that is used.

Consumption expenditures are

$$P_t c_t = P_t^T c_t^T + P_t^N c_t^N, \tag{7.28}$$

$$P_t^T c_t^T = P_t^H c_t^H + P_t^F c_t^F, \tag{7.29}$$

where P_t is both the consumer price level and the general price level, P_t^T and P_t^N are the prices of tradeables and nontradeables, and P_t^H and P_t^F are the prices of home and foreign tradeables. We denote the price of home output by P_t^H and of foreign output by P_t^{H*}.

The terms of trade is now given by

$$Q_t^T = \frac{P_t^F}{P_t^H} = \frac{S_t P_t^{H*}}{P_t^H},$$

as $P_t^F = S_t P_t^{H*}$, where P_t^{H*} is the foreign currency price of foreign tradeables (domestic imports).

Total domestic output y_t, which for simplicity we take as exogenous, satisfies

$$P_t y_t = P_t^H c_t^H + P_t^N c_t^N + P_t^H c_t^{F*}, \tag{7.30}$$

where c_t^{F*} is domestic exports. The nominal balance of payments deflated by the domestic price level P_t is

$$\frac{P_t^H}{P_t} c_t^{F*} - \frac{P_t^F}{P_t} c_t^F + r_t^* f_t = \Delta f_{t+1}.$$

Combining this with equation (7.30) to eliminate exports gives the real resource constraint:

$$y_t = \frac{P_t^H}{P_t} c_t^H + \frac{P_t^N}{P_t} c_t^N + \frac{P_t^F}{P_t} c_t^F + f_{t+1} - (1 + r_t^*) f_t. \tag{7.31}$$

The Lagrangian is

$$\mathcal{L} = \sum_{s=0}^{\infty} \left\{ \beta^s U(c_{t+s}) \right.$$

$$\left. + \lambda_{t+s} \left[y_{t+s} - \frac{P_{t+s}^H}{P_{t+s}} c_{t+s}^H - \frac{P_{t+s}^N}{P_{t+s}} c_t^N - \frac{P_{t+s}^F}{P_{t+s}} c_{t+s}^F - f_{t+s+1} + (1 + r_{t+s}^*) f_{t+s} \right] \right\}.$$

The first-order conditions with respect to $\{c^H_{t+s}, c^F_{t+s}, c^N_{t+s}, f_{t+s+1}; s \geqslant 0\}$ are

$$\frac{\partial \mathcal{L}}{\partial c^H_{t+s}} = (\beta^s c^{-\sigma}_{t+s})\left(\gamma \frac{c_{t+s}}{c^T_{t+s}}\right)\left(\alpha \frac{c^T_{t+s}}{c^H_{t+s}}\right) - \lambda_{t+s}\frac{P^H_{t+s}}{P_{t+s}} = 0, \qquad s \geqslant 0,$$

$$\frac{\partial \mathcal{L}}{\partial c^F_{t+s}} = (\beta^s c^{-\sigma}_{t+s})\left(\gamma \frac{c_{t+s}}{c^T_{t+s}}\right)\left[(1-\alpha)\frac{c^T_{t+s}}{c^F_{t+s}}\right] - \lambda_{t+s}\frac{P^F_{t+s}}{P_{t+s}} = 0, \quad s \geqslant 0,$$

$$\frac{\partial \mathcal{L}}{\partial c^N_{t+s}} = (\beta^s c^{-\sigma}_{t+s})\left[(1-\gamma)\frac{c_{t+s}}{c^N_{t+s}}\right] - \lambda_{t+s}\frac{P^N_{t+s}}{P_{t+s}} = 0, \qquad s \geqslant 0,$$

$$\frac{\partial \mathcal{L}}{\partial f_{t+s}} = \lambda_{t+s}[1 + r^*_{t+s}] - \lambda_{t+s-1} = 0, \qquad s > 0.$$

From the first two conditions and for $s = 0$ the relative consumption of home and foreign goods is a function of the terms of trade Q^T_t and is given by

$$\frac{c^H_t}{c^F_t} = \frac{\alpha}{1-\alpha}Q^T_t. \tag{7.32}$$

Due to the Cobb–Douglas function this has a unit elasticity of substitution. Hence, an increase in the relative price of imported goods causes an equiproportional increase in the consumption of home goods relative to imports.

Substituting equation (7.32) into equation (7.27) gives the demand functions

$$\frac{c^H_t}{c^T_t} = \alpha(Q^T_t)^{1-\alpha}, \tag{7.33}$$

$$\frac{c^F_t}{c^T_t} = (1-\alpha)(Q^T_t)^{\alpha}. \tag{7.34}$$

Substituting equation (7.32) into equation (7.29) gives the share of expenditures on home tradeables in total tradeables expenditures as

$$\frac{P^H_t c^H_t}{P^T_t c^T_t} = \alpha.$$

It then follows from equations (7.27) and (7.29) that the price of tradeables is

$$P^T_t = (P^H_t)^{\alpha}(P^F_t)^{1-\alpha}. \tag{7.35}$$

Intuitively, given the Cobb–Douglas structure, we can derive corresponding results for total consumption, total tradeables, and total nontradeables. From the first-order conditions for c^H_t and c^N_t and for $s = 0$ we obtain

$$\frac{c^H_t}{c^N_t} = \alpha \frac{\gamma}{1-\gamma}\frac{P^N_t}{P^H_t}. \tag{7.36}$$

From this and equations (7.33) and (7.35),

$$\frac{c^T_t}{c^N_t} = \frac{\gamma}{1-\gamma}\frac{P^N_t}{P^T_t}. \tag{7.37}$$

From equations (7.26) and (7.28) the share of tradeables in total consumption is

$$\frac{P_t^T c_t^T}{P_t c_t} = y.$$

It follows that the general price level is

$$P_t = (P_t^T)^y (P_t^N)^{1-y} \tag{7.38}$$

$$= (P_t^H)^{\alpha y} (P_t^F)^{(1-\alpha)y} (P_t^N)^{1-y}. \tag{7.39}$$

Since $P_t^F = S_t P_t^{H*}$ and $P_t^{F*} = S_t^{-1} P_t^H$, the real exchange rate between two countries with identical preferences is

$$
\begin{aligned}
Q_t &= \frac{S_t P_t^*}{P_t} \\
&= \frac{S_t (P_t^{H*})^{\alpha y} (P_t^{F*})^{(1-\alpha)y} (P_t^{N*})^{1-y}}{(P_t^H)^{\alpha y} (P_t^F)^{(1-\alpha)y} (P_t^N)^{1-y}} \\
&= (Q_t^T)^{(2\alpha-1)y} \left(\frac{S_t P_t^{N*}}{P_t^N} \right)^{1-y}. \tag{7.40}
\end{aligned}
$$

Compared with equation (7.24), equation (7.40) shows more clearly the relation between the real exchange rate, the terms of trade, and the relative price of nontradeables. The sign of the effect of an improvement (increase) in the terms of trade—implying greater competitiveness—on the real exchange rate depends on whether the share of home tradeables exceeds that of foreign tradeables: if it does, then there is an increase in the real exchange rate; otherwise, the real exchange rate falls. Why does this occur? Suppose, for example, that the cause of the change in the terms of trade is an increase in the price of foreign tradeables, then because home tradeables have a greater share than imports, the foreign price level rises more than the domestic price level. As before, an increase in the relative price of foreign nontradeables increases the real exchange rate. Finally, we note that when the terms of trade is constant with $Q_t^T = 1$, equation (7.40) reduces to equation (7.25) if y is replaced by α.

The rest of the solution is as before. In particular, the consumption Euler equation is again

$$\beta \left(\frac{c_{t+1}}{c_t} \right)^{-\sigma} (1 + r_{t+1}^*) = 1.$$

And if $r_t^* = r^* = \theta$, then consumption is constant in the long run. From the real resource constraint, equation (7.31), the steady-state net asset position is

$$
\begin{aligned}
f_t &= \frac{1}{r^*} \left(\frac{P_t^H}{P_t} c_t^H + \frac{P_t^N}{P_t} c_t^N + \frac{P_t^F}{P_t} c_t^F - y_t \right) \\
&= \frac{1}{r^*} \left[\left(\frac{P_t^H c_t^H}{P_t^T c_t^T} \frac{P_t^T c_t^T}{P_t c_t} + \frac{P_t^N c_t^N}{P_t c_t} + \frac{P_t^F c_t^F}{P_t^T c_t^T} \frac{P_t^T c_t^T}{P_t c_t} \right) c_t - y_t \right] \\
&= \frac{[\alpha y + 1 - y + (1 - \alpha)y] c_t - y_t}{r^*}
\end{aligned}
$$

$$= \frac{c_t - y_t}{r^*} \tag{7.41}$$

$$= -\frac{(P_t^H/P_t)c_t^{F*} - (P_t^F/P_t)c_t^F}{r^*}. \tag{7.42}$$

Equation (7.42) is the counterpart of equation (7.14) derived earlier. Equation (7.42) relates net assets to trade; equation (7.41) implies that, in the long run,

$$c_t = y_t + r^* f_t,$$

i.e., total consumption equals the permanent income from output and net foreign assets.

7.6 Current-Account Sustainability

Previously we considered the determination of the current account and the net foreign asset position in the long run. We concluded that in the steady state the current account must be in balance but a country may have a permanent trade deficit whose size depends on the interest income from foreign assets. Consequently, a permanent current-account balance is a sustainable situation. In practice, the current-account position will vary over time, sometimes being in surplus and sometimes in deficit. This raises the more general question of whether a sequence of expected future current-account positions is sustainable. We consider two approaches. First, we show how our earlier analysis of the sustainability of the fiscal stance may be applied to the current account. We refer to this as balance of payments sustainability. We then examine a theory known as the intertemporal approach to the current account, which incorporates the optimality of consumption and savings decisions in a dynamic general equilibrium model.

In view of the common perception that a current-account deficit is undesirable, particularly one as large as that of the United States in recent years, we recall at the outset that it may be possible to have a long-run trade deficit and, in certain circumstances yet to be defined, it may even be possible to have a long-run current-account deficit. We also note that an economy whose assets the rest of the world wants to hold may need to run a current-account deficit in order to offset inflows on the capital account of the balance of payments. This has also been the position of the United States in recent years.

7.6.1 Balance of Payments Sustainability

We start with the balance of payments written in nominal terms as

$$CA_t = P_t^T x_t - S_t P_t^{T*} x_t^m + R_t^* S_t B_t^* - R_t B_t^F = S_t \Delta B_{t+1}^* - \Delta B_{t+1}^F,$$

where, as defined earlier, x_t is exports, x_t^m is imports, B_t^* is the domestic nominal holding of foreign assets expressed in foreign currency, B_t^F is the foreign holding of domestic assets expressed in domestic currency, P_t^T is the price of exports, P^{T*} is the foreign currency price of imports, S_t is the nominal effective exchange rate, R_t and R_t^* are the domestic and world nominal interest rates, $F_t = S_t B_t^* - B_t^F$ is the net asset position, and CA_t is the current-account balance expressed in nominal domestic currency terms.

We note that financial assets generally include equity as well as bonds, and equity has a different return due to its higher risk premium. For simplicity, however, we draw no distinction between the two and we ignore any consequent valuation effects.

We now express the balance of payments as a proportion of nominal GDP by dividing through by nominal GDP $P_t y_t$, where P_t is the general price level and y_t is real GDP, to obtain

$$\frac{P_t^T}{P_t}\left(\frac{x_t - Q_t^T x_t^m}{y_t}\right) + (1 + R_t^*)\frac{f_t}{y_t} - (R_t - R_t^*)\frac{b_t^F}{y_t}$$
$$= \left(\frac{(1 + \pi_{t+1})(1 + y_{t+1})}{1 + \Delta s_{t+1}}\right)\left(\frac{f_{t+1}}{y_{t+1}} - \Delta s_{t+1}\frac{b_{t+1}^F}{y_{t+1}}\right), \quad (7.43)$$

where

$$Q_t^T = \frac{S_t P_t^{T*}}{P_t^T}, \quad Q_t = \frac{S_t P_t^*}{P_t}, \quad b_t^F = \frac{B_t^F}{P_t}, \quad b_t^* = \frac{B_t^*}{P_t^*}, \quad f_t = \frac{F_t}{P_t} = Q_t b_t^* - b_t^F,$$

y_t is the rate of growth of GDP, and $s_t = \ln S_t$. This may be rewritten as a difference equation in f_t/y_t:

$$\frac{\tau_t}{y_t} + (1 + R_t^*)\frac{f_t}{y_t} = \left(\frac{(1 + \pi_{t+1})(1 + y_{t+1})}{1 + \Delta s_{t+1}}\right)\frac{f_{t+1}}{y_{t+1}}, \quad (7.44)$$

where

$$\frac{\tau_t}{y_t} = \frac{P^T}{P_t}\left(\frac{x_t - Q_t^T x_t^m}{y_t}\right) - (R_t - R_t^*)\frac{b_t^F}{y_t} + \left(\frac{(1 + \pi_{t+1})(1 + y_{t+1})}{1 + \Delta s_{t+1}}\right)\Delta s_{t+1}\frac{b_{t+1}^F}{y_{t+1}}$$
$$(7.45)$$

can be interpreted as the "primary" current-account surplus expressed as a proportion of GDP. This is analogous to the primary government surplus.

We note that if the domestic equals the world interest rate, which would happen if uncovered interest parity (UIP) holds *ex post* (i.e., if $R_t = R^* + \Delta s_{t+1}$; see chapter 11 for a derivation of UIP) and the exchange rate is constant, or if there is foreign holding of domestic assets, then τ_t is just the trade balance. The two additional terms on the right-hand side of equation (7.45) occur if these conditions do not hold. The first is excess interest payments to foreign holders of domestic debt due to domestic interest rates exceeding foreign rates. The second captures the cost of a revaluation of real foreign holdings of domestic assets due to a depreciation of the exchange rate; the higher the domestic nominal rate of growth, the greater this cost is.

The analysis of balance of payments sustainability depends on whether equation (7.44) is a stable or an unstable difference equation. It is, therefore, similar in form to the analysis of fiscal sustainability in chapter 5. We assume that UIP holds and that π_t, y_t, R_t^*, and Δs_t are constant, taking the values π, y, R^*, and $\Delta s = 0$. It then follows that $R = R^*$. Equation (7.44) becomes

$$\frac{f_t}{y_t} = \frac{(1+\pi)(1+y)}{1+R^*} \frac{f_{t+1}}{y_{t+1}} - \frac{1}{1+R^*} \frac{P_t^T}{P_t}\left(\frac{x_t - Q_t^T x_t^m}{y_t}\right). \tag{7.46}$$

Thus the analysis depends on whether $(1+\pi)(1+y)$ is greater than or less than $1+R^*$. Under long-run UIP this is approximately equivalent to whether $\pi + y$ is greater than or less than R. This is the same condition that arises in the analysis of the sustainability of fiscal policy.

First we consider the case where $R < \pi + y$ when (7.46) is a stable difference equation and is solved backwards. In this case the analysis of balance of payments sustainability consists of determining whether f_t/y_t remains finite. Given our assumptions, it clearly does, whether the trade balance is positive or negative. A trade deficit would therefore be sustainable.

We therefore focus on the unstable case where $R > \pi + y$ when we solve (7.46) forwards. This is how we proceeded earlier when analyzing the optimal solution for the open economy. If $f_t < 0$, we must determine whether the sequence of expected future trade surpluses and deficits is sufficient to repay net debts; and if $f_t > 0$, we must determine whether the sequence of expected future trade surpluses and deficits is sufficient to use up net foreign assets.

Solving equation (7.46) forwards gives

$$\frac{f_t}{y_t} = \left(\frac{(1+\pi)(1+y)}{1+R}\right)^n \frac{f_{t+n}}{y_{t+n}}$$
$$- \frac{1}{1+R} \sum_{i=0}^{n} \left(\frac{(1+\pi)(1+y)}{1+R}\right)^i \frac{P_{t+i}^T}{P_{t+i}}\left(\frac{x_{t+i} - Q_{t+i}^T x_{t+i}^m}{y_{t+i}}\right).$$

Taking limits as $n \to \infty$ gives the transversality condition

$$\lim_{n\to\infty} \left(\frac{(1+\pi)(1+y)}{1+R}\right)^n \frac{f_{t+n}}{y_{t+n}} = 0. \tag{7.47}$$

If this holds then we obtain the intertemporal, or present-value, balance of payments condition expressed as a proportion of GDP:

$$-\frac{f_t}{y_t} \leqslant \frac{1}{1+R} \sum_{i=0}^{\infty} \left(\frac{(1+\pi)(1+y)}{1+R}\right)^i \frac{P_{t+i}^T}{P_{t+i}}\left(\frac{x_{t+i} - Q_{t+i}^T x_{t+i}^m}{y_{t+i}}\right).$$

This can be interpreted as follows. If the economy has a negative net asset position (i.e., if $f_t/y_t < 0$), then it needs the present value of current and expected future real trade surpluses

$$\frac{P_{t+i}^T}{P_{t+i}}\left(\frac{x_{t+i} - Q_{t+i}^T x_{t+i}^m}{y_{t+i}}\right)$$

as a proportion of GDP to be positive and large enough to pay off net debt. And if the economy has a positive net asset position (i.e., if $f_t/y_t > 0$), then the present value of current and future trade deficits must be sufficient to exhaust current net assets, otherwise the economy would be holding an excess level of assets.

In the special case where the real trade surplus is constant and positive, i.e.,

$$\frac{P^{\mathrm{T}}}{P}\left(\frac{x_t - Q^{\mathrm{T}}x^m}{y}\right) > 0,$$

a simple connection emerges between net indebtedness and the long-run real trade surplus that is required to sustain a given level of net indebtedness:

$$-\frac{f}{y} \leqslant \frac{1}{R - (\pi + y)}\frac{P^{\mathrm{T}}}{P}\left(\frac{x_t - Q^{\mathrm{T}}x^m}{y}\right). \tag{7.48}$$

This is an extension of the earlier result, equation (7.14), as it takes account of economic growth, which was previously set to zero. We note that for a given nominal interest rate R, an inflation term is also present. But since higher inflation will tend to result in a correspondingly higher nominal interest rate, thereby leaving the real interest rate $R - \pi$ constant, we may ignore the effect of inflation.

To find the implications of this analysis for the current account, we note from equation (7.43) that in the long run the real current account is the real trade balance plus real net interest earnings, hence

$$\frac{CA}{Py} = \frac{P^{\mathrm{T}}}{P}\left(\frac{x_t - Q^{\mathrm{T}}x^m}{y}\right) + R\frac{f}{y}.$$

Substituting for

$$\frac{P^{\mathrm{T}}}{P}\left(\frac{x_t - Q^{\mathrm{T}}x^m}{y}\right)$$

from equation (7.48) gives

$$-\frac{CA}{Py} \leqslant (\pi + y)\left(-\frac{f}{y}\right).$$

It follows that, if there is nominal economic growth, then it is possible to have a permanent and sustainable current-account deficit ($CA < 0$), even if $f/y < 0$, provided that the current-account deficit does not exceed the right-hand side. The higher the rate of growth of nominal GDP, the more likely it is that a permanent current-account deficit can be sustained without increasing a country's net indebtedness. This contrasts with the earlier result without nominal income growth, when the current account had to be in balance in the long run.

Dynamic efficiency requires that in the long run economic agents (households, government, or the economy) aim to exactly consume their assets. If their spending plans are not sufficient to use up their assets, then they are said to be dynamically inefficient. Unless they have a bequest motive, households should therefore raise consumption. If the economy has a positive net foreign asset position, then it follows that it should have a long-run trade deficit sufficient to run down its assets. Thus the economy should ensure that for $f > 0$ it has a trade deficit that does not exceed the left-hand side of

$$[R - (\pi + y)]\frac{f}{y} \geqslant \frac{P^{\mathrm{T}}}{P}\left(\frac{x_t - Q^{\mathrm{T}}x^m}{y}\right) > 0.$$

It would clearly be a mistake to have a positive net asset position *and* a trade balance or surplus over the long run. This is a position that many oil-producing countries are in; China and Japan, two major manufacturing exporters, also have this problem.

7.6.1.1 The Long-Run Equilibrium Terms of Trade and Real Exchange Rate

The long-run equilibrium terms of trade must satisfy equation (7.48); hence

$$Q^T \leqslant \frac{x + (P/P^T)[R - (\pi + y)]f}{x^m}.$$

Accordingly, the equilibrium terms of trade requires neither a long-run real trade balance nor a long-run current-account balance. Higher exports, lower imports, and $f > 0$, a higher real interest rate, and a lower rate of economic growth will all tend to cause a higher equilibrium terms of trade.

The real exchange rate satisfies

$$Q = Q^T \frac{P^T/P}{P^{T*}/P*}.$$

Consequently, differences between the terms of trade and the real exchange rate are due to differences in the domestic and foreign prices of exports relative to the general price levels. If the terms of trade is constant and $Q^T = 1$, then $Q = (P^T/P)/(P^{T*}/P*)$. More generally, the long-run equilibrium real exchange rate must satisfy

$$Q \leqslant \frac{x + (P/P^T)[R - (\pi + y)]f}{x^m} \frac{P^T/P}{P^{T*}/P*}.$$

We may contrast this result with the concept of the fundamental equilibrium exchange rate (FEER), which is not based on the notion of current sustainability but on long-run current-account balance (see Williamson 1993). The FEER is analogous to requiring a balanced government budget in the long run. Our analysis has shown that in the long run it is possible to have both a permanent trade and current-account deficit; and if there is nominal economic growth, then long-run current-account balance is sufficient, but not necessary, for current-account sustainability.

7.6.1.2 The Twin Deficits

The current account is the consolidation of the accounts of the private and public sectors. It is therefore often of interest to ask whether a current-account deficit is due to the private sector consuming too much (not saving enough) or whether it is due to the public sector consuming too much and borrowing too much. The twin-deficits problem arises when the current-account deficit seems to be due to the government deficit as the private sector is in balance. In the United States at the end of 2003 the annual government deficit was roughly $520 billion, while the current-account balance was around $550 billion. Both were just over 5% of GDP. As a result, the U.S. current-account deficit was often attributed to the government deficit. We reconsider this interpretation below.

Using earlier notation, the national resource constraint is

$$y_t = c_t + i_t + g_t + x_t - Q_t x_t^m.$$

The private-sector budget constraint is

$$\Delta(b_{t+1}^g + b_{t+1}^*) + c_t + i_t - Q_t x_t^m + T_t = y_t + r_t^*(b_t^g + b_t^*),$$

where b_t^g is private-sector real holdings of domestic government debt, b_t^* is private-sector real net holdings of foreign debt, and T_t is taxes. We assume that there is a single world real interest rate r_t^*. The net savings of the private sector are total income less total expenditures:

$$[y_t + r_t^*(b_t^g + b_t^*)] - (c_t + i_t - Q_t x_t^m + T_t) = \Delta(b_{t+1}^g + b_{t+1}^*).$$

The government budget constraint is

$$g_t + r_t^*(b_t^g + b_t^F) = T_t + \Delta(b_{t+1}^g + b_{t+1}^F),$$

where b_t^F is foreign net holdings of domestic government debt. The government deficit is therefore

$$[g_t + r_t^*(b_t^g + b_t^F)] - T_t = \Delta(b_{t+1}^g + b_{t+1}^F).$$

The balance of payments identity can be written as

$$x_t - Q_t x_t^m + r_t^*(b_t^* - b_t^F) = \Delta(b_{t+1}^* - b_{t+1}^F)$$

and the trade balance as

$$\begin{aligned} x_t - Q_t x_t^m &= y_t - (c_t + i_t + g_t) \\ &= \{[y_t + r_t^*(b_t^g + b_t^*)] - (c_t + i_t - Q_t x_t^m + T_t)\} \\ &\quad + \{T_t - [g_t + r_t^*(b_t^g + b_t^F)]\} - r_t^*(b_t^* - b_t^F), \end{aligned}$$

where the first term in braces on the right-hand side is the private-sector balance and the second term in braces is the government balance. Eliminating the trade balance from the balance of payments identity we obtain

$$\{[y_t + r_t^*(b_t^g + b_t^*)] - (c_t + i_t - Q_t x_t^m + T_t)\} + \{T_t - [g_t + r_t^*(b_t^g + b_t^F)]\}$$
$$= \Delta(b_{t+1}^* - b_{t+1}^F).$$

The left-hand side of this equation is the current-account balance. It can be seen to consist of the sum of the private-sector balance and the government balance.

According to the twin-deficits argument, if the private sector is in balance, then a current-account deficit must be due solely to the government deficit. The right-hand side of this equation is the capital account. It consists of increases in the net private holdings of foreign assets and decreases in the net sales of government debt. If the private sector is in balance and the government has a deficit, then the government must sell its debt to the rest of the world, i.e., $\Delta b_{t+1}^F < 0$.

As previously noted, this argument is sometimes used to suggest that a current-account deficit is the fault of government. This ignores the possibility that, due to capital market imperfections, the rest of the world wants to hold so much government debt that the resulting inflow of capital requires an offsetting current-account deficit. This would happen automatically as the increase in the foreign demand for domestic currency would cause an exchange-rate appreciation, which would increase the terms of trade and worsen the trade, and hence the current-account, deficit. The increase in the demand for domestic assets would also cause a revaluation of the private sector's financial wealth and hence raise consumption and imports, which would tend to worsen the current account even more. Further, the government would find it easier to finance a deficit because it could sell more of its debt abroad and less at home, but the worsening of the current-account deficit would not be attributable to the government deficit.

7.6.2 The Intertemporal Approach to the Current Account

The above discussion of current-account sustainability—which we called balance of payments sustainability to distinguish it from the intertemporal approach to the current account—has general applicability irrespective of any particular macroeconomic theory. In a dynamic general equilibrium model of the economy the general argument can be specialized to take account of the optimality of consumption and savings decisions by combining the BOP with a simple intertemporal model of consumption. This special case is known as the intertemporal model of the current account (see Obstfeld and Rogoff 1995b; Sheffrin and Woo 1990).

Consider the balance of payments identity written in real terms as

$$f_{t+1} = (1 + r^*)f_t + \tau_t,$$

where r^* is the world real interest rate, net exports (trade) is

$$\tau_t = y_t - c_t - i_t - g_t,$$

the real current account is

$$ca_t = q_t + r^* f_t - c_t,$$

the national income identity is

$$y_t = c_t + i_t + g_t + \tau_t,$$

and net output is defined as

$$q_t = y_t - i_t - g_t = c_t + \tau_t.$$

It follows from the transversality condition for the BOP that sustainability requires that $\lim_{n\to\infty}(f_{t+n}/(1+r^*)^n) = 0$ and hence

$$f_t = -\sum_{s=0}^{\infty}\frac{1}{(1+r^*)^{s+1}}\tau_{t+s}$$

$$= -\sum_{s=0}^{\infty}\frac{1}{(1+r^*)^{s+1}}(q_{t+s} - c_{t+s}).$$

From earlier results, a representative consumer maximizing the intertemporal utility function $\sum_{s=0}^{\infty}(1/(1+r^*)^s)u(c_{t+s})$ subject to the national income identity sets consumption equal to the permanent income derived from wealth W_t (the "life-cycle theory"):

$$c_t = r^*W_t,$$

where wealth in the open economy is given by

$$W_t = \left\{\frac{1}{1+r^*}\sum_{s=0}^{\infty}\frac{1}{(1+r^*)^s}q_{t+s} + f_t\right\}.$$

Substituting c_t into the expression for the current account gives the following condition for current-account sustainability:

$$ca_t = -\frac{r^*}{1+r^*}\sum_{s=0}^{\infty}\frac{q_{t+s} - q_t}{(1+r^*)^s}$$

$$= -\sum_{s=0}^{\infty}\frac{\Delta q_{t+s}}{(1+r^*)^s}. \tag{7.49}$$

Thus, to be sustainable, a current-account deficit must be offset by the present value of changes in current and future net output.

This result may be compared with our discussion of life-cycle theory in chapter 4. We showed then that current savings s_t should be equal to the present value of current and future changes in income x_t:

$$s_t = -\sum_{s=0}^{\infty}\frac{\Delta x_{t+s}}{(1+r)^s},$$

where r is the rate of return on savings. We interpreted this to mean that savings are undertaken to compensate for expected future falls in income. This suggests that we could also interpret equation (7.49) to mean that a positive current-account position is required to offset expected future falls in net output.

7.7 Conclusions

We have extended the closed-economy model to allow for trade between countries. This has the effect of removing the constraint that a closed economy can only consume in each period what it produces. For example, by borrowing from abroad, the domestic economy can import goods and services, and thereby temporarily increase consumption. The debt incurred must be repaid later by running a current-account surplus and consuming less.

Initially we introduced the open economy simply as a way of removing a constraint on domestic consumption by allowing imports that are perfect substitutes for domestic output. This improved welfare by allowing additional intertemporal substitution. We then generalized this model in two ways. First we noted that not all goods and services are traded internationally and examined the case where there are tradeables and nontradeables. We then relaxed the assumption that there is perfect substitution between domestic and foreign tradeables and allowed them to be imperfect substitutes.

Two common assumptions in open-economy models, especially for the long run, are those of purchasing power parity, which implies a constant real exchange rate, and the law of one price, which under certain circumstances implies a constant terms of trade. The empirical evidence is, however, strongly against these assumptions, particularly in the short run. By introducing a distinction between tradeables and nontradeables we are able to separate the terms of trade from the real exchange rate. Somewhat counterintuitively, we find that it is relative productivity growth in the nontradeable sector that is the main determinant of the real exchange rate in the long run, and hence of the relative costs of living between countries. Consequently there is no reason to expect that, in general, PPP will not hold even in the long run. Throughout this analysis we took the nominal exchange rate as exogenous.

In a closed economy there are two budget constraints: the household and government budget constraints. In an open economy there is an additional budget constraint: the balance of payments. The balance of payments must always be satisfied as it is an accounting identity. As a result, if there is a current-account deficit, there must be a capital outflow to pay for it, and if the rest of the world wants to increase its holdings of domestic assets, then the current account must be in deficit. This raises the question of what constraints there are on the size and persistence of a country's current-account deficit. We have shown that in a static economy, if there are positive net foreign assets, there can be a permanent trade deficit but the current account must be in balance in the long run. In contrast, if the economy is growing, it may be possible to have a permanent current-account deficit. The size of the deficit depends on the size of asset holdings and the rate of growth. It can also be shown that in a general equilibrium model a positive current-account position is required to offset future falls in net output, i.e., output less investment and government expenditures.

In chapter 12, where our focus is on determining the nominal exchange rate, we shall further develop some of the ideas presented in this chapter when we consider the redux model of Obstfeld and Rogoff (1995a).

8

The Monetary Economy

8.1 Introduction

In this chapter we examine the role of money in the macroeconomy. This also allows us to introduce the general price level and inflation. We are then in a position to discuss the economy in nominal terms, and not just in real terms as previously. Although we have previously included money and the price level in the government budget constraint, in order to focus exclusively on fiscal policy we treated them as constant. Similarly, although we mentioned the domestic price level in our discussion of the real exchange rate and the terms of trade, our principal concern was relative prices. Our focus now is on the demand for money, and on some of the implications for the real economy of holding money. We also consider some aspects of the relation between money and inflation. We revert to the closed economy in this discussion.

We start with a brief history of money and its role in the economy. We review the reasons for the emergence of money and why in recent years we have been moving toward a cashless economy. We argue that this has had a profound impact on the way that monetary policy is conducted and how monetary policy affects the economy. We therefore revise our model of the economy so that we can analyze the decisions to hold both money and credit. We consider four theories of money demand. The first is the "cash-in-advance" (CIA) model, in which it is assumed that goods and services can be purchased only in exchange for cash. The second assumes that real-money balances are an independent source of utility and can be treated, in effect, as a commodity—this is the "money-in-utility" (MIU) model. The third model assumes that holding money economizes on shopping time and hence is an intermediate, rather than a final, good. This is called the "money as an intermediate good" (MIG) model. The fourth theory assumes that consumption transactions impose a real resource cost that affects the budget constraint, which can only be lowered by using money. We defer until chapter 13 our detailed discussion of monetary policy and its implications for the real economy and inflation. A more general and detailed discussion of the theory of money can be found in Walsh (2003).

8.2 A Brief History of Money and Its Role

The presence of money in the economy is usually taken for granted. It may therefore come as a surprise that there is no consensus among economists about whether, at least in theory, money is needed at all or, if it is needed, what money is. There are large literatures on both issues which are beyond the scope of this book to discuss. Instead we briefly review the history of money with a view to explaining what the issues are concerning its role.

It is important to distinguish between three roles for money. One is in the use of money in transactions, especially for goods and services. A second is the use of money as a store of wealth in order to transfer consumption across time. The third is money as credit that can be borrowed for consumption today and repaid later. In principle, money is not needed for any of these purposes as there are other means of carrying them out. The case for using money largely rests on convenience and cost.

For example, all transactions could be conducted through barter: exchanging goods and services for goods and services. The disadvantages of barter are well-known: the transactions costs are likely to be very high as barter requires a coincidence of wants among the parties to the exchange, and searching for partners is very time consuming, especially when exchanging large items for small items. Exchanging goods and services for gold and silver (and sometimes other precious commodities) was an early solution to these problems of barter. Gold and silver also solved the problem of providing a store of wealth and a means of creating credit. The main problem with gold and silver is that they are in limited supply. As economies grow they need an increasing supply of these precious metals to finance transactions. This tends to drive up the price of gold and silver, which provides an incentive to economize on their use.

The key to the introduction of money was the need to write contracts when borrowing and lending was involved. Initially, the contracts were to borrow gold and silver today and to repay the gold or silver in the future. There was a charge for borrowing, which usually consisted of an additional gold or silver payment on redemption of the contract. The emergence of secondary markets, in which the contracts themselves were bought and sold for gold, saw the start of replacing gold and silver with paper. In this way, i.e., by receiving gold or silver today for a promise of gold or silver in the future, a creditor could alter the maturity structure of assets and hence make more loans. All that was needed for this to function effectively was confidence that the debt would be redeemed. The principal borrowers were kings and governments, usually in order to finance the prosecution of wars. Large landowners were the main creditors. With the growth of trade, merchants began to dominate both borrowing and lending.

Initially, credit markets were created by money lenders and in the main the sums involved were probably fairly small. Subsequently, successful money lenders institutionalized themselves into banks, but still performed a similar function. This is why we may regard banks simply as firms that specialize in intermediating between savers and borrowers. Savers began to deposit their gold and silver in banks for safekeeping and received an income for doing this. They also sold notes of credit at a discount to the banks in exchange for immediate gold or a gold deposit. The banks made a profit because the discounted purchase price of the credit note was less than its redemption value. As the banks then took on the risk of default, there was a transfer of risk to the bank, which was factored into the discount rate, together with a charge because the bank had to wait for payment.

The larger banks became the main source of credit for kings and government. Some were granted a monopoly of such transactions and became the state or central bank. More recently, most central banks came to be owned by the state. In effect, the state began to borrow from the central bank. The central bank raised the credit by borrowing from the public, issuing promises to repay the debt in the future.

At first, all of this borrowing and lending was denominated in gold or silver. As bank loans and secondary markets for discounting credit notes and loans by other banks developed, the banks observed that they did not need to match their loans (their liabilities) by holding an equal amount of gold and silver provided depositors were confident that they could withdraw their deposits and receive gold or silver at any time of their choosing. Banks therefore started to increase their profits by lending a multiple of their gold and silver holdings.

The state, observing the creation of credit by banks without the need for a 100% backing in gold and silver, began to pay for its purchases of goods and services with standardized notes of credit of small denomination which could be redeemed for gold on application to the central bank. The public, having confidence that they could obtain gold and silver if they wanted, accepted these notes in exchange for providing goods and services to the state. Further, notes began to be accepted in exchange for goods and services for all transactions in the economy, in settling debts, and as deposits in banks.

The final step in the emergence of fiat money was due to the success of this system and occurred when governments suspended the convertibility of these notes into gold and silver and claimed a monopoly on the supply of such credit notes. At this point the notes became pure fiat money. The supply of fiat money by the central bank is called outside money and forms the liabilities of the central bank. This is held by the public mainly in the form of bank deposits. These deposits differ in their accessibility; some are available instantly, others are available only after a time. The deposits are lent in the form of credit to the public; some of this credit takes the form of loans to firms or is the result of purchasing, or discounting, the debt issued by commercial companies. The deposits of the public in the banking system are called inside money and form the liabilities of the rest of the banking system. The sum of outside and inside money is the total supply of money, and forms the liabilities of the whole banking system. Money therefore consists of a broad range of bank liabilities which differ in their degree of liquidity—i.e., their ease of use for instant purchases. Some, such as fiat money is cash in hand and is the most liquid; at the other extreme are time deposits of much longer maturity and bills which are not instantly available.

Two more recent developments may be added to this history. The first is the emergence of "plastic" or "electronic" money, i.e., the use of debit and credit cards. These days some purchases may only be made for cash; they are mainly small ticket items. Increasingly, purchases may be made using a debit or credit card. A debit card allows bank accounts to be debited instantly through electronic communication. A credit card delays payment for a fixed period such as a month, or until the purchaser decides to make repayment. Given that increasingly all bank accounts pay interest, albeit at a low rate for instant access accounts, we are moving toward a cashless economy based on credit.

The second development relates to the activities of banks and the emergence of nonbank financial companies. It is now common for banks to offer mortgages and for building societies and mortgage companies to provide banking facilities. As a result, homeowners are able to borrow against the security of their homes, thereby making one of the most illiquid of assets into an increasingly liquid asset. Further, credit cards, which were initially issued only by banks, are now being offered by a very wide range of companies, including retailers and even charities.

These developments have had a profound impact on the way monetary policy is conducted. No longer can money and credit be controlled effectively by quantity limits or targets based on the supply of money. Controlling highly liquid types of money is no guarantee that less liquid types of money will not be made instantly liquid, or that credit is being controlled. Instead, monetary policy has to rely on the use of interest rates to change the cost of borrowing as this affects all types of credit. Many households have a portfolio of assets ranging from bank accounts to stock market equity and to property. The composition of these portfolios depends on their rates of return as well as their convenience value in use. Debts may be considered as assets with a negative return. By rebalancing their portfolios, including taking on more debt, these households can rapidly generate liquidity.

The new challenge for monetary policy is to establish a reliable link between interest rates and final expenditures on goods and services that takes into account the composition of portfolios and their rebalancing as a result of a change in interest rates. The role of money in this is becoming increasingly unclear as it is just one among many assets. Increasingly, therefore, monetary policy must focus on the whole portfolio of assets.

A classic on the history of money is Friedman and Schwartz (1963). See also Friedman (1968).

8.3 Nominal Household Budget Constraint

In chapter 4, where the decentralized decisions of households were first considered, the household budget constraint was written in real terms as

$$\Delta a_{t+1} + c_t = x_t + r_t a_t,$$

where income x_t was taken to be exogenous, a_t denoted total real assets held at the start of period t, and r_t was the real rate of return. In writing the household budget constraint in nominal terms in chapter 5 we distinguished between two types of assets: M_t, the nominal stock of money held at time t; and B_t, the total expenditure on one-period bonds made at the start of period $t - 1$. We now write the budget constraint in nominal terms as

$$\Delta B_{t+1} + \Delta M_{t+1} + P_t c_t = P_t x_t + R_t B_t, \tag{8.1}$$

where P_t is the general price level, R_t is the nominal rate of return on bonds, and $R_t B_t$ is the interest income from bonds, which is paid at the start of period t. Further details on the definition of bonds and their pricing is provided in chapters 5, 10, and 11.

The real budget constraint is obtained by deflating equation (8.1) by the general price level to give

$$(1 + \pi_{t+1})b_{t+1} - b_t + (1 + \pi_{t+1})m_{t+1} - m_t + c_t = x_t + R_t b_t, \tag{8.2}$$

where $b_t = B_t/P_t$, $m_t = M_t/P_t$, and $\pi_{t+1} = \Delta P_{t+1}/P_t$ is the inflation rate. The real budget constraint can also be written as

$$(1 + \pi_{t+1})[\Delta b_{t+1} + \Delta m_{t+1}] + c_t = x_t + (R_t - \pi_{t+1})b_t - \pi_{t+1}m_t$$
$$= x_t + r_{t+1}b_t - \pi_{t+1}m_t. \tag{8.3}$$

Comparing this with the way the real household budget constraint was written before, we note that total real assets are $a_t = b_t + m_t$, the real rate of return on bonds is $r_{t+1} = ((1 + R_t)/(1 + \pi_{t+1})) - 1 \simeq R_t - \pi_{t+1}$, and the real rate of return on money is $-\pi_{t+1}$. (Here we are continuing to assume perfect foresight. In the absence of perfect foresight the definition of the real interest rate, which is associated with Fisher, is slightly different with expected replacing actual future inflation. We then obtain a new definition of the real interest rate: $r_{t+1} = R_t - E_t \pi_{t+1}$.)

Assuming that inflation is positive, the real rate of return on money is negative. This is because money has a zero nominal return and hence loses its purchasing power due to inflation. The fall in the value of nominal money balances is in effect a tax—the "inflation tax"—and is "seigniorage" income to the issuer of money (the government).

In the static steady state all real stocks are constant, including the real stock of bonds and money. This implies that $\Delta b = \Delta m = 0$, but π is not necessarily zero. If the growth rate of nominal money is $\Delta M/M = \mu$, then

$$\frac{\Delta m}{m} = \frac{\Delta M}{M} - \frac{\Delta P}{P} = \mu - \pi = 0,$$

implying that in equilibrium $\pi = \mu$. This equilibrium condition should be interpreted with some care. If money growth is exogenous, then in the long run inflation will equal the rate of growth of money. But if inflation is determined exogenously, as in inflation targeting, then in the long run money growth equals this rate of inflation, i.e., causation is reversed. We cannot distinguish between these two ways of conducting monetary policy just from the equilibrium condition.

8.4 The Cash-in-Advance Model of Money Demand

We have seen from the household budget constraint that holding money imposes real costs. So why do households hold money? The usual reasons given are that money reduces transactions costs and provides both a store of value and a unit of account. The cash-in-advance (CIA) model focuses exclusively on the transactions demand for money and is the simplest theory of money demand that we examine (see Clower 1967; Lucas 1980a). It assumes that all goods and services must be paid for in full with cash at the time of purchase. In fact, as economies usually operate with less money than total nominal expenditures, the quantity of money required is less than total nominal expenditures. For simplicity, however, we assume that money holdings are equal to total expenditures. In this case, the nominal demand for money is

$$M_t^D = P_t c_t$$

and hence the real demand for money is $m_t^D = M_t^D/P_t = c_t$. We assume that the money supply M_t^S is determined exogenously. Money-market equilibrium implies that $M_t^D = M_t^S = M_t$.

The household's problem is to maximize $\sum_{s=0}^{\infty} \beta^s U(c_{t+s})$ with respect to $\{c_{t+s}, b_{t+s+1}, m_{t+s+1}; s \geqslant 0\}$ subject to its budget constraint, equation (8.2). The Lagrangian is

$$\mathcal{L} = \sum_{s=0}^{\infty} \{\beta^s U(c_{t+s}) + \lambda_{t+s}[x_{t+s} + (1 + R_{t+s})b_{t+s} + m_{t+s}$$
$$- (1 + \pi_{t+s+1})(b_{t+s+1} + m_{t+s+1}) - c_{t+s}]$$
$$+ \mu_{t+s}[m_{t+s} - c_{t+s}]\}.$$

The first-order conditions are

$$\frac{\partial \mathcal{L}}{\partial c_{t+s}} = \beta^s U'(c_{t+s}) - \lambda_{t+s} - \mu_{t+s} = 0, \qquad s \geqslant 0,$$

$$\frac{\partial \mathcal{L}}{\partial b_{t+s}} = \lambda_{t+s}(1 + R_{t+s}) - \lambda_{t+s-1}(1 + \pi_{t+s}) = 0, \quad s > 0,$$

$$\frac{\partial \mathcal{L}}{\partial m_{t+s}} = \lambda_{t+s} - \lambda_{t+s-1}(1 + \pi_{t+s}) + \mu_{t+s} = 0, \qquad s > 0.$$

Subtracting the first-order condition for bonds from that for money gives

$$\mu_{t+s} = \lambda_{t+s} R_{t+s}, \quad s = 1, 2, \dots.$$

Hence, $\beta^s U'(c_{t+s}) = \lambda_{t+s}(1 + R_{t+s})$, and since

$$\frac{\lambda_{t+s+1}}{\lambda_{t+s}} = \frac{1 + \pi_{t+s+1}}{1 + R_{t+s+1}},$$

the Euler equation for period $t + 1$ is

$$\frac{\beta U'(c_{t+1})}{U'(c_t)} \frac{1 + R_t}{1 + \pi_{t+1}} = 1$$

or

$$\frac{\beta U'(c_{t+1})}{U'(c_t)}(1 + r_{t+1}) = 1. \tag{8.4}$$

This is the same as for the real economy.

We now consider the solutions for c_t and m_t. In long-run equilibrium, $\Delta c_t = \Delta m_t = 0$, implying that $r_t = \theta$, where $\beta = 1/(1 + \theta)$, and money demand in both the short and long run is $m_t = c_t$. The solution for consumption in the short run is very similar to our previous analysis. Assuming for convenience that R_t and π_t are constant, the household budget constraint is

$$(1 + \pi)(b_{t+1} + m_{t+1}) + c_t = x_t + (1 + R)b_t + m_t,$$

or, written in terms of $a_t = b_t + m_t$,

$$a_t = \frac{1}{1 + R}(c_t - x_t + Rm_t) + \left(\frac{1 + \pi}{1 + R}\right)a_{t+1}.$$

Eliminating $a_{t+1}, a_{t+2}, \ldots$ gives the intertemporal budget constraint

$$a_t = \frac{1}{1 + R}\sum_{s=0}^{n-1}\left(\frac{1 + \pi}{1 + R}\right)^s (c_{t+s} - x_{t+s} + Rm_{t+s}) + \left(\frac{1 + \pi}{1 + R}\right)^n a_{t+n}.$$

If $r = R - \pi > 0$, then the transversality condition

$$\lim_{n \to \infty}\left(\frac{1 + \pi}{1 + R}\right)^n a_{t+n} = 0$$

is satisfied and hence

$$a_t = \frac{1}{1 + R}\sum_{0}^{\infty}\left(\frac{1 + \pi}{1 + R}\right)^s (c_{t+s} - x_{t+s} + Rm_{t+s}).$$

If we assume that c_t and m_t are in long-run equilibrium, then $c_{t+s} = c_t$ and $m_{t+s} = m_t$ for $s \geqslant 0$; hence

$$c_t \simeq \frac{r}{1 + r}\sum_{0}^{\infty}\frac{x_{t+s}}{(1 + r)^s} + rb_t - \pi m_t.$$

If, in addition, $x_{t+s} = x_t$ for $s \geqslant 0$, then we obtain the long-run consumption function

$$c_t = x_t + rb_t - \pi m_t \tag{8.5}$$

$$= \frac{x_t + rb_t}{1 + \pi}. \tag{8.6}$$

Equation (8.5) shows that, when inflation is positive, the higher the stock of real-money balances, the lower is consumption. This implies that having to pay for consumption expenditures with cash has introduced a nonneutrality into the economy. This is because a nominal variable (inflation) affects a real variable (consumption) due to the loss of the real purchasing power of money holdings when inflation is nonzero. We return to this point later when we consider the super-neutrality of money. Equation (8.6) shows that, due to paying for consumption using cash, the higher is inflation, the lower is consumption for given total income $x_t + rb_t$.

8.5 Money in the Utility Function

We assume now that households consider the broader benefits of holding money by including real-money balances as an argument of their utility function. This is called the "money in the utility" (MIU) model and is due to Sidrauski (1967). In our next money-demand model we offer some justification for this. A feature of the cash-in-advance model is that the demand for money is not interest sensitive. In the MIU model allowance is made for the opportunity cost of holding money in terms of lost interest. We show that this makes the demand for money sensitive to interest rates and encourages households to economize on holding money balances.

We assume that the representative household's utility function is

$$U(c_t, m_t), \quad U_c > 0, \ U_{cc} \leqslant 0, \ U_m > 0, \ U_{mm} \leqslant 0,$$

implying that holding more money improves utility. We also note that m_t is predetermined in period t, whereas m_{t+1} is, in part, the outcome of decisions taken in period t.[1]

We now write the household's problem as that of maximizing

$$V_t = \sum_0^\infty \beta^s U(c_{t+s}, m_{t+s})$$

subject to the household budget constraint. The Lagrangian is

$$\mathcal{L} = \sum_{s=0}^\infty \{\beta^s U(c_{t+s}, m_{t+s}) + \lambda_{t+s}[x_{t+s} + (1 + R_{t+s})b_{t+s} + m_{t+s} \\ - (1 + \pi_{t+s+1})(b_{t+s+1} + m_{t+s+1}) - c_{t+s}]\}.$$

The first-order conditions are

$$\frac{\partial \mathcal{L}}{\partial c_{t+s}} = \beta^s U_{c,t+s} - \lambda_{t+s} = 0, \qquad\qquad s \geqslant 0,$$

$$\frac{\partial \mathcal{L}}{\partial b_{t+s}} = \lambda_{t+s}(1 + R_{t+s}) - \lambda_{t+s-1}(1 + \pi_{t+s}) = 0, \quad s > 0,$$

$$\frac{\partial \mathcal{L}}{\partial m_{t+s}} = \beta^s U_{m,t+s} + \lambda_{t+s} - \lambda_{t+s-1}(1 + \pi_{t+s}) = 0, \quad s > 0.$$

Subtracting the first-order condition for money from that for bonds for $s = 1$ gives

$$U_{m,t+1} = \lambda_{t+1} R_{t+1}.$$

Combining this with the first-order condition for consumption we obtain

$$U_{m,t+1} = U_{c,t+1} R_{t+1}. \tag{8.7}$$

---

[1] An alternative dating convention is sometimes used in which the household budget constraint is written as $\Delta B_{t+1} + \Delta M_t + P_t c_t = P_t x_t + R_t B_t$. In this alternative formulation money is accumulated over period $t - 1$ for use at the start of period t rather than being accumulated during period t for use in period $t + 1$.

The left-hand side measures the additional utility from holding an extra unit of real balances at the start of period $t + 1$. The right-hand side shows the cost of this: the loss of interest over period t through holding money instead of bonds, and hence the loss of consumption in period $t + 1$ evaluated at the marginal utility of period $t + 1$ consumption.

To illustrate what sort of money-demand function may emerge, consider a specific form for the utility function:

$$U(c_t, m_t) = \frac{c_t^{1-\sigma} - 1}{1 - \sigma} + \eta\left(\frac{m_t^{1-\sigma} - 1}{1 - \sigma}\right).$$

Equation (8.7) becomes

$$\eta m_{t+1}^{-\sigma} = c_{t+1}^{-\sigma} R_{t+1}.$$

The real demand for money is therefore

$$m_{t+1} = c_{t+1}\left(\frac{R_{t+1}}{\eta}\right)^{-1/\sigma}.$$

Thus an increase in the *nominal* interest rate reduces the demand for *real* money balances.

The nominal demand for money is

$$M_{t+1} = P_{t+1}c_{t+1}\left(\frac{R_{t+1}}{\eta}\right)^{-1/\sigma}. \tag{8.8}$$

This can be contrasted with the money-demand function in the CIA model, which is just $M_{t+1} = P_{t+1}c_{t+1}$. Thus an increase in the interest rate reduces the nominal demand for money. We note that if the bond is risk free, then R_{t+1} is known at time t. This implies that the risk-free rate at time t affects the quantity of money demanded at the start of period $t + 1$ in order to pay for period $t + 1$ consumption.

The first-order conditions for consumption and bonds give the same Euler equation as for the CIA model, namely equation (8.4). Consequently, apart from the dependence of money on the nominal interest rate, the long-run steady-state solutions for consumption and money demand are similar to those in the CIA model. For a suitable choice of scale factor, so that $(R_{t+1}/\eta)^{-1/\sigma} < 1$, real-money balances in the MIU model can be made less than in the CIA model. Economizing on real-money balances would then reduce the real cost of holding money relative to the CIA model.

Further intuition about these results may be obtained by considering first a small increase in money in period $t + 1$ of $\mathrm{d}m_{t+1}$ that leaves utility in period $t + 1$ unchanged. This implies that

$$\mathrm{d}U_{t+1} = U_{c,t+1}\,\mathrm{d}c_{t+1} + U_{m,t+1}\,\mathrm{d}m_{t+1} = 0,$$

and hence the gain in utility from holding extra money $U_{m,t+1}\,\mathrm{d}m_{t+1}$ equals the loss of utility from a lower level of consumption. This is equal to

$$\mathrm{d}c_{t+1} = -\frac{U_{m,t+1}}{U_{c,t+1}}\,\mathrm{d}m_{t+1}.$$

The two-period intertemporal budget constraint obtained from equation (8.1) is

$$(1 + \pi_{t+1})(1 + \pi_{t+2})(b_{t+2} + m_{t+2}) + (1 + \pi_{t+1})c_{t+1} + (1 + R_t)c_t$$
$$= (1 + \pi_{t+1})x_{t+1} + (1 + R_{t+1})x_t + (1 + R_t)(1 + R_{t+1})(b_t + m_t)$$
$$- (1 + \pi_{t+1})R_{t+1}m_{t+1} - (1 + R_{t+1})R_t m_t.$$

Partial differentiation of this while holding everything except c_{t+1} and m_{t+1} constant gives the change in c_{t+1}:

$$dc_{t+1} = -dm_{t+1}R_{t+1}.$$

Thus

$$U_{m,t+1} = U_{c,t+1}R_{t+1},$$

which is equation (8.7).

Now consider the effect of a small reduction in c_t of dc_t and a change in c_{t+1} and m_{t+1} that leaves V_t constant so that

$$dV_t = U_{c,t}\,dc_t + \beta(U_{c,t+1}\,dc_{t+1} + U_{m,t+1}\,dm_{t+1}) = 0,$$

or

$$-U_{c,t}\,dc_t = \beta(U_{c,t+1}\,dc_{t+1} + U_{m,t+1}\,dm_{t+1}). \tag{8.9}$$

The loss utility in period t must therefore be compensated by a gain in utility in period $t + 1$ from either additional consumption or money holding, or both. Partially differentiating the two-period intertemporal budget constraint gives

$$(1 + \pi_{t+1})\,dc_{t+1} + (1 + R_t)\,dc_t = -(1 + \pi_{t+1})R_{t+1}\,dm_{t+1};$$

hence

$$dc_{t+1} = -\frac{1 + R_t}{1 + \pi_{t+1}}\,dc_t - R_{t+1}\,dm_{t+1}, \tag{8.10}$$

implying that each unit reduction in consumption in period t raises consumption in period $t + 1$ by $1 + r_{t+1}$ minus the interest cost of having to increase money holdings in period $t + 1$. Substituting for dc_{t+1} in equation (8.9) gives

$$-U_{c,t}\,dc_t = -\beta\frac{1 + R_t}{1 + \pi_{t+1}}U_{c,t+1}\,dc_t + \beta(U_{m,t+1} - R_{t+1}U_{c,t+1})\,dm_{t+1}. \tag{8.11}$$

From equation (8.7) the last term is zero. What remains gives the usual Euler equation (8.4).

8.6 Money as an Intermediate Good or the Shopping-Time Model

Microeconomic theories of money explain its existence as a response to the high cost and inefficiency both of barter and of tying up scarce precious metals like gold and silver in transactions. The amount of money that is held for transactions purposes will depend on its convenience in saving time spent on shopping. According to this view, money is an intermediate good that is held to reduce shopping time. We consider a variant of the shopping-time model of money of Ljungqvist and Sargent (2004) that differs primarily in the timing convention used.

We assume that households allocate their total time (normalized to unity) between work n_t, leisure l_t, and shopping s_t to give the time constraint

$$n_t + l_t + s_t = 1.$$

And we suppose that the time spent shopping can be expressed as a function of consumption and real-money balances:

$$s_t = S(c_t, m_t), \tag{8.12}$$

where $S, S_c, S_{cc}, S_{mm} \geqslant 0$ and $S_m, S_{cm} \leqslant 0$.[2] Household utility is now obtained from consumption and leisure (not money), hence

$$U = U(c_t, l_t),$$

where $U_c, U_l, U_{cl} \geqslant 0$ and $U_{cc}, U_{ll} \leqslant 0$.

If we were to substitute s_t from equation (8.12) into the utility function, then we could write it as a derived utility function $V(c_t, n_t, m_t)$ given by

$$V(c_t, n_t, m_t) = U[c_t, 1 - n_t - S(c_t, m_t)].$$

This would provide a justification for the MIU model as a derived utility function. We could then express the household's problem as maximizing $\sum_{s=0}^{\infty} \beta^s V(c_{t+s}, n_{t+s}, m_{t+s})$ subject to the household budget constraint

$$(1 + \pi_{t+1})b_{t+1} + (1 + \pi_{t+1})m_{t+1} + c_t = w_t n_t + (1 + R_t)b_t + m_t.$$

Instead, to emphasize that utility is not directly dependent on money, we formulate the household's problem as maximizing $\sum_{s=0}^{\infty} \beta^s U(c_{t+s}, l_{t+s})$ subject to the household budget constraint and the time constraint. The Lagrangian is then

$$\begin{aligned}
\mathcal{L} = \sum_{s=0}^{\infty} \{ & \beta^s U(c_{t+s}, l_{t+s}) + \lambda_{t+s}[w_{t+s} n_{t+s} + (1 + R_{t+s})b_{t+s} + m_{t+s} \\
& - (1 + \pi_{t+s+1})(b_{t+s+1} + m_{t+s+1}) - c_{t+s}] \\
& + \mu_{t+s}[n_{t+s} + l_{t+s} + S(c_{t+s}, m_{t+s}) - 1] \}.
\end{aligned}$$

---

[2] Ljungqvist and Sargent define their shopping-time cost function with M_{t+1}/P_t replacing m_t. This implies that shopping time is reduced through accumulating money balances in period t. We assume that shopping time is reduced by holding real balances which were accumulated in the previous period.

The first-order conditions are

$$\frac{\partial \mathcal{L}}{\partial c_{t+s}} = \beta^s U_{c,t+s} - \lambda_{t+s} + \mu_{t+s} S_{c,t+s} = 0, \qquad s \geqslant 0,$$

$$\frac{\partial \mathcal{L}}{\partial l_{t+s}} = \beta^s U_{l,t+s} + \mu_{t+s} = 0, \qquad s \geqslant 0,$$

$$\frac{\partial \mathcal{L}}{\partial n_{t+s}} = \lambda_{t+s} w_{t+s} + \mu_{t+s} = 0, \qquad s \geqslant 0,$$

$$\frac{\partial \mathcal{L}}{\partial b_{t+s}} = \lambda_{t+s}(1 + R_{t+s}) - \lambda_{t+s-1}(1 + \pi_{t+s}) = 0, \qquad s > 0,$$

$$\frac{\partial \mathcal{L}}{\partial m_{t+s}} = \lambda_{t+s} - \lambda_{t+s-1}(1 + \pi_{t+s}) + \mu_{t+s} S_{m,t+s} = 0, \quad s > 0.$$

It follows from the first-order conditions for bonds and money that

$$\lambda_{t+s} R_{t+s} = \mu_{t+s} S_{m,t+s}.$$

Combining this with the first-order conditions for consumption and leisure gives, for $s = 1$,

$$-U_{l,t+1} S_{m,t+1} = (U_{c,t+1} - U_{l,t+1} S_{c,t+1}) R_{t+1}. \tag{8.13}$$

$S_{m,t+1}$ measures the saving in shopping time from holding one additional unit of real money. Each unit of time saved provides $U_{l,t+1}$ in extra utility. Thus the left-hand side measures the extra utility from holding one more unit of real-money balances. Each unit of real-money balances that is held costs R_{t+1} in foregone interest and $U_{c,t+1} R_{t+1}$ units of lost utility from having to reduce consumption. However, the lost consumption also saves on shopping time, which adds to utility. The right-hand side therefore measures the net loss of utility from holding one more unit of real-money balances.

Solving equation (8.13) for m_{t+1} gives the demand for real-money balances. In general, due to the functional form of the shopping cost function, this will only give an implicit demand for money, which may be written as

$$m(m_{t+1}, c_{t+1}, l_{t+1}, R_{t+1}) = 0.$$

An example that illustrates an explicit solution is the case where the utility function has the log-linear form

$$U(c_t, l_t) = \ln c_t + \eta \ln l_t$$

and the shopping cost function is

$$s_t = \psi \frac{c_t}{m_t}.$$

In this case,

$$\psi \eta \frac{s_{t+1}}{l_{t+1} m_{t+1}} = \left(\frac{1}{c_{t+1}} - \psi \eta \frac{s_{t+1}}{l_{t+1} c_{t+1}} \right) R_{t+1}.$$

Hence the demand for real-money balances is given by

$$m_{t+1} = c_{t+1} \left[\frac{\psi \eta (s_{t+1}/l_{t+1})}{1 - \psi \eta (s_{t+1}/l_{t+1})} \right] R_{t+1}^{-1}. \tag{8.14}$$

This example has been constructed so that it is easy to compare with the previous money-demand functions. Once again we have a transactions demand and a negative interest rate effect. The additional feature is the dependence of money demand on the ratio of shopping to leisure time. As $\partial m_{t+1}/\partial (s_{t+1}/l_{t+1}) > 0$, an increase in shopping time relative to leisure time raises the demand for money, thereby reducing the cost of shopping. We also note that, compared with the CIA and MIU models, the need to use time for shopping will result in less time for leisure and, probably, work. The latter would mean less income and hence less consumption. In recent years we have observed an increase in online shopping, which has required a greater use of debit and credit cards instead of money. Online shopping reduces both the time spent shopping and the demand for cash in hand. At the same time, it is also highly likely that the holding of broad money will increase due to the increase in credit-card debt. For further discussion of money demand see Walsh (2005, chapters 2 and 3).

8.7 Transactions Costs

So far we have sought to explain the holding of money by arguing either that it is required in order to make transactions, or that it provides utility directly, or that it does so indirectly by increasing leisure by economizing on shopping time. We now assume that there is a real resource cost to making consumption transactions and that using money may be able to reduce this. This idea is associated with Brock (1974, 1990). We consider the formulation of the problem by Feenstra (1986), who showed that various different ways of taking account of transactions costs can be captured by the addition to the household budget constraint of a term representing these costs.

We therefore rewrite the household's real budget constraint, equation (8.2), as

$$(1 + \pi_{t+1})b_{t+1} - b_t + (1 + \pi_{t+1})m_{t+1} - m_t + c_t + T(c_t, m_t) = x_t + R_t b_t, \quad (8.15)$$

where $T(c_t, m_t)$ is the real resource cost of consumption transactions, $T \geqslant 0$, $T(0, m) = 0$, $T_c, T_{cc}, T_{mm} \geqslant 0$, $T_m, T_{mc} \leqslant 0$, and $c + T(c, m)$ is quasi-concave. These assumptions imply that transactions costs increase at an increasing rate as consumption rises, but fall, though at a diminishing rate, as money increases.

The household's problem is to maximize $\sum_{s=0}^{\infty} \beta^s U(c_{t+s})$ with respect to $\{c_{t+s}, b_{t+s+1}, m_{t+s+1}; s \geqslant 0\}$ subject to its budget constraint, equation (8.15). The Lagrangian is

$$\mathcal{L} = \sum_{s=0}^{\infty} \{\beta^s U(c_{t+s}) + \lambda_{t+s}[x_{t+s} + (1 + R_{t+s})b_{t+s} + m_{t+s} - (1 + \pi_{t+s+1})(b_{t+s+1} + m_{t+s+1}) - c_{t+s} - T(c_{t+s}, m_{t+s})]\}.$$

The first-order conditions are

$$\frac{\partial \mathcal{L}}{\partial c_{t+s}} = \beta^s U'(c_{t+s}) - \lambda_{t+s}(1 + T_{c,t+s}) = 0, \qquad s \geqslant 0,$$

$$\frac{\partial \mathcal{L}}{\partial b_{t+s}} = \lambda_{t+s}(1 + R_{t+s}) - \lambda_{t+s-1}(1 + \pi_{t+s}) = 0, \qquad s > 0,$$

$$\frac{\partial \mathcal{L}}{\partial m_{t+s}} = \lambda_{t+s}(1 - T_{m,t+s}) - \lambda_{t+s-1}(1 + \pi_{t+s}) = 0, \quad s > 0.$$

As

$$\frac{\lambda_{t+s+1}}{\lambda_{t+s}} = \frac{1 + \pi_{t+s+1}}{1 + R_{t+s+1}},$$

the Euler equation for period $t + 1$ is

$$\frac{\beta U'(c_{t+1})}{U'(c_t)} \frac{1 + T_{c,t}}{1 + T_{c,t+1}} (1 + r_{t+1}) = 1, \tag{8.16}$$

and

$$T_{m,t+1} = -R_{t+1}. \tag{8.17}$$

In steady state, when $\Delta c_t = \Delta m_t = 0$, we obtain $r_t = \theta$ once more. The steady-state solutions for consumption and money balances are obtained from equation (8.17) and the long-run household budget constraint. Assuming that in the long run $c_t = c$, $m_t = m$, $b_t = b$, $R_t = R$, $\pi_t = \pi$, and $r_t = r$, the long-run household constraint and equation (8.17) become

$$c + \pi m + T(c, m) = x + (1 + \theta)b, \tag{8.18}$$

$$T_m(c, m) = -R, \tag{8.19}$$

which are two nonlinear equations in c and m. Closed-form solutions cannot therefore be obtained.

We consider the effects on the long-run solutions of changes in x, b, and R, where we take all of them as given. Since

$$\begin{bmatrix} T_c + 1 & T_m + \pi \\ T_{mc} & T_{mm} \end{bmatrix} \begin{bmatrix} dc \\ dm \end{bmatrix} = \begin{bmatrix} 1 & 1 + \theta & 0 \\ 0 & 0 & -1 \end{bmatrix} \begin{bmatrix} dx \\ db \\ dR \end{bmatrix},$$

we have

$$\begin{bmatrix} dc \\ dm \end{bmatrix} = \frac{1}{\Delta} \begin{bmatrix} T_{mm} & (1 + \theta)T_{mm} & T_m + \pi \\ -T_{mc} & -(1 + \theta)T_{mc} & -(T_c + 1) \end{bmatrix} \begin{bmatrix} dx \\ db \\ dR \end{bmatrix},$$

where $\Delta = T_{mm}(T_c + 1) - T_{mc}(T_m + \pi)$. Assuming that $\Delta > 0$, and that partial derivatives of $T(c, m)$ are nonzero, the signs of the derivatives are given by

$$\begin{bmatrix} dc \\ dm \end{bmatrix} = \begin{bmatrix} + & + & \pm \\ + & + & - \end{bmatrix} \begin{bmatrix} dx \\ db \\ dR \end{bmatrix}.$$

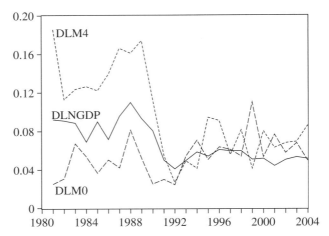

Figure 8.1. Growth rates of nominal GDP, M0, and M4
in the United Kingdom, 1980–2004.

Thus, in the long run, the demand for money increases due to a rise in x and b and a fall in R, as in the MIU and MIG models. We also note that for x, b, and R given, from equation (8.19), $\partial m / \partial c > 0$, implying that higher consumption requires larger real-money holdings.

Since, from equation (8.18), $\partial m / \partial c = -(T_c + 1)/(T_m + \pi)$ and this must be positive, we conclude that $T_m + \pi < 0$, which confirms our assumption that $\Delta > 0$ and shows that $dc/dR < 0$. Hence, the direction of the responses of consumption to increases in x, b, and R are the same as those of money holdings.

8.8 Some Empirical Evidence

What does the evidence reveal about the relation between money and nominal expenditures? Figures 8.1 and 8.2 are based on U.K. data from 1980 to 2004. Figure 8.3 is based on U.S. data from 1959 to 2006. M0 is essentially the money base (outside money that appears in the government budget constraint and consists largely of notes and coins) and M4 is a broad measure of money that includes inside money (money provided by the banking system) and outside money. Currency is notes and coins and M3 is a measure of broad money.

Figure 8.1 shows the rates of growth of nominal GDP, M0, and M4 for the United Kingdom. It shows that there is no close link in the short run between money and expenditures. Figures 8.2 and 8.3 show the velocities of circulation of narrow and broad money for the United Kingdom and the United States. The definition of velocity V_t is derived from the "quantity theory of money":

$$M_t V_t = P_t y_t.$$

Hence V_t is the value required for the quantity theory to hold. It can be interpreted as measuring the number of times each period that a unit of money is

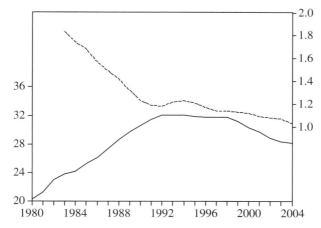

Figure 8.2.   M0 (solid line) and M4 (dashed line)
velocities in the United Kingdom, 1980–2004.

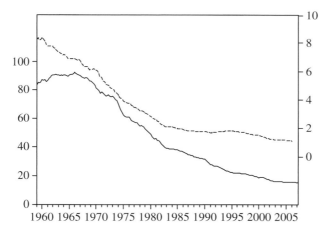

Figure 8.3.   Currency (solid line) and M3 (dashed line)
velocities in the United Kingdom, 1980–2004.

exchanged in transactions. Each type of money will have its own velocity. The
MIU and MIG money-demand functions imply that velocity is a function of the
nominal interest rate.

Figure 8.2 shows that cash or narrow money has behaved very differently
from broad money for the United Kingdom. Whereas M0 (left-hand scale)
increased more slowly than nominal expenditures in the 1980s, M4 (right-hand
scale) has grown faster over the whole period. Figure 8.3, for the United States,
shows that both the currency velocity (left-hand scale) and the M3 velocity
(right-hand scale) have fallen since 1966. The U.K. data show a move away
from using cash for purchases to using credit cards instead. An additional
factor in the growth of M4 is an increase in the use of interest-bearing time
deposits for savings. This evidence offers support for distinguishing between

the demand for transactions balances and for credit when considering the demand for "money." In contrast, the U.S. data show that both currency and broad money have grown faster than nominal expenditures. The growth of broad money supports the argument that credit is increasingly important, but the even faster growth of currency shows the continued importance of cash in the U.S. economy.

8.9 Hyperinflation and Cagan's Money-Demand Model

In a situation of hyperinflation the demand for nominal money simplifies considerably. Real variables have hardly any influence on nominal variables due to their very different rates of growth. Consider the nominal money-demand function

$$M_t = P_t c_t R_t^{-\alpha}$$
$$= P_t c_t (r_t + \pi_{t+1})^{-\alpha}.$$

If consumption and the real interest rate change little, then this can be approximated by

$$M_t = \phi P_t \pi_{t+1}^{-\alpha}, \quad \alpha > 0. \tag{8.20}$$

Cagan (1956) proposed a variant of equation (8.20) in which the logarithm of real-money balances depends only on expected future inflation:

$$\ln M_t - p_t = -\alpha (E_t p_{t+1} - p_t), \tag{8.21}$$

where $p_t = \ln P_t$ and $E_t p_{t+1}$ is the conditional expectation of p_{t+1} given information available at time t, and, for convenience, we ignore the intercept. If the money supply is exogenously determined, then, using successive substitution, p_t is obtained by rewriting (8.21) as

$$p_t = \frac{\alpha}{1+\alpha} E_t p_{t+1} + \frac{1}{1+\alpha} \ln M_t$$
$$= \frac{1}{1+\alpha} \sum_{s=0}^{\infty} \left(\frac{\alpha}{1+\alpha} \right)^s E_t \ln M_{t+s}, \tag{8.22}$$

where it is assumed that

$$\lim_{n \to \infty} \left(\frac{\alpha}{1+\alpha} \right)^n E_t p_{t+n} = 0.$$

If, for example, the money supply grows at the constant rate μ, then

$$\Delta \ln M_t = \mu + \varepsilon_t,$$

where $E_t \varepsilon_{t+1} = 0$. It can then be shown that

$$\ln M_{t+s} = \ln M_t + \mu s + \sum_{i=1}^{s} \varepsilon_{t+i}$$

and hence

$$E_t \ln M_{t+s} = \ln M_t + \mu s.$$

Substituting this into equation (8.22) and simplifying gives

$$p_t = \ln M_t + \alpha\mu.$$

Taking first differences shows that the expected inflation rate equals the rate of growth of money:

$$E_t \pi_{t+1} = E_t \ln M_{t+1} - \ln M_t = \mu.$$

In a period of hyperinflation the astronomical rate of inflation requires a correspondingly high rate of growth of the money supply. For example, during the period of German hyperinflation, between January 1922 and October 1923, the price level grew by a factor of 192 billion and currency grew by 20.2 billion. The inflation rate in October 1923 was 29,720% per month. We have also seen hyperinflation more recently: as previously noted, in the late 1980s to early 1990s in ex-Soviet Union countries, in some South American countries in the mid 1990s, and more recently in Zimbabwe. Within three or four years these countries (Zimbabwe excepted, at the time of writing) were able to reduce inflation to low double-digit numbers at worst.

As explained in chapter 5, in each case the reason for hyperinflation was the failure of tax revenues to meet government expenditures. The ex-Soviet Union countries inherited an inadequate tax base from income and consumption. Until these taxes could be gathered, and in the absence of large-scale borrowing facilities from abroad, they were forced to use seigniorage taxation. In other words, the governments simply printed money to pay for their expenditures. The reader will be able to determine the outcome in Zimbabwe.

To illustrate the order of magnitude of the inflation rate that is required to finance government expenditures, suppose that government expenditures are a proportion α of GDP, tax revenues are sufficient to meet a proportion β of government expenditures, and the money stock is a proportion y of private expenditures. From the government budget constraint seigniorage revenues as a proportion of GDP must satisfy

$$\pi\frac{m}{y} = \frac{g - T}{y}, \tag{8.23}$$

where y is real GDP, g is real government expenditures, and T is real taxes. Solving for the inflation rate we obtain

$$\pi = \frac{(g/y)((g - T)/g)}{(m/c)(c/y)}$$

$$= \frac{\alpha(1 - \beta)}{y(1 - \alpha)},$$

where $\alpha = g/y$, $\beta = T/g$, $y = m/c$, and $y = c + g$. If, for example, $\alpha = 0.5$, $\beta = 0.5$, and $y = 0.1$, then $\pi \equiv 500\%$. In a country where government is more dominant and spends more of GDP so that $\alpha = 0.75$ and the gap between government expenditures and tax revenues is much larger, for example $\beta = 0.2$, the required rate of inflation is $\pi \equiv 2400\%$, a number not dissimilar to the inflation rates experienced by some ex-Soviet countries.

8.10 The Optimal Rate of Inflation

In principle, in the longer term, the rate of inflation for an economy is a matter of government choice. If governments choose the rate of growth of the money supply, then this will result in the long run in a corresponding rate of inflation. Alternatively, if governments choose the rate of inflation, then in the long run this will also be the rate of growth of the money supply. Another option is available in an open economy as domestic inflation can be tied to the rate of inflation of another country by keeping the nominal exchange rate with that country fixed. In practice, there may be considerable difficulties in achieving such objectives through monetary policy. This is particularly true in the short run, but far less so in the long run. We discuss these issues in more detail in chapters 12 and 13. For the moment we assume that inflation is a choice variable for government and we consider what the optimal rate of inflation would be. We assume that the government budget constraint can be satisfied without having to resort to seigniorage taxation and high rates of inflation. First, we consider the Friedman rule, in which the government chooses an optimal nominal interest rate. We then consider whether the Friedman rule is optimal, and what this implies for the optimal rate of inflation.

8.10.1 The Friedman Rule

Friedman (1969) proposed the following (full-liquidity) rule (see also Bailey 1956). Noting that the marginal private return to holding non-interest-bearing money equals $-\pi$ (total cost equals πm), while the marginal social cost of producing money is virtually zero, Friedman proposed eliminating the private cost of holding money by setting $-\pi = \theta$, the rate of time preference, which in our general equilibrium model is also the long-run real interest rate r. Given that r is nonnegative, this implies that the optimal rate of inflation, and hence the optimal rate of growth of nominal money, would be nonpositive. It follows that the Friedman rule gives a nominal interest rate of $R = r + \pi = 0$, i.e., the opportunity cost of holding nominal balances is zero. In this case, U_m, the marginal utility of money, would also be zero. For this to happen, real-money holdings would have to reach saturation level. We also note that a nonpositive inflation rate implies a real yield on money that would be nonnegative and equal to the return on other assets, including bonds.

  A problem with this solution, as pointed out by Phelps (1973), is that it ignores the government budget constraint and the welfare benefits received by households arising from the fact that seigniorage taxation allows other taxes to be cut.

A full solution to the optimal rate of inflation requires choosing π subject to the optimizing decisions of households and the government budget constraint. In effect, therefore, π is treated as one more tax rate, implying that choosing the optimal rate of inflation is another problem in optimal taxation.

8.10.2 General Equilibrium Solution

8.10.2.1 The Household's Problem

Unlike our previous analysis of optimal taxation, our new model includes money in the household utility function, and it includes inflation by allowing the general price level to change. We assume that the household utility function is $U(c_t, l_t, m_t)$, where c_t is consumption, n_t is employment, l_t is leisure ($n_t + l_t = 1$), and m_t is real-money balances. The exact form of the utility function is considered below. At this stage we simply assume that $U_c, U_l, U_m > 0$ and that $U_{cc}, U_{ll}, U_{mm} \leqslant 0$. Households are assumed to maximize $\sum_{s=0}^{\infty} \beta^s U(c_{t+s}, l_{t+s}, m_{t+s})$ with respect to $\{c_{t+s}, l_{t+s}, n_{t+s}, k_{t+s+1}, b_{t+s+1}, m_{t+s+1}; s \geqslant 0\}$ subject to the real budget constraint

$$
\begin{aligned}
c_t + k_{t+1} &+ (1 + \pi_{t+1})(k_{t+1} + b_{t+1} + m_{t+1}) \\
&= (1 - \tau_t) w_t n_t + (1 + R_t^k) k_t + (1 + R_t^b) b_t + m_t,
\end{aligned}
$$

where k_t is equity, b_t is government debt, w_t is the average real-wage rate, R_t^k is the nominal rate of return on equity capital, and R_t^b is the nominal rate of return on government debt. There are two taxes: labor taxes τ_t and seigniorage taxation $\pi_{t+1} m_t$.

The Lagrangian for this problem can be written as

$$
\begin{aligned}
\mathcal{L} = \sum_{s=0}^{\infty} \{ &\beta^s U(c_{t+s}, l_{t+s}, m_{t+s}) \\
&+ \lambda_{t+s}[(1 - \tau_{t+s}) w_{t+s} n_{t+s} + (1 + R_{t+s}^k) k_{t+s} + (1 + R_{t+s}^b) b_{t+s} \\
&+ m_{t+s} - c_{t+s} - (1 + \pi_{t+s+1})(k_{t+s+1} + b_{t+s+1} + m_{t+s+1})]\}.
\end{aligned}
$$

The first-order conditions are

$$
\frac{\partial \mathcal{L}}{\partial c_{t+s}} = \beta^s U_{c,t+s} - \lambda_{t+s} = 0, \qquad\qquad s \geqslant 0,
$$

$$
\frac{\partial \mathcal{L}}{\partial n_{t+s}} = -\beta^s U_{l,t+s} + \lambda_{t+s}(1 - \tau_{t+s}) w_{t+s} = 0, \qquad s \geqslant 0,
$$

$$
\frac{\partial \mathcal{L}}{\partial k_{t+s}} = \lambda_{t+s}(1 + R_{t+s}^k) - \lambda_{t+s-1}(1 + \pi_{t+s+1}) = 0, \quad s > 0,
$$

$$
\frac{\partial \mathcal{L}}{\partial b_{t+s}} = \lambda_{t+s}(1 + R_{t+s}^b) - \lambda_{t+s-1}(1 + \pi_{t+s+1}) = 0, \quad s > 0,
$$

$$
\frac{\partial \mathcal{L}}{\partial m_{t+s}} = \beta^s U_{m,t+s} + \lambda_{t+s} - \lambda_{t+s-1}(1 + \pi_{t+s+1}) = 0, \quad s > 0.
$$

From the first-order conditions for consumption and leisure we obtain

$$\frac{U_{l,t}}{U_{c,t}} = (1 - \tau_t)w_t. \tag{8.24}$$

Labor taxes therefore drive a wedge between the ratio of the marginal utilities and the wage rate. From the first-order conditions for capital and bonds we can show that

$$\frac{\lambda_{t+s-1}}{\lambda_{t+s}} = \frac{1 + R^k_{t+s}}{1 + \pi_{t+s+1}} = 1 + r^k_{t+s} \tag{8.25}$$

$$= \frac{1 + R^b_{t+s}}{1 + \pi_{t+s+1}} = 1 + r^b_{t+s}, \tag{8.26}$$

implying that the real rates of return on capital and bonds satisfy

$$r^k_{t+s} = r^b_{t+s}, \quad s > 0. \tag{8.27}$$

The Euler equation can be obtained from the first-order conditions for consumption and capital as

$$\frac{\beta U_{c,t+1}}{U_{c,t}}(1 + r^k_{t+1}) = 1.$$

Hence, in the long run, $\beta(1 + r^k) = 1$ or $r^k = \theta = r^b$.

From the first-order conditions for consumption, bonds, and money,

$$\frac{U_{m,t+s}}{U_{c,t+s}} = R^b_{t+s}, \quad s > 0. \tag{8.28}$$

If the Friedman rule holds, then $R^b_{t+s} = 0$. This requires that $U_{m,t+s} = 0$; in other words, sufficient money must be held to drive its marginal utility to zero.

As nominal rates are zero in the Friedman rule, real rates must satisfy $r^k = \theta = r^b = -\pi$. And since the real rates of return are nonnegative, inflation must therefore be nonpositive. The next issue is whether the Friedman rule is optimal.

8.10.2.2   *The Optimality of the Friedman Rule*

The government is assumed to maximize household utility subject to the economy's resource constraint and to the optimality conditions of households as expressed through the following implementability condition. This implementability condition is akin to that derived in the analysis of tax policy in chapter 5. Substituting the rates of return for capital and bonds into the household budget constraint, and using the first-order condition for bonds, we obtain

$$c_{t+s} + (1 + \pi_{t+s+1})(k_{t+s+1} + b_{t+s+1} + m_{t+s+1})$$

$$= (1 - \tau_{t+s})w_{t+s}n_{t+s} - (1 + R^b_{t+s})m_{t+s} + (1 + \pi_{t+s+1})\frac{\lambda_{t+s-1}}{\lambda_{t+s}}(k_{t+s} + b_{t+s} + m_{t+s}).$$

Provided the transversality conditions

$$\lim_{n \to \infty} \lambda_{t+n} k_{t+n+1} = 0,$$

$$\lim_{n \to \infty} \lambda_{t+n} b_{t+n+1} = 0,$$

$$\lim_{n \to \infty} \lambda_{t+n} m_{t+n+1} = 0$$

hold, the household budget constraint can be solved forwards to give the intertemporal household budget constraint

$$\lambda_{t-1}(k_t + b_t + m_t) = \sum_{s=0}^{\infty} \lambda_{t+s}[c_{t+s} - (1 - \tau_{t+s})w_{t+s}n_{t+s} + (1 + R_{t+s}^b)m_{t+s}].$$

Using the first-order conditions for consumption, work, and money, the intertemporal budget constraint can be rewritten as the implementability condition

$$\lambda_{t-1}(k_t + b_t + m_t) = \sum_{s=0}^{\infty} \beta^s (U_{c,t+s}c_{t+s} - U_{l,t+s}n_{t+s} + U_{m,t+s}m_{t+s}), \qquad (8.29)$$

where the left-hand side is predetermined at time t.

The government budget constraint is

$$g_t + (1 + R_t^b)b_t + m_t = \tau_t w_t n_t + (1 + \pi_{t+1})(b_{t+1} + m_{t+1}).$$

The economy's usual resource constraint can be derived from the household and government budget constraints as

$$F(k_t, n_t) = c_t - k_{t+1} + (1 - \delta)k_t - g_t.$$

If we assume that the production function has constant returns to scale (and hence is homogeneous of degree one) and that factors are paid their marginal products, then $F_{k,t} - \delta = r_t^k$ and $F_{n,t} = w_t$. Hence,

$$F(k_t, n_t) = F_{k,t}k_t + F_{n,t}n_t$$
$$= (r_t^k + \delta)k_t + w_t n_t.$$

The resource constraint can therefore be written as

$$r_t^k k_t + w_t n_t = c_t + k_{t+1} - k_t + g_t.$$

The government's problem can now be formulated as that of maximizing the intertemporal utility of households subject to the implementability condition and the economy's resource constraint. The Lagrangian for this problem can be written as

$$\mathcal{L} = \sum_{s=0}^{\infty} \{\beta^s U(c_{t+s}, l_{t+s}, m_{t+s})$$
$$+ \phi_{t+s}[r_{t+s}^k k_{t+s} + w_{t+s}n_{t+s} - c_{t+s} - k_{t+s+1} + k_{t+s} - g_{t+s}]\}$$
$$+ \mu \left[\sum_{s=0}^{\infty} \beta^s (U_{c,t+s}c_{t+s}U_{l,t+s}n_{t+s} + U_{m,t+s}m_{t+s}) - \lambda_{t-1}(k_t + b_t + m_t)\right].$$

Or, defining

$$V(c_{t+s}, n_{t+s}, m_{t+s}, \mu)$$
$$= U(c_{t+s}, l_{t+s}, m_{t+s}) + \mu(U_{c,t+s}c_{t+s} - U_{l,t+s}n_{t+s} + U_{m,t+s}m_{t+s}),$$

the Lagrangian becomes

$$\mathcal{L} = \sum_{s=0}^{\infty} \{\beta^s V(c_{t+s}, n_{t+s}, m_{t+s}, \mu)$$
$$+ \phi_{t+s}[r_{t+s}^k k_{t+s} + w_{t+s}n_{t+s} - c_{t+s} - k_{t+s+1} + k_{t+s} - g_{t+s}]\} - \mu\lambda_{t-1}(k_t + b_t).$$

The first-order conditions for consumption, labor, and capital are

$$\frac{\partial \mathcal{L}}{\partial c_{t+s}} = \beta^s V_{c,t+s} - \phi_{t+s} = 0, \qquad\qquad s \geqslant 0,$$

$$\frac{\partial \mathcal{L}}{\partial n_{t+s}} = \beta^s V_{n,t+s} + \phi_{t+s}w_{t+s} = 0, \qquad s \geqslant 0,$$

$$\frac{\partial \mathcal{L}}{\partial k_{t+s}} = \phi_{t+s}(1 + r_{t+s}^k) - \phi_{t+s-1} = 0, \quad s > 0,$$

$$\frac{\partial \mathcal{L}}{\partial m_{t+s}} = \beta^s V_{m,t+s} = 0, \qquad\qquad\qquad s > 0.$$

The first three conditions are the same as before and lead to similar solutions. We therefore focus on the implications for money. The last condition implies that

$$V_{m,t+s} = (1 + \mu)U_{m,t+s} + \mu(U_{cm,t+s}c_{t+s} - U_{lm,t+s}n_{t+s} + U_{mm,t+s}m_{t+s}) = 0.$$

The form of the utility function therefore determines the solution. Consider the separable utility function

$$U(c, l, m) = \frac{c^{1-\sigma}}{1 - \sigma} + \eta\frac{m^{1-\phi}}{1 - \phi} + z(l).$$

The first-order condition for money then becomes

$$\eta(1 + \mu - \mu\phi)m_{t+s}^{-\phi} = 0.$$

Hence, unless by chance $1 + \mu - \mu\phi = 0$ or $\eta = 0$, for $\phi > 0$ it is necessary that $m_{t+s} \to \infty$. But the solution to the household's problem, equation (8.28), gives $U_{m,t+s}/U_{c,t+s} = R_{t+s}^b$, and so if $m_{t+s} \to \infty$, then $U_{m,t+s} \to 0$. But this can only happen if $R_{t+s}^b \to 0$. Thus the Friedman rule would be the optimal policy.

This result may also hold for more general utility functions that are not separable. The key property that the utility function must possess is that it can be written in the form

$$U(c, l, m) = Z[u(c, m), l],$$

where $u(c, m)$ is a homothetic function so that $u_c = u_m$ (see Chari et al. 1994). The Friedman rule can also be shown to be optimal when money is an intermediate good, as in the shopping-time model (see Correia and Teles 1996; Chari et al. 1994; and also Chari et al. 1996).

These results have been challenged by Mulligan and Sala-i-Martin (1997). They argue that the optimality of the Friedman rule depends on taxes not being paid with money, and on the particular assumptions made about the utility function or shopping-time technologies. In particular, they show that optimality depends on there being no economies of scale to holding money, as there could be in the shopping-time model. Given its dependence on the form of preferences and technologies, the conditions required to produce the Friedman rule may therefore seem rather contrived.

The optimality of the Friedman rule also depends on the absence of market imperfections. A negative inflation rate implies that prices must be flexible downward, whereas, in fact, they are well-known to be sticky, particularly downward. As a result, the deflation of prices is likely to have real costs, which would make it an unviable economic policy in practice. Politically, it would almost certainly be rejected. Hence, in practice, monetary policy is not conducted in accordance with the Friedman rule in any country, and inflation and nominal money growth are almost always positive, not negative.

8.11 The Super-Neutrality of Money

The classical dichotomy in macroeconomics is that nominal shocks have no long-run effect on real variables (see Patinkin 1965; Modigliani 1963; Lucas 1980b; Walsh 2005). When these nominal shocks are money shocks this is known as the super-neutrality of money. It implies that proportional changes in nominal money balances, and hence inflation, have no effect on the real variables in the economy such as consumption, output, and capital. From our results on the household demand for money and the presence of nominal money in the household budget constraint, it seems that the existence of nominal money holdings imposes a real cost on the economy, and hence money is not super-neutral. The problem with this interpretation is that it is based solely on the decisions of households. These provide only a partial, and not a general, equilibrium model of the whole economy. To examine the super-neutrality of money we therefore need to consider a complete model of the economy.

The household budget constraint shows that when inflation is positive, holding money causes a decline in household financial wealth and this imposes a real cost on households. Economizing on money balances by taking account of the loss of interest reduces this loss, but does not eliminate it. Moving from the partial view of the economy given by the household sector to a complete view requires that all sectors of the economy are taken into account. In particular, since seigniorage revenues accrue to government, and a government must also satisfy its budget constraint, there must be matching effects on government expenditures or tax revenues.

Consider an economy in which all money is provided by the government, where seigniorage revenues are returned to households in the form of transfers, and where households take such transfers as given when deciding money holdings. The household budget constraint can be written as

$$(1 + \pi_{t+1})(k_{t+1} + m_{t+1}) + c_t + T_t = w_t n_t + m_t + (1 + R_t)k_t, \qquad (8.30)$$

where $T_t < 0$ implies a transfer to households. From the government budget constraint tax revenues are

$$T_t = m_t - (1 + \pi_{t+1})m_{t+1}. \qquad (8.31)$$

Combining the household and government budget constraints gives the consolidated constraint

$$(1 + \pi_{t+1})k_{t+1} + c_t = w_t n_t + (1 + R_t)k_t,$$

in which real-money balances no longer appear.

If the production function is homogeneous of degree one and factors are paid their marginal products so that $F_{k,t} - \delta = r_t$ and $F_{n,t} = w_t$, then the production function will satisfy

$$F(k_t, n_t) = F_{k,t}k_t + F_{n,t}n_t$$
$$= (r_t + \delta)k_t + w_t n_t. \qquad (8.32)$$

If households have a utility function with real-money balances as an argument (for example, an MIU function) and they maximize $\sum_{s=0}^{\infty} \beta^s U(c_{t+s}, l_{t+s}, m_{t+s})$ subject to the household budget constraint and $n_t + l_t = 1$, then the Lagrangian for a centralized economy is

$$\mathcal{L} = \sum_{s=0}^{\infty} \{\beta^s U(c_{t+s}, l_{t+s}, m_{t+s}) + \lambda_{t+s}[w_{t+s}n_{t+s} + m_{t+s} + (1 + R_{t+s})k_{t+s}$$
$$- (1 + \pi_{t+s+1})(k_{t+s+1} + m_{t+s+1}) - c_{t+s} - T_{t+s}]\}.$$

The first-order conditions are therefore

$$\frac{\partial \mathcal{L}}{\partial c_{t+s}} = \beta^s U_{c,t+s} - \lambda_{t+s} = 0,$$

$$\frac{\partial \mathcal{L}}{\partial n_{t+s}} = -\beta^s U_{l,t+s} + \lambda_{t+s}w_{t+s} = 0,$$

$$\frac{\partial \mathcal{L}}{\partial k_{t+s}} = \lambda_{t+s}(1 + R_{t+s}) - \lambda_{t+s-1}(1 + \pi_{t+s+1}) = 0,$$

$$\frac{\partial \mathcal{L}}{\partial m_{t+s}} = \beta^s U_{m,t+s} + \lambda_{t+s} - \lambda_{t+s-1}(1 + \pi_{t+s+1}) = 0.$$

We note that since the real rate of return is $1 + r_{t+s} = (1 + R_{t+s})/(1 + \pi_{t+s+1})$, the first three conditions are identical to those obtained in the basic model without money.

We now examine the long-run solution. From the consumption Euler equation,

$$\frac{\beta U_{c,t+1}}{U_{c,t}}(1 + r_{t+s}) = 1.$$

In the long run we obtain $r = \theta$ and $U_m/U_c = R$. The long-run level of consumption can be obtained from the consolidated constraint and is given by

$$c = rk + wn.$$

Consequently, steady-state consumption is not affected by the level of real-money holdings. Nor will the long-run levels of capital and labor be affected either. As a result, if the government returns seigniorage revenues to households through transfers, then the economy becomes super-neutral with respect to money.

If the idea of government transferring seigniorage revenues back to households seems implausible, consider an alternative in which the government first determines its expenditures and then finances them with a mixture of lump-sum taxes and seigniorage. The government budget constraint can then be written as

$$(1 + \pi_{t+1})m_{t+1} + T_t = g_t + m_t. \tag{8.33}$$

The household budget stays as before but now with $T_t \gtrless 0$ depending on whether the government is giving money to households in lump-sum transfers ($T < 0$) or taking it from them in lump-sum taxes ($T > 0$). The problem for the household therefore remains unchanged and so the solution is the same.

The steady-state level of consumption is obtained from equations (8.30), (8.32), and (8.33) and is given by

$$c = wn + rk - g.$$

Thus, once more, the level of consumption does not depend on the quantity of real money. In steady state the government budget constraint is

$$g = T + \pi m,$$

implying, other things being equal, that the government is indifferent between tax and seigniorage finance. And if $g = 0$ then we revert to the previous formulation. More seigniorage taxation therefore requires less lump-sum taxation and leaves household after-tax income unaffected by the choice. For any given real-money-demand function, the choice between seigniorage and lump-sum taxation may be resolved by predetermining the optimal rate of inflation.

8.12 Conclusions

We have shown how to reformulate the real closed economy to take account of nominal magnitudes. This involves the introduction of money and the general price level. In a brief review of the history of money we noted some of the difficulties that economists have had in providing reasons why money should exist and how to measure it. The irony is that increasingly the need for such an explanation is diminishing as the use of credit in some form is replacing cash holdings, and money is becoming a vehicle for savings.

Historically, the effectiveness of monetary policy has depended on the existence of a stable demand function for money. We have considered three main alternative theories of money holding: the CIA model, the MIU (Sidrauski) model, and the MIG (shopping-time) model. In the first model the demand for money is solely for transactions purposes. In the other two theories the demand for money depends negatively on the nominal interest rate due to households economizing on money holdings in order to reduce forgone interest earnings.

Because a positive rate of inflation reduces the real value of nominal money holdings, it may appear from the household budget constraint that this introduces a nonneutrality into our model of the economy, with a nominal variable affecting real variables even in steady state. We argue that this is a partial, not a general, equilibrium result as, in full general equilibrium, the government budget constraint implies that other forms of taxation would be lower and would offset seigniorage taxation, thereby leaving consumption unaffected in the long run by the quantity of money in the economy. This provides a good example of why macroeconomics should be treated as a general, and not a partial, equilibrium subject. We conclude that one way to resolve the choice between using seigniorage and other forms of taxation is to predetermine the rate of inflation.

We have considered the optimal rate of inflation and shown that Friedman's optimal inflation rate must be negative due to the requirement that the nominal interest rate is zero. This would entail that prices fall continuously—a situation usually associated with deflation and a loss of real output. If there is price and wage inflexibility, then it will usually be optimal for the rate of inflation to be positive, though not large. Taken together, these two drawbacks probably explain why the targeted rate of inflation in nearly all countries is positive, and not negative.

Monetary policy is increasingly conducted through the use of interest rates to target inflation rather than a monetary aggregate. This is due to the observed instabilities in the demand functions for most monetary aggregates that were caused by the increased use of credit and the holding of savings in the form of money balances, plus the ease of borrowing against secured assets. This has generated a new problem for the monetary authorities: namely, to understand the transmission mechanism whereby interest rates affect expenditures on goods and services. One channel is wealth effects caused by changes in interest rates; another is relative price effects on the costs of borrowing and of capital caused directly by the changes in interest rates. Later, in chapter 13, we take up some of these issues again in our discussion of monetary policy.

9

Imperfectly Flexible Prices

9.1 Introduction

A key feature distinguishing neoclassical from Keynesian macroeconomics is the assumed speed of adjustment of prices. Neoclassical macroeconomic models commonly assume that prices are "perfectly" flexible, i.e., they adjust instantaneously to clear goods, labor, and money markets. Keynesian macroeconomic models assume that prices are sticky, or even fixed, and as a result, at best, they adjust to clear markets only slowly; at worst, they fail to clear markets at all, leaving either permanent excess demand (shortages) or excess supply (unemployment). Such market failures provided the main justification for the adoption of active fiscal and monetary policies. The aim was to return the economy to equilibrium (usually interpreted as full employment) faster than would happen without intervention.

Disillusion with the lack of success of stabilization policy and with the weak microeconomic foundations of Keynesian models, particularly the assumption of ad hoc rigidities in nominal prices and wages, which were usually attributed to institutional factors, led to the development of DGE macroeconomic models, with their emphasis on strong microfoundations and flexible prices. Instead of treating the macroeconomy as if it were in a permanent state of disequilibrium with its behavior being explained by ad hoc assumptions, DGE models returned to examining how the economy would behave if it were able to attain equilibrium and how the equilibrium characteristics of the economy would be affected by shocks and by policy changes.

An extensive program of research followed with the aim of investigating whether the dynamic behavior of the economy could be explained by the propagation of shocks in a flexible-price DGE model, or whether it was necessary to restore elements of market failure, including price inflexibility, in order to adequately capture fluctuations in macroeconomic variables over the business cycle. Early work by Kydland and Prescott (1982) focused on whether the business cycle could be explained solely by productivity shocks that were propagated by the internal dynamics of the DGE model to produce serially correlated movements in output. A discussion of the methodology and findings of this research program is provided in chapter 14. Although this research caused a dramatic and far-reaching change in the methodology of macroeconomic analysis, and in the process generated much controversy, the evidence seems to point

to the need for more price inflexibility in macroeconomic models than is provided by a perfectly flexible DGE model. As a result, current research has sought
a way to combine the insights obtained from DGE models with a rigorous treatment of price adjustment based on microfounded price theory. The resulting
models are often called New Keynesian models, though they might be better
described as sticky-price DGE models.

These models usually have three key features. First, they retain the assumption of an optimizing framework. Second, they assume that there is imperfect
competition in either goods or labor markets (or both), which gives monopoly
power to producers. This causes higher prices, and lower output and employment, than under perfect competition. Third, once firms have some control
over their prices, they can choose the rate of adjustment of prices. This allows
the optimal degree of price flexibility for firms to become a strategic, or
endogenous, issue and not an ad hoc additional assumption.

Previously, in our discussion of prices, we focused on the general price level,
not on the prices of individual goods and services or on their relative prices, and
we assumed that the general price level and inflation adjust instantaneously. In
examining imperfect price flexibility, we note that the behaviors of individual
prices differ, with some changing more frequently than others. As a result, the
relative importance of components of the general price level also changes. This
affects the speed of adjustment of both the general price level and inflation,
which are said to be sticky, i.e., to show slow or sluggish adjustment.

A closely related argument is that intermediate outputs are required to produce the final output, but that the price of the final good is not just a weighted
average of the prices of intermediate goods. The difference between final goods
prices and the average price of intermediate goods represents a resource cost;
the greater the dispersion of prices across intermediate goods, possibly initiated by inflation and prolonged by sticky prices, the greater is the resource
cost. The main interest in this argument is that it suggests that inflation may
be costly, and hence provides a reason for controlling inflation.

We now examine optimal price setting when goods and labor markets are
imperfect but prices are flexible. We then analyze the intermediate-goods
model. Next we consider different models that seek to explain why prices may
not adjust instantaneously but may be sticky. The chapter ends by examining
the implications of these theories for the dynamic behavior of prices and inflation. Before developing our theoretical models, we consider some evidence on
the speed of adjustment of prices and wages. Useful surveys on these issues
are Taylor (1999), Rotemberg and Woodford (1999), and Gali (2008).

9.2 Some Stylized "Facts" about Prices and Wages

Information comparing the behavior of different U.S. price series has been
obtained by Bils et al. (2003), Bils and Klenow (2004), and Klenow and Kryvstov (2005). They find that the average time between price changes is around

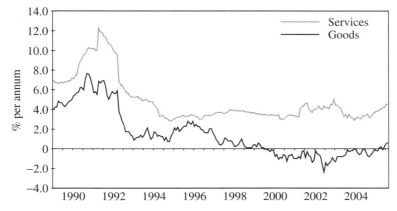

Figure 9.1. U.K. goods and services price inflation 1989.1–2005.8.

six months, whereas Blinder et al. (1998), using data for a much broader range of U.S. industries than Klenow and Kryvstov, found the average to be twelve months and Rumler and Vilmunen (2005) found an average of thirteen months for countries in the euro area.

The frequency of price changes varies across sectors. Bils, Klenow, and Kryvtsov, using unpublished data on 350 categories of goods and services collected by the Bureau of Labor Statistics of the U.S. Department of Labor, report that the median duration between price changes for all items is 4.3 months, that for goods alone (which comprise 30.4% of the CPI) is 3.2 months, and that for services (40.8% of the CPI) is 7.8 months. Individual items differ even more. The median durations between price changes for apparel, food, and home furnishings (37.3%) range between 2.8 and 3.5 months, while for transportation (15.4%) the figure is 1.9 months, for entertainment (3.6%) it is 10.2 months, and for medical services (6.2%) it is 14.9 months. A similar distribution is found by Rumler and Vilmunen for the euro area; there are very frequent changes for energy products and unprocessed food, and relatively frequent changes for processed food, nonenergy industrial goods, and, particularly, services.

In the United Kingdom, the time-series evidence on goods and services price inflation shows very different behavior (see figure 9.1). Services price inflation has been larger and has fluctuated less in the short term. Goods price inflation has been very small—recently even negative—and shows greater short-term variability than services prices. General price inflation is roughly the average of the two.

The rates of change of nominal-wage rates and the general price level in the United Kingdom tend to be similar to each other both in level and volatility, but both the level and the volatility vary considerably over time (see figure 9.2).

More generally, the key stylized "facts" about price and wage changes are the following.

1. Price and wage rigidities are temporary. Hence we expect the DGE model to work in the longer term.

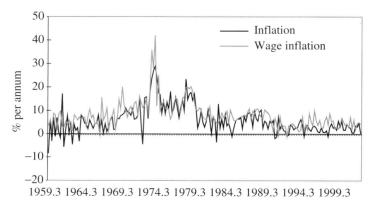

Figure 9.2. U.K. price and wage inflation 1959.3–2005.1.

2. Prices and wages change on average about two or three times a year.

3. The higher inflation is, the more frequently price and wage changes occur.

4. Price and wage changes are not synchronized.

5. Price changes (and to some extent wage changes) occur with different frequencies in different industries (e.g., food/groceries price changes are more frequent than those of manufactures, magazines, or services). Roughly speaking, it seems that changes in the prices of tradeables are more frequent than those of nontradeables.

6. Prices and costs change at different rates at different stages of the business cycle. For example, in the late expansion phase, costs rise more than prices, implying that profit margins fall.

It is clear from this evidence that prices of individual items behave differently: their relative prices change over time, their short-term fluctuations are different, and the frequency with which they change differs. Only for models of the economy with an implicit time period of about one year is it reasonable to assume no lag in the adjustment of prices. Even then, lags elsewhere in the system can delay the completion of price adjustment from one equilibrium to another.

9.3 Price Setting under Imperfect Competition

Under perfect competition in goods markets, firms (or, more generally, suppliers) have no individual power to set prices as consumers, possessing full information, search for the lowest price. Consequently, prices change only when all firms face the same increase in costs. To be able to set prices, firms require a degree of monopoly power. This arises under imperfect competition. Prices are then a markup over costs. The markup depends on the response of demand to prices. As a result, prices may also respond to demand factors.

Similar arguments apply to labor markets. When either the employer or the supplier of labor, whether it be unionized or nonunionized labor, has monopoly power, labor is not paid its marginal product. Depending on who exercises the most monopoly power, real wages will be either below (when employers dominate) or above (when employees dominate) the marginal product of labor. We refer to such discrepancies as wedges. Next we consider some basic results of pricing in imperfectly competitive goods and factor markets.

9.3.1 Theory of Pricing in Imperfect Competition

In the standard theory of pricing in imperfect competition there is a single firm which faces a downward-sloping demand for its product:

$$P = P(Q), \qquad P'(Q) < 0,$$

where P is the price and Q now represents the quantity produced. The firm's production function is

$$Q = F(X_1, \ldots, X_n), \quad F' > 0, \ F'' \leqslant 0,$$

where X_i is the ith factor input, including raw materials. The cost of production is

$$C = \sum_{i=1}^{n} W_i X_i,$$

where, in order to capture monopoly supply features, the factor prices W are a nondecreasing function of the quantity of the factor used, so that

$$W_i = W(X_i), \qquad W'(X_i) > 0.$$

The firm chooses Q and X_i ($i = 1, \ldots, n$) to maximize profits $\Pi = R - C$ subject to the production technology, where $R = PQ$ is total revenue. The Lagrangian for this problem is

$$\mathcal{L} = P(Q)Q - \sum_{i=1}^{n} W(X_i)X_i + \lambda[F(X_1, \ldots, X_n) - Q].$$

The first-order conditions are

$$\frac{\partial \mathcal{L}}{\partial Q} = P + P'(Q)Q - \lambda = 0,$$

$$\frac{\partial \mathcal{L}}{\partial X_i} = -W_i - W'(X_i)X_i + \lambda F'_i = 0.$$

Hence,

$$\lambda = P + P'(Q)Q = MR$$
$$= \frac{W_i + W'(X_i)X_i}{F'_i} = \frac{MC_i}{MP_i} = MC,$$

where MR is marginal revenue, MC_i is the marginal cost, and MP_i the marginal product of the ith factor, and where

$$MC = \frac{\partial C}{\partial Q} = \frac{\partial C}{\partial X_i} \frac{\partial X_i}{\partial Q}$$

is total marginal cost. It follows that

$$p = \frac{1}{1 - (1/\epsilon_\mathrm{D})} MC \tag{9.1}$$

$$= \frac{1}{1 - (1/\epsilon_\mathrm{D})} \frac{MC_i}{MP_i} \tag{9.2}$$

$$= \frac{1 + (1/\epsilon_{X_i})}{1 - (1/\epsilon_\mathrm{D})} \frac{W_i}{MP_i}, \tag{9.3}$$

where

$$\epsilon_\mathrm{D} = -\frac{\partial Q}{\partial P} \frac{P}{Q} > 0$$

is the price elasticity of demand and

$$\epsilon_{X_i} = \frac{\partial X_i}{\partial W} \frac{W}{X_i} > 0$$

is the factor supply elasticity. The labor-supply elasticity may reflect the monopsony power of unionized labor as well as the labor supply of an individual. Hence the price of goods and services is dependent on the unit costs of the factors, their marginal product, the elasticity of their supply, and on the elasticity of demand for the good.

For the Cobb–Douglas production function

$$Q = \prod_{i=1}^{n} X_i^{\alpha_i}, \qquad \sum_{i=1}^{n} \alpha_i = 1,$$

we can obtain the share going to the ith factor, which is

$$\frac{w_i X_i}{pq} = \alpha_i \frac{1 - (1/\epsilon_\mathrm{D})}{1 + (1/\epsilon_{X_i})}.$$

The first-order conditions imply that MC_i/MP_i is equal for each factor. It follows that an increase in the unit cost of a single factor would result in a decrease in its use and hence an increase in its marginal product. If ϵ_{X_i} is constant, then W_i/MP_i, and hence MC_i/MP_i, will remain unchanged. As a result, the price of goods would be unaffected; because this is a relative price change, only the factor proportions have altered. In contrast, if a factor is required in fixed proportion to output, then substitutability between factors is not possible. In this case its marginal product is fixed and so marginal cost, and hence the price of the good, will increase. Output will fall, which will reduce the demand for all factors. This analysis applies to the medium and to the long run; in the short run all factors will tend to be less flexible. Consequently, the case of fixed proportions may also be a good approximation to the short-run response of an increase in the price of a factor.

If all factor prices increase in the same proportion, and their supply elasticities and the price elasticity of demand are constant, then the prices of goods would increase by the same proportion. Accordingly, with constant elasticities, inflation must be due to a general increase in factor prices. We have argued that relative factor price changes would have no effect on prices in the long run; they would only affect relative factor usage. However, they may affect the general price level in the short run.

These elementary principles of pricing are the basis of New Keynesian models of inflation. They underpin the supply side of the economy through new theories of the Phillips curve—a relation between price or wage inflation and a measure of excess supply in the goods or labor market, such as the deviation of output from full capacity (or from trend output) or unemployment. For further discussion of the role of marginal cost pricing and the output gap in the New Keynesian inflation equation see Neiss and Nelson (2005), Batini et al. (2005), and Gali (2008).

9.3.2 Price Determination in the Macroeconomy with Imperfect Competition

Modern macroeconomic theories of price determination emphasize the fact that in the economy a large number of different goods and services are produced. A widely used model of price setting when these goods are imperfect substitutes is that of Dixit and Stiglitz (1977). We consider a variant of this that is closely related to work by Blanchard and Kiyotaki (1987), Ball and Romer (1991), and Dixon and Rankin (1995) (see also Mankiw and Romer (1991) and the articles cited therein). For simplicity, the model is highly stylized.

We assume that the economy is composed of N firms each producing a different good that is an imperfect substitute for the other goods, and that a single factor of production is used, namely, labor that is supplied by N households. The production function for the ith firm is assumed to be

$$y_t(i) = F_i[n_t(i)],$$

where $n_t(i)$ is the labor input of the ith firm. The production function is indexed by i to denote that each good may be produced with a different production function. The profits of the ith firm are

$$\Pi_t(i) = P_t(i)F_i[n_t(i)] - W_t(i)n_t(i), \qquad (9.4)$$

where $P_t(i)$ is the output price and $W_t(i)$ is the wage rate paid by firm i.

9.3.2.1 Households

We assume that there are also N households and these are classified by their type of employment, with each household working for one type of firm i. Households are assumed to have an identical instantaneous utility function:

$$U[c_t, l_t(i)] = u[c_t] + \eta l_t(i)^\varepsilon, \quad \varepsilon \geqslant 1,$$

where c_t is their total consumption, $l_t(i)$ is leisure, and $n_t(i) + l_t(i) = 1$. We assume that $u_c > 0$ and that $u_{cc} < 0$.

We also assume that total consumption c_t is obtained by aggregating over the N different types of goods and services $c_t(i)$ using the constant elasticity of substitution function

$$c_t = \left[\sum_{i=1}^{N} c_t(i)^{(\phi-1)/\phi} \right]^{\phi/(\phi-1)}, \tag{9.5}$$

where $\phi > 1$ is the elasticity of substitution; we recall that a higher value of ϕ implies greater substitutability. Thus goods and services are imperfect substitutes if ϕ is finite.

Total household expenditure on goods and services is

$$P_t c_t = \sum_{i=1}^{N} P_t(i) c_t(i);$$

hence the general price index P_t satisfies

$$P_t = \sum_{i=1}^{N} P_t(i) \frac{c_t(i)}{c_t}. \tag{9.6}$$

The household budget constraint is

$$P_t c_t = \sum_{i=1}^{N} P_t(i) c_t(i) = W_t(i) n_t(i) + \sum_{i=1}^{N} \Pi_t(i),$$

where each household is assumed to hold an equal share in each firm.

In the absence of capital (and trading in shares) the budget constraint is static. Consequently, optimization can be carried out each period without regard to future periods. Thus, in the absence of assets, the intertemporal aspect of the DGE model of the model is eliminated. We assume, therefore, that households maximize utility with respect to $\{c_t(1), \ldots, c_t(N), n_t(i)\}$ subject to their budget constraint and to $n_t(i) + l_t(i) = 1$. The Lagrangian is defined as

$$\mathcal{L} = u\left(\left[\sum_{i=1}^{N} c_t(i)^{(\phi-1)/\phi} \right]^{\phi/(\phi-1)} \right) + \eta l_t(i)^\varepsilon$$
$$+ \lambda_t \left[W_t(i) n_t(i) + \sum_{i=1}^{N} \Pi_t(i) - \sum_{i=1}^{N} P_t(i) c_t(i) \right].$$

The first-order conditions are

$$\frac{\partial \mathcal{L}}{\partial c_t(i)} = u_{c,t} \left[\frac{c_t}{c_t(i)} \right]^{1/\phi} - \lambda_t P_t(i) = 0, \quad i = 1, \ldots, N,$$

$$\frac{\partial \mathcal{L}}{\partial l_t(i)} = \eta \varepsilon l_t(i)^{\varepsilon-1} - \lambda_t W_t(i) = 0,$$

giving

$$\frac{c_t(i)}{c_t} = \left[\frac{\lambda_t P_t(i)}{u_{c,t}} \right]^{-\phi}. \tag{9.7}$$

The household's problem can also be expressed in terms of maximizing utility with respect to aggregate consumption, as the Lagrangian can be rewritten as

$$\mathcal{L} = u(c_t) + \eta l_t(i)^\varepsilon + \lambda_t \left[W_t(i) n_t(i) + \sum_{i=1}^{N} \Pi_t(i) - P_t c_t \right].$$

The first-order condition with respect to c_t is

$$\frac{\partial \mathcal{L}}{\partial c_t} = u_{c,t} - \lambda_t P_t = 0;$$

hence $u_{c,t}/P_t = \lambda_t$ and so equation (9.7) can also be written as

$$\frac{c_t(i)}{c_t} = \left[\frac{P_t(i)}{P_t} \right]^{-\phi}. \tag{9.8}$$

This is the demand function for the ith good.

Substituting (9.8) into (9.6) gives the general price index expressed solely in terms of individual prices:

$$\begin{aligned} P_t &= \sum_{i=1}^{n} P_t(i) \left[\frac{P_t(i)}{P_t} \right]^{-\phi} \\ &= \left[\sum_{i=1}^{n} P_t(i)^{1-\phi} \right]^{1/(1-\phi)}. \end{aligned} \tag{9.9}$$

From the first-order condition with respect to labor, the total supply of labor by the household is

$$n_t(i) = 1 - \left(\frac{u_{c,t} W_t(i)}{\eta \varepsilon P_t} \right)^{1/(\varepsilon-1)}. \tag{9.10}$$

If $\varepsilon \geqslant (\leqslant) 1$, an increase in $W_t(i)$ will raise (reduce) labor supply $n_t(i)$. If labor markets are competitive, households have the same utility function (implying complete markets) and work equally hard (implying firms are indifferent about who they hire), in which case $W_t(i)$ will be equal across firms. We denote the common wage by W_t. If households have different utility functions (or do not work equally hard), then the marginal utilities will differ and so will wages.

9.3.2.2 Firms

The problem for the ith firm is to maximize profits subject to its demand function, equation (9.8). In the absence of investment and government expenditures, we have $c_t(i) = y_t(i) = F_i[n_t(i)]$. The first-order condition of $\Pi_t(i)$, equation (9.4), with respect to $c_t(i)$ is

$$\frac{d\Pi_t(i)}{dc_t(i)} = P_t(i) + \frac{\partial P_t(i)}{\partial c_t(i)} c_t(i) - W_t \frac{dn_t(i)}{dc_t(i)} = 0,$$

where

$$\frac{dc_t(i)}{dn_t(i)} = \frac{dy_t(i)}{dn_t(i)} = F_i'[n_t(i)].$$

It follows that

$$P_t(i) = \frac{\phi}{\phi - 1} \frac{W_t}{F_i'[n_t(i)]}. \tag{9.11}$$

This is a key result. It indicates that price is a markup over W_t/F_i', which is the marginal cost of an extra unit of output; the markup or wedge is $\phi/(\phi-1) > 1$. As $\phi \to \infty$, i.e., as the consumption goods become perfect substitutes, the markup tends to unity and price falls to equal marginal cost. This solution is the standard outcome for monopoly pricing. Prices vary across goods due to differences in the marginal product of labor, $F_i'[n_t(i)]$. Equation (9.11) implies that firms have some control over their prices. This entails a source of inefficiency because output, and hence consumption, are lower than in perfect competition. An increase in the economy-wide wage would therefore cause an increase in the price of each good and in the general price level.

The demand for labor can be obtained from equation (9.11). Suppose that the production function is Cobb–Douglas so that

$$y_t(i) = A_{it} n_t(i)^{\alpha_i}, \quad \alpha_i \leqslant 1,$$

where A_{it} can be interpreted as an efficiency term for the ith firm at time t. Labor demand is then given by

$$n_t(i) = \left(\frac{\phi}{\alpha_i A_{it} (\phi - 1)} \frac{W_t}{P_t(i)} \right)^{-1/(1-\alpha_i)}. \tag{9.12}$$

The greater ϕ is, and hence the lower the markup, the greater labor demand and output are, reflecting once more the inefficiency of monopolies in terms of lost output and employment.

Equating labor demand and supply (equations (9.10) and (9.12)) for firm i gives

$$n_t(i) = \left(\frac{\phi}{\alpha_i A_{it} (\phi - 1)} \frac{W_t}{P_t(i)} \right)^{-1/(1-\alpha_i)} = \left(\frac{u_{c,t} W_t}{\eta \varepsilon P_t} \right)^{1/(\varepsilon-1)}.$$

Hence

$$\frac{P_t(i)}{P_t} = \frac{\phi}{\alpha_i A_{it} (\phi - 1)} \left(\frac{u_{c,t}}{\eta \varepsilon} \right)^{(1-\alpha_i)/(\varepsilon-1)} \left(\frac{W_t}{P_t} \right)^{(\varepsilon-\alpha_i)/(\varepsilon-1)}. \tag{9.13}$$

Thus differences between firm prices are due to A_{it} and α_i. Equation (9.13) implies that, as $\varepsilon \geqslant (\leqslant) 1$, an increase (decrease) in the economy-wide real-wage rate would raise (reduce) the relative price of firm i.

In the special case where the efficiency term A_{it} and the production elasticities are the same, so that $A_{it} = A_t$ and $\alpha_i = \alpha$, firm prices will be identical. In this case we can solve equation (9.13) for the real wage as

$$\frac{W_t}{P_t} = \left(\frac{\phi}{\alpha A_t (\phi - 1)} \right)^{-(\varepsilon-1)/(\varepsilon-\alpha)} \left(\frac{u_{c,t}}{\eta \varepsilon} \right)^{-(1-\alpha)/(\varepsilon-\alpha)}. \tag{9.14}$$

As $u_{c,t}$ is negatively related to c_t ($= y_t$) and $\varepsilon > \alpha$, an increase in the real wage will raise output. Moreover, the lower the markup $\phi/(\phi - 1)$ is, the greater the response of output to the real wage will be. Equation (9.14) also shows that the economy is then neutral with respect to nominal values. An example of this is when each production function is linear in labor when $\alpha_i = 1$. In this case employment is determined by the supply side (equation (9.10)).

More generally, when the α_i are different, we do not obtain a closed-form solution for the real wage. To see this, substitute equation (9.13) into (9.9). An analytic solution for the general price level cannot be derived and hence total output is not a function of the real wage. Nonetheless, the economy remains neutral with respect to a nominal shock. This can be seen by noting that equation (9.13) is still homogeneous of degree zero in wages and prices.

9.3.3 Pricing with Intermediate Goods

Once more our model of the economy is highly stylized for simplicity. The key assumption is that a final good is produced by a profit-maximizing firm using N inputs that are all intermediate goods. It is assumed that the intermediate goods are produced by N monopolistically competitive firms using only one factor of production: labor. Households consume only the final good and supply labor.

9.3.3.1 *Final-Goods Production*

The final good is y_t and the intermediate goods are $y_t(i)$, $i = 1, \ldots, N$. It is assumed that the final output satisfies the CES production function

$$y_t = \left[\sum_{i=1}^{N} y_t(i)^{(\phi-1)/\phi} \right]^{\phi/(\phi-1)}, \quad \phi > 1,$$

and that there are no other factors of production for final output.

The final-output producer is assumed to choose the inputs $y_t(i)$ to maximize profits, which are given by

$$\Pi_t = P_t y_t - \sum_{i=1}^{N} P_t(i) y_t(i)$$

$$= P_t \left[\sum_{i=1}^{N} y_t(i)^{(\phi-1)/\phi} \right]^{\phi/(\phi-1)} - \sum_{i=1}^{N} P_t(i) y_t(i),$$

where P_t is the price of the final output and $P_t(i)$ are the prices of the intermediate inputs. The first-order condition is

$$\frac{\partial \Pi_t}{\partial y_t(i)} = P_t \left(\frac{y_t}{y_t(i)} \right)^{1/\phi} - P_t(i) = 0;$$

hence the demand for the ith input is

$$y_t(i) = \left(\frac{P_t(i)}{P_t} \right)^{-\phi} y_t. \tag{9.15}$$

Since equilibrium profits are zero, the price of the final good is

$$P_t = \sum_{i=1}^{N} P_t(i) \frac{y_t(i)}{y_t}$$

$$= \left[\sum_{i=1}^{N} P_t(i)^{1-\phi} \right]^{1/(1-\phi)}.$$

9.3.3.2   Intermediate-Goods Production

The intermediate goods are assumed to be produced with the constant returns to scale production function

$$y_t(i) = A_i n_t(i),$$

where $n_t(i)$ is labor input. Intermediate-goods firms maximize the profit function

$$\Pi_t(i) = P_t(i) y_t(i) - W_t n_t(i)$$

subject to the demand function, equation (9.15), where W_t is the economy-wide wage rate. The profit function can therefore be written as

$$\Pi_t(i) = P_t \left(\frac{y_t}{y_t(i)} \right)^{1/\phi} y_t(i) - W_t n_t(i)$$

$$= P_t y_t^{1/\phi} y_t(i)^{1-(1/\phi)} - W_t n_t(i)$$

$$= P_t y_t^{1/\phi} [A_i n_t(i)]^{1-(1/\phi)} - W_t n_t(i).$$

Maximizing $\Pi_t(i)$ with respect to $n_t(i)$, taking P_t and y_t as given, yields

$$n_t(i) = A_i^{\phi-1} \left[\frac{\phi-1}{\phi} \frac{P_t}{W_t} \right]^{\phi} y_t,$$

$$y_t(i) = A_i^{\phi} \left[\frac{\phi-1}{\phi} \frac{P_t}{W_t} \right]^{\phi} y_t,$$

$$P_t(i) = \frac{\phi}{A_i(\phi-1)} W_t.$$

9.3.3.3   The Inefficiency Loss

Total output is derived from the outputs of the intermediate goods as

$$y_t(i) = A_i n_t(i) = \left[\frac{P_t(i)}{P_t} \right]^{-\phi} y_t.$$

Total labor is given by

$$n_t = \sum_{i=1}^{N} n_t(i)$$

$$= \sum_{i=1}^{N} \frac{1}{A_i} \left[\frac{P_t(i)}{P_t} \right]^{-\phi} y_t.$$

This gives a relation between the output of the final good and aggregate labor, which can be written as

$$y_t = v_t n_t,$$

$$v_t = \frac{1}{\sum_{i=1}^{N}(1/A_i)[P_t(i)/P_t]^{-\phi}}.$$

If $v_t < 1$, then there is an inefficiency loss in the use of labor in producing the final output but not in producing intermediate outputs. Or, put another way, since it is necessary to use intermediate inputs to produce final output, an inefficiency loss occurs in the use of labor in the economy. Moreover, if $A_i = 1$, then the inefficiency loss is due solely to price dispersion as we can then express v_t as

$$v_t = \left[\frac{\tilde{P}_t}{P_t}\right]^{\phi},$$

$$\tilde{P}_t = \left[\sum_{i=1}^{N} P_t(i)^{-\phi}\right]^{-1/\phi},$$

$$P_t = \left[\sum_{i=1}^{N} P_t(i)^{1-\phi}\right]^{1/(1-\phi)}.$$

This implies that $v_t < 1$.

To see the effect of inflation, totally differentiate P_t to obtain

$$dP_t^{-\phi} = \sum_{i=1}^{N} dP_t(i)^{-\phi}.$$

Hence, the general level of inflation is related to individual intermediate-goods inflation rates through

$$\frac{dP_t}{P_t} = \left\{\sum_{i=1}^{N} \left[\frac{dP_t(i)}{P_t(i)}\frac{P_t(i)}{P_t}\right]^{-\phi}\right\}^{-1/\phi}.$$

Suppose that $dP_t(i)$ is the same for all i, then $dP_t < dP_t(i)$. This implies that if $P_t(i)/P_t$ is the same for i, then

$$\frac{dP_t}{P_t} < \frac{dP_t(i)}{P_t(i)},$$

and so the overall level of inflation for the economy is less than the common individual inflation rate. The presence of intermediate goods therefore ameliorates general inflation.

Putting the two results together, we conclude that the presence of intermediate goods leads to an output loss but also a lower level of inflation for the final good.

9.3.4 Pricing in the Open Economy: Local and Producer-Currency Pricing

Previously, in our discussion of the open economy in chapter 7, we discussed imperfect substitutability between domestic and foreign tradeables. We argued that when they are perfect substitutes, after taking account of transportation costs, the law of one price holds. In other words, there is a single world price for tradeables, which may be expressed in foreign currency, typically the U.S. dollar, or in terms of domestic currency. This relation implies that $P_t^H = P_t^F = S_t P_t^{F*} = S_t P_t^{H*}$, where we are using the notation of chapter 7, i.e., that P_t^H is the domestic currency price of home tradeables, P_t^F is the domestic currency price of imports, S_t is the domestic price of foreign exchange, and an asterisk denotes the foreign equivalent. Not only does this prevent domestic producers from being able to pass on increases in costs that are purely domestic, it also affects the response of prices to changes in the nominal exchange rate, and hence the effectiveness of monetary policy.

Since for a small economy the prices of domestic tradeables are set at the world price, and the world price is given in foreign currency terms, an exchange-rate depreciation—which raises the number of units of domestic currency per unit of foreign currency—would raise the domestic currency price of imports, and hence cause an increase in the price of domestic tradeables sold at home. The foreign currency price of home-country exports would be unaffected as this is set in terms of the world currency price, which is taken as given. Exports therefore become more profitable in terms of domestic currency. An exchange-rate appreciation would reduce the domestic currency price of imports and hence domestic tradeables prices. As the foreign currency price of exports is unchanged, the domestic currency price will decrease; therefore exporting becomes less profitable.

If, instead, domestic and foreign tradeables are imperfect substitutes, then domestic and foreign producers have a measure of monopoly power in setting prices. As previously noted in chapter 7, a situation where producers have monopoly power both at home and abroad has been named producer-currency pricing (PCP) by Betts and Devereux (1996) and Devereux (1997). A situation where producers have monopoly power at home, but not abroad, has been named local-currency pricing (LCP). In this case imports are priced at the domestic producer price; this is known as pricing-to-market.

Consider PCP. In the extreme case of a pure monopoly, the export price is just the domestic currency price expressed in foreign currency, but domestic and foreign tradeables will differ in price. In this case, $P_t^F = S_t P_t^{H*}$ and $P_t^{F*} = S_t^{-1} P_t^H$ but $P_t^H \neq P_t^F$ and $P_t^{H*} \neq P_t^{F*}$. Domestic producers can now pass on cost increases both at home and abroad, and an exchange-rate appreciation would result in an increase in the foreign currency price of exports. If the foreign producer has monopoly power in the domestic market, then a depreciation would raise the domestic currency price of imports.

In contrast, under pure LCP, $P_t^H = P_t^F$ and $P_t^{H*} = P_t^{F*}$ but $P_t^F \neq S_t P_t^{H*}$ and $P_t^{F*} \neq S_t^{-1} P_t^H$. Here the domestic producer would be able to pass on cost increases only in the domestic market and not in the foreign market. An appreciation would have no effect on the foreign currency price of exports, and a depreciation would not affect domestic tradeables prices.

The evidence shows that import prices are relatively sticky and do not fluctuate one-for-one with changes in the nominal exchange rate, or with changes in foreign prices. It is the terms of trade and the real exchange rate that seem to absorb shocks, especially those to the nominal exchange rate. Engel (2000), among others, has found that traded goods prices in Europe are not much influenced by exchange-rate movements. This seems to suggest that either foreign goods are highly substitutable with home goods or they may not be perfect substitutes, but because producers lack monopoly power in foreign markets, the prices of imported goods are priced-to-market, i.e., LCP prevails. This finding has important policy consequences. It implies that a depreciation of the exchange rate tends not to be passed on in the form of higher prices for imported goods. This considerably reduces the effectiveness of an exchange-rate depreciation, a traditional way to stimulate the domestic economy and improve the trade balance.

These arguments apply primarily to a small open economy and are less applicable to the United States, which is a large and relatively closed economy compared with nearly all other countries. By virtue of its size, the U.S. price will often be the principal determinant of the world price. And because world prices are often set in terms of the U.S. dollar, U.S. domestic prices are well-insulated against changes in the value of the dollar. As a result, to a first approximation, it is common to treat the United States as a closed economy. However, this would miss a crucial aspect of the U.S. economy. To the extent that the world prices of commodities are set in dollars, it would be more difficult for the United States to improve its competitiveness through a depreciation. Instead, it would have to rely more on improvements to productive efficiency through technological growth and innovation in new products, which would create, at least for a time, monopoly power in world markets. Thus, in this case, the arguments above concerning pricing under imperfect competition apply to the United States, but those relating to the effect of exchange-rate changes on prices may be less relevant. Like other countries, of course, the United States also exports commodities whose foreign currency price would fall following a dollar depreciation.

9.4 Price Stickiness

We have discussed how optimal prices are determined in the long run. We now consider the dynamic behavior of prices in the short run. This will give us a complete picture of pricing behavior. There are several competing theories of price dynamics adjustment, but they have similar implications for price dynamics. These theories have in common the notion that the general price level is made up of the prices of many individual items, and that the prices of these components adjust at different speeds. Over time the prices of individual items are revised. As a result, the general price level displays inertia. The key distinguishing feature of these theories lies in whether they attribute price changes to chance or to choice: i.e., whether the changes are exogenous or endogenous, optimal or constrained, and hence suboptimal.

We focus on three theories commonly used in modern macroeconomics:

1. The overlapping contracts model of Taylor (1979), where wages are the main cause of price change.

2. The staggered pricing model of Calvo (1983), where price changes occur randomly.

3. The optimal dynamic adjustment model used, for example, by Rotemberg (1982), where the speed of price adjustment is chosen optimally.

We then consider the implications for price dynamics.

9.4.1 Taylor Model of Overlapping Contracts

This model is based on the following assumptions.

1. Price is a markup over marginal cost and the markup may be time-varying and affected in the short-run mainly by the wage rate.

2. The wage rate at any point in time is an average of wage contracts that were set in the past but are still in force, and of those set in the current period.

3. When they were first set, wage contracts were profit maximizing and reflected the prevailing marginal product of labor and the expected future price level.

We define the following variables: P_t is the general price level, $p_t = \ln P_t$, $\pi_t = \Delta p_t$ is the inflation rate, W_t is the economy-wide wage rate, $w_t = \ln W_t$, W_t^N is the new wage contract made in period t, $w_t^N = \ln W_t^N$, v_t is the price markup over costs, and z_t is the logarithm of the marginal product of labor.
Price is assumed to be a markup over wage costs:

$$p_t = w_t + v_t. \tag{9.16}$$

This implies a degree of monopoly power and a single factor, labor. Taylor assumed that wage contracts last for four quarters. For simplicity, we assume that they last for only two periods. The average wage w_t is the geometric mean of the wage contracts w_t^N and w_{t-1}^N made in periods t and $t - 1$:

$$w_t = \tfrac{1}{2}(w_t^N + w_{t-1}^N). \tag{9.17}$$

New wage contracts are assumed to be set to take account of the possibility that the future price level p_{t+1} might differ from the current level p_t; hence the real wage, defined by taking the average of the current and future expected price levels over two periods, equals the current marginal product of labor z_t. The new nominal wage is therefore

$$w_t^N - \tfrac{1}{2}(p_t + E_t p_{t+1}) = z_t. \tag{9.18}$$

Combining equations (9.16), (9.17), and (9.18) gives

$$p_t = \tfrac{1}{2}\{[\tfrac{1}{2}(p_t + E_t p_{t+1}) + z_t] + [\tfrac{1}{2}(p_{t-1} + E_{t-1}p_t) + z_{t-1}]\} + v_t.$$

Consequently, the price level depends on past prices as well as future expected prices. The rate of inflation implied by this equation is

$$\Delta p_t = E_t \Delta p_{t+1} + 2(z_t + z_{t-1}) + 4v_t + \eta_t.$$

And if expectations are rational so that

$$\eta_t = -(p_t - E_{t-1}p_t)$$

with $E_{t-1}\eta_t = 0$, then the inflation rate is given by

$$\pi_t = E_t \pi_{t+1} + 2(z_t + z_{t-1}) + 4v_t + \eta_t. \tag{9.19}$$

This has the forward-looking solution

$$\pi_t = E_t \sum_{s=0}^{\infty} 4(z_{t+s} + v_{t+s}) + 2z_{t-1} + \eta_t. \tag{9.20}$$

Hence, following a temporary unit increase in log marginal productivity z_t, inflation increases in period t by 4 units and in period $t+1$ by 2 units before returning to its initial level in period $t+2$. Equation (9.20) also implies that, following a permanent increase to z_t, inflation instantly increases without bound, which is implausible. The model only makes sense, therefore, if the long-run level of z_t is constrained to be zero but may temporarily depart from this. In this case, the steady-state level of inflation is equal to the logarithm of the markup.

Assuming that wage contracts last longer than n periods results in a price equation of the form

$$p_t = \sum_{s=1}^{n-1} \alpha_s E_t p_{t+s} + \sum_{s=1}^{n} \beta_s p_{t-s} + \frac{1}{n}\sum_{s=0}^{n-1} z_{t-s} + v_t + \xi_t,$$

where ξ_t is a linear combination of innovations in price; hence ξ_t is serially correlated. For each additional period there is an extra forward-looking and lagged price term and an additional lag in productivity.

9.4.2 The Calvo Model of Staggered Price Adjustment

This is perhaps the most popular pricing model as it offers a simple way to derive a theory of dynamic behavior of the general price level while starting from a disaggregated theory of prices. The general price level is the average price of all firms. It is assumed that firms are forward looking and they forecast what the optimal price p_{t+s}^* ($s \geqslant 0$), which is the same for all firms, should be both in the future and in the current period. The crucial distinguishing features of Calvo pricing are that not all firms are able to adjust to the optimal price immediately and that adjustment, when it does occur, is exogenous to the firm and happens randomly. It is assumed that in any period there is a given probability ρ of a firm being able to make an adjustment to its price. Consequently, $(1 - \rho)^s$ is the probability that in period $t + s$ the price is still p_t. The drawback of this theory, therefore, is the restriction that firms have no control over when they can adjust their price.

When firms do adjust their price they set it to minimize the present value of the cost of deviations of the newly adjusted price $p_t^{\#}$ from the optimal price. As soon as the adjustment takes place, given current information, this cost is expected to be zero both for the period of adjustment and for future periods. Thus the aim is to choose $p_t^{\#}$ to minimize

$$\frac{1}{2} \sum_{s=0}^{\infty} \gamma^s E_t [p_t^{\#} - p_{t+s}^*]^2,$$

where $\gamma = \beta(1 - \rho)$.

Differentiating with respect to $p_t^{\#}$ gives the first-order condition

$$\sum_{s=0}^{\infty} \gamma^s E_t [p_t^{\#} - p_{t+s}^*] = 0.$$

Hence, after adjustment, the new price is

$$p_t^{\#} = (1 - \gamma) \sum_{s=0}^{\infty} \gamma^s E_t p_{t+s}^*. \tag{9.21}$$

This can also be written as the recursion

$$p_t^{\#} = (1 - \gamma) p_t^* + \gamma E_t p_{t+1}^{\#}.$$

Consequently, like the Taylor model, the solution is forward looking.

Since the general price level is the average of all prices, and a proportion ρ of firms adjust their price in period t, the actual price level p_t is a weighted average of firms that are able to adjust and those that are not. Thus

$$p_t = \rho p_t^{\#} + (1 - \rho) p_{t-1}. \tag{9.22}$$

Eliminating $p_t^{\#}$ using equation (9.21) gives

$$p_t = \rho(1 - \gamma) \sum_0^{\infty} \gamma^s E_t p_{t+s}^* + (1 - \rho) p_{t-1}.$$

Hence inflation is given by

$$\pi_t = \rho(1 - \gamma) \sum_0^{\infty} \gamma^s E_t [p_{t+s}^* - p_{t+s-1}],$$

or, expressed as a recursion, it is given by

$$\pi_t = \rho(1 - \gamma)(p_t^* - p_{t-1}) + \gamma E_t \pi_{t+1}. \tag{9.23}$$

Once again, therefore, we obtain a forward-looking solution for inflation. At time t, equation (9.23) shows that the actual change in price is related to the "desired" change in price $p_t^* - p_{t-1}$ and to the expected future change in price. In steady state the actual price level equals the desired level and inflation is zero.

A modification of the basic Calvo model assumes that, if firms cannot reset their prices optimally, then they index their current price change to the past inflation rate. As a result, equation (9.22) is replaced by

$$p_t = \rho p_t^\# + (1 - \rho)(\pi_{t-1} + p_{t-1})$$
$$= \rho p_t^\# + (1 - \rho)(2p_{t-1} - p_{t-1}).$$

The auxiliary equation is

$$A(L) = 1 - 2(1 - \rho)L + (1 - \rho)L^2 = 0,$$

where L is the lag operator. As $A(1) = \rho > 0$ and the coefficient of L^2 is less than unity, both roots lie outside the unit circle and so the equation is stable. The solution may therefore be written as

$$\pi_t = \rho(p_t^\# - p_{t-1}) + (1 - \rho)\pi_{t-1}.$$

The inflation equation is then

$$\pi_t = \frac{\rho(1 - y)}{1 + \rho(1 - y)}(p_t^* - p_{t-1}) + \frac{y}{\rho(1 - y)}E_t\pi_{t+1} + \frac{1 - \rho}{\rho(1 - y)}\pi_{t-1}.$$

Hence, there is an additional term in π_{t-1} on the right-hand side of the inflation equation, which implies that inflation takes time to adjust, and the coefficients of the other terms are different.

9.4.3 Optimal Dynamic Adjustment

Here we assume that firms trade off two types of distortion. One arises because changing prices is costly. The other is the cost of being out of equilibrium. The trade-off is expressed in terms of an intertemporal cost function involving the change in the logarithm of the price level, Δp_t, and deviations of the price level from its optimal long-run price p_t^*. The resulting intertemporal cost function is

$$C_t = \sum_{s=0}^{\infty} \beta^s E_t[\alpha(p_{t+s}^* - p_{t+s})^2 + (\Delta p_{t+s})^2].$$

The first term is the cost of being out of long-run equilibrium and the second is the cost of changing the price level. Firms seek to minimize the present value of these costs by a suitable choice of the current price p_t. The solution is the optimal short-run price level, as opposed to the optimal, or equilibrium, long-run price level.

The first-order condition is

$$\frac{\partial C_t}{\partial p_{t+s}} = 2E_t[\beta^s\{-\alpha(p_{t+s}^* - p_{t+s}) + \Delta p_{t+s}\} - \beta^{s+1}\Delta p_{t+s+1}] = 0.$$

For $s = 0$, this implies that

$$\Delta p_t = \alpha(p_t^* - p_t) + \beta E_t \Delta p_{t+1} \tag{9.24}$$

or

$$\pi_t = \frac{\alpha}{1 + \alpha}(p_t^* - p_{t-1}) + \frac{\beta}{1 + \alpha} E_t \pi_{t+1}. \tag{9.25}$$

Once more we have a forward-looking equation for inflation with π_t depending on the desired change in the price level and on $E_t \pi_{t+1}$. The greater is α, the relative cost of being out of equilibrium, the larger is the coefficient on "desired" inflation $\pi_t^* = p_t^* - p_{t-1}$; the greater is the discount factor β, the larger is the coefficient of future expected inflation. In steady state, $p_t^* = p_t$ and $\pi_t = E_t \pi_{t+1}$.

A variant of the optimal dynamic adjustment model that results in π_{t-1} being an additional variable is obtained by assuming that only a fraction λ of firms set their prices in this way and that the rest, $1 - \lambda$, set prices using a rule of thumb based on the previous period's inflation. The resulting inflation equation is

$$\pi_t = \lambda \frac{\beta}{1 + \alpha} E_t \pi_{t+1} + \lambda \frac{\alpha}{1 + \alpha}(p_t^* - p_{t-1}) + (1 - \lambda)\pi_{t-1}.$$

In this way inflation takes time to adjust. An alternative way of adding lagged inflation terms is to include additional terms in the cost function. For example, if it is costly to change the inflation rate, then a term in $(\Delta p_t)^s$, $s \geqslant 3$, can be added. For $s = 3$ the lag in inflation becomes an extra variable in the price equation.

9.4.4 Price Level Dynamics

The Calvo model and the optimal dynamic adjustment model have the same form—only the interpretation of the coefficients differs. The Taylor model has a similar dynamic structure but a different coefficient on expected future inflation. The evidence suggests that additional dynamics may be required in the inflation equations (see, for example, Smith and Wickens 2007). These can be added to the Taylor model by extending the contract period; extra lags can be added to the Calvo model by assuming that firms who are unable to adjust prices optimally index on past inflation; extra lags to the optimal dynamic adjustment model may also be generated by assuming that firms set prices using a rule of thumb or by adding terms to the cost function.

A general formulation of the price equation that captures all three theories is

$$\pi_t = \alpha \pi_t^* + \beta E_t \pi_{t+1}, \quad |\beta| \leqslant 1, \tag{9.26}$$

where $\pi_t = \Delta p_t$ and $\pi_t^* = p_t^* - p_{t-1}$. At first sight, this equation may seem to imply that there is no price stickiness, because it has the forward-looking solution

$$\pi_t = \alpha \sum_{s=0}^{\infty} \beta_s E_t \pi_{t+s}^*.$$

If we rewrite the model in terms of the price level, however, then we obtain

$$\Delta p_t = \alpha(p_t^* - p_{t-1}) + \beta E_t \Delta p_{t+1}, \tag{9.27}$$

or, in terms of the price level,

$$-\beta E_t p_{t+1} + (1 + \beta)p_t - (1 - \alpha)p_{t-1} = \alpha p_t^*, \tag{9.28}$$

which is a second-order difference equation.

Using the lag operator, this can be written as

$$-A(L)L^{-1}p_t = \alpha p_t^*.$$

The auxiliary equation associated with equation (9.28) is

$$A(L) = \beta - (1 + \beta)L + (1 - \alpha)L^2 = 0.$$

As $A(1) = -\alpha < 0$, the solution is a saddlepath. If the roots are denominated $|\lambda_1| \geqslant 1$, $|\lambda_2| < 1$, then the solution can be written as (see the mathematical appendix)

$$(1 - \alpha)\lambda_1 \left(1 - \frac{1}{\lambda_1}L\right)(1 - \lambda_2 L^{-1})p_t = \alpha p_t^*$$

or as the partial adjustment model

$$\Delta p_t = \left(1 - \frac{1}{\lambda_1}\right)(p_t^{\#} - p_{t-1}), \tag{9.29}$$

$$p_t^{\#} = \frac{\alpha}{(1 - \alpha)(\lambda_1 - 1)} \sum_{s=0}^{\infty} \lambda_2^s E_t p_{t+s}^*. \tag{9.30}$$

If expectations are static, so that $E_t p_{t+s}^* = p_t^*$, then

$$p_t^{\#} = \frac{\alpha}{(1 - \alpha)(\lambda_1 - 1)(1 - \lambda_2)}p_t^* = p_t^*.$$

Equations (9.29) and (9.30) show that, following a temporary or permanent disturbance to equilibrium, the adjustment of the price level takes time. In other words, prices are sticky.

For prices to be perfectly flexible—and price adjustment instantaneous—we require that $\lambda_1 = 1$, implying that $\lambda_2 = \beta/(1 - \alpha)$. If we rewrite equation (9.27) as

$$\Delta p_t = \frac{\alpha}{1 - \alpha}(p_t^* - p_t) + \frac{\beta}{1 - \alpha}E_t \Delta p_{t+1}, \tag{9.31}$$

then it is clear that this requires that $\alpha = 1$. Translated in terms of the parameters of the Calvo model, we require that $\rho = 0$, and in the terms of the optimal dynamic adjustment model we require that $\alpha = \infty$.

9.4.4.1 Long-Run Equilibrium

In long-run equilibrium we expect that the solution for the price level is $p_t = p_t^*$. But equation (9.31) does not have this solution unless either the long-run rate of inflation is zero or $\beta/(1-\alpha) = 1$. If $\beta/(1-\alpha) \neq 1$, and long-run inflation is π, then, in order for the long-run solution to be $p_t = p_t^*$, equation (9.31) must include an intercept term so that the equation becomes

$$\Delta p_t = -\left(1 - \frac{\beta}{1-\alpha}\right)\pi + \frac{\alpha}{1-\alpha}(p_t^* - p_t) + \frac{\beta}{1-\alpha}E_t\Delta p_{t+1}. \qquad (9.32)$$

In the Calvo model, $p_t = p_t^*$ in the long run only if $\pi = 0$ or, when $\pi > 0$, if the probability of being able to adjust to equilibrium is unity, i.e., if $\rho = 1$. Similarly, in the optimal adjustment model, we require either that $\pi = 0$ or, for $\pi > 0$, that the discount rate $\beta = 1$.

9.5 The New Keynesian Phillips Curve

The inflation equation is a key relation in models of inflation and monetary-policy analysis. In Keynesian models inflation is determined from the Phillips curve, an ad hoc relation between inflation and unemployment, which we may write in terms of price inflation and unemployment as

$$\pi_t = \alpha - \beta u_t, \qquad (9.33)$$

where u_t is the unemployment rate. Equation (9.33) implies a permanent trade-off between inflation and unemployment. We note that the original Phillips curve used wage inflation and not price inflation.

Observing that the evidence increasingly failed to support a stable negative relation between inflation and unemployment, the Phillips curve came to be replaced by the expectations-augmented Phillips curve (see Friedman 1968; Phelps 1966), which takes the form

$$\pi_t = E_t\pi_{t+1} - \beta(u_t - u_t^n), \qquad (9.34)$$

where u_t^n is the natural (or long-run equilibrium) rate of unemployment (i.e., the "nonaccelerating inflation rate of unemployment" (NAIRU)). In equation (9.34) there is only a short-run trade-off between inflation and unemployment, not a long-run trade-off. This is because unemployment will eventually return to its natural rate. When this happens inflation will equal expected future inflation, and so is not determined within the equation; i.e., equation (9.34) allows inflation to take any value in the long run. (We note that this is also a property of equation (9.31) when $\beta/(1-\alpha) = 1$.) The absence of a long-run trade-off between inflation and unemployment seems to accord better with the evidence during the high-inflation years of the 1970s and 1980s. Figures 13.1–13.3 in chapter 13 plot Phillips curves for the United States and United Kingdom.

Later, in the 1990s, the evidence seemed to show that the natural rate of unemployment varied as much as the actual rate of unemployment, thereby largely destroying any link between inflation and unemployment. This led to the development of the New Keynesian Phillips curve. This is closely related to the NAIRU model, but it has more explicit microfoundations and does not depend on unemployment to provide the link relating the real economy to inflation.

The New Keynesian Phillips curve is based on a model of optimal pricing in imperfect competition and a theory of price stickiness (see Roberts 1995, 1997; Clarida et al. 1999; McCallum and Nelson 1999; Svensson and Woodford 2003, 2004; Woodford 2003; Giannoni and Woodford 2005). From equation (9.32) we may express inflation as

$$\pi_t = -\left(1 - \frac{\beta}{1-\alpha}\right)\pi + \frac{\alpha}{1-\alpha}(p_t^* - p_t) + \frac{\beta}{1-\alpha}E_t\pi_{t+1}, \tag{9.35}$$

where in long-run equilibrium $p_t^* = p_t$ and $\pi_t = \pi$. In equation (9.35) inflation is generated by current expected future deviations of the actual price from the optimal price.

Our previous discussion of pricing in imperfect competition showed that the optimal price is a markup over marginal cost (see equations (9.1)–(9.3)). In this case we may write the logarithm of the optimal price p_t^* as

$$p_t^* = \mu_t + mc_t,$$

where mc_t is the log of marginal cost and μ_t is the markup over marginal cost. The markup depends on the price elasticity of demand. From equation (9.1),

$$\mu_t \simeq -\epsilon_{D,t}.$$

Hence the greater the price elasticity, the smaller the markup. From equation (9.3), and in the case of a single factor, namely, labor,

$$mc_t = -v_t + w_t - mp_t,$$
$$v_t = \epsilon_{X_i,t},$$

where v_t is the labor markup, which depends on the labor-supply elasticity $\epsilon_{X_i,t}$, w_t is the log of the nominal-wage rate, and mp_t is the log of the marginal product of labor. The less elastic the labor-supply function is, the higher the marginal cost. For a Cobb–Douglas production function written in logs

$$y_t = a_t + \phi n_t, \quad 0 < \phi < 1,$$

where y_t is output, n_t is employment, and a_t is technological progress, we have

$$mp_t = \ln\phi + y_t - n_t$$
$$= \ln\phi + \frac{a_t}{\phi} - \frac{1-\phi}{\phi}y_t. \tag{9.36}$$

The optimal price is therefore

$$p_t^* = -\ln\phi + \mu_t - v_t + w_t - \frac{a_t}{\phi} + \frac{1-\phi}{\phi}y_t, \tag{9.37}$$

and so the deviation of the optimal price from the actual price is

$$p_t^* - p_t = -\ln\phi + \mu_t - v_t - \frac{a_t}{\phi} + \frac{1-\phi}{\phi}y_t + (w_t - p_t). \qquad (9.38)$$

Substituting equation (9.38) into (9.35) gives the inflation equation

$$\pi_t = -\left[\left(1 - \frac{\beta}{1-\alpha}\right)\pi + \frac{\alpha\ln\phi}{(1-\alpha)}\right] + \frac{\beta}{1-\alpha}E_t\pi_{t+1} + \frac{\alpha(1-\phi)}{(1-\alpha)\phi}y_t$$
$$+ \frac{\alpha}{(1-\alpha)}(w_t - p_t) - \frac{\alpha}{(1-\alpha)\phi}a_t + \frac{\alpha}{(1-\alpha)}(\mu_t - v_t). \qquad (9.39)$$

By exploiting the fact that in equilibrium $p_t^* = p_t$, we can write the inflation equation (9.39) in another way. Denoting equilibrium values by an asterisk and deviations from equilibrium by a tilde, so that $\tilde{p}_t = p_t^* - p_t$, equation (9.38) implies that

$$0 = -\ln\phi + \mu_t^* - v_t^* - \frac{a_t^*}{\phi} + \frac{1-\phi}{\phi}y_t^* + (w_t^* - p_t^*),$$

and hence

$$\tilde{p}_t = -\tilde{\mu}_t + \tilde{v}_t - \frac{\tilde{a}_t}{\phi} - \frac{1-\phi}{\phi}\tilde{y}_t - (\tilde{w}_t - \tilde{p}_t). \qquad (9.40)$$

It then follows from equations (9.35) and (9.40) that the inflation equation can be written as

$$\pi_t = -\left(1 - \frac{\beta}{1-\alpha}\right)\pi + \frac{\beta}{1-\alpha}E_t\pi_{t+1} - \frac{\alpha}{1-\alpha}\tilde{\mu}_t + \frac{\alpha}{1-\alpha}\tilde{v}_t$$
$$+ \frac{\alpha}{(1-\alpha)\phi}\tilde{a}_t - \frac{\alpha(1-\phi)}{(1-\alpha)\phi}\tilde{y}_t - \frac{\alpha}{1-\alpha}(\tilde{w}_t - \tilde{p}_t). \qquad (9.41)$$

Hence inflation will increase if $y_t > y_t^*$, i.e., if output is above its equilibrium level (which is sometimes measured in empirical work by its trend level), or if the real wage or the price markup exceed their equilibrium levels, or if the labor markup is below its equilibrium level, or if there is a negative technology shock.

A number of observations may be made about equation (9.39). First, it is more complex than the usual specification of the New Keynesian inflation equation, which does not include the real-wage term, the markups, or the productivity shock. Assuming that equation (9.41) is correct, it would, of course, be a specification error to omit these terms. On the other hand, the markup and productivity terms may be small relative to the output and real-wage terms. Second, the equation is based on having a single factor of production: labor. In practice, there are other factors: for example, physical capital and material inputs. There is therefore an argument for deriving a more complete model of inflation that takes these into account. Third, and related to this, we have previously argued that a general increase in the prices of all factors is required for the effect on inflation to be sizeable in the longer term. An increase in the unit cost of a single factor (for example, an oil price increase) may not have a significant effect on inflation for long due to factor substitution in the longer term. Fourth, in equation (9.36) we expressed the marginal product of labor in terms of output. We could, however, have expressed it in terms of labor, in which case the equation would become

$$mp_t = \ln \phi + a_t - (1 - \phi)n_t.$$

The resulting inflation equation would then be

$$\pi_t = -\left(1 - \frac{\beta}{1-\alpha}\right)\pi + \frac{\beta}{1-\alpha}E_t\pi_{t+1} - \frac{\alpha}{1-\alpha}\tilde{\mu}_t + \frac{\alpha}{1-\alpha}\tilde{v}_t$$
$$+ \frac{\alpha}{(1-\alpha)}\tilde{a}_t - \frac{\alpha(1-\phi)}{(1-\alpha)}\tilde{n}_t - \frac{\alpha}{1-\alpha}(\tilde{w}_t - \tilde{p}_t), \quad (9.42)$$

where we may interpret $\tilde{n}_t$, the deviation of employment from its long-run equilibrium value, as unemployment.

9.5.1 The New Keynesian Phillips Curve in an Open Economy

So far we have measured inflation in terms of the GDP deflator. Monetary policy is, however, usually conducted with reference to the consumer price index (CPI). In a closed economy there is little difference between the GDP deflator and the CPI, but in an open economy there is an important difference as the CPI also reflects the price of foreign tradeables. Inflation measured by the GDP deflator is

$$\pi_t = (1 - s_t^{nt})\pi_t^t + s_t^{nt}\pi_t^{nt},$$

where π_t is the inflation rate of domestically produced goods and services and s_t^{nt} is the share of nontraded goods. This is a weighted average of π_t^{nt}, the inflation rate of domestic nontraded goods, and π_t^t, the inflation rate of domestic traded goods. CPI inflation is measured by a weighted average of π_t and the inflation rate of imported goods, π_t^m, and is given by

$$\pi_t^{cpi} = (1 - s_t^m)\pi_t + s_t^m\pi_t^m,$$

where s_t^m is the share of imports.

In an economy where producers have little or no monopoly power—a typical situation for a small economy—domestic traded goods prices are equal to world prices expressed in domestic currency. Thus

$$\pi_t^t = \pi_t^m = \pi_t^w + \Delta s_t,$$

where π_t^w is the world inflation rate and Δs_t is the proportionate rate of change of the exchange rate (the domestic price of foreign exchange). In an open economy in which producers have a degree of monopoly power, such as a large economy, import prices will be fully or partly priced to market. Consequently,

$$\pi_t^m = \varphi(1 - \eta)(\pi_t^w + \Delta s_t) + (1 - \varphi)\eta\pi_t^t,$$

where $\varphi = 1$ for full exchange rate pass through, and $\eta = 1$ for full pricing-to-market (both lie in the interval $[0, 1]$), and π_t^t is determined domestically.

Thus, measured by the GDP deflator, inflation in a small open economy is

$$\pi_t = s_t^{nt}\pi_t^{nt} + (1 - s_t^{nt})(\pi_t^w + \Delta s_t),$$

and in a large open economy it is

$$\pi_t = (1 - s_t^{nt})\pi_t^t + s_t^{nt}\pi_t^{nt}.$$

CPI inflation in a small open economy is given by

$$\pi_t^{cpi} = (1 - s_t^m)s_t^{nt}\pi_t^{nt} + [1 - s_t^m(1 - s_t^{nt})](\pi_t^w + \Delta s_t),$$

and in a large open economy it is given by

$$\pi_t^{cpi} = (1 - s_t^m)s_t^{nt}\pi_t^{nt} + [(1 - s_t^m)(1 - s_t^{nt}) + s_t^m(1 - \varphi)\eta]\pi_t^t + s_t^m\varphi(1 - \eta)(\pi_t^w + \Delta s_t).$$

Consequently, the impact of changes in the exchange rate on inflation depends on how inflation is measured and on the size of the economy. It has little or no effect on the GDP deflator for a large open economy. For a small economy, it has a greater effect on CPI inflation than on GDP inflation.

To complete the model of CPI inflation we need to specify traded and non-traded goods inflation. Suppose that they are identical, and hence equal to GDP inflation, and that they are determined by the New Keynesian Phillips curve. Then, from equation (9.35),

$$\pi_t = \frac{\alpha}{1 - \alpha}\sum_{s=0}^{\infty}\left(\frac{\beta}{1 - \alpha}\right)^s E_t(p_{t+s}^* - p_{t+s}),$$

provided $\beta/(1 - \alpha) < 1$. Hence CPI inflation is given by

$$\begin{aligned}
\pi_t^{cpi} &= [(1 - s_t^m) + s_t^m(1 - \varphi)\eta]\pi_t + s_t^m\varphi(1 - \eta)(\pi_t^w + \Delta s_t) \\
&= \frac{\delta\alpha}{1 - \alpha}(p_t^* - p_t) + \frac{\beta}{1 - \alpha}E_t\pi_{t+1}^{cpi} + s_t^m\delta(1 - \eta)(\pi_t^w + \Delta s_t) \\
&\quad - \frac{\beta}{1 - \alpha}E_t[s_{t+1}^m\varphi(1 - \eta)(\pi_{t+1}^w + \Delta s_{t+1})],
\end{aligned}$$

where p_t is the GDP price level and $\delta = [(1 - s_t^m) + s_t^m(1 - \varphi)\eta]$. Thus, CPI inflation replaces GDP inflation and includes world inflation expressed in domestic currency.

9.6 Conclusions

The evidence shows that prices are not perfectly flexible and that the frequency of price changes varies between different types of goods and services. This suggests that prices are not determined in perfectly competitive markets. Modern theories of price determination adopt an optimizing framework but seek to explain price stickiness by assuming imperfect competition. We have extended this to price determination in the open economy. As a result, prices and output differ from the levels that would prevail in perfect competition.

The three leading theories of price stickiness yield very similar models of inflation. These, together with the assumption of imperfect competition, form the basis of the New Keynesian Phillips curve. In an open economy it is necessary to distinguish between GDP and CPI inflation. The New Keynesian open-economy Phillips curve includes an additional variable: the rate of inflation of world prices measured in domestic currency. As the impact of foreign inflation on domestic inflation is affected by the exchange rate, the exchange rate provides an additional channel in the transmission mechanism of monetary policy. The significance of this channel depends on the degree of imperfect competition in traded goods markets, which affects how the prices of traded goods are set in foreign markets. After including all of the features we have discussed, the resulting price equation has become quite complex. It is therefore common in monetary-policy analysis to use a simplified version of the price equation that is closely related to the basic Calvo model.

10

Asset Pricing and Macroeconomics

10.1 Introduction

Assets—physical, human, and financial capital—play a crucial role in macroeconomics. They are required for production and for generating income, and they are central to the intertemporal allocation of resources through the processes of saving, lending, and borrowing. In this chapter we focus on how financial assets are priced in general equilibrium. In chapter 11 we apply these theories to three financial assets: bonds, equity, and foreign exchange. Each asset has specific features that require the theories to be applied separately.

We began our macroeconomic analysis by discussing the decision about whether to consume today or in the future. This gave us our theories of physical capital accumulation and savings. We argued that people plan their consumption both for today and for the rest of their lives with the aim of maintaining their standard of living even though income may vary through time. During periods when income is low—in retirement or in periods of unemployment, for example—their standard of living would fall unless they had saved some of their income and could draw on this. In order to consume more in the future, people must consume less today, i.e., they substitute intertemporally between consumption today and consumption in the future. The decision of whether to consume or to save depends on the rate of return to savings relative to the rate of time preference: in other words, on the price of financial assets.

Future consumption requires output and hence physical capital. The decision on whether to invest and accumulate capital or to disburse profits depends on the rate of return to capital and the cost of borrowing from households. In general equilibrium, the rate of return to capital and the rate of interest on savings are related because firms will not be willing to borrow at rates higher than their rate of return to capital, and households will not be willing to lend to firms, or anyone else, such as government, unless the rate of return to savings is greater than or equal to their rate of time preference. Moreover, no matter the type of asset, we want to price them in a consistent way. We therefore seek a theory of asset pricing that reflects these intertemporal general equilibrium considerations.

So far we have treated asset returns as though they are all risk free. In practice, however, nearly all assets are risky, having uncertain payoffs in the future and hence risky returns. We therefore need our theory of asset pricing to take account of risk. One way of classifying the various theories of asset pricing is through the way they account for risk, and hence in their measure of the risk premium—the additional expected return in excess of the certain return required to compensate for bearing risk or uncertainty. We consider four theories of asset pricing: contingent-claims analysis, general equilibrium asset pricing, the consumption-based capital-asset-pricing model, and the traditional capital-asset-pricing model. We also show how they are related. As risky returns are random variables, we use stochastic dynamic programming instead of Lagrange multiplier analysis though, as explained, Lagrange multiplier analysis could still be used. We begin by considering some preliminaries: expected utility and risk aversion, the risk premium, arbitrage and no arbitrage, and their implications for efficient market theory. We then consider contingent-claims theory before turning to intertemporal asset pricing. In chapter 11 we apply this theory to the stock, bond, and foreign exchange markets.

A helpful general reference for the basic concepts of the theory of finance covered here is Ingersoll (1987). An excellent recent reference covering asset pricing theory based on the discount-factor approach is Cochrane (2005). For discussion of the links between finance and macroeconomics see Lucas (1978) and Altug and Labadie (1994). In keeping with the rest of this book, our discussion of finance will use discrete time. For an account of the intertemporal capital-asset-pricing model in continuous time see Merton (1973).

10.2 Expected Utility and Risk

10.2.1 Risk Aversion

We begin by establishing a definition of risk aversion. Consider a gamble with a random payoff (value of wealth after the gamble) W in which there are two possible outcomes (payoffs or prospects) x_1 and x_2. Let the probabilities of the two outcomes be π and $(1 - \pi)$, respectively. The issue is whether to avoid the gamble and receive with certainty the actuarial value of the gamble (i.e., its expected or average value), or to take the gamble even though this involves an uncertain outcome.

A person who prefers the gamble is a *risk lover*, one who is indifferent is *risk neutral*, and one who prefers the actuarial value with certainty is *risk averse*. The expected (or actuarial) value of the gamble is

$$E(W) = \pi x_1 + (1 - \pi)x_2.$$

A *fair gamble* is one where $E(W) = 0$.

For the utility function $U(W)$ with $U'(W) \geq 0$ and $U''(W) \leq 0$ we can define attitudes to risk more precisely as follows:

$$\begin{aligned}
\text{risk aversion:} \quad & U[E(W)] > E[U(W)]; \\
\text{risk neutrality:} \quad & U[E(W)] = E[U(W)]; \\
\text{risk loving:} \quad & U[E(W)] < E[U(W)].
\end{aligned}$$

It can be shown that

$$E[U(W)] \gtreqless U[E(W)] \quad \text{as } U'' \gtreqless 0.$$

This is known as Jensen's inequality. To prove this, consider a Taylor series expansion about $E(W)$:

$$E[U(W)] = E(U[E(W)]) + E(W - E[W])U' + \tfrac{1}{2}E[W - E(W)]^2 U''$$

$$= U[E(W)] + \tfrac{1}{2}E[W - E(W)]^2 U''$$

$$\gtreqless U[E(W)] \quad \text{as } U'' \gtreqless 0.$$

Consider now the case where there is a single risky asset with return r and variance $V(r)$ and a risk-free asset with return r^f. If the initial stock of wealth is W_0, then wealth after investing in the risky asset is $W^r = W_0(1 + r)$ and after investing in the risk-free asset it is $W^f = W_0(1 + r^f)$. Expanding $E[U(W^r)]$ about $r = r^f$ we obtain

$$E[U(W^r)] \simeq U[W_0(1 + r^f)] + W_0^2 \tfrac{1}{2} V(r) U''[W_0(1 + r^f)] \qquad (10.1)$$

$$\gtreqless U[W_0(1 + r^f)] = U(E[W^f]) \quad \text{as } U'' \gtreqless 0. \qquad (10.2)$$

Hence, for a risk-averse investor (i.e., $U'' < 0$) the expected utility of investing in the risky asset (taking a gamble) $E[U(W^r)]$ is less than the certain utility of investing in the risk-free asset $U(E[W^f])$. We conclude that when the expected returns are the same, a risk-averse investor would prefer not to take a gamble. On the other hand, the investor who is risk neutral ($U'' = 0$) would be indifferent between the two assets.

10.2.2 Risk Premium

We now ask how much compensation a risk-averse investor would need in order to be willing to take the gamble or hold the risky asset. We assume that this compensation can take the form of a known additional payment, or of a higher expected return than the risk-free rate. The additional (certain) payoff (return) required to compensate for the risk arising from taking the fair gamble is called the risk premium. We consider only the case of a single risky asset and a single risk-free asset.

In equation (10.2) we showed that for a risk-averse investor, $E[U(W^r)] < U(E[W^f])$. We define the risk premium as the certain value of ρ that satisfies $E(r) = r^f + \rho$ and

$$E[U(W^r)] = U(W^f). \qquad (10.3)$$

We now take a Taylor series expansion of $E[U(W^r)]$ about $r = r^f + \rho$ to obtain

$$E[U(W^r)] \simeq U[W_0(1 + r^f + \rho)] + \tfrac{1}{2} W_0^2 E(r - r^f - \rho)^2 U''. \qquad (10.4)$$

Expanding $U[W_0(1 + r^f + \rho)]$ about $\rho = 0$ we obtain

$$U[W_0(1 + r^f + \rho)] \simeq U[W_0(1 + r^f)] + W_0 \rho U'. \qquad (10.5)$$

Combining equations (10.4) and (10.5) gives

$$E[U(W^{\mathrm{r}})] \simeq U(E[W^{\mathrm{f}}]) + W_0 \rho U' + \tfrac{1}{2} W_0^2 V(r) U''. \tag{10.6}$$

It follows that if equation (10.3) is satisfied, then

$$\rho = -\frac{V(r)}{2} \frac{W_0 U''}{U'}.$$

Thus, the risk premium ρ will be larger, the larger the coefficient of relative risk aversion $-(W_0 U''/U')$ (i.e., the curvature of the utility function) and the larger the variance (or volatility) of the risky return, $V(r)$.

10.3 No-Arbitrage and Market Efficiency

10.3.1 Arbitrage and No-Arbitrage

Whether or not assets are correctly priced by a market relates to the concepts of arbitrage and no-arbitrage.

1. An *arbitrage* portfolio is a self-financing portfolio with a zero or negative cost that has a positive payoff.

2. An *arbitrage-free*, or *no-arbitrage*, portfolio is a self-financing portfolio with a zero payoff.

Crudely put, an arbitrage portfolio gives the investor something for nothing. Such opportunities are therefore rare. The financial market, seeing the existence of an arbitrage opportunity, would compete for the assets, thereby raising their price and eliminating the arbitrage opportunity. It is therefore common in the theory of asset pricing to assume that arbitrage opportunities do not exist and to impose this as a restriction. The implication is that if a market is efficient, then it is pricing assets correctly and quickly eliminates arbitrage opportunities.

10.3.2 Market Efficiency

A market is said to be efficient if there are no unexploited arbitrage opportunities. This requires that all new information is instantly impounded in market prices. This is an exacting standard. In practice, fully and correctly reflecting all relevant information so that new information, or new ways of processing this information, have no effect on an asset or any other price is almost impossible to achieve. In principle, the concept should be extended even further to become a criterion of general equilibrium.

The return on an asset may be written as

$$r_{t+1} = \frac{X_{t+1}}{P_t},$$

where P_t is the price of the asset at the start of period t and X_{t+1} is its value or payoff at the start of period $t + 1$. For any risky asset i with return $r_{i,t+1}$ the absence of arbitrage opportunities implies that

$$E_t r_{i,t+1} = r_t^f + \rho_{it}, \tag{10.7}$$

where r_t^f, the return on the risk-free asset, is known with certainty at the start of period t, and ρ_{it} is the risk premium for the ith asset, also known at the start of period t.

Equation (10.7) shows that asset pricing consists of pricing one asset relative to another, namely, the risk-free rate, then adding the risk premium. Traditional finance commonly does this by relating the risk premium to a set of factors determined from the past behavior of asset prices. An example is the use of affine factor models to determine the prices of bonds with different times to maturity, i.e., the term structure of interest rates. In contrast, the general equilibrium theory of asset pricing is based on identifying the fundamental sources of risk generated by macroeconomic fluctuations and their uncertainty. These are due largely to unanticipated fluctuations in output and inflation in both the domestic and the international economies. We begin our discussion of asset pricing by considering contingent-claims analysis.

10.4   Asset Pricing and Contingent Claims

Contingent-claims analysis provides a very general theory of asset pricing to which all other theories may be related. A typical asset can be thought of as comprising a combination of primitive assets called contingent claims. Once we know the prices of the primitive assets we can calculate the price of any other asset. We state the problem of pricing an asset using contingent claims as follows:

1. The price of an asset depends on its payoff.

2. Payoffs are typically unknown today. They depend on the state of the world tomorrow.

3. All assets can be considered as a bundle of primitive assets called *contingent claims*.

4. The difference between assets arises from the way the contingent claims are combined.

5. If we can price each contingent claim, then we can price any combination of them, i.e., any asset.

10.4.1   A Contingent Claim

Suppose there are $s = 1, \ldots, S$ states of the world. A contingent claim is an asset that has a payoff of $1 if state s occurs and a payoff of 0 otherwise. Let $q(s)$ denote today's price of a contingent claim with a payoff of $1 in state s. Also let $x(s)$ be the quantity of this contingent claim that is purchased at date t. Finally, let p denote today's price of an asset whose payoff depends on which state of the world $s = 1, \ldots, S$ occurs.

10.4.2 The Price of an Asset

Provided the state prices exist, the price p of any asset can now be expressed as

$$p = \sum_{s=1}^{S} q(s)x(s). \tag{10.8}$$

The vector $q = [q(1)q(2) \cdots q(S)]'$ is then known as a *state-price* vector. This relation says that the price of the asset is simply equal to the sum of the price in a given state s multiplied by the quantity of contingent claims held in that state.

10.4.3 The Stochastic Discount-Factor Approach to Asset Pricing

Suppose that $\pi(s)$ is the probability of state s occurring. The $\pi(s)$ therefore define the state-density function. Next we define

$$m(s) = \frac{q(s)}{\pi(s)}, \quad s = 1, \ldots, S. \tag{10.9}$$

Thus $m(s)$ is the price in state s divided by the probability of state s occurring; $m(s)$ is nonnegative because state prices and probabilities are both nonnegative. We can now write the price of the asset as

$$p = \sum_{s=1}^{S} \pi(s)m(s)x(s)$$
$$= E(mx). \tag{10.10}$$

$m(s)$ can therefore be interpreted as the value of the stochastic discount factor of \$1 in state s, $x(s)$ can be interpreted as the payoff in state s, and the price of the asset as the average, or expected, discounted value of these payoffs. If $m(s)$ is small, then state s is "cheap" in the sense that investors are unwilling to pay a high price to receive the payoff in state s. An asset that delivers in cheap states tends to have a payoff that covaries negatively with $m(s)$, i.e., $\text{Cov}(m, x) < 0$.

Equation (10.10) is a completely general pricing formula applicable to all assets, including derivatives such as options. It is called the stochastic discount-factor approach. All other asset-pricing theories can be expressed in this form. The differences between them are in the way that the stochastic discount factor m is specified. The reader is referred to Cochrane (2005) for a more detailed treatment of the stochastic discount-factor approach to asset pricing.

10.4.4 Asset Returns

Equation (10.10) can be expressed in terms of returns instead of the asset price. Dividing equation (10.8) through by p and defining $1 + r(s) = x(s)/p$ for $s = 1, \ldots, S$, we can rewrite equation (10.8) as

$$1 = \sum_{s=1}^{S} q(s)[1 + r(s)]. \tag{10.11}$$

It follows that

$$1 = \sum_{s=1}^{S} \pi(s)m(s)[1 + r(s)]$$
$$= E[m(1 + r)], \tag{10.12}$$

where r is the return on the asset. This is the stochastic discount-factor representation of returns, whether risky or risk free.

10.4.5 Risk-Free Return

Since equation (10.12) applies to all assets, it applies to risk-free assets. If the asset is risk free, then it has the same payoff in all states of the world. Thus, $x(s)$ is independent of s, and we can write $x(s) = x$ for all s. The price of the risk-free asset is then

$$p^f = \sum q(s)x = x \sum q(s)$$
$$= x \sum \pi(s)m(s) = xE(m), \tag{10.13}$$

otherwise an arbitrage opportunity would exist.

If, for example, $x = 1$, then the price of an asset today that pays one unit in all states of nature next period is given by

$$p^f = E(m),$$

or

$$1 = \frac{1}{p^f}E(m)$$
$$= (1 + r^f)E(m),$$

where r^f is the risk-free rate. Further,

$$E(m) = \frac{1}{1 + r^f}. \tag{10.14}$$

10.4.6 The No-Arbitrage Relation

We can derive the no-arbitrage relation, equation (10.7), from equations (10.12) and (10.14). From the definition of a covariance between two random variables x and y,

$$\text{Cov}(x, y) = E(xy) - E(x)E(y),$$

and noting that in general m and r are stochastic, we may rewrite equation (10.12) as

$$1 = E(m)E(1 + r) + \text{Cov}(m, 1 + r);$$

hence

$$E(1 + r) = \frac{1}{E(m)} - \frac{\text{Cov}(m, 1 + r)}{E(m)}. \tag{10.15}$$

From equations (10.14) and (10.15) we obtain the no-arbitrage relation:

$$E(r) = r^f - (1 + r^f)\operatorname{Cov}(m, 1 + r). \tag{10.16}$$

Thus the risk premium ρ—the expected return in excess of the risk-free rate—is

$$\rho = -(1 + r^f)\operatorname{Cov}(m, 1 + r). \tag{10.17}$$

For $\rho > 0$ we require that $\operatorname{Cov}(m, 1 + r) = \operatorname{Cov}(m, r) < 0$. In other words, risk arises when low returns coincide with a high discount factor. We will consider how to determine the stochastic discount factor below.

10.4.7 Risk-Neutral Valuation

Having introduced the concept of a risk premium, before pursuing the issue of how to determine it, we consider how to avoid considerations of risk by using risk-neutral valuation. This requires us to use the concept of a risk-neutral probability $\pi^N(s)$ instead of the state probability $\pi(s)$, which is the actual probability of state s occurring. The price of any asset can be represented as the expected value of its future random payoffs using these risk-neutral probabilities. Risk-neutral (or risk-adjusted) probability is crucial to many results in the theory of finance, particularly in pricing options.

10.4.7.1 Risk-Neutral Probability

Given a positive state-price vector $[q(1)q(2)\cdots q(S)]'$, we may define the risk-neutral probability $\pi^*(s)$ as

$$\pi^N(s) = (1 + r^f)\pi(s)m(s)$$
$$= \frac{1}{\sum q(s)}\pi(s)\left(\frac{q(s)}{\pi(s)}\right) = \frac{q(s)}{\sum q(s)},$$

where

$$\sum_{s=1}^{S} \pi^N(s) = 1 \quad \text{and} \quad 0 < \pi^*(s) < 1.$$

10.4.7.2 Asset Pricing Using Risk-Neutral Probabilities

We can convert the price of an asset written in terms of state probabilities into one written in terms of risk-neutral probabilities as follows:

$$p = \sum \pi(s)m(s)x(s)$$
$$= \frac{1}{1 + r^f}\sum \pi^N(s)x(s)$$
$$= \frac{1}{1 + r^f}E^N[x(s)]$$
$$= E(m)E^N(x),$$

where we have substituted $1/E(m)$ for $1 + r^f$ and $E^N(\cdot)$ denotes an expectation taken with respect to the risk-neutral probabilities. Hence, by using risk-neutral probabilities, we can express the price of an asset as

$$p = E[mx] = E(m)E^N(x) \qquad (10.18)$$

$$= \frac{1}{1 + r^f}E^N(x). \qquad (10.19)$$

Equation (10.18) implies that using risk-neutral probabilities, m and x are uncorrelated. Equation (10.19) shows that the price of any asset can be written as the expected discounted value of its future payoffs, where the discounting is done by means of the stochastic discount factor $m(s)$. It then follows that the price of the asset is proportional to the risk-neutral expectation of its random payoff.

From equation (10.19), the no-arbitrage equation for returns can now be written without a risk premium as

$$E^N(r) = r^f. \qquad (10.20)$$

Comparing equation (10.7) or equation (10.16) with (10.20) we deduce that

$$E^N(r) = E(r) - \rho,$$

where ρ is the risk premium. Thus risk-neutral valuation risk-adjusts the risky return. It does not, of course, eliminate the risk itself, which remains. The advantage is that it can simplify asset pricing.

10.5 General Equilibrium Asset Pricing

In general equilibrium, asset prices are determined jointly with all other variables in the economy. Previously in our discussion of the real macroeconomy, we determined the real rate of return to capital jointly with consumption, investment, and capital. But in our discussion of households and life-cycle theory we treated the rate of return to financial assets as given. We now reconsider the analysis of the household, who we take to be the representative investor in financial assets. We begin by examining the problem using contingent-claims analysis. We then extend the discussion to the type of formulation of the macroeconomy that we have used until this chapter.

10.5.1 Using Contingent-Claims Analysis

Consider a representative household that is deciding between consumption today and consumption tomorrow, where current income is known with certainty but income next period is random and hence uncertain. We do not specify the source of this income, which could be from working or from asset income. We assume that the household maximizes the value of current plus discounted expected future utility—both derived from consumption—subject to a budget constraint that depends on the state of the world in the second period. Thus the problem is to maximize

$$V = U(c_t) + \beta E_t U(c_{t+1})$$
$$\equiv U(c) + \beta \sum_s \pi(s) U[c(s)]$$

subject to

$$c + \sum_s q(s)c(s) = y + \sum_s q(s)y(s),$$

where c is current consumption and y is current income and both are known with certainty in the current period, $c(s)$ is next period's consumption and $y(s)$ is next period's income and both are unknown in the current period as s, the state of the economy next period, is unknown. The $q(s)$ are the state prices for contingent claims that are used to value future random consumption and income streams.

Although the problem is stochastic, it can be analyzed using Lagrange multiplier analysis. The problem is to maximize the Lagrangian

$$\mathcal{L} = U(c) + \beta \sum_s \pi(s) U[c(s)] + \lambda \left[y + \sum_s q(s)y(s) - c - \sum_s q(s)c(s) \right].$$

The first-order conditions are given by

$$\frac{\partial \mathcal{L}}{\partial c} = U'(c) - \lambda = 0,$$

$$\frac{\partial \mathcal{L}}{\partial c(s)} = \beta \pi(s) U'[c(s)] - \lambda q(s) = 0, \quad s = 1, \dots, S.$$

Combining these conditions yields the set of conditions

$$q(s) = \beta \pi(s) \frac{U'[c(s)]}{U'(c)}, \quad s = 1, \dots, S.$$

From equation (10.9),

$$q(s) = \pi(s)m(s);$$

hence

$$m(s) = \frac{\beta U'[c(s)]}{U'(c)}. \tag{10.21}$$

Thus, the stochastic discount factor is the intertemporal marginal rate of substitution in consumption between two consecutive periods. As consumption in the second period is a random variable, so is the stochastic discount factor.

It also follows that the state prices $q(s)$ are defined as the product of the state probabilities and the intertemporal marginal rate of substitution in consumption between two consecutive periods. If we are willing to formulate a well-specified underlying economic model, we can then obtain explicit expressions for the state prices $q(s)$. The expected value of any random consumption stream is given by

$$\sum_s q(s)c(s) = \sum_s \pi(s)m(s)c(s) = E(mc).$$

Having determined the stochastic discount factors $m(s)$, we can price any asset in this economy using equation (10.8). The resulting price is

$$p = \sum_s \pi(s)m(s)x(s)$$

$$= \frac{\beta \sum_s \pi(s)U'[c(s)]x(s)}{U'(c)}. \qquad (10.22)$$

In particular, we can price the income stream $y(s)$ by setting $x(s) = y(s)$.

We can also rewrite equation (10.22) in terms of the stochastic rate, or return, $r(s)$ as

$$\sum_s \pi(s)\frac{\beta U'[c(s)]}{U'(c)}[1 + r(s)] = 1, \qquad (10.23)$$

where $1 + r(s) = x(s)/p$. Equation (10.23) is just an Euler equation defined for stochastic returns.

If we denote the current period as time t and the second period as $t + 1$, then we can rewrite the no-arbitrage equation (10.16) for the return on any risky income stream as

$$E(r_{t+1}) = r_t^f - \frac{1}{1 + r_t^f} \, \text{Cov}\left[\frac{\beta U'(c_{t+1})}{U'(c_t)}, r_{t+1}\right]. \qquad (10.24)$$

This will also be the no-arbitrage equation for the return on any asset in the economy. The last term is the risk premium.

10.5.2 Asset Pricing Using the Consumption-Based Capital Asset-Pricing Model (C-CAPM)

Equation (10.24) is commonly known as the asset-pricing equation for the consumption-based capital-asset-pricing model (see Breedon 1979). We now derive this equation using the formulation of the macroeconomy that we have adopted in previous chapters. We demonstrate that the Euler equation that determines the optimal path of consumption is also used to price assets. This result shows that the DGE model provides a single theoretical framework for use in both macroeconomics and finance, and hence unifies the two subjects.

In chapter 4 we defined the household's problem as maximizing

$$V_t = \sum_{s=0}^{\infty} \beta^s U(c_{t+s}) \qquad (10.25)$$

subject to the budget constraint

$$\Delta a_{t+1} + c_t = x_t + r_t a_t, \qquad (10.26)$$

where x_t is income and a_t is the real stock of assets. It was assumed that the future was known with certainty. We now assume that the future is uncertain so that $\{x_{t+s}, r_{t+s}; s > 0\}$ are random variables. We therefore replace equation (10.25) by its conditional expectation based on information available at time t:

$$V_t = \sum_{s=0}^{\infty} \beta^s E_t[U(c_{t+s})]. \qquad (10.27)$$

Previously, we solved the optimization using the method of Lagrange multipliers. As explained in the mathematical appendix, the problem with applying this method to the stochastic case is that the Lagrange multipliers are also random variables. As a result, the Euler equation is expressed in terms of the conditional expectation of the product of the rate of change in the Lagrange multipliers and r_{t+1}, and we are unable to substitute the marginal utility of consumption for the Lagrange multipliers and so solve for consumption. Instead, therefore, we use the method of stochastic dynamic programming, the details of which are given in the mathematical appendix.

First, we rewrite equation (10.27) as the recursion

$$V_t = U(c_t) + \beta E_t[V_{t+1}]. \tag{10.28}$$

More generally, we could have a time-nonseparable utility function

$$V_t = G\{U(c_t), E_t[V_{t+1}]\}.$$

The advantage of such a formulation is that it enables attitudes to risk to be distinguished from attitudes to time (see Kreps and Porteus 1978). For simplicity, we shall confine ourselves to time-separable utility as in equation (10.28). We note that the assumed time horizon in equation (10.27) is infinity. We can justify this by noting that, although people live finite lives, provided their effective time horizon is long enough, the assumption of an infinite horizon will provide a very good approximation. We may also note that people do not know when they will die and act for most of their lives as though they have many more years to live. Further, if reoptimization takes place each period, only the first period (period t) would be carried out. A common reformulation of equation (10.27) with a finite horizon of T is

$$V_t = \sum_{i=0}^{T} \beta^i E_t[U(c_{t+i})] + \beta^T E_t[B(a_T)], \tag{10.29}$$

where $B(a_T)$ can be interpreted as a bequest motive. The familiar capital-asset-pricing model (CAPM) of Sharpe (1964), Lintner (1965), and Mossin (1966) is another special case of equation (10.29) involving only the last term. In other words, in CAPM the aim is to maximize the value of the stock of financial assets at some point in the future, thereby ignoring intermediate consumption.

10.5.2.1 *The Stochastic Dynamic Programming Solution*

The problem is to maximize the value-function equation (10.28) subject to the dynamic-constraint equation (10.26). As shown in the mathematical appendix, provided a solution exists, the first-order condition can be obtained by differentiating with respect to c_t to give

$$\frac{\partial V_t}{\partial c_t} = \frac{\partial U_t}{\partial c_t} - \beta E_t\left(\frac{\partial V_{t+1}}{\partial c_t}\right) = 0 \tag{10.30}$$

with

$$\frac{\partial V_{t+1}}{\partial c_t} = \frac{\partial V_{t+1}}{\partial c_{t+1}} \frac{\partial c_{t+1}}{\partial c_t}.$$

In order to evaluate $E_t(\partial V_{t+1}/\partial c_{t+1})$ we note that

$$V_{t+1} = U(c_{t+1}) + \beta E_{t+1}(V_{t+2});$$

hence,

$$\frac{\partial V_{t+1}}{\partial c_{t+1}} = \frac{\partial U_{t+1}}{\partial c_{t+1}}.$$

To evaluate $\partial c_{t+1}/\partial c_t$ we express c_{t+1} as a function of c_t. This requires using the two-period budget constraint obtained by combining the budget constraints for periods t and $t + 1$ to eliminate a_{t+1} so that

$$c_t + \frac{c_{t+1}}{1 + r_{t+1}} + \frac{a_{t+2}}{1 + r_{t+1}} = x_t + \frac{x_{t+1}}{1 + r_{t+1}} + a_t(1 + r_t).$$

Hence,

$$\frac{\partial c_{t+1}}{\partial c_t} = -(1 + r_{t+1}).$$

The first-order condition (10.30) can now be written as

$$\frac{\partial V_t}{\partial c_t} = \frac{\partial U_t}{\partial c_t} - \beta E_t \left[\frac{\partial U_{t+1}}{\partial c_{t+1}}(1 + r_{t+1}) \right] = 0.$$

We therefore obtain the Euler equation for the stochastic case as

$$E_t \left[\frac{\beta U'_{t+1}}{U'_t}(1 + r_{t+1}) \right] = 1. \tag{10.31}$$

This is equivalent to equations (10.23) and (10.12) with

$$E_t[M_{t+1}(1 + r_{t+1})] = 1 \tag{10.32}$$

and $M_{t+1} \equiv (\beta U'_{t+1}/U'_t)$.

10.5.2.2 Pricing Risky Assets

Previously we solved the Euler equation for consumption, taking the rate of return as given. To obtain the asset price we reverse this by solving instead for r_{t+1} in terms of consumption. In this way we use the same stochastic dynamic general equilibrium model to determine the macroeconomic variables and the asset prices. We therefore unify economics and finance within a single theoretical framework.

   In general, the Euler equation will be highly nonlinear. We therefore take a Taylor series expansion of the Euler equation about $c_{t+1} = c_t$. Expanding $U'(c_{t+1})$ about $c_{t+1} = c_t$ to give

$$U'(c_{t+1}) \simeq U'(c_t) + (c_{t+1} - c_t)U''_t$$

leads to the approximation

$$\frac{\beta U'_{t+1}}{U'_t} \simeq \beta \left[\frac{U'_t + \Delta c_{t+1} U''_t}{U'_t} \right] = \beta \left[1 + \frac{\Delta c_{t+1}}{c_t} \frac{c_t U''_t}{U'_t} \right]$$

$$= \beta \left[1 - \sigma_t \frac{\Delta c_{t+1}}{c_t} \right],$$

where

$$\sigma_t = -\frac{c_t U''_t}{U'_t} \geqslant 0, \quad \text{as } U''_t \leqslant 0,$$

is the coefficient of relative risk aversion (CRRA); the greater the CRRA is, the more risk averse the investor. We recall that in the special case of power utility,

$$U(c_t) = \frac{c_t^{1-\sigma} - 1}{1 - \sigma}, \quad \sigma \geqslant 0;$$

the CRRA is a constant, i.e., $\sigma_t = \sigma$.

We can now write the Euler equation as

$$E_t \left[\beta \left(1 - \sigma_t \frac{\Delta c_{t+1}}{c_t} \right) (1 + r_{t+1}) \right] = 1.$$

Recalling that $\beta = 1/(1 + \theta)$ this can be rewritten as

$$1 - \sigma_t E_t \left(\frac{\Delta c_{t+1}}{c_t} \right) + E_t (r_{t+1}) - \sigma_t E_t \left(\frac{\Delta c_{t+1}}{c_t} r_{t+1} \right) = 1 + \theta.$$

Using the fact that[1]

$$E_t \left(\frac{\Delta c_{t+1}}{c_t} r_{t+1} \right) = \text{Cov}_t \left(\frac{\Delta c_{t+1}}{c_t}, r_{t+1} \right) + E_t \left(\frac{\Delta c_{t+1}}{c_t} \right) E_t (r_{t+1}),$$

we obtain an expression for the expected rate of return:

$$E_t (r_{t+1}) = \frac{\theta + \sigma_t E_t (\Delta c_{t+1}/c_t) + \sigma_t \text{Cov}_t ((\Delta c_{t+1}/c_t), r_{t+1})}{1 - \sigma_t E_t (\Delta c_{t+1}/c_t)}. \tag{10.33}$$

10.5.2.3 Pricing the Risk-Free Asset

Equation (10.33) holds for any asset, whether risky or risk free. But if the asset is risk free, we can replace r_t in the budget constraint by the risk-free rate r^f_{t-1}. Furthermore, r_{t+1} can be replaced in equation (10.33) by r^f_t, which is known at time t. Hence, $E_t(r^f_t) = r^f_t$ and $\text{Cov}_t((\Delta c_{t+1}/c_t), r^f_t) = 0$. Equation (10.33) therefore becomes

$$r^f_t = \frac{\theta + \sigma_t E_t (\Delta c_{t+1}/c_t)}{1 - \sigma_t E_t (\Delta c_{t+1}/c_t)}. \tag{10.34}$$

---

[1] If, for example, X_{t+1} is a vector of random variables with conditional mean AX_t so that $X_{t+1} = AX_t + e_t$, where the e_t are independently distributed with zero mean and variance Σ_t, then for any two elements $x_{i,t+1}$ and $x_{j,t+1}$ we have $\text{Cov}_t(x_{i,t+1}, x_{j,t+1}) = \sigma_{ij,t}$, where $\Sigma_t = \{\sigma_{ij,t}\}$. Thus the conditional covariance is the covariance of the error terms in the forecasting model of X_t based on information available at time t and is itself a forecast of the covariance between $e_{i,t+1}$ and $e_{j,t+1}$. Clearly, a vector autoregressive (VAR) model is a convenient vehicle for constructing the conditional covariance.

For future reference we also note that if z_t is another random variable, then $\text{Cov}_t(a + bx_{t+1}, c + dy_{t+1} + z_t) = bd \, \text{Cov}_t(x_{t+1}, y_{t+1})$.

10.5.2.4 The No-Arbitrage Relation

Combining equations (10.33) and (10.34) yields the no-arbitrage equation

$$E_t r_{t+1} = r_t^f + \frac{\sigma_t \operatorname{Cov}_t((\Delta c_{t+1}/c_t), r_{t+1})}{1 - \sigma_t E_t(\Delta c_{t+1}/c_t)}$$

$$= r_t^f + \beta \sigma_t (1 + r_t^f) \operatorname{Cov}_t \left(\frac{\Delta c_{t+1}}{c_t}, r_{t+1} \right). \tag{10.35}$$

The last term in equation (10.35) is the risk premium. Thus, an asset is risky if for states of nature in which returns are low, the intertemporal marginal rate of substitution in consumption, $M_{t+1} \equiv (\beta U'_{t+1}/U'_t)$, is high. Since M_{t+1} will be high if future consumption is low, a risky asset is one which yields low returns in states for which consumers also have low consumption. This situation is typical of what happens in a business cycle. For example, in the recession phase both returns and consumption growth are low, whereas in the boom phase both are high. This generates a positive correlation between the two and hence a positive risk premium.

We note that we can also write equation (10.35) in terms of the excess return

$$E_t r_{t+1} - r_t^f = \beta \sigma_t (1 + r_t^f) \operatorname{Cov}_t \left(\frac{\Delta c_{t+1}}{c_t}, r_{t+1} - r_t^f \right) \tag{10.36}$$

as

$$\operatorname{Cov}_t \left(\frac{\Delta c_{t+1}}{c_t}, r_{t+1} \right) = \operatorname{Cov}_t \left(\frac{\Delta c_{t+1}}{c_t}, r_{t+1} - r_t^f \right)$$

due to r_t^f being part of the information set at time t.

Taken together, the above results show that in an efficient market risky assets are priced off the risk-free asset plus an asset-specific risk premium that reflects macroeconomic sources of risk.

10.5.2.5 Pricing Nominal Returns

The analysis above assumes that all variables are measured in real terms, including asset returns. This implies that there is a real risk-free asset. In practice, the closest we get to a real risk-free asset is an index-linked bond. As even this is not fully indexed it is not a true risk-free asset. In contrast, if we ignore default risk, there are nominal risk-free bonds. A short-term Treasury bill is an example.

In order to price nominal returns we need to modify our previous analysis a little by restating the budget constraint in nominal terms as

$$P_t c_t + \Delta A_{t+1} = P_t x_t + R_t A_t,$$

where P_t is the price level, A_t is nominal wealth, and R_t is a risky nominal return. It can be shown that the Euler equation is now

$$E_t \left[\frac{\beta U'_{t+1}}{U'_t} \frac{P_t}{P_{t+1}} (1 + R_{t+1}) \right] = 1$$

or

$$E_t\left[\frac{\beta U'_{t+1}}{U'_t}\frac{1+R_{t+1}}{1+\pi_{t+1}}\right] = 1, \tag{10.37}$$

where $\pi_{t+1} = \Delta P_{t+1}/P_t$ is the rate of inflation. Noting that $1 + r_{t+1} = (1 + R_{t+1})/(1+\pi_{t+1})$, where r_{t+1} is the real risky return, equation (10.37) is identical to (10.31).

However, the asset-pricing equation is different because we now have a nominal instead of a real stochastic discount factor. This is $(\beta U'_{t+1}/U'_t)(1/(1+\pi_{t+1}))$. A Taylor series expansion of this gives

$$\frac{\beta U'_{t+1}}{U'_t}\frac{1}{1+\pi_{t+1}} \simeq \beta\left[1 - \sigma_t\frac{\Delta c_{t+1}}{c_t} - \pi_{t+1}\right].$$

The asset-pricing equation for a nominal risky asset is now

$$E_t(R_{t+1})$$
$$= \frac{\theta + \sigma_t E_t(\Delta c_{t+1}/c_t) + E_t\pi_{t+1} + \sigma_t \operatorname{Cov}_t((\Delta c_{t+1}/c_t), R_{t+1}) + \operatorname{Cov}_t(\pi_{t+1}, R_{t+1})}{1 - \sigma_t E_t(\Delta c_{t+1}/c_t) - E_t\pi_{t+1}}.$$
$$\tag{10.38}$$

For a nominal risk-free asset it is

$$E_t(R^{\mathrm{f}}_{t+1}) = \frac{\theta + \sigma_t E_t(\Delta c_{t+1}/c_t) + E_t\pi_{t+1}}{1 - \sigma_t E_t(\Delta c_{t+1}/c_t) - E_t\pi_{t+1}}. \tag{10.39}$$

And the no-arbitrage equation is

$$E_t R_{t+1} = R^{\mathrm{f}}_t + \beta\sigma_t(1 + R^{\mathrm{f}}_t)\left[\operatorname{Cov}_t\left(\frac{\Delta c_{t+1}}{c_t}, R_{t+1}\right) + \operatorname{Cov}_t(\pi_{t+1}, R_{t+1})\right]. \tag{10.40}$$

Thus the risk premium for a nominal risky asset involves two terms: the conditional covariances between the nominal risky rate and consumption growth, and between the nominal risky rate and inflation. If inflation is low when nominal returns are low, as happens in a business cycle caused by negative demand shocks, then the inflation component of the risk premium will be positive. In contrast, a negative supply shock, such as an oil-price shock, would be likely to cause inflation to rise and returns to fall, which would make the inflation component of the risk premium, and possibly even the whole risk premium, negative.

10.5.2.6 *The Assumption of Log-Normality*

An assumption that is widely used, due partly to its convenience and partly to the fact that it is a reasonably good approximation, is that the stochastic discount factor and the gross return have a joint log-normal distribution. We note that a random variable x is said to be log-normally distributed if $\ln(x)$ follows a normal distribution with mean μ and variance σ^2. If $\ln x$ is $N(\mu, \sigma^2)$, then the expected value of x is given by

$$E(x) = \exp(\mu + \tfrac{1}{2}\sigma^2),$$

and hence
$$\ln E(x) = \mu + \tfrac{1}{2}\sigma^2.$$

As a result, equation (10.32) can be written as

$$
\begin{aligned}
1 &= E_t[M_{t+1}(1 + r_{t+1})] \\
  &= \exp\{E_t[\ln(M_{t+1}(1 + r_{t+1}))] + V_t[\ln(M_{t+1}(1 + r_{t+1}))]/2\}.
\end{aligned}
$$

Taking logarithms yields

$$
\begin{aligned}
0 &= \ln E_t[M_{t+1}(1 + r_{t+1})] \\
  &= E_t[\ln(M_{t+1}(1 + r_{t+1}))] + V_t[\ln(M_{t+1}(1 + r_{t+1}))]/2 \\
  &= E_t[\ln M_{t+1} + \ln(1 + r_{t+1})] + V_t[\ln M_{t+1} + \ln(1 + r_{t+1})]/2 \\
  &\simeq E_t(\ln M_{t+1}) + E_t(r_{t+1}) + V_t(\ln M_{t+1})/2 + V_t(r_{t+1})/2 + \mathrm{cov}_t(\ln M_{t+1}, r_{t+1}) \\
  &= 0.
\end{aligned}
\tag{10.41}
$$

When the asset is risk free, equation (10.41) becomes

$$E_t(\ln M_{t+1}) + r_t^{\mathrm{f}} + \tfrac{1}{2}V_t(\ln M_{t+1}) = 0. \tag{10.42}$$

Subtracting (10.42) from (10.41) produces the no-arbitrage condition under log-normality:

$$E_t(r_{t+1} - r_t^{\mathrm{f}}) + \tfrac{1}{2}V_t(r_{t+1}) = -\mathrm{Cov}_t(\ln M_{t+1}, r_{t+1}), \tag{10.43}$$

where $\tfrac{1}{2}V_t(r_{t+1})$ is the Jensen effect, which arises because expectations are being taken of a nonlinear function and $E[f(x)] \neq f[E(x)]$ unless $f(x)$ is linear.

If $M_{t+1} = \beta(U'(c_{t+1})/U'(c_t))$, then

$$\ln M_{t+1} \simeq -(\theta + \sigma_t \Delta \ln c_{t+1}). \tag{10.44}$$

The no-arbitrage condition can now be written as

$$E_t r_{t+1} - r_t^{\mathrm{f}} + \tfrac{1}{2}V_t(r_{t+1}) = \sigma_t \,\mathrm{Cov}_t(\Delta \ln C_{t+1}, r_{t+1}). \tag{10.45}$$

This may be compared with equation (10.36), which does not assume log-normality.

10.5.2.7 Multi-Factor Models

There is a more general way of expressing asset-pricing models: namely, as multi-factor models. If the stochastic discount factor is written as

$$M_{t+1} = a + \sum_i b_i z_{i,t+1},$$

then the no-arbitrage condition becomes

$$
\begin{aligned}
E_t r_{t+1} - r_t^{\mathrm{f}} &= -(1 + r_t^{\mathrm{f}})\,\mathrm{Cov}_t(M_{t+1}, r_{t+1}) \\
&= -(1 + r_t^{\mathrm{f}})\sum_i b_i \,\mathrm{Cov}_t(z_{i,t+1}, r_{t+1}).
\end{aligned}
\tag{10.46}
$$

For example, CAPM assumes that there is a single stochastic discount factor $M_{t+1} = \sigma_t(1 + r_{t+1}^m)$, where r_{t+1}^m, the return on the market, is the single factor; C-CAPM assumes that there is a single stochastic discount factor given by $M_{t+1} = \beta(U_{t+1}'/U_t') \simeq \beta[1 - \sigma_t(\Delta c_{t+1}/c_t)]$ and so consumption growth is the single factor. Thus, for $\sigma_t = \sigma$, a constant,

$$z_{t+1} = \begin{cases} r_{t+1}^m, & \text{CAPM,} \\ \dfrac{\Delta C_{t+1}}{C_t}, & \text{C-CAPM.} \end{cases}$$

Assuming log-normality and that

$$\ln M_{t+1} = a + \sum_i b_i z_{i,t+1},$$

the asset pricing relation is

$$\begin{aligned} E_t(r_{t+1} - r_t^f) + \tfrac{1}{2}V_t(r_{t+1}) &= \sigma_t \operatorname{Cov}_t(\ln M_{t+1}, r_{t+1}) \\ &= \sigma_t \sum_i b_i \operatorname{Cov}_t(z_{i,t+1}, r_{t+1}). \end{aligned} \tag{10.47}$$

Equations (10.46) and (10.47) are known as multi-factor affine models (affine means linear). In practice in finance, often the factors are not chosen to satisfy general equilibrium pricing kernels like the intertemporal marginal rate of substitution but are determined from the data.

10.6 Asset Allocation

We have said that the theory above applies to any asset. If there are several assets in which to hold financial wealth, we must consider in what proportion each asset is to be held in the portfolio. This is the problem of asset allocation or portfolio selection. We begin by examining the case of two assets: a risky and a risk-free asset.

Again the only change that we need to make to the model is to the budget constraint. Let the stocks of risky and risk-free assets be a_t and b_t, respectively, then the budget constraint can be written

$$c_t + a_{t+1} + b_{t+1} = x_t + a_t(1 + r_t) + b_t(1 + r_{t-1}^f).$$

If we define $W_t = a_t + b_t$ and the portfolio shares as $w_t = a_t/W_t$ and $1 - w_t = b_t/W_t$, then the budget constraint can also be written as

$$\begin{aligned} c_t + W_{t+1} &= x_t + W_t[1 + r_{t-1}^f + w_t(r_t - r_{t-1}^f)] \\ &= x_t + W_t(1 + r_t^p), \end{aligned}$$

where $r_t^p = r_{t-1}^f + w_t(r_t - r_{t-1}^f)$ is the return on the portfolio. The problem now is to maximize V_t with respect to $\{c_{t+s}, a_{t+s+1}, b_{t+s+1}; s \geqslant 0\}$ or equivalently $\{c_{t+s}, W_{t+s+1}, w_{t+s+1}; s \geqslant 0\}$.

Using previous results, the first-order conditions are

$$\frac{\partial V_t}{\partial c_t} = U'_t - \beta E_t[U'_{t+1}(1 + r^p_{t+1})] = 0$$

and

$$\frac{\partial V_t}{\partial w_{t+1}} = -\beta E_t\left[\frac{\partial V_{t+1}}{\partial c_{t+1}}\frac{\partial c_{t+1}}{\partial w_{t+1}}\right] = 0$$
$$= -\beta E_t[U'_{t+1}W_{t+1}(r_{t+1} - r^f_t)] = 0.$$

The first condition is the same as before except that r^p_{t+1} replaces r_{t+1}. Thus the consumption/savings decision is unchanged, except that it is now based on the portfolio return. From the budget constraint, W_{t+1} is determined by time t variables, hence the second condition can be written as

$$E_t[U'_{t+1}(r_{t+1} - r^f_t)] = 0. \tag{10.48}$$

We note that

$$U'_{t+1} = U'\{x_{t+1} + W_{t+1}[1 + r^f_t + w_{t+1}(r_{t+1} - r^f_t)] - W_{t+2}\}$$
$$\simeq U'^*_t + W_{t+1}w_{t+1}(r_{t+1} - r^f_t)U''^*_{t+1},$$

where we have used a Taylor series approximation about $w_{t+1} = 0$ and defined $U'^*_t = U'(x_{t+1} + W_{t+1}[1 + r^f_t] - W_{t+2})$. Equation (10.48) can now be written

$$0 = E_t[U'_{t+1}(r_{t+1} - r^f_t)]$$
$$\simeq U'^*_t E_t(r_{t+1} - r^f_t) + W_{t+1}U''^*_{t+1}w_{t+1}E_t(r_{t+1} - r^f_t)^2,$$

and so the share of the risky asset in the portfolio is

$$w_{t+1} = \frac{E_t c_{t+1}}{W_{t+1}}\frac{E_t(r_{t+1} - r^f_t)}{\sigma_t E_t(r_{t+1} - r^f_t)^2}, \tag{10.49}$$

where $\sigma_t = -(E_t c_{t+1}U''^*_{t+1}/U'^*_{t+1})$ is the CRRA. The higher the proportion of total wealth that is consumed, $E_t c_{t+1}/W_{t+1}$, and the expected excess return, $E_t(r_{t+1} - r^f_t)$, and the lower the conditional volatility of the excess return, $E_t(r_{t+1} - r^f_t)^2$, and the degree of aversion to risk, σ_t, the larger the share invested in the risky asset is. If there were no risky asset, then in effect $E_t(r_{t+1} - r^f_t) = 0$ and so $w_{t+1} = 0$, i.e., the portfolio would be completely risk free.

The analysis can be generalized to many risky assets. In this case r_t and w_t become vectors $\boldsymbol{r}_t$ and $\boldsymbol{w}_t$ with the share in the risk-free asset given by $1 - \boldsymbol{\ell}'\boldsymbol{w}_t$, where $\boldsymbol{\ell}' = (1, 1, \ldots, 1)$. The solution has the same form as equation (10.49) and is the vector of shares

$$\boldsymbol{w}_{t+1} = \sigma_t^{-1}\boldsymbol{\Sigma}_t^{-1}E_t(\boldsymbol{r}_{t+1} - \boldsymbol{\ell}r^f_t),$$

where $\boldsymbol{\Sigma}_t$ is the conditional covariance matrix of risky returns.

The excess return on the optimal portfolio is given by premultiplying by $\boldsymbol{w}'_t$,

$$E_t(r^p_{t+1} - r^f_t) = \boldsymbol{w}'_t E_t(\boldsymbol{r}_{t+1} - \boldsymbol{\ell}r^f_t) = \sigma_t \boldsymbol{w}'_t \boldsymbol{\Sigma}_t \boldsymbol{w}_t = \sigma_t V_t(r^p_{t+1}),$$

where $V_t(r_{t+1}^{\mathrm{p}})$ is the conditional variance of the portfolio return. It follows that

$$\frac{E_t(r_{t+1}^{\mathrm{p}} - r_t^{\mathrm{f}})}{V_t(r_{t+1}^{\mathrm{p}})} = \sigma_t. \tag{10.50}$$

Eliminating σ_t using equation (10.50) yields the excess return for each individual asset as

$$E_t(\boldsymbol{r}_{t+1}) - \boldsymbol{\ell}r_t^{\mathrm{f}} = \sigma_t \Sigma_t \boldsymbol{w}_t$$

$$= E_t(r_{t+1}^{\mathrm{p}} - r_t^{\mathrm{f}}) \frac{V_t(\boldsymbol{r}_{t+1})\boldsymbol{w}_t}{V_t(r_{t+1}^{\mathrm{p}})}$$

$$= E_t(r_{t+1}^{\mathrm{p}} - r_t^{\mathrm{f}}) \frac{\mathrm{Cov}_t(\boldsymbol{r}_{t+1}, r_{t+1}^{\mathrm{p}})}{V_t(r_{t+1}^{\mathrm{p}})}. \tag{10.51}$$

Using equation (10.50) we can also write this as

$$E_t(\boldsymbol{r}_{t+1} - \boldsymbol{\ell}r_t^{\mathrm{f}}) = \sigma_t \,\mathrm{Cov}_t(\boldsymbol{r}_{t+1}, r_{t+1}^{\mathrm{p}}). \tag{10.52}$$

For the ith asset this becomes

$$E_t(r_{i,t+1} - r_t^{\mathrm{f}}) = \sigma_t \,\mathrm{Cov}_t(r_{i,t+1}, r_{t+1}^{\mathrm{p}}). \tag{10.53}$$

Equation (10.53) can be shown to be identical to equation (10.36) if $r_t^{\mathrm{f}} = 0$ and if

$$c_{t+1} = r_{t+1}^{\mathrm{p}} W_{t+1}, \tag{10.54}$$

i.e., consumption is equal to the permanent income arising from wealth, as in life-cycle theory.

It is instructive to consider the implications of this solution for expected utility. The conditional expectation of the instantaneous utility function for period $t+1$ may be approximated by a second-order Taylor series expansion about $E_t c_{t+1}$ to give

$$E_t U(c_{t+1}) \simeq U(E_t c_{t+1}) + U_t' E_t(c_{t+1} - E_t c_{t+1}) + U_t'' E_t(c_{t+1} - E_t c_{t+1})^2$$

$$\simeq U_t' \left[E_t c_{t+1} - \frac{\sigma_t}{2} \frac{V_t(c_{t+1})}{E_t c_{t+1}} \right]. \tag{10.55}$$

Thus, expected utility is approximately a trade-off between expected consumption and the expected volatility of consumption evaluated at marginal utility.

This can be rewritten in terms of returns. Since

$$E_t c_{t+1} = W_{t+1} E_t r_{t+1}^{\mathrm{p}},$$

$$V_t(c_{t+1}) = W_{t+1}^2 V_t(r_{t+1}^{\mathrm{p}}),$$

from equations (10.50) and (10.55), the maximized value of $E_t U(c_{t+1})$ is approximately

$$
\max E_t U(c_{t+1}) \simeq U_t' W_{t+1}\left[E_t r_{t+1}^{\mathrm{p}} - \frac{\sigma_t}{2}\frac{V_t(r_{t+1}^{\mathrm{p}})}{E_t r_{t+1}^{\mathrm{p}}} \right]
$$

$$
= U_t' W_{t+1}\left[E_t r_{t+1}^{\mathrm{p}} - \frac{1}{2}\frac{E_t(r_{t+1}^{\mathrm{p}} - r_t^{\mathrm{f}})}{E_t r_{t+1}^{\mathrm{p}}} \right]
$$

$$
= U_t' W_{t+1}\left[r_t^{\mathrm{f}} + \rho_t\left(1 - \frac{1}{2(r_t^{\mathrm{f}} + \rho_t)}\right) \right],
$$

where ρ_t is the risk premium:

$$
\rho_t = \beta\sigma_t(1 + f_t)\,\mathrm{Cov}_t(\Delta \ln c_{t+1}, r_{t+1}^{\mathrm{p}})
$$
$$
= \beta\sigma_t(1 + f_t)W_{t+1}V_t(r_{t+1}^{\mathrm{p}}).
$$

An increase in risk causes the following change in expected utility:

$$
\frac{\partial\{\max E_t U(c_{t+1})\}}{\partial \rho_t} = U_t' W_{t+1}\left(1 - \frac{r_t^{\mathrm{f}}}{2(r_t^{\mathrm{f}} + \rho_t)^2}\right).
$$

Although the sign is ambiguous, it is likely to be negative if r_t^{f} and ρ_t are not large. Usually, therefore, an increase in risk may be expected to reduce utility.

10.6.1   The Capital Asset-Pricing Model (CAPM)

The CAPM, due to Sharpe (1964), Lintner (1965), and Mossin (1966), is a special case of equation (10.51) that assumes that every market investor is identical and will therefore hold identical portfolios. As a result, r_{t+1}^{p} will also be the *market* return r_{t+1}^{m}. Thus

$$
E_t(\boldsymbol{r}_{t+1} - \boldsymbol{\ell} r_t^{\mathrm{f}}) = E_t(r_{t+1}^{\mathrm{m}} - r_t^{\mathrm{f}})\frac{\mathrm{Cov}_t(\boldsymbol{r}_{t+1}, r_{t+1}^{\mathrm{m}})}{V_t(r_{t+1}^{\mathrm{m}})}.
$$

For the ith risky asset we obtain

$$
E_t(r_{i,t+1} - r_t^{\mathrm{f}}) = E_t(r_{t+1}^{\mathrm{m}} - r_t^{\mathrm{f}})\frac{\mathrm{Cov}_t(r_{i,t+1}, r_{t+1}^{\mathrm{m}})}{V_t(r_{t+1}^{\mathrm{m}})}
$$

$$
= E_t(r_{t+1}^{\mathrm{m}} - r_t^{\mathrm{f}})\beta_{it}, \tag{10.56}
$$

where β_{it} is the *market beta* for asset i and is defined by

$$
\beta_{it} = \frac{\mathrm{Cov}_t(r_{i,t+1}, r_{t+1}^{\mathrm{m}})}{V_t(r_{t+1}^{\mathrm{m}})}. \tag{10.57}
$$

Equation (10.56) therefore gives another expression for the risk premium. It says that the expected excess return on a risky asset is proportional to the expected excess return on the market portfolio. The proportionality coefficient beta varies over time and across assets. The beta for the risk-free asset is zero and the beta for the market portfolio is unity. An implication of CAPM is that an investor can hold one unit of asset i, or β_{it} units of the market portfolio. The expected excess return is the same in each case.

Our results also imply that CAPM can be given a general equilibrium interpretation if we define β_{it} as in equation (10.57) and equate the portfolio return with the market return ($r^{p}_{t+1} = r^{m}_{t+1}$) such that the market return satisfies equation (10.54).

10.7 Consumption under Uncertainty

We now examine the implications of the presence of risky assets for the consumption/savings decision. Previously we assumed perfect foresight and no uncertainty so that the return on the financial asset in which savings were held was given. We now assume uncertainty about the future and that savings are held in a risky asset.

In analyzing consumption when the asset is risky we recall our earlier remark that the same model may be used for determining consumption as is used for determination of the price of the risky asset. Hence we use equation (10.35). Solving this equation for consumption gives

$$E_t \frac{\Delta c_{t+1}}{c_t} = \frac{E_t r_{t+1} - \theta}{\sigma_t (1 + E_t r_{t+1})} - \frac{\text{Cov}_t((\Delta c_{t+1}/c_t), r_{t+1})}{1 + E_t r_{t+1}} \tag{10.58}$$

$$\simeq \frac{[E_t r_{t+1} - \sigma_t \text{Cov}_t((\Delta c_{t+1}/c_t), r_{t+1})] - \theta}{\sigma_t}. \tag{10.59}$$

Compared with the case of perfect foresight, the optimal rate of growth of consumption under uncertainty involves an extra term in $\text{cov}_t((\Delta c_{t+1}/c_t), r_{t+1})$. As previously noted, this term is expected to be positive.

If households hold their savings in a risk-free asset with a certain return r^f_t, then, as $\text{cov}_t((\Delta c_{t+1}/c_t), r^f_t) = 0$, from equation (10.58) we obtain

$$E_t \frac{\Delta c_{t+1}}{c_t} \simeq \frac{r^f_t - \theta}{\sigma_t}. \tag{10.60}$$

Thus perfect foresight and investing in a risk-free asset produce exactly the same result.

If we assume that $r^f_t \simeq \theta$, then equation (10.35) may be written as

$$E_t r_{t+1} - r^f_t = \sigma_t \text{cov}_t \left(\frac{\Delta c_{t+1}}{c_t}, r_{t+1} \right). \tag{10.61}$$

The last term is the risk premium for the risky asset. It then follows that equations (10.59) and (10.60) are the same. This implies that in determining consumption it does not matter whether we assume that investors hold the risk-free asset or the risky asset as we have to risk-adjust the risky return in the equation for consumption. This is an important result as it suggests that we may continue to work with the simpler assumption of perfect foresight in our macroeconomic analysis. An alternative would be to evaluate all expectations in the DGE model using risk-neutral probabilities. This would also eliminate the need to take risk into account.

We note, however, that if we assume log-normality, then equation (10.58) is replaced by

$$E_t \Delta \ln c_{t+1} = \frac{r_t^{\mathrm{f}} - \theta}{\sigma_t} + \tfrac{1}{2} \sigma_t V_t (\Delta \ln c_{t+1}).$$

Thus the expected rate of growth of consumption along the optimal path is positively related to the difference between the risk-free rate and the consumer's subjective rate of time preference, and it varies positively with the variance of consumption growth (since σ_t is equal to the CRRA). If consumers are risk averse, higher variability of consumption growth is accompanied by higher expected consumption growth along the optimal path.

10.8 Complete Markets

The concept of a complete market is very important in finance as it determines whether arbitrage opportunities exist, and in macroeconomics it determines whether risk sharing is possible, i.e., whether it is possible to fully insure against risk.

If there is a contingent claim for each possible state of nature, and if there are at least as many assets as states, then the price of each asset is uniquely defined. If not, then there would be arbitrage possibilities. Unfortunately, in practice, there are almost certainly more states of nature than contingent claims.

Let $p(i)$ denote the price of the ith asset and let $x_i(s)$ denote the payoff in state s. It follows that

$$p(i) = \sum_s q(s)x_i(s), \quad i = 1,\ldots,n.$$

Combining these equations for all n assets gives the matrix equation

$$\begin{bmatrix} p(1) \\ \vdots \\ p(n) \end{bmatrix} = \begin{bmatrix} x_1(1) & \cdots & x_1(S) \\ \vdots & \ddots & \vdots \\ x_n(1) & \cdots & x_n(S) \end{bmatrix} \begin{bmatrix} q(1) \\ \vdots \\ q(S) \end{bmatrix}.$$

In vector notation with $\tilde{p} = (p(1), p(2), \ldots, p(n))'$,

$$\tilde{p} = X\tilde{q}.$$

There are three cases to consider.

1. The number of assets equals the number of states, i.e., $n = S$. Thus X is a square matrix and can be inverted to give the contingent-claims prices $q(s)$ for each possible state of nature $s = 1, \ldots, S$:

$$\tilde{q} = X^{-1}\tilde{p}.$$

Given information on the market prices $p(s)$ and payoffs $x(s)$, we can then infer the state prices $q(s)$. In this case markets are said to be complete as market prices contain the complete information needed to obtain the state prices uniquely. Another important implication is that the stochastic discount factors $m(s)$ are uniquely defined and are the same for all investors.

2. The number of assets is greater than the number of states, i.e., $n > S$, and so X is an $n \times S$ matrix. Therefore a unique inverse of X no longer exists, only a generalized inverse. (Note: if X^* is an inverse of X, then $X^*X = I$. If there is a unique inverse, then $X^* = X^{-1}$; this requires X to be a square matrix. But if X is $n \times S$ and $n > S$, then there is more than one X^* matrix that satisfies $X^*X = I$.) It follows that $\tilde{q}$ cannot be obtained uniquely from $\tilde{p}$. In fact there are an infinite number of ways of deriving $\tilde{q}$, and hence an infinite number of pricing functions or stochastic discount factors, $m(s)$.

3. The number of states is greater than the number of contingent claims, i.e., $S > n$ and so X is an $n \times S$ matrix. It follows that now no inverse of X exists. It is not therefore possible to derive $\tilde{q}$ from $\tilde{p}$. This is the case that is considered when pricing derivative securities in terms of the prices of some underlying security.

10.8.1 Risk Sharing and Complete Markets

In practice, investors are heterogeneous. Each investor is subject to different sources of risk, called idiosyncratic risk. Investors may wish to diversify away this risk. In actual markets, however, insurance opportunities are typically imperfect. While there are numerous financial instruments that allow consumers to insure against various types of idiosyncratic shocks, such instruments typically do not allow for the complete diversification of idiosyncratic risk. In contrast, in a complete-markets equilibrium, consumers would be able to purchase contingent claims for each realization of such idiosyncratic shocks and would therefore be able to diversify away all idiosyncratic risk.

We have seen that an implication of the existence of a complete set of contingent claims is that consumers will value future random payoffs using the same pricing function, i.e., they will have the same stochastic discount factors. Suppose that consumer i invests in an asset that has a random payoff $1 + r_{t+1}$ at date $t + 1$. The Euler equation for the ith investor is

$$E_t\left[\frac{\beta_i U'(c^i_{t+1})}{U'(c^i_t)}(1 + r_{t+1})\right] = 1,$$

where β_i is the rate of time preference and c^i_t the consumption of the ith investor. This can be written as

$$E_t[m_{i,t+1}(1 + r_{t+1})] = 1,$$

where $m_{i,t+1} = (\beta_i U'(c^i_{t+1})/U'(c^i_t))$.

In a complete-markets equilibrium, the intertemporal marginal rate of substitution that is used to value future random payoffs will be the same for all consumers, i.e., $m_i = m_j$ for all i, j. Hence,

$$\frac{\beta_i U'_{i,t+1}}{U'_{i,t}} = \frac{\beta_j U'_{j,t+1}}{U'_{j,t}}.$$

If all investors have the same rate of time preference β and the same utility function $U(\cdot)$, then the growth rate of consumption for all consumers will be the same:

$$\frac{c_{i,t+1}}{c_{i,t}} = \frac{c_{j,t+1}}{c_{j,t}} \quad \text{for all } i, j.$$

This implies that in a complete-markets equilibrium only aggregate consumption shocks affect asset prices, and an individual income shock can be insured away through asset markets.

To illustrate this, suppose that there are two consumers in an economy that lasts for one period, and that each consumer $i =$ A, B has the same utility function $U(C) = \ln(C)$ but different income streams. In particular, consumer A is employed when consumer B is unemployed, and vice versa. This gives two (idiosyncratic) states. In state 1 the incomes are $y^A = y$ and $y^B = 0$ with probability π and in state 2 they are $y^A = 0$ and $y^B = y$ with probability $1 - \pi$, where $y > 0$ is a constant. Each consumer maximizes $E[\ln(C^i)]$, the expected value of utility from consumption. The problem is to find the consumption allocations for each consumer in a complete contingent-claims equilibrium.

As there are two possible states of the world, we have two state prices $q(1)$ and $q(2)$. Consumption and income for each consumer are indexed by the state of the world. Thus, the budget constraints for consumers A and B are given by

$$q(1)C^A(1) + q(2)C^A(2) = q(1)y,$$
$$q(1)C^B(1) + q(2)C^B(2) = q(2)y.$$

Each consumer maximizes utility subject to these two budget constraints. The Lagrangian for consumer A is given by

$$\mathcal{L}^A = \pi \ln[C^A(1)] + (1 - \pi) \ln[C^A(2)] + \lambda^A[q(1)y - q(1)C^A(1) - q(2)C^A(2)].$$

The first-order conditions are

$$\frac{\partial \mathcal{L}^A}{\partial C^A(1)} = \frac{\pi}{C^A(1)} - \lambda^A q(1) = 0,$$
$$\frac{\partial \mathcal{L}^A}{\partial C^A(2)} = \frac{1 - \pi}{C^A(2)} - \lambda^A q(2) = 0.$$

Eliminating the Lagrange multipliers from these expressions gives the condition

$$\frac{C^A(2)}{C^A(1)} = \frac{(1 - \pi)q(1)}{\pi q(2)}.$$

Consumer B's problem is similar to that of consumer A: the Lagrangian has the same form, but the budget constraint is different. It follows that

$$\frac{C^B(2)}{C^B(1)} = \frac{(1-\pi)q(1)}{\pi q(2)}.$$

Hence

$$\frac{C^A(2)}{C^A(1)} = \frac{C^B(2)}{C^B(1)} = \bar{c}.$$

Suppose now that y, the income received by each consumer, varies with the aggregate state of the economy. When the economy is in a boom, income is high, and is $\bar{y}$ with probability ϕ. When the economy is in a recession, income is low—perhaps due to unemployment—and is $\underline{y}$ with probability $1 - \phi$, where $\underline{y} < \bar{y}$. Thus there are now four states of the world:

state 1: $y^A = \bar{y}$ and $y^B = 0$ with probability $\pi\phi$;

state 2: $y^A = 0$ and $y^B = \bar{y}$ with probability $(1-\pi)\phi$;

state 3: $y^A = \underline{y}$ and $y^B = 0$ with probability $\pi(1-\phi)$;

state 4: $y^A = 0$ and $y^B = \underline{y}$ with probability $(1-\pi)(1-\phi)$.

The solution could be obtained from the first-order conditions as before. A simpler way is to note that within a given aggregate state, consumers will equate their marginal rates of substitution for consumption across the idiosyncratic states. However, their marginal rates of substitution for consumption across the idiosyncratic states will vary with the aggregate state. Thus, the earlier conditions now become

$$\text{boom state:} \quad \frac{C^A(2)}{C^A(1)} = \frac{C^B(2)}{C^B(1)} = \bar{c}_1,$$

$$\text{recession state:} \quad \frac{C^A(4)}{C^A(3)} = \frac{C^B(4)}{C^B(3)} = \bar{c}_2,$$

where $\bar{c}_1$ and $\bar{c}_2$ differ because there are now different amounts of aggregate resources in the economy depending on whether the economy is in a boom or a recession.

Consider the possibility of insuring against aggregate versus idiosyncratic income shocks. In the absence of aggregate shocks, the ratios of consumption across the employment/unemployment states are equated for both consumers. This is equivalent to insurance against idiosyncratic shocks. However, insurance against variations in the aggregate economy is not possible. Hence, the ratios of consumption across the employment/unemployment states vary with the aggregate state of the economy.

Finally, consider the implications of a complete-markets equilibrium for asset pricing. Suppose that consumer $i = A, B$ invests in an asset that has a random payoff $1 + r_{t+1}$ at date $t + 1$. The consumption/saving problem implies that at the optimum, the ith investor sets

$$E_t\left[\frac{\beta_i U'(c^i_{t+1})}{U'(c^i_t)}(1 + r_{t+1})\right] = 1.$$

But we showed that in a complete-markets equilibrium, the intertemporal marginal rate of substitution that is used to value future random payoffs will be the same for all consumers, i.e., $m^A = m^B$. Hence,

$$\frac{\beta_A U'_{A,t+1}}{U'_{A,t}} = \frac{\beta_B U'_{B,t+1}}{U'_{B,t}}.$$

If all consumers have the same discount factor β and the same utility function $U(\cdot)$, then their rates of consumption growth will be identical:

$$\frac{c_{A,t+1}}{c_{A,t}} = \frac{c_{B,t+1}}{c_{B,t}}.$$

We have shown, therefore, that in a complete-markets equilibrium only aggregate consumption shocks affect asset prices and an individual income shock can be insured away through asset markets. Although in practice we do not have complete markets, this is an important concept in finance and in macroeconomics.

10.8.2 Market Incompleteness

Even if markets are not complete and individuals have different marginal rates of substitution, if there is a risk-free asset to which all consumers have access, then, from equation (10.14), the expected marginal rates of substitution for each investor will be the same and, from equation (10.60), the rates of growth of consumption for all consumers will be the same (see Heaton and Lucas 1995, 1996).

The concept of market completeness is particularly relevant in an open economy as it implies that an economy can insure away its idiosyncratic risk by holding a portfolio of internationally traded assets. In this case the marginal rates of substitution are the same for all countries and all countries have the same rates of growth of consumption. If, however, international markets are incomplete, as countries have different marginal rates of substitution, then, provided each country has access to an internationally traded real risk-free asset at the same rate, expected marginal rates of substitution in each country will be the same, as will consumption growth rates. The problem here is that for the real risk-free rate to be the same in each country, PPP is required, and we have already seen that this does not hold. We return to this point in our discussion of foreign exchange markets.

10.9 Conclusions

Increasingly, asset pricing has become associated exclusively with finance. We have shown that it is, in fact, an important branch of economics, and plays a central role in general equilibrium macroeconomics. In particular, we have demonstrated that the same DGE model used to determine macroeconomic variables also provides a general equilibrium theory of asset pricing. We have therefore unified macroeconomics and finance.

Assets are priced as the discounted value of future payoffs. The key difference between finance and economics is in the choice of discount factor. In traditional finance the risk free rate is often preferred; in general equilibrium economics the marginal rate of substitution M_{t+1} is used. We have shown that the connection between the two is that $E_t M_{t+1} = 1/(1 + r_t^f)$. In finance the risk-free rate is sometimes supplemented with other variables, which are referred to as factors. The problem is how to choose these factors. In economics M_{t+1} is stochastic and is based on the variables that determine marginal utility: typically consumption growth and, for nominal returns, inflation. It will be shown in chapter 11 that, depending on the choice of utility function, other variables may also be used as factors.

We have shown that where each household has the same discount factor, markets are complete, implying that it is then possible to insure against risks and that optimal consumption growth is the same for all households. This can be extended to the open economy when we require that each country has the same discount factor.

We have also shown that returns must satisfy a no-arbitrage condition— otherwise markets would not be efficient and would allow unlimited profit-making opportunities. Given the different characteristics of risky assets, no-arbitrage is brought about by adjusting returns for risk, with the result that, after being risk-adjusted, the expected values of all returns are the same. The problem then is how to determine the risk premium for each asset. We have shown that the answer to this problem is linked to the choice of the discount factor. This presents a problem for traditional finance, as discounting using the risk-free rate does not produce a risk premium; this is why additional factors are sought.

The no-arbitrage condition provides a restriction often ignored in financial econometrics, where univariate time-series methods are commonly used. Testing this restriction enables asset-pricing theories to be evaluated. As it is necessary to jointly model risky returns, the risk-free rate, and the stochastic discount in order to take account of the no-arbitrage condition and model the risk premium, multivariate methods are required. We discuss such tests for particular financial markets in chapter 11.

Although it is necessary to take account of risk when determining asset prices, we have argued that it may not be necessary to include risk premia in stochastic macroeconomic relations. If a real risk-free rate exists, this may be used instead of risky returns because, when they are used in macroeconomic relations, risky returns should be risk-adjusted. An alternative is to evaluate expectations using risk-neutral valuation. This also results in the use of the risk-free rate.

11

Financial Markets

11.1 Introduction

Having considered the general principles of asset pricing in the macroeconomy in chapter 10, we now apply these to three key financial markets: the stock market, the bond market, and the foreign exchange (FOREX) market. Each market has specific features that need to be taken into account which make the analyses very different. Their common feature is that they all satisfy the general equilibrium pricing equation

$$E_t[M_{t+1}(1 + r_{i,t+1})] = 1 \tag{11.1}$$

and hence the no-arbitrage condition

$$E_t r_{i,t+1} - r_t^f = \beta \sigma_t (1 + r_t^f) \operatorname{Cov}_t \left(\frac{\Delta c_{t+1}}{c_t}, r_{i,t+1} - r_t^f \right), \tag{11.2}$$

where r_{it} is the real return on the ith risky asset, which is defined differently for each market, r_t^f is the real risk-free return, $M_{t+1} = (\beta U'(c_{t+1})/U'(c_{t+1}))$ is the stochastic discount factor or marginal rate of substitution, U_t' is marginal utility, c_t is consumption, and σ_t is the coefficient of relative risk aversion.

In general,

$$1 + r_{t+1} = \frac{X_{t+1}}{P_t},$$

where P_t is the price of an asset at the start of period t and X_{t+1} is its payoff at the start of period $t + 1$. The payoffs define the different assets. For example,

1. for a stock which pays a dividend of D_{t+1} and has a resale value of P_{t+1} at $t + 1$, we have $X_{t+1} = P_{t+1} + D_{t+1}$;

2. for a Treasury bill that pays one unit of the consumption good regardless of the state of nature next period, $X_{t+1} = 1$, and the price is then $P_t = 1/(1 + r_t^f)$;

3. for a bond that has a constant coupon payment of C and can be sold for P_{t+1} next period, $X_{t+1} = P_{t+1} + C$;

4. for a bank deposit that pays the risk-free rate of return r_t^f between t and $t + 1$, $X_{t+1} = 1 + r_t^f$, and the price is $P_t = 1$;

5. for a call option that gives the holder the right to purchase a stock at the exercise price K at date T, the future payoff on the asset is $X_T = \max[S_T - K, 0]$, and P_t is the price paid to purchase the option.

For surveys of the general issues discussed here see Ferson (1995), Campbell et al. (1997), Cochrane (2005), and Smith and Wickens (2002).

11.2 The Stock Market

11.2.1 The Present-Value Model

The traditional valuation model for equity is the present-value model (PVM) (see Campbell et al. 1997, chapter 7). This assumes that the marginal rate of substitution $M_{t+1} = 1/(1 + \alpha)$, so that the expected rate of return to equity in period $t + 1$ based on information available in period t is $E_t r_{t+1} = \alpha$, where α is a constant. In terms of the no-arbitrage condition, it is equivalent to assuming that $r_t^f + \rho_t = \alpha$. In effect, therefore, it assumes that there is no risk premium, or that the risk-free rate is constant. The price of equity is then

$$P_t = \frac{1}{1 + \alpha} E_t[P_{t+1} + D_{t+1}] \tag{11.3}$$

$$= \left(\frac{1}{1 + \alpha}\right)^n E_t P_{t+n} + \sum_{i=1}^{n} \frac{E_t D_{t+i}}{(1 + \alpha)^i}. \tag{11.4}$$

Given the transversality condition $\lim_{n \to \infty} (1/(1 + \alpha))^n E_t P_{t+n} = 0$, which requires the average rate of the capital gain on the stock not to exceed the discount rate α, we obtain P_t as the present value of discounted current and future dividends:

$$P_t = \sum_{i=1}^{\infty} \frac{E_t D_{t+i}}{(1 + \alpha)^i}. \tag{11.5}$$

Unsurprisingly, despite its widespread use, the evidence strongly rejects the present-value model.

11.2.1.1 The Gordon Dividend-Growth Model

Gordon's dividend-growth model is a variant of the PVM in which the expected rate of growth of dividends is assumed to be constant but nonzero (Gordon 1962). If

$$g^D = \frac{E_t \Delta D_{t+1}}{D_t},$$

then

$$P_t = D_t \sum_{i=1}^{\infty} \left(\frac{1 + g^D}{1 + \alpha}\right)^i$$

$$= \frac{(1 + g^D) D_t}{\alpha - g^D} \quad \text{if } \alpha > g^D.$$

Thus the dividend–price ratio is

$$\delta_t = \frac{D_t}{P_t} = \alpha - g^{\mathrm{D}}.$$

In practice, the dividend yield is not constant, nor does it fluctuate about a constant.

If dividends are a constant proportion of earnings $\mathcal{E}_t$, then $D_t = \theta\mathcal{E}_t$, where θ is the dividend payout ratio. Earnings per share, e_t, are then defined as

$$e_t = \frac{\mathcal{E}_t}{P_t} = \frac{1}{\theta}\frac{D_t}{P_t} = \frac{\alpha - g^{\mathrm{D}}}{\theta}.$$

It follows that the price of equity can now be written as

$$P_t = \frac{\theta\mathcal{E}_t}{\alpha - g^{\mathrm{D}}}.$$

Hence α, the expected return on equity, is related to average earnings per share e through

$$\alpha = g^{\mathrm{D}} + \theta e.$$

This has been used to decide whether to reinvest earnings or to make a dividend payout. If the dividend payout is $\theta\mathcal{E}_t$, then the amount reinvested is $(1 - \theta)\mathcal{E}_t$. If earnings increase as a result of the investment by $\mathcal{E}_{t+1} - \mathcal{E}_t$, then the rate of return on the investment is

$$\beta = \frac{\mathcal{E}_{t+1} - \mathcal{E}_t}{(1 - \theta)\mathcal{E}_t} = \frac{g^{\mathrm{D}}}{1 - \theta}$$

as the rate of growth of earnings equals that of dividends. The decision of whether to reinvest or make a dividend payout depends on the relative magnitudes of α and β:

$$\text{reinvest if } \beta > \alpha,$$
$$\text{payout if } \beta < \alpha.$$

In practice, however, earnings per share have fallen in recent years and the payout ratio is not constant.

11.2.1.2 *Share Buybacks*

Firms may distribute earnings through share buybacks as well as through distributing dividends. This has become increasingly common in recent years. This may be attractive if the stock price is perceived to be low and if the firm has surplus cash and a dearth of reinvestment incentives. When there are buybacks, the definition of the rate of return on equity needs to be modified.

The price of a share P_t is the market value of a firm V_t divided by the number of shares N_t:

$$P_t = \frac{V_t}{N_t}.$$

Likewise, the dividend per share D_t is total dividends D_t^T divided by the number of shares:

$$D_t = \frac{D_t^T}{N_t}.$$

As a result of share buybacks the number of shares will fall and hence the price per share and the dividend per share will rise. (New issues and stock splits would increase the number of shares and reduce the share price and the dividend.) The rate of return to equity with buybacks r_t^{BB} is given by

$$\begin{aligned} 1 + r_{t+1}^{BB} &= \frac{P_{t+1} + D_{t+1}}{P_t} \\ &= \frac{(V_{t+1}/N_{t+1}) + (D_{t+1}^T/N_{t+1})}{V_t/N_t} \\ &= \frac{V_{t+1} + D_{t+1}^T}{V_t} \frac{N_t}{N_{t+1}}. \end{aligned}$$

Hence, the relation between the rate of return to equity with buybacks and that without (r_t) is

$$r_{t+1}^{BB} \simeq r_{t+1} - \frac{\Delta N_{t+1}}{N_t}.$$

Thus, although the rate of return to equity is correctly measured by the previous formula using price per share and dividend per share, if it is measured using the value of the firm and total dividends—as it is in most published data—then the rate of change in the number of shares needs to be taken into account.

11.2.1.3 Rational Bubbles

When stock prices rise for a period of time in a way that seems inconsistent with the fundamentals, notably the expected behavior of dividends, and then fall very quickly, much is heard about stock market bubbles. A recent example of this phenomenon occurred in the late 1990s when the stock markets of the world were said by some to have suffered a bubble in technology stocks. The existence of a bubble is often interpreted to imply that asset prices are behaving in a completely irrational way compared with what fundamentals would suggest. However, it can be shown that bubbles may reflect perfectly rational behavior.

The present-value model, equation (11.5), may be thought of as giving the fundamentals solution of the stock price. Suppose there is another solution for the stock price P_t^B that also satisfies equation (11.3) and that differs from the fundamentals solution by an amount B_t. Hence, P_t^B is given by

$$\begin{aligned} P_t^B &= P_t + B_t \\ &= \frac{1}{1+\alpha} E_t (P_{t+1}^B + D_{t+1}). \end{aligned} \tag{11.6}$$

Subtracting (11.3) from (11.6) gives the equation of motion that describes B_t:

$$B_t = \frac{1}{1+\alpha} E_t B_{t+1}. \tag{11.7}$$

If expectations are rational, then

$$B_{t+1} = E_t B_{t+1} + \xi_{t+1},$$

where the innovation ξ_{t+1} satisfies $E_t \xi_{t+1} = 0$, the so-called martingale condition. (Roughly, a martingale is like a random walk in that the expected change conditional on information at time t is zero, but it does not have the restriction that the variance of the change is constant.) Thus, B_t would have the equation of motion

$$B_{t+1} = (1 + \alpha)B_t + \xi_{t+1}.$$

As $\alpha > 0$, this is an explosive process. B_t will therefore soon start to dominate the fundamentals, causing P_t^B to explode too. Hence the notion that B_t is a bubble.

We have established that bubbles are explosive, but the connotation of a bubble is also that it bursts, and suddenly disappears. The bubble obtained above requires a single positive innovation ξ_t for it to start to grow. How, then, does it disappear? This question reveals the main weakness of the concept of an asset-price bubble. It takes some ingenuity to think of how to make the bubble disappear and then reappear again some time in the (possibly distant) future.

One way is to assume that in each period there is a very small probability that a bubble will begin, but once begun, a high probability that it will burst. A Markov switching model can be used for this purpose. For example, suppose that the expected asset price in $t + 1$ is a weighted average of the expected fundamentals solution P^F given by equation (11.5) and the bubble P^B. We then have

$$E_t P_{t+1} = \pi(B) E_t P_{t+1}^F + [1 - \pi(B)] E_t P_{t+1}^B,$$

where $\pi(B)$ is the conditional probability of a bubble existing in period $t + 1$ given that a bubble has (or has not) already started. Thus

$$\pi(B) = \begin{cases} \pi(0) & \text{if there is no bubble in period } t, \\ \pi(1) & \text{if there is a bubble in period } t. \end{cases}$$

We expect $\pi(0)$ to be close to unity and $\pi(1)$ to be close to zero. Thus $\pi(B)$ will change depending on whether a bubble is in existence. Other ways of forming these probabilities can also be used. For example, if an asset price starts to accelerate, then the probability of being in a bubble that could burst shortly is much higher. See Campbell et al. (1997) for further discussion of stock market bubbles.

11.2.2   The General Equilibrium Model of Stock Prices

According to the asset pricing theory developed in chapter 10 the general equilibrium real rate of return to equity satisfies

$$E_t \left[\frac{\beta U'(c_{t+1})}{U'(c_t)} (1 + r_{t+1}) \right] = 1,$$

and the no-arbitrage condition is

$$E_t r_{t+1} - r_t^f = \beta \sigma_t (1 + r_t^f) \text{Cov}_t \left(\frac{\Delta c_{t+1}}{c_t}, r_{t+1} - r_t^f \right), \tag{11.8}$$

where $\sigma_t = -(c_t U_t'' / U_t') > 0$ is the coefficient of relative risk aversion.

11.2.2.1 Equity Premium Puzzle

Unfortunately, the evidence does not support this theory either. It shows that the expected excess return to equity greatly exceeds the right-hand side of equation (11.8) unless the value of σ_t is set very high—too high to be acceptable. This is called the *equity premium puzzle* (see Mehra and Prescott 1985). The problem is that $M_{t+1} = (\beta U'(c_{t+1})/U'(c_t))$ must be sufficiently volatile to offset the volatility in the excess return $r_{t+1} - r_t^f$. And as c_{t+1}/c_t on its own is not sufficiently volatile and hence neither is $\text{Cov}_t((\Delta c_{t+1}/c_t), r_{t+1} - r_t^f)$, it is necessary to make σ a large number (see Campbell 2002). Only then is M_{t+1} sufficiently volatile.

11.2.2.2 Responses to the Equity Premium Puzzle

The main response has been to choose a utility function that produces a larger risk premium. Attention has focused on the assumption of time-separable utility. An example of the alternative, time-nonseparable utility, is the habit-persistence model, where $U_t = U(c_t, x_t)$ and x_t is the habitual level of consumption.

Habit Persistence. One example is that of Abel (1990), who assumes that the utility function can be written

$$U_t = \frac{(c_t/x_t)^{1-\sigma} - 1}{1 - \sigma},$$

where x_t is a function of past consumption, for example, $x_t = c_{t-1}^\delta$. The stochastic discount factor then becomes

$$M_{t+1} = \beta \left(\frac{c_{t+1}/x_{t+1}}{c_t/c_t} \right)^{-\sigma}.$$

The no-arbitrage condition now has an extra term:

$$E_t r_{t+1} - r_t^f = \beta(1 + r_t^f)\sigma_t[\text{Cov}_t(\Delta \ln c_{t+1}, r_{t+1}) - \text{Cov}_t(\Delta \ln x_{t+1}, r_{t+1})].$$

The rationale is that if $\text{Cov}_t(\Delta \ln x_{t+1}, r_{t+1}) < 0$ and is large enough, then it can raise the size of the risk premium. There is, however, a logical problem. If x_t is a function of only past consumption (i.e., not of current consumption)—a reasonable assumption given that we are trying to measure habitual consumption—then this extra term must be zero as it is a conditional covariance and $\Delta \ln x_{t+1} = \delta \Delta \ln c_{t+1}$ is known at time t.

Constantinides (1990) has proposed a different habit-persistence utility function: namely,

$$U_t = \frac{(c_t - \lambda x_t)^{1-\sigma} - 1}{1 - \sigma}. \qquad (11.9)$$

This was modified by Campbell and Cochrane (1999), who set $\lambda = 1$ and introduced the concept of surplus consumption, defined as $S_t = (c_t - x_t)/c_t$. If, for example, $x_t = c_{t-1}$, then S_t is roughly the rate of growth of consumption. The stochastic discount factor implied by equation (11.9) with $\lambda = 1$ is

$$M_{t+1} = \beta \left(\frac{c_{t+1} - x_{t+1}}{c_t - x_t} \right)^{-\sigma}$$

$$= \beta \left(\frac{c_{t+1}}{c_t} \frac{S_{t+1}}{S_t} \right)^{-\sigma}.$$

The no-arbitrage condition can then be written

$$E_t(r_{t+1} - r_t^{\mathrm{f}}) = \beta(1 + r_t^{\mathrm{f}})\sigma_t \operatorname{Cov}_t(\Delta \ln c_{t+1}, r_{t+1})$$

$$+ \beta(1 + r_t^{\mathrm{f}})\sigma_t \operatorname{Cov}_t(\Delta \ln S_{t+1}, r_{t+1}).$$

The extra term involves $\Delta \ln S_{t+1}$, which can be interpreted as the proportional change in the rate of growth of excess consumption. This will be much more volatile than consumption itself and hence is likely to raise the risk premium significantly, provided—and it is a large proviso—the correlation between $\Delta \ln S_{t+1}$ and r_{t+1} is not negligible, which it may well be. Campbell and Cochrane claim that the extra term, when measured by the unconditional covariance, does increase the risk premium, but Smith et al. (2006) find that the term is not significant when a conditional covariance is used instead of an unconditional covariance. This shows the importance of the information structure in asset pricing.

Kreps–Porteus Time-Nonseparable Utility.   The previous models were based on time-separable utility. An alternative approach is to assume time-nonseparable utility. The Kreps–Porteus formulation of this is

$$\mathcal{U}_t = \mathcal{U}[c_t, E_t(\mathcal{U}_{t+1})].$$

Epstein and Zin (1989) have implemented a special case based on the constant elasticity of substitution (CES) function

$$\mathcal{U}_t = [(1 - \beta)c_t^{1-1/\gamma} + \beta(E_t(\mathcal{U}_{t+1}^{1-\sigma}))^{(1-(1/\gamma))/(1-\sigma)}]^{1/(1-1/\gamma)},$$

where β is the discount factor, σ is the coefficient of relative risk aversion, and γ is the elasticity of intertemporal substitution. In the additively separable intertemporal utility function the coefficient of relative risk aversion and the elasticity of intertemporal substitution are restricted to be identical, but in the time-nonseparable model they may differ.

Epstein and Zin show that maximizing $\mathcal{U}_t$ subject to the slightly different budget constraint

$$W_{t+1} = (1 + r_{t+1}^{\mathrm{m}})(W_t - c_t),$$

where r_{t+1}^m is the return on the market, gives

$$E_t \left\{ \left[\beta \left(\frac{c_{t+1}}{c_t} \right)^{-1/\gamma} \right]^{(1-\sigma)/(1-(1/\gamma))} (1 + r_{t+1}^m)^{1-((1-\sigma)/(1-(1/\gamma)))} (1 + r_{t+1}) \right\} = 1.$$

Thus the stochastic discount factor is

$$M_{t+1} = \left[\beta \left(\frac{c_{t+1}}{c_t} \right)^{-1/\gamma} \right]^{(1-\sigma)/(1-(1/\gamma))} (1 + r_{t+1}^m)^{1-((1-\sigma)/(1-(1/\gamma)))}.$$

Compared with time-separable utility, this has two additional degrees of freedom, which can boost the size of the risk premium. First, the power index is no longer the coefficient of relative risk aversion, and is therefore free to take on larger values. Second, M_{t+1} now varies with the return on the portfolio.

Assuming log-normality, Campbell et al. (1997) have rewritten the no-arbitrage condition equation as

$$E_t(r_{t+1} - r_t^f) + \tfrac{1}{2} V_t(r_{t+1})$$
$$= \frac{1-\sigma}{1-\gamma} \text{Cov}_t(\Delta \ln c_{t+1}, r_{t+1}) + \left(1 + \frac{\gamma(1-\sigma)}{1-\gamma} \right) \text{Cov}_t(r_{t+1}^m, r_{t+1}). \quad (11.10)$$

This may be compared with the corresponding equation under power utility and log-normality, which is

$$E_t(r_{t+1} - r_t^f) + \tfrac{1}{2} V_t(r_{t+1}) = \sigma \, \text{Cov}_t(\Delta \ln c_{t+1}, r_{t+1}). \quad (11.11)$$

In equation (11.10) the coefficient of the first term on the right-hand side is no longer the coefficient of relative risk aversion and there is a second term that reflects the fact that the market return is an additional factor. The aim in using equation (11.10) is to give more flexibility in the determination of the risk premium. However, the empirical evidence is still equivocal on how well this succeeds—see Smith et al. (2006) for a test of this model.

11.2.3 Comment

It would appear that, in the main, the evidence does not provide very strong support for any of these models of the stock market. As a result, finance has tended to use empirically driven models rather than theoretical models like those we have discussed. The failure of these models is a challenge to economics and finance. Nonetheless, we should still take the connections between macroeconomics and finance seriously, not least because financial evidence provides a valuable new way of testing macroeconomic theories. This has led Cochrane (2008) to conclude that the challenge to both macroeconomics and finance is to understand what macroeconomic risks underlie the "factor risk premia" and the average returns on the special portfolios employed in finance research.

11.3 The Bond Market

Bonds are a widely used vehicle for borrowing. Governments are the main issuers of bonds and these dominate the bond market. Other bonds, such as

corporate bonds, are priced off these. We have assumed so far that all bonds
are issued for a single period, but in practice they have different times to maturity. Short-term government debt (maturities of a year or less) takes the form
of Treasury bills and are held to maturity. Long-term government debt has a
range of maturities, varying from just over one year to up to fifty years, or even
for ever when they are known as perpetuities or consols. As previously noted,
it is still possible to buy debt issued by the U.K. government to finance the
Napoleonic Wars. Long-term debt is not necessarily held to maturity, but may
be bought and sold on secondary markets—as is equity on the stock market.

The value of debt at maturity is usually expressed in nominal terms. This
implies that at maturity it possesses two types of risk: the risk of default and
inflation risk due to the uncertainty about the real value of its purchasing power.
The risk of default is usually judged to be higher for corporate bonds than for
government bonds and is the main reason for the differences in their price.
Most long-term bonds also make annual, or more frequent, payments prior to
maturity. These are called coupons and are usually expressed as a proportion
of the maturity value (or face value) of the debt. Long-term bonds sold before
maturity also have price risk due to the uncertainty about their market price
prior to maturity. Recently, a few governments have started to issue index-
linked debt, where the maturity value (and any interim coupon payments) are
indexed to inflation. Our aim is to analyze how the market price of bonds is
determined. Factors affecting the price are the maturity value of the bond, the
time to maturity, the size of coupon payments, whether it is indexed or not, and
a variety of risks. The price is also affected by the short-term interest rate set as
part of monetary policy. This is the way in which monetary policy is conducted.
The transmission mechanism is through the short rate, which is set by policy,
affecting all bond prices via the term structure of interest rates.

There is a vast literature on the term structure of interest rates or, as it
is sometimes called, fixed-income securities (see, for example, Campbell et al.
1997; Dai and Singleton 2003; Singleton 2006).

11.3.1 The Term Structure of Interest Rates

The price $P_{n,t}$ of a coupon bond with n periods to maturity is the expected
discounted value of the sum of all coupon payments and the value of the bond
at maturity. Thus

$$P_{n,t} = \frac{c}{1 + R_{n,t}^c} + \frac{c}{(1 + R_{n,t}^c)^2} + \cdots + \frac{1 + c}{(1 + R_{n,t}^c)^n}$$

$$= c \sum_{i=1}^{n} (1 + R_{n,t}^c)^{-i} + (1 + R_{n,t}^c)^{-n}$$

$$= \frac{c}{R_{n,t}^c}(1 - (1 + R_{n,t}^c)^{-n}) + (1 + R_{n,t}^c)^{-n}, \tag{11.12}$$

where c is the coupon paid each period expressed as a proportion of the face
value of the bond and $R_{n,t}^c$ is the nominal discount rate for the income stream on

a bond with coupon c. $R_{n,t}^c$ is better known as its yield to maturity. Without loss of generality we have assumed that the payoff at maturity is 1, hence $P_{0,t} = 1$.

We note that a perpetuity has $n = \infty$ and so

$$\lim_{n \to \infty} P_{n,t} = \frac{c}{R_{\infty,t}^c},$$

and a zero-coupon, or pure discount, bond has $c = 0$, which we write as

$$P_{n,t} = \frac{1}{[1 + R_{n,t}^0]^n}.$$

This implies that the zero-coupon yield $R_{n,t}^0$ is approximately

$$R_{n,t}^0 \simeq -\frac{1}{n} \ln P_{n,t}.$$

In practice, in each country usually very few discount bonds are in existence at any point in time, and those that do exist have short maturities. But it is possible to convert a coupon bond into the equivalent discount bond with the same maturity. Again, there are only a limited number of coupon bonds, and so it is not possible to construct a zero-coupon bond for each maturity at every point in time just through converting coupon bonds. It is, however, possible to use interpolation methods to fill in the gaps. In this way we can obtain the equivalent zero-coupon yield to maturity for any maturity. This is called the *term structure of interest rates*. The plot of these zero-coupon yields against the time to maturity is called the yield curve.

11.3.1.1 Converting a Coupon into a Zero-Coupon Bond

An n-period coupon bond can be thought of as a collection of pure discount bonds with payoffs in periods t to $t + n - 1$ that are equal to the coupon value of the bond c, and in period $t + n$ equal to the value of the bond at maturity plus the coupon, $1 + c$. To convert a coupon into a zero-coupon bond each of these payoffs is discounted at the zero-coupon yield $R_{n,t}^0$ corresponding to that maturity. Thus $P_{n,t}$ defined in equation (11.12) may be reexpressed as

$$P_{n,t} = \frac{c}{1 + R_{1,t}^0} + \frac{c}{(1 + R_{2,t}^0)^2} + \cdots + \frac{1 + c}{(1 + R_{n,t}^0)^n}.$$

For each $P_{n,t}$, only $R_{n,t}^0$ is unknown. We solve for $R_{n,t}^0$ from $P_{n,t}$ using the following sequence. For a 1-period bond we know that $R_{1,t}^0 = R_{1,t}$. This can be used to calculate $R_{2,t}^0$ from the price of a 2-period bond. $R_{1,t}^0$ and $R_{2,t}^0$ can then be used to calculate $R_{3,t}^0$ from the price of a 3-period bond. The sequence can be written

$$P_{1,t} = \frac{1}{1 + R_{1,t}^0} \rightarrow R_{1,t}^0,$$

$$P_{2,t} = \frac{c}{1 + R_{1,t}^0} + \frac{1 + c}{(1 + R_{2,t}^0)^2} \rightarrow R_{2,t}^0,$$

$$P_{3,t} = \frac{c}{1 + R_{1,t}^0} + \frac{c}{(1 + R_{2,t}^0)^2} + \frac{1+c}{(1 + R_{3,t}^0)^3} \rightarrow R_{3,t}^0,$$

$$\vdots$$

$$P_{n,t} = \frac{c}{1 + R_{1,t}^0} + \frac{c}{(1 + R_{2,t}^0)^2} + \cdots + \frac{1+c}{(1 + R_{n,t}^0)^n} \rightarrow R_{n,t}^0.$$

In our subsequent analysis of bond prices we will use zero-coupon yields and so, for convenience, we will omit the zero superscript and write $R_{n,t}^0 \equiv R_{n,t}$.

11.3.1.2   Forward Rates

It is possible to enter into an agreement in period t about the one-period rate of interest to be applied during period $t + n$ (i.e., between periods $t + n$ and $t + n + 1$). This is the forward rate, which is denoted by $f_{t,t+n}$. The value in period $t + n$ of an investment of one unit in period t that is compounded using the sequence of forward rates is

$$\frac{1}{P_{n,t}} = (1 + f_{t,t}) \cdots (1 + f_{t,t+n-1}).$$

The present value at time t of one unit in period $t + n$ discounted using the sequence of forward rates is

$$P_{n,t} = \frac{1}{(1 + f_{t,t}) \cdots (1 + f_{t,t+n-1})} = \prod_{i=0}^{n-1} \frac{1}{1 + f_{t,t+i}}. \tag{11.13}$$

It therefore follows that

$$1 + f_{t,t+n} = \frac{P_{n,t}}{P_{n+1,t}}$$

or

$$f_{t,t+n} = p_{n,t} - p_{n+1,t}$$
$$= -nR_{n,t} + (n + 1)R_{n+1,t}. \tag{11.14}$$

Thus the forward rates at time t can be derived from the zero-coupon yields, also at time t.

The no-arbitrage condition for forward rates is that

$$f_{t,t+n} = E_t s_{t+n}, \tag{11.15}$$

i.e., that forward rates are unbiased predictors of future spot rates, where $f_{t,t} = s_t$. The plot of the forward rates $f_{t,t+n}$ against n is called the forward-rate curve. When the forward-rate curve is rising it lies above the yield curve, and when it is falling it lies below. Increasingly, the forward-rate curve is scrutinized by central banks as it tells the bank the market's view of future interest rate expectations. A more formal discussion of forward rates is included in the discussion below of the forward exchange rate and uncovered interest parity.

11.3.1.3 Swap Rates

An interest rate swap is an agreement to exchange the cash flows of bonds in the future. The ownership of the bond is not exchanged, only the cash flows. A "plain vanilla" interest rate swap exchanges cash flows between fixed and variable (floating) interest rate bonds. The floating rate is commonly based on the London Interbank Offer Rate (LIBOR) on one-month eurocurrency deposits and is the sequence of these one-month forward rates until the end of the swap agreement, in period $t + n$, say. The swap rate is the average of the bid and ask (buy and sell) rates. In principle, the n-period fixed interest rate is the yield to maturity on an n-period zero-coupon bond.

The value (or cost) of the swap, assuming no default risk, is the difference between the present values of the two income streams, assuming that they have the same face value at maturity. Thus the value of a swap is

$$V_{n,t}^{\text{swap}} = P_{n,t}^{\text{fl}} - P_{n,t}^{\text{fx}},$$

where

$$P_{n,t}^{\text{fl}} = \prod_{i=0}^{n-1} \frac{1}{1 + f_{t,t+i}},$$

$$P_{n,t}^{\text{fx}} = \frac{1}{(1 + R_{n,t})^n}.$$

In period t, to eliminate arbitrage opportunities $V_{n,t}^{\text{swap}} = 0$. But during its lifetime its value may become positive or negative. The swap rate is the zero-coupon yield obtained by equating $P_{n,t}^{\text{fx}}$ to $P_{n,t}^{\text{fl}}$ at the time when the swap is initiated. Since swap rates exist in the market and zero-coupon yields (a derived yield) do not, swap rates can be used to construct the zero-coupon yields and hence the yield curve. Furthermore, from equation (11.14), swap rates can be used to calculate the forward rates.

11.3.1.4 Holding-Period Returns

The holding-period return is the nominal rate of return to holding a zero-coupon bond for one period. $h_{n,t+1}$ is the holding-period return on an n-period bond between periods t and $t + 1$. It is calculated from

$$1 + h_{n,t+1} = \frac{P_{n-1,t+1}}{P_{n,t}}$$

$$= \frac{(1 + R_{n-1,t+1})^{-(n-1)}}{(1 + R_{n,t})^{-n}}.$$

If $p_{n,t} = \ln P_{n,t}$, then taking logs gives

$$h_{n,t+1} \simeq p_{n-1,t+1} - p_{n,t} = nR_{n,t} - (n - 1)R_{n-1,t+1}.$$

The no-arbitrage condition for bonds is that, after adjusting for risk, investors are indifferent between holding an n-period bond and a risk-free bond for one period. Hence, approximately,

$$E_t h_{n,t+1} = s_t + \rho_{n,t},$$

where $\rho_{n,t}$ is the risk premium on an n-period bond at time t. Noting that

$$s_t = r_t^f = R_{1,t} = -\ln P_{1,t},$$

the no-arbitrage condition may be written either as

$$E_t h_{n,t+1} = n R_{n,t} - (n-1) E_t R_{n-1,t+1} = s_t + \rho_{n,t}$$

or as

$$(n-1)(E_t R_{n-1,t+1} - R_{n,t}) = (R_{n,t} - s_t) - \rho_{n,t}, \qquad (11.16)$$

where $R_{n,t} - s_t$ is called the term spread.

If the risk premium (called, here, the term premium) is omitted, equation (11.16) is known as the "rational-expectations hypothesis of the term structure" (REHTS) (see Cox et al. 1981). There is, however, a vast amount of empirical evidence that rejects the REHTS. This suggests that the term premium should not be omitted.

11.3.1.5 The Yield Curve

The no-arbitrage condition, equation (11.16), is a difference equation. Using successive substitution it can be rewritten as

$$R_{n,t} = \frac{n-1}{n} E_t R_{n-1,t+1} + \frac{1}{n}(s_t + \rho_{n,t})$$

$$= \frac{1}{n} \sum_{i=0}^{n-1} E_t (s_{t+i} + \rho_{n-i,t+i}). \qquad (11.17)$$

Consequently, the nominal yield to maturity is the average of expected future short rates plus the average risk premium on the bond over the rest of its life.

The Fisher equation defines the one-period real interest rate r_t by

$$r_t = s_t - E_t \pi_{t+1},$$

where π_t is inflation. Hence

$$R_{n,t} = \frac{1}{n} \sum_{i=0}^{n-1} E_t (r_{t+i} + \pi_{t+i+1} + \rho_{n-i,t+i}). \qquad (11.18)$$

Accordingly, three variables determine the shape of the yield curve: the real interest rate, inflation, and the risk premium. If the real rate and inflation are constant, the shape will only reflect the risk premium. The longer the time to maturity, the greater the risk component. Hence the yield curve will slope upwards. This is the "normal" shape of a yield curve. If inflation is expected to increase in the future, then this will cause the yield curve to rise more steeply. If inflation is expected to fall, then the yield curve will be flatter, and could even

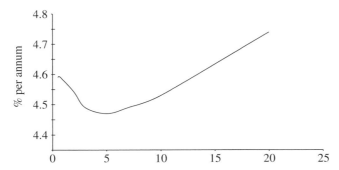

Figure 11.1. The U.S. yield curve, January 31, 2006.

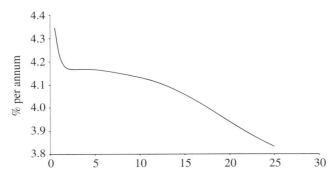

Figure 11.2. The U.K. yield curve, February 15, 2006.

Table 11.1. Bond spreads.

	U.S.	U.K.	EU
Two-year term spread	0.6	−0.1	0.05
Ten-year term spread	2.7	0.6	1.3
Corporate spread	2.2	1.3	0.8

have a negative slope, in which case it is said to be inverted. A hump-shaped yield curve is usually due to an expected temporary increase in inflation.

To illustrate, figures 11.1 and 11.2 give the yield curves for the United States and United Kingdom at the start of 2006. They have very different shapes. The U.S. yield curve suggests that inflation is expected to increase in the short term, then fall over the following five years. The U.K. yield curve is inverted, implying an expected fall in inflation over time.

To give a further idea of the shape of the yield curve and of the orders of magnitude of the risk premia arising from government and corporate bonds, three spreads for November 20, 2002, are reported in table 11.1.

These are based on ten-year, two-year, and three-month government bonds and representative corporate bonds for the United States, the United Kingdom and the European Union. Two yield curve spreads can be calculated from these data: the spread of the two-year over the three-month rate and the ten-year over the three-month rate. These can be thought of for now as measures of price risk for different maturities. Note that in each case this increases with time to maturity. A measure of default risk is given by the spread of corporate bonds over long-term ten-year government bonds. On this date the default risk of corporate bonds was as large as the price risk for ten-year bonds. The yields on corporate bonds are the cumulation of the three-month rate, the ten-year spread, and the corporate spread. The data show that the United States was the most risky investment environment for bonds, but this changes as the spreads vary over time.

11.3.2 The Term Premium

We now consider how to specify the term premium. We focus on two approaches: the latent affine factor approach favored by finance, and the general equilibrium model of risk. The two approaches differ in the choice of intertemporal marginal rates of return. The starting point for both is to express $P_{n,t}$ as the discounted value of $P_{n-1,t+1}$ when the bond has $n-1$ periods to maturity. Thus

$$P_{nt} = E_t[M_{t+1}P_{n-1,t+1}] \tag{11.19}$$

or

$$E_t[M_{t+1}(1 + h_{n,t+1})] = 1.$$

For $n = 1$, the yield is known at time t, hence

$$E_t M_{t+1}(1 + s_t) = 1.$$

Assuming that $P_{n,t}$ and M_{t+1} have a joint log-normal distribution with $p_{n,t} = \ln P_{n,t}$ and $m_{t+1} = \ln M_{t+1}$, taking logarithms of equation (11.19) gives

$$p_{nt} = E_t(m_{t+1} + p_{n-1,t+1}) + \tfrac{1}{2}V_t(m_{t+1} + p_{n-1,t+1}) \tag{11.20}$$

$$= E_t m_{t+1} + E_t p_{n-1,t+1} + \tfrac{1}{2}V_t(m_{t+1})$$

$$+ \tfrac{1}{2}V_t(p_{n-1,t+1}) + \text{Cov}_t(m_{t+1}, p_{n-1,t+1}). \tag{11.21}$$

Hence, as $p_{0,t} = 0$,

$$p_{1,t} = E_t m_{t+1} + \tfrac{1}{2}V_t(m_{t+1}). \tag{11.22}$$

Subtracting (11.22) from (11.21) and rearranging gives the no-arbitrage equation:

$$E_t p_{n-1,t+1} - p_{n,t} + p_{1,t} + \tfrac{1}{2}V_t(p_{n-1,t+1}) = -\text{Cov}_t(m_{t+1}, p_{n-1,t+1}). \tag{11.23}$$

This can be rewritten in terms of yields as

$$-(n-1)E_t R_{n-1,t+1} + nR_{n,t} - s_t + \tfrac{1}{2}(n-1)^2 V_t(R_{n-1,t+1})$$

$$= (n-1)\,\text{Cov}_t(m_{t+1}, R_{n-1,t+1}),$$

and, since $h_{n,t} \simeq -(n-1)R_{n-1,t+1} + nR_{n,t}$, as

$$E_t(h_{n,t+1} - s_t) + \tfrac{1}{2}V_t(h_{n,t+1}) = -\text{Cov}_t(m_{t+1}, h_{n,t+1}). \tag{11.24}$$

This is the fundamental no-arbitrage condition for an n-period bond. The term on the right-hand side is the term premium.

11.3.2.1 Affine Latent Factor Models of the Term Premium

We illustrate this method using a single-factor model and compare two widely used formulations: the Cox–Ingersoll–Ross (CIR) model (Cox et al. 1985a,b) and the Vasicek (1977) model. In a single-factor model we write $p_{n,t}$, the log price, as a linear function of the factor z_t:

$$p_{n,t} = -[A_n + B_n z_t].$$

The coefficients differ for each maturity but are related in such a way that there are no arbitrage opportunities across maturities. Below, we derive the restrictions implied by this. The yield to maturity is

$$R_{n,t} = -\frac{1}{n}p_{n,t} = \frac{A_n}{n} + \frac{B_n}{n}z_t$$

and the one-period risk-free rate is

$$s_t = -p_{1,t} = A_1 + B_1 z_t.$$

In order to derive the restrictions on A_n and B_n we need to introduce an assumption about the process generating z_t.

The Cox-Ingersoll-Ross Model. Cox, Ingersoll, and Ross proposed a model of the term structure that assumes that $m = \ln M$ is defined by

$$-m_{t+1} = z_t + \lambda e_{t+1}, \tag{11.25}$$
$$z_{t+1} - \mu = \phi(z_t - \mu) + e_{t+1}, \tag{11.26}$$

where z_t is unobservable but is assumed to be generated by the above autoregressive process in which $e_{t+1} = \sigma\sqrt{z_t}\varepsilon_{t+1}$ and $\varepsilon_{t+1} \sim$ i.i.d.$(0,1)$, i.e., the ε_{t+1} are independently and identically distributed random variables with zero mean and a unit variance. Thus $V_t(e_{t+1}) = \sigma^2 z_t$. We now evaluate equation (11.20) using these assumptions, noting that

$$E_t[m_{t+1} + p_{n-1,t+1}] = -[z_t + A_{n-1} + B_{n-1}E_t z_{t+1}]$$
$$= -[z_t + A_{n-1} + B_{n-1}(\mu(1-\phi) + \phi z_t)]$$

and

$$V_t[m_{t+1} + p_{n-1,t+1}] = V_t[\lambda e_{t+1} + B_{n-1}e_{t+1}]$$
$$= (\lambda + B_{n-1})^2 V_t(e_{t+1})$$
$$= (\lambda + B_{n-1})^2 \sigma^2 z_t.$$

Hence equation (11.20) becomes

$$-[A_n + B_n z_t] = -[(1 + \phi B_{n-1})z_t + A_{n-1} + B_{n-1}\mu(1 - \phi)] + \tfrac{1}{2}(\lambda + B_{n-1})^2\sigma^2 z_t$$
$$= -[A_{n-1} + B_{n-1}\mu(1 - \phi)] - [1 + \phi B_{n-1} - \tfrac{1}{2}(\lambda + B_{n-1})^2\sigma^2]z_t.$$

Equating terms on the left-hand and right-hand sides (i.e., the intercepts and the coefficients on z_t) gives the recursive formulae

$$A_n = A_{n-1} + B_{n-1}\mu(1 - \phi),$$
$$B_n = 1 + \phi B_{n-1} - \tfrac{1}{2}(\lambda + B_{n-1})^2\sigma^2.$$

Using $P_{0,t} = 1$ implies that $p_{0,t} = 0$ and $A_0 = 0$, $B_0 = 0$. Starting with these values we solve recursively for all A_n, B_n from these two formulae. For $n = 1$, $B_1 = 1 - \tfrac{1}{2}\lambda^2\sigma^2$ and $A_1 = 0$. Hence

$$s_t = -p_{1,t} = A_1 + B_1 z_t$$
$$= (1 - \tfrac{1}{2}\lambda^2\sigma^2)z_t. \tag{11.27}$$

The no-arbitrage condition, equation (11.23), is therefore

$$E_t p_{n-1,t+1} - p_{nt} + p_{1,t} = E_t[h_{n,t+1} - s_t]$$
$$= -[\tfrac{1}{2}V_t(p_{n-1,t+1}) + \text{Cov}_t(m_{t+1}, p_{n-1,t+1})]$$
$$= -\tfrac{1}{2}B_{n-1}^2\sigma^2 z_t + \lambda B_{n-1}\sigma^2 z_t.$$

The first term is the Jensen effect and the second is the risk premium. Thus

$$\text{risk premium} = -\text{Cov}_t(m_{t+1}, p_{n-1,t+1}) = \lambda B_{n-1}\sigma^2 z_t.$$

Both are linear functions of z_t. We note that if $\lambda = 0$ (i.e., if $m_{t+1} = -z_t$ and is nonstochastic), then the risk premium is zero.

So far z_t has been treated as a latent variable and assumed to be unobservable. However, equation (11.27) shows that z_t is a linear function of s_t, which is observable. We can therefore replace z_t everywhere by s_t. As a result, $p_{n,t}$, $R_{n,t}$, and the risk premium can all be shown to be linear functions of s_t, and the model becomes a stochastic discount factor (SDF) model with *observable* factors. Thus

$$p_{n,t} = -[A_n + B_n z_t]$$
$$= -\left[A_n + \frac{B_n}{1 - \tfrac{1}{2}\lambda^2\sigma^2}s_t\right],$$

$$R_{n,t} = \frac{1}{n}[A_n + B_n z_t]$$
$$= \frac{A_n}{n} + \frac{B_n}{n(1 - \tfrac{1}{2}\lambda^2\sigma^2)}s_t,$$

$$\text{risk premium} = \lambda B_{n-1}\sigma^2 z_t$$
$$= \frac{\lambda B_{n-1}\sigma^2}{1 - \tfrac{1}{2}\lambda^2\sigma^2}s_t.$$

This implies that the term structure has the same shape in all time periods, and the curve shifts up and down over time due to movements in the short rate. In practice, however, the shape of the yield curve varies over time, therefore this single-factor CIR model is clearly not an appropriate model of the term structure.

The Vasicek Model. Vasicek's model of the term structure also uses equations (11.25) and (11.26) but assumes that $e_{t+1} = \sigma \varepsilon_{t+1}$. The analysis proceeds as for the CIR model. The first difference is that

$$V_t[m_{t+1} + p_{n-1,t+1}] = (\lambda + B_{n-1})^2 \sigma^2.$$

Equation (11.20) is now evaluated to be

$$-[A_n + B_n z_t] = -[A_{n-1} + B_{n-1}\mu(1 - \phi) + \tfrac{1}{2}(\lambda + B_{n-1})^2\sigma^2] - [1 + \phi B_{n-1}]z_t.$$

Thus

$$A_n = A_{n-1} + B_{n-1}\mu(1 - \phi) + \tfrac{1}{2}(\lambda + B_{n-1})^2\sigma^2,$$
$$B_n = 1 + \phi B_{n-1}.$$

Using $p_{0,t} = A_0 = B_0 = 0$ we obtain $B_1 = 1$ and $A_1 = \tfrac{1}{2}\lambda^2\sigma^2$. Thus

$$s_t = -p_{1,t} = A_1 + B_1 z_t$$
$$= \tfrac{1}{2}\lambda^2\sigma^2 + z_t$$

and

$$p_{n,t} = -[A_n + B_n z_t]$$
$$= -[A_n - \tfrac{1}{2}\lambda^2\sigma^2 B_n] - B_n s_t,$$

$$R_{n,t} = \frac{1}{n}[A_n + B_n z_t]$$
$$= \frac{1}{n}[A_n - \tfrac{1}{2}\lambda^2\sigma^2 B_n] + \frac{B_n}{n} s_t.$$

From the no-arbitrage condition, equation (11.23), as $B_n = (1 - \phi^n)/(1 - \phi)$, we have

$$E_t p_{n-1,t+1} - p_{nt} + p_{1,t} = E_t[h_{n,t+1} - s_t]$$
$$= -\tfrac{1}{2}B_{n-1}^2\sigma^2 + \lambda B_{n-1}\sigma^2$$
$$= -\frac{1}{2}\left(\frac{1 - \phi^n}{1 - \phi}\right)^2\sigma^2 + \frac{\lambda(1 - \phi^{n-1})\sigma^2}{1 - \phi},$$

$$\text{risk premium} = \frac{\lambda(1 - \phi^{n-1})\sigma^2}{1 - \phi}.$$

Thus, as in the CIR model, yields in the Vasicek model are linear functions of the short rate, the shape of the yield curve is constant through time, and the curve shifts due to changes in the short rate. But unlike the CIR model, the risk premium depends only on the time to maturity and not on time itself. The single-factor Vasicek model is, therefore, an even more unsatisfactory way to model the term structure than the single-factor CIR model.

Multi-Factor Affine Models. One of the problems with these particular CIR and Vasicek models is that they are single-factor models. A multi-factor affine CIR model may be better able to capture both changes in the shape of the yield curve over time and shifts in the curve. Dai and Singleton (2000) have proposed the following multi-factor CIR model of the term structure:

$$p_{n,t} = -[A_n + \boldsymbol{B}'_n \boldsymbol{z}_t], \qquad\qquad (11.28)$$

where $\boldsymbol{z}_t$ is a vector of factors:

$$-m_{t+1} = \boldsymbol{\ell}' \boldsymbol{z}_t + \boldsymbol{\lambda}' \boldsymbol{e}_{t+1},$$

$$\boldsymbol{z}_{t+1} - \boldsymbol{\mu} = \boldsymbol{\phi}(\boldsymbol{z}_t - \boldsymbol{\mu}) + \boldsymbol{e}_{t+1},$$

$$\boldsymbol{e}_{t+1} = \Sigma \sqrt{\boldsymbol{S}_t} \boldsymbol{\varepsilon}_{t+1},$$

$$S_{ii,t} = v_i + \boldsymbol{\theta}'_i \boldsymbol{z}_t,$$

where $\boldsymbol{\ell}$ is a vector of 1s, $\boldsymbol{S}_t$ is a diagonal matrix, $\boldsymbol{\varepsilon}_{t+1}$ is i.i.d.$(0, I)$, and $\boldsymbol{\phi}$ and Σ are both square matrices.

To illustrate, we consider the case where the factors are independent, so that $\boldsymbol{\phi}$ and Σ are diagonal matrices. Also we set $S_{ii,t} = z_{it}$. This makes the whole model additive. As result, it can be shown that

$$p_{n,t} = -\left[A_n + \sum_i B_{ni} z_{it}\right],$$

$$-m_{t+1} = \sum_i z_{it} + \sum_i \lambda_i e_{i,t+1},$$

$$z_{i,t+1} - \mu_i = \phi_i(z_{it} - \mu_i) + e_{i,t+1},$$

$$e_{i,t+1} = \sigma_i \sqrt{z_{it}} \varepsilon_{i,t+1}.$$

It then follows that

$$E_t p_{n-1,t+1} - p_{nt} + p_{1,t} = -\frac{1}{2} \sum_i B_{i,n-1}^2 \sigma_i^2 z_{it} + \sum_i \lambda_i B_{i,n-1} \sigma_i^2 z_{it},$$

$$\text{risk premium} = \sum_i \lambda_i B_{i,n-1} \sigma_i^2 z_{it}.$$

Hence the risk premium is the sum of the risk effects associated with each factor. Further, the short rate is a linear function of the factors:

$$s_t = -p_{1,t} = \sum_i (1 - \tfrac{1}{2}\lambda_i^2 \sigma_i^2) z_{it}.$$

Consequently, the yields and the term premia can no longer be written as a linear function of only the short rate. Since every yield is a linear function of the factors, if there are n factors, it would require the short rate plus $n-1$ further yields to represent the factors. If there are more than n yields (including the short rate), then the factors would not be a unique linear function of the yields. And if there were less than n yields, no observable representation of the factors would be possible, and so the model could not be reinterpreted as an observable factor model.

In practice, it has been found that three factors are sufficient to represent the yield curve. They seem to capture the shift or level, the slope, and any curvature in the yield curve. The shift factor is by far the most important, explaining about 90% of the variation in yields; the slope factor explains about 80% of the remaining variation; the curvature factor never explains more than 5% of the total variation. Taken together they explain about 98% of the total variation in yields (see, for example, Marsh 1995). As shifts in the level of the yield curve are due primarily to changes in the short rate, and this is largely an administered rate, this evidence shows the importance of monetary policy in causing changes in yields. The slope and curvature effects, which comprise about 8% of the total variation in yields, may be attributed mainly to the effects of changes in expected future inflation.

11.3.2.2 *General Equilibrium Model of the Term Premium*

In deriving the general equilibrium price of a bond we apply the asset pricing theory of chapter 10 that was developed for nominal returns. All we need to do in addition is to define the excess return for bonds appropriately. Assuming log-normality, the no-arbitrage condition for bond yields can be written

$$E_t(h_{n,t+1} - s_t) + \tfrac{1}{2}V_t(h_{n,t+1}) = -\,\text{Cov}_t(m_{t+1}, h_{n,t+1}),$$

where for C-CAPM with power utility,

$$m_{t+1} = \theta - \sigma \Delta \ln c_{t+1} - \pi_{t+1}. \tag{11.29}$$

Hence

$$E_t(h_{n,t+1} - s_t) + \tfrac{1}{2}V_t(h_{n,t+1}) = \sigma \,\text{Cov}_t(\Delta \ln c_{t+1}, h_{n,t+1},) + \text{Cov}_t(\pi_{t+1}, h_{n,t+1}),$$

or, in terms of yields,

$$E_t[nR_{n,t} - (n-1)R_{n-1,t+1} - s_t] + \tfrac{1}{2}(n-1)^2 V_t(R_{n-1,t+1})$$
$$= -(n-1)\sigma \,\text{Cov}_t(\Delta \ln c_{t+1}, R_{n-1,t+1}) - (n-1)\,\text{Cov}_t(\pi_{t+1}, R_{n-1,t+1}).$$

As the coefficients are the same for each maturity, the term premia can only differ due to different conditional covariance terms. Estimates of this model have been obtained by Balfoussia and Wickens (2007), who found that the coefficient restrictions were rejected. This suggests that this particular general equilibrium model of asset pricing holds for neither equity nor bonds.

11.3.3 Estimating Future Inflation from the Yield Curve

In formulating monetary policy it is becoming common for central banks to extract estimates of future inflation from the yield curve. This either requires an assumption about future real interest rates or, better still, the presence of a yield curve for real yields (i.e., for index-linked yields).

From equation (11.18) the average rate of inflation over the next n periods is given by

$$\frac{1}{n} \sum_{i=1}^{n} E_t \pi_{t+i} = R_{n,t} - \frac{1}{n} \sum_{i=0}^{n-1} E_t (r_{t+i} + \rho_{n-i,t+i}). \tag{11.30}$$

If we assume that $E_t r_{t+i} = r$ for $i > 0$ and ignore the risk premium, we may obtain a rough estimate of average future inflation as

$$\frac{1}{n} \sum_{i=1}^{n} E_t \pi_{t+i} = R_{n,t} - r. \tag{11.31}$$

In other words, average future inflation over different horizons is given by the shape of the yield curve less a constant. In general, therefore, average inflation will differ depending on the horizon. These estimates could be improved a little by making a simple correction for the term premia.

In principle, a better estimate of inflation may be obtained if indexed bonds also exist. Denoting the yield on an n-period indexed bond by r_{nt}, we may construct a theory of the real term structure along the same lines as for nominal yields. This would give us estimates of the real term premia, which we denote by $\rho_{n,t}^r$, where the nominal term premium may be written as

$$\rho_{n,t} = \rho_{n,t}^r + \rho_{n,t}^\pi,$$

and $\rho_{n,t}^\pi$ can be interpreted as the inflation risk premium. From equation (11.18) we may write nominal and real yields as

$$R_{n,t} = \frac{1}{n} \sum_{i=0}^{n-1} E_t (r_{t+i} + \pi_{t+i+1} + \rho_{n-i,t+i}^r + \rho_{n-i,t+i}^\pi), \tag{11.32}$$

$$r_{n,t} = \frac{1}{n} \sum_{i=0}^{n-1} E_t (r_{t+i} + \rho_{n-i,t+i}^r). \tag{11.33}$$

Subtracting (11.33) from (11.32) gives average inflation as

$$\frac{1}{n} \sum_{i=1}^{n} E_t \pi_{t+i} = R_{nt} - r_{nt} - \frac{1}{n} \sum_{i=0}^{n-1} E_t \rho_{n-i,t+i}^\pi. \tag{11.34}$$

If we ignore the last term, which involves the inflation risk premium, the estimate of inflation is simply the difference between the nominal and the indexed yields. This is called the "break-even" estimate of average inflation, and is commonly used by central banks in countries where there are indexed bonds. Strictly speaking, the break-even estimate should be corrected for the inflation risk premium. For the United Kingdom in the 1980s and 1990s this was estimated by Remolona et al. (1998) to be around 1%, a substantial size. More recent evidence after inflation targeting was introduced indicates a lower inflation risk premium. Thus lower rates of inflation so far in the 2000s appear to have reduced the size of this correction.

Finally, we note that it is common to use the term spread in econometric models as an indicator of future economic activity. From equations (11.17) and (11.34) this is

$$R_{n,t} - s_t = \frac{1}{n} \sum_{i=1}^{n-1} E_t(s_{t+i} + \rho_{n-i,t+i})$$

$$= r_{nt} + \frac{1}{n} \sum_{i=1}^{n-1} E_t \pi_{t+i+1} + \frac{1}{n} \sum_{i=1}^{n-1} E_t \rho_{n-i,t+i}^{\pi}. \qquad (11.35)$$

Thus, roughly, the term spread can be regarded as a predictor of the real yield to maturity and average future inflation.

11.3.4 Comment

The theory of bond pricing, fixed-income securities, is the most highly developed of these three financial assets. Although in some ways pricing bonds is the most straightforward of the three, it is also the most technically advanced and it is the most successful. Its success lies in the widespread use of relative asset-pricing techniques rather than fundamentals pricing. Based on fundamentals, pricing bonds is little more successful than pricing equity or FOREX. Recent advances in bond pricing have included attempts to combine the two approaches and to search for a way of incorporating observable macroeconomic factors in the explanation of term premia.

A distinctive feature of the bond market is its close connection with monetary policy. This is both because monetary policy affects the term structure through the short rate, the policy instrument under inflation targeting, and because the term structure possesses information about the market's view of future interest rates, and its view of future inflation. Both are useful to policy makers.

11.4 The FOREX Market

Foreign exchange is required for transactions on the current account (for goods and services) and the capital account (for financial assets). Although the nominal exchange rate is determined by the total demand and supply of a currency, if exchange rates are flexible, then, in the absence of capital controls, the extremely high degree of substitutability between domestic and foreign bonds means that exchange rates are determined primarily by capital-account transactions and not those on the current account. This does not necessarily imply that there will be large net capital-account movements, as the rapid adjustment of home and foreign rates of return expressed in the same currency in response to an excess demand for or supply of currency may be expected to restore FOREX market equilibrium almost instantly. This is what is implied by the uncovered interest parity condition discussed below.

Nonetheless, the volume of FOREX activity has grown hugely in recent years. Nearly half of the world's FOREX activity takes place in London. Over 95% of

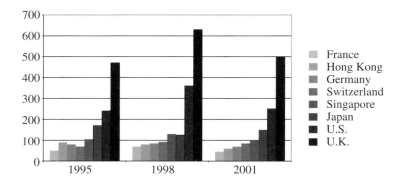

Figure 11.3. FOREX daily turnover ($ bn). Source: *Financial Times*, February 12, 2002.

all U.K. FOREX transactions are associated with the capital account. By 2006 daily FOREX transactions equalled roughly the whole of the United Kingdom's annual GDP. A comparison of FOREX transactions in different countries is given in figure 11.3.

11.4.1 Uncovered and Covered Interest Parity

11.4.1.1 Uncovered Interest Parity (UIP)

Uncovered interest parity is the key no-arbitrage condition in international bond markets. Initially we consider one-period bonds (a one- or a three-month Treasury bill). An investor has two choices: either invest in a domestic bill, which is virtually risk free in the domestic currency in nominal terms, or invest in a foreign bond, which is risk free in terms of the foreign currency but, due to exchange risk, not in domestic currency terms.

We use the following notation in our discussion of FOREX: i_t is the one-period nominal return in domestic currency; i_t^* is the one-period return in foreign currency; and S_t is the domestic price of foreign exchange (the number of units of domestic currency required to purchase one unit of foreign currency). An increase in S_t implies a depreciation of domestic currency.

To compare the two investments we need to measure their payoffs in the same currency. If the domestic investor has X units of domestic currency to invest in the foreign bond, the investor must first convert this into foreign currency at the current (or spot) rate S_t, then invest in the foreign bill, and finally convert the proceeds back into domestic currency. Consider a U.S. investor considering holding U.K. bills. Schematically, we have

$$\$X \to \pounds\frac{X}{S_t} \to \pounds\frac{X}{S_t}(1 + i_t^*) \to \$X\frac{S_{t+1}}{S_t}(1 + i_t^*).$$

The final payoff must be compared with investing in a domestic bill that gives $\$X(1 + i_t)$. Ignoring risk, for the investor to be indifferent between the two investments we require that the expected payoffs are the same, so that for any X,

$$1 + i_t = E_t \left[\frac{S_{t+1}}{S_t} (1 + i_t^*) \right]. \tag{11.36}$$

This is called the uncovered interest parity (UIP) condition.

Taking logarithms, it can be reexpressed to a close approximation as

$$i_t = i_t^* + E_t \left[\frac{\Delta S_{t+1}}{S_t} \right]$$
$$= i_t^* + E_t \Delta s_{t+1}, \tag{11.37}$$

where $s = \ln S$. This can be interpreted as saying that if the domestic exchange rate is expected to depreciate ($E_t \Delta s_{t+1} > 0$), then investors need to be compensated for holding the domestic bond by receiving a higher rate of return on the domestic than the foreign bond.

UIP also implies that domestic and foreign bonds are perfect substitutes and so, when their rates of return are expressed in the same currency, they are equal. If this were not so there would be an arbitrage opportunity. One could borrow at the lower interest rate and invest at the higher interest rate. This would result in extremely large capital flows. We return to this point later when we discuss the carry trade.

11.4.1.2 Covered Interest Parity

The Value of a Forward Contract. The forward contract for any asset, including interest rates and FOREX, may be determined as follows. Using the notation that P_t denotes the spot price of an underlying asset, that $F_{t,T}$ is the forward (or futures) price at t for delivery of the underlying asset at T, and that r^f is the risk-free rate (which is assumed to be constant), we consider two portfolios:

1. A long position in the forward contract. At time T this involves paying $F_{t,T}$ for the asset and selling it for P_T. This yields a profit at time T of

$$\pi^1(T) = P_T - F_{t,T}.$$

2. A long position in the underlying asset and a short position in the risk-free asset. This involves borrowing P_t at the rate of interest r^f to purchase the asset at date t and paying back the amount $e^{r^f(T-t)} P_t$ at date T by selling the asset for P_T. This yields the profit

$$\pi^2(T) = P_T - e^{r^f(T-t)} P_t.$$

The *expected* profits from the two investment strategies must be equal, otherwise an arbitrage opportunity would exist. If the profit from holding portfolio 2 were greater than that from holding portfolio 1, then the investor could borrow to purchase the underlying asset at t, and short (sell) the forward contract. At time T, the investor could close out the position in the forward contract and receive $F_{t,T}$. The profit would be $F_{t,T} - e^{r^f(T-t)} P_t$, which, by assumption, would be positive. Thus the investor would have made a positive profit for an outlay of zero. To rule this out, we require that the *expected* profits are equal, implying that

$$E_t P_T - F_{t,T} = E_t P_T - e^{r^f(T-t)} P_t.$$

From this we can obtain the forward price in terms of information available at time t as

$$F_{t,T} = e^{r^f(T-t)} P_t.$$

Thus the value of the forward contract in period t, the date when it is initiated, is

$$\pi(t) = P_t - e^{-r^f(T-t)} F_{t,T} = 0.$$

For any other period s ($T > s > t$) the profit $\pi(s)$ could of course be zero, positive, or negative.

In the case of FOREX the two investment opportunities are as follows:

1. Invest one unit of domestic currency by buying a domestic risk-free asset with nominal return i. The risk-free payoff in period T is $e^{i(T-t)}$. This is in terms of domestic currency.

2. Invest in a foreign asset whose nominal return i^* is risk free in terms of foreign currency but not in terms of domestic currency.

Purchase of the foreign asset can only be made in foreign currency and so, in order to buy the foreign asset, the investor must first convert the unit of domestic currency into foreign currency. If the spot exchange rate is S_t (i.e., the price of one unit of foreign currency in terms of domestic currency), then the investor receives $1/S_t$ units of foreign currency. The total payoff in foreign currency is therefore $(1/S_t)e^{i^*(T-t)}$. To find the payoff in terms of domestic currency it is necessary to convert it at the spot rate prevailing in period T. The payoff in terms of domestic currency is therefore $(S_T/S_t)e^{i^*(T-t)}$.

The UIP condition is the no-arbitrage condition obtained by equating the expected payoffs (expressed in domestic currency) for the two investments. This gives

$$e^{i(T-t)} = E_t \left[\frac{S_T}{S_t} e^{i^*(T-t)} \right]$$

or

$$S_t = e^{-(i-i^*)(T-t)} E_t S_T. \tag{11.38}$$

Thus the spot exchange rate in period t is determined by the discounted expected future spot rate S_T, where the discount rate is $i - i^*$. Taking logarithms of equation (11.38) and setting $T = t + 1$ gives equation (11.37) once more. Due to the use of continuous time here, equation|(11.37) will hold exactly.

As S_T is unknown at time t, the foreign investment above will be risky even though the payoff in foreign currency terms is not risky. An alternative to converting the proceeds of the foreign investment using the spot exchange rate at time T is to buy a forward contract at time t. This guarantees the exchange rate at which the conversion back into domestic currency takes place.

Let $F_{t,T}$ denote the forward exchange rate at date t for delivery at $T > t$. The payoff in domestic currency terms from the foreign investment is now $(F_{t,T}/S_t)e^{i^*(T-t)}$. As $F_{t,T}$ is known at time t this is a certain payoff. The no-arbitrage condition is now obtained by equating the payoffs from the investments in the domestic asset and in the foreign asset, where conversion takes place using the forward rate. Hence

$$e^{i(T-t)} = \frac{F_{t,T}}{S_t}e^{i^*(T-t)},$$

which gives the forward rate for foreign exchange as

$$F_{t,T} = S_t e^{(i-i^*)(T-t)}. \tag{11.39}$$

Equation (11.39) is called the covered interest parity condition.

If interest rates are time-varying, then taking logarithms of equation (11.39) for $T = t+1$ gives

$$f_t = s_t + i_t - i_t^*,$$

where $f_t = \ln F_{t,t+1}$. If we rewrite the UIP, equation (11.37), as

$$E_t s_{t+1} = s_t + i_t - i_t^*, \tag{11.40}$$

it follows that

$$f_t = E_t s_{t+1}. \tag{11.41}$$

The forward rate is therefore the market's forecast of next period's exchange rate. Equation (11.41) is not the correct no-arbitrage condition, however, unless investors are risk neutral. We return to this point later.

For $T > t+1$ we use the yields on domestic and foreign zero-coupon bonds with maturity $T - t$ as the interest rates. Thus,

$$\ln F_{t,T} = s_t + R_{T-t,t} - R^*_{T-t,t}$$

and $\ln F_{t,T} = E_t s_T$.

11.4.1.3 Implications of UIP for the Exchange Rate

Equation (11.40) is a forward-looking difference equation for s_t:

$$s_t = E_t s_{t+1} + i_t^* - i_t. \tag{11.42}$$

Solving this forwards gives

$$s_t = \sum_{k=0}^{\infty} E_t(i^*_{t+k} - i_{t+k}). \tag{11.43}$$

Consequently, the spot exchange rate is the sum of all expected future interest differentials—and not just the current differential $i_t^* - i_t$.

Equation (11.43) has an important implication for monetary policy. Under inflation targeting, in which the monetary authority controls interest rates, if there is an unanticipated increase in the domestic interest rate, domestic currency appreciates. By how much depends on the market's view of how long the interest differential will last. An increased differential lasting one year will cause the spot exchange rate to increase by twelve times more than if the differential is expected to last only one month. This makes the effectiveness of monetary policy in an open economy more uncertain than is generally realized.

We also note that if the market expects interest rates to change at some point in the future, perhaps due to monetary-policy announcements or hints at future policy, then the spot exchange rate will change today. If, when the time in the future arrives, there is no change in interest rates, then the exchange rate will return to its original level. Subsequently, looking back on the data, it might appear that the market had behaved irrationally, but, given its expectation, which turned out to be false, the market had actually behaved quite rationally throughout. This is known as a peso effect after a notorious episode involving the Mexican peso in the mid 1970s. For many years this had traded at a discount to the U.S. dollar, i.e., the forward rate was less than the spot rate, in the expectation that Mexico would soon have to abandon its policy of maintaining a fixed rate against the dollar. The devaluation eventually occurred in 1976.

An alternative way of expressing the relation between the spot exchange rate and interest rates is to use forward rates together with the result that the forward interest rate is an unbiased forecast of the future spot rate. Thus, if we rewrite the forward interest rate at time t for the spot rate at time $t + k$ as $i_{t,t+k}$, then

$$i_{t,t+k} = E_t i_{t+k}.$$

Hence, equation (11.43) can be written as

$$S_t = \sum_{k=0}^{\infty} (i^*_{t,t+k} - i_{t,t+k}). \tag{11.44}$$

Moreover, because

$$S_t = E_t S_{t+n} + \sum_{k=0}^{n-1} E_t (i^*_{t+k} - i_{t+k}), \tag{11.45}$$

it follows that

$$E_t S_{t+n} = S_t + \sum_{k=0}^{n-1} (i_{t,t+k} - i^*_{t,t+k}). \tag{11.46}$$

Hence, we can use the forward-rate curves together with UIP and the current spot exchange rate to discover the market's implied forecast of the future spot exchange rate.

Alternatively, ignoring risk, as the yield to maturity on an n-period zero-coupon bond satisfies

$$R_{n,t} = \frac{1}{n} \sum_{k=0}^{n-1} i_{t,t+k},$$

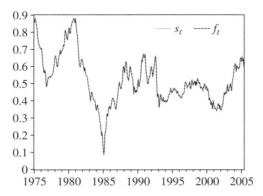

Figure 11.4. U.S. dollar–sterling log spot and log forward exchange rates.

we can combine information about the term structure with the UIP condition to provide a much simpler and more convenient expression for the implied expected future spot exchange rate, namely,

$$E_t s_{t+n} = s_t + n(R_{n,t} - R_{n,t}^*). \tag{11.47}$$

Our discussion of the determination of the exchange rate from the UIP condition was based on the assumption that interest rates are exogenous. More generally, interest rates may be endogenous—for example, if the monetary-policy instrument is the money supply. In this case, the UIP condition becomes a structural equation in the macroeconomic system and the exchange rate is determined within the system, instead of by equations (11.42) or (11.43) alone.

11.4.1.4 Empirical Evidence on UIP

As UIP is so widely used in open-economy macroeconomics, it is perhaps worth briefly considering some empirical evidence on it. See Lewis (1995) for a survey.
An implication of UIP is that

$$s_{t+1} = f_t + \varepsilon_{t+1}, \tag{11.48}$$

where $\varepsilon_{t+1} = s_{t+1} - E_t s_{t+1}$ is an innovation (forecasting) error so that $E_t \varepsilon_{t+1} = 0$. Another implication is that

$$\Delta s_{t+1} = f_t - s_t + \varepsilon_{t+1}, \tag{11.49}$$

where $f_t - s_t$ is the forward premium. Surprisingly, estimates of equations (11.48) and (11.49) typically give very different results: the coefficient on f_t in (11.48) is usually close to unity, as the theory predicts; but the coefficient on $f_t - s_t$ in (11.49) is significantly different from unity and for certain time periods and key currencies can even be significantly negative, which is a clear rejection of the theory.
One of the first tests of UIP was by Fama (1984) using regression analysis. However, much can be learned about the behavior of exchange rates and the

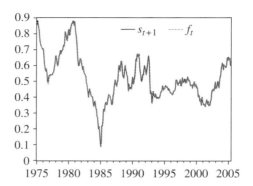

Figure 11.5. U.S. dollar–sterling log future spot and log forward exchange rates.

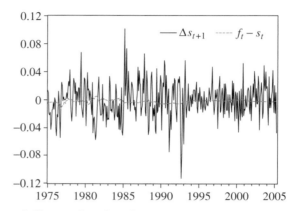

Figure 11.6. U.S. dollar–sterling log change in spot rate and log forward premium.

performance of UIP just by plotting the data. Figures 11.4–11.9 plot the FOREX data for the U.S. dollar–sterling exchange rate. Although it appears that only one series is plotted in figure 11.4, in fact there are two series: s_t and f_t. We conclude from this that $s_t \simeq f_t$. The difference can be seen a little more clearly from figure 11.5, where we plot s_{t+1} and f_t. The intriguing feature here is that UIP would lead us to expect that $E_t s_{t+1} \simeq f_t$ and not that $s_t \simeq f_t$. Putting these two results together we conclude that $E_t s_{t+1} \simeq s_t$. Thus changes in s_t are not predictable. s_t is therefore approximately a martingale (or a random walk if the variance of the shock is constant) and hence is nonstationary. According to UIP, the forward premium is the market prediction of the future change in the spot rate. Figure 11.6 plots Δs_{t+1} and $f_t - s_t$. The forward premium is clearly a very poor predictor of the change in the spot rate. If s_t were indeed a random walk, then the forecast error would be unpredictable from current information. This seems to be what figure 11.6 is showing.

Another way to represent the data is through scatter diagrams. Figure 11.7 plots s_t against f_t. The data lie almost exactly on a 45° line through the origin, indicating once more that $s_t \simeq f_t$. In figure 11.8 we plot s_{t+1} against f_t. According to the UIP condition, equation (11.48), this too should be a 45° line

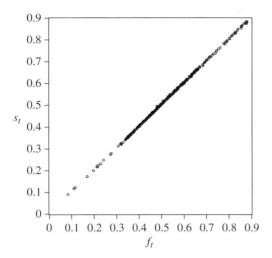

Figure 11.7. Log spot against log forward U.S. dollar–sterling exchange rate.

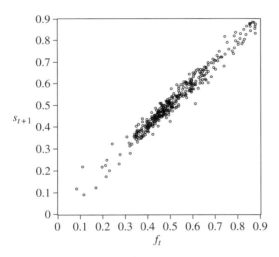

Figure 11.8. Future log spot against current log forward U.S. dollar–sterling exchange rate.

through the origin. We see that it is, but that the fit is far worse than in figure 11.7. Finally, we plot Δs_{t+1} and $f_t - s_t$. According to the UIP condition, equation (11.49), this should again be a $45°$ line through the origin. In fact, it is clear that no line fits these data even approximately.

Similar results hold for other currencies and other time periods. The results of Mark and Wu (1998) reported in table 11.2 are based on monthly data for 1980.1–1994.1 and for 1976.1–1994.1. They provide typical estimates of the coefficient of the forward premium in equation (11.49). Standard errors are in parentheses. Virtually all of the estimates are negative, and most are significantly different from unity, their predicted theoretical value.

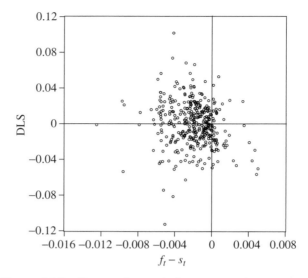

Figure 11.9. Future change in log spot against current log forward premium U.S. dollar—sterling exchange rate.

Table 11.2. Estimates of the coefficients of the forward premium in equation (11.49).

	1976.1–1979.4	1980.1–1994.1	1976.1–1994.1
USD/GBP	1.25 (1.16)	−2.42 (1.08)	−1.52 (0.86)
USD/DEM	−0.03 (1.85)	−0.20 (0.95)	−0.14 (0.89)
USD/YEN	−1.97 (1.56)	−2.67 (1.12)	−2.53 (0.90)
GBP/DEM	0.46 (1.82)	−0.98 (0.98)	−0.60 (0.78)
GBP/YEN	−3.62 (2.36)	−4.55 (1.47)	−4.26 (1.13)
DEM/YEN	−0.90 (3.96)	−1.31 (1.07)	−0.76 (0.62)

Source: Mark and Wu (1998).

These results imply that

$$E_t \Delta s_{t+1} = \lambda(i_t - i_t^*),$$

with $\lambda < 0$ instead of $\lambda = 1$. This can be rewritten as

$$i_t = i_t^* + E_t \Delta s_{t+1} + \left(\frac{1}{\lambda} - 1\right) E_t \Delta s_{t+1}$$

$$\lessgtr \left\{ \begin{array}{l} i_t^* + E_t \Delta s_{t+1} \\ i_t^* \end{array} \right\} \quad \text{as } E_t \Delta s_{t+1} \gtrless 0.$$

Hence, if $\lambda < 0$, then, if the cost of converting the proceeds from investing in the foreign bond back into domestic currency is expected to increase (i.e., if the exchange rate is expected to depreciate), the market sets the domestic interest rate below both i_t^* and $i_t^* + E_t \Delta s_{t+1}$ instead of equal to $i_t^* + E_t \Delta s_{t+1}$. It is therefore better to hold the foreign bond. Conversely, if the exchange rate is expected to appreciate, then the domestic return will be set so that it exceeds both i_t^* and

$i_t^* + E_t\Delta s_{t+1}$. It is then better to hold the domestic bond. In other words, if the market sets the domestic interest rate in this way, then the optimal investment strategy implied by these estimates is to hold the bond with the highest interest rate. Such a strategy is well-known in FOREX markets. It is called the "carry trade." In practice, investors in the carry trade are speculators who borrow in the currency with the low interest rate in order to invest in the currency with the high interest rate, thereby making a profit. The risk in this strategy is that the exchange rate of the currency invested in will eventually depreciate or the exchange rate in the currency borrowed in will appreciate, as predicted by UIP.

We therefore reach the interesting conclusion that UIP appears to hold if we represent the theory by equation (11.48) but is decisively rejected if we use equation (11.49). Why is this? One explanation is that the theory omits a risk premium (see Mark 1985). We have shown that s_t is a nonstationary variable, or behaves like one. And as $s_t \simeq f_t$, the forward rate must be nonstationary too. From the theory of cointegration, if the omitted variables from a relation are stationary, then the estimates of the coefficients associated with the nonstationary variables will not be greatly affected (technically, they will remain super-consistent and hence be very accurate). If, however, there are omitted variables in a model in which all of the variables are stationary, then the estimates are likely to be biased—possibly severely, depending on the size of the correlation between the included and omitted variables. This suggests that if there is an omitted risk premium from the no-arbitrage equation for FOREX, then it is stationary and negatively correlated with the forward premium. This would explain why the estimate of the coefficient on the forward rate in equation (11.48) is consistent with the theory but the estimate of the forward premium in equation (11.49) appears to be heavily biased.

Many other explanations have been offered for these anomalous results (see, for example, Lewis 1995) but there is still no consensus on their cause. We now focus on the need to include a FOREX risk premium and how to formulate it.

11.4.2 The General Equilibrium Model of FOREX

The theory of asset pricing suggests that as investing in the foreign bond is risky we should replace the UIP condition with the no-arbitrage condition

$$i_t + \rho_t = i_t^* + E_t\Delta s_{t+1}, \tag{11.50}$$

where the natural interpretation of ρ_t is that it is the risk premium required to compensate domestic investors for holding the foreign asset. We would therefore expect ρ_t to be nonnegative. However, ρ_t can also be negative. This is because with FOREX the problem of risk is symmetric with respect to domestic investors in a foreign bond and foreign investors in a domestic bond. The risk for the domestic investor in holding the foreign bond is an unexpected appreciation of domestic currency, which would result in a lower payoff than expected for the foreign asset as measured in terms of domestic currency because domestic currency would cost more in terms of foreign currency. But this would not result in risk for the foreign holder of domestic bonds. The converse is also true: namely, the risk for the foreign investor in domestic bonds is that foreign currency would cost more. This is why ρ_t can also be negative.

Another way of looking at this is by expressing UIP from the point of view of the foreign investor. Thus

$$i_t^* + \rho_t^* = i_t + E_t \Delta s_{t+1}^*,$$

where ρ_t^* is the risk premium for the foreign investor and $s_t^* = -s_t$. Hence,

$$i_t - \rho_t^* = i_t^* + E_t \Delta s_{t+1}.$$

Finally, we note that if investors have identical attitudes to risk, i.e., if markets are complete, then $\rho_t = -\rho_t^*$. In other words, only if markets are complete do we obtain the same UIP condition as for the domestic investor. If their attitudes to risk are different, i.e., if markets are not complete, then ρ_t and ρ_t^* will be of opposite sign and different in absolute magnitude.

11.4.2.1   The Domestic-Investor Model

We begin our analysis of the general equilibrium model of the FOREX risk premium by considering domestic investors. We assume that interest rates and the rate of change of FOREX are jointly log-normally distributed. For FOREX the generic no-arbitrage condition

$$E_t(r_{t+1} - r_t^f) + \tfrac{1}{2}V_t(r_{t+1}) = -\operatorname{Cov}_t(m_{t+1}, r_{t+1})$$

therefore becomes

$$E_t(s_{t+1} - f_t) + \tfrac{1}{2}V_t(\Delta s_{t+1}) = -\operatorname{Cov}_t(m_{t+1}, \Delta s_{t+1}), \qquad (11.51)$$

as

$$E_t(r_{t+1} - r_t^f) = E_t(i_t^* + \Delta s_{t+1} - i_t) = E_t(s_{t+1} - f_t),$$
$$-\rho_t = \tfrac{1}{2}V_t(\Delta s_{t+1}) + \operatorname{Cov}_t(m_{t+1}, \Delta s_{t+1}),$$
$$E_t s_{t+1} = f_t + \rho_t.$$

Hence the FOREX risk premium is $-\operatorname{Cov}_t(m_{t+1}, \Delta s_{t+1})$, and this arises from uncertainty about the future spot exchange rate and its conditional covariance with the discount factor m_{t+1}. The higher the rate at which foreign returns are discounted, the larger they must be, and hence the greater the exchange depreciation required.

11.4.2.2   The Foreign-Investor Model

For the foreign investor, excess returns and exchange rates are inverted, or reversed. Denoting foreign variables with an asterisk, and noting that $s_t^* = -s_t$, the excess return is

$$r_{t+1}^* - r_t^{f*} = i_t - \Delta s_{t+1} - i_t^* = -(s_{t+1} - f_t),$$

which leads to the no-arbitrage condition

$$E_t(r^*_{t+1} - r^{f*}_t) + \tfrac{1}{2}V_t(r^*_{t+1}) = -\text{Cov}_t(m^*_{t+1}, r^*_{t+1}),$$

where m^* is measured in foreign currency. Hence,

$$-E_t(s_{t+1} - f_t) + \tfrac{1}{2}V_t(\Delta s_{t+1}) = \text{Cov}_t(m^*_{t+1}, \Delta s_{t+1}). \tag{11.52}$$

11.4.2.3 The Combined Domestic-and-Foreign-Investors Model

Since, in practice, both investors will be conducting FOREX trades, we combine the two no-arbitrage conditions by subtracting (11.52) from (11.51) to obtain

$$E_t(s_{t+1} - f_t) = -\text{Cov}_t[\tfrac{1}{2}(m_{t+1} + m^*_{t+1}), \Delta s_{t+1}], \tag{11.53}$$

where there is now no Jensen effect. The discount factor here is the average of the domestic and foreign investor discount factors. If we add the two no-arbitrage conditions we have

$$V_t(\Delta s_{t+1}) = \text{Cov}_t[(m_{t+1} - m^*_{t+1}), \Delta s_{t+1}].$$

This implies that

$$m_{t+1} = m^*_{t+1} + \Delta s_{t+1} + \eta_{t+1},$$

where either $\eta_{t+1} \equiv 0$ or $\text{Cov}_t[\Delta s_{t+1}, \eta_{t+1}] = 0$. If $\eta_{t+1} \equiv 0$, then the foreign investor's discount factor, when expressed in the same currency, is the same as that of the domestic investor. In other words, we have a complete market. In this case, the domestic and foreign investors' no-arbitrage conditions are identical, and so both can be expressed as equation (11.51). If markets are incomplete, then we should use equation (11.53).

11.4.2.4 The FOREX Risk Premium Based on C-CAPM

As the excess return to FOREX is a nominal return, the log stochastic discount factor for C-CAPM is given by equation (11.29). The no-arbitrage condition for the domestic investor—or the no-arbitrage condition under complete markets—is

$$E_t(s_{t+1} - f_t) + \tfrac{1}{2}V_t(\Delta s_{t+1}) = \sigma\,\text{Cov}_t(\Delta c_{t+1}, \Delta s_{t+1}) + \text{Cov}_t(\pi_{t+1}, \Delta s_{t+1}). \tag{11.54}$$

Thus FOREX risk for the domestic investor in a foreign bond arises from the exchange rate being weak when domestic consumption is low or when domestic inflation is low. In a complete market, the no-arbitrage condition for a foreign investor in domestic bonds can be written as

$$-E_t(s_{t+1} - f_t) + \tfrac{1}{2}V_t(\Delta s_{t+1}) = -\sigma\,\text{Cov}_t(\Delta c^*_{t+1}, \Delta s_{t+1}) - \text{Cov}_t(\pi^*_{t+1}, \Delta s_{t+1}).$$

Hence risk arises for the foreign investor for the same reason as for the domestic investor, with the difference that the excess return to FOREX now has the opposite sign.

Empirical evidence on this general equilibrium model of FOREX produces similar results to those for equity and bonds: namely, the estimate of σ is very high (see Wickens and Smith 2001). Moreover, the contribution of the inflation term in the risk premium appears to be stronger than that of the consumption term. This suggests that FOREX risk arises more from uncertainty about the exchange rate due to unexpected movements in the rate of inflation than from concern about consumption. This may be because most FOREX transactions are undertaken by financial institutions as part of their hedging operations, and these relate more to short-term real returns than to consumption by the ultimate owners of their financial capital, be they shareholders or investors. A further problem is that including a FOREX risk premium defined in this way does not remove the previous problem with UIP as the forward premium still has a negative, though less significant, coefficient. For an alternative approach to modeling the FOREX risk premium using an affine factor pricing model, see Backus et al. (1996).

11.4.3 Comment

The problem of providing an adequate theory of FOREX remains unresolved. UIP suffers from the anomalous result that because the coefficient on the forward premium has the wrong sign it is always best to hold the bond with the highest interest rate. The general equilibrium model for FOREX gives too low a coefficient of relative risk aversion and does not remove the UIP anomaly. A number of explanations have been given for the poor performance of UIP and the general equilibrium model. These include the argument that expectations are not rational, that there are peso effects, that expectations formation is part of a learning process, and that there are threshold effects as arbitrage activity only takes place in FOREX markets when the interest differential is large enough. In practice, none of these theories appears to be sufficiently strongly supported by the evidence.

In our discussion of FOREX there is an implicit assumption that transactions are associated with either trade in goods and services or with capital movements. However, comparing the sizes of trade, of net capital movements, and even of total capital with the huge volume of FOREX transactions shows that something else must be involved too. Hedging operations and FOREX speculation, which may be highly leveraged, are obvious omissions from our discussion. Suppose, for example, that an investor expects the price of foreign exchange in terms of domestic currency to increase by more than is predicted by the forward exchange rate. The investor can speculate on this by entering into a contract to purchase the foreign currency using today's forward rate and converting the currency back into domestic currency at the future spot exchange rate. This gives a profit if the future spot rate is higher than the forward rate and a loss if it is not. It is not, therefore, a riskless strategy.

Alternatively, the investor could buy call options on the foreign currency. This gives the investor the right, but not the obligation, to buy the foreign currency. If the exchange rate depreciates by more than the forward rate, then the investor will exercise this right, but if it does not, then the option may be allowed to expire unexercised. An attraction of this is that the maximum loss is limited to the cost of the option, which is only a small fraction of the size of the full contract. Another major factor is that the speculation is highly leveraged. For any given sum committed to the contract, the investor's command over foreign currency, and hence over the associated potential profit, is a multiple of $1/c$ higher than entering a standard forward contract, where $0 < c \ll 1$ is the cost of a call. The profit for each unit of currency is the difference between the future spot rate and the forward rate less the cost of the call. As a result of using options and leveraging, the size of the FOREX transaction will be greatly increased.

Another example of a FOREX hedge is the use of currency swaps. Here ownership of the currency does not change, only the currency of the interest payments. Swaps may be used both as speculative instruments and as hedging devices. Such purely speculative FOREX transactions will typically not involve trade at all, nor need they be associated with the purchase and sale of nonfinancial foreign assets. Moreover, they can be undertaken by third parties who are based in completely different countries to those whose currencies are being traded.

All of this illustrates why there is a high level of FOREX transactions and why macroeconomic fundamentals may not be an important factor, especially in the short run.

11.5 Conclusions

The behavior of financial markets is crucial for dynamic general equilibrium macroeconomic models. The intertemporal allocation of resources enables consumption to be smoothed and financial markets to channel household savings to borrowers: other households, firms, and government, both home and abroad. This requires well-functioning capital markets. In this chapter we have examined traditional models of financial markets in order to compare them with general equilibrium models. In formulating general equilibrium models for the stock, bond, and FOREX markets we have in each case used the generic theory of no-arbitrage that was derived in chapter 10. This was then specialized to take account of the particular features of each market. The problem in each case was to derive the risk premium and to find out what the macroeconomic sources of this risk were. For equity this was the uncertainty about dividend payments; for bonds it was the need to apply the no-arbitrage condition simultaneously to bonds of all maturities; and for FOREX we had to take into account the presence of both domestic and foreign investors and hence whether markets are complete or incomplete. Thus asset pricing, and the behavior of financial markets, is central to macroeconomics.

Although we have looked at each of these markets separately, households, firms, and government will, either directly or indirectly through third-party investment managers, hold a portfolio of these assets. This requires an equally important asset-allocation decision, the theory of which we touched on in chapter 10.

Finally, we have commented on how well these general equilibrium theories of asset pricing account for the observed behavior of asset prices. The evidence seems to suggest that the theory is unable to provide a satisfactory account of risk for any of the three markets, especially in the short run, as, in each case, the theoretical risk premium turns out to be small in practice. We noted that a large proportion of FOREX transactions may be for purely speculative purposes, and not closely related to macroeconomic fundamentals, especially in the short run. To a lesser extent, this may also be true of stock- and bond-market transactions. Nonetheless, even if an asset price deviates for a time from its fundamental valuation as derived from general equilibrium theory, we still need to know what that fundamental valuation is as we might expect the asset price to fluctuate around it, or mean revert to the fundamental over time. Asset pricing is, therefore, as much a challenge for general equilibrium macroeconomics as it is for finance, where it is currently a highly active area of research. We have also shown that financial data provide another means of testing macroeconomic theories in addition to, or in combination with, the use of macroeconomic data.

12

Nominal Exchange Rates

12.1 Introduction

In our discussion of the open economy in chapter 7, and of pricing in chapter 9, we treated the nominal exchange rate as exogenous, or given. We now examine the case where the nominal exchange rate is freely floating, and hence endogenous. We consider the determination of nominal and real exchange rates and their behavior following shocks to the macroeconomic system. Having a fixed or a floating exchange rate is a policy choice. We therefore examine the relative merits of fixed versus floating exchange rates, particularly as this affects output and inflation and the effectiveness of monetary and fiscal policy. For example, it is widely thought that, compared with a fixed exchange rate, having a floating exchange rate reduces the cost of macroeconomic shocks as it facilitates the adjustment of its real exchange rate and its terms of trade, thereby enabling the economy to return quickly to equilibrium. A contrary view is that because exchange rates are often highly volatile, they amplify the effects of external shocks to the domestic economy. A key factor in this is how prices and wages are set, how flexible they are, and how much they are affected by exchange rate changes.

The nominal exchange rate is the price of an asset: the price of one currency relative to another. In chapter 10 we considered the general problem of pricing assets. We showed that this entails a no-arbitrage condition that relates the expected return on the risky asset to that on a risk-free asset. In chapter 11 we discussed the no-arbitrage equation for FOREX and showed that, under risk neutrality, this is the UIP condition. We demonstrated that UIP provides a theory of bilateral nominal-exchange-rate determination in which the spot exchange rate depends on the current and future interest differentials between two economies.

The macroeconomic problem is how these interest rates are determined. They may be exogenously determined, as in inflation targeting under discretion (see chapter 13); they may be endogenously determined, being set as the result of an interest rate rule that depends on other macroeconomic variables; or they may be the outcome of conducting monetary policy through money-supply targets. Thus, UIP provides a key connection between the nominal exchange rate and the rest of the economy, and is a standard relation in most modern open-economy macroeconomic models with a freely floating exchange rate. And since, in turn, macroeconomic variables may be affected by the exchange rate, the problem is one of general equilibrium.

The principal alternative to having a floating exchange rate is to have some form of fixed exchange rate. An example is the Bretton Woods system in which member countries pegged their currencies to the U.S. dollar and were able to alter the parity only after agreement with the other members. Or a country could be dollarized with a currency board implying, in effect, that it is using the U.S. dollar as its currency. Or it could be part of a monetary union like the euro area and hence share a common currency and monetary policy. Before the Bretton Woods agreement most countries were part of the gold standard, i.e., they fixed their exchange rates to the price of gold instead of to another currency. Currencies could be exchanged for gold usually on application to the central bank; this required central banks to hold sufficient gold reserves to meet demand. Under floating exchange rates there is no need for a central bank to hold exchange reserves or gold, except to clear daily accounts. There is also an intermediate situation where the exchange rate is flexible but changes are managed, perhaps in order to keep the exchange rate within a given band. In this chapter we focus mainly on freely floating exchange rates.

DGE models have not been much used to analyze the exchange rate and so, before embarking on this, we review international monetary arrangements since 1873 (i.e., the choice of exchange-rate system) and the main macroeconomic theories of the exchange rate that were used previously. Each theory reflects the international monetary arrangements that prevailed when they were popular. The aim is not just to explain the historical development of exchange-rate models—although this is of interest—it is to help give a better appreciation of modern theories, and why they emphasize different aspects of the economy from the earlier theories.

In general equilibrium, the determination of any one (endogenous) variable requires consideration of the whole macroeconomic model. Nonetheless, the balance of payments, and how it is specified, is of central importance in the determination of the nominal exchange rate. The various different models of the exchange rate differ, in large part, in their implications for the balance of payments. This, in turn, is related to whether the exchange rate is treated as an asset, or the relative price of goods and services. Key assumptions are whether the exchange rate is determined by the current or the capital account; whether there are capital controls; and whether domestic and foreign bonds are perfect substitutes. A further distinguishing factor is the assumed degree of price and output flexibility.

Due to the very large flows of international capital, modern theories of a flexible exchange rate treat it as an asset price and so assume that it responds almost instantaneously to new information. This creates a considerable problem for macroeconomic models of the exchange rate because the frequency of observation of macroeconomic data is very much lower than that for FOREX.

Occasionally weekly or monthly macroeconomic data exist, but usually the data are quarterly, or even annual. In contrast, FOREX data are available almost continuously. As a result, macroeconomics can only deal with the longer-run response of exchange rates to shocks, which may be very different from their instantaneous response.

There is another problem for macroeconomics. Treating the exchange rate as an asset price focuses attention on bilateral exchange rates. But when it comes to discussing the relation between trade and the exchange rate, it is the effective exchange rate—a trade-weighted average of bilateral rates—that is relevant. As individual bilateral rates will typically respond somewhat differently from each other, the composition of the effective exchange rate will affect its response, which will be different again. Although it is usual in macroeconomic theory to ignore this distinction, it should be borne in mind.

Reflecting the macroeconomic theories prevailing at the time, fixed-exchange-rate models typically use the Keynesian IS–LM–BP framework. We examine a particular version, the "monetary approach to the balance of payments." Floating-exchange-rate models commonly assume uncovered interest parity due to the accompanying removal of capital controls, but differ in their assumptions about the flexibility of prices and output. We consider a number of models: a flexible-exchange-rate version of the IS–LM–BP model; using just the uncovered interest parity condition; the Mundell–Fleming model; the monetary model; the Dornbusch model; and a sticky-price version of the monetary model. None of these models is a DGE model. Their usefulness is that they help in understanding the considerably more complex Obstfeld–Rogoff redux DGE model and some of its recent variants.

12.2 International Monetary Arrangements 1873–2007

> If we look at the most bloody events of modern history, from the French Revolution and the Terror, the great slump, the rise of the Nazis, the Second World War and the holocaust, or to the 70-year Soviet tyranny, we find the mismanagement of currencies among the main causative factors. Incompetent central bankers are more lethal than incompetent generals.
>
> William Rees-Mogg (*The Times*, December 1, 2003)

This remarkably strong statement provides ample justification for starting our discussion of nominal exchange rates with a brief review of international currency arrangements. Over the period 1873–2007 most countries have experienced a number of different exchange-rate systems. These range from floating against gold, to fixed exchange rates, and to a freely floating exchange rate; moreover, currencies may be freely convertible into gold or into other currencies, or they may not be convertible; and there may be controls on capital movements, or capital may be allowed to move freely. The change from one system to another was nearly always forced by circumstances: sometimes it was due to war; sometimes to economic imperatives.

Ideally, the exchange-rate system should permit a country to achieve its economic growth and inflation objectives, to retain competitiveness, and to be able to borrow and lend in international capital markets while maintaining a sustainable current account. The failure to attain any one of these may prove sufficient reason to abandon an exchange-rate system.

12.2.1 The Gold Standard System: 1873–1937

Great Britain adopted the gold standard in 1717. Most other countries who adopted it did not do so until after 1873. Previously they used a bimetallic system involving gold and silver or, in the case of, for example, Austria, France, and Prussia, just silver. The gold rushes in California and Australia in the 1840s and 1850s increased the supply of gold sufficiently for it to be widely used as the payments system of choice. For accounts of the gold standard see Cooper (1982), Eichengreen (1996a,b), and Bordo and Eichengreen (1998). For the period 1873–1914, the gold standard system (GSS) was in operation more or less globally. Gold shipments were suspended during World War I, but countries resumed them afterwards, though at different times. The GSS was eventually abandoned by most countries in the years immediately prior to, or during, World War II, and it was replaced by the Bretton Woods system.

The basic idea behind the GSS is that countries should settle their international transactions in gold or silver. National currencies are convertible into gold, but at a fixed price. In effect, therefore, currencies had fixed parities against each other. Adjustment took place by flows of gold between countries. A country having a balance of payments deficit with another country had to send gold from its reserves to that country. Because the quantity of domestic money supplied was tied to the gold reserves, this caused a reduction in the money supply of the deficit country. As a result, interest rates rose and domestic economic activity and the domestic price level contracted. This led to an improved trade balance and consequent capital inflows, which together were supposed to correct the balance of payments deficit.

For a long period of time the GSS system worked very well, especially for some countries. For example, the United Kingdom, a world economic leader in the latter half of the nineteenth century, had current-account deficits in only four out of a hundred years. There are, however, two main problems with the GSS.

First, as international economic activity grows, it is necessary to increase the supply of gold. However, the supply of newly mined gold to the world is limited, as gold is found in only a few countries. As a result of a shortage of gold, the system required periodic increases in the price of gold in terms of all currencies. This arbitrarily benefited some countries and harmed others, it was disruptive of world trade, and it was inflationary as it increased national money supplies. Worse still, some countries chose to hoard gold. This denied gold to other countries and forced them to adopt "beggar-my-neighbor" policies to promote exports or block imports. Other countries, due to lack of gold reserves, instead of borrowing gold by offering higher interest rates, chose to suspend gold payments, thereby undermining trade. Reparations in the 1920s and 1930s meant that Germany, a major trading nation, had to run a permanent trade surplus. As this was at the expense of trade surpluses by other countries, these countries were denied gold.

Second, and more important, the GSS had a tendency to generate economic recession due to the reductions in output and the price level that were required to correct a current-account deficit. As it took time for balance of payments adjustment to occur, the required contraction in the domestic economy could be of long duration and involve high and severely fluctuating levels of unemployment. When the United Kingdom returned to the GSS after World War I it did so at the prewar parity. This turned out to be too high and the United Kingdom was forced to restore its competitiveness by deflationary policies that reduced its price level. This was a prolonged process that was very harmful to the U.K. economy. Together with German reparations, gold hoarding, economic deflation, and tight monetary policy, notably in the United States, high interest rates caused the severe recessions of the 1920s and the great depression of the 1930s. As a result of this interwar experience, rather than return to the GSS after World War II, a new system was sought.

12.2.2 The Bretton Woods System: 1945–71

We have argued that the two main problems with the GSS were a lack of liquidity to support rising economic activity and the lack of a satisfactory adjustment mechanism for an economy in deficit. These are what the Bretton Woods system aimed to correct, but it succeeded only in providing greater liquidity (see Bordo 1993; Bordo and Eichengreen 1993).

The Bretton Woods agreement was signed in 1944 and was participated in by most of the leading Western economies from 1945. Under the Bretton Woods system only the U.S. dollar remained on the gold standard. The price of the U.S. dollar was fixed in terms of gold, all currencies were fixed in value against the dollar, and all international transactions were settled in dollars. Exchange rates were not completely fixed, but had a small margin of movement of 0.5%. The advantage of the Bretton Woods system was that it was possible to increase international liquidity by supplying more U.S. dollars. However, as the demand for dollars increased, the supply of gold also had to increase.

The adjustment mechanism under Bretton Woods was improved by allowing countries that had large and persistent balance of payments deficits to devalue (i.e., to adopt a lower parity against the dollar). Most exchange parity realignments were small, but occasionally they were large; for example, the devaluations by the United Kingdom in 1949 and 1967 were 30% and 14%, respectively. They were designed to improve competitiveness, thereby helping to speed up the macroeconomic adjustment process and avoiding long periods of recession and high unemployment. At the same time, countries with balance of payments surpluses were expected to revalue their parity upwards. In practice few did, however, and so the burden of adjustment, instead of being shared between countries, fell on the deficit countries alone.

Nonetheless, the system worked tolerably well for about twenty years. In most countries both unemployment and inflation were low—far lower than in the following twenty years, when exchange rates floated. One of the reasons for the system's success was that most countries imposed controls on financial capital movements. This reduced pressure on exchange rates, but meant that capital was not being used where it reaped the highest return. This restricted international development. With the removal of capital controls and the accumulation of large financial resources in private hands it is much more difficult for a country with limited reserves to successfully defend the parity of its currency. In later years, when currencies were floating, capital mobility caused the capital account of the balance of payments to dominate the current account.

Under the Bretton Woods system national monetary policy is assigned to maintaining the fixed parity against the U.S. dollar. A member country therefore has no scope for independent monetary policy. As a result, their domestic price levels were tied to the U.S. price level, and their inflation rates were similar to the U.S. inflation rate. This can only work, however, if the United States is able to control its inflation. This requires the U.S. money supply to increase no faster than is necessary to meet the world demand for dollars. One of the factors that undermined the Bretton Woods system was a U.S. monetary expansion in the late 1960s, partly to finance the Vietnam war. This increased U.S. inflation, raised inflation in the Bretton Woods countries, reduced U.S. competitiveness, and made many countries reluctant to hold dollars and prefer to hold gold instead, which exacerbated an already existing gold shortage.

In order to improve its competitiveness (and to increase international liquidity, and hence economic activity), in 1971 the United States decided to increase the dollar price of gold, i.e., to devalue the dollar against gold. The dollar was allowed to float against gold with the intention of fixing the price of gold again as soon as the market revealed the appropriate rate. In the meantime all other currencies were allowed to float against the dollar. In 1973, after two years in which attempts were made without success to fix the dollar at a new gold price, the Bretton Woods system was abandoned in favor of the generalized floating of exchange rates by most countries.

12.2.3 Floating Exchange Rates: 1973–2007

After 1973 the former Bretton Woods countries adopted a number of different flexible-exchange-rate regimes.

1. Pure floating: where the exchange rate is determined in the world foreign exchange market without intervention by the domestic central bank.
2. Target zones: where the aim is to keep the exchange rate within a range of values against a particular currency; the Exchange Rate Mechanism (ERM) was an example of this in which the reference currency was the deutsche mark.

3. Currency unions: where a group of countries give up their national currencies and adopt a common currency that then floats freely against the currencies of other countries—European Monetary Union (EMU) and the introduction of the euro is the prime example of this.

4. Dollarization: where, in effect, a country adopts the U.S. dollar as its currency by converting its domestic currency at a fixed rate against the dollar. As a result, it cedes all control over its exchange rate.

Under a fixed-exchange-rate system monetary policy is preassigned to maintaining the exchange-rate parity. A crucial consequence of moving to a floating-exchange-rate system is that a country must reformulate its monetary policy. The exception under Bretton Woods was the United States, which had to conduct its monetary policy in such a way as to control its rate of inflation. After the breakdown of Bretton Woods most other countries adopted a similar policy to the United States. This consisted of trying to achieve a chosen constant rate of growth for the money supply—a policy associated with Milton Friedman that is called monetarism.

The adoption of monetarism was strongly criticized in many countries. It was widely seen as abandoning the old methods of monetary policy and importing U.S. ideas instead. This misguided criticism showed a fundamental lack of understanding of the central implication of having a floating exchange rate, namely, that it then becomes necessary to take responsibility for one's own monetary policy, however conducted. Continuing the old style of monetary policy would be equivalent to giving up a floating rate and choosing to peg against the dollar as before. More relevant criticisms of monetarism are that many countries consistently missed their monetary growth targets by a large margin and, as discussed in chapter 8, there was confusion over which monetary aggregate to target: narrow money, which relates more closely to transactions, or broad money, which includes a savings component as well as representing a general measure of liquidity.

Observing that Germany had considerable success with monetary control and was able to achieve a low inflation rate, European countries increasingly tied their currencies to the deutsche mark in an attempt to emulate German rates of inflation. This resulted in the ERM, in which the deutsche mark was the anchor currency. Like the Bretton Woods system, member countries expected to achieve the same inflation rate as the anchor country. The dangers of allowing any single currency to become the benchmark were soon made clear when German unification occurred in 1989. This resulted in huge fiscal transfers from West to East Germany, and an increase in German government debt which caused German interest rates to increase and the deutsche mark to appreciate against the dollar. This presented the other ERM members with a dilemma: should they also raise interest rates in order to maintain parity with the deutsche mark, even though this would harm competitiveness with the rest of the world, or should they leave the ERM? France, for example, deciding to stay in the ERM, had to raise overnight interest rates to astronomical levels. Based on UIP, an expected overnight devaluation by 10% requires an increase in annualized interest rates of 2500% as compensation. This is precisely what happened in France in September 1992.

The United Kingdom, one of the last countries to join the ERM, was willing to raise interest rates to only 15%. The markets therefore speculated on an imminent large devaluation of sterling. In September 1992 the United Kingdom, together with some of its main Scandinavian trading partners, left the ERM and floated their exchange rates once more. Shortly after, following the successful experience of New Zealand, the United Kingdom began experimenting with inflation targeting and controlling interest rates directly.

Meanwhile, the experience with the ERM led its members to look for a better monetary system. In 1999 they formed the EMU and a single currency, the euro. The euro system also adopted an inflation target—the average rate of inflation of member countries—and so allowed the euro to float against other currencies. There is, however, a potential problem with having a single interest rate set by the European Central Bank with the average euro area inflation rate in mind. Countries with higher inflation than the average therefore have negative real interest rates, while countries with lower inflation have positive real interest rates. In other words, monetary policy is the opposite of what is required in each case. High-inflation countries are encouraged to expand and low-inflation countries to contract, thereby exacerbating the inflation differentials between countries rather than eliminating them. The stability of the euro system relies heavily on high-inflation countries losing competitiveness, which causes a loss of demand for their output and hence reduces inflationary pressures, and low-inflation countries gaining competitiveness, which would stimulate their economies and raise inflation. There is some evidence of this occurring as Germany, a low-inflation country, is experiencing a trade-led expansion while Italy, a high-inflation country, has a lower level of economic activity. We analyze these issues in more detail later in chapter 13.

The main benefit of a floating exchange rate is that it allows a country to retain its competitiveness. This is particularly important if prices and wages are inflexible. If prices and wages are flexible, then there is less benefit to having a floating exchange rate. The assumption behind EMU is that, within the euro area, economic activity is best promoted by removing exchange-rate movements entirely. The concern has been that European labor markets are not sufficiently flexible to support this.

Another benefit of floating exchange rates is that they remove the need for capital controls. If capital is used where it brings the best return, in principle, this should raise world economic activity as it would promote economic growth in all countries through trade. One of the main reasons why a government imposes capital controls is to sustain its exchange rates without having high interest rates. This often results in a country having an artificially low interest rate compared with world rates. Although the government can then borrow cheaply from its domestic capital markets, which benefits the taxpayer, it creates a disincentive to save and is eventually likely to harm domestic growth through a lack of savings, and hence investment.

One of the attractions of floating exchange rates over fixed, or even target zones, is that they are best able to cope with the capital movements that accompany an absence of capital controls. Moreover, if a country allows its exchange rate to be determined by market forces, then there is no incentive for private investors to speculate against a currency. Large speculative gains have usually been made by private investors betting against a central bank that is trying to maintain a particular level for the exchange rate but which has only limited reserves of foreign assets with which to do so. An example of this was when George Soros made over a billion pounds sterling in 1992 as a result of the U.K. government's unsuccessful attempt to keep sterling in the ERM in the face of massive international speculation.

Floating exchange rates are not without their problems too. One of the main disadvantages is that they are subject to external shocks and, as they are an asset, they may become volatile and disrupt domestic economic activity. Moreover, if domestic prices and wages are not flexible, then an appreciation could harm competitiveness. Some countries have tried to contain the effects of external shocks by managing their exchange rates within an exchange-rate band. In practice, this has usually proved successful only when the external shocks are not large, in which case the band is unnecessary.

Dollarization, or simply targeting the dollar, is of course a return to fixed exchange rates and monetary dependence. It is not an attractive policy unless a country's economy is tied very closely to, or has converged with, that of the United States. As this is extremely difficult to achieve and to sustain, it is probably only a matter of time before strains start to appear in the domestic economy. Only countries with severe economic problems—for example, with high inflation and a low credibility on international financial markets that causes a large country risk premium—are likely to be willing to swallow such strong medicine while they put their economies in order. Consequently, inflation targeting has often become more viable, and hence more attractive, than full dollarization.

With the removal of capital controls under floating exchange rates, the balance of payments is dominated by the capital account, and fluctuations in exchange rates are dominated by capital-account movements. Some idea of the order of magnitude of foreign exchange transactions was reported in chapter 11. By 2006 daily FOREX transactions through London amounted to more than half of the annual GDP of the United Kingdom. The United States had a slightly lower figure. As the current account is about 10% of U.S. GDP, and 25% of U.K. GDP, this means that each trading day capital movements are over 1250 times greater than current-account transactions for the United States and 500 times greater for the United Kingdom. Unsurprisingly, in the absence of capital controls, the exchange rate is determined by the capital account and, in particular, by interest rates. This is reflected in the specification of models of floating exchange rates because the no-arbitrage equation for FOREX—the UIP condition—replaces the balance of payments.

12.3   The Keynesian IS–LM–BP Model of the Exchange Rate

During the period of the Bretton Woods system the main macroeconomic model in use was the IS–LM model. It was introduced by Hicks as a simple representation of Keynes's "general theory" and was soon widely adopted. A key feature of the IS–LM model is the assumption of fixed prices and wages. One of the most important modifications to the IS–LM model was the addition of the Phillips curve. This gave some flexibility to prices and wages and added a supply side to the model. Previously, the IS–LM model was essentially just a demand-side model. The resulting model, known as the Keynesian model, is familiar to most of those who have taken an undergraduate course in macroeconomics.

Looked at from the perspective of DGE macroeconomic models, the IS–LM model has a number of severe drawbacks. It lacks formal optimizing microeconomic foundations, it does not have an intertemporal framework, and, as explained in chapters 1 and 2, it uses an inappropriate equilibrium concept: namely, flow rather than stock equilibrium. A putative justification for this is that the IS–LM model deals with a period of time sufficiently short that the capital stock remains unchanged. But this would mean that its predictions for the medium to long term would be of dubious validity. As a result, the IS–LM model is often used to conduct a comparative static analysis rather than a dynamic analysis, i.e., it is used for a comparison of flow equilibria for different values of the exogenous variables, and not for providing predictions of the dynamic effects of changes in the exogenous variables. The attraction of the IS–LM model, and perhaps the main reason why it is still widely used, is that it provides a simple representation of the macroeconomy that is easy to work with.

The original IS–LM model was a closed-economy macroeconomic model. It involved two equations: one representing goods-market flow equilibrium (the IS equation), the other representing money-market stock equilibrium (the LM equation). A third equation was added to allow the IS–LM model to be used to analyze the open economy, namely, the balance of payments (or BP equation), and the IS function was modified to reflect the effect on aggregate demand of the real exchange rate and foreign output. The resulting model is known as the IS–LM–BP model. See Rivera-Batiz and Rivera-Batiz (1985) for a discussion of Keynesian models of the open economy, and Branson and Henderson (1985) for a consideration of open-economy macroeconomics with imperfect capital mobility.

The IS–LM–BP model can be used to describe the economy both under the Bretton Woods system of fixed exchange rates and under various models of floating exchange rates. The main distinguishing aspect of these theories is their different specification of the BP equation. The standard fixed-exchange-rate model assumes that due to capital controls the balance of payments is determined by the current account, and that a balance of payments surplus takes the form of an increase in official reserves which, unless sterilized, will increase the money supply. Sterilized intervention involves the sale and purchase of financial assets by the monetary authority in which the aim is to insulate the domestic money supply from reserve changes; unsterilized intervention allows changes in reserves to affect the money supply. The monetary approach to the balance of payments takes this a step further by assuming that the balance of payments can be interpreted as an excess demand for (or supply of) money, and that money-market equilibrium is restored through a change in the supply of money brought about by a foreign exchange reserve inflow or outflow.

Floating-exchange-rate models typically assume that domestic and foreign assets are perfect substitutes (possibly after adjusting for risk) and that, as a result, the balance of payments equation can be replaced by the UIP condition. These models may be distinguished by their assumptions about the flexibility of prices and output. The Mundell–Fleming model assumes that the price level is fixed. The monetary model of the exchange rate assumes that output is fixed. The Dornbusch model draws a contrast between the demand and supply for goods and services. It assumes that output is fixed but that demand is flexible, and that prices are flexible but sticky.

12.3.1 The IS–LM Model

Before turning to the open economy, we consider the closed-economy IS–LM model. Apart from paving the way for a discussion of exchange-rate determination, this analysis of the IS–LM model serves another purpose. It helps bring out more clearly the difference between modern macroeconomic theory based on the DGE framework and traditional macroeconomics with its ad hoc equations.

The IS equation is derived from the national income identity

$$y = c(y, r) + i(y, r) + g, \tag{12.1}$$

where y is output and where consumption and investment are assumed to depend positively on output (income) and negatively on the real interest rate r; g is exogenous government expenditure. If we assume that inflation is zero, then $r = R$, the nominal interest rate. The equation describes goods-market flow equilibrium with the right-hand side giving the demand for goods and services and the left-hand side giving their supply. It is assumed that supply is demand determined. The equation can also be written in implicit form as

$$\text{IS}(y, r, g) = 0. \tag{12.2}$$

This is the IS equation. The name derives from writing goods-market equilibrium as the flow equilibrium condition that national savings $s(y, r)$ equal investment $i(y, r)$, i.e.,

$$s(y, r) = y - c(y, r) - g = i(y, r).$$

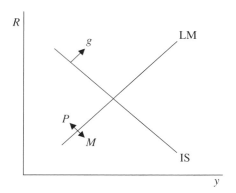

Figure 12.1. A closed-economy IS–LM model.

The IS equation gives the combinations of y and r that are consistent with goods-market flow equilibrium. These are depicted in figure 12.1 by the line IS, which, for simplicity, is assumed to be straight. As inflation is assumed to be zero, we use R instead of r. The line slopes downward because a higher level of output requires a lower interest rate to maintain goods-market equilibrium. A higher level of g implies a higher level of demand for every value of the interest rate. Thus the IS line is shifted up, or to the right (hence the arrow in figure 12.1). Note that here we are dealing here with comparative statics and not dynamics, i.e., we are comparing (static) equilibria and not considering an *increase* in g.

The LM equation is derived from the condition for money-market equilibrium, which we write as

$$M = PL(y, R). \tag{12.3}$$

The right-hand side is the demand function for nominal money balances, which is assumed to depend positively on output and negatively on the nominal interest rate. The left-hand side is the nominal supply of money, which is assumed to be given. Equation (12.3) can be written in implicit form as

$$\mathrm{LM}(y, R, P, M) = 0. \tag{12.4}$$

This describes the values of y and R that are consistent with money-market equilibrium. A higher level of M shifts the LM line down, or to the right.

The intersection of the two lines gives the values of y and R that are consistent with simultaneous equilibrium in both the goods and money markets for given values of g, M, and P. This point represents macroeconomic flow equilibrium in the economy. This equilibrium is different from that obtained for the DGE model because the capital stock may not be in equilibrium at this point. In full static equilibrium, investment is equal to replacement investment ($= \delta k$) and the capital stock is constant. But in a flow equilibrium, capital can take any value, and not necessarily its stock-equilibrium value. Put another way, the IS–LM model describes a temporary (flow) equilibrium that may be changing each period, and not a permanent (stock) equilibrium that may change as a result of changes to g, M, or P, or to an external shock to the system.

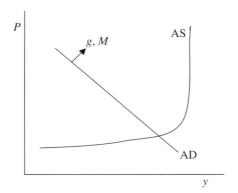

Figure 12.2. A closed-economy AD–AS model.

A higher level of government expenditures is associated with a shift to the right in the IS line. This results in a flow equilibrium with a higher level of output and a higher interest rate. The higher level of output requires a higher level of money balances but, since these are assumed fixed, a higher interest rate is required to make the economy economize on money holdings. A higher level of the money stock shifts the LM line to the right. For P fixed the new equilibrium involves a higher level of output but a lower level of interest rates.

The IS-LM model is clearly a convenient way to analyze fiscal and monetary policy conducted by exogenous changes in government expenditures and the money supply when the price level is fixed. If monetary policy is carried out through exogenous changes in the interest rate, as in inflation targeting, then the money supply becomes endogenous, because, in effect, the monetary authority must supply as much money as is required to sustain the chosen rate of interest. In this case the LM line becomes horizontal at the given rate of interest and price level. In this way a fiscal expansion associated with a higher level of government expenditures would result in a higher level of output than when the money supply is held constant. This is because there must also be an increase in the money supply in order to keep the interest rate constant. Fiscal policy is therefore more effective when monetary policy is conducted through controlling the interest rate than when it is conducted through money-supply targeting.

In the IS-LM model the price level is assumed to be fixed. Put another way, it is assumed that prices are sufficiently slow to adjust compared with output and interest rates that they may be treated as constant over the period of time under consideration. Prices can be made endogenous by adding an output supply function. Instead of supply being demand determined, it is expressed as a positive function of the price level until full capacity is reached, when the line becomes vertical, as in line AS in figure 12.2. Until full capacity is reached, a higher level of output therefore requires a higher price level. The idea here is

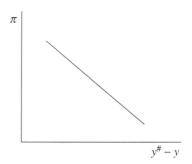

Figure 12.3. The inflation model.

that the period of time is too short for output to be affected by capital accumulation, and therefore it only depends on labor. The other line is the aggregate demand function, AD. This is obtained from the IS–LM model. The AD line is a plot of output against the price level that maintains the savings–investment equality and money-market equilibrium—i.e., is consistent with simultaneously being on both the IS and LM lines—and uses the fact that a higher price level shifts the LM line to the left and results in a lower level of output.

The intersection of the aggregate demand and supply functions relates flow equilibrium in the goods market to the aggregate price level. A higher level of government expenditures or of the money supply shifts the AD line to the right. Below full capacity, this is associated with a higher level of output and aggregate price. At full capacity, output remains unchanged and only the price level is higher. The higher price level in each case shifts the LM line to the left and creates a larger interest rate which reduces the effect on output. At full capacity the interest rate must be high enough to keep output unchanged. Both fiscal and monetary policy are then completely ineffective in bringing about higher output.

As previously noted, this analysis is an exercise in comparative statics. We are asking about the state of the economy in different circumstances, i.e., whether a variable is higher or lower, and not about what happens if a variable increases or decreases over time. We have also assumed that inflation is zero. The IS–LM model is, however, often used to analyze the effects of changes in variables, even though it is not suited to answering this question because it treats capital as fixed and lacks proper dynamics. In particular, it is often used to analyze inflation by adding a Phillips equation. We depict this in figure 12.3 as a negative relation between inflation and the gap between capacity and actual output: π denotes the rate of inflation, $y^{\#} - y$ is the gap from full capacity, and $y^{\#}$ is the capacity level of output.

Having introduced inflation we must distinguish between the nominal and real interest rates in the IS equation. Replacing r by $R - \pi$ in equations (12.1) and (12.2) implies that a higher rate of inflation shifts the IS line to the right in figure 12.1.

We can summarize the resulting IS–LM model by the following simple log-linear model:

$$y = -\beta(R - \pi) + \gamma g,$$
$$m = p + y - \lambda R,$$
$$\pi = \mu - \psi(y^{\#} - y),$$

where output, money, and the price level are in logarithms and $\pi = \Delta p$. The aggregate demand equation is then

$$y = \frac{\gamma\lambda}{\beta + \lambda}g + \frac{\beta}{\beta + \lambda}m - \frac{\beta}{\beta + \lambda}p + \frac{\beta\lambda}{\beta + \lambda}\pi$$

and long-run full-capacity equilibrium inflation is μ.

A further modification, widely used as a result of the high inflation of the 1970s and the breakdown of the Phillips equation in the 1980s, is to assume that inflation also depends on expected inflation. The inflation equation is then written as

$$\pi = \pi^{e} - \psi(y^{\#} - y), \tag{12.5}$$

where π^{e} is expected inflation. Equation (12.5) is known as the expectations-augmented Phillips equation. It implies that the inflation equation shifts to the right when expected inflation is higher. As a result, in the long run, the Phillips equation is vertical and there is no longer a trade-off between inflation and output. Full-capacity equilibrium inflation is now equal to expected inflation, but this rate of inflation is not determined by the model. In particular, it is not determined by output. If money is exogenous, equilibrium inflation is equal to the rate of growth of the money supply.

12.3.2 The BP Equation

In an open economy the IS–LM model needs further modification to take account of the foreign sector. An extra equation—the balance of payments or BP equation—is required, and we must amend the IS function. We consider first the BP equation.

Previously, in chapter 7, we wrote the balance of payments in real terms as

$$x_t - Q_t x_t^{m} + r_t^{*} f_t = \Delta f_{t+1},$$

where x_t is exports, x_t^{m} is imports, Q_t is the terms of trade and, if all goods are tradeables, also the real exchange rate $(S_t P_t^{*})/P_t$, S_t is the nominal exchange rate, P_t and P_t^{*} are the domestic and foreign price levels, f_t is the net stock of foreign assets, r_t^{*} is an exogenous world real rate of interest, $r_t^{*} f_t$ represents net income from foreign asset holding, and we have assumed that inflation is zero. The left-hand side is the real current account and the right-hand side is the capital account.

Exports depend positively on the real exchange rate and world output y_t^*, and imports depend negatively on the real exchange rate and positively on domestic output. The net holding of foreign assets (domestic holding of foreign assets minus foreign holding of domestic assets) depends on the relative rates of return of domestic and foreign assets expressed in the home currency— the portfolio balance decision. An increase in the rate of return on foreign assets increases their holding by domestic residents and hence their income. An increase in the domestic rate of return raises the foreign holding of domestic assets and the outflow of interest income. We approximate the balance of payments by the log-linear model

$$\theta(s + p^* - p) - \phi y + \eta y^* + \mu(R^* + \hat{s} - R) = \Delta f,$$

where p and p^* are the logarithms of the domestic and foreign price levels, y and y^* are the logarithms of domestic and world output, R and R^* are the domestic and the world nominal interest rates, s is the logarithm of the nominal exchange rate, $\hat{s}$ is its expected rate of change, and we assume that $\theta > 0$. $R^* + \hat{s} - R$ represents the effect on net foreign asset income of relative rates of return and $\mu > 0$. The BP equation therefore gives a negatively sloped relation between y and R.

Balance of payments equilibrium implies that $\Delta f = 0$ and hence there is current account, but not trade, balance. Imperfect capital substitutability implies that $0 < \mu < \infty$. If domestic and foreign assets are perfect substitutes, then $\mu = \infty$. In this case the balance of payments equation reduces to the UIP condition discussed in chapter 11, as

$$\lim_{\mu \to \infty} (R - R^* - \hat{s}) = \lim_{\mu \to \infty} \frac{1}{\mu}[\theta(s + p^* - p) - \phi y + \eta y^* - \Delta f] = 0$$

and hence

$$R = R^* + \hat{s}.$$

To complete the model we amend the IS equation to include the effects of trade in the national income identity. In view of the specification of the balance of payments we include the logarithm of the real exchange rate and domestic and foreign output in the IS equation. Thus a weaker real exchange rate and a higher value of world output also shift the IS line to the right. The LM equation is unchanged. The IS–LM–BP model can then be written as

$$y = \alpha(s + p^* - p) - \beta R + \gamma g + \delta y^*, \tag{12.6}$$

$$m = p + y - \lambda R, \tag{12.7}$$

$$\Delta f = \theta(s + p^* - p) - \phi y + \eta y^* + \mu(R^* + \hat{s} - R), \tag{12.8}$$

where $\alpha = \sigma\theta$, $\delta = \sigma\eta$, and $0 < \sigma < 1$ is equal to the share of trade in GDP.

The aggregate demand function obtained by eliminating R from equations (12.6) and (12.7) becomes

$$y = \frac{\gamma\lambda}{\beta + \lambda}g + \frac{\beta}{\beta + \lambda}(m - p) + \frac{\alpha\lambda}{\beta + \lambda}(s + p^* - p) + \frac{\delta\lambda}{\beta + \lambda}y^*$$

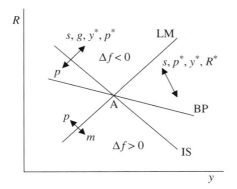

Figure 12.4. The IS–LM–BP model.

and so now depends on the real exchange rate and world output. Thus, in the open economy, a higher real exchange rate and higher world output result in higher aggregate demand. We note that if domestic and foreign goods are perfect substitutes, then $\theta \to \infty$ and hence $\alpha \to \infty$. As a result, the IS and AD equations reduce to PPP:

$$p = s + p^*.$$

The AD line in figure 12.2 is then horizontal at $s + p^*$.

The IS–LM–BP model is represented diagrammatically in figure 12.4. We have assumed that the BP line is flatter than the IS line. The higher the substitutability between domestic and foreign assets, the more likely this is. As they become perfect substitutes ($\mu \to \infty$) the BP line becomes horizontal. Equilibrium occurs at the point of intersection of the three equations at A. Above the BP line we have a current-account deficit and an outflow of capital so that $\Delta f < 0$, and below it, when we have a surplus, we have $\Delta f > 0$. The arrows in figure 12.4 denote the direction of shift of a line to maintain equilibrium following a higher value of the associated variables. These enable us to analyze the effects of shifts in the exogenous variables. As before, it is best to view the analysis as being for the short term, i.e., equilibrium is only temporary.

If there are controls on the movement of private capital so that domestic residents are unable to acquire or sell foreign assets, then $\mu = 0$ and the BP line is vertical. To the left of the vertical BP line we have $\Delta f > 0$ and to the right $\Delta f < 0$. Due to the controls, the change in net foreign assets consists solely of a change in government foreign exchange reserves. These reserves, which we denote as h, form part of the domestic money supply. The total money supply is

$$m = d + h,$$

where d is the domestic component of the money supply. If d is fixed, then

$$\Delta f = \Delta h = \Delta m. \tag{12.9}$$

A current-account surplus therefore increases the money supply and a deficit reduces it. Above the BP line, when we have a current-account deficit, we have

$\Delta f = \Delta m < 0$, and below it, when we have a surplus, we have $\Delta f = \Delta m > 0$. This is indicated in figure 12.4. For points off the BP line the money supply would be changing and hence the LM line would be shifting. Equilibrium requires that the economy is on the BP line as well as on the IS and LM lines, and that the LM line is fixed.

By specializing the IS–LM–BP model it can be used to represent the economy during the Bretton Woods period, and also a number of different flexible-exchange-rate models. Under Bretton Woods, exchange rates were fixed and there was no capital mobility. The capital account of the balance of payments then represented changes in reserves and hence in the money supply. This is the situation captured by the monetary approach to the balance of payments. Turning to flexible-exchange-rate models, the Mundell–Fleming model is obtained by fixing the price level and setting $\mu = \infty$ when UIP holds. If, in addition, $\hat{s} = 0$, then we have the Mundell–Fleming model with static expectations. The Dornbusch model is a variant of the Mundell–Fleming model in which prices are flexible but sticky. The monetary model, which has flexible prices but fixed output, sets $\alpha = \theta = \mu = \infty$.

12.3.3 Fixed Exchange Rates: The Monetary Approach to the Balance of Payments

The monetary approach to the balance of payments (MABP) of Frenkel and Johnson (1976) is a fixed-exchange-rate model with capital controls, hence $\mu = 0$. The MABP assumes that the balance of payments is a monetary phenomenon. A balance of payments surplus, for example, is interpreted as an excess demand for the stock of money where money-market equilibrium is restored through a reserve inflow that increases the supply of money until it equates with the demand for money. The balance of payments is brought back into equilibrium by a correction to the current account that is induced by the monetary expansion.

The model for the MABP consists of equations (12.6), (12.7), and (12.8) of the IS–LM–BP model together with a money-supply equation (12.9). The model can be rewritten as the IS equation (12.6), which determines goods-market equilibrium, plus the following three equations which describe money demand, money supply, and money-market equilibrium:

$$m^{D} = y + p - \lambda R,$$
$$m^{S} = \Delta f + m_0,$$
$$m^{D} = m^{S} = m,$$

where Δf is determined by the balance of payments, equation (12.8), and m_0 is the initial level of money in the economy. Thus, y, p, and m are the endogenous variables; R and s are exogenous variables, as are g, y^*, p^*, and R^*.

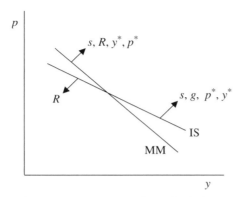

Figure 12.5.   The monetary approach to the balance of payments.

The reduced-form solutions for y and p are

$$y = \sigma\{\alpha(s + p^*) - [\alpha\lambda + \beta(1 + \theta)]R + \delta(1 + \theta)g$$
$$+ [\gamma(1 + \theta) - \alpha\eta]y^* - \alpha m_0\},$$

$$p = \sigma\{[\theta - \alpha(1 + \phi)](s + p^*) + [\lambda + \beta(1 + \phi)]R - \delta(1 + \phi)g$$
$$+ [\gamma(1 + \phi) - \eta]y^* + m_0\},$$

where $\sigma = 1 + \theta - \alpha(1 + \phi) > 0$. All coefficients (or combinations of coefficients) are positive except for that of y^* in the equation for p, which could take either sign. It follows that a depreciation (higher s) and a higher p^* will raise both y and p. A fiscal expansion (higher g) and a domestic monetary easing (lower R) raise y but reduce p. A larger world income y^* raises y but its effect on p is unclear, though it is likely to be negative.

The solution may also be obtained graphically as in figure 12.5. The line IS is still the IS equation but is now drawn in (y, p)-space, instead of (r, y)-space, and the line MM is the money-market equilibrium obtained by equating money demand and money supply to give

$$y = \frac{1 + \theta}{1 + \phi}p + \frac{1 + \theta}{1 + \phi}(s + p^*) + \frac{\lambda}{1 + \phi}R + \frac{1 + \theta}{1 + \phi}y^* + \frac{1}{1 + \phi}m_0.$$

The direction of shift of each line following increases in the values of the exogenous variables is shown by the arrows. The relative slopes of the lines reflects the assumption that $\alpha < (1 + \theta)/(1 + \phi)$.

12.3.4 Exchange-Rate Determination with Imperfect Capital Substitutability

Modern theories of a flexible exchange rate assume that domestic and foreign capital are perfect substitutes. Before discussing these, for the purposes of comparison with modern theories, we consider a situation where they are imperfect substitutes. We base our analysis on the IS–LM–BP model, equations (12.6) and (12.7), partly to reflect the origins of this approach in the Keynesian model. We now treat the analysis as dynamic rather than as an exercise in comparative statics. We assume that there are no capital controls and that the balance of payments determines the net stock of foreign assets. As exchange rates adjust much faster than output and prices, we assume that y and p are exogenous. The model is then used to determine s, f, and R with m, y, p, and R all exogenous. Although the exchange rate is flexible, in the spirit of the Keynesian model, we assume that $\hat{s}$, its expected rate of change, is zero.

The solutions are obtained recursively. First R is determined from the LM equation, then s is obtained from the IS and LM equations (or equivalently from the AD equation) and f is determined from the balance of payments. The solutions are

$$R = \frac{y + p - m}{\lambda},$$

$$s = \frac{\beta + \lambda}{\alpha\lambda}y + \frac{\beta + \alpha\lambda}{\alpha\lambda}p - \frac{\beta}{\alpha\lambda}m - \frac{y}{\alpha}g - \frac{\delta}{\alpha}y^* - p^*,$$

$$f = -\frac{\alpha(\mu + \lambda\phi) - \theta(\beta + \lambda)}{\alpha\lambda}y - \frac{\alpha\mu - \beta\theta}{\alpha\lambda}p + \frac{\alpha\mu - \beta\theta}{\alpha\lambda}m$$
$$- \frac{\theta y}{\alpha}g - \frac{\theta\delta - \alpha\eta}{\alpha}y^* - \mu R^* + f_0.$$

Both a fiscal and a monetary expansion are predicted to cause the exchange rate to appreciate. A fiscal expansion increases domestic demand, and since output and prices are fixed, this requires a corresponding fall in net exports (trade), which is brought about by the exchange-rate appreciation. The weaker trade balance also results in lower net foreign asset holdings. A monetary expansion reduces domestic interest rates and also raises domestic demand, hence the need for an exchange-rate appreciation. The effect on net asset holdings depends on the degree of substitutability of domestic and foreign assets: the higher their substitutability, the more likely are net assets to increase.

This analysis is best suited to the short term. In the longer term, alternative scenarios may be more appropriate, such as also allowing output and prices to adjust. Suppose, that the country is a small open economy and must therefore adopt world interest rates. Moreover, suppose that we impose stock equilibrium so that $\Delta f = 0$. In this case, the model can be written in flow equilibrium as

$$y = \alpha(s + p^* - p) - \beta R^* + yg + \delta y^*,$$
$$m = p + y - \lambda R^*,$$
$$0 = \theta(s + p^* - p) - \phi y + \eta y^*.$$

It now determines s, y, and p instead of s, R, and f. Their solutions are

$$s = m - \frac{y(\theta - \phi)}{\theta - \alpha\phi}g + \left[\lambda + \frac{\beta(\theta - \phi)}{\theta - \alpha\phi}\right]R^* + \frac{\delta(\theta - \phi) - \eta(1 + \alpha)}{\theta - \alpha\phi}y^*,$$

$$y = \frac{\theta y}{\theta - \alpha\phi}g - \frac{\beta\theta}{\theta - \alpha\phi}R^* + \frac{\delta\theta - \alpha\eta}{\theta - \alpha\phi}y^*,$$

$$p = m - \frac{\theta y}{\theta - \alpha\phi}g + \left[\lambda + \frac{\beta\theta}{\theta - \alpha\phi}\right]R^* - \frac{\delta\theta - \alpha\eta}{\theta - \alpha\phi}y^*,$$

where $\theta > \alpha\phi$.

Hence, a fiscal expansion again causes an exchange-rate appreciation, and it raises output and reduces prices. A monetary expansion only has nominal effects as it is passed through into prices and the exchange rate, which rise in the same proportion. As the real exchange rate is unaffected, a monetary expansion has no impact on output.

12.4 UIP and Exchange-Rate Determination

We now assume that domestic and foreign bonds are perfect substitutes. In this case, the balance of payments reduces to the UIP condition. This assumption is a building block for nearly all modern theories of a floating exchange rate. It is also the only equation needed to analyze the exchange rate when the interest rate is the policy instrument, such as in inflation targeting under a policy of discretion where the domestic interest rate is chosen by the monetary authority.

Previously, in our examination of a flexible exchange rate, we used a Keynesian style of model and carried out a comparative-statics analysis. We now revert to a full dynamic analysis of exchange-rate models. Thus, we use the UIP condition derived in chapter 11, which involves forming expectations of the future exchange rate. Using the notation of this chapter, UIP may be written as

$$R_t = R_t^* + E_t \Delta s_{t+1}.$$

Solving this forwards gives

$$s_t = \sum_{i=0}^{\infty} E_t (R_{t+i}^* - R_{t+i}), \qquad (12.10)$$

which implies that the exchange rate responds instantly to new information about current and expected future nominal interest differentials.

In particular, if R_t^* stays constant, then a rise in current R_t, or in expected future R_{t+n} $(n > 0)$, will cause an instantaneous appreciation (fall) in the current spot rate s_t. As noted in chapter 11, a 1% increase in R_t today *that is expected to be sustained for n periods*, will cause an n% appreciation today, and not just a 1% change. Uncertainty about how long the interest differential will last therefore makes it difficult for the FOREX market to price foreign exchange. Since the exchange rate is part of the transmission mechanism of monetary policy in inflation targeting, it is also difficult to assess the impact on inflation of a change in interest rates.

An increase in R_t, with R_t^* constant, is predicted to cause both s_t and $E_t s_{t+1}$ to fall. But because $R_t > R_t^*$, in order to maintain UIP, we require that s_t and $E_t s_{t+1}$ change in such a way that $s_t > E_t s_{t+1}$. This gives rise to the following apparent paradox: an increase in R_t will cause the exchange rate to appreciate, but the market (acting rationally) will expect the exchange rate to depreciate. The paradox is resolved if we note that the expected exchange-rate depreciation is in the future, from period t to period $t+1$, and not from period $t-1$ to period

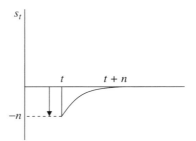

Figure 12.6.   The dynamic response of the
exchange rate to a change in the interest rate.

t. Thus, although $E_t s_{t+1}$ decreases, it does not fall by as much as s_t in order that $E_t \Delta s_{t+1}$ remains positive. If we set $n = 1$, then figure 12.6 shows what happens to the exchange rate between periods t and $t + 1$.

Another implication of the UIP condition is that, if in period t investors acquire the expectation that there will be a change in the domestic interest rate in period $t + n$, then the spot exchange rate s_t would change in period t, and not wait until the interest rate change actually occurred. It would then remain at this level until there was a further change in interest rates. Suppose now that, although the interest rate is expected to change in period $t + n$, when period $t + n$ arrives there is no change in the interest rate. The spot exchange rate would change in period t in anticipation of the change in period $t + n$, but when the mistake is realized, the spot rate would immediately return to its original level. Figure 12.6 depicts the behavior of the exchange rate between periods t and $t + n$. As previously noted in chapter 11, this is called a peso effect, after events in Mexico in the 1980s when it was anticipated that the Mexican interest rate would rise but in fact did not.

Another common occurrence is for the spot exchange rate to depreciate at the same time as interest rates are reduced. Although at first sight this is at variance with UIP, it could in fact be consistent with UIP. If markets expected a larger interest rate cut than was implemented, then the exchange rate, having already depreciated in anticipation of a large cut, would need to appreciate in order to correct for the previous over-depreciation.

Both of these apparently anomalous results illustrate an important feature of exchange rates, or of any asset price, where they are based on forward-looking expectations: news about the future, whether correct or not, will affect the spot price. As a result of this susceptibility to news and shocks, exchange rates are volatile. We also note that when the money stock is chosen as the policy instrument this tends to make interest rates, and hence exchange rates, highly volatile due to their strong response to money shocks. This is another reason for the widespread use of interest rates as the monetary-policy instrument.

We have shown that interest rates are central to the determination of floating exchange rates. For highly traded currencies like the dollar, the euro, sterling, and the yen the volume traded each day is so great that only interest rates can be used to control the currency. Reserves are not large enough to have any significant effect; this is something many central banks have discovered for themselves in recent years as a result of attempts to control the exchange rate through foreign exchange intervention.

In contrast, most macroeconomic theories of the nominal exchange rate focus on the effects of monetary and fiscal policy, where monetary policy is conducted through controlling the money supply. If UIP holds, then monetary and fiscal policy determine the exchange rate through their effect on interest rates. The response of the exchange rate may be instantaneous as in the monetary model of the exchange rate where prices are assumed to be flexible. Or, if prices are fixed, as in the Mundell–Fleming model, or sticky, as in the Dornbusch model, exchange-rate adjustment may be spread over time; moreover, due to the presence of the expected future change in the exchange rate, the spot rate might overshoot its new long-run value.

12.5 The Mundell–Fleming Model of the Exchange Rate

12.5.1 Theory

This model is due to Fleming (1962) and Mundell (1963). Together with the monetary model, it forms the cornerstone of modern nominal-exchange-rate theory. The focus in the Mundell–Fleming model is on the flexibility of the nominal exchange rate in a world of perfect capital mobility and rigid prices. As noted above, the Mundell–Fleming model consists of three equations: the IS equation, the LM equation, and the UIP condition:

$$\text{IS:} \quad y_t = \alpha(s_t + p_t^* - p_t) - \beta R_t + \gamma g_t + \delta y_t^*,$$
$$\text{LM:} \quad m_t = p_t + y_t - \lambda R_t^*,$$
$$\text{UIP:} \quad R_t = R_t^* + E_t(s_{t+1} - s_t),$$

where the price levels are fixed. There are three endogenous variables: the nominal exchange rate, output, and the domestic interest rate.

Solving for the exchange rate we obtain

$$\left. \begin{aligned} s_t &= \frac{\beta + \lambda}{\alpha + \beta + \lambda} E_t s_{t+1} + x_t, \\ x_t &= \frac{1}{\alpha + \beta + \lambda} [(\alpha - 1)p_t + m_t - \gamma g_t - \delta y_t^* - \alpha p_t^* + (\beta + \lambda)R_t^*], \end{aligned} \right\} \quad (12.11)$$

where x_t is exogenous. Solving equation (12.11) forwards gives

$$s_t = \sum_{i=0}^{\infty} \left(\frac{\beta + \lambda}{\alpha + \beta + \lambda} \right)^i E_t x_{t+i}.$$

Thus the exchange rate jumps instantly to its new equilibrium following a change in any of the variables that make up x_t.

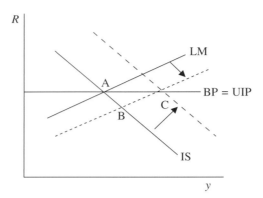

Figure 12.7. Monetary policy.

The long-run solutions for the three endogenous variables can be obtained as follows: output is determined by the LM equation, the exchange rate from the IS equation, and the interest rate from the UIP condition. The long-run reduced forms are

$$s = -\frac{1-\alpha}{\alpha}p + \frac{1}{\alpha}m - \frac{y}{\alpha}g + \frac{\beta+\lambda}{\alpha}y^* + p^*,$$
$$y = m - p + \lambda R^*,$$
$$R = R^*.$$

Hence, in the long run, both a permanent increase in the money supply and a decrease in government expenditures cause the nominal exchange rate to depreciate.

Output is affected only by monetary policy. Fiscal policy has no effect on output, i.e., fiscal policy is entirely crowded out. This is in complete contrast to the effect on output of monetary and fiscal policy when the nominal exchange rate is fixed. In the MABP we showed that monetary policy had no effect on output but that an expansionary fiscal policy caused output to increase. In the Mundell–Fleming model an increase in government expenditures causes an appreciation in the exchange rate, which brings about a switch in private expenditures from domestic to foreign goods. As output is unchanged, this switch must be equal in size to the increase in government expenditures. Thus the government's additional claim on domestic output is at the expense of the claims of the private sector.

Further understanding of the effects of monetary and fiscal policy may be obtained using the IS–LM–BP diagram. A key difference from before is that, as a result of assuming UIP, the BP line is horizontal.

12.5.2 Monetary Policy

In figure 12.7 we depict the effect of a permanent increase in the money supply. The LM line shifts to the right as a result of the monetary expansion. Notionally, the economy moves from point A to point B, where the IS and LM lines intersect.

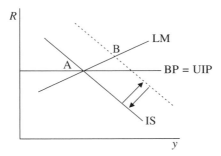

Figure 12.8. Fiscal policy.

At B there is an incipient (notional) capital outflow due to a negative interest differential. This causes an exchange-rate depreciation, which expands trade and shifts the IS line to the right. The depreciation results in the economy attaining a new equilibrium at point C. At this point output has increased, which raises the demand for money and hence the interest rate. This restores the original zero interest differential and so removes any incentive for further changes in the exchange rate or capital movements. Thus a monetary expansion has real effects on output, and causes an exchange-rate depreciation.

From the reduced-form solutions we know that R is unchanged, that $\Delta y = \Delta m$, and that $\Delta s = (1/\alpha)\Delta m$. The exchange rate does not therefore change by the same amount as the money supply; if $\alpha < 1$ it changes by more, and if $\alpha > 1$ it changes by less. This result differs from the previous model with imperfect capital substitutability, and from the monetary and Dornbusch models, which are yet to be considered. In these models the exchanges rate changes by the same percentage as the money supply. The difference is due to the assumption in the Mundell–Fleming model that the price level does not respond to the money supply. If the price level were to increase, then, from the reduced-form exchange-rate equation, s would increase by less than p if $\alpha > \frac{1}{2}$ and by more if $0 < \alpha < \frac{1}{2}$. The solution would then be similar to the other models.

It can be shown that an increase in the foreign interest rate would cause a persistent capital outflow, an exchange-rate depreciation, and a shift to the right in the IS line, which would raise the domestic interest rate. Equilibrium is regained when the original interest differential is restored by an equal increase in the domestic interest rate. From the reduced-form solutions, $\Delta s = ((\beta + \lambda)/\alpha)\Delta R^*$, $\Delta y = \lambda \Delta R^*$, and $\Delta R = \Delta R^*$.

12.5.3 Fiscal Policy

We consider a permanent increase in g. This shifts the IS line to the right as in figure 12.8. Notionally, the economy moves from point A to point B, where the IS and LM lines intersect. At point B there is a positive interest differential. This causes an incipient capital inflow, and hence an exchange-rate appreciation, which reduces trade and shifts the IS line back to the left. The exchange-rate appreciation must be sufficient to restore the IS line to its original position, implying that output is unchanged. In effect, the fiscal expansion has resulted in a reallocation of domestic output from the private to the government sector which was brought about by an exchange-rate appreciation. Fiscal policy therefore has no effect on output; it is completely crowded out by the exchange rate. From the reduced-form equations, $\Delta s = -(\gamma/\alpha)\Delta g$, and y and R are unchanged.

12.6 The Monetary Model of the Exchange Rate

12.6.1 Theory

The key assumptions of the monetary model are that all prices are perfectly flexible, including the exchange rate, and money supplies and output are exogenous (see Frenkel 1976; Mussa 1976, 1982). This is the reverse of the Mundell–Fleming model, where prices were fixed and output was flexible. At best, therefore, both models are best suited to analyzing behavior over a relatively short period of time. Unlike the Mundell–Fleming model, the monetary model can be applied to a large economy as well as a small economy as both the domestic and foreign interest rates are exogenous variables. For a large open economy, the model consists of four equations: UIP, PPP, and domestic and foreign money-demand functions,

$$\text{UIP:} \quad R_t = R_t^* + E_t\Delta s_{t+1}$$
$$\text{PPP:} \quad p_t = p_t^* + s_t,$$
$$M^D: \quad m_t = p_t + y_t - \lambda R_t,$$
$$M^{D*}: \quad m_t^* = p_t^* + y_t^* - \lambda R_t^*.$$

All variables are logarithms except the interest rates, R_t and R_t^*. For a small open economy we assume that R_t^* is exogenous.

UIP is based on no capital controls and a floating exchange rate. PPP implies that the real exchange rate is constant over time as a result of goods arbitrage brought about by flexible goods prices. Our previous discussion of the real open economy and the BOP makes it highly improbable that the real exchange rate is constant, even in the long run. PPP definitely does not hold in the short run. Accordingly, PPP is often replaced by the weaker assumption of relative PPP (RPPP). This implies that PPP holds in terms of first differences (i.e., in terms of proportional rates of change):

$$\text{RPPP:} \quad \Delta p_t = \Delta p_t^* + \Delta s_t.$$

It would then follow that

$$E_t\Delta p_{t+1} = E_t\Delta p_{t+1}^* + E_t\Delta s_{t+1}.$$

Because $E_t\Delta s_{t+1} \simeq 0$ in the short run, we would have $E_t\Delta p_{t+1} \simeq E_t\Delta p_{t+1}^*$, i.e., domestic and foreign inflation rates would be similar. We note that PPP is not strictly required for the monetary model as RPPP will deliver the same analytic results.

The assumption of identical domestic and foreign money-demand functions is made for convenience. This enables us to express the model in terms of the differences between the domestic and foreign money-demand functions. We note that, in practice, money-demand functions may require short-run dynamics, but we omit these. The difference between the two money-demand functions is

$$m_t - m_t^* = (p_t - p_t^*) + (y_t - y_t^*) - \lambda(R_t - R_t^*).$$

We can now eliminate the price and interest differentials using the PPP and UIP conditions. Using a tilde to denote the difference between domestic and foreign, we obtain a difference equation in the logarithm of the nominal exchange rate, namely,

$$\tilde{m}_t = s_t + \tilde{y}_t - \lambda E_t \Delta s_{t+1}.$$

Hence

$$s_t = \frac{\lambda}{1 + \lambda}[\tilde{m}_t - \tilde{y}_t] + \frac{\lambda}{1 + \lambda} E_t s_{t+1}. \tag{12.12}$$

Equation (12.12) has a forward solution, which is

$$s_t = \left(\frac{\lambda}{1 + \lambda}\right)^n E_t s_{t+n} + \frac{\lambda}{1 + \lambda} \sum_{i=0}^{n-1} \left(\frac{\lambda}{1 + \lambda}\right)^i E_t[\tilde{m}_{t+i} - \tilde{y}_{t+i}].$$

Given the transversality condition that $\lim_{n \to \infty}(\lambda/(1 + \lambda))^n E_t s_{t+n} = 0$, the solution is

$$s_t = \frac{\lambda}{1 + \lambda} \sum_{i=0}^{\infty} \left(\frac{\lambda}{1 + \lambda}\right)^i E_t[\tilde{m}_{t+i} - \tilde{y}_{t+i}]. \tag{12.13}$$

Thus, compared with equation (12.10), in equation (12.13) we have replaced the interest differential with the excess holding of money over, in effect, the demand for transactions balances. The exchange rate is forward looking once more: it jumps as a result of new information about $m_{t+i} - m_{t+i}^*$ and $y_{t+i} - y_{t+i}^*$, $i \geq 0$. Moreover, it responds today to expected future values of $\tilde{m}_{t+1}$ and $\tilde{y}_{t+i}$. Due to discounting by the factor $\lambda/(1+\lambda)$, the further ahead the expected future change in the differential, the smaller is the current impact on s_t; the impact effect is $(\lambda/(1 + \lambda))^i$ when the change is expected to occur in period $t + i$.

Comparing this solution with that derived from the UIP condition, we note that s_t still depends on current and expected future interest differentials, but now these are endogenous and not exogenous, and they depend on current and expected future differentials in the money supplies and outputs of the two countries.

12.6.2 Monetary Policy

We now consider the effect on the exchange rate of changes in the money supply. Although our discussion assumes that these changes are due to monetary policy, the analysis also applies to money shocks unconnected with policy. Our discussion of fiscal policy below is subject to the same observation.

Suppose that monetary policy is conducted through money-supply targeting, and that the aim is for the money supply to grow at a constant rate. We wish to distinguish between temporary and permanent money shocks. We interpret temporary money shocks as those affecting the money stock and permanent shocks as those affecting the rate of growth of the money supply. We therefore assume that the domestic and foreign money supplies follow random walks with drift. A change in the drift term, which is the long-run rate of growth of money, is a permanent shock, and a change in the disturbance term is a temporary shock. We also assume that output levels in the two countries satisfy random walks, i.e., the economies are growing in the long run at constant rates. To summarize, we assume that

$$\Delta m_t = \mu + \varepsilon_t, \qquad E_t \varepsilon_{t+1} = 0,$$
$$\Delta m_t^* = \mu^* + \varepsilon_t^*, \qquad E_t \varepsilon_{t+1}^* = 0,$$
$$\Delta y_t = y + \xi_t, \qquad E_t \xi_{t+1} = 0,$$
$$\Delta y_t^* = y^* + \xi_t^*, \qquad E_t \xi_{t+1}^* = 0.$$

Hence, in the long run, the inflation rates in the domestic and foreign economies are μ and μ^*, and the growth rates of GDP are y and y^*.

We note that if $\Delta x_t = \alpha + \varepsilon_t$ and $E_t \varepsilon_{t+1} = 0$, then $x_{t+i} = i\alpha + x_t + \sum_{j=1}^{i} \varepsilon_{t+j}$ and $E_t x_{t+i} = i\alpha + x_t$. We also note that $\sum_{i=0}^{\infty} \theta^i = 1/(1 - \theta)$ and $\sum_{i=0}^{\infty} i\theta^i = \theta/((1 - \theta)^2)$ for $|\theta| < 1$. It follows that

$$E_t \tilde{m}_{t+i} = i\tilde{\mu} + \tilde{m}_t,$$
$$E_t \tilde{y}_{t+i} = i\tilde{y} + \tilde{y}_t,$$

where we recall that a tilde denotes a differential. The solution for the exchange rate is

$$s_t = \frac{1}{1+\lambda} \sum_{i=0}^{\infty} \left(\frac{\lambda}{1+\lambda} \right)^i [i(\tilde{\mu} - \tilde{y}) + \tilde{m}_t - \tilde{y}_t]$$
$$= \lambda(\tilde{\mu} - \tilde{y}) + \tilde{m}_t - \tilde{y}_t.$$

A constant nominal exchange rate requires constant differentials in the money supplies and the output levels, and hence the same rates of growth of money and output. If one country has a permanently higher rate of inflation than another, or a lower rate of output growth, then the exchange rate will depreciate.

A permanent increase in the domestic money growth rate relative to the foreign rate implies that $\Delta\tilde{\mu} > 0$ and hence $\Delta s_t > 0$. Thus there is a jump depreciation in the exchange rate in period t and this change in the exchange rate is permanent. Usually $\lambda > 1$, hence the reaction of the exchange rate is larger than this permanent shock. A related argument applies to output growth rates.

A temporary increase in relative money stocks, or output levels, will not affect the relative growth rates of money and output, but will cause $\tilde{m}_t$ and $\tilde{y}_t$ to change. There will be an equal change in the exchange rate in period t, but this will be temporary. In particular, a temporary increase in the domestic money supply will cause a temporary domestic depreciation.

We can now revisit the paradox mentioned earlier, namely: Why does an increase in the money stock cause a depreciation of the exchange rate, but the market (acting rationally) expects the exchange rate to appreciate? For simplicity, we assume that m_{t+i}^*, y_{t+i}, and $y_{t+i}^* = 0$ for all i. The exchange rate is then determined by

$$s_t = \frac{1}{1+\lambda} m_t + \frac{\lambda}{(1+\lambda)^2} E_t m_{t+1} + \cdots . \tag{12.14}$$

If, in addition, $m_{t+i} = 0$ for all i, then $s_t = 0$. Now consider a one-period unanticipated increase in m_t from zero to $m > 0$. It then follows that

$$s_t = \frac{1}{1+\lambda} m > 0;$$

i.e., the spot exchange rate depreciates. As the exchange rate returns to its original level next period so that $s_{t+i} = 0$ $(i > 0)$,

$$E_t s_{t+1} - s_t = -\frac{1}{1+\lambda} m < 0.$$

Hence there is an expected appreciation of the exchange rate between periods t and $t+1$ and this maintains UIP.

Suppose next that the domestic money stock is expected to increase in period $t+1$, possibly due to an announcement by the monetary authorities, and this announcement is credible, i.e., believed by the market. For simplicity, we continue to assume that m_{t+i}^*, y_{t+i}, and $y_{t+i}^* = 0$ for all i. We consider a temporary and a permanent change. Again we use equation (12.14).

12.6.2.1 A Temporary Change

Let $m_{t+i} = 0$ for all $i > 0$ except for $m_{t+1} = m > 0$. It follows that

$$s_t = \frac{\lambda}{(1+\lambda)^2} E_t m_{t+1} = \frac{\lambda}{(1+\lambda)^2} m > 0,$$

$$E_t s_{t+1} = \frac{1}{1+\lambda} E_t m_{t+1} = \frac{\lambda}{(1+\lambda)^2} m < s_t,$$

$$E_t s_{t+i} = 0, \quad i \geqslant 2,$$

and so

$$E_t[s_{t+1} - s_t] = \frac{1}{(1+\lambda)^2} E_t m_{t+1} > 0.$$

Consequently, the credible announcement of a temporary increase in the money supply in period $t+1$ causes the exchange rate to depreciate in period t, prior to any actual change in the money supply. In period $t+1$, when the money supply

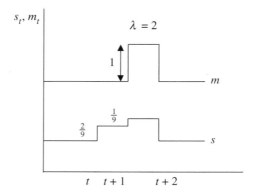

Figure 12.9. An anticipated temporary increase in money in period $t + 1$.

actually increases, the exchange rate appreciates. Seen from the perspective of period $t + 1$, but forgetting what had happened in period t and why it had occurred, this may seem paradoxical. In subsequent periods the exchange rate reverts to its original value as its long-run equilibrium level is unaffected by these events. Once again the explanation for these changes is that at all times the expected change in the exchange rate must satisfy UIP. These exchange-rate movements are depicted in figure 12.9 for $m = 1$.

12.6.2.2 A Permanent Change

We now assume that $m_t = 0$ and that the expectation in period t is that $m_{t+i} = m > 0$ for all $i > 0$. It follows that

$$s_t = \frac{\lambda}{(1 + \lambda)^2} E_t m_{t+1} + \frac{\lambda^2}{(1 + \lambda)^3} E_t m_{t+2} + \cdots$$

$$= \frac{\lambda}{1 + \lambda} m,$$

$$E_t s_{t+1} = \frac{1}{1 + \lambda} E_t m_{t+1} + \frac{\lambda}{(1 + \lambda)^2} E_t m_{t+2} + \cdots$$

$$= m > s_t,$$

$$E_t s_{t+i} = m, \quad i \geqslant 2,$$

and so

$$E_t [s_{t+1} - s_t] = \frac{1}{1 + \lambda} m > 0.$$

Hence, following the announcement in period t of a permanent change in the money supply from period $t + 1$, the spot exchange rate s_t immediately depreciates (increases). It then depreciates again in period $t + 1$ when the money-supply change takes effect. Thereafter, the exchange rate stays at this new equilibrium level until affected by new shocks. This is depicted in figure 12.10 for $m = 1$.

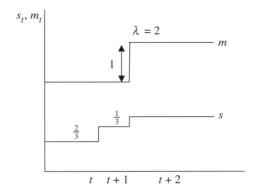

Figure 12.10. An anticipated permanent increase in money from period $t + 1$.

12.6.3 Fiscal Policy

Fiscal variables are not explicitly included in the monetary model. If fiscal policy has any effect on the exchange rate, then it would be through its impact on output. Since output has the opposite sign to money in the solution of the exchange rate, but otherwise has the same impact, we may infer that an increase in current or expected future values of output caused, for example, by a fiscal expansion would bring about an appreciation of the spot exchange rate.

12.7 The Dornbusch Model of the Exchange Rate

12.7.1 Theory

In the Mundell–Fleming model prices were fixed, and in the monetary model they were perfectly flexible. The Dornbusch overshooting model (Dornbusch 1976) assumes that prices are flexible, but sticky. The Dornbusch model was developed from the Mundell-Fleming and the monetary models of the exchange rate with the addition of an equation for the rate of inflation in which inflation is due to the current excess demand for goods and services. Even though there is no lag in the equation, the adjustment of prices is not instantaneous. This is sufficient to cause more variability in the exchange rate and in output in the short run than in the monetary model. After analyzing the Dornbusch model and its implications for monetary and fiscal policy, we return to the monetary model and examine the implications of amending it to include price stickiness. As a result, we come closer to having a general equilibrium model of the exchange rate. We refer to this as the monetary model with sticky prices. We show that in this model the behavior of the nominal exchange rate is similar to that in the Dornbusch model. For a retrospective assessment of the Dornbusch model, see Rogoff (2002).

Like the monetary model, the Dornbusch model is highly stylized. It is essentially an IS-LM-BP model with an aggregate demand function replacing the IS function, with UIP replacing the balance of payments, and with the addition of a price equation. It can be represented by the following equations:

$$d_t = \alpha(s_t + p_t^* - p_t) - \beta R_t + \gamma y_t + g,$$
$$\Delta p_t = \theta(d_t - y_t) + v_t,$$
$$m_t = p_t + y_t - \lambda R_t + u_t,$$
$$R_t = R_t^* + E_t \Delta s_{t+1},$$

where d is aggregate demand, y is domestic output or supply, which is exogenous, s is the nominal exchange rate, p is the price level, R is the domestic nominal interest rate, g is government expenditure, m is the money supply, and u and v are zero-mean serially independent shocks. An asterisk denotes the equivalent foreign variable. All variables are logarithms except the interest rates. Thus the Dornbusch model draws a distinction between aggregate demand, which is endogenous, and aggregate supply, which is exogenous. The first equation is the aggregate demand function. The second equation relates the rate of inflation to aggregate excess demand; in effect, this is the same as the output gap. R_t^* is assumed to be exogenous, hence the Dornbusch model can be considered as suitable for a small open economy. We recall that in the monetary model, R_t^* is an endogenous variable.

Dornbusch's original model was in continuous time. A distinction was therefore made between s_t and the other variables. s_t was assumed to be a jump variable, responding instantly to new information. In contrast, p_t was only allowed to respond with a delay. Such a distinction was vital in producing the exchange rate overshooting property characteristic of the Dornbusch model. In discrete time we do not make such a distinction.

The solution of the model is obtained by first reducing the model to two equations in p_t and s_t. The price equation is obtained from the first three equations and is

$$\left.\begin{aligned} p_t &= \mu p_{t-1} + \phi s_t + a_t, \\ a_t &= \mu\theta\left(\gamma - 1 - \frac{\beta}{\lambda}\right)y_t + \frac{\mu\beta\theta}{\lambda}m_t + \mu\theta g + \mu\alpha\theta p_t^* - \frac{\mu\beta\theta}{\lambda}u_t + \mu v_t, \end{aligned}\right\} \quad (12.15)$$

where $\mu = [1 + \theta(\alpha + (\beta/\lambda))]^{-1}$ and $\phi = \mu\alpha\theta$. The exchange-rate equation is

$$\left.\begin{aligned} s_t &= E_t s_{t+1} - \frac{1}{\lambda}p_t + b_t, \\ b_t &= -\frac{1}{\lambda}y_t + \frac{1}{\lambda}m_t + R_t^* - \frac{1}{\lambda}u_t. \end{aligned}\right\} \quad (12.16)$$

Using the lag operator, and recalling that $L^i z_t = z_{t-i}$ and $L^{-i} z_t = E_t z_{t+i}$, the reduced-form equation for s_t can be written as

$$[\lambda - (\mu\lambda + \lambda + \phi)L + \mu\lambda L^2]L^{-1}s_t = x_t \qquad (12.17)$$

or as

$$\mu\lambda f(L)L^{-1}s_t = x_t, \qquad (12.18)$$

where
$$x_t = a_t - \lambda(1 - \mu L)b_t.$$

The characteristic, or auxiliary, equation is
$$f(L) = \frac{1}{\mu} - \left(1 + \frac{1}{\mu} + \frac{\phi}{\mu\lambda}\right)L + L^2 = 0.$$

This has a saddlepath solution as $f(1) = -(\phi/\mu\lambda) < 0$. We write the roots of the characteristic equation as
$$L = \eta_1 \geqslant 1 \quad \text{and} \quad L = \eta_2 < 1.$$

Hence,
$$f(L) = (L - \eta_1)(L - \eta_2)$$
$$= -\eta_1\left(1 - \frac{1}{\eta_1}L\right)(1 - \eta_2 L^{-1}).$$

The solution for s_t is therefore
$$s_t = \eta_1^{-1}s_{t-1} - \frac{1}{\mu\lambda\eta_1}\sum_{i=0}^{\infty}\eta_2^i E_t x_{t+i}, \tag{12.19}$$

which can be written as the forward-looking partial adjustment model
$$\Delta s_t = \left(1 - \frac{1}{\eta_1}\right)(\bar{s}_t - s_{t-1}), \tag{12.20}$$

$$\bar{s}_t = -\frac{1}{\mu\lambda(\eta_1 - 1)}\sum_{i=0}^{\infty}\eta_2^i E_t x_{t+i}, \tag{12.21}$$

where $\bar{s}_t$ is the "target" value for s_t as well as the steady-state solution. The full solution therefore has both a forward-looking and a backward-looking component. Following a permanent shock to x_t, s_t jumps instantaneously onto the saddlepath, equation (12.19), before proceeding in geometrically declining steps to its new equilibrium $\bar{s}_t$.

The steady-state solution of the exchange rate for constant values of the exogenous variables is
$$\bar{s}_t = m_t - \frac{1}{\alpha}g + \frac{1 - \alpha - \gamma}{\alpha}y_t - p_t^* + \left(\lambda + \frac{\beta}{\alpha}\right)R_t^*. \tag{12.22}$$

It follows that a permanent increase in the money supply m_t causes an equal depreciation in the exchange rate, and a fiscal expansion (increase in w_t) causes an appreciation. An increase in R_t^* and a decrease in p_t^* both cause a depreciation.

The solution for p_t is obtained by substituting equation (12.21) into (12.15) to give
$$p_t = \left(\mu - \frac{1}{\eta_1}\right)p_{t-1} - \frac{\mu}{\eta_1}p_{t-2} - \frac{\phi}{\mu\lambda\eta_1}\sum_{i=0}^{\infty}\eta_2^i E_t x_{t+i} + a_t - \frac{1}{\eta_1}a_{t-1}. \tag{12.23}$$

At first sight it may not appear that the Dornbusch model has sticky prices as there are no lags in the model apart from the change in price, and this depends on current, and not lagged, excess demand. Nonetheless, it is clear from the solution, equation (12.23), that the dynamic behavior of the price level is quite complex and involves second-order lags.

12.7.2 Monetary Policy

First we consider the effect on the exchange rate of a temporary unanticipated increase in the money supply in period t in which m_t increases from m_0 to m_1. In period $t + 1$ the money supply is expected to return permanently to m_0. The money supply appears in both a_t and b_t, and hence in x_t. We set all of the other variables in x_t equal to zero. We can therefore write

$$x_t = \left(\frac{\mu\beta\theta}{\lambda} - 1\right)m_t + \mu m_{t-1}$$

$$= \left(\frac{\mu\beta\theta}{\lambda} - 1\right)m_1 + \mu m_0,$$

$$E_t x_{t+1} = \left(\frac{\mu\beta\theta}{\lambda} - 1\right)m_0 + \mu m_1,$$

$$E_t x_{t+i} = \left(\frac{\mu\beta\theta}{\lambda} - 1\right)m_0 + \mu m_0, \quad i > 1.$$

Prior to period t we set $s_{t-i} = m_0$ $(i > 0)$. Substituting for x_t and $E_t x_{t+i}$ in equation (12.19), the exchange rate in period t is

$$s_t = m_0 + \delta m_1.$$

As $\eta_2 < 1$, we have $\delta = ((1 + \alpha\theta - \eta_2)/\lambda\eta_1) > 0$, and so a temporary change in the level of the money supply in period t causes the exchange rate to depreciate.

We now consider a permanent, but still unanticipated, increase in the money supply in period t. We assume that prior to the policy change it was expected that $s_t = m_0$, its previous long-run value. After the change the new long-run value of the exchange rate is $s = m_1$. We focus on what happens to the exchange rate in period t. In this case,

$$x_t = \left(\frac{\mu\beta\theta}{\lambda} - 1\right)m_1 + \mu m_0,$$

$$E_t x_{t+i} = \left(\frac{\mu\beta\theta}{\lambda} - 1\right)m_1 + \mu m_1, \quad i > 0,$$

$$s_t = \frac{1}{\eta_1}m_0 - \frac{1}{\mu\lambda\eta_1}\left\{\left(\frac{\mu\beta\theta}{\lambda} - 1\right)m_1 + \mu m_0 \right.$$

$$\left. + \sum_{i=1}^{\infty} \eta_2^i\left[\left(\frac{\mu\beta\theta}{\lambda} - 1\right)m_1 + \mu m_1\right]\right\}$$

$$= m_1 + \varphi(m_1 - m_0),$$

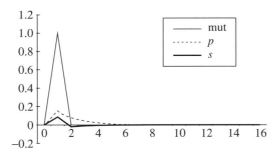

Figure 12.11. An unanticipated temporary money-supply shock.

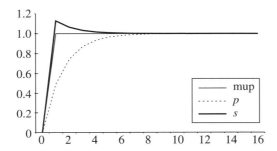

Figure 12.12. An unanticipated permanent money-supply shock.

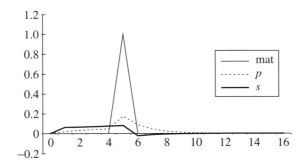

Figure 12.13. An anticipated temporary money-supply shock.

where $\varphi = ((\lambda - 1)/\lambda\eta_1) > 0$ if $\lambda > 1$. Thus, if $\lambda > 1$, in period t the exchange rate overshoots its long-run value of m_1. This is the discrete-time equivalent of the well-known overshooting property of the Dornbusch model. After period t the exchange rate smoothly approaches its new long-run value m_1 in geometrically declining steps.

To illustrate the effect of monetary policy on the exchange rate and on the price level we use numerical simulation. We analyze unanticipated temporary and permanent increases in the money supply, and anticipated temporary and permanent increases in the money supply that we assume occur in period $t + 5$. The outcomes for the exchange rate and the price level are, together with the money supply, shown in figures 12.11–12.14. The notation used in

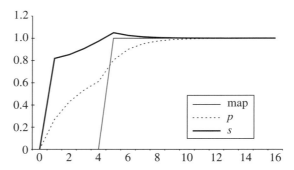

Figure 12.14. An anticipated permanent money-supply shock.

figures 12.11–12.22 is that "m" denotes a money shock and "g" a fiscal shock, "u" denotes unanticipated and "a" anticipated, "t" denotes temporary and "p" permanent. Thus "mut" is a money shock that is unanticipated and temporary.

The money-supply increases cause the exchange rate to depreciate and the price level to increase. The price level adjusts more slowly than the exchange rate. For a permanent shock the exchange rate overshoots its new long-run value, but the price level, being slower to respond, does not. Both the exchange rate and the price level respond instantly to an anticipated future change in the money supply.

12.7.3   Fiscal Policy

This causes a shift in the aggregate demand function and is captured by a change in g. An increase in world demand may be represented by a change in p_t^*. As both variables enter through a_t, when all other variables are constant, we may consider the effect of a change in $x_t = a_t$. If there is a temporary increase in a_t in period t from a_0 to a_1, then, in period t,

$$s_t = a_0 - \frac{1}{\mu\lambda\eta_1}(a_1 - a_0).$$

Hence, there is a temporary appreciation of the exchange rate. After period t the exchange rate slowly returns to a_0 over time.

If the change in a_t is permanent, then $s_t = a_1$, i.e., the exchange rate jumps in period t to its new long-run value. Figures 12.15–12.18 depict simulations of the effect on the exchange rate and price level of temporary and permanent, unanticipated and anticipated positive fiscal shocks.

Following a positive fiscal shock the exchange rate appreciates and the price level increases. The response of the exchange rate is much stronger and faster than that of the price level.

12.7.4   Comparison of the Dornbusch and Monetary Models

The monetary model may be obtained from the Dornbusch model by imposing (i) instantaneous price-level adjustment, which implies that $\theta \to \infty$, and hence

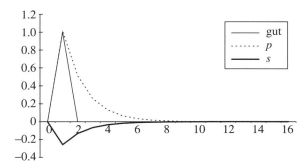

Figure 12.15. An unanticipated temporary fiscal shock.

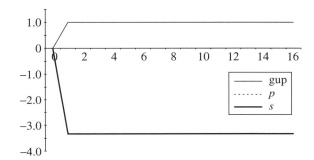

Figure 12.16. An unanticipated permanent fiscal shock.

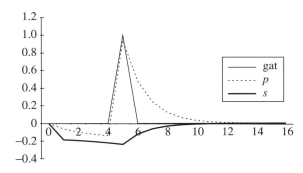

Figure 12.17. An anticipated temporary fiscal shock.

$d_t = y_t$; and (ii) perfect substitutability between domestic and foreign goods, which implies that $\alpha \to \infty$, and reduces the aggregate demand equation to PPP.

It then follows that $\mu \to 0$, $\phi \to 1$, and hence $\eta_1 \to \infty$ and $\eta_2 \to (\lambda/(1+\lambda))$. As a result, the exchange rate in the Dornbusch model would be determined by

$$s_t = -\frac{1}{1+\lambda} \sum_{i=0}^{\infty} \left(\frac{\lambda}{1+\lambda}\right)^i E_t x_{t+i}.$$

Following a permanent change in x_t the exchange rate would now jump instantly to its new long-run equilibrium.

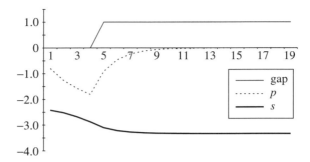

Figure 12.18. An anticipated permanent fiscal shock.

In the monetary model x_t is defined differently. As $\mu = 0$, it is

$$x_t = -\lambda b_t = y_t - m_t - \lambda R_t^* + u_t.$$

Hence, in the absence of a_t, neither fiscal policy nor foreign demand have any explicit effect in the monetary model.

If in the Dornbusch model only $\theta \to \infty$ and not α, so that demand is exogenous, then $\mu \to 0$ but $\phi \to 1 + (\beta/\alpha\lambda)$. As a result, in equation (12.18) we would have

$$f(L) = \lambda - \left(1 + \lambda + \frac{\beta}{\alpha\lambda}\right)L.$$

The single root is $L = 1/(1 + (1/\lambda) + (\beta/\alpha\lambda)) = \eta < 1$, which is unstable. The solution for the exchange rate then becomes

$$s_t = -\frac{1}{1 + (1/\lambda) + (\beta/\alpha\lambda)} \sum_{i=0}^{\infty} \eta^i E_t x_{t+i}.$$

This solution differs only slightly from that of the monetary model, the difference being due to the different parameters.

12.8 The Monetary Model with Sticky Prices

We have seen that the Dornbusch model introduces price stickiness as a result of assuming imperfect substitutability between domestic and foreign goods and an excess-demand price equation. An alternative to the Dornbusch model, which makes the model closer to those considered in earlier chapters, is to introduce price stickiness into the monetary model. This may be achieved by assuming that PPP holds only in the long run and that in the short run prices are determined by an inflation equation like those derived in chapter 9, which are based on the assumption of imperfect price flexibility. We denote the optimal long-run price level for the domestic economy as $p_t^{\#}$, which, due to long-run PPP, satisfies

$$p_t^{\#} = s_t + p_t^*,$$

where p_t^* is the foreign price level. We then replace the optimal price in our earlier inflation equation by $p_t^\#$. The inflation equation for the domestic economy may then be written as

$$\Delta p_t = \alpha(p_t^\# - p_{t-1}) + \beta E_t \Delta p_{t+1}$$
$$= (1 - \alpha - \beta)\pi + \alpha(s_t + p_t^* - p_{t-1}) + \beta E_t \Delta p_{t+1},$$

where π is the long-run rate of inflation in the domestic economy.

Assuming a small open economy, the other equations are the money-demand function and the UIP condition:

$$m_t = p_t + y_t - \lambda R_t,$$
$$R_t = R_t^* + E_t \Delta s_{t+1}.$$

If we eliminate R_t from the money-demand and UIP conditions we obtain

$$p_t + y_t - m_t = \lambda(R_t^* + E_t \Delta s_{t+1}).$$

This gives two dynamic equations in two variables, p_t and s_t; m_t, y_t, and R_t^* are exogenous variables. Rewriting the price equation, the model becomes

$$-\beta E_t p_{t+1} + (1 + \beta)p_t - (1 - \alpha)p_{t-1} - \alpha s_t = (1 - \alpha - \beta)\pi + \alpha p_t^*,$$
$$p_t - \lambda E_t s_{t+1} + \lambda s_t = m_t - y_t + \lambda R_t^*.$$

The long-run solution is the same as for a small-economy version of the monetary model in which R_t^* is treated as an exogenous variable. Hence, the long-run solutions for the price level and the exchange rate are

$$p = s + p^*, \qquad s = y - m + p^* - \lambda(R^* + \pi^* - \pi),$$

where π^* is the foreign long-run rate of inflation.

The short-run solutions may be obtained by using the lag operator and eliminating p_t to give the reduced form of s_t:

$$h(L)s_t = x_t,$$

where

$$x_t = a_t + g(L)b_t,$$
$$a_t = (1 - \alpha - \beta)\pi + \alpha p_t^*,$$
$$b_t = m_t - y_t + \lambda R_t^*,$$
$$h(L) = (1 - \alpha)\lambda L - [\alpha + \lambda(2 - \alpha + \beta)] + \lambda(1 + 2\beta)L^{-1} - \beta\lambda L^{-2}$$
$$= (1 - \alpha)\lambda f(L)L^{-2},$$
$$f(L) = (L - \eta_1)(L - \eta_2)(L - \eta_3),$$
$$g(L) = (1 - \alpha)L - (1 + \beta) + \beta L^{-1},$$

and $\{\eta_i; \ i = 1, 2, 3\}$ are the roots of the characteristic equation $f(L) = 0$. As $f(1) = -(\alpha/((1-\alpha)\lambda)) < 0$, either all three roots must be stable, or only one of

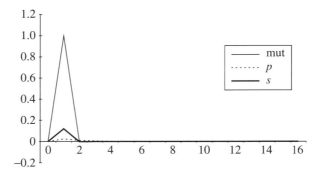

Figure 12.19. An unanticipated temporary money-supply shock.

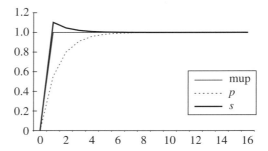

Figure 12.20. An unanticipated permanent money-supply shock.

them is. For all three roots to be stable, and hence greater than unity—assuming they are all positive—we require that their product is greater than unity, but this is $\eta_1\eta_2\eta_3 = \beta/(1 - \alpha)$, which is positive but not necessarily greater than unity. We therefore assume that only one root is stable and two are unstable, i.e., $\eta_1 \geqslant 1$ and $\eta_2, \eta_3 < 1$. The solution for s_t may then be written as

$$s_t = \frac{1}{\eta_1}s_{t-1} - \frac{1}{(1 - \alpha)(\eta_2 - \eta_3)}\left[\eta_2 \sum_{i=0}^{\infty} \eta_2^i E_t x_{t+i} - \eta_3 \sum_{i=0}^{\infty} \eta_3^i E_t x_{t+i}\right].$$

Figures 12.19–12.22 depict simulations of the effect on the exchange rate and price level of temporary and permanent, unanticipated and anticipated increases in the money supply.

These results are very similar to those for the Dornbusch model. Once again the exchange rate overshoots following a permanent unanticipated increase in the money supply, but does not do so for an anticipated permanent increase.

12.9 The Obstfeld–Rogoff Redux Model

The exchange rate models discussed so far have two major limitations: they are all ad hoc without explicit microfoundations; and, in order to make their analysis tractable analytically, they impose restrictions on change in either output or

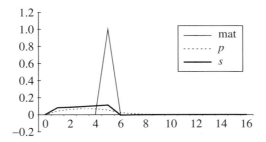

Figure 12.21. An anticipated temporary money-supply shock.

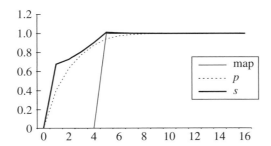

Figure 12.22. An anticipated permanent money-supply shock.

prices. The Obstfeld–Rogoff redux model (1995) is one of the first attempts to provide a model of the exchange rate that is both based on explicit microfoundations and allows output and prices to be flexible. (Redux means revived or brought back; presumably indicating, in this case, that exchange-rate dynamics have been brought back into the DGE framework.) Despite their obvious drawbacks, the previous models help our understanding of the much more complex redux model. The basic redux model is a two-country model with monopolistic competition in goods markets and flexible prices. We consider two variants: one with sticky prices, the other a small-country version. Although we follow closely the analysis of Obstfeld and Rogoff, we keep in mind the need to relate the model to the general framework used in previous chapters. This entails certain unimportant differences from their model.

12.9.1 The Basic Redux Model with Flexible Prices

12.9.1.1 *Preferences, Technology, and Market Structure*

We assume that the world consists of two countries. In this two-country world there is a continuum of individual producer-households each identified by an index $z \in [0, 1]$, and each the sole world producer of a single differentiated good z. The home country consists of producers who are differentiated from each other by their label, which takes a value on the interval $[0, n]$ and the foreign country which consists of the remaining $(n, 1]$ producers. Domestic household consumption is given by $c_t(z)$, foreign household consumption is

$c_t^*(z)$, $p_t(z)$ is the price of good z in terms of domestic currency, and $p_t^*(z)$ is its price in terms of foreign currency. An unusual, but clever, feature of the redux model is the way that the supply side is formulated. Output of good z, which is given by $y_t(z)$, is produced by households who only use labor in production. Instead of specifying a production function explicitly, production is assumed to be negatively related to leisure and capital is implicitly assumed to be fixed, and so is omitted entirely. As a result, neither work nor leisure is included explicitly.

It is assumed that domestic and foreign households have identical preferences and differ only in the good they produce. For a domestic household producing good z but consuming all goods this is given by

$$\mathcal{U}_t = \sum_{j=0}^{\infty} \beta^j \left[\ln c_{t+j} + \frac{\phi}{1-\epsilon} \left(\frac{M_{t+j}}{P_{t+j}} \right)^{1-\epsilon} - \tfrac{1}{2} \gamma y_t(z)^2 \right], \tag{12.24}$$

where $\epsilon > 0$ and c_t is an index of total consumption given by the CES function

$$c_t = \left[\int_0^1 c_t(z)^{(\sigma-1)/\sigma} \right]^{\sigma/(\sigma-1)}, \quad \sigma > 1. \tag{12.25}$$

M_t is the stock of money held by each domestic household and P_t is a general price index given by

$$P_t = \left[\int_0^1 p_t(z)^{1-\sigma} \right]^{1/(1-\sigma)}. \tag{12.26}$$

The last term in the utility function reflects utility from leisure, which is inversely related to the work required to produce good z by a household and is assumed to be proportional to $y_t^s(z)$, the quantity produced. This setup is similar to our discussion of open-economy models in chapter 7, but is based on continuous, instead of discrete, aggregator functions.

Every good is tradeable and is priced in domestic currency. It is also assumed to satisfy the "law of one price" so that there is a single world price,

$$p_t(z) = S_t p_t^*(z),$$

where S_t is the exchange rate (the domestic price of foreign currency). Hence

$$P_t = \left[\int_0^n p_t(z)^{1-\sigma} + \int_0^n S_t p_t^*(z)^{1-\sigma} \right]^{1/(1-\sigma)} \tag{12.27}$$

and

$$P_t = S_t P_t^*,$$

where P_t^* is the foreign general price level. Thus PPP holds for consumer price indices, but only because both countries consume identical commodity baskets.

The budget constraints for domestic and foreign households are

$$B_{t+1} + M_{t+1} + P_t c_t + P_t T_t = p_t(z) y_t(z) + (1 + R_t) B_t + M_t, \tag{12.28}$$

$$B_{t+1}^* + M_{t+1}^* + P_t^* c_t^* + P_t^* T_t^* = p_t^*(z) y_t^*(z) + (1 + R_t^*) B_t^* + M_t^*, \tag{12.29}$$

where B_t is the nominal stock of privately issued bonds in terms of domestic currency, T_t is real taxes paid to the domestic government (or real transfers if $T_t < 0$), and R_t is the nominal interest rate. An asterisk denotes the foreign equivalent. Because there are two countries, bonds are privately issued, and as $P_t = S_t P_t^*$, there is a zero net-supply bond constraint given by

$$nB_t + (1 - n)B_t^* = 0.$$

The domestic and foreign government budget constraints are

$$P_t g_t = P_t T_t + \Delta M_{t+1}, \qquad (12.30)$$
$$P_t^* g_t^* = P_t^* T_t^* + \Delta M_{t+1}^*, \qquad (12.31)$$

where

$$g_t = \left[\int_0^1 g_t(z)^{(\sigma-1)/\sigma} \right]^{\sigma/(\sigma-1)}$$

and $g_t(z)$ is household consumption of the government-provided good z. Government expenditures do not generate household utility. The government budget constraints assume that government expenditures are financed by lump-sum taxes and seigniorage.

Given the CES total consumption index, equation (12.25), and the utility function, it follows from the results in chapter 7 that the domestic household demand for good z is

$$c_t(z) = \left[\frac{p_t(z)}{P_t} \right]^{-\sigma} c_t,$$

and the general price index is determined by equation (12.26). For convenience, government provision of good z is assumed to have the same form. Total world private demand c_t^W is obtained by summing over all households, the n domestic households and the $1 - n$ foreign households, with the result that

$$c_t^W = nc_t + (1 - n)c_t^*. \qquad (12.32)$$

Similarly, total world government demand g_t^W is

$$g_t^W = ng_t + (1 - n)g_t^*.$$

The total world demand for good z is the sum of private household demand and government consumption, i.e., it is

$$y_t(z) = \left[\frac{p_t(z)}{P_t} \right]^{-\sigma} (c_t^W + g_t^W). \qquad (12.33)$$

Due to producer monopoly power, the demand function slopes downward. We note that although PPP holds for consumer price indices due to identical consumer preferences, it does not hold for national output deflators unless $n = \frac{1}{2}$. This is because production in the two countries is different.

Finally, we assume that UIP holds and so

$$1 + R_t = \frac{S_{t+1}}{S_t}(1 + R_t^*).$$

It follows that r_t, the real interest rate, satisfies

$$1 + r_t = \frac{P_t}{P_{t+1}}(1 + R_t)$$

$$= \frac{P_t}{P_{t+1}}\frac{S_{t+1}}{S_t}(1 + R_t^*)$$

$$= \frac{P_t^*}{P_{t+1}^*}(1 + R_t^*)$$

$$= 1 + r_t^*,$$

and hence there is real interest parity.

12.9.1.2 Individual Maximization

The problem for each household is to maximize intertemporal utility, equation (12.24), with respect to $\{c_{t+j}, y_{t+j}(z), B_{t+j}, M_{t+j}, y_{t+j}(z)\}$ subject to the household and government budget constraints, equations (12.28) and (12.30), and aggregate demand, equation (12.33), while taking total world demand, $c_t^W + g_t^W$, as given. Foreign households face a corresponding problem.

The domestic budget constraint can be simplified by eliminating $p(z)$ and $p^*(z)$ to give

$$B_{t+1} + M_{t+1} + P_t c_t + P_t T_t = P_t y_t(z)^{(\sigma-1)/\sigma}(c_t^W + g_t^W)^{1/\sigma} + (1 + R_t)B_t + M_t. \quad (12.34)$$

The Lagrangian for the domestic resident can now be written as

$$\mathcal{L} = \sum_{j=0}^{\infty} \beta^j \left[\ln c_{t+j} + \frac{\phi}{1-\epsilon}\left(\frac{M_{t+j}}{P_{t+j}}\right)^{1-\epsilon} - \tfrac{1}{2}\gamma y_{t+j}(z)^2 \right]$$

$$+ \lambda_{t+j}[P_{t+j} y_{t+j}(z)^{(\sigma-1)/\sigma}(c_{t+j}^W + g_{t+j}^W)^{1/\sigma} + (1 + R_{t+j})B_{t+j}$$

$$- B_{t+j+1} - \Delta M_{t+j+1} - P_{t+j}c_{t+j} - P_{t+j}T_{t+j}].$$

The first-order conditions are

$$\frac{\partial \mathcal{L}}{\partial c_{t+j}} = \beta^j \frac{1}{c_{t+j}} - \lambda_{t+j}P_{t+j} = 0, \qquad\qquad\qquad\qquad j \geqslant 0,$$

$$\frac{\partial \mathcal{L}}{\partial y_{t+j}(z)} = -\beta^j \gamma y_{t+j}(z)$$

$$- \lambda_{t+j}\frac{\sigma-1}{\sigma}P_{t+j}y_{t+j}(z)^{-1/\sigma}(c_{t+j}^W + g_{t+j}^W)^{1/\sigma} = 0, \quad j \geqslant 0,$$

$$\frac{\partial \mathcal{L}}{\partial M_{t+j}} = \beta^j \phi \frac{M_{t+j}^{-\epsilon}}{P_{t+j}^{1-\epsilon}} + \lambda_{t+j} - \lambda_{t+j-1} = 0, \qquad\qquad j > 0,$$

$$\frac{\partial \mathcal{L}}{\partial B_{t+j}} = \lambda_{t+j}(1 + R_{t+j}) - \lambda_{t+j-1} = 0, \qquad\qquad\qquad j > 0.$$

It follows that

$$\frac{\beta c_t (1 + r_{t+1})}{c_{t+1}} = 1,$$

$$\frac{M_{t+1}}{P_{t+1}} = \left[\phi \frac{c_{t+1}}{R_{t+1}} \right]^{1/\epsilon},$$

$$y_t(z)^{(\sigma+1)/\sigma} = \frac{\sigma - 1}{\sigma y} c_t^{-1} (c_t^W + g_t^W)^{1/\sigma}.$$

Similarly, for the foreign country,

$$\frac{\beta c_t^* (1 + r_{t+1})}{c_{t+1}^*} = 1,$$

$$\frac{M_{t+1}^*}{P_{t+1}^*} = \left[\phi \frac{c_{t+1}^*}{R_{t+1}^*} \right]^{1/\epsilon},$$

$$y_t^*(z)^{(\sigma+1)/\sigma} = \frac{\sigma - 1}{\sigma y} c_t^{*-1} (c_t^W + g_t^W)^{1/\sigma}.$$

The consumption Euler equations are familiar, as are the money-demand functions. The output equations reflect the fact that the marginal utility of one extra unit of output equals the marginal disutility of the loss of leisure required to produce it. If goods were perfect substitutes, and hence $\sigma \to \infty$, the home output equation would become

$$\lim_{\sigma \to \infty} y_t(z) = \frac{1}{y c_t} > y_t(z).$$

This exhibits only the supply-side consumption–leisure trade-off and not the effect of world demand on output. It also reveals that, due to monopoly distortions, output is lower than the social optimum.

Consumption is derived from the household and government budget constraints as

$$c_t = (1 + R_t) \frac{B_t}{P_t} - (1 + \pi_{t+1}) \frac{B_{t+1}}{P_{t+1}} + \frac{p_t(z) y_t(z)}{P_t} - g_t, \tag{12.35}$$

$$c_t^* = (1 + R_t^*) \frac{B_t^*}{P_t^*} - (1 + \pi_{t+1}^*) \frac{B_{t+1}^*}{P_{t+1}^*} + \frac{p_t^*(z) y_t^*(z)}{P_t^*} - g_t^*, \tag{12.36}$$

where $1 + \pi_{t+1} = P_{t+1}/P_t$ and $1 + \pi_{t+1}^* = P_{t+1}^*/P_t^*$.

12.9.1.3   The Baseline Long-Run Model

In static equilibrium, consumption, real bonds, and the stock of real money are constant. Consequently, from the Euler equation, the common real rate of return is

$$r = r^* = \theta,$$

where $\beta = 1/(1 + \theta)$. Using the condition that the net supply of bonds is zero to eliminate $B^* = -(n/(1 - n))B$, steady-state consumption in the two countries is

$$c = r\frac{B}{P} + \frac{p(z)y(z)}{P} - g, \qquad (12.37)$$

$$c = -r\frac{nB}{(1-n)P*} + \frac{p*(z)y*(z)}{P*} - g*. \qquad (12.38)$$

In the special case that forms our baseline model, which is to be used below for the purposes of comparison, we impose the restriction that there is neither debt nor government expenditures so that $B = B* = g = g* = 0$. Equations (12.37) and (12.38) then reduce to

$$c_t = \frac{p(z)y(z)}{P},$$

$$c_t* = \frac{p*(z)y*(z)}{P*},$$

and the output equations become

$$y(z)^{(\sigma+1)/\sigma} = \frac{\sigma-1}{\sigma y}c^{-1}[nc + (1-n)c*]^{1/\sigma},$$

$$y*(z)^{(\sigma+1)/\sigma} = \frac{\sigma-1}{\sigma y}c*^{-1}[nc + (1-n)c*]^{1/\sigma}.$$

Further, the balance of payments consists solely of trade, and as this must be in balance, consumption equals income, i.e., $c = y(z)$ and $c* = y*(z)$. It follows that

$$y(z)^{(2\sigma+1)/\sigma} = \frac{\sigma-1}{\sigma y}[ny(z) + (1-n)y*(z)]^{1/\sigma},$$

$$y*(z)^{(2\sigma+1)/\sigma} = \frac{\sigma-1}{\sigma y}[ny(z) + (1-n)y*(z)]^{1/\sigma},$$

from which it can be shown that

$$y(z) = y*(z) = c = c* = c^W = \left[\frac{\sigma-1}{\sigma y}\right]^{1/2}.$$

Hence

$$\frac{M}{P} = \frac{M*}{P*} = \left[\frac{\phi y(z)}{1-\beta}\right]^{1/\epsilon}.$$

Moreover, it also follows that $p(z) = P$ and $p*(z) = P*$ which, given PPP, implies that $p(z) = Sp*(z)$; in other words, the law of one price holds. PPP also implies that

$$S = \frac{M}{M*},$$

i.e., the exchange rate depends on the relative money supplies. Thus the baseline model has different predictions about the long-run determinants of the exchange rate from previous models. For example, in the monetary model relative outputs also affect the exchange rate.

12.9.2 Log-Linear Approximation

A convenient way of analyzing the redux model in more detail is to employ a log-linear approximation about the long-run solution to the baseline model (see also Obstfeld and Rogoff 1996). We denote proportionate deviations from the baseline solution by $x_t^\# = \ln(x_t/x)$, where x is the baseline solution.

Log-linearizing the model gives

- PPP,

$$S_t^\# = P_t^\# - P_t^{*\#};$$

- domestic and foreign general price levels, equation (12.27),

$$P_t^\# = np_t^\#(z) + (1-n)[S_t^\# + p_t^{*\#}],$$
$$P_t^{*\#} = n[p_t^{*\#}(z) - S_t^\#] + (1-n)p_t^{*\#};$$

- world demand functions (12.33), where $\varphi = g^W/c^W$,

$$y_t^\#(z) = \sigma[P_t^\# - p_t^\#(z)] + c_t^{W\#} + \varphi g_t^{W\#},$$
$$y_t^{*\#}(z) = \sigma[P_t^{*\#} - p_t^{*\#}(z)] + c_t^{W\#} + \varphi g_t^{W\#};$$

- output (labor supply),

$$(1+\sigma)y_t^\#(z) = -\sigma c_t^\# + c_t^{W\#} + \varphi g_t^{W\#},$$
$$(1+\sigma)y_t^{*\#}(z) = -\sigma c_t^{*\#} + c_t^{W\#} + \varphi g_t^{W\#};$$

- consumption,

$$c_{t+1}^\# = c_t^\# + (1-\beta)r_t^\#,$$
$$c_{t+1}^{*\#} = c_t^{*\#} + (1-\beta)r_t^\#;$$

and

- money demand,

$$m_t^\# - p_t^\# = \frac{1}{\epsilon}\left[c_t^\# - \beta\left(r_t^\# + \frac{P_{t+1}^\# - P_t^\#}{1-\beta}\right)\right],$$
$$m_t^{*\#} - p_t^{*\#} = \frac{1}{\epsilon}\left[c_t^{*\#} - \beta\left(r_t^\# + \frac{P_{t+1}^{*\#} - P_t^{*\#}}{1-\beta}\right)\right].$$

Finally, we form a consolidated world budget constraint which we log-linearize. Population-weighting the country budget constraints and using equations (12.34) and (12.32) gives the world equilibrium condition:

$$c_t^W = n\frac{p_t(z)y_t(z)}{P_t} + (1-n)\frac{p_t^*(z)y_t^*(z)}{P_t^*} - \varphi g_t^W.$$

Log-linearizing gives

$$\begin{aligned}
c_t^{W\#} &= nc_t^\# + (1-n)c_t^{*\#} \\
&= n[p_t^\#(z) + y_t^\# - P_t^\#] + (1-n)[p_t^{*\#}(z) + y_t^{*\#} - P_t^{*\#}] - \varphi g_t^W.
\end{aligned}$$

12.9.2.1   The Long-Run Solution

First, we form the long-run consolidated budget constraint by population-weighting the log-linearized budget constraints, equations (12.35) and (12.36), where we assume that $b_t = B_t/P_t$, $b_t^* = B_t^*/P_t^*$, $B = B^* = 0$, $\pi = 0$, and $\psi = R(b/c^W)$. This gives

$$c^\# = \psi b^\# + p^\#(z) + y^\#(z) - P^\# - \varphi g^\#,$$
$$c^{*\#} = \psi b^{*\#} + p^{*\#}(z) + y^{*\#}(z) - P^{*\#} - \varphi g^{*\#}.$$

We can now derive the long-run solution in terms of deviations from the baseline solution. This is

$$c^\# = \frac{1}{2\sigma}[(1+\sigma)\psi b^\# - (1-n+\sigma)\varphi g^\# + (1-n)\varphi g^{*\#}],$$

$$c^{*\#} = \frac{1}{2\sigma}\left[-\frac{n(1+\sigma)\psi}{1-n}b^\# + n\varphi g^\# - (n+\sigma)\varphi g^{*\#}\right],$$

$$c^{W\#} = -\tfrac{1}{2}\varphi g^{W\#},$$

$$y^\#(z) = \frac{1}{1+\sigma}(\tfrac{1}{2}\varphi g^{W\#} - \sigma c^\#),$$

$$y^{*\#}(z) = \frac{1}{1+\sigma}(\tfrac{1}{2}\varphi g^{W\#} - \sigma c^{*\#}),$$

$$p^\#(z) - P^\# = -\frac{1}{2\sigma}[(1-n)\varphi(g^\# - g^{*\#}) - \psi b^\#],$$

$$p^{*\#}(z) - P^{*\#} = \frac{n}{2(1-n)\sigma}[(1-n)\varphi(g^\# - g^{*\#}) - \psi b^\#].$$

Further,

$$p^\#(z) - [S^\# + p^{*\#}(z)] = -\frac{1}{\sigma}(y^\# - y^{*\#})$$

$$= \frac{1}{1+\sigma}(c^\# - c^{*\#}),$$

$$P^\# = M^\# - \frac{1}{\epsilon}c^\#,$$

$$P^{*\#} = M^{*\#} - \frac{1}{\epsilon}c^{*\#},$$

$$S^\# = M^\# - M^{*\#} - \frac{1}{\epsilon}(c^\# - c^{*\#}).$$

The last equation shows that in the long run the exchange rate depends on relative money supplies and consumption. This is similar to the monetary model, and differs only because consumption replaces output.

Monetary policy has no effect in the long run on consumption or output, but prices change in equal proportion. A domestic fiscal expansion cuts private domestic consumption but raises foreign consumption. The net effect is to reduce world consumption. World output is unaffected.

12.9.2.2 Short-Run Dynamics

If prices are perfectly flexible, as has been implicitly assumed so far, then the world economy is always in its steady state. If, however, it is assumed that prices are sticky in the short-run due to monopoly power, then it is more profitable to meet an unexpected demand increase by raising output.

Following an unexpected permanent domestic monetary expansion, the domestic interest rate decreases and, despite sticky prices, UIP causes the exchange rate to depreciate to its new long-run value, and not to overshoot this value. This causes the relative price of foreign goods to increase, which generates a temporary increase in the demand for domestic goods, and hence in domestic output. Due to consumption smoothing, domestic residents save part of the increase in income causing a current-account surplus and an increase in foreign asset holding. In the long run there is a shift from work to leisure, which causes a return of output and consumption to their original levels.

12.9.3 The Small-Economy Version of the Redux Model with Sticky Prices

Like the monetary model, the redux model assumes two identical economies. A small-economy version of the redux model with sticky prices akin to the Mundell–Fleming and Dornbusch models has been proposed by Obstfeld and Rogoff. The prices of nontraded goods are assumed to be sticky and those of traded goods are assumed to be flexible. The economy has a nontraded-consumption-goods sector that is monopolistically competitive with preset nominal prices. But there is a single homogeneous perfectly competitive tradable good that sells for the same flexible price in all countries. In each period the representative domestic resident is endowed with a constant quantity y^T of the traded good, and has monopoly power over the production of one of the nontraded goods $y_t^N(z)$, $z \in [0, 1]$.

The utility function of the representative producer is

$$
\mathcal{L} = \sum_{j=0}^{\infty} \beta^j \left[\rho \ln c_{t+j}^T + (1 - \rho) \ln c_{t+j}^N + \frac{\phi}{1 - \epsilon} \left(\frac{M_{t+j}}{P_{t+j}} \right)^{1-\epsilon} - \frac{\gamma}{2} y_{t+j}^N(z)^2 \right],
$$

where now $\beta = 1/(1 + r)$, c_t^T is consumption of the traded good, and c_t^N is an index of consumption of the nontraded good, which is given by

$$
c_t^N = \left[\int_0^1 c_t^N(z)^{(\sigma-1)/\sigma} \right]^{\sigma/(\sigma-1)}, \qquad \sigma > 1. \tag{12.39}
$$

The general price index P_t is

$$
P_t = \frac{(P_t^T)^\rho (P_t^N)^{1-\rho}}{\rho^\rho (1 - \rho)^{1-\rho}}, \tag{12.40}
$$

with $P_t^T = S_t P_t^{T*}$ and

$$
P_t^N = \left[\int_0^1 p_t^N(z)^{1-\sigma} \right]^{1/(1-\sigma)},
$$

where $p_t^N(z)$ is the price of the nontraded good. The demand for the nontraded good is

$$y_t^N(z) = \left[\frac{p_t^N(z)}{P_t^N}\right]^{-\sigma} c_t^{NA}, \tag{12.41}$$

where c_t^{NA} is the aggregate domestic consumption of nontraded goods, which is taken as given, and it is assumed that there are no government expenditures.

The budget constraint is written as

$$P_t^T b_{t+1} + M_{t+1} + P_t^T c_t^T + P_t^N c_t^N + P_t^T T_t = P_t^T y^T + p_t^N(z) y_t^N(z) + (1+r) P_t^T b_t + M_t,$$

where real variables, including the real interest rate r, are denominated in terms of the price of tradeables, and b_t is the real stock of privately issued bonds. As there are no government expenditures, the government budget constraint is

$$0 = P_t^T T_t + \Delta M_{t+1}.$$

The Lagrangian is

$$\mathcal{L} = \sum_{j=0}^{\infty} \beta^j [\rho \ln c_{t+j}^T + (1-\rho) \ln c_{t+j}^N + \frac{\phi}{1-\epsilon} \left(\frac{M_{t+j}}{P_{t+j}}\right)^{1-\epsilon} - \tfrac{1}{2} \gamma y_{t+j}^N(z)^2]$$

$$+ \lambda_{t+j}[P_{t+j}^T y^T + p_{t+j}^N y_{t+j}^N(z)^{(\sigma-1)/\sigma} (c_{t+j}^{NA})^{1/\sigma} + (1+r) P_{t+j}^T b_{t+j}$$

$$+ M_{t+j} - P_{t+j+1}^T b_{t+j+1} - M_{t+j+1} - P_{t+j}^T c_{t+j}^T - P_{t+j}^N c_{t+j}^N - P_{t+j}^T T_{t+j}].$$

The first-order conditions are

$$\frac{\partial \mathcal{L}}{\partial c_{t+j}^T} = \beta^j \frac{\rho}{c_{t+j}^T} - \lambda_{t+j} P_{t+j}^T = 0, \qquad\qquad j \geqslant 0,$$

$$\frac{\partial \mathcal{L}}{\partial c_{t+j}^N} = \beta^j \frac{1-\rho}{c_{t+j}^N} - \lambda_{t+j} P_{t+j}^N = 0, \qquad\qquad j \geqslant 0,$$

$$\frac{\partial \mathcal{L}}{\partial y_{t+j}^N(z)} = -\beta^j \gamma y_{t+j}^N(z) - \lambda_{t+j} \frac{\sigma-1}{\sigma} P_{t+j}^N y_{t+j}^N(z)^{-1/\sigma} (c_{t+j}^{NA})^{1/\sigma} = 0, \quad j \geqslant 0,$$

$$\frac{\partial \mathcal{L}}{\partial M_{t+j}} = \beta^j \phi \frac{M_{t+j}^{-\epsilon}}{P_{t+j}^{1-\epsilon}} + \lambda_{t+j} - \lambda_{t+j-1} = 0, \qquad\qquad j > 0,$$

$$\frac{\partial \mathcal{L}}{\partial b_{t+j}} = \lambda_{t+j}(1+r) P_{t+j}^T - \lambda_{t+j-1} P_{t+j-1}^T = 0, \qquad\qquad j > 0.$$

Hence

$$c_{t+1}^T = c_t^T, \tag{12.42}$$

$$c_t^N = \frac{1-\rho}{\rho} \frac{P_t^T}{P_t^N} c_t^T, \tag{12.43}$$

$$\frac{M_{t+1}}{P_{t+1}} = \left[\phi \frac{P_{t+1}^T c_{t+1}^T}{\rho P_{t+1}}\right]^{1/\epsilon} \left[(1+r)\frac{P_{t+1}^T}{P_t^T} - 1\right]^{-1/\epsilon}, \tag{12.44}$$

$$y_t^N(z)^{(\sigma+1)/\sigma} = \frac{\sigma-1}{\sigma\gamma} (c_t^N)^{-1} (c_t^{NA})^{1/\sigma}. \tag{12.45}$$

As the output of traded goods is fixed, $c^T = y^T$ and hence the current account is in permanent balance regardless of shocks to money or nontraded goods productivity. And as $c_t^N = y_t^N(z) = c_t^{NA}$ for all z, from equations (12.43) and (12.45), in the steady state,

$$c^N = y^N(z) = \left[\frac{(\sigma - 1)(1 - \rho)}{\sigma y} \right]^{1/2}$$

$$= \frac{1 - \rho}{\rho} \frac{P^T}{P^N} y^T.$$

Hence, steady-state consumption and output are unaffected by money. From equations (12.40) and (12.45), in the steady state the price level P is proportional to M and

$$P^T = vM(y^T)^{-(1-\rho)},$$

where $v > 0$. It therefore follows that the steady-state exchange rate is

$$S = v \frac{M}{(y^T)^{(1-\rho)} P^{T*}}.$$

Increases in the stock of money therefore cause an equal depreciation in the exchange rate, and increases in traded goods output and foreign tradeables cause the exchange rate to appreciate.

As nontraded goods' prices are assumed to be fixed in the short run but traded goods prices are flexible, taking a log-linear approximation about the steady state gives the short-run money-demand function

$$M_t^\# - P_t^\# = \frac{1}{\epsilon} \left[P_t^{T\#} - P_t^\# - \frac{1}{r} \Delta P_{t+1}^{T\#} \right],$$

and, from equation (12.40), $P_t^\# = \rho P_t^{T\#}$. We then have

$$P_t^{T\#} = \eta(P_{t+1}^T + r\epsilon M_t^\#),$$

where $0 < \eta = [1 + r + r\rho(\epsilon - 1)]^{-1} < 1$ if $\epsilon > 1$. Hence

$$S_t^\# = P_t^{T\#} - P_t^{T*\#}$$

$$= \eta S_{t+1}^\# + \eta r\epsilon M_t^\# + P_t^{T*\#} - \eta P_{t+1}^{T*\#}. \tag{12.46}$$

Equation (12.46) gives the short-run response of the exchange rate to a temporary change in the money supply and in the foreign price of tradeables. We have shown already that a permanent change in the money stock causes an equal increase in the steady-state exchange rate. Equation (12.46) implies a different long-run solution. This is because the price of nontraded goods is assumed to be fixed, whereas in the correct solution derived previously, nontraded goods' prices were flexible. In order to examine the short-run response to a permanent increase in the money supply, we assume that the exchange rate fully adjusts to its new long-run level by period $t + 1$ as a result of changes in nontraded goods' prices, so that $S_{t+1}^\# = M_t^\#$. In period t, therefore,

$$S_t^\# = \frac{1 + r + r(\epsilon - 1)}{1 + r + r\rho(\epsilon - 1)} M_t^\# > M_t^\#.$$

As $\rho < 1$, the exchange rate initially overshoots its new long-run value.

12.10   Conclusions

In this chapter we have examined the determination of the nominal exchange rate. We began by tracing the emergence of floating exchange rates as a response to the failures of previous international monetary systems. We argued that even in a fixed-exchange-rate system like Bretton Woods it may be necessary to adjust the exchange parity in order to restore competitiveness. The main advantage of flexible exchange rates is that competitiveness is automatically maintained. If prices are perfectly flexible, this occurs very quickly because the exchange rate jumps to its new equilibrium level following a shock to the system. As a result, fiscal and monetary shocks are crowded out. But if prices are sticky, then a theoretical prediction common to these models is that adjustment to a permanent monetary shock is slower, and that the exchange rate is excessively volatile in the sense that initially it overshoots its long-run value. A permanent fiscal expansion is quickly crowded out due to the exchange rate appreciating and causing an equivalent fall in net exports.

Modern flexible-exchange-rate models assume no capital controls and perfect capital flexibility. As a result, the nominal exchange rate is determined in these models by current and future expected interest differentials between countries. The interest differential may be determined directly through monetary policy being conducted via interest rates, or indirectly through money-supply targeting. Most of the models we have discussed assume that monetary policy is conducted via money-supply targeting; they differ over what other variables affect the interest differential.

Another common assumption is PPP. Unlike UIP, this assumption is strongly at variance with the empirical evidence as a consequence of price stickiness. This suggests that, at best, PPP should be a long-run property, as in the sticky-price monetary model proposed in this chapter. Alternatively, a distinction should be drawn between the pricing of tradeables through the law of one price (LOOP), and the pricing of nontradeables as in the redux model. Recent research on pricing to market—which was discussed in chapter 9—has also questioned the LOOP (see Betts and Devereux 1996, 2000; Devereux 1997; Devereux and Engel 2003). For a contrary view see Obstfeld and Rogoff (2000), where it is argued that it is the nontraded component in tradeables that causes the apparent failure of the LOOP. Pricing-to-market is equivalent to making the foreign price of exports in the small-economy version of the redux model (i.e., P_{t+1}^{T*}) an exogenous variable, but this does not change the conclusions we have reached.

The first generation of flexible-exchange-rate models such as the Mundell–Fleming, monetary, and Dornbusch models lack the microfoundations of the new generation of DGE models pioneered by the redux model. Nonetheless, they still act as a valuable benchmark against which to compare the predictions of DGE models, and, given the complexity of open-economy DGE models, they have the advantage of being much easier to work with.

A common feature of all of these models is the assumption that output is fixed. Because the exchange rate adjusts so much faster than output or prices, this is a convenient assumption to make. Accordingly, if the aim is to analyze the behavior of the exchange rate in the short term, then the first-generation models may provide a good approximation. The main advantage of DGE models is their superior treatment of capital accumulation, which affects the dynamic behavior of consumption and output. In the short run this is much less of an advantage. This may partly account for the lack of DGE models with both flexible nominal exchange rates and capital accumulation. A drawback of the redux model is the assumption that the money supplies are exogenous. This makes it less suitable for a world of inflation targeting where money supplies are endogenous. For reviews of the "new open-economy macroeconomics," which attempt to synthesize Keynesian nominal rigidities and intertemporal open-economy sticky-price models, see Lane (2001) and Obstfeld (2001).

In conclusion, we draw attention to the fact that we have not considered target-zone models of the exchange rate. This is when the aim is to constrain movements in a flexible exchange rate to lie within a predetermined band. There are several reasons for this omission. First, target-zone models became popular during the ERM period in the late 1970s and the 1980s. With the demise of the ERM, they have generally fallen out of use except for a few countries tied loosely to the U.S. dollar. Second, it was found that exchange rates did not behave in the manner predicted by the target-zone models. Rather than go outside the target zone, exchange rates are predicted to approach the edge of the zone asymptotically; this is known as the "smooth-pasting" property of target-zone models. The implication is that the exchange rate will tend to lie mainly on the edge of the zone. In practice, however, it has been found that exchange rates tend to lie in the middle of the zone. This may perhaps be due, at least in part, to the vulnerability of the exchange rate to speculative attacks when near the edge of the zone. Third, the mathematics of target-zone models is complex and involves different mathematical methods from the rest of our analysis. For a discussion of target-zone models see Krugman (1991) and Flood and Garber (1984, 1991).

13
Monetary Policy

13.1 Introduction

Initially, in our development of the DGE model, we considered an economy without money. As a result, all prices were relative prices (prices relative to the price of consumption). These included the real wage and the real interest rate and later, when we extended the analysis to the open economy, the terms of trade and the real exchange rate. In general, changes in relative prices have real effects, i.e., they affect quantities. Once we included in the model outside money (money supplied by government, usually through their account at the central bank) and inside money (credit provided by the commercial banking system), we had to include nominal prices and, in particular, the general price level, together with nominal wages and nominal interest rates, etc.

We have argued in chapter 8 that in general equilibrium money is super-neutral in the long run, i.e., permanent money shocks affect nominal variables such as the general price level, but not real variables like output and consumption (see Lucas 1976b). Largely as a result of this, monetary policy is commonly assigned to controlling the general price level or, more commonly, inflation.

We have also argued, in chapter 9, that in the short run, when there is price stickiness, money may have real effects. This would allow monetary policy to be used for short-run output stabilization too. A familiar argument, associated with monetarism and Milton Friedman (1968), is that the short-run effect of money on output is much stronger than that of fiscal policy, but the effect only lasts about eighteen months.

This raises the question of whether monetary policy should be assigned solely to controlling inflation or whether it should also be used for short-term output stabilization. A justification often given is the argument that a policy instrument is required for each target variable and the general price level can only be controlled in the long run by monetary policy. This argument is not strictly correct. In order to achieve n (independent) targets, n policy instruments will be needed. This could be achieved by assigning one instrument to each target. It could also be achieved by using n linear combinations of the instruments. In fact, this would be the general solution to the problem of optimal control. The implication is that monetary policy could also be used in the short run for output stabilization. Nonetheless, since the literature on monetary policy tends to focus on the control of inflation, this will also be our main concern.

There is an even more fundamental question than the assignment issue: how to use monetary policy to maximize social welfare. Our earlier discussion of fiscal policy addressed social welfare. In contrast, the implicit welfare function commonly associated with optimal monetary policy involves minimizing deviations of inflation from target over a given time horizon. This is known as strict inflation targeting. The principal variant on this is to minimize a weighted average of inflation and output deviations. This is called flexible inflation targeting. We consider to what extent either strict or flexible inflation targeting is equivalent to maximizing social welfare as previously defined.

Monetary policy can be conducted in different ways and through the use of different policy instruments. The principal methods are controlling the level or the rate of growth of the money supply, controlling interest rates, or controlling the nominal exchange rate, perhaps by maintaining a fixed exchange rate. The choice depends on whether the aim is to control the price level or the rate of inflation. It also depends on the effectiveness of the instrument: its controllability, the strength and predictability of the transmission mechanism, the time horizon, and any (negative) spillover effects on other variables.

Another issue is whether monetary policy is discretionary or rules-based. In a rules-based monetary policy, the monetary authorities are committed to setting the policy instrument using a publicly known policy rule in which the instrument depends on the current—or possibly the past or the expected future—state of the economy. The Taylor rule is a well-known example of an interest rate rule in which the official interest rate depends on the deviations of inflation and the output gap from their targets. Under discretion, the interest rate is simply announced by the monetary authority. Whether or not the monetary authority is using a rule is, in practice, unknown. We consider which is preferable: discretion or commitment to a rule.

The choice of nominal target—whether it is the price level or the rate of inflation—is important. If we express the price-level target as a path along which the price level grows at a constant rate, the implied rate of inflation would be constant. Although price-level and inflation targeting may then appear to be similar, there is an important difference. A temporary shock to inflation is a permanent shock to the price level. Consequently, under inflation targeting a temporary monetary shock may be accommodated (perhaps even ignored) by monetary policy, but under price-level targeting it would be countered by monetary policy. As a result, price-level targeting is more likely to require deflation, and entail a loss of output, than inflation targeting. Ultimately, of course, the choice of a price-level or an inflation target will depend on the objective function of the policy maker. If this takes account of real effects, then inflation targeting is more likely to be preferred to price-level targeting. For most of this chapter we assume that this is the case.

Monetary policy is strongly affected by the choice of exchange-rate regime—whether the exchange rate is fixed or floating. This is why one must take account of open-economy considerations when studying monetary policy. As we have seen in chapter 12, tying the exchange rate to gold, as under the gold standard, or to another currency like the U.S. dollar, as under the Bretton Woods and, implies that in the longer term the domestic rate of inflation is tied to the price of gold or the U.S. rate of inflation, respectively. In other words, they provide a nominal anchor. The aim of monetary policy then becomes that of managing the currency in order to stay in the exchange-rate regime. In principle, this simply requires monetary policy to be passive or accommodating. Unless deliberately sterilized, a balance of payments deficit, for example, would automatically produce a contraction in the supply of money, which would act to restore current-account balance by raising the price level and improving competitiveness. Were this not the case, sooner or later it would be necessary to realign the exchange-rate parity to correct for the ensuing changes in competitiveness due to an over-expansionary, or over-contractionary, monetary policy. Current-account balance could also be accomplished by fiscal as well as monetary policy. It was in these circumstances that Keynesian economics, with its emphasis on fiscal policy, flourished.

We have argued that the main reason for the eventual breakdown of the Bretton Woods system was high U.S. inflation. This caused a deterioration in U.S. competitiveness and brought about the generalized floating of exchange rates, hence the loss of the nominal anchor. As a result, countries now had to reestablish monetary control by formulating their own monetary policy.

It was at this point that monetarism came to be widely adopted as the preferred monetary policy. In the long run, the general price level is closely related to the domestic quantity of money, and the rate of inflation is closely related to the rate of growth of the money supply. Monetarism consists of controlling the rate of growth of the money supply in order to deliver a corresponding rate of inflation in the longer term. With a floating exchange rate a country may choose its own rate of inflation. According to relative PPP, changes in competitiveness due to differences in inflation rates are, in principle, automatically corrected by the flexibility of the exchange rate.

Support for the emphasis on money in formulating monetary policy was provided by a large body of empirical evidence showing that, in the short term, real variables, in particular real GDP, were strongly affected by monetary shocks. Following initial work at the Federal Reserve Bank of St. Louis by Anderson and Jordon (1968), which showed that monetary policy was far more important than fiscal policy, Friedman (1968) formulated monetarism on the basis that money affected output strongly for the first eighteen months but not thereafter. Forty years of subsequent research into the importance of money shocks has served to confirm these original findings (see, for example, Sims 1980; Christiano et al. 1999; Canova and De Nicolo 2002). However, it does not follow, as initially assumed, that just because money shocks are important, monetary policy is best formulated by targeting the money supply, especially in an open economy with a floating exchange rate.

While monetarism was successful in some countries, it was unsuccessful in others. In part, the outcome depended on a country's banking system and how successfully money was controlled. Some countries, like Germany, were highly successful, but others, such as the United Kingdom, failed to achieve the desired rate of growth of the money supply. Another issue was the choice of which measure of money to control. The most successful countries chose a narrow definition of money closely related to the transactions demand for money. In other countries, a broader measure of money was chosen that included interest-bearing deposits, on the grounds that it better represented the liquid resources available at short notice for expenditure. The problem was that, due to the desire to save more in the form of time deposits, a tightening of monetary policy through higher interest rates could lead to an *increase* in the quantity of money held, rather than a decrease. An increase in money may then presage a decrease rather than an increase in expenditures, and hence inflation.

As Germany was one of the more successful countries in pursuing monetarism in Europe, many of its closest trading partners in Europe decided to fix their currencies to the deutsche mark. This provided these countries with a nominal anchor equal to the German rate of inflation. In effect, a new Bretton Woods had been created based on the deutsche mark. This was called the European Exchange Rate Mechanism (ERM).

As discussed in chapter 12, a complicating factor was that the Bretton Woods system operated with controls on the international flow of capital. The breakdown of this system, and the increased reliance on market-determined prices and quantities, was accompanied by the widespread removal of capital controls. The determination of the exchange rate then came to be associated far more with the capital account of the balance of payments than with the current account. This altered the transmission mechanism of monetary policy and its effect on the exchange rate. Consequently, the link between money growth, competitiveness, and the exchange rate was greatly weakened. Instead, interest differentials, brought about by monetary policy, caused large capital movements that dominated the determination of the exchange rate.

If the money supply is exogenous, then, through the money market, interest rates become endogenous. Consequently, the more successful a country is in controlling its money supply, the more money-demand shocks are absorbed by interest rates. And the more volatile interest rates are, the more volatile the exchange rate becomes, with the consequent destabilizing effect on the real economy. This was vividly illustrated in the United States during the period 1979–81 when monetary policy aimed to control the money supply. As a result, interest rates became extremely volatile.

In practice, the key monetary instrument is the official interest rate, usually the rate at which the central bank is willing to lend short term—mainly to commercial banks—by rediscounting bills. Under monetarism, interest rates were set to achieve the money-supply target. The rate of growth of the money supply was, however, only an intermediate target; the final target of policy was the rate of inflation (or perhaps, in the short term, output). Given the difficulty many countries had in hitting the money-supply target, alternative ways of conducting monetary policy were sought, including inflation targeting.

Inflation targeting first became popular in the 1990s. One of its first exponents was New Zealand, a small open economy. Sweden and the United Kingdom, slightly larger open economies, rapidly followed. The aim is to set interest rates to achieve a target rate of inflation. All three countries are very open economies and have a history of large fluctuations in their exchange rates. It is highly desirable that monetary policy in such countries not only provides an effective nominal anchor, but also avoids increasing exchange-rate volatility through large interest rate fluctuations. This suggests that interest rate changes should be smoothed.

If the interest rate is exogenous, then the money supply becomes endogenous and absorbs shocks to money demand. Nonetheless, a difference of opinion about the significance of the money supply under inflation targeting has emerged between the European Central Bank (ECB) on the one hand and other central banks such as the U.S. Federal Reserve, the Bank of England, and the Riksbank of Sweden on the other hand. The ECB appears to be alone among central banks in still giving importance to the rate of growth of the money supply. It treats the money supply as a second "pillar" in its monetary policy, believing that it still signals spending power either because the money supply represents liquid savings or because it reflects credit that has been extended. In a perfect capital market, money is just one among a number of assets that comprise total wealth. And since life-cycle theory relates consumption to total wealth, there seems little reason in a perfect capital market to single out money from other forms of wealth holding. In the United Kingdom, for example, with the deregulation of capital markets, households increasingly raise credit against their collateral in housing.

In this chapter we focus almost exclusively on monetary policy conducted via inflation targeting. The analysis of inflation targeting is usually conducted using a model based on a simplified form of the DGE model that consists of just two equations: a price equation and an output equation. This is often referred to as the New Keynesian model because, like the Keynesian model, the price equation involves a trade-off between inflation and output. The difference is that the trade-off is temporary, not permanent. The standard New Keynesian model assumes a closed economy. We therefore amend the model to make it suitable for an open economy with a flexible exchange rate.

We begin by considering the role of the Fisher equation in determining inflation and use it to examine the question of price-level versus inflation targeting. We then examine the effectiveness of monetary policy in the Keynesian and New Keynesian models for both closed and open economies with floating exchange rates. We compare a policy of discretion with that of commitment to a rule. We then consider how to formulate an optimal monetary policy based on the New Keynesian model. Finally, we examine inflation targeting in the euro area, where there are many countries but a single currency.

13.2 Inflation and the Fisher Equation

The Fisher equation is a key building block in most models of inflation. It may be written as

$$R_t = r_t + E_t \Delta p_{t+1}, \tag{13.1}$$

where R_t is the nominal interest rate, r_t is the real interest rate, and p_t is the logarithm of the general price level. In the DGE model the long-run real interest rate is θ, the rate of time preference. Thus, in the long run, inflation satisfies

$$\Delta p = R - \theta, \tag{13.2}$$

where R is the nominal interest rate in the long run, or its long-run average value. If the monetary authority has discretion over the choice of the nominal interest rate, then equation (13.2) determines long-run inflation. We note that there is no role for the supply of money in this.

In the short run, when all three variables vary with time, the Fisher equation can be rewritten so that it determines the price level as

$$p_t = E_t p_{t+1} + r_t - R_t$$

$$= \sum_{s=0}^{\infty} E_t (r_{t+s} - R_{t+s}). \tag{13.3}$$

The current price level is therefore determined by current and expected future nominal and real interest rates. If r_t is exogenous and R_t is chosen using discretion, then the money supply is not relevant. More generally, r_t is endogenously determined by the economy, which implies that we need to consider a fuller model. Further, R_t could be determined by an interest rate rule or, under money-supply targeting, through the money market, or, in an open economy, through the UIP condition.

Consider the use of an interest rate rule. Suppose that the monetary authority commits to using the rule

$$R_t = \alpha_0 + \alpha_1 p_t + \alpha_2 \Delta p_t,$$

where, under price-level targeting, $\alpha_2 = 0$, and, under inflation targeting, $\alpha_1 = 0$. It follows from the Fisher equation that the price level is determined from

$$\alpha_1 p_t + \alpha_2 \Delta p_t - E_t \Delta p_{t+1} = r_t - \alpha_0.$$

The solution under price-level targeting is

$$p_t = \frac{1}{1 + \alpha_1} E_t p_{t+1} + \frac{r_t - \alpha_0}{1 + \alpha_1}$$

$$= \sum_{s=0}^{\infty} \frac{E_t r_{t+s} - \alpha_0}{(1 + \alpha_1)^{s+1}}. \tag{13.4}$$

The price level is now the discounted value of current and expected future deviations of real interest rates from α_0.

The solution under inflation targeting is

$$
\begin{aligned}
\Delta p_t &= \frac{1}{\alpha_2} E_t \Delta p_{t+1} + \frac{r_t - \alpha_0}{\alpha_2} \\
&= \sum_{s=0}^{\infty} \frac{E_t r_{t+s} - \alpha_0}{\alpha_2^{s+1}}
\end{aligned}
\tag{13.5}
$$

if $\alpha_2 \geqslant 1$. Here it is the inflation rate, not the price level, that is the discounted value of current and future deviations of real interest rates from α_0; moreover, the price level is no longer determined.

Under the Taylor rule (Taylor 1993),

$$
R_t = \bar{R} + \gamma_1 (\Delta p_t - \pi^*) + \gamma_2 x_t,
$$

where $\bar{R}$ is the long-run target value of R_t, π^* is the target rate of inflation, x_t is the output gap (the deviation of output from trend or long-run equilibrium), $\gamma_1 = 1.5$, and $\gamma_2 = 0.5$. The solution is now

$$
\begin{aligned}
\Delta p_t &= \frac{1}{\gamma_1} E_t \Delta p_{t+1} + \frac{r_t - \gamma_2 x_t - (\bar{R} - \gamma_1 \pi^*)}{\gamma_1} \\
&= \sum_{s=0}^{\infty} \frac{E_t (r_{t+s} - \gamma_2 x_{t+s}) - (\bar{R} - \gamma_1 \pi^*)}{\gamma_1^{s+1}}.
\end{aligned}
\tag{13.6}
$$

Hence inflation is determined by current and expected future values of both the real interest rate and the output gap. It follows that we may now need a model of the output gap and the real interest rate.

These results show how different ways of conducting monetary policy affect inflation (or the price level). The choices about price-level or inflation targeting, about discretion or rules, and about the type of rule employed all affect the solution. They also affect our selection of the economic model required to analyze monetary policy.

We have previously argued that the main objection to price-level targeting is that it may entail greater output costs than inflation targeting because a positive shock to the price level, especially if it is large, may require the price level and hence output to be reduced, whereas under inflation targeting a temporary shock to the price level may be ignored if it is expected to have no subsequent effect on inflation, i.e., if there are no second-round effects through, for example, wages. Price-level targeting also makes inflation more volatile. This is because a shock that raises the price level will temporarily cause inflation, and when the price level returns to its target level, inflation must fall, causing inflation volatility. Taken together, these arguments suggest that targeting inflation is probably preferable to targeting the price level.

13.3   The Keynesian Model of Inflation

13.3.1   Theory

Before considering modern theories of inflation targeting, we examine the determination and control of inflation based on the Keynesian model. One of the most important modifications to Keynes's original macroeconomic framework was the inclusion of an equation describing how prices adjust: the Phillips curve (Phillips 1958). For many years it formed a standard ingredient of the Keynesian model and played an important role in the analysis of inflation (see, for example, Phelps 1968, 1973). Later it was found that this model was unable to provide an adequate explanation for inflation (see Lucas 1976a; Gordon 1997). Nonetheless, modern inflation theory is still based on a modified version of the Phillips curve.

Consider the following stylized Keynesian model of a closed economy. This consists of the expectations-augmented Phillips curve:

$$\Delta w_t = -\alpha(u_t - u_{nt}) + \beta E_{t-1}\Delta p_t, \quad \alpha > 0, \; 1 \geqslant \beta > 0, \tag{13.7}$$

where w_t is the nominal-wage rate and p_t is the price level (both are logarithms), u_t is the unemployment rate, and u_{nt} is the natural rate of unemployment (the rate of unemployment associated with full employment). In the original Phillips curve there was no inflation term. Later, the expected value of current inflation based on information available at time $t - 1$ was added to reflect real-wage bargaining.

Wage inflation is assumed to be passed on to price inflation through a pricing equation based solely on labor costs that ignores labor productivity:

$$\Delta p_t = \Delta w_t. \tag{13.8}$$

The difference between the rate of unemployment and the natural rate is related to the output gap $y_t - y_{nt}$ by

$$u_t - u_{nt} = -\theta(y_t - y_{nt}), \quad \theta > 0, \tag{13.9}$$

where y_t is the logarithm of output and y_{nt} is full-capacity output. This equation is known as Okun's law (Okun 1962). The model is completed by adding the money-demand function

$$m_t - p_t = y_t - \lambda R_t, \quad \lambda > 0, \tag{13.10}$$

where m_t is the logarithm of nominal money balances and R_t is the nominal interest rate, together with the Fisher equation

$$R_t = r_t + E_t\Delta p_{t+1}, \tag{13.11}$$

which defines the real interest rate, r_t. We assume that m_t, r_t, u_{nt}, and y_{nt} are exogenous.

From equations (13.7)–(13.9) inflation is determined by the aggregate supply function

$$\Delta p_t = \alpha\theta(y_t - y_{nt}) + \beta E_{t-1}\Delta p_t. \tag{13.12}$$

It follows that if $\beta < 1$ there is both a long-run and a short-run trade-off between inflation and output. This suggests that, given inflation expectations, the rate of inflation can be controlled through controlling excess capacity; a lower inflation rate requires a higher excess capacity.

We note that if $\beta = 1$ there is no trade-off. Under rational expectations,

$$\Delta p_t = E_{t-1}\Delta p_t + \varepsilon_t,$$

where the innovation ε_t satisfies $E_{t-1}\varepsilon_t = 0$. Hence, if $\beta = 1$, then equation (13.12) becomes

$$y_t = y_{nt} + \frac{1}{\alpha\theta}\varepsilon_t. \tag{13.13}$$

Consequently, inflation is independent of output, and output differs from full-capacity output due to ε_t, the shock or the innovation in inflation, ε_t.

The aggregate demand function is derived from equations (13.10) and (13.11). Combining them to eliminate R_t we obtain

$$y_t = \lambda E_t p_{t+1} - (1 + \lambda)p_t + m_t + \lambda r_t. \tag{13.14}$$

Equations (13.12) and (13.14) determine p_t and y_t. Eliminating y_t gives the reduced-form equation for p_t:

$$[1 + \alpha\theta(1 + \lambda)]p_t - \alpha\theta\lambda E_t p_{t+1} - \beta E_{t-1}p_t - (1 - \beta)p_{t-1} = x_t, \tag{13.15}$$
$$x_t = \alpha\theta(m_t + \lambda r_t - y_{nt}). \tag{13.16}$$

The solution may be obtained using the Whiteman solution procedure described in the mathematical appendix. If we assume that $x_t = \phi(L)e_t$, where e_t is an i.i.d. shock with zero mean, and that the solution takes the form $p_t = A(L)e_t$, then we may rewrite equation (13.15) in terms of the lag operator as

$$p = \{[1+\alpha\theta(1+\lambda)]A(L)-\alpha\theta\lambda[A(L)-a_0]L^{-1}-\beta[A(L)-a_0]-(1-\beta)A(L)L\}e_t.$$

As $A(L) = \phi(L)$, we have

$$A(L) = \frac{-(\alpha\theta\lambda L^{-1} + \beta)a_0 + \phi(L)}{[1 - \beta + \alpha\theta(1 + \lambda)] - \alpha\theta\lambda L^{-1} - (1 - \beta)L}$$
$$= \frac{(\alpha\theta\lambda + \beta L)a_0 - L\phi(L)}{(1 - \beta)f(L)},$$

where

$$f(L) = \frac{\alpha\theta\lambda}{1 - \beta} - \frac{1 - \beta + \alpha\theta(1 + \lambda)}{1 - \beta}L + L^2 = 0.$$

The characteristic equation $f(L) = 0$ has two roots. As $f(1) = -(\alpha\theta/(1-\beta)) < 0$ we have a saddlepath solution. We denote the roots by $\eta_1 \geqslant 1$ and $\eta_2 < 1$.

Hence,

$$f(L) = (L - \eta_1)(L - \eta_2)$$

$$= -\eta_1 L \left(1 - \frac{1}{\eta_1} L\right)(1 - \eta_2 L^{-1}).$$

Using the method of residues for the unstable root η_2, it follows that

$$\lim_{L \to \eta_2} (1 - \beta)(L - \eta_1)(L - \eta_2)A(L) = -(\alpha\theta\lambda\eta_2^{-1} + \beta)a_0 + \phi(\eta_2) = 0$$

and hence a_0 is uniquely determined by

$$a_0 = \frac{\eta_2 \phi(\eta_2)}{\alpha\theta\lambda + \beta\eta_2}.$$

The solution for p_t can therefore be written as

$$(1 - \beta)\eta_1 \left(1 - \frac{1}{\eta_1} L\right) p_t = \frac{\alpha\theta\lambda + \beta L}{\alpha\theta\lambda + \beta\eta_2} \left[\frac{1 - \eta_2 L^{-1}\phi(\eta_2)\phi(L)^{-1}}{1 - \eta_2 L^{-1}} - \beta L\right]\phi(L)e_t$$

or, in terms of x_t, as

$$p_t = \frac{1}{\eta_1} p_{t-1} + \frac{1}{\varphi} \sum_{s=0}^{\infty} \eta_2^s E_t x_{t+s} + \frac{\beta(1 - \alpha\theta\lambda - \beta\eta_2)}{\varphi} x_{t-1}, \qquad (13.17)$$

where $\varphi = (1 - \beta)\eta_1(\alpha\theta\lambda + \beta\eta_2)$.

Equation (13.17) shows that the price level has both forward- and backward-looking components. Increases in the money supply and the real interest rate and decreases in full-capacity output, whether in the current period or expected in the future, would cause the current price level to increase, but the adjustment to a new long-run equilibrium price level takes place over time.

In the long run the solution for the price level is

$$p = m + \lambda r - y_n$$

and so long-run inflation is

$$\Delta p = \Delta m + \lambda\Delta r - \Delta y_n.$$

Since, over the long run, output and inflation tend to be positive, while in comparison the real rate of return is approximately constant, inflation in the Keynesian model requires an accommodating growth in the money supply. Without this, positive output growth would result in negative inflation. Thus, although the emphasis in the Keynesian model is on the control of inflation through demand management (in particular, fiscal policy), an accommodating monetary policy is also required to achieve a stable trade-off between inflation and output. Without this, inflation cannot be controlled in the long run by fiscal policy alone.

13.3.2 Empirical Evidence

The original basis for the Phillips curve was its apparent ability to account for U.K. wage inflation over the previous hundred years. However, as soon as it was used as the basis for policy it appeared to break down, thereby losing its ability to explain inflation. This phenomenon led to a general proposition in economic policy known as "Goodhart's law," which asserts that any economic relation tends to break down when used for policy purposes. Where once there appeared to be a trade-off between wage inflation and unemployment (or output) so that it seemed possible to control inflation by managing output, as soon as this was tried, the trade-off disappeared and inflation appeared to be unconnected with output, especially in the long run.

An explanation for Goodhart's law is that the economic relations being manipulated by policy are not structural; i.e., they are derived from more fundamental behavioral relations, such as the first-order conditions associated with the optimizing decisions of households and firms. These decision rules are determined in terms of the deep structural parameters of the problem, whereas the coefficients of the economic equations being manipulated—like the Phillips curve—are functions of these deep structural parameters and so may change when policy changes. This point was first made by Lucas (1976a) and is known as "the Lucas critique." Further, optimal decision rules, whether those of private economic agents or of a policy maker, and especially if they are intertemporal, are contingent on the state of the economy. If the state of the economy changes, then the decision, and even the decision rule, may change, and hence the derivative economic relations. As we have seen previously, this is the basis of time-inconsistent policy.

Figure 13.1 shows the relation between wage inflation and unemployment in the United Kingdom. The trade-off between wage inflation and unemployment appears to be strong between 1980 and 1985 but weaker up to 1993. After this it disappears, with unemployment falling without any sign of inflation increasing. Figure 13.2 shows the trade-off between inflation and the output gap between 1955 and 2005 based on quarterly data and figure 13.3 uses annual data for greater clarity. It is difficult to detect any stable long-run trade-off between inflation and the output gap in these two figures.

13.4 The New Keynesian Model of Inflation

13.4.1 Theory

Modern monetary economics is based on a dynamic general macroeconomic model with imperfect competition. Like the Keynesian model, it has two equations: an inflation or aggregate supply function, and an IS or aggregate demand function. Due to this resemblance to the Keynesian model, it is usually referred to as the New Keynesian model (NKM) (see Fuhrer and Moore 1995; Roberts

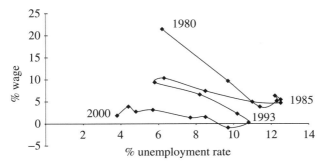

Figure 13.1. U.K. unemployment–wage trade-off.

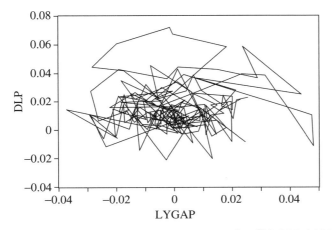

Figure 13.2. U.K. inflation–output gap trade-off (1955–2005).

1995, 1997). The specification of the two equations is, however, very different. As previously noted, particularly in our discussion of imperfect price flexibility in chapter 9 and of exchange rates in chapter 12, the Keynesian model is not derived from a microfounded general equilibrium model, even though it is a model of the whole economy. There is a vast literature on inflation targeting via the NKM. For recent surveys see Clarida et al. (1999), Walsh (2003), Woodford (2003), Bernanke and Woodford (2005), and Gali (2008).

A typical stylized NKM consists of the following two equations:

$$\pi_t = \mu + \beta E_t \pi_{t+1} + \gamma x_t + e_{\pi t}, \tag{13.18}$$

$$x_t = E_t x_{t+1} - \alpha(R_t - E_t \pi_{t+1} - \theta) + e_{xt}, \tag{13.19}$$

where $0 < \beta \leqslant 1$, $\alpha, \gamma, \mu, \theta > 0$, π_t is inflation and is measured either by the CPI or the GDP deflator, $x_t = y_t - y_{nt}$ is the output gap (measured here as output less "steady-state" output and not as capacity output less actual output as in chapter 12), y_t is GDP, y_{nt} is a measure of trend or of equilibrium GDP, R_t is the policy instrument—an official nominal interest rate—and $e_{\pi t}$ and e_{xt} are, respectively, zero mean and serially uncorrelated supply and demand

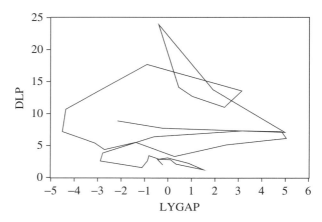

Figure 13.3. U.K. inflation–output gap trade-off 1970–2004.

shocks. Here a positive $e_{\pi t}$ raises inflation if output is fixed. The inflation equation (13.18) is a version of the Phillips equation that is sometimes known as the expectations-augmented or New Keynesian Phillips curve. Equation (13.19) is called the New Keynesian IS function. We continue to relate the real interest rate, r_t, to the nominal interest rate and to inflation through the Fisher equation $r_t = R_t - E_t\pi_{t+1}$, but now r_t is endogenous, and not exogenous as before. This turns out to be an important difference. All variables apart from interest rates are expressed in natural logarithms. Assuming that in equilibrium the rate of inflation is the target rate π^*, the output gap is zero, and the long-run real interest rate is $\bar{r}$, then $\mu = (1-\beta)\pi^*$, the long-run value of i_t is $\bar{r}+\pi^* = \theta+\pi^*$, and hence $\bar{r} = \theta$, where, in general equilibrium, θ is the rate of time preference.

The inflation equation (13.18) is similar to the closed-economy inflation models derived in chapter 9. Its dynamic specification could be made more general by adding a term in π_{t-1}, which would slow down the dynamic adjustment of inflation. This would also accord more with the empirical evidence. Central banks typically target a measure of consumer inflation such as the CPI. For an open economy, further variables may be required in order to capture the effect on domestic CPI inflation of the price of imports and through this the impact of world inflation. The New Keynesian IS function requires more extensive discussion.

13.4.1.1 *The New Keynesian IS Function*

The New Keynesian IS function provides the link between the real interest rate and the output gap. Under inflation targeting, the aim is to use the nominal interest rate to control inflation via its effect on output. Thus the strength of the links between R_t and x_t and between x_t and π_t are crucial to the effectiveness of monetary policy. The intuition is that an increase in the official interest rate raises the real interest rate and hence reduces output and the output gap, which in turn reduces inflation. The New Keynesian IS function is forward looking. The theoretical basis for this in a dynamic general equilibrium model of the economy is the consumption Euler equation. First we consider the derivation of the New Keynesian IS function based on the life-cycle model of the representative household. We then use a full model of the economy.

We have previously represented the household's problem as maximizing

$$E_t \sum_{s=0}^{\infty} \beta^s U(c_{t+s}), \quad \beta = \frac{1}{1+\theta}, \tag{13.20}$$

subject to the real budget constraint

$$a_{t+1} + c_t = y_t + (1 + r_t)a_t, \tag{13.21}$$

where y_t is exogenous income, a_t is the stock of assets held at the start of the period, and r_t is their real return. (If households have net liabilities, we write $b_t = -a_t$.) This gives the Euler equation

$$E_t \left[\beta \frac{U'(c_{t+1})}{U'(c_t)} (1 + r_{t+1}) \right] = 1.$$

Approximating marginal utility by

$$U'(c_{t+1}) \simeq U'(c_t) + U'' \Delta c_{t+1},$$

we obtain the following expression for consumption:

$$E_t \Delta \ln c_{t+1} = \frac{1}{\sigma} (E_t r_{t+1} - \theta), \tag{13.22}$$

where $\sigma = -(C_t U''/U')$ is the coefficient of relative risk aversion. This can be rewritten as

$$\ln c_t = E_t \ln c_{t+1} - \frac{1}{\sigma} (E_t r_{t+1} - \theta) \tag{13.23}$$

or, in terms of deviations around the steady state, as

$$\ln c_t - \ln \bar{c}_t = E_t (\ln c_{t+1} - \ln \bar{c}_{t+1}) - \frac{1}{\sigma} (E_t r_{t+1} - \theta), \tag{13.24}$$

where $\bar{c}_t$ is the steady-state value of consumption, which may be time-varying, and the steady-state value of the real interest rate is θ.

In order to obtain the New Keynesian IS function (13.19) it is necessary to combine the Euler equation with the household budget constraint. A log-linear approximation to the budget constraint is

$$\frac{a}{y} \ln a_{t+1} + \frac{c}{y} \ln c_t = \ln y_t + (1 + \theta) \frac{a}{y} \ln a_t + \frac{a}{y} r_t, \tag{13.25}$$

where we assume that in steady state the ratios of assets and consumption to income are constant. Combining equations (13.24) and (13.25) to eliminate consumption gives

$$\ln y_t - \ln y_{nt} = E_t (\ln y_{t+1} - \ln y_{n,t+1}) - \frac{c}{\sigma y} (E_t r_{t+1} - \theta)$$

$$+ \frac{a}{y} [(1 + \theta) E_t \Delta \ln a_{t+1} - E_t \Delta \ln a_{t+2} + E_t \Delta r_{t+1}]. \tag{13.26}$$

Finally, we note that, for a closed economy, total net assets are zero. If we therefore set $a = 0$, then equation (13.26) reduces to

$$\ln y_t - \ln y_{nt} = E_t (\ln y_{t+1} - \ln y_{n,t+1}) - \frac{c}{\sigma y}(E_t r_{t+1} - \theta). \qquad (13.27)$$

Equation (13.27) is the same as (13.19) if we equate household income with the output of the economy.

More generally, and particularly in an open economy, household net assets are not necessarily equal to zero, and household income is not equal to total output. Moreover, it is then inappropriate to focus on the household sector alone. As a result, we should perhaps regard equation (13.27) as a special case.

A Critique of the NKM. Although we base our subsequent analysis of monetary policy on this formulation of the New Keynesian IS function, before doing so we reflect further on its specification and interpretation. Strictly speaking, the Euler equation describes the future behavior of consumption after having taken into account the information available at time t. New information at time t, whether relating to the current period or the future, causes both c_t and $E_t c_{t+1}$ to change. In contrast, the New Keynesian IS function is interpreted as determining the level of y_t (or c_t).

The first point to make, therefore, is that equation (13.23) is not the same as the consumption function as it describes the expected future change in consumption, not the current level of consumption. In order to obtain the consumption function we must combine equation (13.23) with the budget constraint, equation (13.21). The consumption function may be obtained using the following log-linear approximation to the intertemporal budget constraint:

$$E_t \frac{\ln a_{t+n}}{(1+r)^n} + \frac{c}{a}\sum_{s=0}^{n-1}\frac{E_t \ln c_{t+s}}{(1+r)^s} = \frac{y}{a}\sum_{s=0}^{n-1}\frac{E_t \ln y_{t+s}}{(1+r)^s} + \sum_{s=0}^{n-1}\frac{E_t r_{t+s}}{(1+r)^s} + (1+r)\ln a_t.$$

Taking the limit as $n \to \infty$, assuming that $\lim_{n\to\infty}(\ln a_{t+n}/(1+r)^n) = 0$ and that $E_t r_{t+s} = \theta$, so that $E_t \ln c_{t+s} = \ln c_t$, gives the consumption function as

$$\ln c_t = \frac{r}{1+r}\frac{y}{c}\sum_{s=0}^{\infty}\frac{\ln y_{t+s}}{(1+r)^s} + \frac{r}{1+r}\frac{a}{c}\sum_{s=0}^{\infty}\frac{E_t r_{t+s}}{(1+r)^s} + r\frac{a}{c}\ln a_t. \qquad (13.28)$$

Hence, log consumption depends on the expected present values of log income and the interest rate, and on the log asset stock.

The effect on consumption of a temporary or a permanent change in real interest rates therefore depends on whether households have net assets ($a_t > 0$) or net liabilities ($a_t < 0$). If households have net assets, then, due to the extra interest income, an increase in the real interest rate will increase, not decrease, consumption as the New Keynesian IS function, equation (13.19), assumes. If, on the other hand, households hold net liabilities (i.e., $b_t > 0$), then the log-linear approximation becomes

$$\ln c_t = \frac{r}{1+r}\frac{y}{c}\sum_{s=0}^{\infty}\frac{\ln y_{t+s}}{(1+r)^s} - \frac{r}{1+r}\frac{b}{c}\sum_{s=0}^{\infty}\frac{E_t r_{t+s}}{(1+r)^s} - r\frac{b}{c}\ln b_t. \qquad (13.29)$$

Thus it is only if households have net liabilities that an increase in the real interest rate reduces consumption and hence aggregate demand. For example, a tightening of current monetary policy by a one-period unit increase in the current interest rate r_t will increase $\ln c_t$ by $(r/(1+r))(a/c)$ if households have net assets, and decrease $\ln c_t$ by this amount if they have net liabilities, but $E_t \ln c_{t+1}$ would be unchanged in both cases. In other words, if households have net assets, a temporary tightening of monetary policy would be a stimulus to the economy, not a depressive as assumed in the New Keynesian inflation-targeting model. Since at any point in time there will be some households with net assets and others with net liabilities, the strength of the interest rate effect on consumption may be quite weak, or even zero for a closed economy, where, in the aggregate, net financial assets must be zero as one person's assets are another's liabilities.

Further understanding of the different implications of the consumption Euler equation and the consumption function may be obtained by considering what happens when the future real interest rate is expected to change. As a result of a unit increase in $E_t r_{t+1}$ from its initial value of θ, such that real interest rates in all other periods are assumed unchanged, c_t becomes c_t^* and $E_t \ln c_{t+1}$ becomes $E_t \ln c_{t+1}^*$. From the consumption functions for periods t and $t+1$ with income fixed, equation (13.29), we then have

$$E_t \Delta \ln c_{t+1} = -\frac{r}{1+r}\frac{a}{c}r_t + \frac{r}{1+r}\frac{a}{c}\left(1 - \frac{1}{1+r}\right)E_t r_{t+1} + r\frac{a}{c}E_t \Delta \ln a_{t+1}.$$

Hence, as a result of the unit increase in $E_t r_{t+1}$, the expected rate of growth of consumption becomes

$$E_t \Delta \ln c_{t+1}^* = E_t \Delta \ln c_{t+1} + \frac{r}{1+r}\frac{a}{c}\left(1 - \frac{1}{1+r}\right) + r\frac{a}{c}E_t(\ln a_{t+1}^* - \ln a_{t+1}).$$

From the Euler equation (13.22),

$$E_t(\Delta \ln c_{t+1}^* - \Delta \ln c_{t+1}) = \frac{1}{\sigma} > 0$$

and

$$E_t(\ln a_{t+1}^* - \ln a_{t+1}) = -\frac{1}{\sigma}\frac{r}{(1+r)^2} < 0.$$

An increase in the interest rate has therefore led to an increase in the expected rate of growth of consumption, but a fall in current consumption and a fall in asset holding. A corresponding result can be derived when households have net liabilities. The implication is that, in order to determine the effect on consumption of a change in the real interest rate, either we should use the consumption function instead of the consumption Euler equation, or we should include the budget constraint in the model as well as the Euler equation.

Even then there is a further difficulty. Our derivation of the New Keynesian IS function is based on the decisions of the household, and not on a model of the full economy. We now rectify this. We assume that in the full closed economy the problem is to maximize expected discounted utility

$$E_t \sum_{s=0}^{\infty} \beta^s U(c_{t+s}, l_{t+s}), \quad \beta = \frac{1}{1+\theta},$$

subject to

$$y_t = c_t + i_t + g_t,$$
$$y_t = A_t k_t^{\alpha} n_t^{1-\alpha},$$
$$\Delta k_{t+1} = i_t - \delta k_t,$$
$$n_t + l_t = 1,$$

where y is output, c is consumption, l is leisure, n is work, i is investment, k is capital, g is government expenditure, and A is technical progress.

The solution is

$$E_t \Delta \ln c_{t+1} = \frac{1}{\sigma}(E_t r_{t+1} - \theta),$$
$$U_{l,t} n_t = (1-\alpha) U_{c,t} y_t,$$
$$r_{t+1} = \alpha \frac{y_{t+1}}{k_{t+1}} - \delta.$$

A log-linear approximation to the resource constraint is

$$\ln y_t = \frac{c}{y} \ln c_t + \frac{k}{y}[\ln k_{t+1} - (1-\delta)\ln k_t] + \frac{g}{y} \ln g_t.$$

Eliminating $\ln c_t$ using the Euler equation and noting that $r = \alpha(y/k) - \delta$ and $1 - (c/y) - (g/y) = \delta(k/y)$ we obtain the IS function:

$$\ln y_t = E_t \ln y_{t+1} + \left(1 - \delta \frac{k}{y} - \frac{g}{y}\right)\frac{1}{\sigma}(E_t r_{t+1} - \theta)$$
$$+ \frac{k}{y}[E_t \Delta \ln k_{t+2} - (1-\delta)E_t \Delta \ln k_{t+1}] - \frac{g}{y} E_t \Delta \ln g_{t+1}.$$

Thus, in the full economy model, output depends on the capital stock and on government expenditures, and the capital stock depends on output and on the real interest rate. Since an increase in the real interest rate reduces the capital stock and hence output, the direct response of output to a change in the real interest rate, which is positive, may be partly, or fully, offset by the real interest rate's negative effect on capital.

The general conclusion to emerge from this discussion is that the New Keynesian IS function does not provide a secure theoretical basis for the part of the monetary transmission mechanism that links interest rates to output. We have shown that the New Keynesian IS function may give a completely misleading signal of the effects of monetary policy, even to the extent of giving the wrong sign. We have suggested that it is better to carry out the analysis using the consumption function or to include the budget constraint as an extra equation in the model. We have also argued that the New Keynesian IS function derived solely from the behavior of households may be misspecified due to not being based on a model of the full economy. A more secure way to proceed is, therefore, to use the Euler equation together with the economy's resource constraint. For further discussion on the theoretical underpinnings of the NKM see Smith and Wickens (2007). Despite these misgivings, we will continue to use the New Keynesian IS function found in the literature on inflation targeting.

13.4.2 The Effectiveness of Inflation Targeting in the New Keynesian Model

We consider the response of inflation and output to a change in interest rates under both a policy of discretion and commitment to a Taylor rule. The analysis is based on the New Keynesian model, equations (13.18) and (13.19), which for convenience we repeat:

$$\pi_t = \mu + \beta E_t \pi_{t+1} + \gamma x_t + e_{\pi t}, \tag{13.30}$$

$$x_t = E_t x_{t+1} - \alpha(R_t - E_t \pi_{t+1} - \theta) + e_{xt}. \tag{13.31}$$

13.4.2.1 Using Discretion

The monetary instrument is the nominal interest rate R_t, which is chosen at the discretion of the central bank. Intuitively, an increase in the nominal interest rate reduces output and hence inflation. However, in the NKM a surprising result occurs.

Eliminating x_t from the model gives the following reduced-form dynamic equation for π_t:

$$\left. \begin{aligned} \pi_t - (1 + \beta + \alpha\gamma)E_t\pi_{t+1} + \beta E_t\pi_{t+2} &= \alpha\gamma\theta + z_t, \\ z_t &= -\alpha\gamma R_t + e_{\pi t} + \gamma e_{xt}. \end{aligned} \right\} \tag{13.32}$$

The long-run solution is

$$\pi_t = R_t - \theta.$$

Using Whiteman's solution method to analyze the short-run dynamics we write equation (13.32) as

$$\{A(L) - (1 + \beta + \alpha\gamma)L^{-1}(A(L) - a_0) + \beta L^{-2}[A(L) - a_0 - a_1 L]\}\varepsilon_t = \phi(L)\varepsilon_t,$$

where $\pi_t = a + A(L)\varepsilon_t$ and $z_t = \phi(L)\varepsilon_t$. Hence

$$A(L) = \frac{[\beta - (1 + \beta + \alpha\gamma)L]a_0 + \beta L a_1 + L^2\phi(L)}{\beta - (1 + \beta + \alpha\gamma)L + L^2}$$

and the characteristic equation is

$$f(L) = \beta - (1 + \beta + \alpha\gamma)L + L^2 = 0.$$

Since $f(1) = -\alpha\gamma < 0$ we have a saddlepath solution. We denote the roots by $\eta_1 \geq 1$ and $\eta_2 < 1$. As there is only one unstable root η_2, but two undetermined coefficients a_0 and a_1, the solution will not be unique. Using the method of residues gives

$$\lim_{L \to \eta_2} (L - \eta_1)(L - \eta_2)A(L) = [\beta - (1 + \beta + \alpha y)\eta_2]a_0 + \beta\eta_2 a_1 + \eta_2^2 \phi(\eta_2) = 0.$$
(13.33)

This shows that a_0 and a_1 cannot be uniquely determined; we can only eliminate one as a function of the other.

Noting that

$$f(L) = (L - \eta_1)(L - \eta_2)$$

$$= -\eta_1 L \left(1 - \frac{1}{\eta_1}L\right)(1 - \eta_2 L^{-1})$$

from equation (13.33),

$$\left(1 - \frac{1}{\eta_1}L\right)A(L)$$

$$= \frac{[(1 + \beta + \alpha y)a_0 - \beta a_1](L - \eta_2) - L^2\phi(L) + \eta_2^2\phi(\eta_2)}{\eta_1 L(1 - \eta_2 L^{-1})}$$

$$= \frac{(1 + \beta + \alpha y)a_0 - \beta a_1}{\eta_1} - \left[\frac{\eta_2}{\eta_1}\frac{1 - \eta_2 L^{-1}\phi(\eta_2)\phi(L)^{-1}}{1 - \eta_2 L^{-1}} + \frac{1}{\eta_1}L\right]\phi(L).$$

The solution for inflation is therefore

$$\pi_t = -\frac{\alpha y \theta}{\eta_1(1 - \eta_2)} + \frac{1}{\eta_1}\pi_{t-1} - \frac{\eta_2}{\eta_1}\sum_{s=0}^{\infty}\eta_2^s E_t z_{t+s}$$

$$- \frac{1}{\eta_1}z_{t-1} + \frac{(1 + \beta + \alpha y)a_0 - \beta a_1}{\eta_1}\varepsilon_t$$

$$= -\frac{\alpha y \theta}{\eta_1(1 - \eta_2)} + \frac{1}{\eta_1}\pi_{t-1} + \frac{\alpha y \eta_2}{\eta_1}\sum_{s=0}^{\infty}\eta_2^s E_t R_{t+s} + \frac{\alpha y}{\eta_1}R_{t-1}$$

$$+ \delta(e_{\pi t} + y e_{xt}) + \frac{\alpha y}{\eta_1}(e_{\pi,t-1} + y e_{x,t-1}), \quad (13.34)$$

where δ is an arbitrary constant, implying that the solution is not unique.

It follows that a discretionary increase in interest rates either in the previous period, the current period, or in the future is expected to increase, not decrease, inflation, which is contrary to what the earlier intuition might lead one to expect. Moreover, the appropriate setting for the interest rate so that it counteracts current supply and demand shocks is unclear as the effects of the shocks on inflation are indeterminate. It would seem, therefore, that a policy of discretion, based on this specification of the NKM, does not provide a satisfactory basis for inflation targeting.

The solution for the output gap is obtained by rewriting equation (13.19) using the lag operator and then substituting for $E_t\pi_{t+1} = L^{-1}\pi_t$ from the solution for π_t. This can be shown to give

$$\Delta x_t = \frac{1}{\eta_1} \Delta x_{t-1} - \frac{\alpha^2 \gamma \eta_2}{\eta_1} \sum_{s=0}^{\infty} \eta_2^s E_t R_{t+s} + \alpha\left(1 - \frac{\alpha \gamma}{\eta_1}\right) R_{t-1} - \frac{\alpha}{\eta_1} R_{t-2}$$
$$- \alpha\delta(e_{\pi t} + \gamma e_{xt}) - \frac{\alpha^2 \gamma}{\eta_1} e_{\pi,t-1} - \left(1 + \frac{\alpha \gamma^2}{\eta_1}\right) e_{x,t-1} + \frac{1}{\eta_1} e_{x,t-2}.$$

$$\text{(13.35)}$$

The interest rate therefore affects the change in the output gap, but not its level. Furthermore, this change persists over time.

13.4.2.2 Rules-Based Policy

It is informative to compare the solutions for inflation and the effectiveness of monetary policy under a policy of discretion with one of commitment to a Taylor rule. We now write the Taylor rule as

$$R_t = \theta + \pi^* + \mu(\pi_t - \pi^*) + \nu x_t + e_{Rt} \qquad \text{(13.36)}$$

with $\mu = 1.5$ and $\nu = 0.5$. The random variable e_{Rt} is introduced to allow for unexpected departures from the rule. Solving the NKM together with the Taylor rule results in both x_t and R_t being eliminated and gives

$$\left.\begin{array}{l} \pi_t - [1 + \beta(1 + \alpha\nu) + \alpha\gamma]E_t\pi_{t+1} + \beta E_t\pi_{t+2} = z_t, \\ z_t = \alpha\pi^*[\nu(1 - \beta) + \gamma(\mu - 1)] + (1 + \alpha\nu)e_{\pi t} + \gamma e_{xt} - \alpha\gamma e_{Rt}. \end{array}\right\} \quad \text{(13.37)}$$

Equation (13.37) can be written as

$$\{[1 + \alpha(\nu + \mu\gamma)]A(L) - [1 + \beta(1 + \alpha\nu) + \alpha\gamma]L^{-1}[A(L) - a_0]$$
$$+ \beta L^{-2}[A(L) - a_0 - a_1 L]\}\varepsilon_t = \phi(L)\varepsilon_t,$$

where $\pi_t = a + A(L)\varepsilon_t$ and $z_t = \phi(L)\varepsilon_t$. Hence

$$A(L) = \frac{[\beta - (1 + \beta(1 + \alpha\nu) + \alpha\gamma)L]a_0 + \beta L a_1 + L^2 \phi(L)}{\beta - [1 + \beta(1 + \alpha\nu) + \alpha\gamma]L + [1 + \alpha(\nu + \mu\gamma)]L^2}$$

and the characteristic equation is

$$f(L) = \beta - [1 + \beta(1 + \alpha\nu) + \alpha\gamma]L + [1 + \alpha(\nu + \mu\gamma)]L^2 = 0.$$

As $f(1) = \alpha[\nu(1 - \beta) + \gamma(\mu - 1)] > 0$ both roots are either stable or unstable. As $1 > \beta/(1 + \alpha(\nu + \mu\gamma)) > 0$, the roots must be less than unity and positive. Hence they are unstable. We denote the roots by $0 < \eta_1, \eta_2 < 1$.

Using the method of residues gives, for $i = 1, 2$,

$$\lim_{L \to \eta_i} f(L)A(L) = \lim_{L \to \eta_i} [1 + \alpha(\nu + \mu\gamma)](L - \eta_1)(L - \eta_2)A(L)$$
$$= [\beta - (1 + \beta(1 + \alpha\nu) + \alpha\gamma)\eta_i]a_0 + \beta\eta_i a_1 + \eta_i^2 \phi(\eta_i)$$
$$= 0.$$

This gives two equations in the two unknowns a_0 and a_1. Hence a_0 and a_1 are uniquely determined.

The solution for π_t can therefore be obtained directly from equation (13.37) as

$$
\begin{aligned}
\pi_t &= \frac{1}{[1 + \alpha(v + \mu y)]L^{-2}(L - \eta_1)(L - \eta_2)}z_t \\
&= \frac{1}{[1 + \alpha(v + \mu y)](1 - \eta_1 L^{-1})(1 - \eta_2 L^{-1})}z_t \\
&= \frac{1}{[1 + \alpha(v + \mu y)](\eta_1 - \eta_2)}\left[\frac{\eta_1}{1 - \eta_1 L^{-1}} - \frac{\eta_2}{1 - \eta_2 L^{-1}}\right]z_t \\
&= \frac{1}{1 + \alpha(v + \mu y)}\left[\frac{\eta_1}{\eta_1 - \eta_2}\sum_{s=0}^{\infty}\eta_1^s E_t z_{t+s} - \frac{\eta_2}{\eta_1 - \eta_2}\sum_{s=0}^{\infty}\eta_2^s E_t z_{t+s}\right] \\
&= \pi^* + \frac{1}{1 + \alpha(v + \mu y)}[(1 + \alpha v)e_{\pi t} + y e_{xt} - \alpha y e_{Rt}]. \qquad (13.38)
\end{aligned}
$$

Thus the average inflation rate equals the target rate π^*. Inflation deviates from target due to the three shocks. Positive inflation and output shocks cause inflation to rise above target, but positive interest rate shocks cause inflation to fall below target. We note that a forward-looking Taylor rule in which $E_t \pi_{t+1}$ replaces π_t and $E_t x_{t+1}$ replaces x_t gives a similar result.

It is possible to choose the parameters of the Taylor rule μ and v in an optimal way. For example, we could choose μ and v to minimize the variance of inflation. From equation (13.38), and assuming that the shocks are uncorrelated,

$$
\text{var}_t(\pi_t) = \frac{1}{[1 + \alpha(v + \mu y)]^2}[(1 + \alpha v)^2 \sigma_\pi^2 + y^2 \sigma_x^2 - (\alpha y)^2 \sigma_R^2],
$$

where the σ_i^2 ($i = \pi, x, R$) are the variances of the shocks. As $\mu \to \infty$ the variance of inflation goes to zero; and, for any finite value of μ, as $v \to 0$ the variance of inflation decreases. This suggests that if the policy objective is to minimize the variation of inflation about the target level π^*, which is equivalent to minimizing the variance of inflation as $E\pi_t = \pi^*$, then strict inflation targeting ($v = 0$) is preferable to flexible inflation targeting ($v > 0$).

The solution for the output gap is obtained from equation (13.19) by substituting for π_t from equation (13.38), for R_t from equation (13.36), and for $E_t \pi_{t+1} = \pi^*$. Consequently,

$$
\begin{aligned}
x_t &= E_t x_{t+1} - \alpha(R_t - \pi^* - \theta) + e_{xt} \\
&= E_t x_{t+1} - \alpha\mu(\pi_t - \pi^*) - \alpha\mu v x_t + e_{xt} - \alpha e_{Rt} \\
&= E_t x_{t+1} - \frac{\alpha\mu}{1 + \alpha(v + \mu y)}[(1 + \alpha v)e_{\pi t} + y e_{xt} - \alpha y e_{Rt}] \\
&\qquad\qquad\qquad\qquad\qquad\qquad\qquad - \alpha\mu v x_t + e_{xt} - \alpha e_{Rt} \\
&= \frac{1}{1 + \alpha\mu v}E_t x_{t+1} - \frac{1}{1 + \alpha(v + \mu y)}(\alpha\mu e_{\pi t} + e_{xt} - e_{Rt}). \qquad (13.39)
\end{aligned}
$$

Solving equation (13.39) forwards gives the solution for x_t as

$$x_t = -\frac{1}{1 + \alpha(v + \mu y)}(\alpha\mu e_{\pi t} + e_{xt} - e_{Rt}). \qquad (13.40)$$

Hence the expected output gap is zero.

To summarize, inflation targeting based on the New Keynesian model and a policy of discretion results in an increase in the interest rate causing inflation to rise, but does not uniquely determine inflation. In contrast, under commitment to a rule, average inflation is equal to its target value. Moreover, by fine-tuning the parameters of the Taylor rule, it is possible to minimize the fluctuations of inflation about target. We return to this point later. Under discretion, interest rates affect the change in the output gap and this change is persistent, but, under commitment, on average the output gap is zero and deviations of the output gap from zero are not persistent.

13.4.3 Inflation Targeting with a Flexible Exchange Rate

Having a flexible exchange rate provides an additional channel to the real interest rate in the transmission mechanism of interest rates to inflation, which makes monetary policy more powerful than relying on the real interest rate (cost of capital) channel alone. This is because, given UIP, an increase in interest rates causes an exchange-rate appreciation, which worsens the trade balance and hence reduces domestic demand. We illustrate this using the following modified New Keynesian model:

$$\pi_t = (1 - \beta)\pi^* + \beta E_t \pi_{t+1} + \gamma x_t + e_{\pi t}, \qquad (13.41)$$

$$x_t = -\alpha(R_t - E_t \pi_{t+1} - \theta) + \delta(s_t + p_t^* - p_t) + e_{xt}, \qquad (13.42)$$

$$R_t = R_t^* + E_t \Delta s_{t+1}, \qquad (13.43)$$

where all coefficients are nonnegative. Note that although π^* denotes target inflation, R_t^* and P_t^* denote the foreign interest rate and price level, respectively. The main changes from the previous New Keynesian model are the omission of the forward-looking term in $E_t x_{t+1}$ from the aggregate demand equation and the inclusion of the real exchange rate and the UIP condition, which is an extra equation. The reason for omitting $E_t x_{t+1}$ is to simplify the dynamics.

13.4.3.1 Using Discretion

If we assume that the central bank sets R_t through a policy of discretion, then, using the lag operator, it can be shown that the resulting reduced-form equation for the price level can be written as

$$[1 + \beta + \gamma(\alpha + \delta) - L - (\beta + \alpha\gamma)L^{-1}]p_t = z_t,$$

$$z_t = -\gamma\left(\frac{\alpha + \delta - \alpha L^{-1}}{1 - L^{-1}}\right)R_t + \gamma\delta p_t^* + e_{\pi t} + \gamma e_{xt}.$$

The characteristic equation

$$f(L) = \beta + \alpha y + [1 + \beta + y(\alpha + \delta)]L + L^2 = 0$$

satisfies $f(1) = -y\delta < 0$ and so has a saddlepath solution. We denote the roots by $\eta_1 \geqslant 1$ and $\eta_2 < 1$. The solution for the price level can be written as

$$p_t = \frac{1}{\eta_1}p_{t-1} - \frac{y}{\eta_1(1 - \eta_2)}\sum_{i=0}^{\infty}\{\delta + [\alpha(1 - \eta_2) + \delta\eta_2]\eta_2^2\}E_t R_{t+i}$$

$$+ \frac{y\delta}{\eta_1}\sum_{i=0}^{\infty}\eta_2^2 E_t p_{t+i}^* + \frac{1}{\eta_1}(e_{\pi t} + y e_{xt}). \quad (13.44)$$

Equation (13.44) shows that domestic inflation is driven by foreign inflation, but this may be offset by discretionary changes in the domestic interest rate as an increase in R_t reduces the domestic price level. The equation also shows that the larger is δ (i.e., the effect of the real exchange rate on domestic output), the stronger is the exchange-rate channel. Consequently, having a floating exchange rate makes monetary policy more effective.

We may compare this result with our earlier result on the effectiveness of inflation targeting where we found that an increase in the interest rate raised, instead of reduced, inflation. The reason for this difference is that the output equation (13.19) previously included the term $E_t x_{t+1}$, whereas in equation (13.42) we have omitted it. And the reason why the solution in equation (13.44) is for the price level rather than the inflation rate is because we have included the real exchange rate in equation (13.42).

13.4.3.2 *Rules-Based Policy*

We assume now that the central bank commits to setting interest rates using the Taylor rule, equation (13.36). As a result, R_t is also an endogenous variable, together with p_t, x_t, and s_t.

The model may be written using the lag operator as

$$A(L)\begin{bmatrix} p_t \\ x_t \\ s_t \\ R_t \end{bmatrix} = \begin{bmatrix} (1 - \beta)\pi^* + e_{\pi t} \\ \alpha\theta + \delta p_t^* + e_{xt} \\ R_t^* \\ \theta + (1 - \mu)\pi^* + e_{Rt} \end{bmatrix},$$

where

$$A(L) = \begin{bmatrix} 1 + \beta - L - \beta L^{-1} & -y & 0 & 0 \\ \alpha + \delta - \alpha L^{-1} & 1 & -\delta & \alpha \\ 0 & 0 & L^{-1} - 1 & -1 \\ -\mu & -\nu & 0 & 1 \end{bmatrix}.$$

The characteristic equation is

$$|A(L)| = 0.$$

It can be shown that

$$|A(L)| = [1 + \nu(\alpha + \delta)]L^{-2}f(L),$$
$$f(L) = (L - \eta_1)(L - \eta_2)(L - \eta_3),$$

where $\eta_1 \geqslant 1$ and $\eta_2, \eta_3 < 1$. Thus there is one stable root and two unstable roots. It then follows that the solution is

$$\begin{bmatrix} p_t \\ x_t \\ s_t \\ R_t \end{bmatrix} = \frac{1}{|A(L)|} \operatorname{adj}[A(L)] \begin{bmatrix} (1 - \beta)\pi^* + e_{\pi t} \\ \alpha\theta + \delta p_t^* + e_{xt} \\ R_t^* \\ \theta + (1 - \mu)\pi^* + e_{Rt} \end{bmatrix},$$

where $\operatorname{adj}[A(L)]$ is the adjoint matrix of $A(L)$. The solution for the price level has the general form

$$p_t = \frac{1}{\eta_1} p_{t-1} + \sum_{k=0}^{\infty} \eta_2^k (\varphi_2 E_t p_{t+k}^* + \varphi_3 E_t R_{t+k}^*)$$

$$+ \sum_{k=0}^{\infty} \eta_3^k (\varphi_4 E_t p_{t+k}^* + \varphi_5 E_t R_{t+k}^*) + \varphi_\pi e_{\pi t} + \varphi_x e_{xt} + \varphi_R e_{Rt},$$

where φ_π, φ_x, and φ_R are all positive. Consequently, like a policy of discretion, domestic inflation is determined by foreign inflation, but, unlike discretion, following a Taylor rule does not necessarily eliminate the effect of foreign inflation, nor does it deal with the additional presence of the foreign interest rate. This suggests that for the model defined by equations (13.41), (13.42), and (13.43) a policy of discretion may be preferable to one of commitment to a Taylor rule. Intuitively, the obvious way to improve the outcome for domestic inflation is to modify the Taylor rule by including in it additional variables such as foreign inflation and the foreign interest rate.

Taken together, these results on inflation targeting based on the NKM reveal their sensitivity to different specifications of the model and to the choice of discretion versus rules. For further discussion of monetary policy in an open economy see Clarida et al. (2001).

13.5 Optimal Inflation Targeting

So far we have examined the effect on inflation of changing the interest rate, but without having any particular objective in mind. The aim of optimal inflation targeting is to set interest rates to minimize a given objective function subject to the constraints provided by the structure of the economy. The central bank could choose its own objective function or it could try to maximize social welfare. A common assumption is that the central bank seeks to minimize the intertemporal quadratic objective function

$$E_t \sum_{s=0}^{\infty} \beta^s [(\pi_{t+s} - \pi^*)^2 + \alpha(y_t - y_t^*)^2], \tag{13.45}$$

where π^* is the target level of inflation, y_t is output, and y_t^* is the target level of output—typically full-capacity or equilibrium output. Thus the aim is to minimize the present value of deviations of inflation and output from their target levels; α is the weight attached to the output objective relative to that for the inflation objective. The constraint is a model of the determination of inflation and output such as the New Keynesian model.

13.5.1 Social Welfare and the Inflation Objective Function

Originally, the choice of equation (13.45) as the objective function was purely ad hoc, though intuitively reasonable. In particular, it was not based explicitly on considerations of social welfare. The relation between social welfare and a quadratic loss function like equation (13.45) has been analyzed by Rotemberg and Woodford (1997) and Woodford (2003, chapter 6). They show that intertemporal social welfare can be approximated by equation (13.45). This is the basis of our discussion. The difference is that we use a setup related to our previous discussion which is similar to a closed-economy version of the Obstfeld–Rogoff redux model.

We have previously defined social welfare in terms of the representative household intertemporal utility function, which depends on real variables such as consumption, real-money balances, and leisure. In contrast, equation (13.45) has a nominal as well as a real component. In reconciling the two objective functions we need to show how a nominal objective is consistent with seeking to maximize a social welfare function based only on real variables. The answer lies in the real costs imposed through prices being slow to adjust and not being perfectly flexible.

Suppose that the social welfare function for the representative household in period t is

$$U_t = \ln c_t - \gamma \ln y_t(z), \tag{13.46}$$

where c_t is an index of total household consumption given by the CES function

$$c_t = \left[\int_0^1 c_t(z)^{(\sigma-1)/\sigma} \right]^{\sigma/(\sigma-1)}, \quad \sigma > 1, \tag{13.47}$$

and the last term reflects utility from leisure. which is inversely related to the work required to produce $y_t(z)$ of good z. Let P_t be a general price index given by

$$P_t = \left[\int_0^1 p_t(z)^{1-\sigma} \right]^{1/(1-\sigma)}. \tag{13.48}$$

The budget constraint for the representative household is

$$P_t c_t = p_t(z) y_t(z).$$

It follows from the results in chapters 8 and 12 that the demand for good z is

$$c_t(z) = \left[\frac{p_t(z)}{P_t} \right]^{-\sigma} c_t.$$

As $c_t(z) = y_t(z)$ and $c_t = y_t$,

$$y_t(z) = \left[\frac{p_t(z)}{P_t}\right]^{-\sigma} y_t. \qquad (13.49)$$

Next consider a second-order approximation to the utility function taken about the steady-state values of c_t and $y_t(z)$, which we denote by c_t^* and $y_t^*(z)$. This gives

$$E_t U_t \simeq \ln c_t^* - \gamma \ln y_t^*(z) - \tfrac{1}{2} E_t \left[\frac{c_t - c_t^*}{c_t^*}\right]^2 - \tfrac{1}{2}\gamma E_t \left[\frac{y_t(z) - y_t^*(z)}{y_t^*(z)}\right]^2$$

$$= U_t^* - \tfrac{1}{2}V_t(\ln c_t) - \tfrac{1}{2}\gamma V_t[\ln y_t(z)]$$

$$= U_t^* - \tfrac{1}{2}V_t(\ln y_t) - \tfrac{1}{2}\gamma V_t[\ln y_t(z)],$$

where $V_t(\ln y_t)$ can be interpreted as the variance of total output about the steady state or, approximately, by the squared deviation about the steady state:

$$V_t(\ln y_t) \simeq E_t(y_t - y_t^*)^2.$$

$V_t[\ln y_t(z)]$ can be interpreted as the variance of output *across* households/firms from the steady state. Thus dispersion of output across firms is assumed to cause a real welfare loss.

From equation (13.49),

$$\ln y_t(z) = -\sigma(\ln p_t(z) - \ln P_t) + \ln y_t,$$

where we interpret $\ln y_t$ as the expected value of $\ln y_t(z)$ in the steady state and $\ln P_t$ as the expected value of $\ln p_t(z)$ in the steady state. We can then interpret $\ln y_t(z) - \ln y_t$ and $\ln p_t(z) - \ln P_t$ as deviations from the expected steady state. Hence,

$$V_t[\ln y_t(z)] = \sigma^2 V_t[\ln p_t(z)],$$

implying that the variance of output across firms is caused by the variance of their prices. It is, therefore, variations in prices across firms from their steady-state values that causes a loss of real welfare.

At this point we take account of price stickiness by invoking the Calvo model assumption (discussed in chapter 9) that at any point in time only a proportion of firms are able to adjust prices fully and the rest keep their prices fixed or adjust them using a rule of thumb. Distinguishing between the steady-state price level, which is common to all firms, and the average price level across firms, if all prices were fully flexible, then the variance of prices across firms would just be the squared deviation of the average price level from its steady-state value. The reason that $V_t[\ln p_t(z)]$ differs from this is price stickiness.

Reinterpreting the Calvo model using the notation here, a proportion ρ of firms are assumed to adjust their price to the optimal level in period t. The rest do not adjust at all. The general price level is a weighted average of the two. Thus

$$\ln P_t = \rho \ln P_t^\# + (1 - \rho) \ln p_{t-1}(z),$$

where $\ln P_t^{\#}$ is the optimal price. Hence, as a proportion $1 - \rho$ of firms do not change price,

$$\ln p_t(z) - \ln P_t = \rho(\ln p_t(z) - \ln P_t^{\#}) + (1 - \rho)\Delta \ln p_t(z)$$
$$= \rho(\ln p_t(z) - \ln P_t^{\#}). \qquad (13.50)$$

Recalling that the aim in the Calvo model is to choose $\ln p_t(z)$ to minimize

$$\frac{1}{2}\sum_{s=0}^{\infty} \delta^s E_t[\ln p_t(z) - \ln P_{t+s}^{\#}]^2,$$

where $\delta = \beta(1 - \rho)$, we obtain the solution

$$\ln p_t(z) = (1 - \delta)\ln P_t^{\#} + \delta E_t \ln p_{t+1}(z).$$

Hence

$$\ln p_t(z) - \ln P_t^{\#} = \delta[E_t \ln p_{t+1}(z) - \ln P_t^{\#}]$$
$$= \frac{\delta}{1 - \delta} E_t \Delta \ln p_{t+1}(z). \qquad (13.51)$$

Consequently, from equations (13.50) and (13.51),

$$\ln p_t(z) - \ln P_t = \rho\frac{\delta}{1 - \delta} E_t \Delta \ln p_{t+1}(z).$$

Accordingly,

$$V_t[\ln p_t(z)] = \left(\frac{\rho\delta}{1 - \delta}\right)^2 [E_t \pi_{t+1}(z) - \pi]^2, \qquad (13.52)$$

where $\pi_t(z) = \Delta \ln p_t(z)$ and π is the average value of $E_t \pi_{t+1}(z)$.

Putting these results together, and noting that all firms who change prices do so by the same amount, which implies that $\pi_{t+1}(z) = \pi_{t+1}$, we can approximate the social welfare function by

$$E_t U_t \simeq U_t^* - \frac{1}{2}V_t(\ln y_t) - \frac{1}{2}\gamma\left(\frac{\sigma\rho\delta}{1 - \delta}\right)^2 [E_t \pi_{t+1}(z) - \pi]^2$$
$$\simeq U_t^* - \frac{1}{2}E_t(y_t - y_t^*)^2 - \frac{1}{2}\alpha[E_t \pi_{t+1} - \pi]^2. \qquad (13.53)$$

Equation (13.53) is a reassuring result. It suggests that equation (13.45) can be regarded as an approximation to the intertemporal utility function based on a utility function defined by equation (13.46). The closeness of the approximation is, of course, dependent on the validity of the many assumptions that we have made.

13.5.2   Optimal Inflation Policy under Discretion

13.5.2.1   The Barro-Gordon Model

The seminal paper on optimal inflation targeting is that of Barro and Gordon (1983). This will form the basis of our analysis. For the sake of simplicity, Barro and Gordon use a highly stylized model of the economy. They also use a policy objective function that is slightly different from equation (13.45).

We assume that the economy faces a trade-off between inflation and output in the short run but not in the long run. The connection between the two is given by the following stylized version of the Phillips equation, which is rewritten as a supply function:

$$y = y_n + \alpha(\pi - \pi^e) + \varepsilon, \tag{13.54}$$

where y_n is capacity or equilibrium output, π^e is the economy's rational expectation of inflation, and ε is an output shock. An important, but arguably somewhat implausible, assumption is that the output shock is observed by the monetary authority—which we take to be the central bank—but not by the public. This gives an informational advantage to the central bank.

The monetary-policy instrument is denoted by z. At present we assume that this is chosen using discretion rather than a rule. z could be the official interest rate, R, or the rate of growth of the money supply, Δm. A simplifying assumption is that the effect of z on the inflation rate is stochastic and can be captured by the stylized transmission mechanism

$$\pi = z + v, \tag{13.55}$$

where v is a shock not observable by the central bank and has a zero mean, $E(v) = 0$. Consequently, z controls π imperfectly. Another simplifying assumption is that the transmission mechanism is instantaneous and involves no lags. It follows that the rational expectation of inflation is

$$E\pi = \pi^e = z. \tag{13.56}$$

Barro and Gordon specify the central bank's objective function as

$$U = \lambda(y - y_n) - \tfrac{1}{2}(\pi - \pi^*)^2, \tag{13.57}$$

where π^* is the target rate of inflation, rather than as a quadratic objective function. As the model of the economy involves no lags, the objective function can be formulated for a single period. The solution is the same as using an intertemporal utility function. The implication of equation (13.57) is that the central bank prefers output to be above its natural level (i.e., $y > y_n$) but dislikes inflation deviating from target, whether above or below target. Thus, while the inflation objective is symmetric, the output objective is not. A possible justification for the output target asymmetry is that the government chooses the objective function and prefers output to be above target rather than below it, but fears that the central bank might have a tendency to conservatism, i.e., the central bank might have a preference for keeping output below its equilibrium level in order to better achieve its inflation objective.

The central bank's problem is to choose z to maximize U subject to the constraints provided by the economy, namely, equations (13.54) and (13.55). We recall that ε is known to the central bank but that v is not, and that y_n, π^e, and π^* are given.

Eliminating $y - y_n$ using the supply function, equation (13.54), and π using the transmission mechanism, equation (13.55), gives

$$U = \lambda[\alpha(\pi - \pi^e) + \varepsilon] - \tfrac{1}{2}(\pi - \pi^*)^2$$
$$= \lambda[\alpha(z + v - \pi^e) + \varepsilon] - \tfrac{1}{2}(z + v - \pi^*)^2.$$

The first-order condition is

$$\frac{\partial U}{\partial z} = \alpha\lambda - (z + v - \pi^*) = 0.$$

Hence the solution for the policy instrument z is

$$z = \alpha\lambda + \pi^* - v.$$

As the central bank does not know v, it uses its best guess, namely that $E(v) = 0$. The optimal setting of z is therefore

$$z^* = \alpha\lambda + \pi^*.$$

Actual inflation is then

$$\pi = \alpha\lambda + \pi^* + v$$

and so the public's rational expectation of inflation is

$$\pi^e = E\pi = \alpha\lambda + \pi^* > \pi^*. \tag{13.58}$$

Equation (13.58) is the key result. It shows that expected inflation is greater than target inflation. In other words, there is an inflation bias. Why is this? Because the central bank likes y to be greater than y_n. Consequently, if $\lambda = 0$ then the inflation bias is zero.

Does the extra inflation that results from the central bank's concern for output confer any benefit on the economy in terms of extra actual output, i.e., is $y > y_n$? From the supply function, equation (13.54),

$$y = y_n + \alpha(\pi - \pi^e) + \varepsilon$$
$$= y_n + \alpha(\alpha\lambda + \pi^* + v - \pi^e) + \varepsilon$$
$$= y_n + \alpha v + \varepsilon.$$

Hence $Ey = y_n$, implying that no output gain is to be expected as a result of the central bank preferring output to exceed its equilibrium level. Moreover, there is no output benefit to the public arising from having excessive inflation. If the central bank sets $\lambda = 0$ in the objective function and, as a result, acts like a strict rather than a flexible inflation targeter, inflation would be lower and expected output would be unaffected.

Although the extra inflation does not generate additional output, does it improve expected utility? This can be evaluated from

$$U = \lambda(y - y_n) - \tfrac{1}{2}(\pi - \pi^*)^2$$
$$= \lambda(\alpha v + \varepsilon) - \tfrac{1}{2}(\alpha\lambda + v)^2.$$

Expected utility is therefore

$$E(U) = -\tfrac{1}{2}[(\alpha\lambda)^2 + \sigma_v^2],$$

where σ_v^2 is the variance of v. The value of λ that maximizes $E(U)$ is $\lambda = 0$. Hence, there is no benefit, i.e., expected gain in utility, arising from the central bank's concern about output. In fact, there is an expected utility loss that is eliminated when $\lambda = 0$. We conclude, therefore, that it is optimal for a central bank pursuing a policy of discretion to be a strict inflation targeter, i.e., to eschew any output objectives.

13.5.2.2 *Using a Quadratic Loss Function*

A question that arises is whether this strong conclusion is due to the choice of objective function. To answer this we reexamine the problem using a single-period quadratic objective function Q where

$$
\begin{aligned}
Q &= \tfrac{1}{2}\lambda(y - y_n - k)^2 + \tfrac{1}{2}(\pi - \pi^*)^2 \\
&= \tfrac{1}{2}\lambda[\alpha(\pi - \pi^e) + \varepsilon - k]^2 + \tfrac{1}{2}(\pi - \pi^*)^2 \\
&= \tfrac{1}{2}\lambda[\alpha(z + v - \pi^e) + \varepsilon - k]^2 + \tfrac{1}{2}(z + v - \pi^*)^2.
\end{aligned}
\tag{13.59}
$$

The reason for including k is so that the central bank still prefers $y > y_n$.

The problem is to choose z to minimize Q. The first-order condition is

$$\frac{\partial Q}{\partial z} = \alpha\lambda[\alpha(z + v - \pi^e) + \varepsilon - k] + (z + v - \pi^*) = 0;$$

hence the solution for z is

$$z = \frac{\alpha^2\lambda\pi^e + \pi^* + \alpha\lambda(k - \varepsilon)}{1 + \alpha^2\lambda} - v.$$

Setting $E(v) = 0$ gives the optimal z as

$$z^* = \frac{\alpha^2\lambda\pi^e + \pi^* + \alpha\lambda(k - \varepsilon)}{1 + \alpha^2\lambda}.$$

As a result, inflation is

$$\pi = z^* + v$$

and so expected inflation is

$$
\begin{aligned}
\pi^e = E\pi &= E(z^* + v) \\
&= \frac{\alpha^2\lambda\pi^e + \pi^* + \alpha\lambda k}{1 + \alpha^2\lambda} \\
&= \pi^* + \alpha\lambda k > \pi^*.
\end{aligned}
\tag{13.60}
$$

Once again, therefore, there is an inflation bias. This disappears if either $\lambda = 0$ or $k = 0$, i.e., if either the central bank is a strict inflation targeter or if it discards its preference for having $y > y_n$. Is there an output gain to justify the inflation bias? Using the result that $\pi^e = \pi^* + \alpha\lambda k$, the optimal setting for z is

$$z^* = \frac{\alpha^2\lambda\pi^e + \pi^* + \alpha\lambda(k - \varepsilon)}{1 + \alpha^2\lambda}$$

$$= \pi^e - \frac{\alpha\lambda\varepsilon}{1 + \alpha^2\lambda}.$$

Hence, the actual values of inflation and output are

$$\pi = \pi^e - \frac{\alpha\lambda\varepsilon}{1 + \alpha^2\lambda} + v,$$

$$y = y_n + \alpha v + \frac{\varepsilon}{1 + \alpha^2\lambda}.$$

This implies that the expected level of output is

$$E(y) = y_n.$$

Thus, setting $\lambda, k > 0$ is not expected to lead to any output gain.

Is there a welfare benefit from the inflation bias? Substituting the solutions for inflation and output into the quadratic objective function gives

$$Q = \tfrac{1}{2}\lambda(y - y_n - k)^2 + \tfrac{1}{2}(\pi - \pi^*)^2$$

$$= \tfrac{1}{2}\lambda\left[\alpha v + \frac{\varepsilon}{1 + \alpha^2\lambda} - k\right]^2 + \frac{1}{2}\left(v - \frac{\alpha\lambda\varepsilon}{1 + \alpha^2\lambda} + \alpha\lambda k\right)^2.$$

Hence expected welfare is

$$E(Q) = \tfrac{1}{2}\lambda\left[\alpha^2\sigma_v^2 + \left(\frac{1}{1 + \alpha^2\lambda}\right)^2\sigma_\varepsilon^2 + k^2\right] + \frac{1}{2}\left(\sigma_v^2 + \left(\frac{\alpha\lambda}{1 + \alpha^2\lambda}\right)^2\sigma_\varepsilon^2 + (\alpha\lambda)^2 k^2\right).$$

To minimize $E(Q)$ we must set $\lambda = 0$, i.e., give no weight to output. Consequently, as in the Barro-Gordon model, there is neither an output nor a welfare gain from having $\lambda > 0$. A strict ranking of expected welfare costs is possible as

$$E(Q) > E(Q)|_{\lambda>0, k=0} > E(Q)|_{\lambda=0, k>0} = E(Q)|_{\lambda=0, k=0}.$$

Thus, welfare costs are minimized solely by setting $\lambda = 0$; the choice of k is immaterial. Nonetheless, a central bank following a policy of discretion might as well be a strict inflation targeter as there is no advantage to having $\lambda > 0$. The choice of objective function does not affect this conclusion.

13.5.3 Optimal Inflation Policy under Commitment to a Rule

Instead of allowing the monetary authority to have complete discretion in their choice of z as above, we now consider the case where the central bank publicly commits itself to following the rule

$$z = z^* = \pi^*,$$

where the rule is known to the public. As z is chosen through a rule, the central bank does not need to refer to its objective function.

It follows that

$$\pi = z + v = \pi^* + v,$$
$$E\pi = \pi^e = \pi^*,$$
$$y = y_n + \alpha(\pi - \pi^*) + \varepsilon$$
$$= y_n + \alpha v + \varepsilon,$$
$$Ey = y_n.$$

We now find that there is no inflation bias and that expected output is the same as under a policy of discretion.

The welfare implications of commitment can be derived by evaluating the Barro-Gordon and the quadratic loss functions, equations (13.57) and (13.59). We can then compare these with their values under discretion.

13.5.3.1 The Barro-Gordon Model

We denote the value of U under commitment by U^C. From equation (13.57),

$$U^C = \lambda(\alpha v + \varepsilon) - \tfrac{1}{2}v^2,$$
$$E(U^C) = -\tfrac{1}{2}\sigma_v^2.$$

By comparison, under discretion, expected welfare is

$$E(U^D) = -\tfrac{1}{2}(\alpha^2\lambda^2 + \sigma_v^2) < E(U^C).$$

Thus, expected welfare is higher under commitment than discretion. It appears, therefore, that allowing the central bank to exercise discretion is costly to society.

13.5.3.2 Quadratic Loss

Similarly, from equation (13.59), actual and expected losses under commitment are

$$Q^C = \tfrac{1}{2}\lambda(\alpha V + \varepsilon - k)^2 + \tfrac{1}{2}V^2,$$
$$E(Q^C) = \tfrac{1}{2}(1 + \alpha^2\lambda)\sigma_V^2 + \tfrac{1}{2}\lambda(\sigma_\varepsilon^2 + k^2).$$

Expected loss under discretion is

$$E(Q^D) = E(Q^C) + \tfrac{1}{2}\lambda\left(1 - \frac{\alpha^2}{1 + \alpha^2\lambda}\right)\sigma_\varepsilon^2.$$

It follows that if $\lambda > 1 - (1/\alpha^2) > 0$, then

$$E(Q^D) > E(Q^C).$$

In other words, a policy of commitment gives a lower expected loss than one of discretion. We recall that when $\lambda = 0$ cost is minimized under discretion. In addition, $E(Q^D) = E(Q^C)$.

We conclude that the public would prefer a rules-based policy to one of discretion in which the central bank is a strict inflation targeter. Although a policy of commitment is preferred by the public, if it is not also preferred by the central bank, then the temptation for the central bank is to abandon the rule and use discretion instead. If the public knows what the rule is, they would know that it had been broken. Having once reneged on their commitment, the public would be unlikely to believe any future promises by the central bank to commit to using a rule. The public would then act on the assumption that the central bank is using discretion even if it says it is not. In other words, once the central bank loses its reputation, it would be very difficult to restore. We examine these issues further by considering intertemporal optimization. In practice, of course, matters will not be so clear-cut due to probable public ignorance of the correct economic structure and, even if this were known, to the impact of unpredictable shocks.

13.5.4 Intertemporal Optimization and Time-Consistent Inflation Targeting

As noted in our discussion of fiscal policy in chapter 6, a situation where a policy maker announces one policy for a given point in time but switches to a different policy when that time comes is called time inconsistency. We now carry out a more formal analysis of this problem as it applies to inflation targeting in the Barro–Gordon model under discretion and commitment.

We assume that prior to period t the central bank commits to using a rule and hence sets $z = \pi^*$. As a result, the public's expectation of inflation is $\pi^e = \pi^*$. However, the central bank prefers to use discretionary policy and so in period t decides to switch to this without warning the public of the change. In particular, we assume that from period t the central bank sets z to minimize the intertemporal objective function

$$\mathcal{U}_t = E_t \sum_0^\infty \beta^s U_{t+s}, \quad 0 < \beta < 1,$$

subject to

$$U_t = \lambda(y_t - y_n) - \tfrac{1}{2}(\pi_t - \pi^*)^2,$$
$$y_t = y_n + \alpha(\pi_t - \pi_t^e) + \varepsilon_t,$$
$$\pi_t = z_t + v_t.$$

As a result, the central bank switches to $z_t = \alpha\lambda + \pi^* - v_t$.

Once the central bank is perceived to have switched its policy to discretion, the public believes this will continue and so revises its expectation of inflation to $E_t\pi_{t+s} = \pi_{t+s}^e = \pi^* + \alpha\lambda$ for $s > 0$. Thus

$$\pi_{t+s}^e = z_{t+s} = \begin{cases} \pi^* & \text{if } \pi_t = \pi^*, \\ \pi^* + \alpha\lambda & \text{if } \pi_t \neq \pi^*, \end{cases} \quad s > 0.$$

We now compare the value of the intertemporal objective function when the central bank does not switch policy with that when it does.

13.5.4.1 No Switch (NS)

If $z = \pi^*$ in each period, then

$$\pi_t = \pi^* + v,$$
$$\pi_t^e = \pi^*,$$
$$y_t = y_n + \varepsilon_t,$$
$$U_t^{NS} = \lambda\varepsilon_t - \tfrac{1}{2}v_t^2,$$
$$E(U_t^{NS}) = \tfrac{1}{2}\sigma_v^2.$$

Hence the expected value of welfare as evaluated using the central bank's welfare function is

$$E\mathcal{U}_t^{NS} = \frac{\tfrac{1}{2}\sigma_v^2}{1-\beta}.$$

Only unavoidable shocks v_t in the transmission mechanism cause a loss of welfare.

13.5.4.2 Switching (S)

We assume that a switch to discretion occurs in period t but that this is not apparent to the public until after they have formed their inflation expectations for period t. Thus, although

$$\pi_t = \pi^* + \alpha\lambda + v_t,$$

as the public were not expecting the switch, their expectation of inflation is π^*. As a consequence of the switch, output in period t is

$$y_t = y_n + \alpha(\pi^* + \alpha\lambda + v_t - \pi^*) + \varepsilon_t$$
$$= y_n + \alpha^2\lambda + \alpha v_t + \varepsilon_t,$$
$$Ey_t = y_n + \alpha^2\lambda.$$

Thus there is an output gain due to switching. The welfare implications for period t are

$$U_t^S = \lambda(\alpha^2\lambda + \alpha v_t + \varepsilon_t) - \tfrac{1}{2}(\alpha\lambda + v_t)^2,$$
$$E(U_t^S) = \tfrac{1}{2}(\alpha\lambda)^2 - \tfrac{1}{2}\sigma_v^2 > E(U_t^{NS}) = -\tfrac{1}{2}\sigma_v^2.$$

Through causing higher output in period t, there is, therefore, also a welfare gain to the central bank.

This is only temporary as the public's expectations will change when they realize that a switch has occurred. Having observed the switch of policy in period t, the public then assumes that discretion will be employed in the future. Consequently, for $s > 1$,

$$E(U^S_{t+s}) = -\tfrac{1}{2}[(\alpha\lambda)^2 + \sigma^2_v] < E(U^{NS}_{t+s}) = -\tfrac{1}{2}\sigma^2_v.$$

It follows that

$$E(\mathcal{U}^S_t) = \tfrac{1}{2}(\alpha\lambda)^2 - \tfrac{1}{2}\sigma^2_v - \sum_{s=1}^{\infty} \beta^s[\tfrac{1}{2}(\alpha\lambda)^2 + \tfrac{1}{2}\sigma^2_v]$$

$$= (\alpha\lambda)^2 - \frac{1}{2}\frac{(\alpha\lambda)^2 + \sigma^2_v}{1 - \beta}$$

$$= E(\mathcal{U}^{NS}_t) + (\alpha\lambda)^2\left[1 - \frac{1}{2(1 - \beta)}\right]$$

$$\lessgtr E(\mathcal{U}^{NS}_t) \quad \text{as } 1 > \beta \gtrless \tfrac{1}{2}.$$

The greater the discount factor β, the greater the intertemporal loss of welfare caused by switching. It is only when the future is heavily discounted ($\beta < \tfrac{1}{2}$) that the output gain, which occurs only in period t, is sufficient to cause an increase in intertemporal welfare. In the longer run, welfare is lower in each period. Moreover, both the central bank and the public are worse off. This suggests that although switching policy produces immediate gains, it is not a welfare-improving strategy in the long run. In practice, the public may find it difficult to identify whether the central bank has switched policy, or whether both inflation and z have been affected by the shock v.

13.5.5   Central Bank versus Public Preferences

So far we have taken account only of the preferences of the central bank. Suppose that these are different from those of the public. In particular, suppose that the central bank gives more weight to achieving the inflation objective than does the public, or the central bank has a lower target level of inflation π^* than the public. In other words, the central bank is more conservative about inflation than the public.

To illustrate, we assume that the welfare function of the central bank is

$$U^{CB} = \lambda(y - y_n) - \tfrac{1}{2}(1 + \delta)(\pi - \pi^*)^2 \tag{13.61}$$

with $\delta > 0$, but the public prefers $\delta = 0$. Thus the central bank gives more weight to the inflation objective than the public. Equation (13.61) can be rewritten as

$$U^{CB} = (1 + \delta)\left\{\frac{\lambda}{1 + \delta}(y - y_n) - \tfrac{1}{2}(\pi - \pi^*)^2\right\}.$$

Thus, in effect, we have simply replaced λ in the original formulation by $\lambda/(1 + \delta)$. We can therefore just reinterpret the previous results.

It follows that the optimal setting for policy is

$$z^* = \frac{\alpha\lambda}{1 + \delta} + \pi^* = \pi^e$$

and inflation is

$$\pi = \frac{\alpha\lambda}{1+\delta} + \pi^* + v,$$

$$\pi^{e} = \frac{\alpha\lambda}{1+\delta} + \pi^*.$$

Consequently, the effect of introducing δ, which is positive, is to reduce both z and the inflation bias. Output is

$$y = y_n + \alpha\left[\frac{\alpha\lambda}{1+\delta} + \pi^* + v - \pi^{e}\right] + \varepsilon$$

$$= y_n + \alpha v + \varepsilon,$$

which implies that, as before, $Ey = y_n$.

The measure of welfare will depend on whose welfare function is being used. The central bank's level of welfare is

$$U^{CB} = \lambda(\alpha v + \varepsilon) - \tfrac{1}{2}(1+\delta)\left(\frac{\alpha\lambda}{1+\delta} + v\right)^2,$$

$$E(U^{CB}) = -\frac{1}{2}\left[\frac{(\alpha\lambda)^2}{1+\delta} + (1+\delta)\sigma_v^2\right]$$

$$= (1+\delta)E(U^P)$$

$$> E(U^{CB}),$$

where U^P is the public's welfare.

For the central bank the optimal value of δ is obtained from

$$\frac{\partial EU^{CB}}{\partial\delta} = \frac{1}{2}\left[\left(\frac{\alpha\lambda}{1+\delta}\right)^2 - \sigma_v^2\right] = 0.$$

The optimal value of δ is therefore

$$\delta = \frac{\alpha\lambda}{\sigma_v} - 1.$$

Thus, the greater σ_v is and the smaller α is, the smaller δ should be. The cost of shocks in the transmission mechanism are increased by having a large δ. But for the public

$$\frac{\partial E(U^P)}{\partial\delta} = \left(\frac{\alpha\lambda}{1+\delta}\right)^2 > 0,$$

implying that the more conservative the central bank, the better off is the public.

These results were derived under the assumption that the central bank is using discretion. Do they hold under commitment, i.e., when the central bank commits itself to setting $z = \pi^*$? In this case there is no inflation bias and no expected output gain. Further,

$$E(U^{CB}) = -\tfrac{1}{2}(1+\delta)\sigma_v^2,$$

$$E(U^P) = -\tfrac{1}{2}\sigma_v^2,$$

implying, once more, that there is no gain to the public from having a more conservative central bank.

The expected welfare of the public and the central bank can be compared under commitment to a rule and discretion. For the public we get the same result as before that commitment is preferable as

$$E(U^{\mathrm{P}})|_{\mathrm{C}} = E(U^{\mathrm{P}})|_{\mathrm{D}} + \frac{1}{2}\left(\frac{\alpha\lambda}{1+\delta}\right)^2 > E(U^{\mathrm{P}})|_{\mathrm{D}}.$$

Commitment is also better for the central bank, as

$$E(U^{\mathrm{CB}})|_{\mathrm{C}} = E(U^{\mathrm{CB}})|_{\mathrm{D}} + \frac{1}{2}\frac{(\alpha\lambda)^2}{1+\delta} > E(U^{\mathrm{CB}})|_{\mathrm{D}}.$$

There is, therefore, no reason to alter our previous conclusion that, as far as the public is concerned, the central bank should pursue a policy of strict inflation targeting with commitment. We can now add another condition: the central bank should not switch policy.

13.6   Optimal Monetary Policy using the New Keynesian Model

13.6.1   Using Discretion

The Barro–Gordon model is a stylized version of the New Keynesian model. Next we now consider optimal monetary policy using the New Keynesian model derived earlier and given by equations (13.30) and (13.31). We repeat these equations for ease of reference:

$$\pi_t = (1 - \beta)\pi^* + \beta E_t \pi_{t+1} + \gamma x_t + e_{\pi t}, \tag{13.62}$$

$$x_t = E_t x_{t+1} - \alpha(R_t - E_t \pi_{t+1} - \theta) + e_{xt}. \tag{13.63}$$

We recall that $x_t = y_t - y_n$ is the output gap and $e_{\pi t}$ and e_{xt} are independent, zero-mean, and serially uncorrelated shocks unknown to the central bank. A key difference between this model and the Barro–Gordon model is that this model possesses a dynamic structure.

We assume that in using its discretion the central bank chooses the interest rate R_t to minimize the single-period quadratic cost function:

$$E(Q_t) = \tfrac{1}{2}E[(\pi_t - \pi^*)^2 + \varphi(x_t - k)^2], \tag{13.64}$$

where other variables are as defined previously. It can be shown that

$$E\left(\frac{\partial Q_t}{\partial R_t}\right) = E\left[\frac{\partial \pi_t}{\partial R_t}(\pi_t - \pi^*) + \frac{\partial x_t}{\partial R_t}\varphi(x_t - k)\right] = 0.$$

In order to evaluate the two derivatives we must use the solutions derived earlier, namely equations (13.34) and (13.35), which are also repeated:

$$\pi_t = -\frac{\alpha\gamma\theta}{\eta_1(1-\eta_2)} + \frac{1}{\eta_1}\pi_{t-1} + \frac{\alpha\gamma\eta_2}{\eta_1}\sum_{s=0}^{\infty}\eta_2^s E_t R_{t+s} + \frac{\alpha\gamma}{\eta_1}R_{t-1}$$
$$+ \delta(e_{\pi t} + \gamma e_{xt}) + \frac{\alpha\gamma}{\eta_1}(e_{\pi,t-1} + \gamma e_{x,t-1}),$$

$$\Delta x_t = \frac{1}{\eta_1}\Delta x_{t-1} - \frac{\alpha^2\gamma\eta_2}{\eta_1}\sum_{s=0}^{\infty}\eta_2^s E_t R_{t+s} + \alpha\left(1 - \frac{\alpha\gamma}{\eta_1}\right)R_{t-1} - \frac{\alpha}{\eta_1}R_{t-2}$$
$$- \alpha\delta(e_{\pi t} + \gamma e_{xt}) - \frac{\alpha^2\gamma}{\eta_1}e_{\pi,t-1} - \left(1 + \frac{\alpha\gamma^2}{\eta_1}\right)e_{x,t-1} + \frac{1}{\eta_1}e_{x,t-2}.$$

If the change in the interest rate in period t is temporary, and is just for that single period, then

$$\frac{\partial\pi_t}{\partial R_t} = \frac{\alpha\gamma\eta_2}{\eta_1},$$
$$\frac{\partial x_t}{\partial R_t} = -\frac{\alpha^2\gamma\eta_2}{\eta_1}.$$

Hence,

$$E(\pi_t - \pi^*) - \alpha\varphi E(x_t - k) = 0.$$

The relation between inflation and output is therefore

$$E\pi_t = \pi^* + \alpha\varphi E(x_t - k).$$

Solving this for Ex_t and substituting into equation (13.62) gives the solution for expected inflation:

$$E\pi_t = (1-\beta)\pi^* + \beta E\pi_{t+1} + \gamma\left[k + \frac{1}{\alpha\varphi}E(\pi_t - \pi^*)\right]$$
$$= \frac{\beta}{1-(\gamma/\alpha\varphi)}E\pi_{t+1} + \frac{(1-\beta-(\gamma/\alpha\varphi))\pi^* + \gamma k}{1-(\gamma/\alpha\varphi)}.$$

The solution therefore depends on the values of the parameters. Suppose that

$$\left|\frac{\beta}{1-(\gamma/\alpha\varphi)}\right| < 1.$$

The solution is then

$$E\pi_t = \pi^* + \frac{\gamma k}{1-\beta-(\gamma/\alpha\varphi)}.$$

Thus $E\pi_t \gtrless \pi^*$ depending on $\beta + (\gamma/\alpha\varphi) \lessgtr 1$. And if $\varphi = 0$, or if $k = 0$, then $E\pi_t = \pi^*$.

The solution for expected output is

$$Ex_t = k + \frac{1}{\alpha\varphi}E(\pi_t - \pi^*)$$
$$= k + \frac{1}{\alpha\varphi}\frac{\gamma k}{1-\beta-(\gamma/\alpha\varphi)}.$$

Hence

$$Ex_t = \frac{(1-\beta)}{1-\beta-(\gamma/\alpha\varphi)}k,$$

and so, for $\beta < 1$, we have $Ex_t \gtrless 0$ depending on $\beta + (\gamma/\alpha\varphi) \lessgtr 1$. And if $\varphi = 0$, or if $k = 0$, then $Ex_t = 0$.

To summarize, optimal inflation policy based on the NKM will achieve its target if either the central bank is a strict inflation targeter, and so sets $\varphi = 0$, or if $k = 0$. In both the cases the expected output gap is zero as $Ex_t = 0$. The interest rate that achieves this may be obtained from equation (13.63) or, since $Ex_t = 0$, from the Fisher equation, and is given by

$$R_t = E_t\pi_{t+1} + \theta$$
$$= \pi^* + \theta.$$

Consequently, the optimal choice is to set the nominal interest rate equal to the long-run value consistent with the inflation target.

13.6.2 Rules-Based Policy

Previously we considered the behavior of inflation and output when monetary policy was conducted using the rule

$$R_t = \theta + \pi^* + \mu(\pi_t - \pi^*) + \nu x_t + e_{Rt}. \tag{13.65}$$

We found that the solutions for inflation and output were

$$\pi_t = \pi^* + \frac{1}{1+\alpha(\nu+\mu\gamma)}[(1+\alpha\nu)e_{\pi t} + \gamma e_{xt} - \alpha\gamma e_{Rt}], \tag{13.66}$$

$$x_t = -\frac{1}{1+\alpha(\nu+\mu\gamma)}(\alpha\mu e_{\pi t} + e_{xt} - e_{Rt}). \tag{13.67}$$

We treated the values of μ and ν as given. For example, the Taylor rule chooses them as $\mu = 1.5$ and $\nu = 0.5$. We now consider the optimum choice of μ and ν.

From equations (13.66) and (13.67), the larger μ is, the smaller the impact of all three shocks on inflation, and the output and interest rate shocks on output, but the greater the impact of inflation shocks on output. The larger ν is, the smaller the impact of all three shocks on output, and the output and interest rate shocks on inflation, but the greater the impact of inflation shocks on inflation.

To find the optimal values of μ and ν we evaluate $E(Q_t)$ by substituting the solutions given by equations (13.66) and (13.67) into equation (13.64). As the shocks are assumed to be independent of each other, we obtain

$$E(Q_t)$$
$$= \frac{1}{2[1+\alpha(\nu+\mu\gamma)]^2}\{[(1+\alpha\nu)^2 + \varphi(\alpha\mu)^2]\sigma_\pi^2 + (\varphi+\gamma^2)\sigma_x^2 + [\varphi+(\alpha\gamma)^2]\sigma_R^2\}$$
$$+ \tfrac{1}{2}\varphi k^2,$$

where σ_π^2, σ_x^2, and σ_R^2 are the variances of $e_{\pi t}$, e_{xt}, and e_{Rt}, respectively. We now minimize $E(Q_t)$ with respect to μ and ν. The general solution can only be obtained numerically for specific values of the model parameters due to the nonlinearities of the first-order conditions. But we can obtain a closed-form solution with respect to one parameter of the rule, given the others. For example, with $\nu = 0$, minimizing $E(Q_t)$ with respect to μ gives

$$\mu = \frac{y}{\varphi\alpha}\left\{1 + (\varphi + y^2)\frac{\sigma_x^2}{\sigma_\pi^2} + [\varphi + (\alpha y)^2]\frac{\sigma_R^2}{\sigma_\pi^2}\right\}.$$

Hence, the greater the variances of the shocks to output and interest rates relative to that of inflation shocks (i.e., σ_x^2/σ_π^2 and σ_R^2/σ_π^2), the greater the interest rate response to inflation in excess of its target.

Alternatively, under strict inflation targeting, when $\varphi = 0$,

$$E(Q_t) = \frac{1}{2[1 + \alpha(\nu + \mu y)]^2}[(1 + \alpha\nu)^2\sigma_\pi^2 + y^2\sigma_x^2 + (\alpha y)^2\sigma_R^2].$$

The optimal value of μ is therefore infinity. In this case $E(Q_t) = 0$, irrespective of the choice of ν. However, choosing $\mu = \infty$ would make interest rates extremely volatile.

This identifies a new problem, namely, the economic cost of instrument volatility. One way to deal with this is to modify the objective function by penalizing variations in interest rates, for example, by adding a term in $(R_t - \theta - \pi^*)^2$. Since this may still result in frequent, though smaller, changes in interest rates, a further modification could be to include in the objective function a term in $(\Delta R_t)^2$. This would have the effect of smoothing interest rate changes. Taken together, the objective function would then be of the form

$$E(Q_t) = \tfrac{1}{2}E[(\pi_t - \pi^*)^2 + \varphi(x_t - k)^2 + \eta(R_t - \theta - \pi^*)^2 + \psi(\Delta R_t)^2]. \quad (13.68)$$

For further discussion of the conduct of monetary policy and other issues related to optimal inflation targeting, see Clarida et al. (1999, 2000, 2001), Gali et al. (2004b), Gali (2008), Giannoni and Woodford (2005), Leeper et al. (1996), Leeper and Zha (2001), McCallum and Nelson (1999), Svensson and Woodford (2003, 2004), Walsh (2003), and Woodford (2003).

13.7 Monetary Policy in the Euro Area

The European Central Bank sets a common interest rate for the whole euro area. We consider the consequences of this for inflation and output in individual countries. Our analysis is based on a simple stylized New Keynesian model adapted for open economies that share a common currency.

At first sight, a country with a higher inflation rate requires a higher interest rate in order to reduce the output pressure on inflation. But this rate would then be too high for a country with a lower inflation rate, which may need an output stimulus. Choosing an interest rate somewhere between the two—which is the

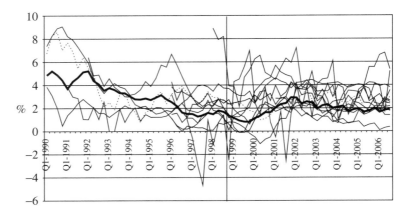

Figure 13.4. EU annual inflation (year-on-year) 1990–2006.

result of having a common interest rate—may also pose a problem. A country with inflation higher than the common nominal interest rate would have a negative real interest rate. This would be expected to stimulate the economy and tend to increase inflation in that country. Whereas a country with an inflation rate below the nominal interest rate would have a positive real interest rate, which would tend to deflate the economy and decrease inflation. This suggests that a common interest rate for countries with widely differing inflation rates could cause individual country inflation rates to diverge from each other.

There is, however, a factor that may offset this. The higher-inflation countries would suffer a loss of competitiveness to the lower-inflation countries. This would tend to reduce output, and hence the inflationary pressure, in the higher-inflation countries, and raise output, and hence inflation, in the lower-inflation countries. The issue, therefore, is whether this competitiveness effect is strong enough to bring about the convergence of individual country inflation rates, and hence lead to balanced economic activity in the currency union.

In figures 13.4 and 13.5 we consider the recent inflation experience of euro area members together with Denmark and the United Kingdom, who are not members of the euro area. Figure 13.4 plots the year-on-year inflation rates for each country together with EU inflation (the heavier line) for the period 1990–2006. The corresponding U.K. inflation rate is the dotted line. EU inflation was on a falling trend prior to the launch of the euro in 1999; afterwards the EU inflation rate has fluctuated close to 2%. Convergence of individual country inflation rates seemed to occur until around 1993, but after that inflation appears to show no tendency for any further convergence; in fact, since 2005, inflation rates appear to have diverged somewhat.

Figure 13.5 plots the natural logarithms of the price levels of these EU countries from the start of 1999, the base for each series. Since the natural logarithm of the price level for each country is zero in the first quarter of 1999, the data depict cumulative inflation rates since 1999. Again the average EU price level is the heavier line and the United Kingdom is the dotted line. The slopes of the

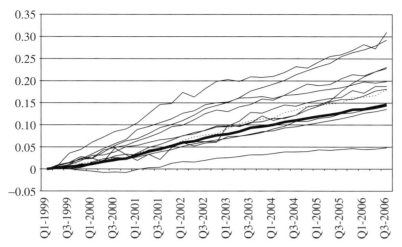

Figure 13.5. The natural logarithm of EU price levels 1999–2006 (1999 = 0).

lines therefore measure the average inflation rates over the period 1999–2006. (The increase in the dispersion of the lines is partly an artifact of the choice of base period. Had the base period been the last period of 2006, the lines would be shown converging at the end and not the start, but the slopes of the lines would still convey the same information about average inflation.) The top line is Ireland, which has had the highest inflation, and the bottom line is Germany, which has had the lowest inflation. Thus price levels have steadily diverged, implying a relative gain in competitiveness for countries below the EU line and a loss in competitiveness for countries above the EU. In order of the size of the gain in competitiveness we have Germany, France, and then Belgium.

The evidence seems to indicate that inflation rates have not diverged, but neither have they converged, with the result that there has been a steady loss of competitiveness by the high-inflation countries and a gain of competitiveness by the low-inflation countries.

13.7.1 New Keynesian Model of the Euro Area

We now examine these issues more formally by constructing a model of the euro area with a common monetary policy and with real interest rate, competitiveness, and absorbtion effects. The absorbtion effects are captured by the output of foreign countries, including of course other euro area countries. We then derive the optimal discretionary monetary policy for the euro area subject to this model. We wish to determine whether in theory competitiveness and absorbtion effects bring about inflation convergence.

13.7.2 Model

The model for the euro area is based on a stylized open-economy version of the New Keynesian model. It is sufficient to assume that the euro area consists of only two countries. We assume that each economy is described by two equations: open-economy aggregate demand and supply functions. These are

AD: $x_{it} = -\beta(R_t - E_t \pi_{i,t+1}) + \gamma(p_{jt} - p_{it})$
$$+ \phi(s_t + p_t^* - p_{it}) + \delta x_{jt} + z_{it} + e_{xi,t}, \qquad (13.69)$$

AS: $\pi_{i,t+1} = E_t \pi_{it} + \alpha(x_{it} - x_{n,it}) + e_{\pi i,t+1}, \qquad (13.70)$

for $i, j = 1, 2$, where $0 < \delta, \gamma < 1$, x_{it} is the output of country i at time t, $x_{n,it}$ is its long-run equilibrium (or natural) level of output, which is assumed to be exogenous, p_{it} is the price level of country i, $p_{jt} - p_{it}$ is the terms of trade for country i in trade with country j, $s_t + p_t^* - p_{it}$ is the terms of trade for country i in trade with the rest of the world, s_t is the exchange rate, which is taken as given, p_t^* is the rest of the world's price level, and z_{it} is an exogenous variable affecting country i. $e_{\pi i,t}$ and $e_{xi,t}$ are independent serially uncorrelated shocks that are unknown to the central bank and are not part of the time t information set, hence $E_t e_{\pi,it} = E_t e_{x,it} = 0$. Thus aggregate demand depends on the real interest rate, the price differential (competitiveness), and foreign demand (absorbtion effects). Output differs between the two countries due to different inflation expectations, price levels, real rates of return, export demand, and country-specific shocks. Inflation differs due to different inflation expectations, output gaps, and country-specific inflation shocks. We note that taking the conditional expectation of equation (13.70) gives $E_t x_{it} = x_{ni,t}$. Thus output is expected to be at its natural rate in each country.

We assume that the monetary authority—in the case of the euro, the European Central Bank (ECB)—chooses the common interest rate R_t to minimize a single-period quadratic cost function, which is defined for the entire euro area as

$$E_t(Q_t) = \tfrac{1}{2}\lambda E_t(\bar{x}_t - \bar{x}_{nt} - k)^2 + \tfrac{1}{2}E_t(\bar{\pi}_{t+1} - \pi^*)^2, \qquad (13.71)$$

where $\bar{a}_t$ denotes the average of a_{1t} and a_{2t} so that

$$\bar{a}_t = \theta a_{1t} + (1 - \theta)a_{2t}$$

and θ is the relative size of the economies. Thus the aim is to choose the common nominal interest rate R_t to minimize the deviations of average EU inflation $\bar{\pi}_{t+1}$ from the target level π^* and average output $\bar{x}_t$ from the target $\bar{x}_{nt} + k$, $k \geqslant 0$. If the ECB were a strict inflation targeter, then $\lambda = 0$.

13.7.3 Optimal Monetary Policy

First we derive the optimal common nominal interest rate for this model and the implications for expected EU inflation and output. We then derive the inflation and price-level differentials between euro area countries and examine whether the model implies that either or both diverge. By specializing the model through removing the two potential automatic stabilizers in the aggregated demand function—namely the effects of competitiveness and absorbtion—we may examine what happens to inflation and price-level divergence in the absence of these two effects.

For convenience, we assume that the two economies are of equal size, hence $\theta = \frac{1}{2}$. Average EU inflation and output are then

$$\bar{\pi}_t = \tfrac{1}{2}(\pi_{1t} + \pi_{2t}),$$

$$\bar{x}_t = \tfrac{1}{2}(x_{1t} + x_{2t}).$$

Target EU inflation is π^*. The aggregate model for the euro area is therefore

$$\bar{x}_t = -\frac{\beta}{1-\delta}(R_t - E_t\bar{\pi}_{t+1}) + \frac{\phi}{1-\delta}(s_t + p_t^* - \bar{p}_t) + \frac{1}{1-\delta}\bar{z}_t + \frac{1}{1-\delta}\bar{e}_{xt},$$

$$\tag{13.72}$$

$$\bar{\pi}_{t+1} = E_t\bar{\pi}_{t+1} + \alpha(\bar{x}_t - \bar{x}_{nt}) + \bar{e}_{\pi,t+1}, \tag{13.73}$$

which does not involve the price differential. Taking conditional expectations of the aggregate model,

$$E_t\bar{x}_t = -\frac{\beta}{1-\delta}(R_t - E_t\bar{\pi}_{t+1}) + \frac{\phi}{1-\delta}(s_t + p_t^* - \bar{p}_t) + \frac{1}{1-\delta}\bar{z}_t, \tag{13.74}$$

$$E_t\bar{\pi}_{t+1} = E_t\bar{\pi}_{t+1} + \alpha(E_t\bar{x}_t - \bar{x}_{nt}). \tag{13.75}$$

Hence $E_t\bar{x}_t = \bar{x}_{nt}$.

Choosing R_t to minimize $E_t(Q_t)$ gives the first-order condition

$$E_t\left(\frac{\partial Q_t}{\partial R_t}\right) = -\frac{\beta\lambda}{1-\delta}(E_t\bar{x}_t - \bar{x}_{nt} - k) - \frac{\alpha\beta}{1-\delta}E_t(\bar{\pi}_{t+1} - \pi^*) = 0.$$

This implies that the optimal rate of inflation for the euro area is

$$E_t\bar{\pi}_{t+1} = \pi^* - \frac{\lambda}{\alpha}(E_t\bar{x}_t - \bar{x}_{nt} - k)$$

$$= \pi^* + \frac{\lambda}{\alpha}k. \tag{13.76}$$

This is the familiar result derived above that in optimal inflation targeting under discretion there is an aggregate inflation bias if both λ and k are positive, i.e., if the ECB is a flexible inflation targeter and seeks to achieve a higher level of euro area output than the natural level. We note that none of the additional variables in the aggregate demand function has affected this result.

In order to achieve the optimal level of inflation, from equation (13.74), the ECB should set the common nominal interest rate equal to

$$R_t = \pi^* + \frac{\lambda}{\alpha}k - \frac{1-\delta}{\beta}\bar{x}_{nt} - \frac{\phi}{\beta}(\bar{p}_t - s_t - p_t^*) + \frac{1}{\beta}\bar{z}_t. \tag{13.77}$$

Hence, monetary policy would respond negatively to higher aggregate output and to a loss of euro area competitiveness with the rest of the world, and positively to exogenous effects such as an increase in euro area exports to the rest of the world.

We now consider the implications for the two countries of this choice of nominal interest rate. Substituting the nominal interest rate given by equation (13.77) into equation (13.69) and taking expectations gives the expected output for country i as

$$E_t x_{it} - \bar{x}_{nt} = -\beta \left(\pi^* + \frac{\lambda}{\alpha} k - E_t \pi_{i,t+1} \right) - \gamma E_t (p_{it} - p_{jt})$$
$$- \phi E_t (p_{it} - \bar{p}_t) + \delta (E_t x_{jt} - \bar{x}_{nt}) + (z_{it} - \bar{z}_t). \quad (13.78)$$

Recalling that $E_t x_{it} = x_{ni,t}$ and subtracting from equation (13.78) the corresponding equation for country j gives the following equation for the expected country inflation differential:

$$E_t (\pi_{i,t+1} - \pi_{j,t+1}) = \frac{\phi + 2\gamma}{\beta} E_t (p_{it} - p_{jt}) + \frac{1 + \delta}{\beta} (x_{ni,t} - x_{nj,t}) - \frac{1}{\beta} (z_{it} - z_{jt}).$$
$$(13.79)$$

This is our key equation. It identifies the factors that cause a country inflation differential.

13.7.4 Competitiveness and Absorbtion

If there are no competitiveness or absorbtion effects so that $\gamma = \phi = \delta = 0$, then the price-level and natural output terms vanish and the inflation differential depends on only exogenous individual country effects. If these effects are different (and remain constant), then the inflation differential will persist. The price levels would then diverge over time without bound. This is consistent with our earlier intuition.

Now assume that there are competitiveness and absorbtion effects so that $\gamma, \phi, \delta > 0$. Equation (13.79) shows that the inflation differential may still persist. A higher initial price level, a higher natural rate of output, and a smaller response to world trade all cause inflation in country i to exceed that in country j. Moreover, the difference is greater, the stronger are the two competitiveness coefficients γ and ϕ, the larger is the absorbtion coefficient δ, and the smaller is the response to the real interest rate β. Thus if country i starts with a higher price level than country j, then the stronger the effect of competitiveness, the larger the resulting inflation differential. The competitiveness gap would then be expected to increase over time.

This can be shown more formally by noting that $E_t \pi_{i,t+1} = E_t p_{i,t+1} - p_{it}$. Hence equation (13.79) can be rewritten as

$$E_t (p_{it} - p_{jt}) = \frac{\beta}{\beta + \phi + 2\gamma} E_t (p_{i,t+1} - p_{j,t+1})$$
$$- \frac{1 + \delta}{\beta + \phi + 2\gamma} (x_{ni,t} - x_{nj,t}) + \frac{1}{\beta + \phi + 2\gamma} (z_{it} - z_{jt}), \quad (13.80)$$

which is an unstable difference equation. Thus, any initial price differential would grow without bound unless corrected by a reversal in sign, at some point in the future, of the country differentials in the natural output levels or the world trade effects. Consequently, the presence of the competitiveness effect in the model does not prevent the price levels from diverging. And since the other two variables in equation (13.80) are assumed to be exogenous, they are unable to alter this unless, by chance, they offset each other.

13.7.5 Is There Another Solution?

We have assumed that the natural output levels are exogenous. If instead they are endogenous and if capital accumulation in each country is affected by its real interest rate, then higher-inflation countries, which have lower real interest rates, would also have higher natural rates of output. From equation (13.79) this would raise the country inflation differential.

Despite these problems at the individual country level, euro area inflation is unaffected. As its remit is euro area inflation, and not inflation in individual euro area countries, there would be no incentive for the ECB to react to the price divergence by changing interest rates. In fact, the ECB is powerless to do anything about widening country price-level differentials using just monetary policy.

In the absence of any countervailing forces, the divergence of country price levels may pose a threat to the sustainability of the euro. At a minimum it imposes a real cost to some member countries. How, then, might the single currency be sustained? From equations (13.79) and (13.80), the solution appears to lie in finding offsetting effects that operate through either the natural output differential or the exogenous variables. The long-run solution requires an improvement in competitiveness that raises the natural output of the country with lower inflation relative to that of the higher-inflation country. In the short run, a fiscal transfer from the high-inflation to the low-inflation country would help. This may be captured by the exogenous variables. In effect, this would be a tax on inflation. This is what happens within a single country where high-activity (and high-inflation) regions make net fiscal transfers to low-activity (and low-inflation) regions. Often these take the form of unemployment benefits. For further discussion of these issues see Wickens (2007).

13.8 Conclusions

In this chapter we have analyzed monetary policy in a closed economy based on inflation targeting in which the monetary-policy instrument is an official short-term nominal interest rate under the control of the monetary authority (commonly the central bank). The interest rate may be chosen either at the discretion of the central bank or through commitment to a publicly known rule. We have considered the implications for the economy based on the assumption that the economy is described by some form of New Keynesian model of inflation and output.

Our main finding is that the objectives of policy, as expressed in terms of inflation, output, and social welfare, are best achieved through a central bank that uses a rule rather than discretion and that focuses on targeting only inflation and not output. Under a policy of discretion there appears to be little or no gain to either including output in the central bank's objective function, or to trying to achieve a level of output in excess of its natural (i.e., full-employment/

long-run equilibrium) level as inflation ends up above target without any compensating extra output. Whereas, by following a rule it is possible on average to achieve the inflation target and to maintain output at its natural level.

We have considered whether it is possible to choose the rule in an optimal way (i.e., a way that maximizes social welfare). We found that this required giving an extremely high weight to inflation in the rule and would result in making the interest rate very volatile. Smoothing interest rates avoids this, and may be accomplished by including the level and changes in the interest rate in the objective function, together with inflation.

We extended the analysis to an open economy with a flexible exchange rate. Under UIP, an increase in the domestic interest rate, for example, would cause an appreciation in the exchange rate, which would reduce competitiveness, and so reinforce the negative effect on output caused by a higher real interest rate. In other words, having a flexible exchange rate would create an extra channel in the transmission mechanism of interest rates to inflation. We found that under both discretion and commitment to a rule, domestic inflation is determined primarily by foreign inflation. The difference is that, by using discretion, it may be possible to eliminate the influence of foreign inflation, whereas under a Taylor rule there is in general only a partial offset of foreign inflation. This suggests either the use of discretion or a different rule to the Taylor rule.

A consequence of having a fixed nominal exchange rate is that inflation in the domestic economy is tied to that of the country to whose currency the exchange rate is pegged. The role of domestic monetary policy is to maintain the exchange-rate parity. Matters are somewhat different in the euro area. Member countries achieve a fixed exchange-rate parity through sharing a common currency. The ECB sets a single interest rate for the whole euro area by targeting the average inflation rate in the euro area. We have argued that even though euro area inflation may be on target, differences in country inflation rates may make the common interest rate too high for low-inflation countries and too low for high-inflation countries. Due to the offsetting effects of competitiveness, we have shown that individual country inflation rates are unlikely to diverge, but individual country price levels may.

Although this chapter has reflected the concerns of modern monetary policy, with its focus on an independent central bank using a single policy instrument (its interest rate) to control inflation, we should bear in mind that other solutions to the policy assignment issue are possible. As, in the short run, interest rates affect output and fiscal policy affects inflation, a less restrictive approach would be to combine monetary and fiscal policy to simultaneously achieve the two major policy goals: the control of inflation and output stabilization. In the long run, of course, we expect monetary policy to have no effect on output and, in the absence of monetary accommodation, fiscal policy to have no effect on inflation.

One of the main reasons for preferring to assign interest rates to the control of inflation through an independent central bank is that it gives monetary policy

greater credibility and transparency, which makes it more publicly accountable and less open to short-term political pressures. There may, however, be a price for this strict assignment: policy may be less effective, especially in the short term, and there may be unwanted spillover effects elsewhere in the economy, such as to the exchange rate, output, and unemployment. To set against this, it has proved difficult to fine-tune fiscal policy in the short run: expenditures take time to have an effect and are likely to be crowded out in the longer term and, following the tax-smoothing arguments made in chapter 5, it is costly to be continually altering taxes due to the disruptions to private decisions that this causes. Hence, although, in principle, inflation targeting may not be the best way to control inflation, in practice, it is so far proving to be the most effective.

14

Real Business Cycles, DGE Models, and Economic Fluctuations

14.1 Introduction

The aim in this book has been to explain how modern macroeconomic theory has evolved in recent years. The main distinguishing features of this development are the use at all times of models that describe the whole economy rather than a part of the economy, an emphasis on intertemporal rather than single-period models, and a focus on the macroeconomic consequences of individual decisions, i.e., microfoundations, rather than theorizing directly about aggregates. This has led to models of increasing complexity—often too complex to be analyzed without the use of numerical simulation. We started with a small centralized, centrally planned, or representative-agent model of the economy which we then extended in various ways to include growth, decentralized decisions and markets, government, the open economy, and money. When we included additional features of observed economies, to simplify the analysis, we tried where possible to revert to the original basic model. Nonetheless, in the process, it became increasingly difficult to analyze their full general equilibrium consequences, and we have often had to restrict our analysis to the long-run properties of the model. Since our interest also includes the short-run behavior of the models, we need to find another way to perform the analysis. In addition we would like to know which features of the economy are important to include in our models, how the economy responds to different types of shocks, and what sorts of policy are effective.

  These issues form part of the agenda of real-business-cycle (RBC) analysis, which was initiated by the work of Lucas (1975), Kydland and Prescott (1982), Long and Plosser (1983), and Prescott (1986). For a survey of RBC analysis see King and Rebelo (1999). The first RBC empirical studies examined the effects of productivity (technology) shocks on the main macroeconomic aggregates using the basic DGE model of chapter 2, or closely related models. Subsequently, this methodology has been extended to the study of a variety of shocks. In order to represent these shocks, more complicated models were required. In this chapter we explain how to perform such an analysis, we report the evidence obtained in some of the more influential studies, and we consider what this implies for the specification of DGE models. In the process we extend the range of shocks considered to other types of supply shock, to demand shocks (in particular, to monetary and fiscal shocks), and to foreign shocks. We stress that our aim here is to examine evidence on the general equilibrium properties of macroeconomic models.

In RBC analysis, the parameter values of the model are typically calibrated and not estimated. This has proved a matter of contention, as the traditional way to obtain parameter values is to estimate the model using standard econometric estimation methods. We discuss the reasons why calibration methods have been used instead.

Next we describe the methodology of RBC analysis using the growth model of chapter 3 as the basis for the model. We then consider the empirical evidence on various RBC models, including a real open-economy model. Finally, we examine at some length a very general DGE macroeconomic model of the monetary economy that is estimated using Bayesian methods. This model enables us to consider the effects of a variety of shocks, including monetary shocks.

14.2 The Methodology of RBC Analysis

We illustrate the analysis of real business cycles using the basic centralized growth model of chapter 3. We choose a model with growth because we wish to explain observed data. The model assumes that the economy is seeking to choose aggregate consumption C_t, total labor N_t, and total capital K_t to maximize

$$E_t \sum_{s=0}^{\infty} \beta^s U(C_{t+s}),$$

where $U(C_t) = C_t^{1-\sigma}/(1 - \sigma)$ and $\beta = 1/(1 + \theta)$, subject to the economy's resource constraint. This is derived from the national income identity, the production function, and the capital accumulation equation, namely from

$$Y_t = C_t + I_t,$$
$$Y_t = A_t K_t^{\alpha} N_t^{1-\alpha},$$
$$\Delta K_{t+1} = I_t - \delta K_t.$$

The resulting resource constraint is

$$A_t K_t^{\alpha} N_t^{1-\alpha} = K_{t+1} + C_t - (1 - \delta)K_t.$$

We assume that labor is growing at the constant rate n, implying that

$$N_t = (1 + n)^t N_0. \tag{14.1}$$

The aim in RBC analysis is to determine the dynamic response of the economy to productivity shocks. A_t denotes technological change. We assume that the logarithm of A_t is a random walk with drift. Hence,

$$A_t = (1 + \mu)^t Z_t,$$

$$\ln Z_t = z_t,$$

$$\Delta z_t = e_t \sim \text{i.i.d.}(0, \omega^2).$$

The drift term μ is the long-run rate of growth of technological change. e_t represents a serially uncorrelated productivity shock, which, through the economy's dynamic structure, generates serially correlated behavior in the economy's main aggregates: output, consumption, capital, investment, and employment. These assumptions imply that technological change consists of two components: a deterministic exponential trend $(1 + \mu)^t$ and a stochastic trend Z_t, where $z_t = z_0 + \sum_{s=0}^{t} e_s$. As a result, output, consumption, capital, and investment are all nonstationary variables, even when measured as deviations about their growth path.

   In order to obtain the solution to the model, first we redefine all variables in terms of deviations about their long-run growth paths. As in chapter 3, we redefine the variables in per capita terms as

$$y_t = \frac{Y_t}{N_t^\#} = \frac{Y_t}{[(1+\mu)^{1/(1-\alpha)}]^t N_t} = \frac{Y_t}{(1+\eta)^t N_0},$$

$$k_t = \frac{K_t}{N_t^\#} = \frac{K_t}{[(1+\mu)^{1/(1-\alpha)}]^t N_t} = \frac{K_t}{(1+\eta)^t N_0},$$

$$N_t^\# = (1+\mu)^{t/(1-\alpha)} N_t = [(1+\mu)^{1/(1-\alpha)}]^t (1+n)^t N_0 = (1+\eta)^t N_0,$$

where we have used the approximation

$$[(1+\mu)^{1/(1-\alpha)}]^t (1+n)^t \simeq (1+\eta)^t,$$

$$\eta \simeq n + \frac{\mu}{1-\alpha}.$$

The national income identity is now

$$y_t = c_t + i_t,$$

where

$$c_t = \frac{C_t}{N_t^\#} = \frac{C_t}{(1+\eta)^t N_0},$$

$$i_t = \frac{I_t}{N_t^\#} = \frac{I_t}{(1+\eta)^t N_0}.$$

The production function becomes

$$y_t = Z_t k_t^\alpha$$

and, since $N_{t+1}^\#/N_t^\# = 1 + \eta$, the capital accumulation equation can be written as

$$\Delta K_{t+1} = I_t - \delta K_t,$$

$$\frac{K_{t+1}}{N_{t+1}^\#}\frac{N_{t+1}^\#}{N_t^\#} = \frac{I_t}{N_t^\#} + (1 - \delta)\frac{K_t}{N_t^\#},$$

$$(1 + \eta)k_{t+1} = i_t + (1 - \delta)k_t.$$

Consequently, the economy's resource constraint becomes

$$Z_t k_t^\alpha = c_t + (1 + \eta)k_{t+1} - (1 - \delta)k_t. \tag{14.2}$$

Finally, normalizing $N_0 = 1$, we rewrite the utility function as

$$U(C_t) = \frac{C_t^{1-\sigma}}{1 - \sigma}$$

$$= \frac{[(1 + \eta)^t c_t]^{1-\sigma}}{1 - \sigma}.$$

As technological change has made the problem stochastic, we maximize the value function

$$V_t = U(C_t) + \beta E_t(V_{t+1})$$

$$= \frac{[(1 + \eta)^t c_t]^{1-\sigma}}{1 - \sigma} + \beta E_t(V_{t+1}),$$

subject to the resource constraint (14.2). The first-order condition for this stochastic dynamic programming problem is

$$\frac{\partial V_t}{\partial c_t} = (1 + \eta)^{(1-\sigma)t}c_t^{-\sigma} + \beta E_t\left[\frac{\partial V_{t+1}}{\partial c_{t+1}}\frac{\partial c_{t+1}}{\partial c_t}\right] = 0.$$

Noting that

$$V_{t+1} = U(C_{t+1}) + \beta E_{t+1}(V_{t+2})$$

and hence

$$\frac{\partial V_{t+1}}{\partial c_{t+1}} = (1 + \eta)^{(1-\sigma)(t+1)}c_{t+1}^{-\sigma},$$

and that

$$\frac{\partial c_{t+1}}{\partial c_t} = \frac{\partial c_{t+1}/\partial k_{t+1}}{\partial c_t/\partial k_{t+1}}$$

from the budget constraints for periods t and $t + 1$, we can show that

$$\frac{\partial c_{t+1}}{\partial c_t} = \frac{\alpha Z_{t+1}k_{t+1}^{\alpha-1} + 1 - \delta}{-(1 + \eta)}.$$

Hence

$$\frac{\partial V_t}{\partial c_t} = (1 + \eta)^{(1-\sigma)t}c_t^{-\sigma} - \beta E_t\left[(1 + \eta)^{(1-\sigma)(t+1)}c_{t+1}^{-\sigma}\frac{\alpha Z_{t+1}k_{t+1}^{\alpha-1} + 1 - \delta}{1 + \eta}\right]$$

$$= (1 + \eta)^{(1-\sigma)t}\{c_t^{-\sigma} - \beta E_t[(1 + \eta)^{-\sigma}c_{t+1}^{-\sigma}(\alpha Z_{t+1}k_{t+1}^{\alpha-1} + 1 - \delta)]\} = 0.$$

This gives the Euler equation

$$E_t\left[\beta\left[(1+\eta)\frac{c_{t+1}}{c_t}\right]^{-\sigma}(\alpha Z_{t+1}k_{t+1}^{\alpha-1}+1-\delta)\right]=1. \qquad (14.3)$$

In deriving the solution to the model it is usual in RBC analysis to invoke certainty equivalence. This allows all random variables to be replaced by their conditional expectations. As there is no risk-free rate in this model, in the Euler equation, we should, strictly speaking, take account of the conditional covariance terms involving c_{t+1}, k_{t+1}, and Z_{t+1} and, in particular, $\text{cov}_t(c_{t+1}, k_{t+1})$.

14.2.1 Steady-State Solution

Assuming a steady-state solution exists, it satisfies $\Delta c_{t+1} = \Delta k_{t+1} = 0$ and $Z_t = 1$ for each time period. Hence we can drop the time subscript in the steady state to obtain

$$\beta(1+\eta)^{-\sigma}[\alpha k^{\alpha-1}+1-\delta]=1.$$

As first shown in chapter 3, this implies that in equilibrium

$$k \simeq \left(\frac{\delta+\theta+\sigma(n+(\mu/(1-\alpha)))}{\alpha}\right)^{-1/(1-\alpha)},$$

$$c = k^\alpha - (\eta+\delta)k.$$

Although k_t is constant in equilibrium, K_t/N_t, the per capita capital stock of the economy, is growing through time. As $k_t = K_t/([(1+\mu)^{1/(1-\alpha)}]^t N_t)$, the optimal path for per capita capital is

$$\frac{K_t}{N_t} = \left[\frac{\delta+\theta+\sigma(n+(\mu/(1-a)))}{\alpha}\right]^{-1/(1-\alpha)}[(1+\mu)^{1/(1-\alpha)}]^t.$$

Hence K_t/N_t grows at approximately the rate $\mu/(1-\alpha)$.

The optimal growth rate of per capita output Y_t/N_t is determined from

$$y_t = Y_t/([(1+\mu)^{1/(1-\alpha)}]^t N_t).$$

As $y_t = k_t^\alpha$ and $\Delta k_{t+1} = 0$, it follows that $\Delta y_{t+1} = 0$. Thus, the growth rate of Y_t/N_t is also approximately $\mu/(1-\alpha)$. The optimal growth rate of per capita consumption C_t/N_t is obtained from the condition that $\Delta c_{t+1} = 0$ and $c_t = C_t/([(1+\mu)^{1/(1-\alpha)}]^t N_t)$. Thus the growth rate of C_t/N_t is also approximately $\mu/(1-\alpha)$. The optimal growth rates of total output, total capital, and total consumption are obtained by taking into account population growth. By adding the growth rate of the population, we obtain their common rate of growth $\eta = n + (\mu/(1-\alpha))$.

14.2.2 Short-Run Dynamics

We now consider short-run deviations about the logarithm of the growth path. The model reduces to two equations: the Euler equation and the resource constraint. As they are nonlinear we linearize them by taking logarithmic approximations of each based on the Taylor series approximation

$$f(x_t) \simeq f(x_t^*) + f'(x_t^*) \left[\frac{\partial x_t}{\partial \ln x_t} \right]_{x_t^*} [\ln x_t - \ln x_t^*]$$

$$\simeq f(x_t^*) + f'(x_t^*) x_t^* [\ln x_t - \ln x_t^*].$$

Omitting the intercept, invoking certainty equivalence, and noting that $E_t \ln Z_{t+1} = \ln Z_t = z_t$ and that, in equilibrium, $z_t = 0$, the log-linear approximation to the Euler equation can be shown to be

$$E_t \Delta \ln c_{t+1} \simeq -\left(\eta + \frac{\delta + \theta}{\sigma} \right)(1 - \alpha) E_t \ln k_{t+1} + \left(\eta + \frac{\delta + \theta}{\sigma} \right) z_t. \qquad (14.4)$$

Omitting the intercept once again, the log-linearized resource constraint is

$$\ln k_{t+1} \simeq -\frac{\theta + \eta(\sigma - \alpha - 2) + (1 - \alpha)\delta}{\alpha} \ln c_t$$

$$+ [1 + \theta + (\sigma - 1)\eta] \ln k_t + \frac{\theta + \delta + \eta(\sigma - 1)}{\alpha} z_t. \qquad (14.5)$$

From equations (14.4) and (14.5) we obtain the linear system

$$\begin{bmatrix} 1 + \theta + (\sigma - 1)\eta & -\dfrac{\theta + \eta(\sigma - \alpha - 2) + (1 - \alpha)\delta}{\alpha} \\ 0 & 1 \end{bmatrix} \begin{bmatrix} \ln k_t \\ \ln c_t \end{bmatrix}$$

$$= \begin{bmatrix} 1 & 0 \\ \left(\eta + \dfrac{\delta + \theta}{\sigma} \right)(1 - \alpha) & 1 \end{bmatrix} E_t \begin{bmatrix} \ln k_{t+1} \\ \ln c_{t+1} \end{bmatrix} - \begin{bmatrix} \dfrac{\theta + \delta + \eta(\sigma - 1)}{\alpha} \\ \eta + \dfrac{\delta + \theta}{\sigma} \end{bmatrix} z_t. \qquad (14.6)$$

Denoting equation (14.6) by the matrix equation

$$Bx_t = CE_t x_{t+1} + Dz_t, \qquad (14.7)$$

where $x_t' = (\ln k_t, \ln c_t)$, B and C are 2×2 matrices, and D is a 2×1 vector, we can rewrite equation (14.7) as

$$x_t = AE_t x_{t+1} + Fz_t, \qquad (14.8)$$

where $A = B^{-1}C$ and $F = B^{-1}D$.

We now introduce the lag operator L. Recalling that $E_t x_{t+1} = L^{-1} x_t$, we write equation (14.8) as

$$(I - AL^{-1})x_t = Fz_t. \qquad (14.9)$$

The dynamic solution of equation (14.9) depends on the roots of the determinantal equation

$$|A| - (\text{tr } A)L + L^2 = 0.$$

There are two roots. Setting $L = 1$ gives three cases:

(i) $|A| - (\text{tr}\,A) + 1 > 0$ implies that both roots are either stable or unstable;

(ii) $|A| - (\text{tr}\,A) + 1 < 0$ implies a saddlepath solution (one root is stable and the other is unstable);

(iii) if $|A| - (\text{tr}\,A) + 1 = 0$, then at least one root is 1.

Assuming that $\sigma \geqslant \alpha + 2$, which is a sufficient but not a necessary condition, it can be shown that

$$|A| - (\text{tr}\,A) + 1 = -\frac{[\theta + \eta(\sigma - \alpha - 2) + (1 - \alpha)\delta](\eta + ((\delta + \theta)/\sigma))(1 - \alpha)}{\alpha[1 + \theta + (\sigma - 1)\eta]} < 0.$$

Thus, the two roots satisfy $\eta_1 > 1$ and $\eta_2 < 1$, and so the short-run dynamics about the steady-state growth path follow a saddlepath. Equation (14.9) can therefore be written as

$$\eta_1\left(1 - \frac{1}{\eta_1}L\right)(1 - \eta_2 L^{-1})x_t = \text{adj}(A - L)Fz_t.$$

Hence,

$$x_t = \frac{1}{\eta_1}x_{t-1} + \frac{1}{\eta_1}(1 - \eta_2 L^{-1})^{-1}\,\text{adj}(A - L)Fz_t. \tag{14.10}$$

Noting that $E_t z_{t+s} = z_t$ for $s \geqslant 0$, and $\Delta z_t = e_t$, equation (14.10) can be shown to simplify to

$$\Delta x_t = \frac{1}{\eta_1}\Delta x_{t-1} + G_0 e_t + G_1 e_{t-1}, \tag{14.11}$$

which is a vector autoregressive/moving average model in the change in x_t.

Equation (14.11) describes the dynamic behavior of changes in $\ln c_t$ and $\ln k_t$ following a technology shock e_t. The precise path followed by the economy depends on the (deep) structural parameters of the model. The equation implies that the system returns to its steady-state growth path following a temporary technology shock, but not to its original steady state as the temporary shock e_t has a permanent effect on technology z_t and hence on $\ln c_t$ and $\ln k_t$.

From the solutions for $\ln c_t$ and $\ln k_t$ we can derive the corresponding solutions for C_t and K_t, and hence for Y_t and I_t. As $\ln c_t$ and $\ln k_t$ are log deviations about their steady-state growth paths, we must first add back their growth paths. As the resulting variables are in per capita terms, we must then convert them back to total consumption and capital, and then solve for total output and investment from the national income identity and the capital accumulation equation. We can also derive the implied wage rate from the marginal product of labor, and the implied real interest rate from the net marginal product of capital. If we include labor, this would give us the dynamic behavior of seven macroeconomic variables.

The original purpose of RBC analysis was to see whether it was possible to match data generated by the model as a result of a technology shock to the observed macroeconomic data. It is common in this literature to focus on matching the variances, covariances, and autocorrelations. The data generated by the model have only one source of randomness, the technology shock, but the observed data have seven independent sources of randomness. As a result, there is a singularity in the variance-covariance matrix of the outputs of the model that is not present in the observed data. One of the problems for RBC models, therefore, is to specify additional sources of randomness in the model. We could, for example, add a random shock to equation (14.1) to make the labor supply stochastic. There would then be two random shocks in the solution, equation (14.11). Other potential sources of shocks are preference shocks to the instantaneous utility function, shocks to the capital accumulation equation, possibly reflecting, among other things, random depreciation effects, shocks to the relations between the two marginal productivity relations associated with wages and the real interest rate, and random shocks to the national income identity to reflect wasted output or inventories. Incorporating all of these would entail seven independent shocks generating the seven outputs of the model.

The variance-covariance matrix and the autocorrelations of the model outputs can be derived analytically by rewriting equation (14.11) as a vector moving average model:

$$x_t = \sum_{s=0}^{\infty} \eta_1^{-s} (G_0 e_{t-s} + G_1 e_{t-s-1}) = \sum_{s=0}^{\infty} H_s e_{t-s}.$$

It follows that

$$V(x_t) = \sigma^2 H(1) H(1)',$$

where $V(e_t) = \sigma^2$ with $H(L) = \sum_{s=0}^{\infty} H_s L^s$ and $H(1) = H(L)|_{L=1}$. Hence, with just one shock, $V(x_t)$ is a singular matrix. H_s defines both the autocorrelation functions and the impulse response functions to a unit shock in e_t. These are derived from the production function using

$$e_t = \Delta \ln Z_t$$
$$= \Delta \ln Y_t - \alpha \Delta \ln K_t - (1 - \alpha) \Delta \ln N_t - (1 + \mu),$$

where $\Delta \ln Y_t$, $\Delta \ln K_t$, and $\Delta \ln N_t$ are observed data and α and μ are calibrated or estimated. The variance of e_t is σ^2.

In practice, in most RBC studies, these moments are calculated using numerical simulation, rather than analytically. It is not then necessary to linearize the model. The numerical simulation can be carried out in several ways. One way is to generate the shocks by drawing independent random samples from a distribution with a zero mean and given variance, and then to calculate the outputs of the model. This requires a nonlinear rational-expectations solution procedure. There are now a large number of these: see Canova (2005) and De Jong and Dave (2007). The outputs are then detrended using a Hodrick–Prescott (HP) filter and the sample moments are calculated. This can be repeated a large number of times and the numerical distribution of each of the moments constructed. The means (or medians) of these distributions of the moments are then calculated. Finally, the calculated means of the generated sample moments are compared with the sample moments of the observed detrended data.

The main variant on this procedure concerns the way the random samples of shocks are generated. Most studies estimate the technology shocks using the Solow residuals. These are derived from the observed data after first detrending them with the HP filter. Thus the estimated shocks are

$$\hat{e}_t = \ln \tilde{Z}_t$$
$$= \ln \tilde{Y}_t - \alpha \ln \tilde{K}_t - (1 - \alpha) \ln \tilde{N}_t - (1 + \mu),$$

where $\ln \tilde{X}_t$ $(X = Z, Y, K, N)$ are the corresponding detrended data, and α and μ are calibrated, or estimated. The variance of the shocks used in the first method is the variance of the $\hat{e}_t$. The next step in this alternative approach is to draw a random sample from the estimated residuals and to use this sample to generate the outputs of the model and their moments. Repeated sampling from the same estimated shocks, and calculating the corresponding model outputs and their sample moments, gives the numerical distributions of these moments, from which the means may be calculated. This second procedure is known as bootstrapping.

The use of calibration instead of conventional econometric estimation has proved highly controversial. Kydland and Prescott (1982) explain their use of calibration as the result of seeking to calibrate the model *to* the situation of interest. They argue that the selection of the parameter values should reflect the specifications of preferences and technology that are used in applied studies, and that they should be those values for which the model's steady-state values are near the average values for the economy over the period being explained. In other words, they want parameter values appropriate for the problem at hand.

The danger in using conventional econometric estimation methods is that the model is often then judged solely on statistical criteria, such as the model's fit to the data or the significance of the coefficient estimates. As a result, any apparent misspecification is often dealt with by generalizing the dynamic structure rather than by rethinking the underlying macroeconomic theory. The temptation to add dynamics is because corresponding to any complete simultaneous-equation model of the economy, for each endogenous variable there exists a specific univariate time-series representation or, for a group of variables, a vector autoregressive representation. These representations are either exact or can be made very close approximations by including sufficient lags. Accordingly, omitting variables that are serially correlated from a structural model can usually be largely compensated for by specifying a longer lag structure. Moreover, without explicitly including the omitted variables, this misspecification would be difficult, or even impossible, to detect. As calibrated DGE models usually have simple dynamic structures, they tend to have a worse fit than estimated models. A better way of judging a model is probably to focus more on its long-run solution, as the long-run parameter values are usually something that we are better informed about. When calibrating a model, this knowledge can be exploited directly by imposing it on the model. In evaluating an estimated structural model it is possible to test the estimates of long-run parameters against such prior knowledge. It is more difficult to carry out such a test on a calibrated model, though not impossible.

Recently, methods of optimizing calibration have been proposed. One of these is known as indirect inference. The attraction of this approach is that the calibrated model can be evaluated using standard methods of statistical inference. Another advantage occurs when the model is nonlinear. Often it is difficult to estimate such models using conventional econometric methods without first having to linearize the model. Linearization is not usually required for optimal calibration.

The idea is first to fit the data to a model using conventional estimation. This model is called an auxiliary model and could be a vector autoregression or an equation like (14.11). Second, the RBC model is calibrated and then simulated to produce artificial data. (We do not usually need to linearize the model in order to obtain the simulation values.) Third, the auxiliary model is estimated using the simulation data. The second and third steps are then repeated for different calibrations of the RBC model. The optimal calibration is that for which the estimated auxiliary model based on simulated data is closest to the estimated auxiliary model obtained from the observed data. The comparison of the two data sets may be made in many ways: by comparing the estimated coefficients of the auxiliary model (Gregory and Smith 1993) or by comparing the ratio of the likelihood functions or the scores of the likelihood functions. For an account of the evaluation, optimal calibration, and simulation of macroeconomic models, see Canova (2005), De Jong and Dave (2007), Gourieroux et al. (1993), and Gourieroux and Monfort (1996).

Although widely used, it is not clear that the HP filter is the best way to detrend the data. According to the theory above we should detrend the logarithms of the data using a linear trend. A problem with the HP filter is its greater flexibility, which depends on the choice of the parameter λ, which is the weight given to having a smooth trend. It controls whether, at one extreme, the trend follows the original data exactly or, at the other extreme, it follows a linear trend. Although specific values of λ are commonly chosen, any choice between the two extremes is in fact arbitrary. We note that by deviating from a linear trend, the HP filter reduces the volatility of the shocks that result.

We have described the methodology used to evaluate RBC models. In principle, it is straightforward to modify this so that it can deal with the more general DGE macroeconomic models considered in earlier chapters. We would, however, need to give more thought to the sources of randomness in the economy than we have previously and to whether we estimate or calibrate the model. The properties of the resulting numerical model can then be derived.

14.3 Empirical Evidence on the RBC Model

Most of the empirical evidence on DGE macroeconomic models is concerned with RBC models. There are a large number of these. Rather than attempt to

Table 14.1. Calibration of baseline RBC model.

σ	β	ϕ	γ	η	α	δ	ρ	ω
1	0.984	3.48	1	0.004	0.667	0.025	0.979	0.0072

present each RBC model and each data set, as nearly all are versions of the model discussed above and the findings do not alter greatly for different time periods, we focus on summarizing their principal findings. Our aim is to identify the main factors that explain business cycles and, more generally, fluctuations in key macroeconomic variables. Most of this evidence relates to the United States. Our initial discussion concerns the basic RBC model and some extensions of it. We then consider an RBC model of the open economy and, finally, a DGE model of the monetary economy. A useful general source of information on RBC models is the Web site of the Euro Area Business Cycle Network: www.eabcn.org.

14.3.1 The Basic RBC Model

Our discussion of the basic RBC model derived above draws heavily on King and Rebelo (1999) and Rebelo (2005), but see also King and Plosser (1988), King et al. (1988a,b), Cooley (1995), and Marimon and Scott (1999). The only significant difference between King and Rebelo's model and the RBC model above lies in the treatment of labor. Population growth is ignored and the utility function includes leisure as an argument. Their utility function is defined as

$$U(c_t, L_t) = \frac{c_t^{1-\sigma}}{1-\sigma} + \frac{\phi}{1-\gamma}(L_t^{1-\gamma} - 1),$$

where L_t is leisure and N_t is work, with $L_t + N_t = 1$. All of the other equations are defined as above. Technological progress is specified as

$$\ln A_t = \alpha \ln \Psi_t + \ln \Gamma_t,$$
$$\ln \Psi_t = \ln \Psi_{t-1} + \ln \xi,$$
$$\ln \Gamma_t = \rho \ln \Gamma_{t-1} + \varepsilon_t,$$

where ε_t is an i.i.d.$(0, \omega^2)$ shock. Thus, there is both a permanent and a temporary component to the technology shock and they are defined, respectively, by $\ln \Psi_t$ and $\ln \Gamma_t$. As a result, there is an extra first-order condition for leisure. Nonetheless, apart from the specification of the technology shock, the model solution is the same as for the growth model. This is a point made in chapter 3. The parameter values chosen to calibrate King and Rebelo's baseline RBC model are given in table 14.1.

The aim is see how well the baseline model can reproduce the business-cycle statistics for the U.S. economy for the period 1947.1–1996.4. These numbers are those not in parentheses in table 14.2. With exception of the real interest rate, all variables are in per capita terms and are logarithms, and have been detrended

Table 14.2. U.S. business cycle and baseline model statistics 1947.1–1996.4. (The numbers in parentheses are model statistics.)

	Standard deviation	Relative standard deviation	First-order autocorrelation	Correlation with output
Y	1.81 (1.39)	1.00 (1.00)	0.84 (0.72)	1.00 (1.00)
C	1.35 (0.61)	0.74 (0.44)	0.80 (0.79)	0.88 (0.94)
I	5.30 (4.09)	2.93 (2.95)	0.87 (0.71)	0.80 (0.99)
N	1.79 (0.67)	0.99 (0.48)	0.88 (0.71)	0.88 (0.97)
Y/N	1.02 (0.75)	0.56 (0.54)	0.74 (0.76)	0.55 (0.98)
w	0.68 (0.75)	0.38 (0.54)	0.66 (0.76)	0.12 (0.98)
r	0.30 (0.05)	0.16 (0.04)	0.60 (0.71)	−0.35 (0.95)
A	0.98 (0.94)	0.54 (0.68)	0.74 (0.72)	0.78 (1.00)

with the HP filter. The numbers in parentheses in table 14.2 are calculated from the baseline model.

The observed data show that per capita consumption is highly contemporaneously correlated with per capita output, has three-quarters of the volatility of per capita output, and a similar first-order autocorrelation. (We may interpret the correlation coefficients as representing long-run comovements with output.) Per capita investment is nearly three times as volatile as per capita output and has a slightly lower correlation. Labor (per capita hours) has the same volatility as per capita output and is highly correlated with per capita output, but output per hour has a lower volatility and correlation. This suggests that short-term variations in employment are largely the result of fluctuations in output. The real-wage rate (compensation per hour) is much less volatile than per capita output and has a very low correlation with per capita output, which shows the relative stickiness of real wages. The real interest rate has an even lower volatility and has a negative correlation with per capita output. Finally, (total factor) productivity has half the volatility of per capita output, but has a high correlation.

The corresponding results for the baseline RBC model are in parentheses. Broadly, the simulated variables have lower volatilities and higher correlations with output than the observed variables. The autocorrelations reveal little. Consumption and investment are too smooth. But the main discrepancies are the very high correlations with output of labor productivity, wages, and the real interest rate; the real interest rate is also far too smooth. In King and Rebelo's view, the baseline RBC model does a surprisingly good job for such a simple model.

What can we learn from these results about the adequacy of the baseline RBC model? One problem is the labor market. In the model, the variability of employment is far too low, and the correlation of wages with output is much too high, as is labor productivity. This suggests that, in practice, wages are much less flexible, and employment more flexible, than in the model. Furthermore, in practice, wages seem to be less closely tied to their marginal product and employment responds slightly less to output. These findings are consistent with a higher degree of wage stickiness and the presence of additional shocks, perhaps on the supply side, which raise the volatility of all of the main macroeconomic aggregates and reduce the correlations with output.

The greatest discrepancy is in the correlation between the real interest rate and output. In the observed data it is negative and in the simulated data it is close to unity. This suggests that market real interest rates are not closely related to the marginal product of capital. This indicates a gap between the equity price and the fundamental value of a firm. It also reflects the fact that real interest rates are determined in financial markets and are affected by monetary policy, and do not simply represent the real return to capital.

Consumption poses another conundrum. It is far more volatile in practice than in the model, and nearer to the volatility of output, but has a slightly lower correlation with output. Again this suggests that there is a separate shock, and this affects consumption differently from output. According to life-cycle theory, consumption depends on after-tax income and wealth, not on output. Furthermore, wages are sticky but employment is more variable than in the model. This indicates that there may be other factors that affect consumption besides output, such as taxes, financial and other sources of wealth, and income from employment fluctuations—perhaps due to unemployment.

The main problem with the RBC model is that it is based on just one type of shock, a technology shock. It is not difficult to conceive that a positive shock (such as a new invention like computers) will raise output, and that a negative supply shock (such as harvest failure) would reduce output in an economy (particularly one heavily dependent on agriculture). It is much more difficult to see how a negative technology shock could cause a recession; it is even less likely that an extreme event like the Great Depression can be attributed to a negative technology shock. Moreover, the estimate of the technology shock, which is based on the Solow residual, is, in reality, likely to be a mixture of effects, including the under-utilization of factor inputs. The production function assumes that capital and labor are fully used, but in practice they are likely to be underused in downturns, and not written off or made redundant. The Solow residual will therefore include the effects of other shocks.

However well the simple RBC model is thought to perform, these findings point strongly to the need for a more general model of the economy. The DGE macroeconomic framework that we have developed in this book has sufficient richness and flexibility to generate a model of the economy that overcomes the failings that we have identified in the basic RBC model.

14.3.2 Extensions to the Basic RBC Model

Attempts to improve on the RBC model have focused on additional types of shocks. Demand shocks are an obvious candidate. These include monetary and fiscal shocks—such as the interest rate, government expenditures, and tax changes—preference shocks, and external trade shocks. Other types of shocks include labor-supply shocks arising from changing labor participation and population changes, raw material price shocks, such as oil price changes, terms-of-trade effects due to foreign productivity shocks, and exchange-rate shocks. Another line of research has focused on the internal structure of the model—such as the degree of substitutability between consumption and leisure—and indivisibilities in labor inputs, which constrain the choice of the number of hours to work and permit flexibility only in the decision of whether or not to participate in the labor force. Apart from preference shocks, these are all issues we have considered previously.

One of the first extensions considered in the literature was an attempt to enhance the response of the aggregate labor supply. Noting that the evidence pointed more to the potential role of substitution between work and leisure (the extensive margin) than to variations in the number of hours worked (the intensive margin), two strategies were adopted. One assumed that households have reservation wages below which they are unwilling to work, and these differ across households: see Cho and Rogerson (1988). The other assumed that households are identical, but some people work a given number of hours while others work none (the indivisible labor model): see Hansen (1985), Rogerson (1988), and Hansen and Wright (1992). The allocation between work and unemployment is assumed to be random. Hansen finds that this leads to a higher labor elasticity, which increases the standard deviation of employment (total hours) relative to productivity compared with the baseline model.

Another early extension of the basic model was the inclusion of government spending shocks (see Christiano and Eichenbaum 1992; Baxter and King 1993; McGrattan 1994). The argument used was that a positive shock to the labor-supply function, i.e., a shift outwards, would increase employment and wages while reducing the size of the response of wages. McGrattan suggests that households substitute between taxable and nontaxable activities in response to changes in tax rates introduced to finance government expenditures, and this alters the variability of consumption, investment, hours worked, and productivity. The result is a lower correlation between hours worked and productivity. Although producing results that are closer to the data, fiscal shocks are probably too small to be a major source of business cycles.

Baxter and King study the effects of different fiscal policy shocks based on a DGE model calibrated on U.S. data from 1930 to 1985. In contrast to the RBC model above, their model allows government expenditures to affect utility and productivity, and includes the government budget constraint and fiscal transfers. Their main findings are (i) that permanent changes in government purchases have important effects on macroeconomic activity when financed by lump-sum taxes—they suggest that the long-run multiplier may even be greater than unity; (ii) that the method of financing is more important than the direct resource cost of the purchases—for example, when financed by income taxes, output falls in response to higher government purchases; and (iii) that the effect of government purchases also depends on whether they influence private marginal product decisions—for example, by augmenting the productivity of private capital and labor, and by affecting private investment.

Following the analysis of the Great Depression by Friedman and Schwartz (1963)—which attributed the depression largely to a tightening of U.S. monetary policy—and Friedman's (1968) lecture on monetary policy, a monetary shock is thought to have a strong impact on output for about eighteen months. It may therefore appear somewhat surprising to find that until recently monetary shocks did not have a prominent role in RBC models (see Dotsey et al. 1999; Clarida et al. 1999; Christiano et al. 1999). It is clear from our earlier discussion that imperfect price and nominal-wage flexibility could easily be calibrated to produce the sort of business-cycle responses found in observed data. It has also been found that a technology shock only produces a large expansionary effect on output in the short run if monetary policy is accommodative (see Altig et al. 2004; Gali et al. 2004a). We return to these issues later.

14.3.3 The Open-Economy RBC Model

Most of the research on real business cycles relates to the United States, which, in many respects, is almost a closed economy. In comparison, most other countries are small open economies strongly affected by the rest of the world and, in particular, by the United States, which is likely to be a major source of shocks for most other economies. There are few studies of open-economy RBC models. Perhaps the first, and still the best known, are those by Backus, Kehoe, and Kydland (Backus et al. 1992, 1995), who investigate international business cycles. Backus et al. (1995) apply the baseline RBC model to ten OECD countries and examine their comovements with the United States and the effects of terms-of-trade shocks.

Their benchmark model is essentially the baseline model above with the addition in the national income identity of government expenditures and net exports. Government expenditures are assumed to be generated by an autoregressive process and net exports are treated as a residual in the national income identity, i.e., output less consumption, investment, and government expenditures. The utility function is

$$U(c_t, l_t) = \frac{(c_t^\nu l_t^{1-\nu})^{1-\sigma}}{1 - \sigma},$$

which implies that consumption and leisure are nonseparable.

They also consider a modification to the benchmark model designed to endogenize net exports in order to examine the effects of terms-of-trade shocks. A two-country model is constructed in which each country specializes in the production of a single good labeled *a* for country 1 and *b* for country 2. The resource constraints for the two countries are

$$y_{1t} = a_{1t} + a_{2t} = F(k_{1t}, n_{1t}),$$
$$y_{2t} = b_{1t} + b_{2t} = F(k_{2t}, n_{2t}),$$

where a_{2t} and b_{2t} are exports. The production functions are

$$F(k_{it}, n_{it}) = Z_{it} k_{it}^\alpha n_{it}^{1-\alpha}$$

and there are time-to-build effects, so investment is

$$i_{it} = \sum_{j=1}^{J} \phi_j i_{t-j}^s,$$

where i_{t-j}^s are investment starts begun in period $t - j$.

In order to introduce imperfect substitutability between domestic and foreign goods, in each country total expenditures on consumption and investment plus government expenditures are specified as composites of domestic and foreign goods as follows:

$$c_{1t} + i_{it} + g_{it} = G(a_{1t}, b_{1t}) = (wa_{1t}^{1-\varphi} + b_{1t}^{1-\varphi})^{1/(1-\varphi)},$$
$$c_{2t} + i_{2t} + g_{2t} = G(b_{2t}, a_{2t}) = (wb_{2t}^{1-\varphi} + a_{2t}^{1-\varphi})^{1/(1-\varphi)}.$$

The elasticity of substitution between domestic and foreign goods is given by $1/\varphi$. If q_{1t} and q_{2t} are the prices of domestic and foreign goods, then, in equilibrium, their relative price—the terms of trade—is

$$Q_t = \frac{q_{2t}}{q_{1t}} = \frac{\partial G/\partial b_{1t}}{\partial G/\partial a_{1t}}$$
$$= \frac{1}{w}\left(\frac{a_{1t}}{b_{1t}}\right)^\varphi.$$

The trade balance of country 1, expressed in units of the domestic good, is

$$x_{1t} = a_{2t} - Q_t b_{1t}.$$

The shocks to the two economies are productivity and government expenditure shocks which satisfy the VARs:

$$Z_{t+1} = AZ_t + e_{t+1},$$
$$g_{t+1} = Bg_t + \varepsilon_{t+1},$$

where $Z_t = (Z_{1t}, Z_{2t})'$, $g_t = (g_{1t}, g_{2t})'$, and the government expenditure shocks are uncorrelated but the technology shocks are correlated across the two countries.

Using calibration, the parameters are chosen to be $\beta = 0.99$, $\sigma = 2$, $v = 0.34$, $\alpha = 0.36$, $\delta = 0.025$, corr$(e_1, e_2) = 0.258$, $J = 4$, and

$$A = \begin{bmatrix} 0.906 & 0.088 \\ 0.088 & 0.906 \end{bmatrix}.$$

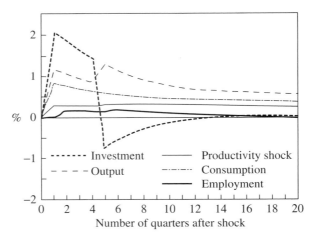

Figure 14.1. Effects in the home country.

Consequently, $\text{corr}(Z_1, Z_2) = 0.015$.

For several countries we now compare various moments calculated from the observed data with simulated data obtained from the benchmark economy and from variants on the benchmark economy. We report only a selection of Backus et al.'s results.

Table 14.3 shows sample statistics based on observed data for the United States, Canada, Germany, Japan, and the United Kingdom for different versions of the model. The data are detrended using the HP filter and the model statistics are based on twenty stochastic simulations for one hundred periods which are then HP filtered. For the most part the observed statistics across countries are not too dissimilar. We therefore concentrate our discussion on comparing the statistics across the various models with those of the observed data.

In the benchmark model, government expenditures are constrained to be zero and there are no terms-of-trade effects. The model data refer to domestic productivity shocks. The main differences with the observed data are the lower volatility in consumption and the low correlation of investment with output. Figures 14.1 and 14.2, which are reproduced from Backus et al. (1995), show the impulse response functions of the home and foreign countries to a domestic technology shock.

The largest effect is that on investment. It also leads to a deficit in net exports, which is not shown. Eventually the home productivity shock affects the foreign economy causing an increase in its productivity. Despite this, foreign output and investment fall initially, but consumption rises a little. The correlations between corresponding variables in each country are shown in table 14.4. The Europe column refers to the observed correlation between the United States and Europe. Thus, in the benchmark model the consumption correlations are high and positive, which reflects consumption risk sharing (under complete markets this correlation would be unity), the productivity shocks are positively correlated, but the other three correlations are negative. This is in contrast to the

Table 14.3. International business cycle and model statistics, 1970 to mid 1990.

		United States	Canada	Germany	Japan	United Kingdom	Benchmark	Autarky
Standard deviation (%)	Output	1.92	1.50	1.51	1.35	1.61	1.50	1.26
	Terms of trade	3.68	2.99	2.66	7.24	3.14	0.48	—
Ratio of standard deviation with standard deviation of output	Consumption	0.75	0.85	0.90	1.09	1.15	0.42	0.54
	Investment	3.27	2.80	2.93	2.41	2.29	10.99	2.65
	Government expenditures	0.75	0.77	0.81	0.79	0.69	—	—
	Employment	0.61	0.86	0.61	0.36	0.68	0.50	0.91
	Productivity	0.68	0.74	0.83	0.88	0.88	0.67	0.99
Correlation with output	Consumption	0.82	0.83	0.66	0.80	0.74	0.77	0.90
	Investment	0.94	0.52	0.84	0.90	0.59	0.27	0.96
	Government expenditures	0.12	−0.23	0.26	−0.02	0.05	—	—
	Employment	0.88	0.69	0.59	0.60	0.47	0.93	0.91
	Productivity	0.96	0.84	0.93	0.98	0.90	0.89	0.99
	Net exports	−0.37	−0.26	−0.11	−0.22	−0.19	0.01	—
	Terms of trade	−0.20	−0.05	−0.11	−0.22	0.09	0.49	—
Correlation with net exports	Terms of trade	0.30	0.05	−0.08	−0.56	−0.58	−0.41	—

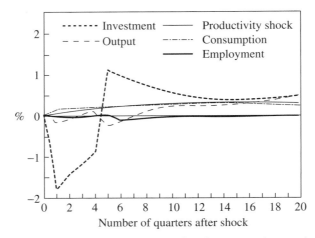

Figure 14.2. Effects in the foreign country. The change in the productivity shock is measured as a percentage of its steady-state value. Changes in other variables are measured as percentages of the steady-state value of output.

Table 14.4. Correlation of home and foreign variables.

	Europe	Benchmark	Autarky
Output	0.66	−0.21	0.08
Consumption	0.51	0.88	0.56
Investment	0.53	−0.94	−0.31
Employment	0.33	−0.78	−0.51
Productivity	0.56	0.25	0.25

observed data where all are positively correlated. Backus et al. interpret these differences in the signs of the correlations between output, investment, and employment as being due to a shift of resources from the foreign to the home economy as a result of the greater productivity boost to the home economy. They call this a quantity anomaly.

Backus et al. examine the effects of adding transport costs. This substantially reduces the variability of net exports, from 3.77 in the benchmark model to only 0.37, and the variability of investment relative to output, but makes little difference otherwise.

If all trade is prohibited, then we have autarky. Unsurprisingly, this reduces the correlation of consumption between countries and, ignoring the sign, of output, investment, and employment. One way to raise these correlations is to increase the correlation between the productivity shocks. Backus et al. say that this does not simultaneously raise both the output and consumption correlations: if one rises, the other does not.

In the modified benchmark model, which is designed to take account of changes in the terms of trade, $\varphi = 0.67$, ω is chosen to set the share of imports in GDP equal to 0.15, and $J = 1$. The results are summarized in table 14.3 in the last three rows. In the modified benchmark model the correlation of output with net exports is close to zero and much lower than in the data, but the correlation with the terms of trade is much higher than in the data. The obvious explanation is that productivity shocks have a large terms-of-trade effect and this offsets the effect on net exports. However, with the exceptions of Canada and Germany, the correlation between the terms of trade and net exports in the theoretical model is not dissimilar to the original data. Backus et al. describe this as a price anomaly. In other experiments, government expenditure shocks and a larger share of imports in GDP are examined. The results differ little from those above.

The Backus et al. study marked a large step forward in the use of RBC models to study the open economy. The results raise a number of problems with the theoretical model that are yet to be resolved. One obvious flaw in the theoretical model is that it is for the real economy and ignores nominal-exchange-rate effects. We have argued in chapter 7 that variation in the terms of trade (and in the real exchange rate) are dominated in the short run by nominal-exchange-rate movements. This is reflected in the second row of table 14.2: for the modified benchmark model the standard deviation is only 0.48, whereas in the data it is much greater.

14.4 DGE Models of the Monetary Economy

We began our study of DGE models with the real closed economy; we then extended this to the open economy; finally, we considered a monetary economy. Much of the empirical evidence about the monetary economy relates to the New Keynesian model (see, for example, Batini et al. 2005; Gali et al. 2001, 2005; King and Plosser 2005; Leeper and Zha 2001; Roberts 1995; Smith and Wickens 2007) or to VAR models of the economy for which there is a vast literature (see, for example, Canova and De Nicolo 2002; Christiano et al. 1999, 2005; Leeper et al. 1996). This evidence indicates that monetary shocks have important real effects in the short run. The main weakness of the VAR studies is their identification of monetary shocks (see Canova 1995; Wickens and Motto 2000). Our present interest is, however, in the general equilibrium implications of a monetary economy as characterized in a DGE macroeconomic model.

In an ambitious study, Smets and Wouters (2003) estimated a closed-economy DGE model for the euro area using Bayesian methods rather than calibration. Their model incorporates many of the New Keynesian features discussed previously, notably, sticky nominal prices and wages generated by a Calvo staggered-adjustment model. It also includes two supply shocks (a productivity and a labor-supply shock), three demand shocks (a preference shock, a shock to investment demand, and a government expenditure shock), three cost-push shocks (to the markups in the goods and labor markets and to the capital risk premium), and two monetary-policy shocks.

Unsurprisingly, in view of the number of issues addressed, the specification of the model is considerably more complex than the models we have considered before. Part of its interest is that it incorporates many of the features described in previous chapters. It shows how they can be fitted together to form a model of the economy, albeit of a closed one. Our exposition of their model keeps closely to their notation and consequently differs somewhat from the models and notation used in previous chapters.

14.4.1 The Smets–Wouters Model

14.4.1.1 Households

The household utility function is

$$U\left(c_{it}, n_{it}, \frac{M_{it}}{P_t}\right) = \left[\frac{(c_{it} - hc_{i,t-1})^{1-\sigma_c}}{1 - \sigma_c} - \frac{n_{it}^{1+\sigma_n}\varepsilon_t^{\mathrm{n}}}{1 + \sigma_n} + \frac{(M_{it}/P_t)^{1-\sigma_m}\varepsilon_t^{\mathrm{m}}}{1 - \sigma_m}\right]\varepsilon_t^{\mathrm{B}},$$

where c_{it}, n_{it}, and M_{it}/P_{it} denote the consumption, work, and real-money balances of the ith household, the ε_t^i (i = B, n, m) are preference shocks, and P_t is the general price level. The term hc_{t-1} is to capture consumption habits, where c_t is aggregate consumption. The real household budget constraint is

$$\frac{M_{it}}{P_t} + p_t^{\mathrm{B}}\frac{B_{it}}{P_t} = \frac{M_{t-1}}{P_{t-1}} + \frac{B_{i,t-1}}{P_{t-1}} + y_{it} - c_{it} - i_{it},$$

where bonds B_{it} are one-period securities with a price of p_t^{B}. Total household income is

$$y_{it} = w_{it}n_{it} + a_{it} + r_t^{\mathrm{k}}z_{it}k_{i,t-1} - \Psi(z_{it})k_{i,t-1} + d_{it},$$

where w_{it} is the real-wage rate, k_{it} is the capital stock, r_t^{k} is the rate of return to capital, the term $r_t^{\mathrm{k}}z_{it}k_{i,t-1} - \Psi(z_{it})k_{i,t-1}$ represents income from capital after depreciation, z_{it} is capacity utilization, and d_{it} is dividend income.

The resulting Euler equation is

$$E_t\left[\beta\frac{\lambda_{t+1}}{\lambda_t}\frac{R_t P_t}{P_{t+1}}\right] = 1,$$

where R_t is the gross nominal rate of return on bonds ($R_t = 1/p_t^{\mathrm{B}}$) and λ_t is the marginal utility of consumption:

$$\lambda_t = (c_t - hc_{t-1})^{-\sigma_c}\varepsilon_t^{\mathrm{B}}.$$

The demand for money is

$$\left(\frac{M_t}{P_t}\right)^{-\sigma_m}\varepsilon_t^{\mathrm{m}} = (c_t - hc_{t-1})^{-\sigma_c} - \frac{1}{R_t}.$$

Households are assumed to act as price setters in the labor market. Their nominal wages are given by

$$W_{it} = \left(\frac{P_{t-1}}{P_{t-2}}\right)^{\gamma}W_{i,t-1}.$$

Households set their nominal wages to maximize their intertemporal objective function subject to their budget constraint and the demand for labor, which is given by

$$n_{it} = \left(\frac{W_{it}}{W_t}\right)^{-(1+\lambda_w,t)/\lambda_{w,t}} n_t,$$

where n_t, the aggregate labor demand, and W_t, the aggregate nominal wage, are given by

$$n_t = \left[\int_0^1 n_{it}^{1/(1+\lambda_{w,t})}\, di\right]^{1+\lambda_{w,t}},$$

$$W_t = \left[\int_0^1 W_{it}^{-1/\lambda_{w,t}}\, di\right]^{-\lambda_{w,t}},$$

and

$$\lambda_{w,t} = \lambda_w + \eta_t^w,$$

where η_t^w is an i.i.d. shock.

The result of this maximization is the following markup equation for the reoptimized wage:

$$\frac{\tilde{w}_t}{P_t} E_t \sum_{s=0}^{\infty} \beta^s \xi_w^s \left(\frac{P_t/P_{t-1}}{P_{t+s}/P_{t+s-1}}\right)^\gamma \frac{n_{i,t+s} U_{c,t+s}}{1+\lambda_{w,t+s}} = E_t \sum_{s=0}^{\infty} \beta^s \xi_w^s n_{i,t+s} U_{n,t+s},$$

where $\tilde{w}_t$ is the new optimal nominal wage and $\xi_w = 0$ if wages are perfectly flexible. The real wage is a markup $1+\lambda_{w,t}$ over the current ratio of the marginal disutility of labor to the marginal utility of an additional unit of consumption. As a result, the aggregate wage satisfies

$$W_t^{-1/\lambda_w} = \xi \left[W_{t-1}\left(\frac{P_{t-1}}{P_{t-2}}\right)^\gamma \right]^{-1/\lambda_w} + (1-\xi)\tilde{w}_t^{-1/\lambda_w}.$$

Households, who own firms, choose the capital stock and investment to maximize their intertemporal utility subject to their budget constraint and the capital accumulation condition

$$k_t = (1-\delta)k_{t-1} + I\left(\frac{i_t \varepsilon_t^i}{i_{t-1}}\right) i_t,$$

where $I(i_t \varepsilon_t^i/i_{t-1})$ is an adjustment cost function and ε_t^i is an investment shock determined by the autoregression

$$\varepsilon_t^i = \rho \varepsilon_{t-1}^i + \eta_t^i.$$

The first-order conditions give

$$Q_t = E_t\left[\beta \frac{\lambda_{t+1}}{\lambda_t}[Q_{t+1}(1-\delta) + z_{t+1}r_{t+1}^k - \Psi(z_{t+1})]\right],$$

$$1 = Q_t I'\left(\frac{i_t \varepsilon_t^i}{i_{t-1}}\right)\left(\frac{i_t \varepsilon_t^i}{i_{t-1}}\right) + \beta E_t Q_{t+1}\frac{\lambda_{t+1}}{\lambda_t}\left(\frac{i_{t+1}\varepsilon_{t+1}^i}{i_t}\right)\left(\frac{i_{t+1}\varepsilon_{t+1}^i}{i_t}\right)\left(\frac{i_{t+1}}{i_t}\right),$$

$$r_{t+1}^k = \Psi'(z_t),$$

where Q_t is the value of installed capital.

14.4.1.2 Firms

It is assumed that there is a single final competitive good and a continuum of monopolistically produced intermediate goods indexed by j, where j is distributed over the unit interval ($j \in [0,1]$). The final good is produced from intermediate goods by

$$y_t = \left[\int_0^1 y_t^{j(1/(1+\lambda_{p,t}))} \, dj \right]^{1+\lambda_{p,t}},$$

where y_t^j is the intermediate good and ν_t is a markup generated by

$$\lambda_{p,t} = \lambda_p + \eta_t^p,$$

where η_t^p is an i.i.d. shock. Cost minimization gives the demand function for intermediate goods as

$$y_{jt} = \left(\frac{p_{jt}}{P_t} \right)^{-(1+\lambda_{p,t})/\lambda_{p,t}} y_t$$

and the final goods price level as

$$P_t = \left[\int_0^1 (p_{jt})^{-1/\lambda_{p,t}} \, dj \right]^{-\lambda_{p,t}},$$

where p_{jt} are the prices of intermediate goods.

The production functions for intermediate goods are

$$y_{jt} = (z_t k_{j,t-1})^\alpha N_{j,t}^{1-\alpha} \varepsilon_t^a - \Phi,$$

where $N_{j,t}$ is an index of different types of labor used by firms, Φ is a fixed cost, and ε_t^a is the productivity shock. Cost minimization implies that

$$\frac{W_t N_{j,t}}{r_t^k z_t k_{j,t-1}} = \frac{1-\alpha}{\alpha}.$$

The firm's marginal cost is

$$MC_t = \frac{1}{\varepsilon_t^a} W_t^{1-\alpha} (r_t^k)^a [\alpha^{-\alpha}(1-\alpha)^{-(1-\alpha)}],$$

which is independent of the intermediate good produced. The firm's nominal profits are

$$\pi_{j,t} = (p_{jt} - MC_t) \left(\frac{p_{jt}}{P_t} \right)^{-(1+\lambda_{p,t})/\lambda_{p,t}} y_t - MC_t \Phi.$$

Firms are assumed to be able to reoptimize their price randomly with probability $1 - \xi_p$, as in the Calvo model. The optimal price $\tilde{p}_t$ is obtained from the first-order condition

$$E_t \sum_{s=0}^\infty \beta^s \xi_p^s \lambda_{t+s} y_{j,t+s} \left[\frac{\tilde{p}_t}{P_t} \left(\frac{P_{t+s-1}/P_{t-1}}{P_{t+s}/P_t} \right)^\gamma - (1+\lambda_{p,t+s}) \frac{MC_{t+s}}{P_{t+s}} \right] = 0,$$

which shows that the optimal price is a function of future marginal costs and is a markup over them unless $\lambda_p = 0$. The general price index therefore satisfies

$$P_t^{-1/\lambda_{p,t}} = \xi_p \left(P_{t-1} \left(\frac{P_{t-1}}{P_{t-2}} \right)^{\lambda_p} \right)^{-1/\lambda_{p,t}} + (1-\xi_p) \tilde{p}_t^{-1/\lambda_{p,t}}.$$

14.4.1.3 Market Equilibrium

Final goods-market equilibrium satisfies the national income constraint

$$y_t = c_t + i_t + g_t + \Psi(z_t)k_{t-1}.$$

14.4.1.4 The Log-Linearized Model

For the empirical analysis the model is log-linearized around its nonstochastic steady state. Denoting log-deviations about equilibrium by a caret (or hat), and noting that variables dated $t + 1$ are rational expectations, the log-linearized model is

$$\hat{c}_t = \frac{h}{1+h}\hat{c}_{t-1} + \frac{1}{1+h}\hat{c}_{t+1} - \frac{1-h}{(1+h)\sigma_c}[(\hat{R}_t - \hat{\pi}_{t+1}) + (\hat{\varepsilon}_t^b - \hat{\varepsilon}_{t+1}^b)],$$

$$\hat{i}_t = \frac{1}{1+\beta}\hat{i}_{t-1} + \frac{\beta}{1+\beta}\hat{i}_{t+1} + \frac{\varphi}{1+\beta}\hat{Q}_t + \beta\hat{\varepsilon}_t^i - \hat{\varepsilon}_t^i,$$

$$\hat{Q}_t = -(\hat{R}_t - \hat{\pi}_{t+1}) + \frac{1-\delta}{1-\delta+\bar{r}^k}\hat{Q}_{t+1} + \frac{\bar{r}^k}{1-\delta+\bar{r}^k}\hat{r}_t^k + \eta_t^Q,$$

$$\hat{\pi}_t = \frac{\nu}{1+\beta\gamma_p}\hat{\pi}_{t-1} + \frac{\beta}{1+\beta\gamma_p}\hat{\pi}_{t+1}$$
$$+ \frac{(1-\beta\xi_p)(1-\xi_p)}{(1+\beta\gamma_p)\xi_p}[\alpha\hat{r}_t^k + (1-\alpha)\hat{w}_t - \hat{\varepsilon}_t^a + \eta_t^p],$$

$$\hat{w}_t = \frac{1}{1+\beta}\hat{w}_{t-1} + \frac{\beta}{1+\beta}\hat{w}_{t+1} + \frac{\gamma_w}{1+\beta}\hat{\pi}_{t-1} - \frac{1+\beta\gamma_w}{1+\beta}\hat{\pi}_t + \frac{\beta}{1+\beta}\hat{\pi}_{t+1}$$
$$- \frac{(1-\beta\xi_w)(1-\xi_w)}{(1+\beta)[1+((1+\lambda_w)\sigma_n/\lambda_w)]\xi_w}$$
$$\times \left[\hat{w}_t - \sigma_n\hat{N}_t - \frac{\sigma_c}{1-h}(\hat{c}_t - h\hat{c}_{t-1}) - \hat{\varepsilon}_t^n - \eta_t^w\right],$$

$$\hat{N}_t = -\hat{w}_t + (1+\Psi)\hat{r}_t^k + \hat{k}_{t-1},$$

$$\hat{y}_t = (1 - \delta k_y - g_y)\hat{c}_t + \delta k_y\hat{i}_t + g_y\varepsilon_t^g$$
$$= \phi[\hat{\varepsilon}_t^g + \alpha\hat{k}_{t-1} + \alpha\psi\hat{r}_t^k + (1-\alpha)\hat{N}_t],$$

$$\hat{R}_t = \rho\hat{R}_{t-1} + (1-\rho)[\bar{\pi}_t + r_\pi(\hat{\pi}_{t-1} - \bar{\pi}_t) + r_y\hat{y}_t]$$
$$+ r_{\Delta\pi}(\hat{\pi}_t - \hat{\pi}_{t-1}) + r_{\Delta y}(\hat{y}_t - \hat{y}_{t-1}) - r_a\eta_t^a - r_n\eta_t^n + \eta_t^R,$$

where $\varphi = I''^{-1}$, $\beta = (1 - \delta + \bar{r}^k)^{-1}$, $\psi = \Psi'(1)/\Psi''(1)$, $\bar{\pi}_t$ is the inflation target, and the equations include various parameters that are long-run average values. Thus, there are nine endogenous variables and ten independent shocks. Five of the shocks arise from technology and preferences (ε_t^a, ε_t^i, ε_t^b, ε_t^n, ε_t^g), which are assumed to be generated by first-order autoregressive processes, three are cost-push i.i.d. shocks (η_t^w, η_t^p, η_t^Q), and two are monetary shocks ($\bar{\pi}_t$ and η_t^R).

14.4.2 Empirical Results

The model is estimated using Bayesian procedures on quarterly data for the period 1970.1–1999.4 for seven euro area macroeconomic variables: GDP, consumption, investment, employment, the GDP deflator, real wages, and the nominal interest rate. It is assumed that neither capital nor the rental rate of capital are observed. By using Bayesian methods it is possible to combine key calibrated parameters with sample information. Rather than evaluate the DGE model based only on its sample moment statistics, impulse response functions are also used. The moments and the impulse response functions for the estimated DGE model are based on the median of ten thousand simulations of the estimated model. A third-order VAR is fitted to the original data and is used to provide the impulse response functions for the original data. We now summarize the main findings.

Comparing the autocovariances of the VAR and the simulated DGE model, those from the VAR are generally quite close to those of the DGE model: the VAR autocovariances lie within the confidence bands of those for the DGE model; the bands are, however, quite wide, indicating parameter uncertainty. The main discrepancy concerns the autocovariances between output and the expected real interest rate. These are higher in the VAR, but the differences are not significant. These results, while satisfactory, leave open the question of the extent to which they are due to allowing the various shocks to be generated by an unrestricted VAR, freely estimated to fit the data.

Turning to the impulse response functions for the DGE model, first we consider the responses to a positive productivity shock, ε_t^a. This causes output, consumption, and investment to rise, but employment and the utilization of capital to fall. The real wage also rises, but only gradually. The fall in employment is consistent with evidence on the impulse responses to U.S. productivity shocks, but is in contrast to the predictions of the standard RBC model without nominal rigidities. A possible explanation is that, due to the rise in productivity, marginal cost falls on impact and, as monetary policy does not respond strongly enough to offset this fall, inflation declines gradually. The estimated reaction of monetary policy to a productivity shock is comparable with results for the United States.

A positive labor-supply shock has a similar effect on output, inflation, and the interest rate to a positive productivity shock. Due to the strong persistence of the labor-supply shock, the real interest rate is not greatly affected. The main differences are that employment also rises in line with output and that the real wage falls significantly. This fall in the real wage leads to a fall in marginal cost and in inflation. A negative wage-markup shock has similar effects, except that the real interest rate rises, and real wages and marginal costs fall more on impact. The effects of a negative price-markup shock on output, inflation, and interest rates are also similar, but the effects on real marginal cost, real wages, and the rental rate of capital are opposite in sign.

Positive demand shocks generally cause real interest rates to rise. A positive preference shock, while increasing consumption and output, crowds out investment. The increase in capacity necessary to satisfy increased demand is delivered by an increase in the utilization of installed capital and an increase in employment. Increased consumption demand puts pressure on the prices of the factors of production, and both the rental rate on capital and the real wage rise, thereby putting upward pressure on marginal cost and inflation.

A positive government expenditure shock raises output initially but crowds out consumption, which, due to increases in the marginal utility of working, leads to a greater willingness of households to work. As a result, the effects on real wages, marginal costs, and prices are small.

A negative monetary-policy shock (increase in the interest rate shock η_t^R) has temporary effects on all variables apart from the price level, which falls permanently. For the first few periods, nominal and real short-term interest rates rise, and output, consumption, investment, and real wages fall. The maximum effect on investment is about three times as large as that on consumption. Overall, these effects are consistent with other evidence on the euro area, though the price effects in the model are somewhat larger than those estimated in some identified VARs.

A permanent increase in target inflation ($\bar{\pi}_t$) does not have a strong effect on output, consumption, employment, the real wage, or the real interest rate, although all rise quickly. It has a larger effect on investment and, of course, causes the price level to rise permanently.

The contribution of each of the structural shocks to variations in the endogenous variables may be obtained from the forecast error variances at various horizons. At the one-year horizon, output variations are driven primarily by the preference shock and the monetary-policy shock. In the medium term, both of these shocks continue to dominate, but the two supply shocks (productivity and labor supply) account for about 20% of the forecast error variance. In the long run, the labor-supply shock dominates, but the monetary-policy shock still accounts for about a quarter of the forecast error in output. The monetary-policy shock is transmitted mainly through investment. The price- and wage-markup shocks make little contribution to output variability. Taken together, the two supply shocks, the productivity and the labor shock, account for only 37% of the long-run forecast error variance of output, which is less than is found in most VAR studies. The limited importance of productivity shocks, which explain a maximum of 12% of the forecast error variance of output, is probably due to the negative correlation between output and employment.

In the short run, variations in inflation are mainly driven by price-markup shocks. This appears to be a very sluggish process, with inflation only gradually responding to current and expected changes in marginal cost. In the medium and long run, preference shocks and labor-supply shocks account for about 20% of the variation in inflation, whereas monetary-policy shocks account for about 15%.

In summary, in this study by Smets and Wouters three structural shocks explain a significant fraction of variations in output, inflation, and interest rates at the medium- to long-term horizon: these are the preference shock, the labor-supply shock, and the monetary-policy shock. In addition, the price-markup shock is an important determinant of inflation, but not of output, while the productivity shock determines about 10% of output variations but does not affect inflation. Smets and Wouters do not report corresponding results for government expenditure shocks, though these shocks appear to have a strong temporary effect on output. This supports our earlier conclusion that RBC models, with their focus on productivity shocks, do not give an adequate representation of the economy, or even of output, and that the effects of monetary and, possibly, fiscal policy should also be represented in a DGE macroeconomic model together with labor-supply effects.

14.5 Conclusions

Our main purpose in seeking empirical evidence on DGE models is to improve the underlying macroeconomic theory, and hence our knowledge of the economy. This is one of the main attractions of the form of analysis discussed in this chapter. We have argued that any shortcomings in the ability of our DGE model to account for observed data should be addressed by rethinking the theory rather than by propping up the model with, for example, additional dynamic terms. A frequent weakness of time-series econometrics is that it is too concerned with obtaining models with acceptable statistical properties, and too little concerned with contributing to better macroeconomic theory. The unfortunate consequence is that increasingly macroeconomists have ignored empirical evidence on their models and, where they have used data, they have adopted poor statistical practices. The challenge for econometrics is to retain its relevance to macroeconomic theory; the challenge for macroeconomic theory is to bring evidence to bear in a way that is consistent with the principles of statistical inference without compromising its general equilibrium agenda.

A corollary is that allowing the disturbances in a DGE model to have a dynamic structure may improve the fit to the observed data but it is also vulnerable to the criticism that this too may be data-mining. This is one reason why the contemporaneous covariance structure between variables is a valuable guide to the adequacy of a DGE model.

In this final chapter we have selected a small number of key articles for a close scrutiny of their empirical properties. These covered RBC models for closed and open economies and a DGE model of the monetary economy. The principal findings are that although fluctuations in output (i.e., business cycles) are affected by productivity shocks, other shocks also affect output: notably, monetary shocks. There is also evidence of the importance of preference and labor-supply shocks. Inflation seems to be driven both by monetary shocks and by price-markup shocks, but the response is sluggish. This supports the arguments made earlier concerning the inflexibility of prices and the role of monopolistic competition in causing this inflexibility. Imperfectly flexible prices also affect the dynamic adjustment of real variables.

The more complex the model, the greater the reliance on numerical procedures to analyze the dynamic response of the model to shocks and policy changes. However, even for complex models it is often relatively straightforward to derive their long-run general equilibrium properties analytically. And by carefully simplifying the DGE model, it is often also possible to derive their short-run properties analytically. Taken together, this may provide a close approximation to how the economy behaves.

15
Mathematical Appendix

15.1 Introduction

In this appendix, for easy reference, we explain the mathematical methods that we use in our macroeconomic analysis. As far as possible, discussion will be brief and to the point, and the derivations are heuristic rather than rigorous. For a more detailed and rigorous analysis of the issues the reader is referred to the mathematical literature: see, for example, Bellman and Dreyfus (1962), Intriligator (1971), Leonard and Long (1992), Dixit (1990), Chiang (1992), and Chow (1975, 1981, 1997). As the macroeconomic models in this book are specified in discrete time, we focus throughout almost entirely on discrete-time methods. First, we consider dynamic optimization, and then we discuss solution methods for linear rational-expectations models.

15.2 Dynamic Optimization

The generic mathematical problem in intertemporal macroeconomics is to maximize an objective function defined over multiple periods subject to constraints, at least one of which is dynamic, and to given boundary conditions. This may be called intertemporal or, more commonly, dynamic optimization. Often the objective function is a present-value relation defined in terms of the choice or control variables and other noncontrollable variables, and the dynamic constraint describes a dynamic relation between these variables. The problem may have an infinite or a finite horizon, and there may be a constraint on the outcome in the last period of the finite horizon, or at the start. Such boundary conditions may be exogenously given, or be choice variables. The problem may be nonstochastic, implying perfect foresight, or stochastic, implying uncertainty about future outcomes. And it may be defined in continuous or discrete time. We focus mainly on nonstochastic dynamic optimization in discrete time with an infinite horizon, but we also consider the case of continuous time, stochastic optimization, and a finite horizon.

Dynamic optimization may be carried out in several ways: by the use of Lagrange multipliers, the calculus of variations, the maximum principle, or dynamic programming. The choice of method will depend in part on the particular problem. Whichever feasible optimization method is chosen, the solution will be the same.

The general nonstochastic discrete-time intertemporal problem takes the form: choose $\{x_t, z_t; t = 0, 1, \ldots, T\}$ to maximize the concave scalar objective function

$$V(x_0, x_1, \ldots, x_T; z_0, z_1, \ldots, z_T)$$

subject to the $N \times 1$ vector of constraints F, where the ith constraint is

$$F_i(x_0, x_1, \ldots, x_T; z_0, z_1, \ldots, z_T) \geqslant 0, \quad i = 1, \ldots, N,$$

x_t is an $n \times 1$ vector of state variables, and z_t is an $m \times 1$ vector of control variables. The control variables are the instruments (under the control of the optimizer) and the state variables are related to the instruments through the constraints. Without specifying them precisely, we assume that appropriate regularity conditions are satisfied so that an interior solution exists. For example, we assume throughout that whatever functional form V takes, it exists over the domain under consideration and has at least continuous first- and second-order derivatives. We also assume that F is differentiable. This problem may be solved using the method of Lagrange multipliers or, for particular functional forms, using other methods.

A particular case of the general problem commonly occurs in intertemporal macroeconomics. The function V is often additively separable over time so that

$$V(x_0, x_1, \ldots, x_T; z_0, z_1, \ldots, z_T) = U(x_0, z_0) + \beta U(x_1, z_1) + \cdots + \beta^T U(x_T, z_T)$$

$$= \sum_{t=0}^{T} \beta^t U(x_t, z_t),$$

where $0 < \beta \leqslant 1$ has the interpretation of a discount factor; $\beta = 0$ would imply static optimization. V then has the interpretation of a present-value function. If we also define

$$V \equiv V_0 = \sum_{t=0}^{T} \beta^t U(x_t, z_t),$$

$$V_1 = \sum_{t=1}^{T} \beta^t U(x_t, z_t),$$

then we can rewrite V as the recursion

$$V_0 = U(x_0, z_0) + \beta V_1.$$

In other words, V can be derived by successive substitution for V_1, V_2, etc. Typically, at least one of the constraints takes the form of a difference equation such as

$$x_{t+1} = f(x_t, z_t), \quad t = 0, \ldots, T,$$

which provides $T + 1$ constraints, one for each period, and optimization takes place with respect to $\{x_t, z_t; t = 0, 1, \ldots, T\}$.

Implicitly, it has been assumed that the future values of state variables are known. In practice this will not usually be the situation. As a result, intertemporal problems in economics and finance often take the form: maximize

$$E_t[V(x_t)] = U(z_t) + \beta E_t[V(x_{t+1})]$$

subject to a dynamic constraint, where $E_t[\cdot]$ denotes the expectation conditional on information available up to and including period t. This reflects the fact that x_t and z_t may be stochastic variables whose future values are unknown at time t and so must be forecast from current information. This problem is called stochastic dynamic programming. The Lagrange multiplier technique can be used for this problem, but has major drawbacks.

The optimal solutions to these problems are defined over the entire planning horizon. This raises the question of whether it is best to carry out the entire plan as initially conceived or to reoptimize at some point in the future and abandon the initial plan. The plan could even be reoptimized each period, so that only the first period is ever implemented. The notion that it is optimal to reoptimize a dynamic program in this way is called the problem of time inconsistency. The inconsistency is that the plan announced for the given time horizon is replaced by a new plan. One reason why reoptimization may be optimal is the later arrival of new information about the future. A more common argument in economics relates to the fact that decisions are often decentralized so that the optimality of one person's decision depends on the expected decisions of others.

15.3   The Method of Lagrange Multipliers

15.3.1   Equality Constraints

To illustrate the method of Lagrange multipliers consider the static optimization problem: maximize $V(x, z)$ subject to the constraint

$$f(x, z) = c,$$

where x and z are nonnegative scalars and c is a constant. The problem is depicted in figure 15.1. All values on the line $V(x, z)$ give the same value of V, and V increases in the direction of the arrow.

(i) Graphical Solution.   The constraint is a given line in $\{x, z\}$-space; the aim is to choose the maximum value of the function $V(x, z)$ that satisfies the constraint. This occurs at the point of tangency of V with that of the constraint. At this point the slopes of the tangents are the same. The solutions for x and z can be obtained by solving the equations for these slopes simultaneously.

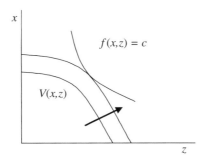

Figure 15.1. Constrained optimization.

(ii) Substitution. Assuming that the constraint holds exactly and that we can write the constraint as $x = g(z)$, we can eliminate x to give $V[g(z), z]$. Hence the first-order condition for a maximum is

$$\frac{dV}{dz} = \frac{\partial V}{\partial g}\frac{\partial g}{\partial z} + \frac{\partial V}{\partial z}$$
$$= \frac{\partial V}{\partial x}\frac{\partial x}{\partial z} + \frac{\partial V}{\partial z} = 0.$$

This can be solved for z, and x can then be obtained from the constraint. More generally, we note that the slope of the tangent to the constraint is

$$\frac{dx}{dz} = -\frac{\partial f/\partial z}{\partial f/\partial x}.$$

(iii) Lagrange Multipliers. Define the function (called the Lagrangian)

$$\mathcal{L}(x, z, \lambda) = V(x, z) + \lambda[c - f(x, z)],$$

where λ is called the Lagrange multiplier. Now maximize $\mathcal{L}$ with respect to x, z, and λ. The first-order conditions are

$$\frac{\partial \mathcal{L}}{\partial x} = \frac{\partial V}{\partial x} - \lambda\frac{\partial f}{\partial x} = 0, \tag{15.1}$$

$$\frac{\partial \mathcal{L}}{\partial z} = \frac{\partial V}{\partial z} - \lambda\frac{\partial f}{\partial z} = 0, \tag{15.2}$$

$$\frac{\partial \mathcal{L}}{\partial \lambda} = f(x, z) - c = 0. \tag{15.3}$$

From equation (15.1), $\lambda = (\partial V/\partial x)/(\partial f/\partial x)$. Substituting this into equation (15.2) gives

$$\frac{\partial V}{\partial z} - \frac{\partial V/\partial x}{\partial f/\partial x}\frac{\partial f}{\partial z} = \frac{\partial V}{\partial z} - \frac{\partial V}{\partial x}\frac{\partial f/\partial z}{\partial f/\partial x}$$
$$= \frac{\partial V}{\partial z} + \frac{\partial V}{\partial x}\frac{\partial x}{\partial z} = 0;$$

the same as the solution obtained by substitution.

We can give the following interpretation of Lagrange multipliers. The optimal solutions can be written $x^* = x^*(c)$, $z^* = z^*(c)$, $\lambda^* = \lambda^*(c)$, as they are functions of c, and the maximized value of V can be written $V^*(c) = V[x^*, z^*]$. Hence the Lagrangian function at the optimum can be written

$$\mathcal{L}^*(c) = V^*(c) + \lambda^*(c)\{c - f^*[x^*(c), z^*(c)]\}.$$

It follows that

$$\frac{\partial \mathcal{L}^*(c)}{\partial c} = \frac{\partial V^*(c)}{\partial x^*}\frac{\partial x^*}{\partial c} + \frac{\partial V^*(c)}{\partial z^*}\frac{\partial z^*}{\partial c} + \frac{\partial \lambda^*(c)}{\partial c}\{c - f^*[x^*(c), z^*(c)]\}$$

$$+ \lambda^*(c)\left(1 - \frac{\partial f^*}{\partial x^*}\frac{\partial x^*}{\partial c} - \frac{\partial f^*}{\partial z^*}\frac{\partial z^*}{\partial c}\right)$$

$$= \left[\frac{\partial V^*(c)}{\partial x^*} - \lambda^*(c)\frac{\partial f^*}{\partial x^*}\right]\frac{\partial x^*}{\partial c} + \left[\frac{\partial V^*(c)}{\partial z^*} - \lambda^*(c)\frac{\partial f^*}{\partial z^*}\right]\frac{\partial z^*}{\partial c}$$

$$+ \frac{\partial \lambda^*(c)}{\partial c}\{c - f^*[x^*(c), z^*(c)]\} + \lambda^*(c)$$

$$= \lambda^*(c)$$

where we have used the fact that, from the previous first-order conditions,

$$\frac{\partial V^*}{\partial x^*} - \lambda^*\frac{\partial f^*}{\partial x^*} = \frac{\partial V^*}{\partial z^*} - \lambda^*\frac{\partial f^*}{\partial z^*} = 0$$

and that from the constraint, $c - f^*(x^*, z^*) = 0$. Hence,

$$\frac{\partial \mathcal{L}^*(c)}{\partial c} = \frac{\partial V^*(c)}{\partial c} = \lambda^*(c).$$

The Lagrange multiplier can therefore be interpreted as the change in V^*, the maximized value of V, of a unit change in the constraint c.

If the constraint is not binding, then a small change in the constraint would have no effect on V^*. In this case $\lambda = 0$. It is only when the constraint is binding that $\lambda \neq 0$ and an easing or tightening of the constraint would affect V^*.

Example 15.1. Minimize $V = x^2 + cz^2$ subject to the constraint $x = a + bz$.

(i) The substitution method:

$$V = (a + bz)^2 + cz^2,$$

$$\frac{\partial V}{\partial z} = 2b(a + bz) + 2cz = 0,$$

$$z = -\frac{ab}{b^2 + c}.$$

(ii) Lagrange multipliers:

$$\mathcal{L} = x^2 + cz^2 + \lambda(a + bz - x),$$

$$\frac{\partial V}{\partial x} = 2x - \lambda = 0,$$

$$\frac{\partial V}{\partial z} = 2cz + \lambda b = 0,$$

$$z = -\frac{b}{c}x = -\frac{b}{c}(a + bz) = -\frac{ab}{b^2 + c}.$$

Applying the method of Lagrange multipliers to the general problem we define the Lagrangian as

$$\mathcal{L} = V(x_0, x_1, \ldots, x_T; z_0, z_1, \ldots, z_T) + \lambda' F(x_0, x_1, \ldots, x_T; z_0, z_1, \ldots, z_T),$$

where λ is an $N \times 1$ vector of Lagrange multipliers. The first-order conditions for $t = 0, \ldots, T$ are

$$\frac{\partial \mathcal{L}}{\partial x_t} = \frac{\partial V}{\partial x_t} + \frac{\partial F}{\partial x_t} \lambda = 0,$$

$$\frac{\partial \mathcal{L}}{\partial z} = \frac{\partial V}{\partial z_t} + \frac{\partial F}{\partial z_t} \lambda = 0,$$

$$\frac{\partial \mathcal{L}}{\partial \lambda} = F(x_0, x_1, \ldots, x_T; z_0, z_1, \ldots, z_T) = 0.$$

In principle these equations can be solved for $x_0, x_1, \ldots, x_T$, $z_0, z_1, \ldots, z_T$, and λ.

Finally, consider the special case where V is a present value and the constraints are given by the difference equation. The Lagrangian can be written as

$$
\begin{aligned}
\mathcal{L} &= \sum_{t=0}^{T} \beta^t U(x_t, z_t) + \lambda_1 [f(x_0, z_0) - x_1] \\
&\quad + \lambda_2 [f(x_1, z_1) - x_2] + \cdots + \lambda_T [f(x_T, z_T) - x_{T+1}] \\
&= \sum_{t=0}^{T} \{ \beta^t U(x_t, z_t) + \lambda_t [f(x_t, z_t) - x_{t+1}] \} \\
&= \sum_{t=0}^{T} H(x_t, z_t, \lambda_t),
\end{aligned}
$$

where

$$H(x_t, z_t, \lambda_t) = \beta^t U(x_t, z_t) + \lambda_t [f(x_t, z_t) - x_{t+1}].$$

As there are $T + 1$ constraints, the problem requires $T + 1$ Lagrange multipliers. We note that time $T + 1$ variables, notably x_{T+1}, are present in the optimand but optimization is assumed to take place only for periods $0, 1, \ldots, T$. The implication is that x_{T+1} must be prespecified. We also assume that, being a state variable, x_0 is given. The first-order conditions are

$$\frac{\partial \mathcal{L}}{\partial x_t} = \frac{\partial H(x_t, z_t, \lambda_t)}{\partial x_t} = \beta^t \frac{\partial U(x_t, z_t)}{\partial x_t} + \lambda_t \frac{\partial f(x_t, z_t)}{\partial x_t} - \lambda_{t-1} = 0,$$
$$t = 1, 2, \ldots, T,$$

$$\frac{\partial \mathcal{L}}{\partial z_t} = \frac{\partial H(x_t, z_t, \lambda_t)}{\partial z_t} = \beta^t \frac{\partial U(x_t, z_t)}{\partial z_t} + \lambda_t \frac{\partial f(x_t, z_t)}{\partial z_t} = 0, \quad t = 0, \ldots, T,$$

$$\frac{\partial \mathcal{L}}{\partial \lambda_t} = \frac{\partial H(x_t, z_t, \lambda_t)}{\partial \lambda_t} = f(x_t, z_t) - x_{t+1} = 0, \qquad t = 0, \ldots, T.$$

We note that the first-order condition for $\partial \mathcal{L}/\partial x_t$ defines a set of difference equations in λ_t. This is because x_t appears in two constraints for each t. In principle, we can now solve for $\{x_t, z_t, \lambda_t; t = 0, \ldots, T\}$ taking x_{T+1} and x_0 as given.

Example 15.2. Maximize

$$V = \sum_{t=0}^{T} \beta^t U(c_t), \quad U' > 0, \ U'' < 0,$$

$$U(c_t) = \ln c_t,$$

subject to

$$s_{t+1} - s_t = \alpha(s_t - c_t), \quad s_{T+1} = 0, \quad 0 < a < 1, \tag{15.4}$$

where $\beta = 1/(1 + \theta)$ can be interpreted as a discount factor and θ is the implied discount rate. The Lagrangian is

$$\mathcal{L} = \sum_{t=0}^{T} \{\beta^t \ln c_t + \lambda_t[(1 + \alpha)s_t - \alpha c_t - s_{t+1}]\}.$$

The first-order conditions for $t = 0, \ldots, T$ are

$$\frac{\partial \mathcal{L}}{\partial c_t} = \beta^t \frac{1}{c_t} - \alpha \lambda_t = 0,$$

$$\frac{\partial \mathcal{L}}{\partial s_t} = (1 + \alpha)\lambda_t - \lambda_{t-1} = 0.$$

Hence, $\lambda_t = \beta^t / (\alpha c_t)$ and

$$c_{t+1} = (1 + \alpha)\beta c_t, \tag{15.5}$$

$$= \frac{1 + \alpha}{1 + \theta} c_t, \tag{15.6}$$

implying that the growth rate of c_t is positive or negative depending on whether $\alpha \gtrless \theta$.

The solution for s_t may be obtained by solving this simultaneously with the constraint. It can be shown that the resulting solution of s_t can be written

$$s_{t+2} - (1 + \alpha)(1 + \beta)s_{t+1} + (1 + \alpha)^2 \beta s_t = 0. \tag{15.7}$$

It is clear, therefore, that knowledge of s_{T+1} is not sufficient; we also need one more piece of information. This could be knowledge either of one of the other values of s_t, for example s_{T+2}, s_T, or s_0, or of c_{T+1}.

In intertemporal macroeconomics it is common for the dynamic solution to be a saddlepath. This is characterized by having both stable and unstable roots and has a solution that can be interpreted as a partial adjustment model with a forward-looking long-run target. The condition that s_t has a saddlepath solution is that the auxiliary equation satisfies

$$[1 - (1 + \alpha)(1 + \beta)L + (1 + \alpha)^2 \beta L^2]_{L=1} < 0. \tag{15.8}$$

This requires that $\alpha[(1 + \alpha)\beta - 1] < 0$. If $\beta = 1/(1 + \theta)$, then for a saddlepath solution we require that $\theta > \alpha$.

If $T \to \infty$, then we can show that the constraint, equation (15.4), implies that

$$s_t = \frac{\alpha}{1+\alpha} \sum_{i=0}^{\infty} \left(\frac{1}{1+\alpha}\right)^i c_{t+i}. \tag{15.9}$$

From equation (15.5), $c_{t+i} = [(1+\alpha)\beta]^i c_t$, hence substituting in (15.9) gives

$$c_t = \frac{(1+\alpha)(1-\beta)}{\alpha} s_t. \tag{15.10}$$

15.3.2 Inequality Constraints

Consider the following problem:

$$\max_x V(x) \text{ subject to } f(x) \geqslant 0, \ x \geqslant 0,$$

where $V(x)$ is a concave function, x is an $n \times 1$ vector of variables and f is a vector of k constraints, some of which are equality or binding constraints and some of which are inequality constraints. The inequality constraints allow for slack such as free disposable, where, for example, not all of the output necessarily needs to be purchased. This is known as a nonlinear programming problem.

The first-order conditions for this problem are a modification of those for Lagrange multipliers and are called the Kuhn–Tucker conditions. In order to state these, first we define the Lagrangian as

$$\mathcal{L}(x,\lambda) = V(x) + \lambda' f(x)$$

$$= V(x) + \sum_{i=1}^{k} \lambda_i f_i(x),$$

where λ is a $k \times 1$ vector of Lagrange multipliers and $f_i(x)$ is the ith constraint. If $\{x^*, \lambda^*\}$ is a solution to this problem, then the first-order conditions are

$$\frac{\partial \mathcal{L}(x^*, \lambda^*)}{\partial x^*} \leqslant 0, \quad x^* \geqslant 0, \quad x^{*\prime} \frac{\partial \mathcal{L}(x^*, \lambda^*)}{\partial x^*} = 0,$$

$$\frac{\partial \mathcal{L}(x^*, \lambda^*)}{\partial \lambda^*} \geqslant 0, \quad \lambda^* \geqslant 0, \quad \lambda^{*\prime} \frac{\partial \mathcal{L}(x^*, \lambda^*)}{\partial \lambda^*} = 0.$$

The condition $\partial \mathcal{L}(x^*, \lambda^*)/\partial x^* \leqslant 0$ reflects the fact that any departure from the unconstrained maximum due to the inequality constraints must be below the unconstrained maximum. The condition $x^{*\prime}(\partial \mathcal{L}(x^*, \lambda^*)/\partial x^*) = 0$ reflects the fact that sign restrictions on the ith elements of x^* and $\partial \mathcal{L}(x^*, \lambda^*)/\partial x^*$ may cause both to be nonnegative, but the product must be zero for each i. For example, if $x_i^* > 0$ then $\partial \mathcal{L}(x^*, \lambda^*)/\partial x_i^* = 0$ (the usual case for binding constraints), but if $x_i^* = 0$ then $\partial \mathcal{L}(x^*, \lambda^*)/\partial x_i^* < 0$. Similar arguments apply to the conditions involving λ^*. We also note that the condition $\lambda^{*\prime}(\partial \mathcal{L}(x^*, \lambda^*)/\partial \lambda^*) = 0$ holds when the constraint is nonbinding and $\lambda^* = 0$; in this case, $\partial \mathcal{L}(x^*, \lambda^*)/\partial \lambda^*$ may be positive. If $\lambda^* > 0$, we have $\partial \mathcal{L}(x^*, \lambda^*)/\partial \lambda^* = 0$.

We note that this solution applies only in the precise conditions stated. If the inequality constraints are different, then the problem must be reformulated as above for these conditions to apply.

Example 15.3. Consider the following problem

$$\max_{x,z} V(x,z) \text{ subject to } f(x,z) \leqslant c, \ x, z \geqslant 0.$$

The solution can be obtained by defining a new variable y such that

$$f(x,z) + y = c, \quad x, z, y \geqslant 0.$$

We now maximize $V(x,z)$ subject to x, z, and y and the new equality constraint. The Lagrangian is

$$\mathcal{L}^*(x,z,y,\lambda) = V(x,z) + \lambda[c - f(x,z) - y]$$
$$= \mathcal{L} - \lambda y,$$

where the usual Lagrangian is

$$\mathcal{L}(x,z,\lambda) = V(x,z) + \lambda[c - f(x,z)].$$

The Kuhn–Tucker first-order conditions are

$$\frac{\partial \mathcal{L}^*}{\partial x} = \frac{\partial V}{\partial x} - \lambda \frac{\partial f}{\partial x} = \frac{\partial \mathcal{L}}{\partial x} \leqslant 0,$$

$$\frac{\partial \mathcal{L}^*}{\partial z} = \frac{\partial V}{\partial z} - \lambda \frac{\partial f}{\partial z} = \frac{\partial \mathcal{L}}{\partial z} \leqslant 0,$$

$$\frac{\partial \mathcal{L}^*}{\partial y} = -\lambda \leqslant 0,$$

$$\frac{\partial \mathcal{L}^*}{\partial \lambda} = \frac{\partial \mathcal{L}}{\partial \lambda} - y \geqslant 0$$
$$= c - f(x,z) - y = 0.$$

The last equation follows from the fact that the inequality constraint has been converted into an equality constraint. Eliminating y gives

$$\frac{\partial V}{\partial x} - \lambda \frac{\partial f}{\partial x} \leqslant 0,$$

$$\frac{\partial V}{\partial z} - \lambda \frac{\partial f}{\partial z} \leqslant 0,$$

$$c - f(x,z) \geqslant 0,$$

$$x, z, \lambda \geqslant 0.$$

15.4 Continuous-Time Optimization

We can compare the method of Lagrange multipliers in discrete time with two standard continuous-time methods: the "calculus of variations" and the "maximum principle." As we do not use continuous-time optimization in this book, we sketch only sufficient details for the comparison to be made (see, for example, Intriligator (1971) for more details).

15.4.1 Calculus of Variations

The calculus of variations is concerned with choosing a path for $y(t)$ that maximizes

$$\int_0^T f[y(t), \dot{y}(t), t]\, dt,$$

where $\dot{y}(t) = dy/dt$ and $y(t)$ may be a vector. We note that not all elements of $\dot{y}(t)$ may be present in $f[y(t), \dot{y}(t), t]$ and there may be constraints on $y(0)$ and $y(T)$. The first-order conditions are

$$\frac{\partial f(t)}{\partial y(t)} - \frac{d}{dt}\left(\frac{\partial f(t)}{\partial \dot{y}(t)}\right) = 0.$$

These are called the Euler equations.

Example 15.4. Consider a continuous-time version of example 15.2 with an infinite horizon in which the objective function is

$$V = \int_0^\infty e^{-\theta t} \ln c_t,$$

where the constraint is the differential equation

$$\dot{s}(t) = \alpha[s(t) - c(t)].$$

Replacing $\dot{s}(t)$ by Δs_{t+1} gives the previous difference equation.
  Let $y(t) = \{s(t), c(t), \lambda(t)\}$ and let

$$f[y(t), \dot{y}(t), t] = e^{-\theta t} \ln c(t) + \lambda(t)[\alpha(s(t) - c(t)) - \dot{s}(t)].$$

Applying the calculus of variations gives the Euler equations

$$\frac{\partial f}{\partial s} - \frac{d}{dt}\left(\frac{\partial f}{\partial \dot{s}}\right) = \alpha\lambda + \dot{\lambda} = 0,$$

$$\frac{\partial f}{\partial c} = e^{-\theta t}\frac{1}{c} - \alpha\lambda = 0,$$

$$\frac{\partial f}{\partial \lambda} = \alpha(s - c) - \dot{s} = 0.$$

It follows that $\lambda = e^{-\theta t}/\alpha c$ and $\dot{\lambda} = -\lambda((\dot{c}/c) + \theta)$; hence the first condition implies that

$$\frac{\dot{c}}{c} = \alpha - \theta.$$

This and the constraint form a differential equation system that can be solved for x_t and z.

  Comparing this solution with the discrete-time solution we note that the discrete-time solution can be written

$$\frac{c_{t+1} - c_t}{c_t} = \frac{1 + \alpha}{1 + \theta} - 1$$

$$\simeq \alpha - \theta.$$

15.4.2 The Maximum Principle

The maximum principle is concerned with choosing $\{x(t), z(t)\}$ to maximize $\int_0^T f[x(t), z(t), t] \, dt$ subject to the constraint

$$\dot{x}(t)\left(= \frac{dx(t)}{dt} \right) = g[x(t), z(t), t]$$

and possible constraints at $t = 0$ and $t = T$. First we define the function (called the Hamiltonian)

$$h[x(t), z(t), \lambda(t)] = f[x(t), z(t), t] + \lambda(t) g[x(t), z(t), t].$$

The first-order conditions are

$$\frac{\partial h}{\partial x} = -\dot{\lambda},$$

$$\frac{\partial h}{\partial z} = 0,$$

$$\frac{\partial h}{\partial \lambda} = \dot{x}.$$

Example 15.5. Consider example 15.3 once more. We now define

$$h[x(t), z(t), \lambda(t)] = e^{-\theta t} \ln c(t) + \lambda(t) \alpha[s(t) - c(t)].$$

The first-order conditions are

$$\frac{\partial h}{\partial s} = \alpha \lambda = -\dot{\lambda},$$

$$\frac{\partial h}{\partial c} = e^{-\theta t} \frac{1}{c} - \alpha \lambda = 0,$$

$$\frac{\partial h}{\partial \lambda} = \alpha(s - c) = \dot{s}.$$

These first-order conditions are identical to those obtained from the calculus of variations.

15.5 Dynamic Programming

When the intertemporal problem in discrete time has a time-separable objective function that can be represented as a recursive structure, it can be solved using the "principle of optimality" due to Bellman (1957). This method is also known as dynamic programming.

The basic idea of the principle of optimality is to solve the optimization period by period—starting with the final period, taking the previous periods' solutions as given, and then working back sequentially to the first period. Having optimized the final period, period T say, this solution is substituted into the period $T - 1$ problem and then period $T - 1$ is optimized. Substituting the previous solutions, the solutions for periods $T - 2, T - 3, \ldots, 0$ are obtained in sequence in the same way.

Suppose that the problem is to maximize

$$V(x_t) = U(x_t, z_t) + \beta V(x_{t+1}) \tag{15.11}$$

for $t, t+1, \ldots, T$ subject to

$$x_{t+1} = f(x_t, z_t) \tag{15.12}$$

and to $x_{T+1} = x$. z_t is called the control variable in the optimal control literature and x_t is called the state variable.

Consider the problem for period T. First we maximize

$$V(x_T) = U(x_T, z_T) + \beta V(x_{T+1}) \tag{15.13}$$

with respect to z_T subject to $x_{T+1} = f(x_T, z_T)$ and *taking x_T as given*. Thus we maximize

$$V(x_T) = U(x_T, z_T) + \beta V[f(x_T, z_T)]. \tag{15.14}$$

The first-order condition is

$$\frac{\partial V(x_T)}{\partial z_T} = \frac{\partial U(x_T, z_T)}{\partial z_T} + \beta \frac{\partial V_{T+1}[f(x_T, z_T)]}{\partial z_T} = 0. \tag{15.15}$$

The solution for z_T has the form

$$z_T = g_T(x_T). \tag{15.16}$$

Strictly speaking we should write $z_T = g_T(x_T, x)$ but we omit x for convenience. Substituting this solution for z_T into $V(x_T)$ gives

$$
\begin{aligned}
V(x_T) &= U(x_T, z_T) + \beta V[f(x_T, z_T)] \\
&= U\{f(x_{T-1}, z_{T-1}), g_T[f(x_{T-1}, z_{T-1})]\} \\
&\quad + \beta V\{f[f(x_{T-1}, z_{T-1})], g_T[f(x_{T-1}, z_{T-1})]\} \\
&= V_T(x_{T-1}, z_{T-1}).
\end{aligned}
\tag{15.17}
$$

Turning next to period $T - 1$, we maximize

$$V(x_{T-1}) = U(x_{T-1}, z_{T-1}) + \beta V(x_T) \tag{15.18}$$

with respect to z_{T-1} subject to $x_T = f(x_{T-1}, z_{T-1})$, taking x_{T-1} as given. The first-order condition is

$$\frac{\partial V(x_{T-1})}{\partial z_{T-1}} = \frac{\partial U(x_{T-1}, z_{T-1})}{\partial z_{T-1}} + \beta \frac{\partial V_T(x_{T-1}, z_{T-1})}{\partial z_{T-1}} = 0. \tag{15.19}$$

We write the solution for z_{T-1} as

$$z_{T-1} = g_{T-1}(x_{T-1}). \tag{15.20}$$

Substituting this solution into $V(x_{T-1})$ gives

$$V(x_{T-1}) = U[x_{T-1}, g_{T-1}(x_{T-1})] + \beta V_T[x_{T-1}, g_{T-1}(x_{T-1})] \tag{15.21}$$

$$= V_{T-1}(x_{T-2}, z_{T-2}). \tag{15.22}$$

We proceed similarly in periods $T - 2, T - 3, \ldots, 0$.

The general solution for period t has the first-order condition

$$\frac{\partial V(x_t)}{\partial z_t} = \frac{\partial U(x_t, z_t)}{\partial z_t} + \beta \frac{\partial V_{t+1}(x_t, z_t)}{\partial z_t} = 0 \qquad (15.23)$$

and the solution

$$z_t = g_t(x_t). \qquad (15.24)$$

The solution given by equation (15.24) is known in the optimal control literature as a *closed-loop* solution because the optimal value of the control variable z_t during period t is given as a function of the state variable x_t at the start of that period. This is in contrast to *open-loop* control, in which the solution is given as a function of time only. Typically, dynamic programming provides a closed-loop solution whereas the maximum principle gives an open-loop solution.

In the case where $T \to \infty$ we can also derive the solution given by equation (15.24) by noting that

$$\frac{\partial V_{t+1}(x_t, z_t)}{\partial z_t} = \frac{\partial V(x_{t+1}, z_{t+1})}{\partial z_{t+1}} \frac{\partial z_{t+1}}{\partial z_t},$$

where

$$\frac{\partial z_{t+1}}{\partial z_t} = \frac{\partial z_{t+1}}{\partial x_{t+1}} \frac{\partial x_{t+1}}{\partial z_t}$$

is obtained directly from the constraint, equation (15.12), or by expressing the constraint as the two-period intertemporal constraint

$$\begin{aligned} x_{t+2} &= f(x_{t+1}, z_{t+1}) \\ &= f[f(x_t, z_t), z_{t+1}] \\ &= h(x_t, z_t, z_{t+1}). \end{aligned}$$

Taking the total differential of $x_{t+2} - h(x_t, z_t, z_{t+1}) = 0$, and taking x_{t+2} and x_t as given, yields

$$\frac{\partial z_{t+1}}{\partial z_t} = -\frac{\partial h / \partial z_t}{\partial h / \partial z_{t+1}}.$$

Hence

$$\frac{\partial V(x_t)}{\partial z_t} = \frac{\partial U(x_t, z_t)}{\partial z_t} + \beta \frac{\partial V(x_{t+1}, z_{t+1})}{\partial z_{t+1}} \frac{\partial z_{t+1}}{\partial x_{t+1}} \frac{\partial x_{t+1}}{\partial z_t} = 0 \qquad (15.25)$$

or

$$\frac{\partial V(x_t)}{\partial z_t} = \frac{\partial U(x_t, z_t)}{\partial z_t} - \beta \frac{\partial V(x_{t+1}, z_{t+1})}{\partial z_{t+1}} \frac{\partial z_{t+1}}{\partial h} \frac{\partial h}{\partial z_t} = 0. \qquad (15.26)$$

Example 15.6. Reconsider example 15.2. This can be rewritten as: maximize

$$\begin{aligned} V_0 &= \sum_{t=0}^{T} \beta^t U(c_t), \quad U(c_t) = \ln c_t \\ &= \ln c_0 + \beta V_1 \end{aligned}$$

subject to

$$s_{t+1} = (1 + \alpha)s_t - \alpha c_t, \quad s_{T+1} = 0, \quad 0 < a < 1,$$

with respect to s_t and c_t for periods $t = 0, 1, \ldots, T$. Compared with the general problem we note that $x_t \equiv s_t$ and $z_t \equiv c_t$.

First we consider the solution for period T. This requires us to maximize

$$V(s_T) = U(c_T) + \beta V(s_{T+1})$$

with respect to c_T subject to $s_{T+1} = (1 + \alpha)s_T - \alpha c_T$ and $s_{T+1} = 0$, *taking s_T as given.* Thus we maximize $V(s_T) = U(c_T)$. On this occasion no maximization is required. The solution is obtained from the constraint as

$$c_T = \frac{(1 + \alpha)s_T}{\alpha};$$

hence

$$V(s_T) = \ln\left[\frac{(1 + \alpha)s_T}{\alpha}\right] + \beta V(0).$$

The period $T - 1$ problem is to maximize

$$V(s_{T-1}) = \ln c_{T-1} + \beta V(s_T)$$

$$= \ln c_{T-1} + \beta \ln\left[\frac{(1 + \alpha)s_T}{\alpha} + \beta V(0)\right]$$

with respect to c_{T-1} subject to $s_T = (1 + \alpha)s_{T-1} - \alpha c_{T-1}$, taking s_{T-1} as given. The first-order condition is

$$\frac{\partial V(s_{T-1})}{\partial c_{T-1}} = \frac{1}{c_{T-1}} - \beta \frac{\alpha}{(1 + \alpha)s_{T-1} - \alpha c_{T-1}} = 0.$$

Hence,

$$c_{T-1} = \frac{1 + \alpha}{\alpha(1 + \beta)} s_{T-1}$$

and so

$$V(s_{T-1}) = \ln\left[\frac{1 + \alpha}{\alpha(1 + \beta)} s_{T-1}\right] + \beta \ln\left[\frac{(1 + \alpha)^2 \beta}{\alpha(1 + \beta)} s_{T-1}\right].$$

Similarly, the period $T - 2$ problem is to maximize

$$V(s_{T-2}) = \ln c_{T-2} + \beta V(s_{T-1})$$

$$= \ln c_{T-2} + \beta \ln\left[\frac{1 + \alpha}{\alpha(1 + \beta)} s_{T-1}\right] + \beta^2 \ln\left[\frac{(1 + \alpha)^2 \beta}{\alpha(1 + \beta)} s_{T-1}\right]$$

with respect to c_{T-2} subject to $s_{T-1} = (1 + \alpha)s_{T-2} - \alpha c_{T-2}$, taking s_{T-2} as given. The first-order condition is

$$\frac{\partial V(s_{T-2})}{\partial c_{T-2}} = \frac{1}{c_{T-2}} - (\beta + \beta^2) \frac{\alpha}{(1 + \alpha)s_{T-2} - \alpha c_{T-2}} = 0.$$

Hence,

$$c_{T-2} = \frac{1 + \alpha}{\alpha(1 + \beta + \beta^2)} s_{T-2}.$$

It is now clear that the general solution for periods $t = 0, \ldots, T$ takes the form

$$c_t = \frac{1 + \alpha}{\alpha(1 + \beta + \cdots + \beta^{T-t})} s_t$$
$$= \frac{(1 + \alpha)(1 - \beta)}{\alpha(1 - \beta^{T-t+1})} s_t.$$

We note that as $T \to \infty$ this becomes

$$c_t = \frac{(1 + \alpha)(1 - \beta)}{\alpha} s_t,$$

which is identical to the corresponding solution based on Lagrange multipliers, equation (15.10).

We also note that in this case we can obtain the solution using equation (15.25). This gives

$$\frac{\partial V(s_t)}{\partial c_t} = \frac{\partial \ln c_t}{\partial c_t} + \beta \frac{\partial \ln c_{t+1}}{\partial c_{t+1}} \frac{\partial c_{t+1}}{\partial s_{t+1}} \frac{\partial s_{t+1}}{\partial c_t}$$
$$= \frac{1}{c_t} + \beta \frac{1}{c_{t+1}} \frac{1 + \alpha}{\alpha} (-\alpha) = 0. \tag{15.27}$$

This implies that

$$c_{t+1} = (1 + \alpha)\beta c_t, \tag{15.28}$$

which is the same solution that was derived using Lagrange multipliers in equation (15.5).

15.6 Stochastic Dynamic Optimization

Intertemporal problems in economics and finance often take the form of maximizing the *expected* present value

$$E_t[V(x_t)] = E_t\left[\sum_{s=0}^{\infty} \beta^s U(z_{t+s}) \right] \tag{15.29}$$

subject to the constraint

$$x_{t+1} = f(x_t, z_t), \tag{15.30}$$

where $E_t[\cdot]$ denotes the expectation conditional on information available up to and including period t. This reflects the fact that x_t and z_t may be stochastic variables whose future values are unknown at time t and so must be forecast from current information. Previously, we have implicitly assumed that future values are known, i.e., that we have perfect foresight.

The stochastic problem can be solved using the method of Lagrange multipliers, but there is a problem with this solution. We can write the Lagrangian as

$$\mathcal{L} = E_t \sum_{s=0}^{\infty} \{\beta^s U(z_{t+s}) + \lambda_{t+s}[f(x_{t+s}, z_{t+s}) - x_{t+s+1}]\}.$$

The first-order conditions are

$$\frac{\partial \mathcal{L}}{\partial x_{t+s}} = E_t \left\{ \lambda_{t+s} \frac{\partial f(x_{t+s}, z_{t+s})}{\partial x_{t+s}} - \lambda_{t+s-1} \right\} = 0, \qquad s > 0,$$

$$\frac{\partial \mathcal{L}}{\partial z_{t+s}} = E_t \left\{ \beta^s \frac{\partial U(z_{t+s})}{\partial z_{t+s}} + \lambda_{t+s} \frac{\partial f(x_{t+s}, z_{t+s})}{\partial z_{t+s}} \right\} = 0, \quad s \geqslant 0,$$

$$\frac{\partial \mathcal{L}}{\partial \lambda_{t+s}} = E_t [f(x_{t+s}, z_{t+s}) - x_{t+s+1}] = 0, \qquad s \geqslant 0.$$

Unless the conditional covariance is zero, in solving these equations for the optimal values we encounter the term

$$E_t \left[\lambda_{t+s} \frac{\partial f(x_{t+s}, z_{t+s})}{\partial z_{t+s}} \right]$$

$$= \mathrm{Cov}_t \left[\lambda_{t+s}, \frac{\partial f(x_{t+s}, z_{t+s})}{\partial z_{t+s}} \right] + E_t[\lambda_{t+s}] E_t \left[\frac{\partial f(x_{t+s}, z_{t+s})}{\partial x_{t+s}} \right]$$

$$\neq E_t[\lambda_{t+s}] E_t \left[\frac{\partial f(x_{t+s}, z_{t+s})}{\partial x_{t+s}} \right],$$

which implies that λ_{t+s} and $\partial f(x_{t+s}, z_{t+s})/\partial z_{t+s}$ are conditionally uncorrelated. As a result, we are unable to eliminate λ_{t+s} in the way that we did before.

Instead of using Lagrange multipliers we therefore use the method of dynamic programming. This entails writing the present-value relation as the recursion (also known as the Bellman equation)

$$E_t[V(x_t)] = U(z_t) + \beta E_t[V(x_{t+1})] \tag{15.31}$$

and maximizing this directly subject to the constraint, equation (15.30).

In view of example 15.6 and, in particular, equation (15.27), we obtain the first-order condition

$$E_t \left[\frac{\partial V(x_t)}{\partial z_t} \right] = \frac{\partial U(z_t)}{\partial z_t} + \beta E_t \left[\frac{\partial V(x_{t+1})}{\partial z_{t+1}} \frac{\partial z_{t+1}}{\partial x_{t+1}} \frac{\partial x_{t+1}}{\partial z_t} \right] = 0. \tag{15.32}$$

Hence

$$\frac{\partial V(x_{t+1})}{\partial z_{t+1}} = \frac{\partial U(z_{t+1})}{\partial z_{t+1}},$$

$$\frac{\partial z_{t+1}}{\partial x_{t+1}} = -\frac{\partial f_{t+1}/\partial x_{t+1}}{\partial f_{t+1}/\partial z_{t+1}},$$

$$\frac{\partial x_{t+1}}{\partial z_t} = \frac{\partial f_t}{\partial z_t},$$

where the last two derivatives are obtained from the constraint, equation (15.30). Consequently, the solution satisfies

$$\frac{\partial U(z_t)}{\partial z_t} - \beta E_t \left[\frac{\partial U(z_{t+1})}{\partial z_{t+1}} \frac{\partial f_{t+1}/\partial x_{t+1}}{\partial f_{t+1}/\partial z_{t+1}} \frac{\partial f_t}{\partial z_t} \right] = 0. \tag{15.33}$$

The optimal solutions can be obtained from equations (15.33) and (15.30).

Example 15.7. Consider a stochastic version of example 15.6. We rewrite this as

$$\max E_t[V(s_t)] = U(c_t) + \beta E_t[V(s_{t+1})], \quad U(c_t) = \ln c_t,$$

subject to

$$s_{t+1} = (1 + \alpha)s_t - \alpha c_t, \quad s_{T+1} = 0, \quad 0 < a < 1.$$

The first-order condition is

$$E_t\left[\frac{\partial V(s_t)}{\partial c_t}\right] = \frac{\partial \ln c_t}{\partial c_t} + \beta E_t\left[\frac{\partial \ln c_{t+1}}{\partial c_{t+1}}\frac{\partial c_{t+1}}{\partial s_{t+1}}\frac{\partial s_{t+1}}{\partial c_t}\right]$$

$$= \frac{1}{c_t} - \beta E_t\left[\frac{1+\alpha}{c_{t+1}}\right] = 0.$$

It follows that

$$\frac{1}{c_t} = \beta(1 + \alpha)E_t\left[\frac{1}{c_{t+1}}\right].$$

As $E_t[c_{t+1}] \neq 1/(E_t[c_{t+1}])$, we cannot obtain the solution from that of example 15.6 by simply replacing c_{t+1} in equation (15.28) by $E_t[c_{t+1}]$, i.e., by invoking the certainty equivalence principle. A second-order Taylor series expansion about c_t gives

$$E_t\left[\frac{1}{c_{t+1}}\right] \simeq \frac{1}{c_t} - \frac{1}{c_t}E_t\left[\frac{\Delta c_{t+1}}{c_t}\right] + \frac{1}{c_t}E_t\left[\left(\frac{\Delta c_{t+1}}{c_t}\right)^2\right];$$

hence,

$$E_t\left[\frac{\Delta c_{t+1}}{c_t}\right] = [\beta(1 + \alpha) - 1] + E_t\left[\left(\frac{\Delta c_{t+1}}{c_t}\right)^2\right].$$

Consequently, compared with equation (15.28) there is an extra term in the implied optimal rate of growth of c_t.

15.7 Time Consistency and Time Inconsistency

Time inconsistency may arise in multiperiod optimization problems. Having formulated the optimal plan for the current period and for future time periods, next period it may prove better to reoptimize and carry out the new plan rather than the earlier plan. This is called time inconsistency. In contrast, a time-consistent policy is one that retains its optimality in the future. The ensuing discussion of time-consistent and time-inconsistent policies is based on the seminal paper by Kydland and Prescott (1977).

Consider the following two-period problem for periods t and $t + 1$. Suppose that in period t social welfare is defined by

$$V_t = V(x_t, x_{t+1}, z_t, z_{t+1}), \tag{15.34}$$

where z_t and z_{t+1} are the values of the single policy instrument in periods t and $t + 1$, and x_t and x_{t+1} satisfy the constraints

$$x_t = C(x_{t-1}, z_t, z_{t+1}), \tag{15.35}$$

$$x_{t+1} = C(x_t, z_t, z_{t+1}), \tag{15.36}$$

with x_{t-1} given at time t. We note that the period t constraint is forward looking due to the presence of z_{t+1}. The problem is to choose z_t and z_{t+1} to maximize V_t. An example of V_t is the time-separable function

$$V_t = U(x_t, z_t) + \beta U(x_{t+1}, z_{t+1}). \tag{15.37}$$

At time t the policy maker can choose z_t and z_{t+1} to satisfy the first-order conditions

$$\frac{\partial V_t}{\partial z_t} = \frac{\partial V}{\partial z_t} + \frac{\partial V}{\partial x_{t+1}}\left[\frac{\partial x_{t+1}}{\partial z_t} + \frac{\partial x_{t+1}}{\partial x_t}\frac{\partial x_t}{\partial z_t}\right] + \frac{\partial V}{\partial x_t}\frac{\partial x_t}{\partial z_t} = 0,$$

$$\frac{\partial V_t}{\partial z_{t+1}} = \frac{\partial V}{\partial z_{t+1}} + \frac{\partial V}{\partial x_{t+1}}\left[\frac{\partial x_{t+1}}{\partial z_{t+1}} + \frac{\partial x_{t+1}}{\partial x_t}\frac{\partial x_t}{\partial z_{t+1}}\right] + \frac{\partial V}{\partial x_t}\frac{\partial x_t}{\partial z_{t+1}} = 0.$$

These can be rewritten as

$$\frac{\partial V}{\partial z_t} + \frac{\partial V}{\partial x_{t+1}}\frac{\partial x_{t+1}}{\partial z_t} + \left[\frac{\partial V}{\partial x_t} + \frac{\partial V}{\partial x_{t+1}}\frac{\partial x_{t+1}}{\partial x_t}\right]\frac{\partial x_t}{\partial z_t} = 0, \tag{15.38}$$

$$\frac{\partial V}{\partial z_{t+1}} + \frac{\partial V}{\partial x_{t+1}}\frac{\partial x_{t+1}}{\partial z_{t+1}} + \left[\frac{\partial V}{\partial x_t} + \frac{\partial V}{\partial x_{t+1}}\frac{\partial x_{t+1}}{\partial x_t}\right]\frac{\partial x_t}{\partial z_{t+1}} = 0. \tag{15.39}$$

The optimal values of x_t, x_{t+1}, z_t, and z_{t+1} can be solved from these two conditions together with the two constraints and the given value of x_{t-1}.

At time $t + 1$ the policy maker is able to reoptimize the choice of z_{t+1}, but must now take x_t and z_t as given. This value of x_t will depend on the choice of z_{t+1} made in period t. The first-order condition with respect to z_{t+1} is now

$$\frac{\partial V}{\partial z_{t+1}} + \frac{\partial V}{\partial x_{t+1}}\frac{\partial x_{t+1}}{\partial z_{t+1}} = 0. \tag{15.40}$$

This can be solved for x_{t+1} and z_{t+1} for given values of x_t and z_t. We denote the new solutions by x_{t+1}^* and z_{t+1}^*. If the policy is time consistent, then $z_{t+1} = z_{t+1}^*$, and hence $x_{t+1} = x_{t+1}^*$. But if it is time inconsistent, then $z_{t+1} \neq z_{t+1}^*$, and hence $x_{t+1} \neq x_{t+1}^*$.

In order for the solution to be time consistent, i.e., for equations (15.39) and (15.40) to be the same, it is necessary that either

$$\frac{\partial x_t}{\partial z_{t+1}} = 0,$$

i.e., x_t is unaffected by the choice of z_{t+1}, or

$$\frac{\partial V}{\partial x_t} + \frac{\partial V}{\partial x_{t+1}}\frac{\partial x_{t+1}}{\partial x_t} = 0,$$

i.e., the total effect of x_t on V is zero. As the latter is less plausible, we conclude that time inconsistency is most likely to arise when expectations of the future choice of z_{t+1} affect the current choice of x_t.

Example 15.8. Consider the problem

$$\max V_t = U(x_t, z_t) + U(x_{t+1}, z_{t+1}),$$

$$U(x_t, z_t) = -\tfrac{1}{2}[x_t^2 + yz_t^2],$$

subject to

$$x_t = \alpha x_{t-1} + \theta z_{t+1},$$
$$x_{t+1} = \alpha x_t + \theta z_{t+1},$$
$$x_{t-1} = x > 0.$$

The unconstrained optimal solution is where U is maximized by setting $x_t = x_{t+1} = z_t = z_{t+1} = 0$. The initial condition prevents this from being realized. The two first-order conditions (15.38) and (15.39) are

$$-\gamma z_t = 0,$$
$$-\gamma z_{t+1} - (1 + \alpha)\theta x_{t+1} - \theta x_t = 0.$$

It follows that the optimal solution at time t is

$$z_t = 0,$$
$$z_{t+1} = -\alpha\phi x,$$
$$x_t = \alpha(1 - \theta\phi)x,$$
$$x_{t+1} = \alpha[\alpha - (1 + \alpha)\theta\phi]x,$$
$$\phi = \frac{[1 + \alpha(1 + \alpha)]\theta}{\gamma + [1 + (1 + \alpha)^2]\theta^2}.$$

At time $t + 1$, from (15.40) the optimal solution satisfies

$$-\gamma z_{t+1}^* - \theta x_{t+1}^* = 0;$$

hence, given the constraint and the previous solutions for x_t and z_t, the new optimal solution for period $t + 1$ is

$$z_{t+1}^* = -\frac{\alpha^2\theta(1 - \theta\phi)}{\gamma + \theta^2}x,$$
$$x_{t+1}^* = \frac{\alpha^2\gamma(1 - \theta\phi)}{\gamma + \theta^2}x.$$

Thus, in general, z_{t+1}^* differs from z_{t+1} and policy is time inconsistent.

Consider a numerical example where $\alpha = \gamma = \theta = \frac{1}{2}$. It follows that $\phi = \frac{2}{3}$. Hence, $z_t = 0$, $z_{t+1} = -\frac{1}{3}x$, $z_{t+1}^* = -\frac{1}{18}x$, $x_t = \frac{1}{3}x$, $x_{t+1} = 0$, $x_{t+1}^* = \frac{1}{18}x$, $U_t = -\frac{1}{18}x^2$, $U_{t+1} = -\frac{1}{36}x^2$, $U_{t+1}^* = -\frac{1}{216}x^2$. We note that $z_{t+1}^* > z_{t+1}$, hence policy is time inconsistent. Since $U_{t+1}^* > U_{t+1}$, there has been an improvement in welfare as a result of the reoptimization of policy. Had the initial condition been $x = 0$, policy would not have been time inconsistent.

15.8 The Linear Rational-Expectations Models

For simplicity, we have more often than not suppressed the fact that our intertemporal macroeconomic models are stochastic and the future is uncertain and instead treated them as though the future is known with certainty. However, in solving the dynamic equations that emerge, we should take account of the fact that they are usually stochastic and, where there are future variables, we should treat them as rational expectations of the future that are based on current information. We therefore consider the solutions to linear rational-expectations models rather than nonstochastic difference equations.

15.8.1 Rational Expectations

The rational expectation of x_{t+1} conditional on information available at time t may be written

$$E_t(x_{t+1}) = E(x_{t+1} \mid \Phi_t),$$

where Φ_t is the set of information available at time t. It is therefore the mean of the conditional distribution of x_{t+1} given Φ_t.

Two pieces of information are involved here: Φ_t and the conditional probability distribution of x_{t+1}. In economics, under full rationality, we require complete knowledge of the macroeconomic model, which must be a correct representation of the economy, the variables that enter the model, and the underlying stochastic structure. This is a very demanding interpretation of rationality and is best treated as a limiting case. In practice, probably the most we should hope for is that we do not repeat mistakes—in other words, the forecast error of x_{t+1} is uncorrelated with past forecast errors.

Formally, if expectations are rational with respect to Φ_t, then the forecast error is

$$\varepsilon_{t+1} = x_{t+1} - E_t(x_{t+1})$$

and has the property

$$E_t(\varepsilon_{t+1}) = 0.$$

In other words, the best forecast of ε_{t+1} based on the information Φ_t is that it will be zero. Since Φ_t contains current and past information, including knowledge of past forecast errors $\{\varepsilon_{t-s}, s \geqslant 0\}$,

$$E_t(\varepsilon_{t+1}\varepsilon_{t-s}) = 0, \quad s \geqslant 0.$$

Thus, future forecast errors are uncorrelated with past errors. For this reason the forecast errors are sometimes called innovations, implying that they are always new, and unanticipated, events. We note that if Φ_t consists solely of current and past values of x_t, i.e., $\{\Phi_t : x_{t-s}, s \geqslant 0\}$, then the expectation is said to be weakly rational.

The solution method that we describe for rational-expectations models is that of Whiteman (1983). This is an extension of Muth's (1961) method of undermined coefficients and Lucas's (1972) variant on this. There are a number of other solution methods too. The advantage of Whiteman's method is that it helps clarify what is happening when the solution is not unique. The disadvantage is that it is not a completely general solution.

Using Whiteman's extension of the method of undetermined coefficients, we derive the solutions to the two rational-expectations models that appear most often in dynamic general equilibrium macroeconomic models. We can then draw on these solutions in the main text. We show that where there is a unique solution, there is a simpler, and more direct, way of deriving the solution. We complete our discussion by considering the solution to systems of rational equations and how to determine whether or not they are unique. This is related to the alternative solution method of Blanchard and Kahn (1980).

15.8.2   The First-Order Nonstochastic Equation

We begin by considering the solution to a simple, nonstochastic, first-order, single, difference equation. Consider the model

$$x_t = \alpha x_{t-1} + z_t. \tag{15.41}$$

We introduce the lag operator L, which has the property of converting x_t to either a lag or a lead:

$$L^s x_t = x_{t-s},$$
$$L^{-s} x_t = x_{t+s}.$$

The difference equation can therefore be rewritten as

$$(1 - \alpha L)x_t = z_t$$

or as

$$\alpha(L)x_t = z_t.$$

We introduce the auxiliary polynomial equation

$$\alpha(L) = 1 - \alpha L = 0.$$

This determines the dynamic behavior of x_t. Solving this for L provides the (single) root of the polynomial as

$$L = \frac{1}{\alpha}.$$

If this root is greater than or equal to unity in absolute value, then the difference equation is stable; if it is less than unity in absolute value, then it is unstable.

15.8.2.1   *The Stable Case: $|\alpha| \leqslant 1$*

In this case the root $|1/\alpha| \geqslant 1$ and it is said to lie outside the unit circle. Equation (15.41) can then be solved for x_t as follows:

$$x_t = \frac{z_t}{1 - \alpha L}$$

$$= \left(\sum_{s=0}^{\infty} \alpha^s L^s \right) z_t$$

$$= \sum_{s=0}^{\infty} \alpha^s z_{t-s}.$$

(Note that $\lim_{s \to \infty} \alpha^s L^s = 0$ if $|\alpha| < 1$.) x_t is therefore determined by current and past values of z_t. A change to z_t would result in x_t converging back to equilibrium at the geometric rate α.

This solution can also be obtained without using the lag operator by successive substitution of $x_{t-1}, x_{t-2}, \ldots$ in (15.41). Thus,

$$
\begin{aligned}
x_t &= \alpha(\alpha x_{t-2} + z_{t-1}) + z_t \\
&= \alpha^2 x_{t-2} + z_t + \alpha z_{t-1} \\
&\vdots \\
&= \sum_{s=0}^{\infty} \alpha^s z_{t-s},
\end{aligned}
$$

provided $\lim_{s \to \infty} \alpha^s x_{t-s} = 0$.

15.8.2.2 *The Unstable Case:* $|\alpha| > 1$

In this case $\lim_{s \to \infty} \alpha^s L^s$ explodes and hence does not exist. It is therefore no longer possible to solve the equation backwards (i.e., to solve x_t as a function of past z_t). Consider instead, therefore, solving the difference equation forwards. First, we rewrite the difference equation for period $t + 1$, and then premultiply by $-(1/\alpha)L^{-1}$ to obtain

$$
\left(1 - \frac{1}{\alpha}L^{-1}\right)x_t = -\frac{1}{\alpha}L^{-1}z_t.
$$

This may now be written

$$
\begin{aligned}
x_t &= \frac{-(1/\alpha)L^{-1}z_t}{1 - (1/\alpha)L^{-1}} \\
&= -\left(\sum_{s=0}^{\infty} \alpha^{-s} L^{-s}\right)\frac{1}{\alpha}L^{-1}z_t \\
&= \sum_{s=1}^{\infty} \alpha^{-s} z_{t+s}, \tag{15.42}
\end{aligned}
$$

where we have used $\lim_{s \to \infty} \alpha^{-s} L^{-s} = 0$. Thus, in this unstable case, x_t can be expressed as a function of future values of z_t. Given knowledge of these future values, by solving equation (15.42) we can arrive at the value x_t. According to this solution, changes in future values of z_t (i.e., in z_{t+s}; $s > 0$) will cause a change in x_t even before they occur in z_t. In a world of perfect knowledge this implies that there is a unique value of z_{t+s} ($s > 0$); it cannot therefore be changed—by future policy for example. We also note that we need z_{t+s} ($s > 0$) not to increase faster than α^{-1} in order for the solution to equation (15.42) to exist.

In effect, in obtaining equation (15.42) we have rewritten equation (15.41) as

$$
x_t = \frac{1}{\alpha}x_{t+1} - \frac{1}{\alpha}z_{t+1}
$$

and, noting that $|1/\alpha| < 1$, we have solved this forwards.

15.8.3 Whiteman's Solution Method for Linear Rational-Expectations Models

Whiteman's solution method can be used for a large number of different types of rational-expectations (RE) models. We derive the solutions for two models that appear frequently in our macroeconomic analysis. These are

$$x_t = \alpha E_t x_{t+1} + \gamma z_t + e_t, \quad |\alpha| < 1, \tag{15.43}$$

$$x_t = \alpha E_t x_{t+1} + \beta x_{t-1} + \gamma z_t + e_t, \tag{15.44}$$

where z_t satisfies

$$z_t = \sum_{s=0}^{\infty} \phi_s e_{t-s} + \sum_{s=0}^{\infty} \theta_s \varepsilon_{t-s}$$
$$= \phi(L) e_t + \theta(L) \varepsilon_t \tag{15.45}$$

with $\phi_0 = 1$, $\theta_0 = 1$, $\sum_{s=0}^{\infty} \phi_s^2 < \infty$, $\sum_{s=0}^{\infty} \theta_s^2 < \infty$, $\phi(L) = \sum_{s=0}^{\infty} \phi_s L^s$, and $\theta(L) = \sum_{s=0}^{\infty} \theta_s L^s$ are analytic functions (this roughly means that they exist and have continuous derivatives when evaluated at their roots) where e_t and ε_t are uncorrelated zero-mean i.i.d. processes, and L is the lag operator such that $L^s x_t = x_{t-s}$ and $L^{-s} x_t = E_t x_{t+s}$. This implies that x_t and z_t are stationary zero-mean processes. If they contain a unit root, then we replace x_t and z_t by Δx_t and Δz_t. We can also add nonzero means. If $\theta_s = 0$, then z_t would be a strongly exogenous process.

We also note that Whiteman's solution method can be applied to models where the rational expectation takes the form $E_{t-p} x_{t-q}$ $(p > q)$: for example,

$$x_t = \alpha E_{t-1} x_t + \gamma z_t + e_t.$$

It is assumed that the general solution has the form

$$x_t = \sum_{s=0}^{\infty} a_s e_{t-s} + \sum_{s=0}^{\infty} b_s \varepsilon_{t-s}$$
$$= A(L) e_t + B(L) \varepsilon_t, \tag{15.46}$$

where $A(L) = \sum_{s=0}^{\infty} a_s L^s$ and $B(L) = \sum_{s=0}^{\infty} b_s L^s$ contain no roots inside the unit circle. The problem is how to determine the values of $\{a_s, b_s; s \geqslant 0\}$; hence the notion of undetermined coefficients.

We will need to use the following Weiner–Kolmogorov prediction formula for stationary processes that have the Wold (moving average) representation:

$$y_t = \sum_{s=0}^{\infty} c_s e_{t-s}$$
$$= C(L) e_t,$$

where e_t is a zero-mean i.i.d. process. Thus

$$E_t y_{t+n} = E_t(c_0 e_{t+n} + c_1 e_{t+n-1} + \cdots + c_n e_t + c_{n+1} e_{t-1} + \cdots)$$

$$= c_n e_t + c_{n+1} e_{t-1} + \cdots$$

$$= L^{-n}\left[C(L) - \sum_{s=0}^{n-1} c_s L^s\right] e_t.$$

We also note that

$$\frac{1 - \alpha L^{-1} C(\alpha) C(L)^{-1}}{1 - \alpha L^{-1}} y_t = \sum_{s=0}^{\infty} \alpha^s E_t y_{t+s}. \tag{15.47}$$

We now consider the solutions to equations (15.43) and (15.44).

15.8.3.1   The Solution to Equation (15.43)

Using the Weiner–Kolmogorov formula and taking note of equations (15.46) and (15.45), equation (15.43) can be written as

$$A(L)e_t + B(L)\varepsilon_t = \alpha L^{-1}\{[A(L) - a_0]e_t + [B(L) - b_0]\varepsilon_t\}$$
$$+ \gamma[\phi(L)e_t + \theta(L)\varepsilon_t] + e_t.$$

Equating terms in e_t and ε_t gives

$$A(L) = \frac{L + \gamma L \phi(L) - \alpha a_0}{L - \alpha}, \tag{15.48}$$

$$B(L) = \frac{\gamma L \theta(L) - \alpha b_0}{L - \alpha}, \tag{15.49}$$

where a_0 and b_0 are free coefficients.

Equations (15.48) and (15.49) are analytic for $|L| < 1$ if and only if the roots of the auxiliary equation

$$L - \alpha = 0$$

lie on or outside the unit circle (i.e., if $|\alpha| \geqslant 1$). This is known as the stable case. When $|\alpha| < 1$ we have an unstable solution.

(i) The Stable Case.   We obtain this by substituting equations (15.48) and (15.49) into (15.46), which gives

$$x_t = \frac{L + \gamma L \phi(L) - \alpha a_0}{L - \alpha} e_t + \frac{\gamma L \theta(L) - \alpha b_0}{L - \alpha} \varepsilon_t.$$

Hence

$$-\alpha\left(1 - \frac{1}{\alpha}L\right)x_t = \gamma L[\phi(L)e_t + \theta(L)\varepsilon_t] + (L - \alpha a_0)e_t - \alpha b_0 \varepsilon_t$$

or

$$x_t = \frac{1}{\alpha}x_{t-1} - \frac{\gamma}{\alpha}z_{t-1} - \frac{1}{\alpha}e_{t-1} + a_0 e_t + b_0 \varepsilon_t. \tag{15.50}$$

As the coefficients a_0 and b_0 are undetermined, this solution is not unique. We note from equation (15.46) that the last two terms comprise the innovation in x_t based on information available at time $t - 1$, i.e.,

$$x_t - E_{t-1}x_t = a_0 e_t + b_0 \varepsilon_t.$$

Suppose instead that we simply invert equation (15.43) as

$$x_{t+1} = \frac{1}{\alpha}x_t - \frac{\gamma}{\alpha}z_t + \frac{1}{\alpha}e_t + (x_{t+1} - E_t x_{t+1}), \qquad (15.51)$$

where, from (15.46), the innovation in x_{t+1} is

$$x_{t+1} - E_t x_{t+1} = a_0 e_{t+1} + b_0 \varepsilon_{t+1}.$$

This is exactly the same as equation (15.50). We conclude, at least in this stable case, that we can obtain the solution just by inverting equation (15.43). We note, however, that because the innovation in time $t + 1$ is unknown at time t, this is not a unique solution; any innovation in $t + 1$ would give a valid solution. It is of course tempting to obtain a unique solution by setting this innovation equal to zero on the grounds that this would be the best estimate of it given the information available at time t even though it is not likely to be zero when it is realized at time $t + 1$.

The difference between the solution of the rational-expectations model and that of the nonstochastic first-order difference equation is the presence of the innovation in the RE solution, which makes the RE solution nonunique.

(ii) The Unstable Case. We now consider the case where $|\alpha| < 1$. This is in fact what we assumed in specifying equation (15.43). The solution procedure is now more complicated. In this case a singularity occurs in the $A(L)$ and $B(L)$ functions at $L = \alpha$. In order to remove this singularity we require that the residues of these functions at $L = \alpha$ be zero. Thus we require that

$$\lim_{L \to \alpha} (L - \alpha)A(L) = \alpha + \gamma\alpha\phi(\alpha) - \alpha a_0 = 0.$$

This determines the free coefficient a_0 as

$$a_0 = 1 + \gamma\phi(\alpha).$$

Thus

$$A(L) = 1 + \frac{\gamma L\phi(L) - \alpha\gamma\phi(\alpha)}{L - \alpha}$$

$$= 1 + \gamma\phi(L)\frac{1 - \alpha L^{-1}\phi(\alpha)\phi(L)^{-1}}{1 - \alpha L^{-1}}.$$

By a similar argument, $b_0 = \gamma\theta(\alpha)$ and

$$B(L) = \frac{\gamma L\theta(L) - \alpha\gamma\theta(\alpha)}{L - \alpha}$$

$$= \gamma\theta(L)\frac{1 - \alpha L^{-1}\theta(\alpha)\theta(L)^{-1}}{1 - \alpha L^{-1}}.$$

From (15.47) we may write the solution for x_t as

$$x_t = \gamma \left\{ \sum_{s=0}^{\infty} \alpha^s E_t[\phi(L)e_{t+s} + \theta(L)\varepsilon_{t+s}] \right\} + e_t$$

$$= \gamma \sum_{s=0}^{\infty} \alpha^s E_t z_{t+s} + e_t. \tag{15.52}$$

Thus, in this unstable case, x_t is determined uniquely by the expected discounted value of current and future values of z_t.

Suppose now that we derive a solution directly from equation (15.43) by solving it forwards. Thus we rewrite (15.43) as

$$x_t = \alpha L^{-1} x_t + \gamma z_t + e_t$$

$$= \frac{\gamma z_t + e_t}{1 - \alpha L^{-1}}$$

$$= \sum_{s=0}^{\infty} \alpha^s L^{-s} (\gamma z_t + e_t)$$

$$= \sum_{s=0}^{\infty} \alpha^s E_t (\gamma z_{t+s} + e_{t+s})$$

$$= \gamma \sum_{s=0}^{\infty} \alpha^s E_t z_{t+s} + e_t.$$

This is identical to the full solution using the extended method of undetermined coefficients, equation (15.52).

Finally, this solution may be compared with the nonstochastic case, equation (15.42). The key difference between equations (15.52) and (15.42) is that in the nonstochastic case expectations of z_{t+s} replace actual values; whereas the value of z in future periods cannot change, its expectation based on contemporaneous information can.

15.8.3.2 *The Solution to Equation (15.44)*

Using the Weiner–Kolmogorov formula enables us to write equation (15.44) as

$$A(L)e_t + B(L)\varepsilon_t = \alpha L^{-1}\{[A(L) - a_0]e_t + [B(L) - b_0]\varepsilon_t\}$$
$$+ \beta L[A(L)e_t + B(L)\varepsilon_t] + \gamma[\phi(L)e_t + \theta(L)\varepsilon_t] + e_t.$$

Equating terms in e_t and ε_t gives

$$A(L) = -\frac{L + \gamma L\phi(L) - \alpha a_0}{\beta L^2 - L + \alpha}, \tag{15.53}$$

$$B(L) = -\frac{\gamma L\theta(L) - \alpha b_0}{\beta L^2 - L + \alpha}, \tag{15.54}$$

where a_0 and b_0 are free coefficients. Denoting the roots of the auxiliary equation

$$\beta L^2 - L + \alpha = 0$$

by λ_1 and λ_2 (and for convenience assuming that they are real), we obtain

$$(L - \lambda_1)(L - \lambda_2) = 0, \tag{15.55}$$

$$L^2 - (\lambda_1 + \lambda_2)L + \lambda_1\lambda_2 = 0. \tag{15.56}$$

Hence $\lambda_1 + \lambda_2 = 1/\beta$ and $\lambda_1\lambda_2 = \alpha/\beta$.

There are three cases to consider:

(i) $|\lambda_1|, |\lambda_2| \geqslant 1$, when the model is said to be stable;

(ii) $|\lambda_1|, |\lambda_2| < 1$, when the model is said to be unstable;

(iii) $|\lambda_1| \geqslant 1, |\lambda_2| < 1$, when the model is said to have a saddlepath solution.

If both roots are either stable or unstable, then the evaluation of the polynomial at $L = 1$ is

$$(L - \lambda_1)(L - \lambda_2)|_{L=1} = (1 - \lambda_1)(1 - \lambda_2) \geqslant 0,$$

i.e., $\alpha + \beta \geqslant 1$. But if the solution is a saddlepath, then

$$(L - \lambda_1)(L - \lambda_2)|_{L=1} \leqslant 0,$$

i.e., $\alpha + \beta \leqslant 1$. Equality occurs when there is a unit root. These inequalities provide a quick way of checking the type of solution. We now consider the solution of x_t.

(i) The Stable Case: $|\lambda_1|, |\lambda_2| \geqslant 1$.   The solution for x_t is

$$x_t = -\frac{L + \gamma L\phi(L) - \alpha a_0}{\beta L^2 - L + \alpha}e_t - \frac{\gamma L\theta(L) - \alpha b_0}{\beta L^2 - L + \alpha}\varepsilon_t,$$

which may be written as

$$(\beta L^2 - L + \alpha)x_t = -\gamma L[\phi(L)e_t + \theta(L)\varepsilon_t] - (L - \alpha a_0)e_t + \alpha b_0\varepsilon_t \tag{15.57}$$

or as

$$x_t = \frac{1}{\beta}x_{t-1} - \frac{\alpha}{\beta}x_{t-2} - \frac{\gamma}{\beta}z_{t-1} - \frac{1}{\beta}e_{t-1} + \frac{\alpha}{\beta}(a_0 e_t + b_0\varepsilon_t)$$

$$= \frac{1}{\beta}x_{t-1} - \frac{\alpha}{\beta}x_{t-2} - \frac{\gamma}{\beta}z_{t-1} - \frac{1}{\beta}e_{t-1} + \frac{\alpha}{\beta}(x_{t+1} - E_t x_{t+1}),$$

which is nonunique as a_0 and b_0 are undetermined.

The corresponding solution obtained simply by inverting equation (15.44) is

$$x_{t+1} = \frac{1}{\beta}x_t - \frac{\alpha}{\beta}x_{t-1} - \frac{\gamma}{\beta}z_t - \frac{1}{\beta}e_t + \frac{\alpha}{\beta}(x_{t+1} - E_t x_{t+1}).$$

(ii) The Unstable Case: $|\lambda_1|, |\lambda_2| < 1$. As both roots are unstable, a singularity occurs in the $A(L)$ and $B(L)$ functions at $L = \lambda_1$ and $L = \lambda_2$. In order to remove these singularities we require that

$$\lim_{L \to \lambda_i} (L - \lambda_i) A(L) = \lambda_i + \gamma \lambda_i \phi(\lambda_i) - \alpha a_0 = 0, \quad i = 1, 2.$$

This gives

$$a_0 = \frac{\lambda_i + \gamma \lambda_i \phi(\lambda_i)}{\alpha}$$

for both λ_1 and λ_2. Hence the solution is overdetermined; we do not know which value of a_0 to choose. A similar result is obtained for b_0, namely

$$b_0 = \frac{\gamma \lambda_i \phi(\lambda_i)}{\alpha}.$$

Proceeding despite this we can show that the solution for x_t is again equation (15.57). Noting that

$$\beta L^2 - L + \alpha = \beta(L - \lambda_1)(L - \lambda_2)$$
$$= \alpha L^2 (1 - \lambda_1 L^{-1})(1 - \lambda_2 L^{-1})$$

and that

$$\frac{1}{(1 - \lambda_1 L^{-1})(1 - \lambda_2 L^{-1})} = \frac{1}{\lambda_1 - \lambda_2} \left(\frac{\lambda_1}{1 - \lambda_1 L^{-1}} - \frac{\lambda_2}{1 - \lambda_2 L^{-1}} \right)$$
$$= \frac{1}{\lambda_1 - \lambda_2} \sum_{s=0}^{\infty} (\lambda_1^{s+1} - \lambda_2^{s+1}) L^{-s},$$

the solution may be written as

$$x_t = -\frac{L^{-2}}{\alpha(\lambda_1 - \lambda_2)} \sum_{s=0}^{\infty} (\lambda_1^{s+1} - \lambda_2^{s+1}) L^{-s} \{\gamma L [\phi(L) e_t + \theta(L) \varepsilon_t]$$
$$+ (L - \alpha a_0) e_t - \alpha b_0 \varepsilon_t\}$$
$$= -\frac{\gamma}{\alpha(\lambda_1 - \lambda_2)} \sum_{s=1}^{\infty} (\lambda_1^s - \lambda_2^s) E_t z_{t+s} + \frac{1}{\lambda_1 - \lambda_2} (a_0 e_t + b_0 \varepsilon_t), \quad (15.58)$$

where there are two choices for each of a_0 and b_0. This is a purely forward-looking solution.

Had we adopted the more direct approach, we would have written equation (15.44) as

$$(\beta L^2 - L + \alpha) x_{t+1} = \alpha L^2 (1 - \lambda_1 L^{-1})(1 - \lambda_2 L^{-1}) x_{t+1}$$
$$= -\gamma z_t - e_t,$$

where we have used $E_t x_{t+1} = L^{-1} x_t$ instead of $E_t x_{t+1} = x_{t+1} - (x_{t+1} - E_t x_{t+1})$. This gives the solution

$$x_{t+1} = -\frac{\gamma}{\alpha(\lambda_1 - \lambda_2)} \sum_{s=1}^{\infty} (\lambda_1^s - \lambda_2^s) E_t z_{t+s+1},$$

which omits the innovation term in equation (15.58) and is therefore an incomplete solution.

(iii) The Saddlepath Case: $|\lambda_1| \geqslant 1$, $|\lambda_2| < 1$. This type of solution is very common in DGE macroeconomic models and is therefore of most interest to us. We now have one stable root λ_1 and one unstable root λ_2. Here there is one singularity in the $A(L)$ and $B(L)$ functions. This occurs at $L = \lambda_2$. In order to remove this singularity we require that

$$\lim_{L \to \lambda_2} (L - \lambda_2)A(L) = \lambda_2 + \gamma\lambda_2\phi(\lambda_2) - \alpha a_0 = 0.$$

This gives

$$a_0 = \frac{\lambda_2 + \gamma\lambda_2\phi(\lambda_2)}{\alpha}.$$

Similarly, for b_0 we obtain

$$b_0 = \frac{\gamma\lambda_2\phi(\lambda_2)}{\alpha}.$$

The solution for x_t is therefore

$$(\beta L^2 - L + \alpha)x_t = -[L + \gamma L\phi(L) - \lambda_2 - \gamma\lambda_2\phi(\lambda_2)]e_t - [\gamma L\theta(L) - \gamma\lambda_2\phi(\lambda_2)]\varepsilon_t.$$

Noting that

$$\beta L^2 - L + \alpha = -\alpha\lambda_1 L\left(1 - \frac{1}{\lambda_1}L\right)(1 - \lambda_2 L^{-1})$$

we have

$$\alpha\lambda_1\left(1 - \frac{1}{\lambda_1}L\right)x_t$$
$$= \gamma\left[\phi(L)\frac{1 - \lambda_2 L^{-1}\phi(\lambda_2)\phi(L)^{-1}}{1 - \lambda_2 L^{-1}}e_t + \theta(L)\frac{1 - \lambda_2 L^{-1}\theta(\lambda_2)\theta(L)^{-1}}{1 - \lambda_2 L^{-1}}\varepsilon_t\right] + e_t$$

or

$$x_t = \frac{1}{\lambda_1}x_{t-1} + \frac{\gamma}{\alpha\lambda_1}\sum_{s=0}^{\infty}\lambda_2^s E_t z_{t+s} + \frac{1}{\alpha\lambda_1}e_t, \qquad (15.59)$$

which is a unique solution involving both forward- and backward-looking terms.

   Suppose that we now apply the more direct method to equation (15.44). Thus first we rewrite it as

$$(\beta L^2 - L + \alpha)x_t = -\gamma z_t - e_t.$$

Hence

$$\alpha\lambda_1 L\left(1 - \frac{1}{\lambda_1}L\right)(1 - \lambda_2 L^{-1})x_t = \gamma z_t + e_t$$

or

$$x_t = \frac{1}{\lambda_1}x_{t-1} + \frac{1}{\alpha\lambda_1}\frac{\gamma z_t + e_t}{1 - \lambda_2 L^{-1}}$$

$$= \frac{1}{\lambda_1}x_{t-1} + \frac{\gamma}{\alpha\lambda_1}\sum_{s=0}^{\infty}\lambda_2^s E_t z_{t+s} + \frac{1}{\alpha\lambda_1}e_t, \qquad (15.60)$$

which is the same solution as (15.59). Thus, once more, when the solution is unique, we have an alternative and simpler way of deriving the solution.

Equation (15.59) may also be written as

$$\Delta x_t = \left(1 - \frac{1}{\lambda_1}\right)(x_t^* - x_{t-1}),$$ (15.61)

$$x_t^* = \frac{\gamma}{\alpha(\lambda_1 - 1)} \sum_{s=0}^{\infty} \lambda_2^s E_t z_{t+s} + \frac{1}{\alpha(\lambda_1 - 1)} e_t.$$ (15.62)

This is a partial adjustment model in which the dynamic adjustment of x_t following a change in the long-run equilibrium value x_t^* (which is brought about by changes in current or expected future z_t) may be considered in two parts. At time t, x_t adjusts by a proportion $1 - (1/\lambda_1)$ of the gap between x_t^* and x_{t-1}; in subsequent periods it adjusts by a proportion $1/\lambda_1$ of the change in the previous period until the new equilibrium is reached. The former is often referred to as x_t jumping onto the saddlepath; the latter as x_t moving along the saddlepath to equilibrium.

The saddlepath is sometimes portrayed as a knife-edge solution in which a failure of x_t to jump onto the saddlepath may cause it to diverge for ever, possibly exploding. This is misleading. This interpretation derives from the associated phase diagram of the solution in which points off the saddlepath are depicted as leading to increased divergence from both the saddlepath and the new equilibrium. In fact, x_t must always lie on the saddlepath and cannot deviate from it. This is because x_t must satisfy both the original model and the saddlepath. Equation (15.61) is just another representation of equation (15.59); and the precise characteristics of the saddlepath depend on the parameters of equation (15.59).

15.8.3.3 *Summary of Results*

We have demonstrated how to obtain the solutions of rational-expectations models like equations (15.43) and (15.44). Some of the solutions are not unique (typically where the solution is stable), some are overdetermined (in equation (15.44), where there is more than one unstable root), and some are unique. We have shown how to determine which of these types of solutions occurs. A unique solution occurs for an equation with a single forward expectation without a lag, like (15.43), when the single root is unstable, and for an equation with a lag in addition, like (15.44), which has two roots, one stable and one unstable, giving a saddlepath. We have also shown that where the solution is unique there is a simpler and more direct way of obtaining the solution. We now extend this discussion to systems of rational-expectations equations with a view to determining what type of solution occurs and how to derive the solution when it is unique.

15.8.4 **Systems of Rational-Expectations Equations**

We consider the system

$$\begin{bmatrix} x_{t+1} \\ E_t y_{t+1} \end{bmatrix} = \begin{bmatrix} A_{xx} & A_{xy} \\ A_{yx} & A_{yy} \end{bmatrix} \begin{bmatrix} x_t \\ y_t \end{bmatrix} + \begin{bmatrix} C_x \\ C_y \end{bmatrix} z_t,$$ (15.63)

where x_{t+1} is a vector of n variables that are predetermined at time t, y_{t+1} is a vector of m variables that are not predetermined at t, and z_t are exogenous variables. We wish to find the solution for y_t. We gives examples of how to represent models in this form below.

We denote the size $n + m$ matrix A by

$$A = \begin{bmatrix} A_{xx} & A_{xy} \\ A_{yx} & A_{yy} \end{bmatrix}.$$

Its Jordan canonical form is

$$A = Q\Gamma Q^{-1},$$

where Γ is a diagonal matrix of eigenvalues ordered by size:

$$\Gamma = \begin{bmatrix} \Gamma_{xx} & 0 \\ 0 & \Gamma_{yy} \end{bmatrix}.$$

Proposition. *There is a unique solution to this system if Γ_{xx} has n eigenvalues all either on or inside the unit circle and Γ_{yy} has m eigenvalues all outside the unit circle.*

The solution may be obtained by first taking expectations of the system (15.63) to give

$$\begin{bmatrix} E_t x_{t+1} \\ E_t y_{t+1} \end{bmatrix} = \begin{bmatrix} A_{xx} & A_{xy} \\ A_{yx} & A_{yy} \end{bmatrix} \begin{bmatrix} x_t \\ y_t \end{bmatrix} + \begin{bmatrix} C_x \\ C_y \end{bmatrix} z_t, \tag{15.64}$$

and then defining

$$Z_t = \begin{bmatrix} X_t \\ Y_t \end{bmatrix} = Q^{-1} \begin{bmatrix} x_t \\ y_t \end{bmatrix}$$

so that the system can be written as

$$\begin{aligned} E_t Z_{t+1} &= Q^{-1} A Q Z_t + Q^{-1} C z_t \\ &= \Gamma Z_t + Q^{-1} C z_t, \end{aligned} \tag{15.65}$$

where

$$C = \begin{bmatrix} C_x \\ C_y \end{bmatrix}.$$

Thus (15.65) consists of $n + m$ equations of the form

$$E_t Z_{i,t+1} = \gamma_i Z_{it} + P_i z_t, \quad i = 1, \dots, n + m,$$

where γ_i are the individual eigenvalues of Λ and P_i is the ith row of $Q^{-1} C$.

We can now apply the results derived above to each of these equations, noting that γ_i is an inversion of the earlier eigenvalues so that $\gamma_i \equiv \lambda_i^{-1}$. We have previously argued that a unique solution occurs if λ_i lies inside the unit circle, which implies that γ_i must lie outside, as noted in the proposition. This implies that there is a unique solution for Z_{it} $(i = n + 1, \dots, m)$ and it is given by

$$Z_{it} = -\sum_{s=0}^{\infty} \gamma_i^{-s} P_i E_t z_{t+s},$$

and hence

$$Y_t = -\sum_{s=0}^{\infty} \Gamma_{yy}^{-s} P_i E_t z_{t+s}.$$

We are interested in the solution for y_t. This is obtained from

$$\begin{bmatrix} x_t \\ y_t \end{bmatrix} = Q \begin{bmatrix} X_t \\ Y_t \end{bmatrix};$$

hence, as $X_t = x_t$,

$$y_t = Q_{yx} x_t - \sum_{s=0}^{\infty} Q_{yy} \Gamma_{yy}^{-s} P E_t z_{t+s}. \tag{15.66}$$

We now give some examples of how to write a rational-expectations model in the form of equation (15.63).

Example 15.9. Consider the solution to the model

$$E_t \Delta y_{t+1} = y_t - x_t + e_t, \tag{15.67}$$

$$x_t = 0.25 x_{t-1} + \varepsilon_t, \tag{15.68}$$

where e_t and ε_t are zero-mean innovation processes.

The model can be written in the form of (15.63) as

$$\begin{bmatrix} x_{t+1} \\ E_t y_{t+1} \end{bmatrix} = \begin{bmatrix} 0.25 & 0 \\ -1 & 2 \end{bmatrix} \begin{bmatrix} x_t \\ y_t \end{bmatrix} + \begin{bmatrix} \varepsilon_{t+1} \\ e_t \end{bmatrix}. \tag{15.69}$$

Using the lag operator, the system (15.69) can be rewritten using the notation of (15.65) as

$$B(L) Z_{t+1} = Z_t, \tag{15.70}$$

where $B(L) = I - AL$. The eigenvalues can be obtained from

$$\det B(L) = 0.$$

We note that

$$\det(I - AL) = (1 - \lambda_1 L)(1 - \lambda_2 L)$$
$$= 1 - (\lambda_1 + \lambda_2)L + \lambda_1 \lambda_2 L^2$$
$$= 1 - (\operatorname{tr} A)L + (\det A)L^2,$$

where the roots are $\gamma_i = 1/\lambda_i$ and are obtained from

$$\{\lambda_1, \lambda_2\} = \tfrac{1}{2} \operatorname{tr} A \pm \tfrac{1}{2} [(\operatorname{tr} A)^2 - 4(\det A)]^{1/2}.$$

Hence the roots satisfy

$$\{\lambda_1, \lambda_2\} = \tfrac{1}{2} \operatorname{tr} A \pm \tfrac{1}{2} [(\operatorname{tr} A)^2 - 4(\det A)]^{1/2}.$$

Using a first-order Taylor series approximation to the term in the square root gives a result that is sometimes useful, especially for local approximations to nonlinear systems, namely

$$\{\lambda_1, \lambda_2\} \simeq \left\{ \frac{\det A}{\operatorname{tr} A}, \operatorname{tr} A - \frac{\det A}{\operatorname{tr} A} \right\}.$$

Using a first-order Taylor series approximation to the term in the square root gives a result that is sometimes useful, especially for local approximations to nonlinear systems, namely

$$\{\lambda_1, \lambda_2\} \simeq \left\{ \frac{\det A}{\operatorname{tr} A}, \operatorname{tr} A - \frac{\det A}{\operatorname{tr} A} \right\}.$$

Hence

$$\left| I - \begin{bmatrix} 0.25 & 0 \\ -1 & 2 \end{bmatrix} L \right| = (1 - 2L)(1 - 0.25L) = 0,$$

and the roots are $1/\lambda_1 = 4$ and $1/\lambda_2 = 0.5$, implying a saddlepath solution.

The inverse of $B(L)$ is the adjoint matrix of $B(L)$ divided by the determinant of $B(L)$:

$$B(L)^{-1} = \frac{\operatorname{adj} B(L)}{\det B(L)},$$

where

$$\det B(L) = (1 - 2L)(1 - 0.25L).$$

Hence

$$[\det B(L)] Z_t = [\operatorname{adj} B(L)] L z_t$$

or

$$(1 - 2L)(1 - 0.25L) Z_t = -2(1 - 0.5L^{-1})(1 - 0.25L) L Z_t$$

$$= \begin{bmatrix} 1 - 2L & 0 \\ L & 1 - 0.25L \end{bmatrix} L z_t.$$

The solution for y_t is therefore

$$(1 - 0.25L) y_t = -\frac{1}{2(1 - 0.5L^{-1})} [\varepsilon_t + (1 - 0.25L) e_t]$$

or

$$y_t = 0.25 y_{t-1} - \sum_{s=0}^{\infty} 0.5^{s+1} E_t [\varepsilon_{t+s} + (1 - 0.25L) e_{t+s}]$$

$$= 0.25 y_{t-1} - 0.5\varepsilon_t - 0.375 e_t + 0.25 e_{t-1}.$$

Example 15.10. Consider the single equation

$$y_t = \alpha E_t y_{t+1} + \beta y_{t-1} + \gamma z_t + e_t.$$

We can rewrite this as the two-equation system

$$\begin{bmatrix} 1 & 0 \\ 0 & \alpha \end{bmatrix} \begin{bmatrix} y_t \\ E_t y_{t+1} \end{bmatrix} = \begin{bmatrix} 0 & 1 \\ -\beta & 1 \end{bmatrix} \begin{bmatrix} y_{t-1} \\ y_t \end{bmatrix} + \begin{bmatrix} 0 \\ -1 \end{bmatrix} (\gamma z_t + e_t),$$

or, in the form of (15.63), as

$$\begin{bmatrix} y_t \\ E_t y_{t+1} \end{bmatrix} = \begin{bmatrix} 0 & 1 \\ -\beta/\alpha & 1/\alpha \end{bmatrix} \begin{bmatrix} y_{t-1} \\ y_t \end{bmatrix} + \begin{bmatrix} 0 \\ -1/\alpha \end{bmatrix} (\gamma z_t + e_t).$$

The roots of this system are obtained from

$$\det(I - AL) = 1 - \frac{1}{\alpha}L + \frac{\beta}{\alpha}L^2$$
$$= (1 - \lambda_1 L)(1 - \lambda_2 L) = 0,$$

where the roots are $1/\lambda_1$ and $1/\lambda_2$. Assuming that we have a unique saddlepath solution with $|\lambda_1| \leqslant 1$ and $|\lambda_2| > 1$,

$$\det(I - AL) = -\lambda_2 L(1 - \lambda_1 L)(1 - \lambda_2^{-1}L^{-1}).$$

Writing the solution in the form

$$[\det B(L)]Z_t = [\operatorname{adj} B(L)]L \begin{bmatrix} 0 \\ -1/\alpha \end{bmatrix} (\gamma z_t + e_t),$$

$$-\lambda_2 L(1 - \lambda_1 L)(1 - \lambda_2^{-1}L^{-1})Z_t = \begin{bmatrix} 1 - (1/\alpha)L & -(\beta/\alpha)L \\ L & 1 \end{bmatrix} \begin{bmatrix} 0 \\ -1/\alpha \end{bmatrix} (\gamma z_t + e_t),$$

we obtain

$$(1 - \lambda_1 L)Z_t = -\frac{1}{\lambda_2(1 - \lambda_2^{-1}L^{-1})} \begin{bmatrix} 1 - (1/\alpha)L & -(\beta/\alpha)L \\ L & 1 \end{bmatrix} \begin{bmatrix} 0 \\ -1/\alpha \end{bmatrix} (\gamma z_t + e_t).$$

Hence

$$y_t = \lambda_1 y_{t-1} + \frac{\gamma}{\alpha\lambda_2} \sum_{s=0}^{\infty} \lambda_2^{-s} E_t z_{t+s} + \frac{1}{\alpha\lambda_2} e_t,$$

which is the same as the previous solution, equation (15.60), apart from the inversion of the names of the roots.

Finally, we note that we have focused on unique solutions in our discussion of systems in which there are as many unstable roots as there are nonpredetermined variables. If there are less unstable roots (more stable roots) than there are nonpredetermined variables, then we have an infinity of solutions, and if there are more unstable roots than nonpredetermined variables, then there is no solution. The former is the case of a stable model.

References

Abel, A. B. 1990. Asset prices under habit formation and catching up with the Joneses. *American Economic Review* 80:38–42.

Aghion, P., and P. Howitt. 1998. *Endogenous Growth Theory*. Cambridge, MA: MIT Press.

Altig, D., L. J. Christiano, M. Eichenbaum, and J. Linde. 2004. Firm-specific capital, nominal rigidities and the business cycle. Mimeo, Northwestern University.

Altug, S. 1989. Time-to-build and aggregate fluctuations: some new evidence. *International Economic Review* 30:889–920.

Altug, S., and P. Labadie. 1994. *Dynamic Choice and Asset Markets*. San Diego, CA: Academic Press.

Anderson, L., and J. Jordon. 1968. Monetary and fiscal actions: a test of their relative importance in economic stabilization. *Federal Reserve Bank of St. Louis Review* 50: 11–24.

Backus, D. K., P. J. Kehoe, and F. E. Kydland. 1992. International real business cycles? *Journal of Political Economy* 100:745–75.

———. 1995. International business cycles: theory vs evidence. In *Frontiers of Business Cycle Research* (ed. T. F. Cooley). Princeton University Press.

Backus, D. K., S. Foresi, and C. Telmer. 1996. Affine models of currency pricing. NBER Working Paper 5623.

Bailey, M. J. 1956. The welfare costs of inflationary finance. *Journal of Political Economy* 64:93–110.

Balassa, B. 1964. The purchasing power parity doctrine: a reappraisal. *Journal of Political Economy* 72:584–96.

Balfoussia, H., and M. R. Wickens. 2007. Macroeconomic sources of risk in the term structure. *Journal of Money, Credit and Banking* 39:205–36.

Ball, L., and D. Romer. 1991. Sticky prices as coordination failure. *American Economic Review* 81:539–52.

Barro, R. J. 1974. Are government bonds net wealth? *Journal of Political Economy* 82: 1095–117.

———. 1979. On the determination of the public debt. *Journal of Political Economy* 87: 940–71.

———. 1989. The Ricardian approach to budget deficits. *Journal of Economic Perspectives* 3:37–54.

———. 1997. *Macroeconomics*, 5th edn. New York: Wiley.

Barro, R. J., and D. B. Gordon. 1983. Rules, discretion and reputation in a model of monetary policy. *Journal of Monetary Economics* 12:101–21.

Barro, R. J., and X. Sala-i-Martin. 2004. *Economic Growth*, 2nd edn. Cambridge, MA: MIT Press.

Batini, N., B. Jackson, and S. Nickell. 2005. Inflation dynamics and the labour share in the UK. *Journal of Monetary Economics* 52:1061–71.

Baxter, M., and R. G. King. 1993. Fiscal policy in general equilibrium. *American Economic Review* 83:315–34.

Bellman, R. 1957. *Dynamic Programming*. Princeton University Press.

Bellman, R., and S. E. Dreyfus. 1962. *Applied Dynamic Programming*. Princeton University Press.

Bernanke, B., and M. Woodford (eds). 2005. *The Inflation-Targeting Debate.* Chicago University Press.

Betts, C., and M. B. Devereux. 1996. The exchange rate in a model of pricing-to-market. *European Economic Review* 40:1007–22.

——. 2000. Exchange rate dynamics in a model with pricing-to-market. *Journal of International Economics* 50:215–44.

Bils, M., and P. J. Klenow. 2004. Some evidence on the importance of sticky prices. *Journal of Political Economy* 112:947–85.

Bils, M., P. J. Klenow, and O. Kryvtsov. 2003. Sticky prices and monetary policy shocks. *Federal Reserve Bank of Minneapolis Quarterly Review* 27:2–9.

Blanchard, O. J., and S. Fischer. 1989. *Lectures on Macroeconomics.* Cambridge, MA: MIT Press.

Blanchard, O. J., and C. M. Kahn. 1980. The solution of linear difference models under rational expectations. *Econometrica* 48:1305–11.

Blanchard, O. J., and N. Kiyotaki. 1987. Monopolistic competition and the effects of aggregate demand. *American Economic Review* 77:647–66.

Blinder, A. S., E. R. D. Canetti, D. E Lebow, and J. B. Rudd. 1998. *Asking About Prices: A New Approach to Understanding Price Stickiness.* New York: Russell Sage Foundation.

Bohn, H. 1995. The sustainability of budget deficits in a stochastic economy. *Journal of Money, Credit and Banking* 27:257–71.

Bordo, M. 1993. The Bretton Woods international monetary system: an historical overview. NBER Working Paper 4033.

Bordo, M., and B. J. Eichengreen. 1993. *A Retrospective on the Bretton Woods System: Lessons for the International Monetary System.* University of Chicago Press.

——. 1998. The rise and fall of a barbarous relic: the role of gold in the international monetary system. NBER Working Paper 6436.

Branson, W. H., and D. W. Henderson. 1985. The specification and influence of asset markets. In *Handbook of International Economics* (ed. R. W. Jones and P. B. Kenen), volume 2. Amsterdam: North-Holland.

Breedon, D. 1979. An intertemporal asset pricing model with stochastic consumption and investment. *Journal of Financial Economics* 7:265–96.

Brock, W. A. 1974. Money and growth: the case of long run perfect foresight. *International Economic Review* 15:750–77.

——. 1990. Overlapping generations models with money and transactions costs. In *Handbook of Monetary Economics* (ed. B. M. Friedman and F. H. Hahn), volume 1, pp. 263–95. Amsterdam: North-Holland.

Buchanan, J. M. 1976. Barro on the Ricardian equivalence theorem. *Journal of Political Economy* 84:337–42.

Cagan, P. 1956. The monetary dynamics of hyperinflation. In *Studies in the Quantity Theory of Money* (ed. M. Friedman), pp. 25–117. University of Chicago Press.

Calvo, G. 1983. Staggered prices in a utility-maximizing framework. *Journal of Monetary Economics* 12:383–98.

Campbell, J. Y. 2002. Consumption-based asset pricing. In *Handbook of the Economics of Finance* (ed. G. Constantinides, M. Harris, and R. Stulz). Amsterdam: Elsevier.

Campbell, J. Y., and J. H. Cochrane. 1999. By force of habit: a consumption-based explanation of aggregate stock market behavior. *Journal of Political Economy* 107:205–51.

Campbell, J. Y., A. W. Lo, and A. C. MacKinlay. 1997. *The Econometrics of Financial Markets.* Princeton University Press.

Canova, F. 1995. VAR models: specification, estimation, inference and forecasting. In *Handbook of Applied Econometrics* (ed. H. M. Pesaran and M. R. Wickens). Oxford: Blackwell.

Canova, F. 2005. *Methods for Applied Macroeconomic Research*. Princeton University Press.

Canova, F., and G. De Nicolo. 2002. Money matters for business cycle fluctuations in the G7. *Journal of Monetary Economics* 49:1131–59.

Cass, D. 1965. Optimal growth in an aggregate model of capital accumulation. *Review of Economic Studies* 32:233–40.

Chamley, C. 1986. Optimal taxation of capital income in general equilibrium with infinite lives. *Econometrica* 54:607–22.

Chari, V. V., and P. J. Kehoe. 1999. Optimal fiscal and monetary policy. In *Handbook of Macroeconomics* (ed. J. B. Taylor and M. Woodford), volume 1C, pp. 1671–745. Amsterdam: Elsevier.

——. 2006. Modern macroeconomics in practice: how theory is shaping policy. *Journal of Economic Perspectives* 20:3–28.

Chari, V. V., P. J. Kehoe, and E. C. Prescott. 1989. Time consistency and policy. In *Modern Business Cycle Theory* (ed. R. Barro), pp. 265–305. Cambridge, MA: Harvard University Press.

Chari, V. V., L. J. Christiano, and P. J. Kehoe. 1994. Optimal fiscal policy in a business cycle model. *Journal of Political Economy* 102:617–52.

——. 1996. Optimality of the Friedman rule in economies with distorting taxes. *Journal of Monetary Economics* 37:203–23.

Chiang, A. C. 1992. *Elements of Dynamic Optimization*. New York: McGraw-Hill.

Cho, J. O., and R. Rogerson. 1988. Family labor supply and aggregate fluctuations. *Journal of Monetary Economics* 21:233–45.

Chow, G. C. 1975. *Analysis and Control of Dynamic Economic Systems*. New York: Wiley.

——. 1981. *Econometric Analysis by Control Methods*. New York: Wiley.

——. 1997. *Dynamic Economics: Optimization by the Lagrange Method*. Oxford University Press.

Christiano, L. J., and M. Eichenbaum. 1992. Current real business cycle theories and aggregate labor market fluctuations. *American Economic Review* 82:430–50.

Christiano, L. J., M. Eichenbaum, and C. L. Evans. 1999. Monetary policy shocks: what have we learned and to what end? In *Handbook of Macroeconomics* (ed. J. B. Taylor and M. Woodford), volume 1A, pp. 65–148. Amsterdam: Elsevier.

——. 2005. Nominal rigidities and the dynamic effects of a shock to monetary policy. *Journal of Political Economy* 113:1–45.

Clarida, R., J. Gali, and M. Gertler. 1999. The science of monetary policy: a New Keynesian perspective. *Journal of Economic Perspectives* 37:1661–707.

——. 2000. Monetary policy rules and macroeconomic stability: evidence and some theory. *Quarterly Journal of Economics* 115:147–80.

——. 2001. Optimal monetary policy in open vs. closed economies. *American Economic Review* 91:253–57.

Clower, R. W. 1967. A reconsideration of the microfoundations of monetary theory. *Western Economic Journal* 6:1–8.

Cochrane, J. H. 2005. *Asset Pricing*, 2nd edn. Princeton University Press.

——. 2008. Financial markets and the real economy. In *Handbook of The Equity Premium*, pp. 237–325. Amsterdam: Elsevier.

Constantinides, G. M. 1990. Habit formation: a resolution of the equity premium puzzle. *Journal of Political Economy* 98:519–43.

Cooley, T. F. (ed.). 1995. *Frontiers of Business Cycle Research*. Princeton University Press.

Cooper, R. N. 1982. The gold standard: historical facts and future prospects. *Brookings Papers on Economic Activity* 1:1–45.

Correia, I., and P. Teles. 1996. Is the Friedman rule optimal when money is an intermediate good? *Journal of Monetary Economics* 38:223–44.

Cox, J. C., J. E. Ingersoll, and S. A. Ross. 1981. A reexamination of traditional hypotheses about the term strucure. *Journal of Finance* 36:769–99.

——. 1985a. An intertermporal general equilibrium model of asset prices. *Econometrica* 53:363–84.

——. 1985b. A theory of the term structure of interest rates. *Econometrica* 53:385–408.

Dai, Q., and K. Singleton. 2000. Specification analysis of affine term structure models. *Journal of Finance* 55:1943–78.

——. 2003. Fixed income pricing. In *Handbook of the Economics of Finance* (ed. G. M Constantinides, M. Harris, and R. M Stulz), volume 1B, pp. 1207–46. Amsterdam: Elsevier.

De Jong, D. N., and C. Dave. 2007. *Structural Macroeconometrics*. Princeton University Press.

Devereux, M. 1997. Real exchange rates and macroeconomics: evidence and theory. *Canadian Journal of Economics* 30:773–808.

Devereux, M., and C. M. Engel. 2003. Endogenous exchange rate pass-through when nominal prices are set in advance. NBER Working Paper 9543.

Diamond, P. A. 1965. National debt in a neoclassical growth model. *American Economic Review* 55:1126–50.

Dixit, A. K. 1990. *Optimization in Economic Theory*, 2nd edn. Oxford University Press.

Dixit, A. K., and J. E. Stiglitz. 1977. Monopolistic competition and optimum product diversity. *American Economic Review* 67:297–308.

Dixon, H. D., and N. Rankin (eds). 1995. *The New Macroeconomics, Imperfect Markets and Policy Effectiveness*. Cambridge University Press.

Dornbusch, R. 1976. Expectations and exchange rate dynamics. *Journal of Political Economy* 84:1161–76.

Dotsey, M., R. G. King, and A. L. Wolman. 1999. State-dependent pricing and the general equilibrium dynamics of money and output. *Quarterly Journal of Economics* 114: 655–90.

Duesenberry, J. S. (ed.). 1965. *The Brookings Quarterly Econometric Model of the United States*. Washington, DC: Brookings Institution/Amsterdam: North-Holland.

Eichengreen, B. J. 1996a. *Globalizing Capital: A History of the International Monetary System*. Princeton University Press.

——. 1996b. *Golden Fetters: The Gold Standard and the Great Depression, 1913–1939*. Oxford University Press.

Engel, C. M. 2000. Long-run PPP may not hold after all. *Journal of International Economics* 51:243–73.

Epstein, L. G., and S. E. Zin. 1989. Substitution, risk aversion, and the temporal behavior of consumption and asset returns: a theoretical framework. *Econometrica* 46:937–69.

Fama, E. 1984. Forward and spot exchange rates. *Journal of Monetary Economics* 14: 319–38.

Feenstra, R. C. 1986. Functional equivalence between liquidity costs and the utility of money. *Journal of Monetary Economics* 17:271–91.

Ferson, W. E. 1995. Theory and empirical testing of asset pricing models. In *Finance* (ed. R. A. Jarrow, V. Maksimovic, and W. T. Ziemba). Handbooks in Operational Research and Management Science, volume 9. Amsterdam: North-Holland.

Fischer, S. 1980. Dynamic inconsistency, cooperation and the benevolent dissembling government. *Journal of Economic Dynamics and Control* 2:93–107.

Fleming, J. M. 1962. Domestic financial policies under fixed and under floating exchange rates. *International Monetary Fund Staff Papers* 9:369–79.

Flood, R. P., and P. M. Garber. 1984. Collapsing exchange rate regimes: some linear examples. *Journal of International Economics* 17:1–13.

Flood, R. P., and P. M. Garber. 1991. The linkage between speculative attack and target zone models of exchange rates. *Quarterly Journal of Economics* 106:1367–72.

Frenkel, J. A. 1976. A monetary approach to the exchange rate: doctrinal aspects and empirical evidence. *Scandinavian Journal of Economics* 78:200–24.

Frenkel, J. A., and H. Johnson. 1976. The monetary approach to the balance of payments: essential concepts and historical origins. In *The Monetary Approach to the Balance of Payments* (ed. J. A. Frenkel and H. Johnson). University of Toronto Press.

Friedman, M. 1957. *A Theory of the Consumption Function*. Princeton University Press.

——. 1968. The role of monetary policy. *American Economic Review* 58:1–17.

——. 1969. The optimum quantity of money. In *The Optimum Quantity of Money and Other Essays*, pp. 1–50. Chicago, IL: Aldine.

Friedman, M., and A. J. Schwartz. 1963. *A Monetary History of the United States, 1867–1960*. Princeton University Press.

Froot, K. A, and K. Rogoff. 1995. Perspectives on PPP and long-run real exchange rates. In *Handbook of International Economics* (ed. G. M. Grossman and K. Rogoff), volume 3, pp. 1647–88. Amsterdam: Elsevier.

Froot, K. A, M. Kim, and K. Rogoff. 1995. The law of one price over seven hundred years. NBER Working Paper 5132.

Fuhrer, J. C., and G. R. Moore. 1995. Inflation persistence. *Quarterly Journal of Economics* 110:127–59.

Gali, J. 2008. *Monetary Policy, Inflation, and the Business Cycle*. Princeton University Press.

Gali, J., M. Gertler, and J. D. Lopez-Salido. 2001. European inflation dynamics: a structural econometric analysis. *European Economic Review* 45:1237–70.

Gali, J., J. D. Lopez-Salido, and J. Valles. 2004a. Technology shocks and aggregate fluctuations: assessing the Fed's performance. *Journal of Monetary Economics* 50:723–43.

——. 2004b. Rule-of-thumb consumers and the design of interest rules. *Journal of Money, Credit and Banking* 36:739–63.

Gali, J., M. Gertler, and J. D. Lopez-Salido. 2005. Robustness of the estimates of the hybrid New Keynesian Phillips curve. *Journal of Monetary Economics* 52:1107–18.

Giannoni, M. P., and M. Woodford. 2005. Optimal inflation targeting rules. In *Inflation Targeting* (ed. B. S. Bernanke and M. Woodford). University of Chicago Press.

Goldberg, P. K., and M. M. Knetter. 1997. Goods prices and exchange rates: what have we learned? *Journal of Economic Literature* 35:1243–72.

Gordon, M. 1962. *The Investment, Financing and Valuation of the Corporation*. Homewood, IL: Irwin.

Gordon, R. J. 1997. The time-varying NAIRU and its implications for policy. *Journal of Economic Perspectives* 11:11–32.

Gourieroux, C., and A. Monfort. 1996. *Simulation-Based Econometric Methods*. Oxford University Press.

Gourieroux, C., A. Monfort, and E. Renault. 1993. Indirect inference. *Journal of Applied Econometrics* 8:S85–S118.

Gregory, A., and G. Smith. 1993. Calibration in macoeconomics. In *Handbook in Statistics* (ed. G. S. Maddala), pp. 703–19. Amsterdam: North-Holland.

Hall, R. E. 1978. Stochastic implications of the life cycle–permanent income hypothesis: theory and evidence. *Journal of Political Economy* 86:971–87.

Hansen, G. D. 1985. Indivisible labor and the business cycle. *Journal of Monetary Economics* 16:309–27.

Hansen, G. D., and R. Wright. 1992. The labor market in real business cycle theory. *Federal Reserve Bank of Minneapolis Quarterly Review* 16:2–12.

Hayashi, F. 1982. Tobin's marginal Q and average Q: a neoclassical interpretation. *Econometrica* 50:213–24.

Heaton, J., and D. J. Lucas. 1995. The importance of investor heterogeneity and financial market imperfections for the behavior of asset prices. *Carnegie-Rochester Conference Series on Public Policy* 42:1–32.

———. 1996. Evaluating the effects of incomplete markets on risk sharing and asset pricing. *Journal of Political Economy* 104:443–87.

Howitt, P. 1999. Steady endogenous growth with population and R&D inputs growing. *Journal of Political Economy* 107:715–30.

Inada, K. 1964. Some structural characteristics of turnpike theorems. *Review of Economic Studies* 31:43–58.

Ingersoll, J. E. 1987. *Theory of Financial Decision Making*. New York: Rowman and Littlefield.

Intriligator, M. D. 1971. *Mathematical Optimisation and Economic Theory*. Englewood Cliffs, NJ: Prentice Hall.

Isard, P. 1977. How far can we push the law of one price? *American Economic Review* 67:942–48.

Jones, L. E., and R. Manuelli. 1990. A convex model of equilibrium growth: theory and policy implications. *Journal of Political Economy* 98:1008–38.

Judd, K. L. 1985. Redistributive taxation in a simple perfect foresight model. *Journal of Public Economics* 28:59–83.

Keynes, J. M. 1930. *A Treatise on Money*. London: Macmillan.

———. 1936. *The General Theory of Employment, Interest and Money*. London: Macmillan.

King, R. G., and C. I. Plosser. 1988. Real business cycles: introduction. *Journal of Monetary Economics* 21:191–93.

———. 2005. The econometrics of the New Keynesian price equation. *Journal of Monetary Economics* 52:1059–60.

King, R. G., and S. T. Rebelo. 1999. Resuscitating real business cycles. In *Handbook of Macroeconomics* (ed. J. B. Taylor and M. Woodford), volume 1B, pp. 927–1008. Amsterdam: Elsevier.

King, R. G., C. I. Plosser, and S. T. Rebelo. 1988a. Production, growth and business cycles. I. The basic neoclassical model. *Journal of Monetary Economics* 21:195–232.

———. 1988b. Production, growth and business cycles. II. New directions. *Journal of Monetary Economics* 21:309–41.

Klenow, P. J., and O. Kryvstov. 2005. State-dependent vs time-dependent pricing: does it matter for recent US inflation? Mimeo, Stanford University.

Knetter, M. M. 1993. International comparisons of pricing to market behavior. *American Economic Review* 83:473–86.

Koopmans, T. J. 1967. Objectives, constraints and outcomes in optimal growth models. *Econometrica* 67:1–18.

Kreps, D., and E. Porteus. 1978. Temporal resolution of uncertainty and dynamic choice theory. *Econometrica* 46:185–200.

Krugman, P. R. 1991. Target zones and exchange rate dynamics. *Quarterly Journal of Economics* 116:669–82.

Kydland, F. E., and E. C Prescott. 1977. Rules rather than discretion: the inconsistency of optimal plans. *Journal of Political Economy* 85:473–91.

———. 1982. Time to build and aggregate fluctuations. *Econometrica* 50:1345–70.

Lane, P. 2001. The new open economy macroeconomics: a survey. *Journal of International Economics* 54:235–66.

Leeper, E. M., C. A. Sims, and T. Zha. 1996. What does monetary policy do? *Brookings Papers on Economic Activity* 2:1–63.

Leonard, D., and N. V. Long. 1992. *Optimal Control Theory and Static Optimisation in Economics*. Cambridge University Press.

Kreps, D., and E. Porteus. 1978. Temporal resolution of uncertainty and dynamic choice theory. *Econometrica* 46:185–200.

Leeper, E. M., and T. Zha. 2001. Assessing simple policy rules: a view from a complete macroeconomic model. *Federal Reserve Bank of St. Louis Review* 83:83–110.

Leeper, E. M., C. A. Sims, T. Zha, R. E. Hall, and B. S. Bernanke. 1996. What does monetary policy do? *Brookings Papers in Economic Activity* 2:1–78.

Lewis, K. K. 1995. Puzzles in international financial markets. In *Handbook of International Economics* (ed. G. Grossman and K. Rogoff), volume 3, pp. 1913–71. Amsterdam: Elsevier.

Lintner, J. 1965. The valuation of risky assets and the selection of risky investments in stock portfolios and capital budgets. *Review of Economics and Statistics* 47:13–37.

Ljungqvist, L., and T. J. Sargent. 2004. *Recursive Macroeconomic Theory*, 2nd edn. Cambridge, MA: MIT Press.

Long, J. B., and C. I. Plosser. 1983. Real business cycles. *Journal of Political Economy* 91:31–69.

Lucas, R. E. 1972. Expectations and the neutrality of money. *Journal of Economic Theory* 4:103–24.

——. 1975. An equilibrium model of the business cycle. *Journal of Political Economy* 83:1113–44.

——. 1976a. Econometric policy evaluation: a critique. In *The Phillips Curve and Labor Markets* (ed. K. Brunner and A. H. Meltzer), pp. 19–46. Amsterdam: North-Holland.

——. 1976b. Nobel lecture: monetary neutrality. *Journal of Political Economy* 104:661–82.

——. 1978. Asset prices in an exchange economy. *Econometrica* 46:1429–46.

——. 1980a. Equilibrium in a pure currency economy. In *Models of Monetary Economies* (ed. J. H. Karaken and N. Wallace), pp. 131–45. Federal Reserve Bank of Minneapolis.

——. 1980b. Two illustrations of the quantity theory of money. *American Economic Review* 70:1005–14.

Mankiw, N. G. 2006. The macroeconomist as scientist and engineer. *Journal of Economic Perspectives* 20:29–46.

Mankiw, N. G., and D. Romer (eds). 1991. *New Keynesian Economics*. Cambridge, MA: MIT Press.

Marimon, R., and A. Scott. 1999. *Computational Methods for the Study of Dynamic Economies*. Oxford University Press.

Mark, N. 1985. On time-varying risk premia in the foreign exchange market: an econometric analysis. *Journal of Monetary Economics* 16:3–18.

Mark, N., and Y. Wu. 1998. Rethinking deviations from uncovered interest parity: the role of covariance risk and noise. *Economic Journal* 108:1686–706.

Marsh, T. A. 1995. Term structure of interest rates and the pricing of fixed income claims and bonds. In *Finance* (ed. R. A. Jarrow, V. Maksimovic, and W. T. Ziemba), pp. 273–314. Handbooks in Operations Research and Management Science, volume 9. Amsterdam: Elsevier.

McCallum, B. T., and E. Nelson. 1999. An optimizing IS–LM specification for monetary policy and business cycle analysis. *Journal of Money, Credit and Banking* 31:296–316.

McGrattan, E. R. 1994. A progress report on business cycle models. *Federal Reserve Bank of Minneapolis Quarterly Review* 18:2–16.

——. 1998. A defense of AK growth models. *Federal Reserve Bank of Minneapolis Quarterly Review* 22:13–27.

Mehra, R., and E. C. Prescott. 1985. The equity premium: a puzzle. *Journal of Monetary Economics* 15:145–61.

Merton, R. C. 1973. An intertemporal capital asset pricing model. *Econometrica* 41: 867-87.

Michel, P., and D. de la Croix. 2002. *A Theory of Economic Growth: Dynamics and Policy in Overlapping Generations*. Cambridge University Press.

Modigliani, F. 1963. The monetary mechanism and its interaction with real phenomena. *Review of Economics and Statistics* 45:79-107.

——. 1970. The life cycle hypothesis of saving and intercountry differences in the saving ratio. In *Induction, Growth and Trade: Essays in Honour of Sir Roy Harrod* (ed. W. A. Eltis, M. G. Scott, and J. N. Wolfe). Oxford: Clarendon Press.

Modigliani, F., and R. Brumberg. 1954. Utility analysis and the consumption function: an interpretation of cross-section data. In *Post Keynesian Economics* (ed. K. K. Kurihara). New Brunswick, NJ: Rutgers University Press.

Modigliani, F., and M. H. Miller. 1958. The cost of capital, corporation finance and the theory of investment. *American Economic Review* 48:261-97.

Mossin, J. 1966. Equilibrium in a capital asset market. *Econometrica* 35:768-83.

Mulligan, C. B., and X. Sala-i-Martin. 1997. The optimum quantity of money: theory and evidence. *Journal of Money, Credit and Banking* 24:687-715.

Mundell, R. A. 1963. Capital mobility and stabilization policy under fixed and flexible exchange rates. *Canadian Journal of Economics and Political Science* 29:475-85.

Mussa, M. 1976. The exchange rate, the balance of payments, and monetary and fiscal policy under a regime of controlled floating. *Scandinavian Journal of Economics* 78: 229-48.

——. 1982. A model of exchange rate dynamics. *Journal of Political Economy* 90:74-104.

Muth, J. F. 1960. Optimal properties of exponentially weighted forecasts. *Journal of the American Statistical Association* 55:299-306.

——. 1961. Rational expectations and the theory of price movements. *Econometrica* 29: 315-35.

Neiss, K. S., and E. Nelson. 2005. Inflation dynamics, marginal cost, and the output gap: evidence from three countries. *Journal of Money, Credit and Banking* 37:1019-45.

Obstfeld, M. 2001. International macroeconomics: beyond the Mundell-Fleming model. *First Annual Conference, International Monetary Fund Mundell-Fleming Lecture 2001*. NBER Working Paper 8369.

Obstfeld, M., and K. Rogoff. 1995a. Exchange rate dynamics redux. *Journal of Political Economy* 103:624-60.

——. 1995b. The intertemporal approach to the current account. In *Handbook of International Economics* (ed. G. M. Grossman and K. Rogoff), volume 3, pp. 1731-99. Amsterdam: Elsevier.

——. 1996. *Foundations of International Macroeconomics*. Cambridge, MA: MIT Press.

——. 2000. The six major puzzles in international macroeconomics: is there a common cause? *NBER Macroeconomics Annual* 15:339-90.

O'Driscoll, G. P. 1977. The Ricardian nonequivalence theorem. *Journal of Political Economy* 85:207-10.

Okun, A. M. 1962. Potential GNP: its measurement and significance. In *Proceedings of the Business and Economics Statistics Section, American Statistical Association*, pp. 98-103. Washington, DC: American Statistical Association.

Patinkin, D. 1965. *Money, Interest, and Prices: An Integration of Monetary and Value Theory*, 2nd edn. New York: Harper & Row.

Phelps, E. S. 1966. *Golden Rules of Economic Growth*. New York: Norton.

——. 1968. Money-wage dynamics and labor market equilibrium. *Journal of Political Economy* 76:678-711.

——. 1973. Inflation in the theory of public finance. *Swedish Journal of Economics* 75: 67-82.

Phillips, A. W. 1958. The relationship between unemployment and the rate of change of money wages in the United Kingdom, 1861-1957. *Economica* 25:283-99.

Polito, V., and M. R. Wickens. 2007. Measuring the fiscal stance. University of York Discussion Paper 07/14.

Prescott, E. C. 1986. Theory ahead of business-cycle measurement. *Carnegie-Rochester Conference Series on Public Policy* 25:11-44.

Ramsey, F. P. 1927. A contribution to the theory of taxation. *Economic Journal* 37:47-61.

——. 1928. A mathematical theory of saving. *Economic Journal* 38:543-59.

Rebelo, S. 1991. Long-run policy analysis and long-run growth. *Journal of Political Economy* 99:500-21.

——. 2005. Real business cycle models: past, present, and future. *Scandanavian Journal of Economics* 107:217-38.

Remolona, E., M. R. Wickens, and F. Gong. 1998. What was the market's view of UK monetary policy? Estimating inflation risk and expected inflation with indexed bonds. Federal Reserve Bank of New York, Staff Report 57 (December).

Rivera-Batiz, F. L., and L. Rivera-Batiz. 1985. *International Finance and Open Economy Macroeconomics.* New York: Macmillan.

Roberts, J. M. 1995. New Keynesian economics and the Phillips curve. *Journal of Money, Credit and Banking* 27:975-84.

——. 1997. Is inflation sticky? *Journal of Monetary Economics* 39:173-96.

Rogerson, R. 1988. Indivisible labor, lotteries and equilibrium. *Journal of Monetary Economics* 21:3-16.

Rogoff, K. 2002. Dornbusch's overshooting model after twenty-five years. *Second Annual Conference, International Monetary Fund Mundell-Fleming Lecture 2001.* IMF Working Paper 02/39.

Romer, P. M. 1986. Increasing returns and long-run growth. *Journal of Political Economy* 94:1002-37.

——. 1987. Growth based on increasing returns due to specialization. *American Economic Review* 77:56-62.

——. 1990. Endogenous technological change. *Journal of Political Economy* 98:S71-S102.

Rotemberg, J. J. 1982. Sticky prices in the United States. *Journal of Political Economy* 90:1187-211.

Rotemberg, J. J., and M. Woodford. 1997. An optimization-based econometric framework for the evaluation of monetary policy. *NBER Macroeconomics Annual* 2:297-346.

——. 1999. The cyclical behavior of prices and costs. In *Handbook of Macroeconomics* (ed. J. B. Taylor and M. Woodford), volume 1B, pp. 1052-1135. Amsterdam: Elsevier.

Rumler, F., and J. Vilmunen. 2005. Price setting in the euro area: some stylised facts from micro consumer data. ECB Working Paper 524.

Samuelson, P. A. 1958. An exact consumption-loan model of interest with or without the social contrivance of money. *Journal of Political Economy* 66:467-82.

Sargent, T., and N. Wallace. 1981. Some unpleasant monetarist arithmetic. *Federal Reserve Bank of Minneapolis Quarterly Review* 3:1-19.

Sharpe, W. F. 1964. Capital asset prices: a theory of market equilibrium under conditions of risk. *Journal of Finance* 19:425-42.

Sheffrin, S. M., and W. T. Woo. 1990. Present value tests of an intertemporal model of the current account. *Journal of International Economics* 29:237-53.

Shell, K. 1967. A model of inventive activity and capital accumulation. In *Essays on the Theory of Optimal Economic Growth* (ed. K. Shell), pp. 67-85. Cambridge, MA: MIT Press.

Sidrauski, M. 1967. Rational choice and patterns of growth in a monetary economy. *American Economic Review* 57:534-44.

Sims, C. A. 1980. Macroeconomics and reality. *Econometrica* 48:1-48.

Sims, C. A. 1994. A simple model for the study of the determination of the price level and the interaction of monetary and fiscal policy. *Economic Theory* 4:381-99.

Singleton, K. J. 2006. *Empirical Dynamic Asset Pricing.* Princeton University Press.

Skidelski, R. 1992. *John Maynard Keynes. Volume 2: The Economist as Saviour 1920-1937.* London: Macmillan.

Smets, F., and R. Wouters. 2003. An estimated dynamic stochastic general equilibrium model of the euro area. *Journal of the European Economic Association* 1:1123-75.

Smith, P. N., and M. R. Wickens. 2002. Asset pricing with observable stochastic discount factors. *Journal of Economic Surveys* 16:397-446.

——. 2007. The new consensus in monetary policy: is the NKM fit for the purpose of inflation targeting. In *The New Consensus in Monetary Policy* (ed. P. Arestis), pp. 97-127. New York: Palgrave Macmillan.

Smith, P. N., S. Sorensen, and M. R. Wickens. 2006. General equilibrium theories of the equity risk premium: estimates and tests. Mimeo, University of York.

Solow, R. 1956. A contribution to the theory of economic growth. *Quarterly Journal of Economics* 70:65-94.

Svensson, L. E. O., and M. Woodford. 2003. Indicator variables for optimal policy. *Journal of Monetary Economics* 50:691-720.

——. 2004. Indicator variables for optimal policy under asymmetric information. *Journal of Economic Dynamics and Control* 28:661-90.

Swan, T. W. 1956. Economic growth and capital accumulation. *Economic Record* 32:334-61.

Taylor, J. B. 1979. Staggered wage setting in a macro model. *American Economic Review* 69:108-13.

——. 1993. Discretion versus policy rules in practice. *Carnegie-Rochester Conferences Series on Public Policy* 39:195-214.

——. 1999. Staggered price and wage setting in macroeconomics. In *Handbook of Macroeconomics* (e.d J. B. Taylor and M. Woodford), volume 1B, pp. 1009-50. Amsterdam: Elsevier.

Tobin, J. 1969. A general equilibrium approach to monetary theory. *Journal of Money, Credit and Banking* 1:15-29.

Vasicek, O. 1977. An equilibrium characterization of the term structure. *Journal of Financial Economics* 5:177-88.

Walsh, C. E. 2003. *Monetary Theory and Policy*, 2nd edn. Cambridge, MA: MIT Press.

Wickens, M. R. 2007. Is the euro sustainable? CEPR Discussion Paper 6337.

Wickens, M. R., and R. Motto. 2000. Estimating shocks and impulse response functions. *Journal of Applied Econometrics* 16:371-87.

Wickens, M. R., and P. N. Smith. 2001. Macroeconomic sources of FOREX risk. Mimeo, University of York.

Wilcox, D. W. 1989. The sustainability of government deficits: implications of the present-value borrowing constraint. *Journal of Money, Credit and Banking* 21:291-306.

Williamson, J. 1993. Exchange rate management. *Economic Journal* 103:188-97.

Whiteman, C. H. 1983. *Linear Rational Expectations Models: A User's Guide.* Minneapolis, MN: University of Minnesota Press.

Woodford, M. 1995. Price level determinacy without control of a monetary aggregate. *Carnegie-Rochester Conference Series on Public Policy* 43:1-46.

Woodford, M. 2001. Fiscal requirements for price stability? *Journal of Money, Credit and Banking* 33:669–728.

——. 2003. *Interest and Prices.* Princeton University Press.

Yaari, M. E. 1965. Uncertain lifetime, life insurance, and the theory of the consumer. *Review of Economic Studies* 32:137–150.

Index